DATE DUE		DEC 8 1981	

Sotheby's

By the same author

The English as Collectors

Sotheby's

PORTRAIT OF
AN AUCTION HOUSE

by

FRANK HERRMANN
F.S.A.

1981

W W NORTON & COMPANY
NEW YORK · LONDON

Published by
W. W. Norton & Company, Inc.
500 Fifth Avenue
New York, NY 10110

ISBN 0 393 01424 X

© Frank Herrmann 1980
First American Edition, 1981

Printed in Great Britain by
Ebenezer Baylis and Son Ltd
The Trinity Press
Worcester, and London

To

JIM KIDDELL

who knew more of the answers
than anyone else

CONTENTS

Part Four
THE GREAT SURGE

Illustrations

Colour plates appear following pages 358, 390, 422 and 438; and monochrome plates following pages 54, 182, 342 and 406.

ACKNOWLEDGEMENTS

This portrait of Sotheby's could never have come into being without the help and information I received from a very large number of people who have either been associated with the firm in the past or are still connected with it today. A few have asked to remain anonymous. I would like to express my gratitude to them all. I am sorry if it has not always been possible to use the specific items of information they supplied, but, as it is, the book has turned out much longer than planned. I would also apologise to anyone whom inadvertently I have omitted to mention.

My particular gratitude must go to the late John Carter who asked me to write the book and forged my early links with Sotheby's; to the late Tim Munby who assisted greatly with information on the early sales held by the firm; to Peter Wilson who gave unfailing encouragement throughout the many years of work on the project, and to Katherine MacLean, his secretary for much of that time; to the late A. J. B. Kiddell, with whom for three years I shared an office whenever we coincided at Bond Street, for the most unstinting help and encouragement of every kind; to Tim Wilder who unravelled the mysteries of the last years of Tom Hodge and the advent of Barlow, Hobson and Warre; to David MacKitterick who checked the early chapters after Tim Munby's death; to Joe Och for invaluable help with documentation; and on the other side of the Atlantic to Jesse Wolff, also for magnificently useful documentation and searing objectivity; to John Marion, Tom Norton and Nancy Forster for support during numerous visits to New York; to E. M. Dring, Nicholas Poole-Wilson and Lord Parmoor of Quaritch for the generous use of that firm's records.

There were more people within Sotheby's who helped in one way or another than those who did not, but I would like specifically to thank Lord Westmorland, Peregrine Pollen, Graham Llewellyn, Marcus Linell, Peter Spira, Derek Johns, Julian Thompson, Lord John Kerr, Michel Strauss, the late Tony Holloway, Stanley Clark, Tim Clarke, Wilfrid Hodgson, Fred Snelling, Neil Davey, Philip Pouncey, Richard Came, Julien Stock, David Battie, Christopher de Hamel, John Collins, Jock Palmer, Paul Mack, Liz Wilson, Roy Davids, John Somerville, Derrick Crowther, Michael Naxton, Peter Hinks, David Jeffcoat, John Cann, the late Ernie Collman, Jonathan Franklin (the modest maestro of 'General File'), the late Andreas Mayer, Jock Campbell, Jan Pieter Glerum, Bruce Rutherford (in Australia), Dr. Ernst Behrens, Dr. S. N. Cristea, Reinhold Cassirer and Sue Bond.

Again in New York my task would have been much harder without the help of Edward Lee Cave, David Nash, Hugh Hildesley, Tom Clarke, the late Paul Rewald, Rose Kissel, Armin Allen, Betsy Pinover, Martin Stansfield (particularly on jewellery sales) and Charles Seilheimer.

Of those who had once worked for Sotheby's and had either retired or moved elsewhere I would like to thank particularly Sam Patch (also for the loan of much useful material), Vere Pilkington, Miss Edith Bourne, Tom Lumley, and Temple Williams (who with Jim Kiddell had once constituted Sotheby's 'Flying Squad'), Howard Ricketts, Paul Thompson, Carmen Gronau, Anthony Hobson, Billy Winkworth, Kate Foster, Dr. Feisenberger, Mrs. Eldridge, Miss de la Torre, Jerry Patterson, Bonny Prandato, Barbara Evans, Clifford Barclay and Herman Robinow (on matters corporate and financial).

There were many related to one-time members of the staff who gave me most useful information. They included Lady Montague-Barlow, Canon Barlow, the late Mrs. Tancred Borenius and her daughter Mrs. Clarissa Lada-Grodzicki, Mrs. Rham, Mrs. Helen Ballard, Philip Wilson, Colin Rich, Mrs. Sheila Munby and Mrs. Ernestine Carter.

Finally there were a large group of experts in many fields and institutions who helped with difficult problems, vital facts and general knowledge, who included Dr. F. G. Emmison, Frank Simpson, Sir Ellis Waterhouse, Dr. David Rogers, Michael Turner, Nicolas Barker, Mrs. Miller (on Natural History Sales), Sir Geoffrey Keynes, Dr. Christopher Sotheby Pitcher (on the genealogy of the Sotheby family), Geraldine Norman, Kenneth Snowman, Sir Nikolaus Pevsner, the late Benedict Nicholson, David Foxon, William LeFanu, Jean Fürstenberg, Clifford Maggs, W. Forster (who often had in stock all the catalogues that no one else could find), the late Francis Matthiessen (who first took me into Sotheby's many years ago), H. P. Kraus, John Fleming, the late Lou Feldman, David Howard, Peter Mimpress, Miss Olwen Hall (for transliteration of vital but wholly illegible letters), and Julia Shaw (for translations from the French).

My most particular thanks are due to my secretary, Mrs. Sheila Phillips, who has the fastest and most accurate shorthand I have encountered in thirty years of dictation, for endless patience with drafts and revisions of the manuscript.

I would like to thank the following publishers and copyright authors for permission to reprint extracts from the following works: *English Collectors of Books and Manuscripts (1530–1903) and their Marks of Ownership* by Seymour de Ricci (Cambridge University Press); *Rare People and Rare Books* by Millicent Sowerby (Constable & Co.); *Letters of Thomas J. Wise to John Henry Wrenn, a further inquiry into the skill of certain nineteenth-century forgers* by Fannie E. Ratchford (A. Knopf Inc. and Texas University); the Barlow-Yates Thompson correspondence (The Librarian of the Lilly Library, Indiana University, Bloomington, U.S.A.); *Bibliotheca Osleriana* (The Osler Library Board of Curators as the Literary Executors of Sir William Osler).

Finally, I am grateful to the following for permission to reproduce illustrations:

The Metropolitan Museum of Art, New York; The National Gallery, London; King's College, Cambridge; Times Newspapers Ltd.; Country Life; Pierre Boulat/Life © Time Inc. 1963; London News Agency Photos Ltd.; Sport and General; United Press International UK Ltd.; and Fox Photos Ltd.

A

LIST

OF THE

ORIGINAL CATALOGUES

OF

THE PRINCIPAL LIBRARIES

𝔚𝔥𝔦𝔠𝔥 𝔥𝔞𝔳𝔢 𝔟𝔢𝔢𝔫 𝔖𝔬𝔩𝔡 𝔟𝔶 𝔄𝔲𝔠𝔱𝔦𝔬𝔫

BY

Mr. SAMUEL BAKER, from 1744 to 1774.

Messrs. S. BAKER and G. LEIGH, from 1775 to 1777.

Mr. GEORGE LEIGH, 1778;

Messrs. LEIGH and SOTHEBY, from 1780 to 1800.

Messrs. LEIGH, SOTHEBY and SON, from 1800 to 1803

Messrs. LEIGH and S. SOTHEBY, from 1804 to 1816:

And Mr. SOTHEBY, from 1816 to 1828.

*The whole forming a Series of One Hundred and Forty-six Volumes
in Quarto, with Prices and Purchasers' Names.*

𝔏𝔬𝔫𝔡𝔬𝔫:

PRINTED BY COMPTON & RITCHIE, MIDDLE STREET CLOTH FAIR

MDCCCXXVIII.

Title page of a catalogue that constitutes an invaluable source book on early auctioneering
history.

INTRODUCTION

i *A Quarter of a Millennium*

IT comes as a surprise to many people that Sotheby's has been in business for almost 250 years. It is an unusual record. Inevitably very little is known about the firm's early days: the first part of this book brings together as many of the facts as it has been possible to garner after a great deal of probing. Thus the foundation of the firm has been pushed back some eleven years and the long established myth of what really was Samuel Baker's first auction sale has been finally exploded. We discover something of the personalities of Baker himself, of his first partner George Leigh; of his nephew, John Sotheby, and of the latter's son, Samuel Sotheby; and of his grandson, Samuel Leigh Sotheby, a scholar and picture collector and the first head of the firm to make a determined effort to mingle the auctioneering of books with other artistic property. With his death the family connection ended.

John Wilkinson, who dominated the business in the second half of the nineteenth century, had entered it as an accountant. He and Edward Grose Hodge, who succeeded him, worked in the firm for more than 120 years between them. Though its style, SOTHEBY, WILKINSON and HODGE, remained unchanged between 1864 and 1924 (when it became SOTHEBY & CO.), Tom Hodge, who succeeded his father as sole proprietor, sold the business in 1909 to a triumvirate of partners who laid the foundations of the Sotheby's we know today.

Readers who are interested principally in the expansion of the company in the present century may well be advised to skip Part I and turn at once to Part II. There they will learn that in 1908 a friendly rival firm of book auctioneers, Hodgson's of Chancery Lane, were given an opportunity of buying Sotheby's for a down payment of only £6,500 but after long deliberation they considered this too great a risk.

Instead the firm was acquired by a partnership of a barrister, a banker and a former Foreign Office official. The first had extraordinary political acumen and wide-ranging ambition; the second infinite charm and a formidable talent for auctioneering; the third exquisite taste and a gift for scholarship. The combination of Sir Montague Barlow's drive, Felix Warre's integrity and Geoffrey Hobson's brain power became a force to be reckoned with in the art market on both sides of the Atlantic, and by the early 1930s Sotheby's profits had overtaken those of their long established and much larger rivals, Christie, Manson & Woods. By the time the Second World War was approaching, Sotheby's had finally shaken off the reputation of being mainly 'Auctioneers of Literary

Property' and was principally engaged in selling works of art and paintings. By 1944, in fact, books only represented about 15 per cent of Sotheby's turnover.

The fierce decline in domestic business as a result of the Slump had generated a more active search for business from abroad. By the mid-1930s London had begun to overtake Paris as Europe's most important international art centre. But business was severely impeded for the first few years after 1945 by oppressive government restrictions on free trading between Britain and countries overseas. As soon as new legislation permitted the free flow of goods and money both in and out of the country, things began to look up. An era of fresh opportunity came into being. The directors of Sotheby's, in common with those of many other businesses, had worked hard to have the restrictions on trade removed and were quick to see their opportunities, particularly in the United States. More than anyone else, Peter Wilson became the architect of Sotheby's great global expansion during the last thirty years. The fact that he has recently retired after forty-two years within the firm, twenty-two of them as Chairman (and moved the centre of his working life to Sotheby's in France), sees this book appearing quite fortuitously at the end of a particular era: one that has witnessed an unprecedented growth of interest in the arts, as well as a sweeping advance of scholarship in all its branches, and in the number of people who enjoy collecting.

Inevitably this has brought in its train a fundamental re-assessment of values attached to works of art and an almost constant upward surge of prices. The latter is something quite new. There have been long periods in the history of Sotheby's when prices remained completely stable and in general the fear always was that they would decline, which, of course, at times they did. The most notable downturns in recent times occurred in 1930 and again in 1940. Inflation on the scale of the last fifteen years is an altogether novel experience which has, if anything, strengthened the demand for possession of works of art in preference to more conventional and seemingly volatile financial assets, and added vigour to the appeal of the auction room.

ii *A People Business*

Art auctioneering as an occupation represents a life of perpetual anticipation, often unfulfilled. The participants create the pressures, the tensions, the gossip, the emotions, the conflict of the rational and the irrational. They give to it that extra intangible dimension of mystique, of excitement, discovery, uncertainty and significance in cultural life, that exercises such fascination both inside and outside the business.

The history of an auction house such as Sotheby's is therefore principally about the people involved; the management, the cataloguers, the clerks and the porters, those who send their goods to be sold, charmingly known in the auction world as 'proprietors', the dealers who support the sales and the collectors, who both buy and sell. I make no apology for having concentrated on these personalities.

One of the rewards of delving into this background has been to bring to prominence within the narrative little-known men and women who worked long and lovingly, often with the minimum of personal recognition, to bring about a public – and, of course, a commercial – awareness of particular items among a seemingly unlimited variety of objects. The social historians have so far overlooked men like George Leigh, Samuel Leigh Sotheby and Tom Hodge who had considerable influence on their own generations. Certainly those who still remember Sir Montague Barlow, Geoffrey Hobson and Charles des Graz frequently refer to them as Olympians or Titans. They were men apart; often, let us face it, rather aloof and autocratic but they gained enormous respect, even veneration, from those who came into contact with them. Since their day management has learned to become a great deal more approachable. Admiration must also go to the many cataloguers and experts whose skill, anonymous scholarship and enthusiasm have often throughout the present century helped to bring about what has now become universal appreciation. Within the context of specialisation, the most immediately arresting area has been in the long tradition of sales of autograph material – letters, manuscripts and documents, the very stuff of history. Our knowledge of Samuel Pepys, Isaac Newton, Napoleon, Nelson or the Brownings would be a good deal poorer for a lack of their letters sold at Sotheby's.

In general my aim has been to attempt a reconstruction of what Sotheby's was through the ages. I have tried to get beneath the outer skin of the public image, often by concentrating on sales that made a particular impact in their own time. The story reveals all the human failings that occur in every business: it reveals in particular a mean streak and tight-fistedness among the firm's owners which may have been typical of its time and lasted until well after the Second World War. Possibly it was the relaxation of this attitude that helped to trigger off the expansion of more recent years. Certainly one has to bear in mind that from 1929 to 1945 there was an obsessive tradition in the outlook of senior management that the morrow would always bring disaster.

The sales that stay in the mind over the years are usually those of single-owner collections and very often the personality of the collector shines through the dry print of the catalogues. Such sales tend to set new standards of appreciation and values in whatever speciality they happen to be, whether Roman glass, gold coins, English delftware, netsuke, Japanese engravings, chess sets, French furniture or miniature paintings. The cataloguers make an extra effort because the collectors concerned will often have assembled unusually useful source material; prices are higher because competition for objects with well known and respected provenances is greater; private buyers attend such sales in larger numbers.

There is a long history of divided opinion, both within the firm and outside it, of whether collectors should attend sales and bid in person, or give their commissions to professional dealers to do it for them. Sir Montague Barlow and Felix Warre encouraged all their friends to come and bid for themselves. For one thing it helped to defeat 'rings' of dealers, a much more common phenomenon in their day; for another it was highly enjoyable. Geoffrey Hobson opposed this practice. He advised *his* friends to get dealers to bid for them because they would probably get their books more cheaply that way, and his son, Anthony Hobson, who ran the book department, shared this view. Jim Kiddell went to great lengths to encourage collectors of Chinese porcelain to bid in person, but the bankers and city merchants who collected such things before the war had neither the time nor the inclination to do so and were served by particularly able dealers. Vere Pilkington and Peter Wilson encouraged collectors of drawings and pictures to do their own bidding; indeed Pilkington lays claim to having made it an important and regular feature of Sotheby sales. This increasing presence of the private buyer and his willingness to bid beyond an accepted trade price has greatly eroded the once almost exclusive wholesaling or clearing house function of the fine art auction house.

An auctioneer's catalogues are all important: they are the firm's ambassadors, salesmen and recording angels all in one. The information conveyed has become steadily more sophisticated as knowledge has improved. Much more is known today about, say, the individual carvers of netsuke or English furniture makers of the eighteenth century than before the war. Indeed some members of the book and art trade have reproached Sotheby's for over-cataloguing: there is little else beyond the sale descriptions which they can add when selling objects to their own customers. A great number of people, however, find it difficult to view sales in person, so accurate catalogue descriptions are all important. Attractive catalogues certainly help to stoke the fires of demand. Illustrations are a great aid in this respect and together with the relatively recent introduction of printed estimates and subsequent price lists, catalogues are the tangible evidence for posterity of the art market's activities.

While there is great joy and satisfaction for a collector who is a regular subscriber to a specialist range of catalogues in settling down in a comfortable armchair of a weekend in the contemplation of possible purchases, it has to be remembered that the primary function of the auctioneer is to turn goods into money. It is difficult for the public to imagine the protracted negotiations that often go on before some major piece is finally put on view in the main gallery in Bond Street or Madison Avenue. The volume of correspondence that accumulates for some major sales has to be seen to be believed. On the rare occasions when this has survived from the more distant past, it has been highly useful source material. Things are usually much simpler where an active collector is involved. A close relationship – rather as between an author and his editor in a publisher's office – often exists between a client who sells (and buys) regularly and his expert contact in the auctioneer's office. But such relationships only constitute a minor source of business.

Those who have not had to face the problem of suddenly disposing of the entire contents of a house, a library or a massive collection of art and antiques may not appreciate the difficulties of doing so. Belongings are very personal; tastes of successive generations rarely coincide; often there is more material than a fully-fledged family can additionally accommodate at one bite. This is where an auction is the most practical means of disposal. Furthermore the recirculation of a collection of works of art or books is the life blood of the collecting community. A well-publicised sale, by one of the foremost houses, brings together a multitude of potential buyers, presents the objects systematically and accurately described, and establishes realistic values in a way that no alternative can rival. Indeed many people attribute the success of the London and New York auction houses since the last war to the fact that their sales have provided much better and fairer prices than individual dealers could or would offer for similar property.

Taste, fashion, demand, scarcity, eternal economic ups and downs are the provender of variety and excitement. There is no certainty about success at auction. The skill has become to reduce the variables to a minimum. This can improve the statistical averages, but people do not buy or sell statistics. Their concern is with the fate of the individual lot. Of course the auctioneer can influence circumstances. Sotheby's have often been taunted with overdoing the theatricality of sales, but ultimately the market is not a force any single firm can control.

Foreigners sometimes accuse the British of having become auction mad. They marvelled for years at that surprising characteristic of English collectors, their complete candour about the prices they paid for the objects they bought.[1] If one looks at the auction room pages of the *Daily Telegraph* on Monday or *The Times* on a Tuesday in mid-season, the four leading auction houses – Sotheby's, Christie's, Phillips' and Bonham's – are found to be holding around sixty to seventy auction sale sessions a week in their various sale-rooms – that is twelve to fifteen on an average working day. It highlights the much enhanced degree of specialisation that has become a feature of the London fine art auctioneers. Sotheby's greatest strength is its expertise. Major errors of judgement soon tend to attract adverse publicity. With almost two hundred specialists employed just in England, training has become of great importance. The firm initiated its own training course some years ago. Once an apprentice cataloguer has finished this course, the constant handling and sight of pieces of all kinds in each department, plus the benefit and experience of established authorities around him, soon leads to confidence and assurance.

The auctioneering vocabulary needs a word of explanation. Sotheby's strong aversion to a plethora of adjectival superlatives has been in strong contrast to some of its competitors during its long history. The one word that is wheeled out with apparent frequency is *important*, but analysis soon establishes that its use in general is appropriate in differentiating the unusual from the run-of-the-mill. The distinction between different house sales in the 1930s was particularly finely tuned. In the case of the Old Court House, Hampton Court, it was 'the interesting contents'; Cam House, Camden Hill included 'the important contents' while 47 Belgrave Square consisted of 'the valuable contents' and 148 Piccadilly, the Rothschild family home, 'the magnificent contents'. The

1. Alas, it is now only in the world of books that the printed, post-sale price lists still include the purchaser's name.

watersheds have appeared under plain labels: 'Catalogue of seven paintings by Cézanne, Manet, Renoir and van Gogh – the property of the Estate of the late Jakob Goldschmidt of New York City', or 'The Robert von Hirsch Collection'.

Nowadays the printed estimates supplied with each catalogue speak much more directly than any amount of subtlety in verbal descriptions. Even though such figures must represent an approximation, they have eliminated a minor industry of advisers – from articulate sale-room porters to 'sale-room consultants' to whom intending private purchasers could turn for counsel. However, in order to impart information to intending buyers as dependably as possible – particularly in the case of paintings and drawings – many of the firm's catalogues, both in the USA and in the UK, today contain glossaries of definitions about the extent to which the attribution to authorship of a work of art may be taken as reliable in the cataloguer's judgement.

I have made no attempt within the text to translate contemporary hammer prices into present day sterling or dollar equivalents. Fluctuation is so rapid that efforts to do this can become meaningless within weeks of publication.[1] What I have endeavoured to do instead is occasionally to include some details of what the purchase of goods and services would cost contemporaneously. As mentioned earlier it is really quite difficult to believe how stable prices remained over long periods in the past. This was of course reflected in wages and salaries. A competent secretary who joined Sotheby's in 1919 might have expected to earn £2 15s. per week, and she would probably have earned £3 15s. in 1939 after two decades of loyal service. This figure would conceal the fact that, in common with the rest of the staff, she would have accepted a 10 per cent cut in her weekly wages which Major Warre was forced to impose on everyone in 1931 at the time of the depression, and which he was very loath to remove later. Perhaps it should be added that if that secretary happened to be unmarried and to live with her widowed mother (there are records of a number of such instances) she could probably save sufficient from her earnings to buy the freehold of a small house in a quiet London suburb at between £250 and £350.

For the first thirty years of this century a good cataloguer in the book department would expect to earn £5 a week and stay there. A really senior man might get up to £9 10s. a week. £10 a week was a magic barrier that was not often breached. As it happened the directors often chose expert staff whom they knew to have an additional private income. Even the senior partners only paid themselves a basic £700 to £1,000 a year between 1909 and 1939, and a share of the profits when there was one. As will be seen, the Slump hit Geoffrey Hobson so hard that he had to sell up a sumptuous home in Bedford Square in 1931. By 1939 he and Major Warre were back to £500 a year after much higher levels of income ten years earlier, and after working thirty years in the business.

1. It is perhaps of interest, but no special significance should be attached to the fact, that an ounce of pure gold (24 carats) cost £4.25 in July 1920 and reached a peak of £410 briefly in February 1980.

One has to remember that the partners also had to supply the entire capital required by the business. Although it is always dangerous to generalise, because life was so relatively cheap in the first forty years of the present century there genuinely was much less striving for profits than is the case in commerce or business today. Certainly in the UK it was a much less materialistic era than the present, where everything has a value and a price. How otherwise could a competent porter (they were usually ex-guardsmen) and his family live on 30 shillings a week – this sum might admittedly be augmented by tips – and retire on a pension of £1 a week, with virtually no grumbling? Sales clerks always were a race apart. Clients who could not attend sales in person were advised to leave their bids with them. They were highly expert and experienced analysts of the market. They knew the value of every sort of commodity; they had a shrewd idea who would be bidding and they often even knew the identity of the client for whom specific dealers were acting. They were thus the eyes and ears of the auctioneer and they benefited with a handsome supplementary income.

Price increases, it must be stressed, are not a mere matter of inflation. The factors of greater desirability, often because of greater knowledge, followed in due course by changing taste; interest not simply from a limited English clientele but from a globally extended dealing fraternity; the knowledge that an object is one of the few of its kind remaining in private ownership – all these play their part. A telling but by no means uncommon example of the dramatic change in value between the pre-war and the post-war eras concerns a Chelsea boar's head tureen which Jim Kiddell had included in a porcelain sale in 1936. A dealer had had it in stock for a good many years and had been unable to sell it at an asking price of £40. The £28 it fetched at Bond Street was regarded as very satisfactory. In December 1973 the identical piece came up again in a porcelain sale taken on this occasion by Tim Clarke, a post-war pupil of Jim Kiddell's. Jim stood beside the rostrum and his normally impassive face was a study in perplexity as the piece was knocked down – at a price of £32,000.

iii *Background to Authorship*

It may be thought extraordinary that no full account of Sotheby's history has previously appeared. When I began the long adventure of chronicling the firm's past, I was astonished to find that there was no archive and a minimum of preserved documentation on which to base such a work. A great fire in 1865 had destroyed all the early records and John Wilkinson and Edward Grose Hodge either felt too daunted by such a disaster to start re-assembling them or, more likely, they were the sort of people who were more concerned with the present and the future. Of the three partners who bought the business in 1909, Geoffrey Hobson was in embryo a great historian. He did, in fact, compile and publish the only brief outline of the firm's history ever to have appeared, which was published in 1917 when the firm moved to Bond Street from Wellington Street, where it had been for almost exactly a hundred years. This very move no doubt accounted for the jettisoning of more material that might have proved useful. At least Hobson assembled and preserved detailed statistical records of his own time, some of which survive to the present day.

It is not surprising therefore that I was the fifth putative author who had agreed to undertake the task. The last of them before me was the redoubtable John Carter. He never got beyond a cockshy at the Sotheby family's genealogy and a draft for a preface. He wrote in the latter, 'When on 23 March 1972 the diarist of *The Times* stated that Sotheby's had "opened its archives" to the present writer for the compilation of this history, he was putting his own gloss on the firm's modestly worded press release announcing the semi-retirement, after seventeen years' service, of one of its Associate Directors. The fact is that, extraordinary as it may seem, *there are no archives to open* . . . and it remains the case that Sotheby's has always, apparently, been wholly, and scandalously inattentive to its long and distinguished history – nothing has been systematic- ally preserved and very little, even of quite recent date, has survived by accident. (This is in sharp contrast to our friendly rivals in King Street, St. James's whose well-kept records from their foundation twenty-two years later[1] have furnished the material for half a dozen histories of Christie's.)'

John Carter also dwelt at some length on the difficulty of doing justice to the founding fathers of the firm while delaying the general reader from reaching the dramatic episodes of the last fifty years which probably interested him more. But he felt it was essential not to ignore the long succession of historic book sales from Dr. Richard Mead, Richard Heber and Thomas Corser down to the Hamilton Palace Library which included William Beckford's and the monu- mental Henry Huth and Britwell Sales which occupied the best part of a decade. Carter also counselled the reader to start with Part II and to return later to the as yet unwritten Part I, in 'the hope that he may be sufficiently curious to turn back to the origins, earlier years and gradual development of what has long been one of the country's proudest and most widely respected institutions'.

Soon after drafting this, however, John must have realised that he was mortally ill and asked me to take over from him. I had assigned to me as adviser on the early history, about which I knew very little, Dr. Tim Munby, Librarian of King's College, Cambridge, certainly the most knowledgeable and erudite student of early book trade history in the world. There followed a marvellous collaborative programme in Cambridge's best tutorial tradition, when I spent the occasional whole day (snatched from a busy life in publishing) in the dream-like setting of Tim's room in King's College, the walls lined with desirable bibliographical treasures, overlooking the three most beautiful buildings in England. I had the free use of Tim's library and each time I left Cambridge after such a visit I took with me an armful of volumes of essential reading. Alas, John Carter and Tim Munby died within three weeks of each other after some eighteen months of spasmodic collaboration, and I was left to find my own way.

Thus my first three years on the job (it was very much a part-time occupa- tion) were spent in becoming familiar with the firm as it was in its many and

1. We now know it to be thirty-three years later.

varied activities; in talking to existing and retired members of the staff; in studying and familiarising myself with the most important sales during a period of two-and-a-half centuries. The first essential was to find out which *were* the important sales and events. I constructed a detailed chronology which became a sort of bible. I read my way through the existing literature. I searched through libraries and record offices all over the country (and indeed in America) for useful source material and references. I combed booksellers' catalogues for likely annotated catalogues and letters. Persistence led to lucky breaks. Someone remembered an old file that should have been thrown away and was not; someone else had preserved an ancient bundle of letters. Invaluable newspaper cuttings, memoranda and pencilled drafts fell out of old catalogues in the innumerable departmental libraries at Bond Street. Those were the red letter days. I became familiar with gauging the age of perished rubber bands, rusty pins and paperclips that held together undated documentation. I also began to appreciate the appalling disparity between personal memories and documented records of the same events, with which professional historians of the contemporary scene must be all too familiar. Like some interrogator from an intelligence organisation I recorded diverse recollections of identical occasions and learned to sift out the facts they had in common and to evaluate the inevitable discrepancies. Sometimes it was simply a difference in emphasis (the Goldschmidt Sale); sometimes there was a total conflict of views (the acquisition of Parke-Bernet). The sale-room is a fine breeding ground of anecdote, but anecdote is a great enemy of accuracy, particularly where figures are concerned. It is astonishing how important sales, which take place in public in the full blaze of promotional activity, can so soon be forgotten. For the participants, one exciting sale merges into another. It becomes difficult to recall dates and to isolate the sequence of events.

In the end, however, I found at least three collections of source material that were of primary importance (all, of course, within Sotheby's) and a host of minor ones that gradually provided the basis of the story. My very presence acted as a sort of magnet. When members of the firm came across an old document or letter, a copy of it found its way on to my desk. Before they threw away dusty files I was asked to look through them. If Sotheby's ever establishes an archive, it will consist largely of items which I saved for posterity at short notice before they were thrown away to make room for material of more recent vintage. More than three hundred interviews gave human substance to dry fact. Eventually I became so familiar with the more prominent but long departed personalities in the story that I got to know their habits, their idiosyncracies and occasionally even discovered the skeletons in their cupboards: I could positively understand how their minds worked in the face of the problems they had to solve.

In the end it took some seven years to complete the work for publication. As a result of the strenuous search for supporting documentation, a dramatic change of circumstance occurred about two-thirds of the way through that period: where at first there had only been a great void, there was now a plethora of information. Sotheby's had, in a manner of speaking, retrieved its past.

iv *Source Material*

References to published sources are included throughout the text. While there is a good deal on the early book collectors and the dispersal of their collections, there is relatively little that gives much information on Sotheby's itself. For anyone who wishes to know more of the history of book collecting, Seymour de Ricci's *English Collectors of Books and Manuscripts (1530–1930) and their Marks of Ownership*, first published from the text of de Ricci's Sandars Lectures in 1921 and re-published in 1960, is an admirably succinct introduction to the subject. De Ricci shows with startling clarity the importance of the book auctioneer in redistributing libraries since the early eighteenth century. A. N. L. Munby's various works are all immensely useful and remarkably readable. The five volumes of *Phillipps' Studies* go much further than delineating the activities of the great collector: they are the best available description of the whole book trade of the period. His *Cult of the Autograph Letter* and *Connoisseurs and Medieval Miniatures* are each invaluable in their own field. Mention should also be made of the series of twelve volumes entitled *Sale Catalogues of Libraries of Eminent Persons* of which Tim Munby was the general editor (London, 1971–1975), which reproduce a number of important Sotheby sale catalogues in facsimile, each with a useful introduction.

Lugt is remarkable in plotting as complete a range of sales as one is likely to get. There are 58,704 separate catalogues listed in the first three volumes of his *Repertoire des Catalogues de Ventes Publiques interessant l'Art ou la Curiosité*. But these are dry bones which can only act as a checklist. George Redford's *Art Sales* has some very useful information on picture sales up to 1887. Redford was *The Times* sale-room correspondent. It seems that he rarely included Sotheby's in his ambit. His descriptions are almost exclusively of Christie's sales. Algernon Graves refined Redford in his own *Art Sales* (three volumes, 1918 to 1921) but only helps in tracing the history of individual paintings. In his *Economics of Taste* (three volumes, 1961, 1963 and 1970) Gerald Reitlinger valiantly attempted a complete survey of the art market, principally in Britain, and based it largely on Christie's records. The American auction scene in the present century has been magnificently described in Wesley Towner's *The Elegant Auctioneers* (New York, 1970). Despite the author's death a few years earlier his papers were preserved for some time. To my infinite regret they had been destroyed only weeks before I learned of their whereabouts.

The great bulk of the information on which this book is based is taken from Sotheby's own catalogues and from primary source material that came to light during its compilation. The firm's own annotated copies of sale catalogues are reasonably complete only from the 1920s onwards. A useful but patchy run of eighteenth- and nineteenth-century catalogues (of which a detailed index exists) were acquired from the Robinson Brothers after they had purchased the

Phillipps' Collection. An almost complete run of the firm's catalogues from the beginning to the present time is in the British Library. I must confess I did not have the courage to look at the literally miles of shelving in the British Museum Iron Gallery until the work was practically completed. The sight is so daunting as to stop any putative author in his tracks. Tim Munby calculated that there were about 2,300 catalogues between 1733–1850, 2,700 between 1851–1900 and some 5,000 between 1901–1945, making some 10,000 in all. If one includes Parke-Bernet, Belgravia and the firm's various other sale-rooms, the total number by 1980 must be well in excess of 30,000. Catalogues of the period 1733–1945 were put on microfilm under the editorship of Tim Munby, assisted by Lenore Coral, in 1971. Sir Francis Watson acted as consultant on the sale of pictures and works of art and estimated that 1,544 sales out of 4,480 by 1900 had been devoted to works of art of some sort or another. The firm possesses a complete run of picture sale catalogues from 1870–1938 that had been accumulated by Vicars Bros., art dealers, and A. C. R. Carter's fully annotated set of picture sale catalogues from 1913–1935 which Carter assembled and grangerised while he was sale-room correspondent of the *Daily Telegraph* and editor of *The Year's Art* (the annual ran from 1882 to 1947). I have drawn a great deal of valuable information from Sotheby's own annual which appeared as *Sotheby's Season* from 1957 to 1962, as *The Ivory Hammer* from 1963 to 1966 and as *Art at Auction* from 1967 to the present. Most departments have their own extensive photographic reference libraries.

Two of the three deed boxes of material that eventually came to light – at different times and in different places – contained the papers which Tom Hodge, Barlow, Hobson and des Graz had each regarded as their most important private papers. These included the 1919 sale document between Hodge and Barlow, Hobson and Warre; the letters relating to private sales, in particular those from Pierpont Morgan; the file on Lord Crawford's collection of French Revolution documents; Barlow's letters offering employment to des Graz, and later chastising him, and the quarrel between Hobson and Warre about the Russian visit. Another box was filled with the staff files relating to the period between the wars. Wilfrid Hodgson produced the invaluable correspondence between Hodge and the Hodgsons on the sale of the business, which had been preserved at Chancery Lane. Messrs. Quaritch were kind enough to allow me the free run of all their material at Golden Square relating to their early history, which, as will be seen from Chapter 5, was inextricably linked with Sotheby's, and Mr. E. M. Dring found correspondence between his father and Tom Hodge. Anthony Hobson helped enormously by passing on to me many of his father's working papers which had been preserved, as well as his own. Jock Campbell never ceased to discover invaluable documentation from odd corners of Bond Street where they had come to light, and also from sales of autograph material as they went on view. Joe Och, the firm's own legal consultant, must take more credit than any other single individual for producing a seemingly endless stream of material once he knew what would be of value. It was acutely tantalising that while I discovered a complete index of the subjects in Major Warre's 'private file', which had always apparently been locked away even from his own secretary, the documents in question were never found, despite the most diligent searches. It was Ernie Collman who first drew my attention to the forgotten proprietors' ledgers from the beginning of the century that filled an entire broom cupboard at the top of St. George Street. Ledgers were for many years the backbone of the business. They included all the vital information of *which* owners had sold *what*, and all the miscellaneous expenses involved, such as the cab fares of the cataloguers, the exact catalogue production costs and even such details as the price of the string for tying up the parcels. There were other ledgers which held riveting information on what dealers had bought, and when, and what they paid for it, and when they hadn't *and* needed to be chastised for taking too long over settling their accounts. I hasten to add that these all relate to the pre-war period. Such detail was recorded in painstaking, beautiful copperplate, embellishing the bare facts with an inextinguishable life and personality – an astonishing contrast to today's arid computer print-outs.

Various family papers eventually came to light: long correspondences with Tancred Borenius, Charles Bell and some of Sir Montague Barlow's personal memorabilia. Tom Norton unearthed a whole cache of documents relating to the founding of Parke-Bernet. No one helped more than Jim Kiddell in locating unique copies of catalogues, biographical information on dealers and collectors, and in producing his own files of special sales – such as the Wilton Armour Sale – without which the book would have been infinitely poorer.

Contemporary newspaper accounts are an invaluable aid to sale-room history. Those of the late nineteenth century and early twentieth century often included a spirited re-telling of what the auctioneer had said and between whom the bidding duels had been fought. I spent many weary hours tracking them down for individual sales. It was only when the book was almost finished that Sotheby's virtually complete press-cuttings books from between 1911 and 1950 came to light in a boarded-up loft, though it took nearly three months to clean them.

Finally of course there were personal recollections. I filled some fifteen note-books with details of interviews and taped a great many more. It would have been quite possible to write two companion volumes to the present work: one entitled 'How Sotheby's Did Me', and the other 'How I Did Sotheby's'. There was a wonderful mixture of veneration and irreverence from some of the leading *personae*. One of the most delightful comments was Tim Munby's reaction when asked by Geoffrey Hobson whether he would take over the cherished post from Rham of being Dr. Rosenbach's London liaison man. 'What!' said Tim 'Work for that pickled old ruin. Never!'.

v *Future Indicative*

At the time of the Von Hirsch sale in June 1978 Queen Elizabeth, the Queen Mother came to lunch at Bond Street and a number of directors showed her round the collection afterwards. Like a bevy of senior officers in the Praetorian Guard the group consisting of Peter Wilson, Peregrine Pollen, Graham Llewellyn, Lord Westmorland and Peter Spira made an impressive sight as they accompanied Her Majesty, a tiny figure in bright green, around the galleries. 'What will happen', asked a visitor standing beside me, 'when Peter Wilson goes?' It was a pertinent question. Late in 1979 he announced that he would retire in the following February. David Westmorland, his first cousin, a fact of which few people were aware, took over as chairman at the firm's annual general meeting in 1980. He had been a director for fourteen years; he was also Master of the Horse and for many years a Lord-in-Waiting to the Queen.

It is perhaps germane to summarise the extent of Lord Westmorland's responsibilities. He now heads a globe-encircling group with three busy sale-rooms in London, four more in the English provinces, two in New York, one in Los Angeles, another in Amsterdam. In Europe there are offices in Florence, Rome, Milan, Paris, Monte Carlo, Munich, Frankfurt, Hamburg, Brussels, Madrid, Stockholm, Zurich and Geneva. Many hold their own local sales. There are further regional offices in Dublin, Edinburgh, Harrogate, Cheltenham, Cambridge and Bournemouth. In the US the following cities have offices: Boston, Chicago, Connecticut, Houston, Palm Beach, Philadelphia, Washington, San Francisco and Honolulu. There is a new sale-room in Toronto and an office in Vancouver. Offices in Johannesburg and Hong Kong regularly stage sales. Finally there is a representative in Argentina, two in Brazil and another in Melbourne, Australia. All of them handle consignments in every field of connoisseurship from medieval manuscripts to vintage motor cars.

A recent development is a new-style link between East and West consisting of offices in two branches of Japan's leading department store, Seibu. The Sotheby Parke Bernet Group includes what has after four years become a major real estate company in the USA, a shipping firm in the UK, and it employs rather more than 1,500 people worldwide, among them probably 300 with expert knowledge in specialist fields.

On assuming office, Lord Westmorland forecast a period of consolidation. Sotheby's has been blessed with a mixture of brilliant innovators and outstanding consolidators. The firm could never have survived so long without the exceptional talents of Samuel Baker, Samuel Leigh Sotheby, Sir Montagu Barlow and Peter Wilson, each of whom gave the company a new identity. Equally the firm's character has been enriched by men like George Leigh, John Wilkinson, Tom Hodge, Geoffrey Hobson, Charles des Graz and, latterly, Jim Kiddell. The principal test of the 1980s will be to maintain a fluent dialogue at all levels between London and New York.

The group is headed by a lively and responsive senior management. Over recent years the command structure has tended to be fluid. The chairman and his deputies in London constitute what is called the 'Office of Chairman', recently renamed the Executive Committee. Areas of responsibility are very clearly defined. New York is now completely autonomous, but is answerable to the group board. John Marion is President and has as his recently appointed chief operating officer Frederick H. Scholtz. There is a local board and a local executive committee. On both sides of the Atlantic the firm has made, and continues to make, intelligent use of new technological development, by dint of such aids as computerised accounts control and in-house television links between the public counters and expert departments. It has perforce to learn unceasingly about security. There are plans for greatly extended capital investment. But so far neither corporate ambition nor technical adjuncts have been allowed to interfere with what the firm's long tradition has established as the two most vital elements of its business: personal relationships with clients of every kind and the unceasing application of scholarship and expertise to what passes through the sale-room.

As specialisation has grown, departments within the firm have, to all intents and purposes, become a multitude of smaller businesses linked by centralised services (not always that: in London each department has its own administrators) and a common management. Thus each cell is dependent for its success on the skill and vigour of the man or woman at the head of it.

Proof perhaps of ultimate self-confidence is the fact that New York – as it divides its business between York Avenue and Madison Avenue – will simply call itself 'Sotheby's' in the future. Farewell Hiram Parke; farewell Otto Bernet.

If anyone should ever seek an example of an activity where competition has proved a spur to endeavour, he could not do better than to study the fine art auction field. It is a tough, often cut-throat business today. Determination and brains are essential ingredients for success in a world where haste and bustle, and rapid reaction to constantly changing circumstances, are the norm. What has become particularly clear with the growth of all the contenders in this field is the importance of sound financial management of a highly international kind and – just as important from the client's point of view – thoughtful and efficient administration. There are few greater frustrations than mislaid goods and lost opportunities.

Economic crises, even inflation, have now become a way of life. It seems that only a satisfactory resolution of the future of the world's energy supplies will order things differently, so it is unlikely that such factors will change in the short term. Sotheby's have led the way in showing that great art can be a sound form of investment. In one way this has begun to be counter-productive. People have become reluctant to let go of objects they enjoy owning when money is constantly losing its value. In contrast there are parts of the world where the firm or its rivals have barely begun to scratch the surface of the potential markets. That is where the future will lie. For the outsider the next few years may reveal a fascinating spectacle if sales by the group in America for the first time surpass those in Europe. The reader will learn from the pages that follow that the past has frequently produced precedents for what are later regarded as fresh developments, but if the balance of power comes down in favour of America, that for Sotheby's may well inaugurate a testing period for the rules of the game learned in the previous two hundred and fifty years.

PART ONE

From Samuel Baker
to Tom Hodge

A

CATALOGUE

Of a Choice

LIBRARY of BOOKS,

Consisting of

History, Antiquity, Divinity, Physick, Mathe-
maticks, Law, Novels, Romances, &c. &c.

In most LANGUAGES,

Most of them neatly bound :

Among which are the following ;

FOLIO.
Campbell's Vitruvius, L.P.
Echard's Hist. of England, 3 vol.
Ashmole's Order of the Garter.
Montfaucon's Antiquities, 5 vol.
Dryden's Plays, 2 vol.
Leybourn's Mathemat. Sciences.
Ben Johnson's Works, best.
Collier's Eccles. Hist. 2 vol.
Dr. Hammond's Works, 4 vol.
Fidde's Body of Divinity, 2 vol.
Kettlewell's Works, 2 vol.
Machiaveli's Works, best.

S. Chrysostomi Opera, 8 tom. Etom.
Buchanani Opera, a Ruddimanno.
Brady's History of England.
Dryden's Virgil, Cuts.
Cambden's Britannia, by Gibson.
Madox's Firma Burgi.
QUARTO.
Addison's Works, 4 vol.
Wright's Travels, 2 vol.
Thomson's Seasons.
Bentley's Milton.
Tyson's Anatomy of a Pigmie.
Tournefort Voy. de Levant, 2 tom.

Which will be sold Cheap (the Lowest Price mark'd to each
Book in the Catalogue) on Tuesday the 19th of this Instant
February, 1733-4, at SAMUEL BAKER's, Bookseller, at
the Angel and Crown, in Russel-street, Covent-Garden; and
to continue every Day till all are sold.

CATALOGUES may be had gratis at the Place of Sale; at Mr.
Osborne's, Bookseller, at the Golden-Ball, in Pater-noster Row;
and at Mr. Huddleston's, Bookseller, in St. Martin's Court, Leicester-
Fields.

A
CATALOGUE
Of the GENUINE and ELEGANT
LIBRARY
OF
JOHN BABER, Esq;
Of SUNNING-HILL PARK,
Lately Deceased,
CONTAINING
A good Collection of Classicks and Miscellaneous
Books; with the greatest Number of the best and
scarcest ITALIAN Books that were ever sold in any
one Collection in this Kingdom, and in the
finest Condition;
LIKEWISE
Many of the best and rarest SPANISH Authors;

Which will begin to be sold by AUCTION,

By SAMUEL BAKER,
At his House in York-street, Covent Garden,

On Monday, the 31st of March, 1766, and to continue the ten following Evenings.

Beginning each Evening at Six o'Clock.

N. B. The Books may be viewed on Monday,
March the 24th, and every Day after to the Time of
Sale.

CATALOGUES to be had of the following Booksellers:
Mr. DODSLEY's, Pall-Mall; Mr. ROBSON's, Bond-Street;
Mr. WALTER's, Charing-Cross; Mr. BROTHERTON's, Corn-
hill; Mr. OWEN's, Temple Bar; and at the Place of
SALE.

(Price Six-pence)

CONDITIONS of SALE.

I. THAT he who bids most is the Buyer; but
if any Dispute arises, the Book or Books
be put up to Sale again.

II. That no Person advances less than Six-pence
each Bidding; and after the Book arises to One
Pound, not less than One Shilling.

III. The Books are supposed to be perfect;
but if any appear otherwise before taken away,
the Buyer is at his Choice to take or leave them.

IV. That each Person give in his Name, and
pay Five Shillings in the Pound (if demanded) for
what he buys; and that no Book be deliver'd in
Time of Selling, unless first paid for.

V. The Books must be taken away at the Buyer's
Expence, and the Money paid at the Place of Sale,
within three Days after the Sale is ended.

Any Gentleman who cannot attend the Sale,
may have their Commissions receiv'd, and
faithfully executed,

By their most Humble Servant,

SAMUEL BAKER.

A
Catalogue
OF THE
GENUINE AND VALUABLE COLLECTION
OF
COINS AND MEDALS;
CONSISTING OF
GREEK, ROMAN, SAXON, ENGLISH AND SCOTCH;
Many very Rare, and in a high State of Preservation:
TOGETHER WITH A
FEW CHOICE ANTIQUE RINGS,
Bronzes, Marbles, Raphael's Ware, &c. &c.
THE PROPERTY OF THE LATE
MR. JOHN THANE,
Author and Editor of the British Autography, in 3 vol. quarto.

Which will be Sold by Auction,

By MR. SOTHEBY,
At his new and more extensive Premises,
No. 3, WELLINGTON-STREET, STRAND,
On MONDAY, the 19th of APRIL, 1819,
And Five following Days, at Twelve o'Clock.

To be Viewed till the Sale, and Catalogues (price 1s. 6d.) had at
the Place of Sale.

Printed by J. DAVY, Queen Street, Seven Dials.

Overleaf – The first known catalogue issued by Samuel Baker; *top left* – A typical Baker book-auction catalogue; *top right* – Baker's 'Conditions of Sale' were delightfully simple; *bottom left* – One of the few catalogues issued by John Sotheby at a time when he had no partners. The firm had recently moved to Wellington Street and remained there for almost a hundred years.

I

Father of our Tribe

WE know exactly what the founder looks like because there is an excellent portrait of him hanging in Sotheby's to this day. It shows a serious, sedate man in middle age in a bob-wig and a plum-coloured coat. Naturally he is holding a book in his hand. He has the appearance of a man with an orderly mind, well used to exercising authority, who can look back on life with some satisfaction. As it happens he bears an uncanny resemblance to Dr. Johnson as he was painted by Joshua Reynolds in 1756. In fact this is Samuel Baker at sixty. We know this precisely because Dibdin, a famous nineteenth-century bibliographer, records a conversation with Samuel Sotheby[1] in which the latter says: 'he was as fine a fellow as ever broke a crust of bread and we have a portrait of him up stairs taken not long before he died in his sixtieth year and with every tooth in his head as sound as a roach'.[2]

At twenty-two, when Baker's name first appears on a sale catalogue of books, we have to imagine him as a bright, cheerful, busy and remarkably efficient individual[3] who knew the intricacies of his trade sufficiently well to produce a catalogue that compares very favourably with others of its time. It was a *bookseller's* catalogue listing mostly old books, which states the price of every title, and so one must assume that he had probably learned his job as an apprentice to another bookseller.[4] The first such catalogue is dated 19 February 1733-34[5] and two others followed in the same year on 30 April and 14 November. We know of ten more which had appeared by 1744. In 1745 Baker issued his first *auction* catalogue. Here the phrase 'which will be sold by auction' has replaced the phrase 'which will be sold cheap'.

1. Baker's great-nephew (see page 19).
2. *Bibliographical Decameron*, Tenth Day, p.446, 1817.
3. Dibdin says: 'a hale, healthy, joyous fellow'.
4. On 14 April 1760 Baker sold the library of John King, Bookseller. A copy of this catalogue in the Bodleian contains a hand-written note that King was the uncle of the auctioneer. It may well be that Baker learned his trade under John King. He was also registered – at the tender age of fifteen – as an apprentice to Richard Mallard of St. John's Lane, for an annual wage of £5.
5. Some dates at this period are bedevilled by the inclusion of double years, i.e. 1733-34. The explanation is that until 1751, the legal new year in England began on March 25, though New Year's Day was popularly celebrated on 1 January, as it is now. For all dates between 1 January and 24 March, it was therefore quite usual to print two year dates: the legal and popular years.
   In Samuel Baker's time, the matter was further complicated by two other facts: the legal new year in Scotland had been changed to 1 January since 1600; but the whole of Britain was eleven days ahead of the rest of Europe, since we still followed the Julian Calendar. Parliament finally sorted out the confusion by passing an act making the legal new year start on 1 January from 1751, and changing to the Gregorian calendar by losing eleven days in September 1752.

For generations the sale of the library of a Dr. Thomas Pellet was thought to have been Sam Baker's first auction sale. This story was put about by Dibdin because he tells us that there is a note on the flyleaf of a copy of the relevant catalogue in Baker's own hand which reads, 'The first Auction sold by Sam Baker, 1744'.[1] But close comparison of this note which Dibdin reproduces shows that it is not in fact in Baker's hand at all. Furthermore the conditions of sale, usually signed by the auctioneer, are signed by one Joseph Brigstock, a lesser-known auctioneer, together with John Atkinson, 'writer'; writer in this context seems to indicate that he was the cataloguer, for he signed a number of book catalogues issued by other auctioneers at about this period. Finally, the entire presentation of the Pellet sale catalogue, looked at from a typographical, linguistic and promotional point of view, is not that usually adopted by Baker.

Our Sam's incontrovertible first auction was of the valuable library of the Rt. Hon. Sir John Stanley, Bart, 'containing several Hundred scarce and valuable Books in all branches of Polite Literature'. The catalogue announced that the sale was to be held over ten nights in the Great Room, over Exeter Exchange in the Strand beginning on Monday, 11 March 1744–45. The conditions of sale are signed by Samuel Baker, Auctioneer, and again by John Atkinson, Writer. There were some 457 lots (every book was sold as a separate lot in those days), so each evening's sale sessions must have been quite short.

Baker's next recorded sale of the library of the Rev. William Stuart, D.D., late Chancellor of the diocese of Exeter, was moved to Paul's Coffee House, near St. Paul's churchyard. Its first session was on the evening of 3 February 1746 and it continued for nineteen nights. In fact, it was a joint effort with John Whiston of Fleet Street, whose career as a book auctioneer continued for another thirty years. One gains the impression that Whiston was a man who did not like working on his own. When later he and Baker ceased to collaborate, Whiston joined forces with Benjamin White, another auctioneer and bookseller. They continued together for fourteen years though towards the end of their respective careers each again found himself another partner, in White's case his own son.

Baker's next – and solo[2] – auction sale, of which a catalogue has survived, took him into the realm of the fine arts. (It is, in fact, recorded that he was an early member of the Royal Society of Arts.)[3] It consisted of the 'Scarce and Curious Books of Sculpture, Prints and Architecture being the Collection of Sir Thomas

1. Sotheby's presented its entire run of annotated sale catalogues from 1733 up to the end of the 1842–43 season to the British Museum in March 1848. These contained both the prices which the books had fetched and the purchaser's name of each lot. The marked Pellet catalogue was certainly among them but has disappeared in recent years. Further batches continuously up-dating the series followed in September 1860 and have done so ever since.
2. Curiously the conditions are again signed jointly by Baker and Whiston. Whiston is also listed as the first bookseller whose catalogues of this particular sale 'may be had *gratis*'. The fact that most such catalogues were given away free makes it the more surprising that so many have survived.
3. He was proposed for the Society by the clockmaker brothers, Daniel and Thomas Grignion who were related to the painter.

Franklands, Bart, Deceased' and lasted two days on 18 and 19 June 1747. There were many art and architectural books copiously illustrated with engravings as well as collections of loose prints, a large number after famous Italian Masters. Thus lot 45, which sold for £1 10s., contained 'a collection of prints by Caracci, Dominichini, Ra. Urbin, Vasari, Titian, Marat &c, bound in blue Turkey'; lot 108 consisted of 'views of Venice and other very curious Prints by Palma Tintorett, Zucchi, Basan &c'. The catalogue was printed in a rather more lavish format than any that Baker had issued previously.

The terms and conditions under which Baker organised his sales were the simplest and the briefest in the business. They were usually printed on the back of the title page or the page following. They made those of other contemporary auctioneers look positively legalistic. The first stated that: 'He who bids most is the Buyer; but if any Dispute arise the Book or Books be put to Sale again'. At first Condition II stated that 'No Person advances less than Threepence each bid; Six-pence after Five Shillings; and after the Book arises to One Pound no less than a Shilling'. But after a few years the threepenny bids were banished, although they returned later in the century.

The other conditions related to the right to reject books if they were found to be imperfect, the need for a part payment immediately after the sale and to the fact that lots had to be removed at the buyer's expense and paid for within three days. In Baker's later years, inexplicably the conditions of sale were omitted and only re-appeared after Leigh had joined him.

Book sales were organised by size: the octavos came first; then the quartos; finally the folios. In the fixed-price catalogues there were also sections of duodecimos, a small size which was very popular for collected, multi-volume sets of established authors and thus ideal for libraries. They were also known as 'Twelves'. The titles given were short. They were rarely longer than a single line and usually included the author, thus – Birch's Life of Boyle, Terry's Sermons, Sprigg's England's Recovery under Sir T. Fairfax, Gordon's History of Amphitheatres. Dates of publication were always included, presumably because they pinpointed the edition of a book; sometimes the city in which the book had been published was also given. In the fixed-price sales the order of authors was alphabetical: in the early auction catalogues it seems completely random. The preliminary matter and descriptive detail supplied by the auctioneer of catalogues of especially important sales were often, infuriatingly, in Latin. This was because Latin was very much an international language, and understood by continental bidders like the French and the Dutch, though there can be no doubt that it also lent a spurious air of scholarship.

In Baker's early days, important and particularly expensive titles were set in italics. Thus lot 186 of the library of a Dr. Richard Rawlinson, sold on 29 March 1756, is printed as *A Treatyse Dyalogue of Dives and Paupers, that is to saye, the Ryche and the Poore. Emprinted by me Wynken de Worde at Westmonstre, 1486.*

Major sales continued remorselessly for days on end: forty, even fifty, continuous sessions were not uncommon. It must have required the patience of Job to sit right through them, particularly when one remembers the hard, wooden benches provided for buyers attending the sale, which are shown in contemporary drawings.

The Rawlinson Library was indeed the most celebrated and extensive that had come Samuel Baker's way and it was a feather in his cap that he was asked to dispose of it, for there was no shortage of competing auctioneers. Rawlinson was the son of a former Lord Mayor of London and, like his brother (whose library had contained more than 200,000 volumes), he was an enthusiastic bibliophile, specialising in history and topography. We learn from the eighteenth-century diarist, Thomas Hearne, that Rawlinson, who was called to the Bar in 1705 and applied himself especially to the study of Municipal Law, had four rooms in Grays Inn which were so filled with books that he was obliged to sleep in the passage. Even though he bequeathed over five thousand manuscripts and many particularly valuable books to the Bodleian Library at Oxford, it took Baker no less than fifty days to sell the remaining books alone. There were 9405 lots which fetched £1161 18s. 6d. A second sale devoted principally to 'upwards of Twenty Thousand Pamphlets, reduced into lots under proper heads' took only nine days starting on 3 March 1757, and realised £203 13s. 6d. The cataloguing here was sometimes of the sketchiest kind. Thus lot 82 reads 'Seventeen Tracts on Various useful subjects'; and lot 143 reads 'Twenty-one Voyages and Travels, *chiefly old*'; and lot 144 'Six Voyages and Travels, *black letter*'. There was a further sale of Rawlinson's 'Prints, Books of Prints and Drawings' which lasted eight evenings and the catalogue speaks of 'upwards of Ten Thousand Prints'. One hundred and three of them by Dürer fetched a mere £1 10s. 6d. and a large collection of woodcuts by the same artist only 2s. 6d. Twenty-four etchings by Rembrandt, sold as four lots, realised £3 5s. The total came to £163 10s. 3d. It was quite clear that here was too much for the market to absorb at one time and Baker endeavoured to take care not to make the same mistake again.

In view of these results it is not surprising that he pursued the bookselling side of the business vigorously. From the rare survival of some correspondence we learn of Baker's appointment in 1739 as one of six leading booksellers designated to act as official agents for the Society for the Encouragement of Learning. This body had come into being three years earlier to assist authors in the publication of their works. There were about a hundred members, and the Duke of Richmond was President. After a number of years, however, it became clear that there was a conflict of interest between the Society's objectives and the commercial activities of the booksellers (who were also, of course, publishers) which was bound to doom it to failure.

One of Baker's five fellow agents for the Society was the veteran bookseller, Thomas Osborne (who was not an auctioneer himself but used Christopher Cock when he needed the services of one), who had recently bought the largest private library to have come on the market, that of Edward Harley, Earl of Oxford, for £14,000. Osborne felt that this called for a special catalogue and indeed for special cataloguing with more explicit descriptions of each book than was usual. The man he employed for this immense task (for there were 40,000 titles) was the son of a country bookseller, Samuel Johnson.[1] This detailed scrutiny of so much diverse literature was to stand Dr. Johnson, with his marvellously retentive memory, in good stead all his life. His model cataloguing was certainly closely studied by his contemporaries.

Baker's activities were even more diverse, for he also sold stationery. The catalogue of 21 June 1743 includes a note that 'All Sorts of STATIONERY WARE sold by Samuel Baker, Bookseller . . .'. From a letter written early in the nineteenth century by a relative of the Sotheby family we learn that the writer's grandparents bought their stationery from the firm of booksellers started by Samuel Baker. Additionally, Baker also acted as a publisher. In his very first catalogue of 1733 he advertised:

A Treatise of Arithmetick, in Whole Numbers and Fractions, where in all the necessary practical rules are laid down in the plainest and most familiar Terms and the Truth of each Rule demonstrated . . . the whole being designed and compos'd, not only for the Benefit of young Students, but of those who are desirous of being rationally skilful in the Science of Arithmetick. By *Thomas Weston*, late Master of the Academy of Greenwich. . . . Price 6s. Printed and sold by Samuel Baker, Bookseller at the Angel and Crown, in Russel-street, Covent Garden.

Similarly, at the end of the catalogue of Dr. Rawlinson's Library he advertises that 'This day is publish'd, Price 5s. sew'd, An Essay towards a new English Translation of the Book of Job, from the Original Hebrew; with a Commentary and some Account of his Life; by *Thomas Heath* Esq; of Exeter' (whose library Baker was to sell only four years later).

The advertisements in early sale catalogues are fascinating for the detailed insight they provide into the world of books. They not only describe forthcoming sales, but also books published by the auctioneer himself and by his fellow booksellers. Presumably in return for this favour they stocked and distributed the catalogues of Baker's own forthcoming sales. Thus the first 1733 catalogue contains the following note at the foot of the title page, 'Catalogues may be had *gratis* at the Place of Sale, at Mr. *Osborne's*, Bookseller, at the *Golden-balls* in *Paternoster Row* and Mr. *Huddlestone's*, Bookseller, in *St. Martin's Court, Leicester Fields'*. Other trade friends who gave this service were Mr. Strahan in Cornhill, Tom Ballard in Little Britain, Mr. Dodsley in Pall Mall, Mr. Chapelle in Grosvenor Street, Mr. Merrills at Cambridge and Mrs. Fletcher at Oxford. Many held auctions of their own, but rarely on their own premises. Taverns and coffee houses had large rooms available for such functions (and, of course, for more festive occasions) and throughout the eighteenth century they were the popular centres of social life for meeting friends, exchanging the latest gossip, reading the newspapers, collecting post, wining and dining, or merely places where one could drink coffee, cocoa and ale or consume bread and cheese.

1. It should be added that Johnson received valiant assistance from William Oldys, who had been the Earl of Oxford's secretary.

Baker advertised sales widely in the newspapers. On 13 April 1742 one could read in *The Daily Advertiser* that 'this day is published a catalogue of A VERY LARGE COLLECTION of Books, containing several Libraries and Parcels lately purchas'd, consisting of upwards of five thousand Volumes in all Parts of Polite Literature with some Italian and Spanish. Which will begin to be sold cheap, the lowest price being mark'd to each Book, on Thursday next, the 10th instant, At Samuel Baker's, Bookseller. At Chaucer's Head, Russel-street, Covent Garden'. Baker regularly used *The Daily Advertiser* for announcements of sales between 1740 and 1750. Another journal he favoured was the *Whitehall Evening Post*.

As his business prospered he moved into new premises of his own in York Street, Covent Garden and there he remained for many years. The first and most memorable sale from the new premises was of the library of Dr. Richard Mead. This sale had preceded Rawlinson's by two years in 1754. Mead was the most brilliant physician of his time. He had studied at the universities of Utrecht, Leyden and Naples before returning to the house where he was born in Stepney, and building up an immensely successful practice there. He moved to Great Ormond Street in 1720. His house there[1] became so full of books, pictures and antiquities that he had to construct a private museum in the garden at the rear of the house. His income was said to have exceeded £7,000 a year, an enormous sum at that time, but he devoted his wealth to the patronage of science, literature and the arts. When Watteau was unwell during a visit to London, for example, he came to Dr. Mead to be cured and painted him two fine pictures in gratitude. Mead bought other canvases direct from Canaletto and Pannini. His large circle of close friends included Newton, Halley, Pope and Dr. Johnson. In 1727 he was appointed Physician-in-Ordinary to King George II, but declined the post of President of the College of Physicians in 1734 because he wanted to retire. Dr. Mead had an insatiable curiosity. He was an omnivorous reader and became a great scholar. His library exceeded ten thousand printed volumes and many rare manuscripts. Not surprisingly his collection was especially rich in medical works and also in the earliest editions of the classics. Until well into the nineteenth century the latter were, of course, the principal staple of the devoted bibliophile; Mead, for example, owned the Spira Virgil of 1470 on vellum and the 1469 and 1472 editions of the *Historia Naturalis* of Pliny.[2]

Baker organised the sale in two parts. The first began on 18 November 1754

1. It was the original site of the famous children's hospital.
2. The 1469 edition was bought at Mead's sale by the King of France for eleven guineas, an early instance of a continental collector buying in London; the 1742 edition was sold for eighteen guineas to a dealer. One of the most beautiful of Mead's manuscripts was a missal said to have been illuminated by Raphael and his pupils for a Queen of France. Horace Walpole bought it for £48 6s. At the sale of his own Strawberry Hill Collection in 1842 it was bought by the Earl of Waldegrave for £115 10s. It was later in Alfred de Rothschild's collection and was sold in the Countess of Carnarvon sale at Christie's in 1925 for £2,100 and made its final appearance in the sale-room at Lord Rothermere's sale at Sotheby's in 1942 when it realised £2,500.

and lasted twenty-eight days; the second part began on 7 April 1755 and lasted twenty-nine days. Most of Mead's books were in particularly fine condition and the two sales realised £5,508 10s. 11d.

His collection of pictures, drawings, prints, cameos, coins and classical sculpture were sold separately as the *Museum Meadianum*[1] by the foremost art auctioneer of his time, Abraham Langford (who had taken over the business from Christopher Cock, equally well-known until his retirement shortly before) in three series of sales in 1754 and 1755, and they fetched £10,550 18s. 0d. The pictures alone raised £3,417 11s. in three days. The two Watteaus sold for £42 and £52 10s.; Rubens's portrait of that other great collector, the Earl of Arundel, £36 15s.; David Teniers's the *Inside of the Gallery at Brussels*, £73 10s. The total for Dr. Mead's Collection came to £16,069 8s. 11d., one of the highest sums ever recorded at auction up to the middle of the eighteenth century.

If Mead and Rawlinson were early highlights, Baker continued to be entrusted with the sale of major libraries – that of the novelist Henry Fielding in 1755, of Martin Folkes, President of the Royal Society in 1756, of Sir Uvedale Price, one of the theorists of the Picturesque in 1761. 1764 was something of an *annus mirabilis* because it brought four major sales: Sir Clement Cottrell Dormer's library (twenty nights of sales for 3,082 lots: the catalogue repeatedly states in large type 'N.B. The Books in this Collection are in general of the best Editions, and in the finest Condition, many of them in *large* Paper, bound in *Morocco*, *gilt leaves*, &c, &c');[2] the books, and particularly the manuscripts of the Earl of Clarendon; the library of John Wilkes, M.P. after his arrest and of Richard Mead (the doctor's son). In 1765 there were four sales in the first half of the year (an extensive bookseller's catalogue came out in the second half, as had happened regularly every year since 1758); in 1766 there were five sales including 'the Genuine and Elegant Library of John Baber of Sunning-Hill Park . . . containing the greatest number of the best and scarcest Italian Books that were ever sold in any one collection in this Kingdom'. They cannot have been too popular. 2,069 lots sold for £603 15s. 9d., though we know that Baker made rather a point of dealing in foreign books, because some of his fixed-price sale catalogues contained the advice on the title page that his was the business '*where Books in all Languages are bought and sold*'. A number of these catalogues contained a sub-section headed *Livres Francois et Italien*.

Clearly Baker's successful career was not without its critics. In 1766 the London bookseller, Henry Dell, wrote and published a poem about his world simply called *The Bookseller*. He comments on a hundred members of the trade in 427 lines, and of Baker he says:

---

1. Baker sold this catalogue (the bigger catalogues were not distributed gratis) at the time of the Langford Sale and continued to advertise it in stock for many years.
2. A series of catalogues of famous Continental libraries, i.e. early bibliographies (lots 2362–67), consistently fetched the lowest prices in the sale – 6d. each!

Oh! – waddling like a duck,
To public auctions 'tis you owe your luck,
By them enrich'd, now grown so stiff and proud,
You're like a bashaw, o'er th'inferior croud;
The muse could tell, but prudence stops her tongue,
From what mean trick your vast importance sprung;
I wish *Cervantes* were alive to see,
His Sancho Pancha fresh reviv'd in thee.[1]

We have little knowledge of the staff employed by Baker, though there was certainly a clerical factotum called James Gardener at York Street who frequently signed receipts in Baker's absence, and a journeyman called Andrew Edwards whom Baker mentions in his will. By 1767 though, when Baker was fifty-five and he had run the business on his own for thirty-four years, he must have felt the need to take a young man into the firm, not only to assist him but also perhaps to carry on after his own death. The young man he chose was George Leigh, the ninth son of the Rev. Egerton Leigh, LL.D., former rector of Lymme and Middle, and at the time one of the canons residentiary of Hereford Cathedral and possessor of the West Hall of High Leigh in Cheshire.

At the age of twenty-five, Leigh was clearly too old to have become an apprentice in the normal sense and the fact that the style of the firm changed to BAKER AND LEIGH almost immediately after the young man's arrival implies that he must have had some knowledge of the job. Certainly there becomes discernible very soon a subtle change in the style of the cataloguing.[2] For the first time we see lots which include more than one title – a habit other book auctioneers had adopted some time earlier. Also we find occasional bibliographical comments on particularly noteworthy aspects of books included. The first sale to be catalogued under the joint imprint of both Baker and Leigh is that of the Library of John Hadley, Physician to the Charter House, on 5 February 1767; and the first Baker and Leigh fixed-price catalogue was issued on 31 March in the same year.

Baker's wife, born Rebecca Flitcroft, who was seven years older than Sam, died at the age of sixty-three in the year after Leigh joined forces with him and

1. Quoted by Terry Belanger in *Publishing History*, Vol. I, 1978. Dell's offering was generally panned on publication and neither Belanger nor I have been able to find any details about 'the mean trick' alluded to.
   The best cataloguer of Baker's generation was Samuel Paterson (1728–1802), who was famed in his day for his prodigious knowledge of the *contents* of books. He issued 'digested' catalogues, where titles were grouped together under subject matter, a practice he is said to have learned from the Paris bookseller, Gabriel Martin. Paterson was also one of the first cataloguers to identify varying editions and issues of the same title, particularly by English writers, in proper chronological sequence. He acted as auctioneer for many years but after going bankrupt took to cataloguing for other booksellers and for many years he acted as librarian to the 1st Marquis of Lansdowne (see page 24). He is probably best remembered for his fine catalogue of the wide-ranging and scholarly library of John Strange, which was used as a bibliographical model by others for many years – including presumably Leigh – because of its completeness of eighteenth-century publications.

was buried in the churchyard of St. Paul's, Covent Garden. It appears that thereafter Sam began to take things easier, and in the contemplation of a long retirement he built himself what was described as a 'delightful villa' at Woodford Bridge, near Chigwell in Essex. The firm's reputation must now have been well established, despite growing competition, because there was an increasing number of sales. The diversity of interests of some of the people whose libraries were sold is fascinating – Chinese history, Provençal linguistics, Rites of the Greek Orthodox Church in Russia, Danish antiquities. It was scholars, divines, lawyers, officers of State and the generally learned who looked upon Baker and Leigh – or rather their executors did – as the obvious firm to dispose of major libraries. In April 1769 came the accolade of being asked to dispose of the duplicates from the library of the British Museum. 1772 saw the sale of the library of the painter, Jonathan Richardson, the Younger, which also included a large number of his equally celebrated father's books. In 1778 Sam had spent some weeks at Woburn Abbey, presumably cataloguing the library there. Two letters to his 'niece' Betsy survive from this period. He complains that there is so much work that he cannot find the time to walk in the Duke of Bedford's magnificent park. Sam and Rebecca had had no children and Betsy was obviously Sam's favourite niece-by-marriage. Born Elizabeth Cotton, she was the wife of John Sotheby. John's parents were Sam's sister, Anne, and John Sotheby the elder, who hailed from York. After the death of Sam's wife it seems that Betsy looked after the household at Baker's London residence as well as doing so occasionally at Woodford Bridge. A later letter from Sam asks her to prepare a particularly fine meal for the following Sunday when a number of guests are coming to dine with Sam. Included among them are a Mr. & Mrs. Grignion. This was the same Charles Grignion who had recently painted Sam's portrait. On another occasion he writes to Betsy that he has just had dinner with Dr. Anthony Askew (a great book collector whose library was eventually sold by the firm) and that Askew is prepared to act as godfather to her new-born child. Several times in these letters, Baker asks Betsy to look into York Street to see whether the business is running smoothly and to ask George Leigh to write to him. Almost every letter concludes with particular greetings to John Sotheby, of whom the old man was evidently very fond.

On 24 April 1778 Samuel Baker died at the age of sixty-six, and was buried alongside his wife and his mother in St. Paul's churchyard in Covent Garden. He had made George Leigh a full partner in 1774 and the sale catalogue of the library of Sir William Duncan (Physician-in-Ordinary to George III) now appeared under the sole imprint of George Leigh. In the event it was the only one that did so, for in his will Baker left twenty pounds apiece to Thomas Payne of Castle Street, Westminster and to Lockyer Davis of Holborn to repay their kindness in assisting his nephew, John Sotheby, in dividing his 'stock in trade' with his partner, George Leigh. Both these men were well-known booksellers whom Baker termed 'two worthy friends' in his will. John Sotheby was thirty-eight when he joined the firm and it appears that he looked after the administration while George Leigh became the auctioneer. The changeover must have been reasonably swift for the first fixed-price list published under the names of LEIGH AND SOTHEBY appeared as soon as 23 July 1778. Thus the business acquired the name it has borne ever since. Ultimately three generations of the Sotheby family were at its helm until 1861.

The Sotheby family came from the delightfully sleepy little market town of Pocklington near Scarborough which lies in open, rolling Yorkshire countryside of rich, chocolate-brown soil that makes wonderful farmland. A wall plaque in Pocklington's eleventh-century parish church, put up by a Victorian descendant of the family, commemorates Robert Sothebee of Birdsall Hall, who took out the family's patent of arms in 1563. He had two wives and nineteen children and died aged eighty in July 1594. The church also contains a fine piece of fourteenth-century stone sculpture known as the Sotheby Cross, donated by the family. It appears to have been a well-kept family secret that our John's grandfather, James (1682–1742), one of five children of an earlier James, and an army officer, never married but was, in fact, the father of twins whose mother died in childbirth, and that John (our John's father) and his sister Mary may have been brought up by an uncle.

Baker's choice of Leigh as helpmate, successor and tutor to John Sotheby was brilliantly contrived. Leigh was universally liked. He was a good auctioneer and it seems evident that he gave the business the additional sophistication and expertise it needed at a time when, under a particularly enlightened monarch, George III, the interest in collecting, literature and the arts received unusual encouragement. Leigh and Sotheby's catalogues became noticeably more elegant in the Eighties and Nineties of the eighteenth century. The detail of the cataloguing improved also, and the prices, particularly of manuscript material and prints, rose gently, but none of this would have been possible without the solid foundations laid by Samuel Baker. His energy and integrity stood out prominently in the cut and thrust of London's vigorous book trade of that period, and he survived and thrived where so many others went to the wall. It seemed particularly apt, therefore, that Samuel Sotheby should refer to Baker, the leading book auctioneer of his time, as the 'Father of our Tribe' when he discussed him with Dibdin years later.

2

The Era of George Leigh and the three Sothebys – John, Samuel and Samuel Leigh

GEORGE LEIGH died in 1816, still in harness after nearly fifty years in the business. He seems to have been an amusing, lively, fair-minded man who gave the relatively dull commerce of book auctioneering an extra dimension of pleasurable anticipation and continuous excitement. The era from 1770 to 1816 was important in the history of book collecting. It saw an increasing interest in early English and Elizabethan literature and a waning in the obsession with the Greek and Roman classics, as well as with the Italian books which had been so highly regarded in the middle of the previous century. A greater interest in manuscripts of all kinds – particularly as historical source material – became discernible and the detail of books began to be more closely studied with corresponding advances in bibliographical description. Book prices too began to rise, but up to the third quarter of the eighteenth century it is difficult to make out any rationale in the value of antiquarian books.

Up to that time most books published during the century sold for ten shillings or less, and the more esoteric books from earlier eras sold at between ten shillings and £1, but in all matters concerning the book trade at this stage there were exceptions to every rule and very little true conformity. It was a rare lot indeed that rose above two guineas and as a rule that would be a heavily illustrated work of reference in many volumes. After 1780 a price of £20 was not that exceptional. Leigh and John Sotheby were well aware of these trends and their catalogues mirrored them conscientiously, though the number of auctions held was still very limited. As far as one can judge from surviving catalogues, up to 1784 the firm rarely staged more than four sales a year; in 1786 the number went up to eight for the first time. This was probably one-fifth of the total number of book auctions held each year in the London area and the principal cities in Britain – again to judge from what has remained extant in the way of catalogues – though a study of contemporary newspaper advertisements leads one to believe that far more sales were held for which no catalogues survive.

As far as a pattern of trading becomes perceptible, Leigh and Sotheby liked to hold the bulk of their sales in the first half of the year, with the occasional sale in December. Presumably the second part of the year was devoted to selling the contents of their fixed-price bookseller's catalogue (it included nearly ten thousand items by 1799) and to the firm's publishing activities which seem to have grown extensively by the end of the century. There were no fewer than seven pages of titles advertised in the same 1799 catalogue. In many cases, as was usual at the time, the copyright was shared with other bookseller/ publishers, but in a number of instances the Leigh and Sotheby imprint is the only one given on the title pages. The complexity and quantity of illustration in some of the titles must have involved the investment of considerable capital – for example, the seven quarto volumes of *A General Synopsis of Birds* by John Latham,[1] which included 119 plates 'beautifully coloured', sold for £9 3s. 6d. in boards.

In a number of instances the libraries of the authors whose work had been published by Leigh and Sotheby were subsequently auctioned by the firm (e.g. Samuel Pegge). There is an amusing satirical sketch by one of the firm's own authors[2] of his dealings with Leigh as a publisher. Leigh is lampooned as *The Financial Bookseller*, 'who had many good points about him, and independent of the peculiar interests of his profession, had a taste for literature and a friendly disposition towards literary men'. The work in question was commissioned and things went well, but when the author had completed his labours, the resulting text turned out much longer than had been agreed. The publisher made threatening noises, the author remonstrated, but matters were resolved amicably and 'the parties brought their *opus magnum* to desirable termination'. It is then that Beloe makes the point that when Leigh became agitated, excited or merely carried away by his conversation he makes 'adroit and whimsical exercise of his snuffbox'.

The omnipresence of Leigh's snuff-box was also something which the antiquarian, Richard Gough, commented on in 1812 when discoursing about Leigh:

> ... this genuine disciple of the *elder* Sam [Baker] is still at the head of his profession, assisted by a *younger* Sam [Sotheby]; and of the Auctioneers of Books may not improperly be styled *facile princeps*. His pleasant disposition, his skill and his integrity, are as well known as his famous *snuff-box*, described by Mr. Dibdin as having a not less imposing air than the remarkable periwig of Sir Fopling of old, which, according to the piquant note of Dr. Warburton, usually made its entrance upon the stage in a Sedan chair, brought in by two chairmen, with infinite satisfaction to the audience. When a high price book is balancing between £15 and £20, it is a fearful sign of its reaching an additional sum if Mr. Leigh should lay down his hammer and delve into this said crumple-horn-shaped snuff-box.

In fact, it was Dibdin who had bestowed upon Leigh the soubriquet, the 'Raffaelle of Auctioneers'. But shortly before Leigh's death, William Gardiner, a bookseller of Pall Mall, felt that Dibdin had not done justice to Leigh and, in a passage which is particularly illuminating about the profession of book auctioneering, wrote as follows:

> Mr. Leigh, to the birth, person, and manners of a gentleman, adds, in the autumn of life, the cheerfulness, the bloom, and the gentle, friendly warmth of spring;

---

1. He became a very well-known ornithologist and was, in fact, a cousin of John Sotheby's.
2. The Rev. William Beloe, in the 'Sexagenarian', Vol. II, 1817; he was the author of the firm's *The History of Herodotus* translated from the Greek with notes, in four volumes and priced at £1 1s. in boards or £1 4s. bound.

and, during a space of forty years devoted to the service of the publick, has attended to its interests, whatever might be the magnitude, with the utmost vigilance, impartiality, and success; and, in a profession accompanied by much trouble, perplexity, confusion, and uncertainty, has spared neither his person nor purse, to introduce regularity, method, and precision; and has preserved a character not only unstained and unsuspected, but highly honourable. His discharge of duty during the hour of sale cannot be too highly praised, whether for a gracefulness of delivery that adds interest to such a correct enunciation of his articles as each of their Authors would approve or for that polished suavity with which he moderates the occasional asperity of contending parties – whether he checks with a *bon mot* the Doctor's[1] rarely unchristian want of benevolence to an unfortunate Classick, or with irresistable politeness induces Dom. Atticus[2] to indulge the room with a slight glance of the contended prize – whether he reinvigorates the declining powers of the combatants with the effluvia of his 'spirit-stirring horn', or crowns glorious victory with a triumphant laurel of brown *rappee*.-[3] The Battle ended, a gentlemanly attention to the wounds of every unfortunate hero, from whatever cause they arise, furnishes a rude index to a few, and only a few, of the virtues and accomplishments of Mr. Leigh.

Dibdin actually described Leigh's technique in the auctioneer's rostrum:

His voice was soft, and he had a sort of jirk in its *cadenza* – somewhere between the affettuoso and adagio. Now and then his hammer came down with a sharp and startling thump; but in general it moved mechanically, and dropt in a sort of 'dying, dying fall'.

The story of the hammer is interesting. It has even been celebrated in verse:[4]

> And down
> Th'important hammer drops.
> This instrument
> Had wielded been of old by Langford. He
> With dying breath to Baker had bequeath'd
> This sceptre of dominion; which now decks
> The courteous hand of Leigh.

Langford was the auctioneer who had sold the fine arts portion of Dr. Mead's possessions and was evidently a good friend of Samuel Baker's. After Leigh's

1. This was the noted Rev. Dr. Isaac Gossett (1735–1812), the most regular attendant at book sales of his generation, who bought more bibliographical treasures for 6d. than any man before or since. 'He also had a fad for milk-white vellum.' His health, 'which was delicate even to deformity, prevented him from pursuing an active clerical career.' He was said to have taught Richard Heber the rudiments of bibliography. His library was sold by LEIGH AND SOTHEBY in June 1813. The sale lasted 23 days and realised £3,141. There is an amusing reference to Dr. Gossett in *A Book for a Rainy Day*, *Recollections of the Events of the Years 1766 to 1833* by John Thomas Smith, edited by Wilfred Whitten, London, 1905, which contains a lively description of 'the frequenters of print sales' in the 1780s.
2. The reference here is to Richard Heber.
3. A coarse form of snuff.
4. Dibdin, *Bibliography, a Poem*, 1812, quoted by G. D. Hobson in his *Notes on the History of Sotheby's*, 1917.

death the hammer passed to Benjamin Wheatley, at one time senior clerk at Sotheby's, who became a partner in another auctioneering firm in 1826.[1] He died in 1837 and through his son, B. R. Wheatley, the hammer found its way back to Sotheby's where it has remained ever since.

Leigh used the hammer in many particularly interesting sales, no longer all – by any means – confined to books. There were more frequent sales of prints,[2] also of drawings, of coins and medals and various forms of antiquities, and these began to constitute an increasing proportion of the firm's turnover. The brevity of the cataloguing of many items makes reading them today particularly tantalizing. Presumably at the time this was compensated by Leigh's appropriate and amusing commentary. Thus the manuscript and missal section of the library of Edward Jacob Esq. F.S.A. (13 February 1789 and seven following days), includes 'A large Parcel of Manuscripts English and Modern on Physic, Law, Divinity, History, etc., Fol. Quarto, Duod', (lot 1460); 'Four Manuscripts of Conchology, with Drawings of Shells', (lot 1461); 'A Book of Surgery written in the Year 1392, Fol.', (lot 1463) and finishes with four illuminated Books of Hours.

Enter Sam Sotheby

In 1794 the firm held its first sale devoted to natural history (the Earl of Bute's botanical collection) and a smaller collection belonging to the Rev. Richard Southgate, on 12 May 1795.[3] Another interesting such collection was sold on 13 February 1800, the property of Mr. Walker, Surgeon (Deceased). But here there was also a fine collection of surgical instruments. From its earliest days the firm had sold scientific instruments and navigational devices, and this continued at irregular intervals. There were also occasional sales of music and

1. The firm was Stewart, Wheatley & Adlard who held regular auctions at 191 Piccadilly from 1794 to 1837; it then became Fletcher & Wheatley and in 1841 its premises and goodwill were acquired by Thomas Puttick and William Simpson. Puttick & Simpson continued in business as auctioneers for rather more than a century. In 1954 they were taken over by Phillips, Son & Neale who have in recent years – with a new wave of dynamic, and trading simply as Phillips – emerged as a powerful third force in the London auction room.

2. A particularly interesting sale of this sort was that of a Dr. Michael Lort, Regius Professor of Greek at Cambridge, on 26 May 1791, which went on for seven days and included engravings of all kinds, a great number of maps, a sizeable collection of Chinese and Indian paintings and engravings (including large scrolls) and concluded with a copy of Abraham van der Doort's inventory of the collections of Charles I.

3. The most important dispersal in this field was of the Herbarium of Aylmer Bourke Lambert, a Vice President of the Linnean Society, in June 1842. It was one of the largest collections of its kind with over 50,000 specimens built up from some 130 collections including the celebrated one of the Duchess of Portland. For a detailed account of its formation and dispersal see Hortense Miller's 'The Herbarium of A. B. Lambert', in *Taxon* 19(4), pages 489–553, August 1970; for a complete list of botanical and other natural history seals see J. M. Chalmers-Hunt's *Natural History Auctions 1700–1972*, London, 1976 and in particular E. G. Allingham's *Romance of the Rostrum*, London, 1924, an account of the firm of Henry Stevens whose origins were in one of Baker's rivals, Samuel Paterson, which in turn became King and Lochée. Stevens specialised in natural history and ethnological sales and dominated this sphere for rather more than a century until 1939.

musical instruments, though there were other auctioneers who made a speciality of this.

Links with the British Museum became ever closer at this period too. In 1788 came the sale of duplicate coins and medals as well as books, and there were further such sales in 1805, 1807, 1811, 1816, 1818 and 1819. When the Museum's Assistant Librarian, the Rev. Richard Southgate, died, Leigh and Sotheby was entrusted with the dispersal of his coins, drawings and, as we have already mentioned, shells and natural curiosities, as well as his library, in 1795. Southgate had led an estimable but relatively uneventful life, mostly in dire poverty, as assistant curate in a number of parishes, and even though he was known to have parted with much of his tiny income for charitable purposes, he assembled an important and scholarly library and a fine collection of coins, which shows that such things could be done at that period with very small financial resources. He was widely admired and esteemed for his astonishingly retentive memory. His unique knowledge of medieval history and expertise on Anglo-Saxon coins led to his appointment to the British Museum. Although the last few years of his life were made more comfortable by an inheritance from a distant relative, he was killed when already in poor health by the extreme winter of 1795 'when the thermometer at Clapham Common was 6° below zero, and in other places lower, a degree of cold hitherto unknown in this country'.

On 10 March 1800 Sotheby's dispersed the library of Dr. Charles Morton, the British Museum's principal, if rather idle, Librarian. The firm also sold the library and a major collection of prints and drawings belonging to William Alexander,[1] Keeper of the Museum's Department of Prints and Drawings, in November 1816. It also dispersed posthumously, first, the collection of manuscript music and later the entire library and antiquities of William Young Ottley, a particularly distinguished successor of Alexander's who had been a connoisseur and *marchand amateur* of Old Master drawings most of his life and had advised Sir Thomas Lawrence in the formation of his unique and enormous collection of them.

The sale of collections of prints expanded in its own right and drew the firm more and more into the sale of other aspects of the fine arts. One of the most important early collections of this kind which aroused widespread interest in March 1802 was the 'Valuable and Extensive Collection of *English Portraits* of the late Samuel Tyssen, F.A.S., of Narborough Hall, in the County of Norfolk'. The sale included everything which a cultivated man with a strong interest in the arts could assemble in the eighteenth century. Apart from the prints and books of engravings, there were antique bronzes, paintings, coins, gems and cameos and 'curiosities'. The prize item was a copy of Grainger's

1. It is astonishing how early links with a firm continue. In his younger days Alexander, who was a competent artist particularly in watercolours, had accompanied Lord Macartney's embassy to the Chinese Emperor Ch'ien Lung in 1792–94. It was Britain's first attempt to establish diplomatic relations with China. Alexander's many sketches and paintings of the long journey provided a unique contemporary record and formed a special sale at Sotheby's on 1 April 1976.

Biographical History of England in thirty-three volumes with extra illustrations amounting to more than seven thousand portraits in number. The whole took fifteen days to disperse.[1]

From the number of catalogues that have survived one gains the impression that there were, in fact, more collectors of engravings than was the case. The Rev. J. Maberley writing in his anonymously published book *The Print Collector: an Introduction to the Knowledge Necessary for Forming a Collection of Ancient Prints* (1844), mentions that there were 'not in all London above half a dozen dealers in Ancient Prints'. He went on to say:

> It is a common habit of collectors to attend the auction sales of prints; but there is a certain temptation in a saleroom, and a certain excitement which stimulates that temptation, which make it absolutely dangerous for anyone, who is not of the most phlegmatic disposition or who has not been made callous by long practise or become apathetic by the years rolled over his head, to indulge his curiosity or idle away an hour in this amusing occupation. Old collectors are aware of this, and, though they may attend, they are not very frequently seen to bid. It will often happen indeed, that there is nothing to tempt them; but, if otherwise, their most usual course is to commission a print dealer to bid for them.

Maberley's own collection was dispersed by Sotheby's in May 1851 in a five-day sale and, like a number of similarly mouth-watering collections of prints and engravings later in the century, included 'a nearly complete set of the Works of Albert Dürer and almost every important work by Rembrandt, the whole being of matchless quality, both as to impression and condition'.

Another interesting development was the sale of the library of Prince Talleyrand on 11 April 1793 (there were to be two further sales of his *Bibliotheca Splendidissima* on 8 May 1816 and 18 April 1817). The unsettled state of Europe and the French Revolution brought a good deal of property for sale to England. In fact, on 27 July 1823, Sotheby's had the distinction, after Napoleon's death, of selling the books he had taken with him to St. Helena. A real flood of importations from the Continent only began with the library of the Abbé Celotti. The first of his sales was in April 1819: there were three more in 1821, 1825 and 1826.

A dramatic change of tempo in staging sales occurred in the year 1796. The number increased to fourteen, with four sizeable sales taking place in the autumn for the first time. From 1798 to 1800 there were no fewer than twenty-three sales in each year. Poor George Leigh had had to auction his own father's library in February 1799, but in contrast there were also the libraries of two very eminent men of his time, Joseph Addison, the essayist, and John Wilkes, M.P., the great pamphleteer and champion of liberty. There was another new venture for the firm when they held what was virtually the studio sale of Thomas Sandby, draughtsman and architect brother of the more famous Paul, which included all his drawings and prints, as well as his library. Clearly all this additional work called for extra assistance. It arrived in the

---

1. There had been an earlier thirteen-day sale of Tyssen's vast library in December 1801.

form of John Sotheby's son, Samuel,[1] in the late summer of the year 1800, and the firm now changed its style to LEIGH, SOTHEBY AND SON. We know remarkably little of John Sotheby, the father, who lived much of his married life in Charlotte Street, Bloomsbury, before inheriting Samuel Baker's house in Chigwell, though a portrait of him – unsurprisingly also by Charles Grignion – came to light in 1964.[2] His dress in the portrait is a little old-fashioned for the period, and one cannot help reflecting that he looks a much more serious man than George Leigh. For some reason that has never come to light, the two older partners had a major altercation in 1804 and George Leigh and young Sam took themselves off to new premises at 145 The Strand, the first move for exactly fifty years, and for the time being called themselves LEIGH AND S. SOTHEBY. John Sotheby remained at York Street and held another two sales there before closing the premises and going into retirement. He died four years later. The schism between the families must have been pretty deep-seated because we find that John Sotheby's extensive library was sold by a neighbour in York Street, W. Richardson, over twenty-five days in May 1808 and not by the family firm. In fact, 1808 must have been rather a traumatic year for the younger Sotheby, Sam, now thirty-seven, for not only was there the row with his father and the sundering of the business, but he also lost his first wife, Harriet, to whom he had been married for five years. They had lived in Hampstead and in that time she had borne him four children, two sons and two daughters. He did not marry again for nine years and though his second wife had two children, both died in infancy.

The premises at 145 The Strand obviously became too cramped for the firm very quickly for it moved again in 1818 to No. 3 Waterloo Bridge Street, which soon after was re-named 13 Wellington Street, and there it remained for almost exactly a century. Soon after Leigh's death, Samuel Sotheby took his second son, Samuel Leigh Sotheby,[3] into the business at an early age. It was a happy partnership, for father and son shared many interests. One of the strongest was in the study of early printing and typography; in fact, Samuel Leigh completed and published a number of books on which his father had spent years of research.[4] If he did not actually retire, Samuel began to take things easier after 1827 and his son firmly took over the reins of the business in that year.

Samuel Leigh Sotheby was decidedly the most scholarly of any of the partners associated with the firm since its foundation. He also took an interest in its early history and a strong interest in the history of book collecting generally. In 1828 he published *A List of the Original Catalogues of the Principal Libraries which have been sold by Auction. . . .* The early part is neither very accurate nor very complete, but it was a useful record of the firm's

1. Samuel Baker had been his godfather.
2. A replica of the portrait is in the possession of Dr. Christopher Sotheby Pitcher, a descendant through the female line, who has taken a vigorous genealogical interest in the Sotheby family.
3. George Leigh had been Samuel Leigh Sotheby's godfather.
4. See page 27.

activities nevertheless. Rather sadly, the Sothebys decided in July 1831 to part
with some of the source material used for this compilation.[1] Samuel already had
experience of such a sale of catalogue material from the largely numismatic
library of Thomas Dimsdale[2] (it was sold anonymously) which had done
reasonably well in June 1824. As early as May 1828 Samuel Leigh Sotheby had
written to Sir Thomas Phillipps to offer him a complete set of Sotheby catalogues from 1802 to 1825 annotated personally by George Leigh and Samuel
Sotheby. (Rather tantalisingly Samuel Leigh Sotheby refers to a *second* set of
such catalogues which his father had bought in 1826 when Sir Thomas had
stood aside to enable him to do so.) But Sir Thomas must have refused again,[3]
for Sotheby's staged an auction of the 'Bibliographical and other Collections
of Eminent Literary Men forming a most interesting and curious series of Sale
and Privately Printed Catalogues of Literary Property, from the commence-
ment of the last Century [1700] to the present time; collected together with the
greatest difficulty: the whole in the choicest condition'. It was probably the
most complete conspectus of the history of all aspects of English collecting
then extant, and the Sothebys' made the catalogue a very useful scholars'
working tool by adding extensive indexes of the collections of books (408),[4]
privately printed catalogues (42), pictures and drawings (144), coins and medals
(142) and pictures (65). One section of the sale includes 'literary Collections
sold by various Auctioneers' and is again of interest as representing Sotheby's
major competitors up to 1831. These consisted of Messrs Hutchins (1785 to
1798[5] – mostly 'museums'); Greenwood (1784 to 1806, mostly drawings and
pictures, including those of William Hogarth, Paul Sandby and Sir Joshua
Reynolds); Thomas Philipe (1798 to 1814, mostly prints and drawings – Philipe
often sold the graphic property when Sotheby's were selling the library of the
same owner); Richardson (1791 to 1815, mostly prints); Christie (1777 to 1816,
drawings, prints, curiosities, 'museums', also some libraries; James Christie,
having started his business in 1766, began to compete particularly strongly in
the field of books after his partner, Robert Ansell, joined him in 1777);
Vallance & Jones of Dublin (1796 to 1816) and Lewis of Dublin (1812 to 1816) –
both specialised in libraries; King & Lochée (1790 to 1816) of King Street,

1. It was a period of considerable economic hardship which hit the book trade as severely as
other forms of commerce, and one assumes that father and son felt that this was one asset that
could be turned into ready money.
2. Thomas Dimsdale's coin collection was dispersed separately and was one of the largest
the firm had ever handled.
3. Through an ironic twist of fate Sir Thomas Phillipps's own bound but incomplete set of
Sotheby catalogues from about 1810 to the 1870s came into the firm's possession in the
1950s after the brothers Philip and Lionel Robinson had acquired the Phillipps Collection;
and it now constitutes the principal in-house source of information of its own early history
at Bond Street. It usefully supplements the *complete microfilm* of all known Sotheby sales
compiled under the editorship of Dr. A. N. L. Munby (Xerox University Microfilms in
association with Sotheby Parke Bernet Publications) which became available in 1973.
4. The figures in brackets represent numbers of collections included.
5. The dates refer to the period from which representative catalogues were included in
the Sotheby's collection.

Covent Garden, very active auctioneers mostly of prints and books; Dodd & Jones (1806 to 1823, again, seemingly very active); and – preceding Leigh and Sotheby's own long list – came that of R. H. Evans (1812 to 1831 in thirty-three bound volumes).

Robert Harding Evans, born in the year of Samuel Baker's death (1778), became Leigh and Sotheby's greatest competitor and although they were never short of auctions, Evans disposed of the cream of what was going. The highlight of his career was the sale of the collection of the Duke of Roxburghe in the summer of 1812. It probably ranks as the most influential book sale of the nineteenth century, and its effect on Sotheby's immediately afterwards and for generations to come was such that it is worth considering it in some detail.

The 3rd Duke of Roxburghe (1740–1804) fell in love with Christina, the eldest daughter of the Duke of Mecklenburg and Strelitz while travelling on the Continent, but as George III wanted to marry the younger daughter, the Roxburghe marriage was called off, and neither the Duke nor the Princess ever married. The Duke consoled himself with collecting books and amassed an enormous library in his house in St. James's Square. It was especially rich in *incunabula*, choice editions of the French Chivalry Romances, Italian literature, and, as a later authority wrote, 'to him old English literature, with all its roughness, was more precious than any other, and a very large number of his English books were things so rare that no individual of today can hope to make a similar collection even if he possessed the wealth of Fortunatus'.[1] Evans, who had a large sale-room in Pall Mall, sold the library eight years after the Duke's death, in the St. James's Square dining-room. The books had been catalogued by Messrs. G. & W. Nicol who had been the Duke's favourite booksellers (as they were for George III) during his lifetime. The sale was remarkably well attended and unbelievably successful. In many ways it ushered in a new era of book collecting. 'From the hobby of a scholar or the whim of an eccentric commoner, the collecting of rare books became once more, as in Harley's and Sunderland's days, the favourite pastime of the wealthy nobleman. Fine bindings too again became the fashion. . . .'[2] The sale lasted forty-two days, consisted of 9,533 lots (representing some 30,000 volumes), and raised the remarkable total of £23,341. The most outstanding event was the purchase by the Marquess of Blandford of the celebrated Valdarfer Boccaccio, of 1471, for £2,260, a record price which remained unequalled, let alone broken, until 1884. The Duke of Devonshire also caused a great stir by giving £1,060 10s. for Caxton's *Recuyell of the Historyes of Troye*. Such four-figure prices for mere books were very hard to understand in 1812. It is almost impossible for us today, accustomed to £1 million objects, to imagine the impact such events made. It was certainly the competition between Lord Blandford, the Duke of Devonshire and a third bibliophile aristocrat, Lord Spencer, that made the Roxburghe sale so successful. Of the three it was ultimately Lord Spencer who built up the greatest library at Althorp with the help of the Rev. Thomas

1. Bernard Quaritch in his *Dictionary of English Book-Collectors*, 1892.
2. Seymour de Ricci, *English Collectors of Books and Manuscripts*, 1930.

Frognall Dibdin whom we have already quoted extensively and whom he had made his librarian.

De Ricci wrote of Lord Spencer's library: 'for incunabula and Aldines it equalled – when it did not surpass them – the greatest public libraries of the world. No other collector ever owned *all* the first editions of the classics, both the Mayence (Gutenberg) Bibles (42 line and 36 line editions), both the Fust and Schoeffer Psalters (1457 and 1459), nearly all the rarest incunabula, including impressions by Pfister, no less than fifty-six Caxtons [more than the British Museum had until 1929], the finest Bibles, the first editions of all the great Italian authors, books in splendid bindings, the rarest English Bibles, fourteen block-books, about a hundred books printed on vellum, beautiful Elzeviers and the choicest collection of Aldines existing in any library'. De Ricci is rarely so fulsome.

Spencer, and all his rivals, of course, bought large parts of their collections at Sotheby's. A new generation of collectors bred a new generation of book-sellers to help them to find what they wanted. James Edwards made a speciality of buying libraries on the Continent and selling them in London; Payne and Foss, started in 1740 by 'Honest Tom Payne', and then run by his son and later still by that son's nephew; Thomas Thorpe whose 'success was not commensurate with his exertions';[1] Thomas Rodd (1796 to 1849), a particular friend of the Sotheby family – in fact, John Wilkinson was one of the executors of Rodd's (rather meagre) estate; John Bohn of Henrietta Street, Covent Garden, who issued the most remarkable and extensive catalogues; John Cochran of the Strand – another Sotheby family friend; and Robert Triphook who issued particularly elegant catalogues between 1806 and 1824.

When a collector bought on Spencer's scale there was a fairly frequent shedding of duplicates and unwanted books. He sold these at Sotheby's in 1798, 1800, 1802, 1804 and 1811. Evans took over in 1813, 1815, 1821 and 1823. Such events must have been galling for Sotheby's, but by the 1840s when they were gaining greater strength, Evans's business was on the wane. He went bankrupt in 1846 and Sotheby's purchased his goodwill and stock. It is for this reason that at that time Sotheby's staged a number of sales at 106 New Bond Street, Evans's last premises.

A second major sale staged by Evans is important because it marked the end of the great post-Napoleonic War boom and heralded a levelling down of the extremes of the Roxburghe Sale. The Marquess of Blandford (his title afterwards became George Spencer Churchill, fifth Duke of Marlborough) had spent vast sums on the library which he had built up in his mansion, White Knights, near Reading. Its principal treasure was the Bedford Book of Hours, now in the British Museum.[2] The collector's profligate extravagance, however, compelled him to put the library up for sale in the summer of 1819. Even though it was

1. Quoted from his obituary in the *Gentleman's Magazine,* an invaluable source of biographical information of the period.
2. For a full and amusing account of how it got there, see A. N. L. Munby's *Connoisseurs and Medieval Miniatures 1750–1850,* 1972, chapter 1.

very well attended, the much-vaunted 'Valdarfer Boccaccio' now brought only £918 15s. and other prices dropped correspondingly. They were to remain at a depressed level for another twenty years although interesting sales increased rather than diminished, and there was now a group of very active collectors who began to assemble the major libraries that in their turn were the subject of the most important sales in the second half of the century.

In fact, there is hardly a year throughout the nineteenth century which does not contain one or more sales of particular interest at Sotheby's because the owner of the library or the property concerned had played a role of some importance in the history of the nation in a political, cultural, scientific or commercial sense. But this volume would swell to totally unmanageable dimensions if one referred to more than a seminal minority of such sales. All an author can do is to stress the real sense of scholarship, the diversity of special interest and the variety of collections – both of traditional and previously unassembled material – reflected by the seemingly endless concatenation of catalogues. It would probably not be unfair to assert that by the time George Leigh had died, the vast majority of books of value in private possession in Britain had passed through the hands of known collectors or the sale-room, though, of course, exciting discoveries continued (and continue) to be made particularly in old, established libraries. The point cannot be made too strongly that it was primarily the book collectors of the eighteenth and first half of the nineteenth century who amassed and saved from oblivion the bulk of the literature of earlier periods that followed the invention of printing, which scholars have studied and readers have enjoyed in modern times. It was truly the devotion of bibliophiles, like Robert Harley, Thomas Rawlinson, Dr. Anthony Askew and the Rev. Clayton Mordaunt Cracherode (and Dawson Turner, Upcott, Douce and later Sir Thomas Phillipps in the case of unpublished manuscript material) who were regarded as eccentric almost to the point of insanity in their own day, who garnered not only printed books but pamphlets and manuscripts of all kinds which were not then regarded as worth preserving, and saved what was only considered suitable for burning or the rag-and-bone man. Many members of this lunatic fringe bequeathed their entire lives' collections to the Bodleian and the British Museum and these institutions often owe the still under-explored richness of their resources to such men to an extent which is largely forgotten today. While some libraries were retained in large country houses and urban ancestral homes by the collectors' immediate descendants and their successors, the vast preponderance almost inevitably finished up in the auction room for dispersal to the next generation of collectors.

We do not know much about the clerical staff at Sotheby's, who undertook the cataloguing or their mode of working at this time, although a document made out for Samuel Leigh Sotheby in 1828 by Joseph Haslewood (1769–1833) has survived which sets out some sort of guide to policy. Entitled *Hints for a Young Auctioneer of Books* its first paragraph is as true today as it was then: 'Consider your catalogue as the foundation of your eminence and make its perfection of character an important study'. Its second paragraph stressed the importance of describing each item separately, and there is an interesting reference to the 'rig and knock out crew' found at furniture sales. The full document is given as an Appendix on page 445. Its author was a self-educated and very successful solicitor, antiquary and book collector who, because of his friendship with Dibdin, became one of the founder members of the Roxburghe Club. He was an auction room habitué and made something of a speciality of perfecting imperfect books and selling them at high prices, particularly in the fields of *incunabula*, Elizabethan poetry and books on angling, hawking and field sports. King and Lochée sold a substantial collection of Haslewood books in 1809 and Evans sold his library after his death. Even so, Samuel Leigh Sotheby noted at the end of the document, 'The foregoing was written by my excellent friend Mr. Haslewood and is deserving of every attention on every point, save part of No. II', where Sotheby expresses a preference for listing in a single alphabetical sequence books that might belong to a number of proprietors rather than endorsing Haslewood's suggested procedure of separately listing each owner's collection in alphabetical order.

Two examples of cataloguing come to mind, even though they are some years apart, where love of the job and recognition of the genuine importance of the collections concerned must have completely outweighed commercial considerations by the auctioneers. In 1805 the 1st Marquis of Lansdowne died. Also titled the 2nd Earl of Shelburne, he was a courageous soldier and an effective though unpopular politician who had held high office as President of the Board of Trade, Home Secretary and even, briefly, as Prime Minister. For the last twenty-two years of his life he had shunned politics and devoted his energies to forming an art collection and a fine library. Understandably he had a particular passion for the acquisition of State papers. Leigh and Sotheby were asked to dispose of his books, charts, maps, prints and documents and held two long sales early in 1806. The State papers were to be dispersed at a separate sale in 1807. There were two volumes of the catalogue. The first stated that the papers were to be sold 'early in the Spring, 1807'; the second gave the date as 27 April 1807. The first volume alone consisted of 444 closely set pages, which listed almost every document in the collection. The early issue of the catalogue was presumably intended to give possible buyers every chance to digest its remarkable contents. An introduction explained:

> The late Marquis of Lansdowne's Manuscripts unquestionably form one of the noblest and most valuable private Collections in the kingdom. They were principally accumulated by the industry of the two celebrated Collectors, Mr. James West and Mr. Ph. Carteret Webb, whose favourite study and amusement it was, to procure and preserve all the original Papers and Records, which they could meet with, relative to the laws, customs, government, topography, and history, both civil and ecclesiastical, of England and Ireland.
>
> Mr. James West's Collection[1] includes one hundred and fifteen volumes, in

1. James West was President of the Royal Society: his library was sold over 24 days in his own house in King Street, Covent Garden, by Samuel Paterson (see page 10*n*).

folio, of original Cecil Papers, with materials sufficient to make up the number one hundred and twenty. These Papers were bought in 1682 by Mr. Richard Chiswell, a stationer of London, of Sir William Hickes, the great grandson of Sir Michael Hickes, who was Secretary both to Lord Burleigh, and to his Son, the Earl of Salisbury. They were afterwards sold to Mr. John Strype, Vicar of Low Leighton, of whose Executor they were purchased by Mr. West. These Manuscripts were scarcely, if at all known, to Collins, Murdin, Jones, Birch, and other publishers of State Papers; and yet, if we except those of the Earl of Hardwick, no papers were more deserving of publication. In Mr. J. West's Collection there are also Bishop Kennet's historical Papers, which are very voluminous and valuable; – likewise Surveys, and other materials for the histories of the different counties of England, particularly Sussex and Yorkshire, which were collected by Warburton, Anstis, and other Antiquaries; – also considerable treasures in the department of Family History, and Pedigree, with Heraldical Collections of Le Neve, and most of the Heralds and Kings at Arms, back to the time of Glover and Camden; – and many original Abbey Registers of great value, as Records in tythe causes, &c. – and finally, every Paper and Volume that could be procured, relative to the office of Secretary of the Treasury, which Mr. West enjoyed for many years. His intimacy with the second Harley, Earl of Oxford, seems to have contributed much to enrich him in several of the aforementioned particulars.

Mr. Ph. Carteret Webb's Collection,[1] consisting chiefly of Parliamentary and Revenue History, contains numberless curious articles relative to the Chancery, Exchequer, and Treasury, the Spiritual and the Admiralty Courts, Wards and Livery, Star Chamber, &c. Among these are above thirty volumes of the Papers of Sir Julius Caesar, Judge of the Admiralty in Queen Elizabeth's time, and Chancellor of the Exchequer, and Master of the Rolls in the time of James I. and Charles I. From them may be gained almost a complete History of the Finances of those Reigns, together with much secret information, and many curious unpublished State Papers, connected with the general history of those times. Sir Julius Caesar's Manuscripts were exposed to sale many years ago,[2] at an auction in St. Paul's Church Yard, where Mr. West and Mr. Webb became the principal purchasers of them. Mr. Webb, being Solicitor to the Treasury, was likewise attentive to collect all memorials of the business of that office down to his own time. Several volumes of his Manuscripts belonged to Lord Somers; and many, not the least curious, relative to Law business, were the property of Mr. Umfreville,[3] who, having incurred an extraordinary expense in carrying his election as Coroner for Middlesex, was under the necessity of selling his Collection.

In addition to the two Collections which have been already described, there are many Volumes of Copies, done at a great expence, from the Tower and Cottonian Records. Many of them are of singular value, as they preserve the contents of some originals, which are obliterated, burnt, or lost. There is likewise a very considerable Collection of original letters to and from the Kings and Queens of England and Scotland, from the time of Henry VIII. to that of George II.

For the extent of the present Catalogue no apology is deemed necessary. If any manuscripts ever deserved a circumstantial Catalogue, these surely do. The

1. It was sold by Baker and Leigh in February 1771.
2. By Samuel Paterson in December 1757.
3. Also sold by Paterson, in February 1758.

trouble which it has cost, and the expence which it has incurred, are far out-weighed by the single consideration, that a Catalogue of this description will not only improve the value of the property, but, it is hoped, confer an important and permanent advantage upon the Republic of Letters.

However, the collection never came up for sale. The British Museum stepped in and bought it in its entirety for £4,925, granted for that purpose by Parliament.

If it was Samuel Sotheby who had been excited by the importance of handling the Burleigh Papers, his son, Samuel Leigh Sotheby, became even more bemused when he received from Frankfurt the library of the 5,000 volumes of Dr. Georg Franz Burkhard Kloss (1787–1854), a medical practitioner and pro-fessor at Frankfurt University. They were mostly books printed before 1536 and had been collected by Kloss from all parts of Germany, largely, one gathers, in order to complement G. W. Panzer's *Annales Typographici*. During the course of cataloguing the books Samuel Leigh Sotheby became more and more intrigued by the marginal annotations he found in many of Dr. Kloss's volumes and he became convinced, on what subsequently turned out to be rather flimsy evidence, that these were in the handwriting of Philip Melanchthon, the friend of Martin Luther. He pursued this theory with a zeal that almost amounted to an obsession and prefaced the catalogue for the sale with a detailed explanation of his views (which Dr. Kloss does not seem to have shared). '. . . the compilers of this volume, who have prepared the collection for sale, and who were the first to make the discovery of this feature in its contents, have thought it encumbent upon them to support, by the best testimony they can adduce, the position which they have ventured to take up on the subject. For at the same time they feel confident in their own minds of the correctness of the views they have taken, they would not presume to dictate a ready concurrence in their opinions by the public without advancing some more solid arguments beyond mere declarations in their support.' Sotheby consulted scholars, experts on hand-writing and knowledgeable friends. He larded the catalogue with expensive facsimiles of selected annotations. Some of his detective work was well ahead of its time. In the case of the manuscript material he went to his friend, Young Ottley, to compare the watermarks of the paper used to establish the accuracy of his dating. Thus the note to lot 4669 reads:

The periods of the execution of manuscripts upon paper are often to be more correctly ascertained from the water-marks of the paper, than from the peculiar character of their writing, as the style of writing continued with little difference from one century to another, more particularly in Monasteries or Colleges, from whence a great portion of the manuscripts existing have emanated; so that, judging from the writing alone, a MS. of the fourteenth century might often-times be ascribed to the fifteenth, and *vice versa*.

Being anxious to ascertain the date, as far as possible, of the present volume, and not agreeing with Dr. Kloss as to the period to which he had placed it, we addressed ourselves to our friend, Mr. Ottley, whom, we knew, had made this subject his particular study; and in answer to our enquiry, he writes as follows:-

'I have found this paper-mark in a leaf coming from a book of accounts at the Hague, of the year 1518; and I am of opinion that, as nearly as may be, this is the true date of this specimen.'

Samuel Leigh Sotheby bought twenty-two volumes, mostly with what he considered Melanchthon's annotations, during the twenty-day Kloss Sale in May 1835 and a larger quantity afterwards from dealers who had attended the sale. A few he thought actually to be in the hand of Martin Luther. By and large, however, collectors of the early printed books preferred clean, unmarked copies, and the marginalia seem, if anything, to have detracted from the prices in this case. Be that as it may, Samuel Leigh Sotheby continued to work on his discoveries and published a formidable array of books on this and related subjects.[1] They display much industry and enthusiasm, and earnest rather than very penetrating scholarship. The audience for them in Samuel Leigh Sotheby's lifetime was small, and John Wilkinson, his partner, had on several occasions to organise auctions of the surplus stock. The titles concerned were:

UNPUBLISHED DOCUMENTS, Marginal Notes, and Memoranda in the Autographs of Philip Melancthon and Martin Luther, with numerous Fac-similes; accompanied with Observations upon the Varieties of Style in the Handwriting of these illustrious Reformers, 1840.

THE TYPOGRAPHY OF THE FIFTEENTH CENTURY: being Specimens of the Productions of the Early Continental Printers, exemplified in a Collection of Fac-similes from One Hundred Works, together with their Water-marks. Arranged and edited from the Bibliographical Collections of the late Samuel Sotheby, by his son, S. Leigh Sotheby, 1845.

PRINCIPIA TYPOGRAPHICA. The Block Books; or, Xylographic Delineations of Scripture History, issued in Holland, Flanders, and Germany during the Fifteenth Century; exemplified and considered in connection with the Origin of Printing. To which is added an Attempt to Elucidate the Character of the Paper-marks of the Period: a work contemplated by the late Samuel Sotheby, and carried out by his son Samuel Leigh Sotheby, 1858. 3 vols., Imperial 4to.

MEMORANDA RELATING TO THE BLOCK BOOKS preserved in the Bibliotheque Imperiale, Paris, made October, 1858, by Samuel Leigh Sotheby, Author of the 'Principia Typographica', London, printed for the Author by I. Richards, 1859. Not for sale.

In a different vein, Sotheby produced *Ramblings in the Elucidation of the Autograph of Milton* which was to be sold in aid of the Booksellers' Provident Society and Retreat,[2] and for nearly forty years he was at work on a *Bibliographical Account of the English Poets to the Period of Restoration* which contained full records of all copies described in sale catalogues. But the work

1. For a detailed account of Sotheby's work on the Kloss Sale and other of his interests which later led to publications, see Cecil H. Clough, 'Samuel Leigh Sotheby und seine Bibliothek' in *Librarium*, Volume II, August 1976, which is mostly based on relevant material in the John Rylands Library in Manchester.
2. 330 were offered at £3 3s. each, but only 51 were sold.

remained unpublished even though Mrs. Julia Emma Sotheby, the auctioneer's widow, continued to work on it for a long time. For many years it seemed to have disappeared. It was, in fact, sold to what was the library of the Humphrey Chetham School in Manchester (now a separate institution) by Thomas Hayes (apparently of Sotheby's) for £85 in 1874, and still remains in the library.

Completing the first century

A form of exotic cataloguing which had already started in Samuel Baker's day and must have caused a good deal of head scratching, was of oriental and Islamic books and manuscripts. In the early part of the nineteenth century such descriptions became increasingly detailed and showed a much better understanding of the material. A good example is the 'Catalogue and Detailed Account of the very valuable and curious Collection of Manuscripts collected in Hindostan . . . collected by the late Dr. Samuel Guise', sold in July 1812, and an 'Advertisement' – essentially an explanatory introduction about the material – said that 'This Collection was made at Surat, from the Year 1788 till the End of 1795, with great Trouble and Expence. It is necessary to observe, that in any Country where the Art of Printing has not been introduced, Books will be multiplied slowly; and, there being no Booksellers, or particularly Scribes, at Surat, the Opportunities to purchase Manuscripts, of any Kind, rarely occur; and they are always sold very dear.' We learn that the Emperor Akbar had a library of no fewer than 24,000 volumes, roughly valued at £34 sterling each; that among the Sanscrit Manuscripts, the Mahabharat is particularly valuable, and that a translation of it into Persian cost a French collector one thousand rupees; also, the Advertisement tells us that there are no Pehlavic Manuscripts in England apart from those in the proffered collection and probably no more than four or five in Zend. Furthermore, 'however rich in Arabick and Persian Works of Merit, the chief Value consists in the numerous *Zend* and *Pehlavi* MSS. treating of the antient Religion and History of the *Parsees*, or Disciples of the celebrated Zoroaster'. It would be interesting to know how well such a sale was attended, though interest in the Middle and Near East was surprisingly widespread. What we do know is that that most omnivorous of manuscript collectors, Sir Thomas Phillipps, was represented and bought some of the most important items at the sale. Slightly less unusual books followed on the second, third and fourth days and mixed in with them was a small collection of coins, a number of antique and oriental rings and a collection of various sorts of ivory chessmen.

By 1824 the firm had evidently found someone who was fully conversant with oriental languages, and book titles are now fully accented, hyphenated and more systematically arranged. A catalogue of 5 July that year stated that there was 'a very choice collection of Manuscripts and Printed Books, in the Persian, Hindostani, Mahratta, Sanscrit, Afghan, Tamil and Canara Dialects in fine condition'. A high watermark in the area of exotica occurred in 1835 when Sotheby's sold the antiquities collection of Henry Salt, a former British Consul

General in Egypt.[1] It was due to Salt's momentous efforts that the British Museum had acquired its major Egyptian sculptures and antiquities. Salt had already disposed of two vast collections of antiquities, but just before his death he had instituted a further wide range of excavations, and Sotheby's persuaded Salt's principal assistant and interpreter, a Greek named Giovanni D'Athanasi (universally known as 'Yanni' for short) to undertake the sorting out, identification and cataloguing of the nine-day sale, which caused an enormous amount of public interest at the time. It included numerous excavated sculptures and statues in stone and bronze, inscribed tablets, vases, furniture, ornaments of all kinds including jewellery, sarcophagi, several perfectly preserved mummies, a very great deal of funerary furnishings including models of boats and a complete Egyptian house with its courtyard, galleries and staircases and a figure of the master of the house seated in an elaborate chair, and a huge collection of rolls of papyrus inscribed in a host of different languages and characters. We learn from Samuel Leigh Sotheby's introduction to the catalogue that it was to have contained engraved illustrations of the most beautiful objects in the sale, but that it was felt that D'Athanasi should have priority to include these in a publication of his own which he was seeing through the press. This described his eighteen years of research and excavation in Egypt, but apparently there were snags in the translation of 'Yanni's' Greek text into French which delayed its publication. However, in 1836 Samuel Leigh Sotheby compiled the descriptive material for an 'Exhibition Catalogue of Giovanni D'Athanasi's Collection of Egyptian Antiquities' which went on show at the Exeter Hall in the Strand in London following the *éclat* of the Salt Sale.

In fact, more and more frequently the firm was now departing from its role of being mainly auctioneers of literary property. Sales of pictures, watercolours and even artists' materials became very common. In November 1824, for example, mixed in with the property of Charles Muss, Enamel Painter to the King, were a host of pictures and sketches by John Martin. There were four major sales devoted to paintings, drawings and sketches by Richard Parkes Bonington, the brilliant young artist whose family had emigrated from Nottingham to France. R. P. Bonington died aged only twenty-six and his father arranged a sale at Sotheby's of the contents of the young man's Paris studio in June 1829, and other family descendants arranged a further such sale in February 1838. There were also two sales of the collections of 'eminent collectors' in July 1834 and 1835 which contained many examples of Bonington's work. As we shall see later, the Bonington sales caused Samuel Leigh Sotheby quite a number of problems. In July 1825 the firm sold the library of Henry Fuseli and in June 1830[2] that of Sir Thomas Lawrence, late President of the Royal Academy, while Christie's sold his pictures in a series of sales at the same time.

21 May 1819 seems to have been the date of the first sale by Sotheby's devoted entirely to a collection of autograph letters. It belonged to John Thane, an

1. See also page 229. 2. It was dispersed over four days.

elderly print-seller in the Haymarket who had died in the previous year, and was the author of *British Autography: a collection of facsimiles of the Handwriting of Royal and Illustrious Personages with their Authentic Portraits*. The book seems to have acted as catalyst for a new fashion in collecting which spread very rapidly because it was enjoyable, cheap and historically engrossing. One or two particularly enthusiastic collectors helped to spread the craze and to stimulate interest in it. William Upcott (1779-1845), who had once worked for Evans, the auctioneer,[1] and was employed as deputy librarian at the London Institution from 1806 to 1834 and was therefore constantly in touch with likely collectors, and bought and sold autographs in enormous quantities on behalf of a large circle of acquaintances. One of them was Dawson Turner, a wealthy banker who lived an idyllic, industrious and fruitful life with his charming family in a fine house in Yarmouth. He was deeply interested in botany and topography, and with the help of his several daughters pursued the collection and arrangement of autographs with almost unparalleled zeal. The ordering of letters, grouped alphabetically, chronologically, by the writer's occupation or by content, was very much a personal discipline, perfected to bring out the collector's own standard of completeness in a way that has affinities with stamp collecting. But the collation and combination of letters, engraved illustrations, legal documents, play bills, theatre tickets, receipts and other printed ephemera lent itself to endless variety – and of course skilful captioning. The material was pasted into large, blank volumes, annotated, indexed and then beautifully bound – often in uniform style – by the skilled craftsmen of the day. The cost of this was so low that fine leather, complex tooling, endless special guards for extraneous items and folding plates enabled the ambitious autograph collector to encapsulate his prizes in permanent and attractive form for a relatively small outlay.

This growing interest in autographs was on a countrywide scale and represented a new area of trade for Sotheby's, though prices for autographs in the 1830s were as depressed as they were for almost everything else. In fact, though Sotheby's sold part of Dawson Turner's library in 1853, most of the autographs went to Puttick & Simpson. Upcott's collection was taken over from Evans by Sotheby's after his bankruptcy in June 1846. Much of Upcott's collection which had passed to Thomas Rodd and other collectors, was dispersed by Sotheby's in February 1850 and April 1851.[2] The firm had disposed of more than fifty major collections of autograph material by 1900.

Above all the tempo of book sales continued unremittingly. Mere numbers of sales only tell part of the story because so many of the firm's library sales encompassed enormous numbers of volumes, which had to be auctioned over

1. Upcott did not care for his former employer. A character sketch in a volume of his diary in the British Library readily explains why Evans went bankrupt in 1846: he was idle, at times offensive to his clients and administratively inefficient, even though he had an excellent memory and a first class knowledge of books.

2. For a learned, detailed but most readable account of autograph collecting during the nineteenth century, see A. N. L. Munby's *The Cult of the Autograph Letter in England*, 1962, an unduly neglected not-so-minor classic in the field of bibliographical studies.

many days' sessions, but the sales statistics do reflect the nature of the firm's activities to some extent. Of the twenty-six sales held in the year of the first move, 1804, seventeen were of books. In 1808 the total number of sales had increased to forty-four, and twenty-six were of books. By 1816 the ratio was twenty-nine book sales out of a total of fifty and there it more or less remained with minor fluctuations until 1845. Samuel Sotheby had died in 1842. In rather a strange way (that was to be repeated many years later in the case of the Hodges) father and son – that is Samuel and Samuel Leigh – had for many years been regarded as almost a single personality, though both were popular with booksellers and collectors. The *Gentleman's Magazine* wrote rather charmingly in a long obituary at the time of Sam's death at the age of seventy, 'The character of the late Mr. Sotheby was strictly exemplary in all the relations of private life; and though not so happy as he deserved in realising his fortune in a very arduous profession he retired from it with the good wishes and regret of very many who had long known and highly respected him'.

There were many comments on his interest in and studies of 'literary antiquities, and particularly the history of the origin and progress of the art of printing, on the subject of which he had long been engaged in preparing a work for the press, an undertaking for which, indeed, the circumstances of his profession afforded him peculiar facilities. His collections for this purpose are known to have been most extensive, and were so far advanced that he anticipated, had not the hand of death arrested its progress, to have brought it before the public during the ensuing year.' Presumably Sam had spent much of his long retirement on this work. He was buried alongside Samuel Baker in St. Paul's churchyard. The bulk of his library had been sold (anonymously) by the firm in February 1837 and, in fact, that was the year in which – after his total withdrawal from it – his son had changed the firm's title to S. L. SOTHEBY. The *Gentleman's Magazine* went on to state that 'since his father's retirement, Mr. Samuel Leigh Sotheby has, with great credit to himself, and advantage to his employers, kept up the credit of this long established mart for the sale of books, coins and objects of *vertu*'. Perhaps a word is due here to the reference 'long established'. The firm had now been going for a century. As we have seen, in a fickle world it never lacked for competitors. They came and went surprisingly rapidly and at times overtook the firm Samuel Baker had founded and became much more successful, but ultimately, with a few honourable exceptions, such supremacy was short-lived. So by the time Samuel Leigh Sotheby faced the world alone, the business, though small, had an enviable reputation and now began to enter an era which during the greater part of the next sixty years gave it a very firmly consolidated place as the premier auctioneer of antiquarian books, or what it later termed 'Auctioneers of Literary Property and Works Illustrative of the Fine Arts'.[1]

1. The first use of this phrase occurs in a catalogue dated 18 December 1843.

3

Sotheby, Wilkinson and Hodge

SOME years before he found himself in sole charge of the firm, Samuel Leigh Sotheby had taken into his employment John Wilkinson, a young Yorkshireman who had left his native village, Huggate, in 1821 to seek his fortune in London. Like George Leigh, Wilkinson was the son of a clergyman. He was supremely good at figures and soon became the firm's senior accountant. He was a most dependable and conscientious man and Samuel Leigh Sotheby moved him out of the counting house and made him a partner in the year after his father's death, when Wilkinson acquired a quarter share in the business. We know little about him, considering his very long service in the firm, though again we have his portrait and certainly he looks the very epitome of a shrewd and successful Victorian businessman. It seems clear that he soon began to take auctions himself and personally conducted some of Sotheby's greatest sales during his long service with the firm. (He retired about 1885.) He became a Fellow of the Society of Antiquaries in 1856 and also belonged to the Numismatic Society. He was on terms of close friendship with many literary figures of his time and had a particular liking for the theatre. He had greatly admired and got to know when he was a young man the famous Shakespearian actor, Edmund Kean.

A contemporary[1] mentions that he 'was conspicuous by his raven–black locks' (another sale-room commentator refers to Wilkinson's beautiful silver hair much later in the century). 'Mr. Wilkinson', says the first, 'was the principal seller . . . in my early days. His appearance as it is impressed on my mind, when I became a habitual frequenter of the rooms about 1858, was very agreeable, and his manner highly prepossessing; he was then in the full vigour of life. Halliwell[2] and he were very intimate, and I dined with him at Halliwell's table. One not very unreasonable idiosyncracy on his part was his tenacious resistance to the admission of anyone else in the conduct of the sales; he persisted in keeping Mr. Hodge out, so long as he physically could. He liked to lord over the whole show to the very last', and Hazlitt concludes rather pointedly, 'I think that the spirit of *monarchy* remains rather strong in Wellington Street'.

As soon as Samuel Leigh Sotheby realised how good Wilkinson was in the

1. W. Carew Hazlitt in *The Bookworm*, No. 7, 1894.
2. James Orchard Halliwell, who had been something of a child prodigy, was an enthusiastic collector, particularly of English literature, but also of scientific and mathematical books and manuscripts, which Sotheby's sold (sometimes anonymously) in 1840, 1856–59, 1863, 1889, 1891 and 1895. He was suspected of having stolen books from the Trinity College Library in Cambridge as an undergraduate. He married Sir Thomas Phillipps's oldest daughter and the older man eventually learned to hate his son-in-law and always scribbled disparaging comments into his copies of the sale catalogues of Halliwell's books.

rostrum, he left the selling to his partner and concentrated on the supervision of the cataloguing.

From their partnership accounts of 1843-44,[1] it seems that they had an excellent first year in harness together. The total cash income was £40,196 os. 8d.; wages amounted to £469. The production of catalogues cost £466 5s. 3d.; Excise duty paid came to £1,973 17s. 10d. This consisted of a 5 per cent auction tax (introduced in 1777 and soon to be abolished) which could be recovered from customers. At the end of the day there was a net profit of £2,136 of which Samuel Leigh Sotheby took £1,602 and John Wilkinson received £534. This was each man's sole income: they did not pay themselves a basic salary, though Sotheby had drawn £621 from the firm in anticipation of his share of the profits and Wilkinson took £130. The firm's bankers were Prescott's, who had begun in business as early as 1766 and merged in 1903 with what is now the National Westminster Bank (which must therefore constitute one of the longest London banking associations on record). There was no capital account. Samuel Leigh Sotheby seems to have paid £1,000 into Prescott's at the beginning of the year to start off the partnership accounts. This had been repaid by the end of the year, and the partners still had £1,400 in cash at the bank. It seems to have been a most satisfactory year's trading.[2]

There had been forty-one sales in the first 'season' of the new partnership, that is, between November 1843 and July 1844, which happened to be a pretty thin year. Probably the most exciting year after a fairly flat patch was 1847, a year which initiated a new period of growth. The end had now arrived of a decade of sales forced by the general shortage of money, which had also meant that anonymity veiled the identity of very many of the owners of property being sent to the sale-room. The ingenuity and variety used in concealment deserves a passing mention: 'A catalogue of books detached from a Library in the environs of London'; 'a catalogue of a collection of autograph letters formed by an eminent collector'; 'a rare and uncommon collection of choicest books chiefly formed by a foreign nobleman'; 'a small but choice library of a gentleman removed from the Isle of Wight'; 'a valuable library of an eminent Orientalist'; 'a Valuable and well selected law library of a barrister', but by and large Sotheby's were more successful than most of the firm's rivals in persuading proprietors to allow their names to be used. The title page of one catalogue that must have given great pleasure to the partners was 'William IV, King of Britain and Ireland: Duplicates of a Library' (24 August 1837), and on 8 May 1844 the firm sold the library of the Poet Laureate, Robert Southey.

Before we leave financial and economic considerations we must record a debt

1. The only nineteenth-century set of partnership accounts to survive: they were presented to the firm in 1938 by a Mrs. Simpson, and as they are signed only by Samuel Leigh Sotheby it is probably fair to deduce that they were a set that belonged to Wilkinson.

2. Some years ago an opportunity seems to have arisen to study Sotheby's earlier bank 'Signature Book Records' and it appears that, under the aegis of Leigh and Sotheby, there had only once been a borrowing of £1,000 on 12 February 1807. Although it was designated a three-months loan, the sum was repaid within a fortnight and no other loan was ever requested before 1816 when George Leigh died.

of gratitude to the Rev. Michael Wodhull who seems to have attended every London book sale between 1764 and 1800, and less regularly thereafter until 1816. He was a notable classical scholar and the first translator into English of the complete works of Euripides. Understandably, therefore, fifteenth-century editions of the greatest works of the Greek and Roman authors were his particular passion. He annotated each volume he bought with its peculiarities of collation and condition, and also recorded where and at what price he had bought the book. Frequently he made up a good copy out of two or more imperfect ones and then had it rebound by his favourite binder, Roger Payne, or alternatively by a Mrs. Weir, usually in full Morocco or in Russia leather, and always embossed with the Wodhull arms. In this way he accumulated a large number of duplicates, which he dispersed at Sotheby's in 1801 and 1803. In the first sale 1,059 lots fetched £361 10s.; in the second 1,613 lots realised £815. Some volumes fetched more than Wodhull had paid; others brought less. In his usual methodical way, he had both sale catalogues mounted in quarto and rebound, and then added the figures himself of the cost of each item and what it had fetched. The result was a loss on the first sale of £103 12s. 5d., and a gain of £127 9s. on the second, and thus a profit of £23 16s. 7d. in all. For students of the period, Frederick Clarke has recorded a host of financial detail about individual prices in Quaritch's *Dictionary of English Book-Collectors*, but the story becomes even more intriguing because Wodhull's principal library (and his house, Thenford House, Banbury, Northamptonshire) passed by inheritance and re-inheritance to J. E. Severne, M.P., who decided to sell the collection at Sotheby's in January 1886. The sale lasted ten days, and the catalogue contains one of the most uninspired introductions Sotheby's ever appended to a distinguished library. Such dullness was rare; often these prefatory notes give us riveting biographical and bibliographical information about the collector which is not obtainable from any other source, and one infinitely regrets their virtual disappearance in catalogues of single-owner collections when these come up for sale today. Frequently the writing of such introductory material gives the impression that it was a welcome opportunity both for cataloguers and partners (up to the time of the Second World War) to escape from the compressed telegraphese of mere catalogue entries, and that it allowed them to give vent to a polished prose style that often deserved a much wider readership than it ever eventually received.

Be that as it may, the Wodhull sale was a success and attracted collectors from all over the world. De Ricci tells us that two famous American bibliophiles, Robert Hoe and William Loring Andrews, pooled their bids and divided their purchases. Hoe's acquisitions appeared in his own celebrated sale (see page 117), and the *incunabula* secured by Andrews are now at Yale University. The 2,804 lots realised £11,972 14s. 6d., or almost exactly ten times the sum for about the same number of duplicates sold by Wodhull eighty-five years earlier. Even though the prices were regarded as satisfactory then, they seem laughable ninety years later. Caxton's Cicero of 1481 fetched £250; Aesop's Fables printed in 1480, £20; Sweynheim and Pannaertz's Apuleius printed in Rome in

1469, £14 10s.; the Works of Aristotle in six folio volumes printed by Aldus between 1496–98, £19; Ovid's Metamorphosis with fine woodcuts, printed in Venice in 1497, £36. But it is also of interest that many titles in 1886 actually fetched *less* than Wodhull had given for them generations earlier. The last word should be left to Frederick Clark, because it is so easy to overlook the fact he stresses: 'Should anyone find fault with these little jottings, or with other small details written above, a reason for giving them may be urged in that Wodhull's habit of life as a booklover was very minute and full of little particulars, and that he was exact in his study and noting. *Moreover, it was a day of small things.*'

If Wodhull was exceptional in recording the detailed cost of books at auction, we are just as short of general contemporary descriptions of the book auction scene in the 1840s. Indeed there has long been an almost total paucity of personal detail of Sotheby's partners in the whole era spanned by the dynasty of Samuel Leigh Sotheby, John Wilkinson and the elder Hodge. Within Sotheby's it has often been referred to as 'The Dark Ages',[1] though a visiting journalist in 1843 reported on it in the *Morgenblatt für Gebildete Leser* (the same piece was also translated into French and appeared in book form). It is worth quoting at some length for the insight it gives into the procedure of the contemporary book auctions:

> The London book auctions offer considerable food for thought on the subject of the misfortunes and frailty of human life for, whenever an eminent person dies, or goes bankrupt, his library is usually destined for the public auction rooms. These auction sales are also often very entertaining, and in a city like London, they take on a greater importance and a very particular interest. It might be thought strange that these sales are sparsely attended, not only by foreigners but even by leisured Londoners. The fact is that this inconceivable indifference can only be explained by the words 'ce n'est pas la mode'.
>
> If one considers the size of London the main book auction rooms are relatively close to each other. An hour's brisk walk will take one from Piccadilly, along Pall Mall and the Strand as far as Fleet Street. Within this area can be found the premises of the principal book auctioneers, Messrs. Evans, Sotheby, Fletcher, Hodgson and Southgate. At the beginning of Spring these gentlemen announce their sales in the newspapers and publish sale catalogues. One or other of them will almost certainly hold a sale towards the end of July or August, at a time when 'the Season' which exerts such an incredible influence on all branches of business, is drawing to a close. They come to mutual agreement on the dates for sales and it is only in an emergency that two or three sales might take place on the same day.
>
> Like most businessmen these gentlemen specialise. Evans has pride of place, as had his father who was well known in the literary world as editor of a collection of English ballades which filled several of the gaps left by Percy. And like his father before him Evans has been granted the privilege of presiding, as auctioneer,

---

1. Not only within the firm: out of forty-eight letters requesting information which the author sent to national libraries, record offices and similar archival repositories, only three responded with positive information and none had any biographical detail of the three partners concerned.

over the sale of the valuable libraries of noblemen and the wealthy middle classes. His knowledge of books has become almost proverbial in London. After Evans comes Sotheby who is often the choice of the aristocracy and the rich when antiques, coins, engravings, literary curiosities and other similar objects, as well as books, are to be auctioned. The other three gentlemen share among themselves the sales entrusted to them by the middle classes, and are none the less esteemed for that.

The duties of a London book auctioneer demand various talents not given to all. He must be gifted with excellent eyesight and physical and moral discernment. He must also, by tireless effort, have acquired a wide circle of acquaintances. He must be able to recognise, at a glance, the enthusiast on whom the words 'a tall copy' will have an electrifying effect, the one who cannot resist an 'uncut copy', the one whose imagination will be fired by the words 'first edition', or who will respond to the announcement 'bound by Lewis'. Everyone who sells books constantly has on his lips the words 'a desirable copy', 'a pic-nic [*sic* ... working?] copy', 'a sweetly bound volume', 'a glorious black-letter', and the terms and phraseology can easily be learned. The art of using them at exactly the right moment and of fixing one's gaze on the appropriate listener, however, demands tact and a profound knowledge of one's fellow men. At the same time the auctioneer has to be on the alert for anyone who from his place in a corner to right or left, in front of his rostrum, on the benches at the long table, at the back of the room, or in the furthest doorway might wish, with a nod of the head, to raise the bidding. A slight inclination of the head indicates a bid of sixpence, a more obvious nod means a shilling. A smile from the auctioneer will encourage one man, a frown will urge on another, while a shrug will embolden a third. The auctioneer must be able to judge which method has the greatest effect on each potential buyer. He must be able to read the minds of those present and help them to translate their thoughts into action. Genius is not always needed when one writes a book but genius alone can sell books at a public auction in London. For this reason I would accord the auctioneer's hammer as much respect as the writer's pen.

The auction rooms are open a few hours before the sale so that the books can be viewed. The behaviour of enthusiasts is amusing even then. They stand in front of the table or shelves where the books are displayed, with catalogue and pencil in hand. Sometimes serious, sometimes smiling, they pick up and leaf through a book then put it down with a show of disinterest. They nonetheless mark the lot number carefully in the catalogue before looking round to make sure that no one has noticed and they eye anyone else who stretches out a hand for the book in a challenging manner. Many people leave the room as soon as the auctioneer takes his place. This is not always because they have found nothing of interest. Often it is because they know themselves too well and cannot trust themselves if they stay. Hard won experience has taught them that, difficult though it may always be to exercise restraint once the bidding starts, for them it is impossible. If a man whose appearance or triumphant expression annoys you bids a shilling more than your limit, you cannot help bidding another shilling. If he then gives up you will have nothing more to regret than the loss of two shillings, or, if you are sensible enough to stop bidding you will be able to congratulate yourself on your will-power. There are even some secondhand booksellers, whose enthusiasm has not been tempered by their trade, who have to send messenger

Mrs E Valler

1846.

May 1 & 9   By Gross Amount of Sale   1678. 5. 6

                                £. s. d.

Feby 20th   Cartage, String &c removing Town Library   1. 19. 6
      Cartage, Paper, String &c removing Library
          from Bromley   } 1. 15. 6
      Mr Blundell cleaning "Purchas" &c   . 9. 6
      Selling at 12½ per cent   209. 16. 0
          Books returned Imperfect:
  Impft 89 -1/. 1239 -1/3/. 1953 -10/. 1948 -1/2/. 733 -2/3/.
  933 -13/. 1786 -19/. 1129 -1/2/. 419 -5/. 692 -6/8/. 693 -6/8/
  98 -7/6 201 -1/6 613 -5/6 725 -3/6/. 914 -8/6. 561 -3/. 568 -1/ } 30. 3. 6
  2013 allᵈ 9/. 845 -5/6 2002 -2/3/. 1288 -10/ allowed 10/—

      Mr Elkins bill in safe, as agreed   100. 0. 0   349. 4. 0

27 July 1846 — Cheque of receipt   Balance £1329. 1. 6
of Bank of England £1329. 1. 6

Balance, Payable July 24th

S. Leigh Sotheby & Co

This decorative billhead figured on all the firm's stationery for many years.

boys to represent them at sales. These lads are often excellent representatives who can calculate the bidding with a skill unexpected in boys of twelve to fourteen. They have often reduced more experienced and important buyers to despair.

Usually not a year passes without at least one sale which attracts the interest of all the London bibliophiles. In 1842 it was the sale of the Marquess of Wellesley's library which was said to contain the best collection of Latin and Greek works in the whole of England. Many of the volumes were sold at ten or twelve times the trade price because of the annotations made by their owner. The highest price of all was paid for a pamphlet on the last war in the East Indies, solely because, although insignificant in itself, it had two or three comments in the Marquess's own hand on the subject of certain events which took place in those countries while he was Governor General. The price of the pamphlet, whose face value was about one franc, was pushed up beyond eleven hundred francs. Last year the most prestigious sale was that of Lord Berwick's library [26 April 1843] which contained some splendid heraldic works, manuscripts and autographs. All the collectors were in a state of excitement because, among the documents was a deed relating to Shakespeare's house in Blackfriars which bore his signature, and as everyone knows there are only four signatures of the great playwright still in existence.

When Sotheby raised the precious document the room was overflowing with interested spectators. The auctioneer himself hesitated to break the sudden silence. Finally after a short preamble he started the sale. After five minutes of bidding the sum offered had reached one hundred guineas. This seemed to be the limit for most people. On the faces of many a frown, a twist of a lip or an expression of defeat revealed the fading of hope, or an inner conflict between desire to continue bidding and determination to stop. There was a long pause before the next bid. The bidders withdrew one after another. Excitement was running high and Sotheby's voice as he announced each new bid became more deliberate. When he had said one hundred and fifty guineas for the third time everyone held his breath. Only when the hammer fell and the auctioneer solemnly said 'gone' was the silence broken and the spectators who had been motionless as statues became men again. The City Library had won the day.

1848 may be remembered as the year of revolutions by the world in general, but in England it brought about a bankruptcy that shook all ranks of society to the core. One of the saddest events in the annals of great sales in the middle of the nineteenth century was the dispersal of the property of Richard Plantagenet Temple Nugent Brydges Chandos Grenville, 2nd Duke of Buckingham and Chandos. His was an accumulation of property, works of art, books and manuscripts garnered by many generations of one illustrious family. The Duke had been left heavy debts by an extravagant father. But despite this he indulged extensively in buying land on borrowed money, at a level of interest greater than the resultant rent. The crash was finally precipitated by the expenses of a visit to Stowe by Queen Victoria and Prince Albert. The special building that took place and the preparations for the visit cost vast sums and in August 1847 the bailiffs (who were said to have been present even at the time of the royal visit, but had donned the uniforms of the Duke's staff for the occasion) took possession of the effects of Stowe and the Duke's other residences. A fortnight later he left England with debts said to exceed £1,000,000. His estates in Buckinghamshire, Oxfordshire and Northamptonshire were sold for £262,000. Christie's sold the contents of Stowe House over forty days for a mere £75,562. There was simply too much to absorb at one time. Every collector of note attended. The occasion was described at the time as the greatest bargain hunt of the era. On the day before the Christie's sale began *The Times* wrote:

> During the past week the British public has been admitted to a spectacle of painful interest and gravely historical import. One of the most splendid abodes of our almost regal aristocracy has thrown open its portals to an endless succession of visitors who, from morning to night have flowed in an uninterrupted stream from room to room, and floor to floor – not to enjoy the hospitality of the lord or to congratulate him on his countless treasures of art, but to see an ancient family ruined, their palace marked for destruction,[1] and its contents scattered to the four winds of Heaven. We are only saying what is notorious and what therefore it is neither a novelty or a cruelty to repeat, that the most notable and puissant prince, his Grace the Duke of Buckingham and Chandos, is at this moment an absolutely ruined and destitute man. Our advertising columns have introduced to the public the long list of assets, properties, and interests which are no longer his, and will not revert to his heirs. The last crash of this mighty ruin is that which now sounds. Stowe is no more. This morning the tumultuous invasion of sight-seers will once again be endured and tomorrow the auctioneer will begin his work.

Samuel Leigh Sotheby was one of the hundreds of subscribers whose name is printed in a special edition of a priced and annotated catalogue which was published to commemorate the event. Sotheby's also advertised in this the fact that they were to sell the highly important and extensive library removed from Stowe, at their house, 3 Wellington Street, Strand, over two 12-day sales planned for January 1849. In the event the sale of the Stowe library did not occur till March, June and August of 1849, and what was probably the most important part of the library was never exposed to public sale at all. This was the truly remarkable collection of ancient manuscripts and unpublished State papers. These included the vast accumulation of the manuscripts acquired by the Duke's father in 1804 from Thomas Astle, Keeper of the Records in the Tower, which contained not only 'the matchless volume of Original Anglo-Saxon Charters, a collection hitherto unrivalled in number, beauty and preservation'; but also the Psalter of King Alfred the Great; the original inventory of Queen Elizabeth I's Wardrobe, Plate and Jewels; the Hanoverian State Papers; a host of letters and accounts by Wolsey about the extravagances of Henry VIII and innumerable other collections of correspondence, as well as the original work of many antiquaries. They were offered to the Duke of Buckingham under the terms of Astle's will (and to the Trustees of the British Museum if he did not want to acquire them, but he did). In fact, he had at once commissioned the most original architect of his time, Sir John Soane, to

1. The buildings have, of course, been the home of a distinguished public school since 1923.

3

prepare a suitable apartment for the reception of the papers at Stowe, 'and the result of his labours was the very beautiful Gothic room in which the collection has been up to a very recent period, very carefully preserved'. Later, a vastly important collection of early Irish manuscripts also arrived at Stowe, and with it the collector's grandson who spent many years at Stowe cataloguing it, as well as the various other manuscript collections that were already there or added later. These later additions included the Earl of Essex's State papers and those of Sir Thomas Edmondes, ambassador in the reign of Elizabeth I and James I to the courts of France and the Netherlands. The most famous letter among them was Cecil's detailed and dramatic description of the Gunpowder Plot, dated 9 November 1605.

Sir Frederick Madden, Keeper of the Department of Manuscripts of the British Museum, and a most assiduous and shrewd purchaser on its behalf for forty years, at once realised the importance of the collection and called on Samuel Leigh Sotheby at Wellington Street to find out whether it could be bought *en bloc*. He discovered that the same thought had already occurred to other collectors and Sotheby's had received a number of tentative and one firm offer. Madden reported at once to his Trustees but they displayed a marked lack of enthusiasm to find the necessary money. So the manuscripts went instead to Bertram, the 4th Earl of Ashburnham, who had recently become the most powerful purchaser in this sphere of collecting. His first offer was £7,000. After some negotiations with Samuel Leigh Sotheby, he increased it to £8,000 which was accepted. (Madden had valued the collection at £8,360.) Ashburnham insisted on buying not only the manuscripts in their entirety but also every available copy of the printed sale catalogue. The one which remains at Sotheby's to this day is a file copy which the firm's faithful printers over many years, J. Davy, sent to Samuel Leigh Sotheby because there were no copies left within the firm itself, even for reference purposes. Sotheby wrote inside the cover some years later, 'I believe this to be the only copy not in the possession of the Earl of Ashburnham'.

The 4th Earl was one of those English aristocrats who might have been the very model for the aloof, cold, autocratic, arrogant eccentrics that figured so prominently in French and German romantic novels around the end of the nineteenth century. In the pursuit of his own interests, Ashburnham did not care a rap what others thought of him but this was rather in the nature of a public front. He was a firm though fair-minded manager of his large family estate; he was an adventurous traveller who went far beyond the confines of the conventional Grand Tour; and he was a considerable scholar who employed particularly scholarly librarians to catalogue his acquisitions, and then distributed such catalogues generously both to public libraries and to fellow collectors. Having been a collector of books since he was a schoolboy at Westminster he had ample funds from the 1830s onwards to make purchases on a scale hardly known in his day. He walked into the book shop of Payne and Foss one day, for example, and put on the counter £472 10s. in return for which he took away a copy of the forty-two line Gutenberg Bible on paper, the 1462 Bible on vellum and the famous block-book, *Biblia Pauperum*. All the same, another bookseller said of him that he was 'a man rather calculated to inspire fear than love or respect'. He was a constant purchaser at Sotheby sales and one way or another his family interests were to be linked with the history of Sotheby's for several generations.

Manuscripts of all kinds, illuminated missals and books of hours became his particular penchant and he accelerated the building up of his library between 1847 and 1849 by the wholesale purchase of several entire collections. One of these was from a genial, naturalised Frenchman, born in Paris, whose full name was Guglielmo Bruto Icilio Timoleone, Conte Libri Carucci della Sommaia. Libri was brilliant but crooked, and he became the centre of a *cause célèbre* that went on for years. Having studied law and science, he occupied the Chair of Mathematics at the University of Pisa at the age of twenty. He escaped to France as a political refugee in 1830 and not long afterwards was appointed to a professorship in the Faculty of Science at the University of Paris. He was one of the first scholars to interest himself in the history of mathematics and science. It was through this that he devoted himself to a study of bibliography and palaeography, and with his discerning genius he soon showed a grasp of these subjects in which he had few rivals. By 1835 he was already spending more time trading in books and manuscripts than on his academic duties. Although he twice failed to get an appointment to the staff of the Bibliothèque du Roi, he was made secretary to an official commission to oversee the publication of a Union Catalogue of manuscripts in French public libraries. In this capacity, armed with impressive letters of introduction, he had free and unsupervised entry to go anywhere he wanted, and during his travels around France he did indeed find an awesome state of neglect among those responsible for the administration of many provincial libraries. With brazen audacity and total assurance he used every opportunity of helping himself to any manuscript of great antiquity which he found desirable. Some he stole entire; others he rendered imperfect by simply ripping out leaves or quires, presumably on the assumption that this would never be detected. Later, with the assistance of some of the many Paris bookbinders and facsimile-artists (who carried on a profitable sideline in the 1840s of forging the then fashionable genealogies and documents to prove descent from the Crusaders), he removed or altered the marks of provenance and renewed the bindings.

Libri's library 'grew' so rapidly that he began wholesale disposals by auction: as many as eleven such sales took place in Paris between 1835 and 1846, and after a particularly extensive one in 1847 ugly rumours about the origin of fine, rare books in such quantities began to circulate in Paris. Libri began to look for buyers further afield. He offered a marvellous selection of manuscripts to the British Museum. Madden and an assistant went over to study it and to prepare a report for their principals, but once again the latter failed to act. Eventually, tipped off by Madden's assistant and advised by Payne and Foss, the Earl of Ashburnham acquired the selection for £8,000. Among the 1,923 items there were forty-five ancient Biblical manuscripts, all before the eleventh century, and ten of them of the eighth and earlier; a number of Latin classics of the ninth and tenth centuries; an immense selection of Dante MSS; a good series of early French Romances; many important Italian texts; much Florentine correspondence of the fourteenth and fifteenth centuries; important scientific papers of the seventeenth and eighteenth and a fine collection of Napoleonic letters. On top of all this there were a considerable number of richly illuminated manuscripts. It soon emerged, however, that Ashburnham's purchase contained many stolen items and the restoration of these to the French State was a matter that was to haunt both the 4th and the 5th Earl of Ashburnham like a veritable albatross for forty years.[1]

In the meantime, serious and painstaking investigations into Libri's activities began to take place, though he defended himself vigorously as soon as he was officially accused – he was, as Munby so charmingly put it, 'in the highest degree combative by nature'. When it looked, however, as if he might really be in serious trouble, Libri fled to London with his library. Naturally he turned to Sotheby's for a continuation of its dispersal. The partners must have had some misgivings about accepting the books for sale, though relatively little was known about Libri in England at this stage, and the first Libri catalogue was brought out anonymously, which was by no means unusual. During the 1850s there was a massive return to anonymous sales, except in the case of very well-known collections. It was indeed also the period when sales made up of the properties of several owners became the norm rather than the exception.

The first Libri Sale, which took place on 19 February 1849 and for the four following days, was quaintly entitled as of 'very fine, important and valuable books selected from the library of an eminent literary character'. It was a mixed bag with some superb items, and the results seem to have come up to Libri's expectations. Sotheby's association with him continued for many years thereafter. He usually catalogued the sales himself. There were further sales in 1853 and 1857 but in fact the principal dispersals of Libri's library, at a time when he had become a well-known and much disputed figure in England, took place, under his full name, between 1859 and 1865.

The Libri association had an unhappy ending from Sotheby's point of view. Libri became so dissatisfied with the prices obtained in the later sales that he bought in a large number of lots and subsequently brought a Chancery suit against the firm. Finally, one day Libri came into the Wellington Street premises and physically removed the cream of what had remained unsold. After his death in 1869 his suit came to an end, and Sotheby's had to pay £1,500 in costs. The bill appears to have been met personally by John Wilkinson, as senior partner. In part compensation he appropriated the books Libri had left behind but never sold them for fear of litigation. They were still in his possession at the time of his death exactly twenty-five years later. Wilkinson's heirs, who felt with some justification that the firm should have shared the burden of

1. Much of the information on Libri is taken, with his permission, from A. N. L. Munby's two lectures on Libri called *The Earl and the Thief* which describe the acquisition of the Libri manuscripts by Ashburnham and the subsequent history of the collection.

the legal costs with him, took the books to Christie's where they were sold in February 1895.

If a single sale were to epitomise the firm's activities in the lifetime of the last of the Sotheby's, it is the long sale of the library of Benjamin Heywood Bright in 1845. Bright, unlike Heber and Corser and other distinguished book collectors, has never been made much of by the great pundits of book trade history, and there seems a simple reason. Bright was an amateur: a man who loved books in their own right and bought them wherever and whenever he could, and the Sotheby cataloguers had the devil's own job in divining any sort of system in Bright's jackdaw assemblage. Again there was a reason: Bright actually read all his books. Although he was well known in his own day as a prolific book collector, he resented being approached by scholars and students who wanted to research in his library, because it caused worry and endless exploration of cluttered shelves in dusty nooks and crannies to find the volume in question, and generally interfered with the collector's peace of mind.

The exceedingly acid note on Bright's sale (after his death, of course), which appeared in the *Gentleman's Magazine*, was probably written by one of them. This author said of the library that 'it had been formed silently and secretly by the late Benjamin Heywood Bright, esq., who appears to have had a mercenary pleasure in accumulating articles of admitted and increasing value, and keeping them unknown to those who might have employed them to a more general benefit'. He goes on to cite two instances of rather esoteric works of scholarship which would have greatly benefited from collation with manuscripts which Bright owned, and thunders, 'We wish such a man, or his survivors who are like-minded, were capable of a blush'.

In fact, Bright seems to have been generous to a degree in lending his books to fellow collectors – thus Lord Spencer printed one of Bright's rarest volumes (a sixteenth-century poem about the Battle of Flodden in Italian) as a contribution to the Roxburghe Club – and Bright also gave books and manuscripts to various libraries, but did it so quietly that this was hardly known.

The introduction to the Bright catalogue goes some way towards explaining the old man's outlook. 'Like some other eminent philological scholars, he was a collector from his schoolboy days, and in whatever situation he was, the same passion possessed him. At home there was not an obscure recess in which old books were to be found that was unknown to him; and when he travelled abroad, one of his main objects was to collect those rare volumes of which so many are to be found in this catalogue, in which Foreign writers have treated of English affairs or English writers have printed their works at Foreign presses. Like other collectors, he had at the beginning no particular plan, and no particular object. . . .'

He bought liberally from book shops and at auction, and price did not worry him. 'This habit', the catalogue continues, 'continued through forty years and more, and being at the same time under the guidance of admirable taste and surprising knowledge, cannot but have created a library of great curiosity and value.' Bright annotated whatever he had read with pencilled notes 'pointing to the curious facts, the singular opinions, the remarkable words, the parallel passages, the reference to other writings, or to the lines of other persons, which he observed in the perusal, intended only for himself and his own particular pursuits and objects, but useful to all'. This, one feels, is what genuine book collecting is all about and, incidentally, the proficiency of the cataloguing shows the experienced book auctioneer at his best, in creating order out of chaos to his client's great advantage and lasting benefit. The sale was divided into two parts, each of twelve-day sessions, in March and April 1845. There were well over 6,000 lots and the total they fetched was £3,916 15s. 6d.

It was an astonishingly diverse library, from the French volume printed in Caen in 1699 ('on the Origin and Progress of Coffee'), which now sold for 6d., to *Caesar's Commentaryes* translated by the Earl of Worcester in 1530 ('A Book of the GREATEST RARITY') which occurred two lots earlier and fetched £26 10s. What, one wonders, would the great Italian painters of altar-pieces have made of 'A treatise declaryng and shewing dyvers causes taken out of the holy scriptures . . . that pyctures and other ymages which were wont to be worshypped are in no wise to be suffred in the temples or churches of Christen men. *Black letter'*? It was bought by Thomas Rodd (perhaps for the British Museum, whose official agent he was) for £1 15s. and it was followed by the more convential *Pictures exhibited at the British Institution* (1824) (1s. 6d.), and the *Picturesque Annual* (with plates, Morocco, Gilt leaves) of 1832 which fetched 3s. 6d. Bright also owned copies of the funeral orations of Michelangelo and Carracci, but these came in the section on theology.

His books on law and jurisprudence had already been the subject of a big, earlier sale in two parts (3 and 18 June 1844); the second also included a great mass of manuscripts. A special catalogue on natural history, geography and mining was to follow the main sale. Bright's most famous possession was an enormous collection of Broadside Ballads, which he had bought at the Roxburghe Sale in 1813 for £477 15s. There were over 1,300 of them and they were now acquired for the British Museum for £535 by Rodd, as indeed were five smaller collections of ballads in the sale. The Roxburghe Ballads, which had originally been brought together by the Earl of Oxford, occupied eight full pages of the catalogue.

The whole process of Sotheby's cataloguing had now become much more sophisticated, though the compiler apologises that because all the books are in alphabetical sequence of authors, the Bright catalogue does not seem to do justice to the wealth of the individual subject areas covered. In a final paragraph he advises clients that 'in forming the catalogue, several errors and oversights have been committed, which, so far as they have been noticed, or may be discovered before the day of the sale, will be corrected. Care has been taken, as far as possible, to point out any defects in order to prevent disappointment to persons who may not have an opportunity of examining the books: and wherever a more minute description of the condition may be desired, Messrs. Sotheby and Wilkinson will be ready to answer every enquiry.'

If the Bright catalogue is a worthy monument to Sotheby's around the middle of the century, it also exemplifies the enormous labours that were involved in the preparation of such material for the printer; and, of course, the sale itself – curiously broken into two '*divisions*' – took up rather more than one-tenth of Sotheby's selling time in a single year. Again more manpower was needed, and in 1847 the firm took on a young man, Edward Grose Hodge, who was to play a most important role in its history. He had recently arrived in London from his native Cornwall (he was born at Angarrach) and it seems as if employment at Sotheby's was his first job. He had married a Cornish girl and they had five children, but sadly we do not have much biographical detail about him. Though it seems quite clear from the many brief references both to John Wilkinson and to Hodge – both individually and jointly – that the London book trade regarded them as pillars of the establishment, and as they were both so long-lived their pre-eminence in the sale-room tended to be taken for granted. Hodge became a partner in 1864, but right to the end of Wilkinson's life they addressed each other in surviving correspondence as 'Dear *Mr.* Wilkinson' and 'Dear *Mr.* Hodge'. Between them they put in more than a hundred and twenty years of service to the firm, and each – but particularly Wilkinson – outlived most of his contemporaries, so that by the time they died each had become something of a living legend.

At that time too the firm acquired the services, as senior sales clerk, of Arthur Nattali, member of a bookselling family[1] which had premises in 13 Bedford Street, Covent Garden and specialised in books on art and architecture. Nattali's advertised their catalogue rather quaintly as '*Nattali's Post Circular of Books*, forwarded on the receipt of two postage stamps'. The senior sales clerk seems to have acted at that time as sale-room manager and to have supervised all forms of work in progress when the partners were absent. Arthur Nattali's place as senior sales clerk was taken by F. J. du Pasquier – a nephew of John Wilkinson's – in the mid-1860s, and he was renowned for his impeccable dress. One contemporary account of the firm's activities refers to 'Pasquier's sartorial embellishments which were the despair and envy of many a younger member of the only trade which had been dignified by the sub-title of profession'. (His name is variously spelled in auction reports of his day.)

Hodge's arrival more or less coincided with a period when an unusually large number of booksellers, not only of new, but also of specialist and antiquarian stock, were going out of business. Sotheby's was merely one of several firms of auctioneers who undertook the dispersal of their stock: Puttick & Simpson, as well as Southgate & Barratt and L. A. Lewis, both of Fleet Street, all played a prominent part in this melancholy task. It seems that the trade was hit both in London and the provinces. The three major businesses whose stock came under the hammer in Wellington Street were Longman, Brown, Green & Longman 'giving up that branch of their business [second-hand bookselling] for the convenience of their publishing and wholesale trade'; Payne & Foss, after a long,

1. Another Nattali, Henry, was a professional book cataloguer who worked for both Christie's and Puttick & Simpson's in a freelance capacity later in the century.

distinguished and gallant reign, and Thomas Rodd (there was enough for *eight* multi-session sales).[1] Presumably young Hodge had to do his share of the endless, monotonous cataloguing involved.

After his father's death in 1842, Samuel Leigh Sotheby, now universally referred to as 'Young Mr. Sotheby' even in advancing middle-age, changed the style of the firm from S. L. SOTHEBY to S. L. SOTHEBY & CO. In 1850 the importance of Wilkinson's role was more fully acknowledged and it became S. LEIGH SOTHEBY AND JOHN WILKINSON which it remained until 1864. Even before the death of the elder Sotheby, Samuel Leigh had moved himself and his family to 'Woodlands', a delightful residence in spacious grounds in Norwood, away from the centre of London. It happened to be close to the spot in Sydenham where the Crystal Palace was to be re-erected after its transfer from Hyde Park in 1852, and Sotheby took an enormous interest in the event and the subsequent management of the building. History does not record whether he was acquainted with its designer, the great Joseph Paxton, but Samuel Leigh published two papers on the future of the erstwhile home of the Great Exhibition: *A few Words by Way of a Letter addressed to the Directors* in 1855, and a *Postscript* to that letter in the same year. Within 'Woodlands' Sotheby not only had a sizeable library, but also a considerable gallery of cabinet paintings.

By the end of the 1850s the number of sales, particularly of engravings, pictures and the decorative arts, was increasing rapidly and the partners decided to build a large, new gallery for the display and sale of such objects in North Wellington Street at No. 21, adjoining the Lyceum Theatre, 'as an addition to their house of business, for the more advantageous disposal by public auction of cabinet pictures, drawings, engravings, antiquities and all works of art'. Its accompanying offices also relieved the pressure on space for the staff that had gradually built up at No. 3 Wellington Street. In February 1861, when Samuel Leigh Sotheby had already more than half retired – he had been in an indifferent state of health for some years – and had rented the castellated neo-Gothic Buckfastleigh Abbey in Devonshire with the intention of seeing out his days there,[2] he organised an exhibition of his own collection to celebrate the opening of the new premises. He produced an elaborate catalogue entitled 'List of a few Specimens of Art, chiefly the productions of English artists in oil and watercolours; collected during the last twenty-five years by S. Leigh Sotheby, F.S.A.'. There were 267 exhibits. Many of the artists' names mean little to us today but there were works by Beechey, Bonington, George Cattermole, William Collins, John Constable, David Cox, William Etty, J. F. Herring, John

1. Three further enormously long booksellers' stock sales were handled by Sotheby's in the ensuing years: firstly Henry George Bohn's, which began in February 1868 (24 days) and continued in May 1870 (21 days); secondly Joseph Lilly's in March, June and November of 1871 (35 days in all) as well as April 1872 and January and July 1873, and finally that of F. S. Ellis who had earlier merged with the long-established family firm of William Boone, which began in November 1885.
2. He was very fond of fishing, particularly for Dartmoor trout.

Martin, George Morland, Samuel Prout, Benjamin West and Sir David Wilkie.

He states to the reader, somewhat apologetically one feels, that 'intuitively fond of Works of Art, I have not considered my peculiar position in business to have been such as to have deterred me from indulging my taste, as far as my means have permitted me', and then explains rather charmingly the background of his acquisitions:

> Some of the Drawings have been presented to me by the Relatives of Deceased Artists and Executors as Reminiscences of Departed Friends. I may conscientiously feel, that in all cases where I have purchased Specimens at the Sales entrusted to the care of my Partner and myself, I have invariably paid more than other persons would have done; and therefore, by the commissions which I have given generally to some dealer, I feel that my taste for collecting Works of Art has materially benefited the interest of the Proprietors. At the same time, when aware of it, I have made a point of withdrawing my commission when any Collectors have desired the possession of the same object. I think it also right to state that I have never purchased any Work of Art as a matter of commerce.

It rather looks, therefore, as if some of the paintings were in the nature of left-overs from the firm's sales; Sotheby bought others at what appears to have been an annual exhibition at the Crystal Palace Picture Gallery.

The collection included a portrait, a landscape with St. Paul's in the distance and *A Study after Rembrandt*, all by Bonington. To the latter Sotheby appended the following note:

> The works of this distinguished Artist were sold, on his decease, by auction in Wellington Street. No sale, the production of any artist, caused greater interest, and though the pictures and drawings sold at unprecedented prices, they have, – which is not often the case after the excitement of a well supported sale is over, – maintained their then estimated value, notwithstanding the injury that was afterwards done to the memory of the artist by his Father, most unfairly attempting to impose upon the public by making sales of his own and other persons' COPIES of the beautiful productions of HIS SON, who, had he lived, bid fair to rank as one of England's Brightest Stars in the Circle of Art. On the death of the Father, the Sister of the deceased artist placed the remaining works of her brother and those left by her father in my hands, for sale by auction. With her consent, *I then had all the copies stamped as such.* Among the original sketches, however, was the present '*Study after Rembrandt*', marked at the back in the autograph of the artist, 'R. P. B. COPY'.

In the case of a *View of Windsor Castle with the Thames in the Foreground* by John Constable, Sotheby notes 'Presented to me in 1846, as inscribed at the back, by William Smith Esq., the Executor of the eminent print-seller, John Thane as a memorial of his collection of drawings'. Of *A Storm at Sea* by Cotman, he writes that it was bought at the studio sale held by Christie's.

Perhaps the painting one would most like to see is No. 133 by E. Marcin. It is an outdoor family portrait showing the Essex countryside in the background with Samuel Baker in the year before his death, 'the old gentleman, booted and spurred, with his favourite horse in the adjoining field. In the foreground are

Mr. and Mrs. John Sotheby, with their infant son, the late Mr. Samuel Sotheby'. The infant, of course, was the collector's father. It must be one of the very few representations of three generations of the great auctioneering family.[1]

Sotheby included a number of additional items in the catalogue which he had brought more recently. Among them were a number of set pieces (*Morning, Noon, Evening and Night, Sunset, From the Tempest, Elegance,* etc.) produced by members of the Sketching Society who met at each others' houses and within a given time all would produce their rendering of a set theme. Sotheby bought examples by the brothers Alfred E. and John James Chalon as well as by C. Leslie and Clarkson Stanfield, all Royal Academicians.

Our portrait of him shows the collector holding another late entry to the exhibition. This was the subject of a four-page addendum which he included in a limited number of copies of the catalogue. The item in question was 'a vase in terra-cotta with Bacchanalian figures in alto relievo'. He had spotted it at Colnaghi's, fallen in love with it and bought it at once 'lest it be taken out of the country'. It was such a perfect specimen that many knowledgeable experts puzzled their heads over its origin. Sotheby publishes a letter from such a one,[2] but a more practical nephew, one Arthur Rich, thought he had seen a similar vase elsewhere. He tracked it down and bought it, and found the number 954 embossed on its base. Further research showed that Sotheby's 'antique' specimen had, in fact, been made by Josiah Wedgwood.[3] 'A thought of the possibility of the vase being a modern production, *in imitation or style of an antique in a state of dilapidation,* never for a moment entered my head.'

There were slight similarities in the decoration with Wedgwood's reproduction of the Portland Vase. The nephew seems to have suggested that nobody would notice. Sotheby now wrote him an admonitory epistle (also published in the catalogue) as to why a man in his position could never stoop to such deception, even though 'proving it to be the work of the celebrated Wedgwood Emporium of Ceramic Art at once takes away the *pecuniary* value it would merit had it been a work created during the Roman period by a Greek Artist, which it had all the appearance of being'. '*Concealment*', Sotheby goes on, 'WILL BE IMPOSSIBLE'. (The phrase is set in capital letters in the catalogue.) 'I have lived nearly sixty years and know sufficiently of the world to be aware *that matters most desired and specially agreed to be kept secret are not so kept.*' The vase was put back on show with the letter inside it to attest to anyone else who discovered the truth that its owner was already well aware of it.

The letter was one of the last published documents written by this lovable if slightly dotty character, a man of enormous and diverse enthusiasms[4] who had

1. The picture probably passed to Arthur Rich, a nephew of Samuel Leigh Sotheby. It seems to have been sold at auction with other family chattels at Tunbridge Wells in 1934.
2. The artist J. L. Tupper. It was he who made the sketch of Samuel Leigh Sotheby's small, dapper figure admiring it shown in Plate 5.
3. Sotheby's sold Wedgwood's prints and drawings in a two-day sale on 11 November 1846 and his library over six days in the following week.
4. He was a Fellow of the Society of Antiquaries as well as of the Royal Geographical, the Numismatic and a host of other bodies.

changed the character of the firm's establishment in Wellington Street into an altogether more interesting and wide-ranging business. He was fortunate in having a partner whose solid but intelligent objectivity tempered his own idiosyncracies and who was also able to consolidate profitably the innovations the last of the Sothebys had brought about.

Samuel Leigh died suddenly and completely unexpectedly in June 1861. The *Gentleman's Magazine* wrote, 'The circumstances of the death of this gentleman are very distressing. After lunching in good spirits with his family, he started, as was his custom, for a ramble near the [Buckfastleigh] Abbey ruins; not returning his absence caused intense anxiety; but it was not till the next morning that his body was found in the River Dart in very shallow water. From evidence before the Coroner, it appeared that Mr. Sotheby was subject to fainting fits, and it is supposed that he was suddenly seized with heart disease when near the brink of the river. The verdict was "Found Drowned". Mr. Sotheby had recently taken a lease of the Abbey where he anticipated much enjoyment from the beauties of the scenery, and from leisurely occupations'.

In an extremely short will, Sotheby left everything to his wife, Julia Emma, but the will contained a major error: the date of its signature had been given as 1057 instead of 1857, and a good many legal complications were involved to set this right. The estate amounted to some £14,000. Julia Emma outlived her husband by nearly half a century. From her own will it seems quite evident that she was on the friendliest terms with the Hodge family. A Hodge sister, Edith, was her executor and Julia Emma left many individual bequests to Edward Grose Hodge,[1] his son Tom and other Hodge relations. She and Samuel Leigh had had four children – two daughters and two sons. One son died in infancy; the other was sub-normal and, in the manner of the times, was sent to live with a doctor in Ireland who had other such children in his care. It probably demonstrates how close was the relationship between Samuel Leigh Sotheby and John Wilkinson that the son was christened Frederick Petit *Wilkinson* Sotheby. The residue of Julia Emma Sotheby's estate went to her niece, Rose Emma Rich. A part of Samuel Leigh Sotheby's library was sold at Wellington Street on 8 February 1862. Most of the books relating to his researches on Melanchthon and Luther, and his notes and unpublished documents on the subject were included in the sale.[2] The bulk of his collection of pictures and drawings had been sold in the previous two days.

John Wilkinson was now left in charge, though it appears to have taken nearly two years for him to effect the transfer of the ownership of the business to himself from the Sotheby family. As we have seen, it was to be another year before he appointed Edward Grose Hodge his partner. It was clear that both appreciated how important it was that the name of Sotheby's should not disappear from the firm, for the new style, SOTHEBY, WILKINSON AND HODGE began to appear on catalogues from 1864 onwards, and remained unchanged until 1924.

1. Including the famous office desk that Tom Hodge so treasured all his life.
2. The majority of them was bought by the Manchester bookseller, John Gray Bell, who issued a special catalogue of them.

4

Fire!

PROBABLY the most memorable sale of the year in which the firm began to call itself SOTHEBY, WILKINSON & HODGE began on 20 July and continued for ten days. The occasion was the sale of a library of a book collector whom all the world knew to have belonged to an occupation that rarely concerned itself with such matters as Elizabethan literature and drama. This was George Daniel of 18 Canonbury Square, Islington. He had begun life in a stockbroker's office, and afterwards followed the profession of an accountant, and a very successful accountant at that. He had started writing at a tender age and had a number of substantial satirical works to his credit by the time he was twenty. The story goes that he composed in 1812 a poetical squib on the reputed horse-whipping of the Prince of Wales by Lord Yarmouth, entitled *R-y-l Stripes; or a Kick from Yar---th to Wa--s,* for the suppression of which the Prince Regent paid a very sizeable sum. Daniel continued to write and to act as textual editor and critic all his life, but his principal pastime was the collecting of books. Thirty years after it had gone out of fashion he still affected the faintly foppish dress of the days of the Prince Regent. Though his portly figure and florid, good-humoured countenance were familiar to every auctioneer and dealer in old books, he was by no means universally popular and all too often people remembered the less lovable traits of Dickens's Mr. Turveydrop Senior from *Bleak House* when they thought of Daniel. 'His manner', says F. S. Ellis,[1] 'was too supercilious, condescending and pompous to inspire any very warm hearted remembrances in those who knew him . . . it may be safely said that he rarely bought a book at any important price which his judgement did not assure him was a good investment and rarely was his judgement at fault.' He had bought extensively from Thomas Thorpe, Thomas Rodd, Joseph Lilly and particularly from William Pickering 'though a cautious buyer and a hard-mouthed bargainer, as any of those he dealt with could have testified. Still, he had a real love of books and could tell many a good anecdote concerning the prizes he had secured from time to time.'

These included his favourite story of his 'acute management of the purchase of a roll of black letter Elizabethan Ballads from Mr. Fitch, postmaster at Ipswich, who obtained them from the housekeeper at Helmingham Hall, Suffolk, the family mansion of the Tollemaches, for £50; another concerned the first folio Shakespeare in particularly fine condition from Mr. Pickering for £100 (which he insisted that the bookseller should wrap up in one of his best silk handkerchiefs), and so on, and so on.'

After a thoroughly convivial life Daniel died, as one might have expected, of

1. A well-known antiquarian bookseller in his day, who was also a major contributor to Quaritch's *Contributions Towards a Dictionary of English Book-Collectors.*

apoplexy, in March 1864. He was making his purchases, wrote W. Carew Hazlitt, 'at a fortunate and peculiar juncture, just when prices were depressed, about the time of the great Heber Sales. The marvellous gleanings came to the hammer precisely when the quarto Shakespear, the black-letter romance, the unique book of Elizabethan verse, had grown to ten times their weight in sovereigns. Sir William Tite, J. O. Halliwell and Henry Huth were to the front [at the sale]. What a wonderful sight it was! No living man had ever witnessed the like. Copies of Shakespear printed from the prompters' MSS. and published at 4d., now fetched £300 or £400'.

Indeed the Daniel sale in 1864 was something of a bridge between one generation of collectors and another. Daniel had bought at the sale of the great bibliophiles of the Twenties, Thirties and Forties when money was tight, and particularly because of the Heber Sales there were far more antiquarian books about than the small body of collectors could digest. It was now the turn of Henry Huth, Sir William Tite, the Earl of Ashburnham, the Baroness Burdett-Coutts[1] (all of whose libraries were subsequently to be dispersed by Sotheby's) to compete for Daniel's most treasured items for their own collections, and naturally this drove up prices so that for this reason alone the Daniel sale was something of a landmark. There were fierce auction room duels, mostly between booksellers with commissions from important clients (such as Lilly acting on behalf of Huth, and Henry Stevens of Vermont, a distinguished American bookseller, as agent for the Lenox Library), and as Ellis mused subsequently 'What the choicer volumes of Daniel's library would bring now [that is, in 1892] it is idle to speculate; but in 1864 there was much less money afloat, and some of the prices that were then thought monstrously high would now be regarded almost as pence compared to pounds'. He could not get over the fact that a very fine copy of Walton's *Compleat Angler* went for £27 10s., that the still rarer second edition only fetched £4 6s. (1980 prices would be £8,000 and £1,000), while the third, fourth and fifth editions brought only £10 11s. between them; or that Herrick's *Poems* of 1648 was knocked down for a mere £6 10s. (1980 price £3,000).

On the other hand, Chute's *Beautie Dishonoured*, which Daniel had bought at the Bright Sale in 1845 for £35, was now bought for Huth by Lilly at £96. Great too, says Ellis, 'was the fight over the unique volume (Lot 1154), between Sir William Tite's commission and Lilly, as Mr. Huth's agent, *A Banquet of Daintie Conceits. Furnished with verie delicate and choyce inventions, to delight their mindes, who take pleasure in musique, and therewithall to sing sweet Ditties, either to the Lute, Bandora, Virginalles, or any other instrument, &c., 1588*. Even though the copy were not unique such a book could not fail to be attractive in itself, and long and determined was the contest for it. Lilly was a slow and cautious bidder, advancing, not by leaps and bounds, but by sums of 10s. or £1 only, and at last it was knocked down to him for £225'.

1. She was by no means the first woman collector of books. In 1862 Sotheby's had sold the fine library of Miss Richardson Currer, whom Heber had considered marrying on account of her bibliographical talents. See also page 304.

Most of the sale was a curious mixture of highs and lows, 'but it was in the sixth day of the Sale that the chief interest centred, the day that was to see the contest for the Folio Editions of Shakespeare and the first editions of several of the quartos in unmatchable condition, for the first editions of the *Rape of Lucrece* and the *Sonnets*, and the editions of 1594 and 1596 of the *Venus and Adonis*. It was a hot July day, and those who were present had reason to remember it for the rest of their lives; the atmosphere of the black hole of Calcutta, added to the excitement of the particular occasion, was such as one would not willingly undergo again. Among the 119 lots sold on that day a large proportion were of the greatest interest and value, and by the time that Lot 1416 (the Shakespeare of 1623) was reached, the room was crowded to suffocation, crammed to a degree that the writer has never witnessed anywhere before or since (except at a boxing match in New York); every corner of the room was packed and vantage ground made of piles of books, stools, and what not. Mr. Wilkinson, the veteran auctioneer, always remarkable alike for his insensibility to heat or cold when he wielded the hammer, was as cool and collected as usual.'

The Baroness Burdett-Coutts paid 682 guineas for a first folio Shakespeare in exceptional condition. It was the highest price by far ever paid for the book: the record was to stand until July 1899 when a Mr. M'George of Glasgow paid £1,700 for a copy, and two years after that 'young' Mr. Quaritch gave £1,720 for another copy at Christie's (1980 price £25,000).

As Ellis concludes, 'there may have been many another sale of greater importance, but during an experience of forty years the present writer never remembers any that created equal excitement and interest'. Daniel's library raised nearly £14,000, a remarkable sum for its day, and together with his prints, watercolours, paintings, coins and porcelain the total came to almost £16,000. It was one of the most valuable collections that Sotheby's had sold until that time.

The sales in the rest of the year were standard in comparison, and indeed 1865 was relatively unspectacular, though there was an amusing mixture of works of art and natural history on 2 March which included nine complete suits of armour among a great mass of such material, Etruscan vases of fine quality, a Madonna by Rafaelle – 'a very fine work confidently attributed by Connoisseurs of Repute to the pencil of the great painter', fine Sèvres porcelain, the skull and thighbone of Lord Darnley, as well as an immense collection of 'the Butterfly and Beetle Tribes' and a large mass of fossils and minerals formed by the Hon. Archd. Fraser of Lovat in the previous century. The sale that started on the following day consisted principally of a large number of prints and engravings, many of musical celebrities, but there was 'an extraordinary collection of old concert tickets', and a portrait of Henry Purcell by Verjolke (*sic*, perhaps Verkolje), 'said upon good authority to be the only known oil painting of this immortal English Composer'.

There were now constant sales of every form of the decorative arts. The

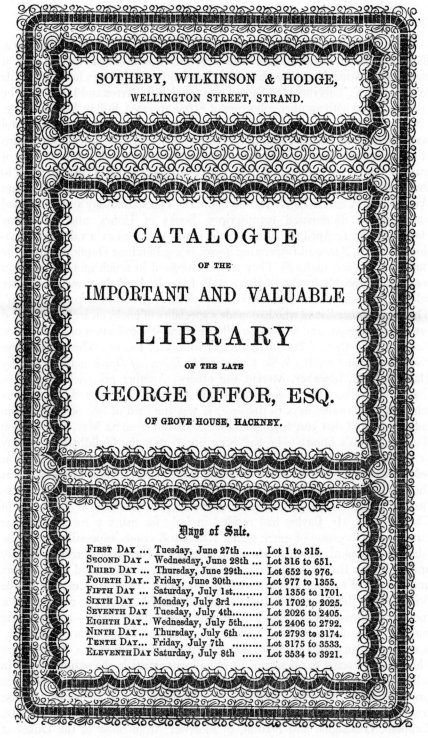

SOTHEBY, WILKINSON & HODGE,

WELLINGTON STREET, STRAND.

CATALOGUE

OF THE

IMPORTANT AND VALUABLE

LIBRARY

OF THE LATE

GEORGE OFFOR, ESQ.

OF GROVE HOUSE, HACKNEY.

Days of Sale.

FIRST DAY ...	Tuesday, June 27th	Lot 1 to 315.
SECOND DAY ..	Wednesday, June 28th ...	Lot 316 to 651.
THIRD DAY ...	Thursday, June 29th......	Lot 652 to 976.
FOURTH DAY..	Friday, June 30th.........	Lot 977 to 1355.
FIFTH DAY ...	Saturday, July 1st.........	Lot 1356 to 1701.
SIXTH DAY ...	Monday, July 3rd	Lot 1702 to 2025.
SEVENTH DAY	Tuesday, July 4th.........	Lot 2026 to 2405.
EIGHTH DAY..	Wednesday, July 5th......	Lot 2406 to 2792.
NINTH DAY...	Thursday, July 6th	Lot 2793 to 3174.
TENTH DAY...	Friday, July 7th	Lot 3175 to 3533.
ELEVENTH DAY	Saturday, July 8th	Lot 3534 to 3921.

A typical catalogue cover of its time. In fact, much of the Offor Library perished in a fire that destroyed Sotheby's premises in 1865.

7 March sale included a great number of Saxon and Celtic antiquities, Roman glass, cameos and intaglios, silver and tortoiseshell snuff-boxes, various ancient marble sculptures, Venetian glass, and then followed what was headed 'Fictile Manufactures'. This included Palissy ware, maiolica, Sèvres and Dresden. The sale concluded with another collection of Etruscan vases. Still in March, on the 13th and 14th, Sotheby's auctioned the Literary Correspondence of a Bristol bookseller, Joseph Cottle, who had been one of the first to publish the poems of Coleridge and Southey. The sale included the original holograph versions of many of their early poems, and there were letters from both of them to attest to their authenticity, as well as correspondence from William Cowper, William Wordsworth, Charles Lamb and de Quincey. The second day's sale included some superb illuminated manuscripts, Books of Hours, and an *Album Amicorum*. On 12 April the firm sold 362 items described as 'a valuable collection of Curios, Rare and Interesting Books, being Purchase Duplicates from the Bodleian Library, Oxford'. They were catalogued in much more detail than was usual, probably by the Bodleian staff. Later in April there was a four-day sale of the stock of an 'eminent Book and Print Seller retired from Business'. This was another Evans who had made a speciality of books on architecture and ornamental design, and was a marvellously complete collection of such works. Early in May there followed the 'select library of the late Thomas Holbein Esq., comprising a remarkable series of *The Dances of Death* as illustrated by Hans Holbein, Macaber, Merian and others'. Another print-seller's stock – that of 'an eminent firm' – followed in mid-May, which consisted of 2,254 lots which it took twelve days to disperse. It was the turn of one of several coin collections sold that year to come under the hammer on 22 May, and William Turner Alchin's library – he had been librarian at the Guildhall for twenty years – took three days from 24 to 26 May. Another print-seller's collection was sold on 27 May, but what today would probably cause the most excitement was the sale which followed on 29 and 30 May, the residue of a magnificent collection of Italian drawings and some paintings, the property of J. Bayley of Cheltenham.[1] Mr. Bayley had resided in Italy for many years and his was largely an aggregation of much earlier Italian collections, especially that of the Marquis Niccolini, which was brought together in the mid-eighteenth century and who, says the catalogue, 'was one of the most distinguished connoisseurs and patrons of the fine arts in Italy'. It continues, 'the interest excited by the possession of these beautiful designs naturally led Mr. Bayley to researches for more, and thus their acquirement became a prevailing study – an absorbing pursuit – and, in the course of fifteen or sixteen years of devotion to it in Italy, it resulted in an accumulation of many thousand drawings. Some of these were obtained by tracing out descendants of eminent artists in the various places in which they had chiefly lived, or pursued their studies; but a greater portion was procured from the cabinets of eminent connoisseurs and collectors of these treasures in Italy in former times, as the Riccardi, Buonarotti, Rinuccini, Capponi, Guadagna, and Piattoli, in Florence; from those of the Dukes of

1. Lugt, *Répertoire des Catalogues de Ventes*, No. 28557.

1. The view that everybody knows. Sotheby's main entrance in 34–35 New Bond Street after restoration in the late 1960s. Note the strange Egyptian sculpture (Sekhmet) above the newspaper kiosk.

2. Samuel Baker, the founder of the firm – bookseller, publisher, auctioneer and outstanding man of business.

3. John Sotheby, Baker's nephew, who inherited the business from his uncle.

4. George Leigh, Baker's first partner, and a much loved auctioneer in his day.

5. Samuel Leigh Sotheby, the third and last member of the family connected with the firm.

6. Thomas Rowlandson's impression of a book sale, possibly that of the library of Dr. Richard Mead.

7. Samuel Leigh Sotheby's splendid country seat, which housed his library and considerable collection of English paintings. It was not far from the site of the Crystal Palace.

8. The firm's premises, the second from the right, were in Wellington Street for almost a hundred years. Waterloo Bridge is seen in the distance.

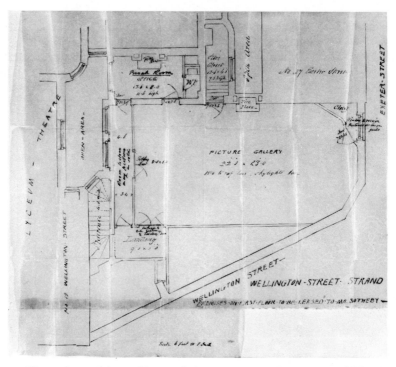

9. The only surviving evidence of the occupation of the large additional galleries in 21 Wellington Street. Samuel Leigh Sotheby took over the building for the firm's increasing number of art sales in the 1840s. The entire business functioned from these premises after fire had destroyed the principal buildings in 1865.

17. When the painter, R.W.B. ('Pen') Browning, the only child of the poets Robert and Elizabeth Barrett Browning, died, Sotheby's undertook the dispersal of the contents of his family's several houses in Italy in a six-day sale. The painting shows the Browning's drawing-room at the Casa Guidi.

18. A portrait of his father by 'Pen'. It fetched £77 in the sale. Most of the painter's other works fetched much less.

9 hote the dreadful hollow behind the little wood

19. One item in the sale (lot 11) showed Dante Gabriel Rossetti's sketch of Tennyson reading the manuscript of *Maud* to the Brownings.

20 & 21. In 1917 the firm moved to Bond Street. The premises had previously housed a firm of wine merchants called Basil Woodd in the extensive basement. Basil Woodd's cellarage, now converted into store rooms for Sotheby's paintings department, and a view of the original 'sampling corner'.

22. The upper parts of the new premises were formerly occupied by Messrs. Fairless & Beesforth who used the gallery to display and sell the works of Gustave Doré.

23. Extensive structural alterations were necessary to improve the display facilities. The original Doré gallery was much enlarged.

10. John Wilkinson worked at Sotheby's from 1825 to about 1885. He took over as senior partner after Samuel Leigh Sotheby's death in 1861. He was the architect of Sotheby's supremacy in the book auction field throughout the second half of the nineteenth century.

11. Bernard Quaritch, one of the world's greatest booksellers, and Sotheby's principal customer for forty years.

12. 'Young' Mr. Quaritch (Bernard Alfred) consolidated his father's success. A great ladies' man, he died young.

13. E. H. Dring – trained by the Quaritches, father and son – continued to expand the business after their deaths and rarely missed a sale at Sotheby's.

14. A famous engraving of a book sale at Sotheby's being taken by Edward Grose Hodge, Wilkinson's successor as head of the firm. It first appeared in the *Illustrated London News* in the 1880s. Most of the buyers present can be identified as the principal antiquarian booksellers of their day.

15. The bookshop of James Tregaskis, a Cornishman like Edward Grose Hodge. He married twice and both his wives were active booksellers. He was a faithful Sotheby customer for many years and his firm issued well over a thousand catalogues.

16. The ground floor at 34 and 35 Conduit Street where the Maggs Bros. had their lavish premises between the wars. The firm was founded in 1860 and is still going strong, and has thus been a client of Sotheby's for 120 years.

Modena and D'Alva, and the Marquis Antaldi; from the Altieri, Giustiniani, Ghigi, Borghese, Barberini, and other palaces in Rome; and from smaller private collections in different parts of Central Italy'.

The largest collection of material came from the Piattoli Collection in Florence, assembled by several generations of that family, which Bayley had purchased in 1844. Apparently a considerable portion of it had been deposited at one time in the lower apartments of a house near the Arno and had been badly damaged in a great flood some years earlier. It seems that subsequently the drawings had been lovingly and painstakingly restored. Again, the catalogue explains that in the eighteenth century, 'Signori Gaetano, and, after him, his son, Giuseppe Piattoli were directors of the Royal and Imperial Academy of the Fine Arts in Florence, and, consequently, had a perfect knowledge of the works of the great masters, and very superior advantages in forming such a collection'. It had apparently comprised sixteen folio volumes before the flood, containing several thousand drawings. The cataloguer writes rather mysteriously that much that had been damaged had been discarded and the collection greatly 'reduced from its former numbers, and the surplus has partly been disposed of in various ways, but chiefly in donations for the promotion of art'.

Even so, enough was left to make a fascinating sale of representative works of most fifteenth- and sixteenth-century Italian masters of any note, including several attributed with apparent certainty to Titian, Caravaggio, Correggio, Botticelli, Mantegna, Michelangelo, Raphael and Veronese. In addition to the loose sheets there were three volumes into which the drawings had been pasted – one of forty-five mixed drawings; a second said to contain only designs from the studio of Michelangelo, and a third with 160 drawings including thirty attributed to Raphael. There were also paintings said to be by Ghirlandaio, Mantegna, Leonardo and Rembrandt.

There were no fewer than sixteen sales in June, and the firm was reaching a completely new level of activity, when disaster struck. In the early hours of the morning of 29 June, some time between 3.30 a.m. and 4.00 a.m., Edward Moore, housekeeper of *The Globe* newspaper offices, was wakened by the crackling sound of burning wood. He jumped out of bed and saw flames coming from the back portion of the adjoining house, No. 13 Wellington Street, and sought at once to remove his family to a place of safety. Even before he had done so 'the flames had spread right through the five-storey building, and rising high above it had been seen from all the fire-engine houses in London. A large number of land-steamers and manual engines were soon on the spot, and a good supply of water having been procured they were at once set to work. The firemen succeeded in pouring water upon the flames from all sides, and were enabled to confine them to the building in which the fire broke out. It was nearly destroyed before the flames were extinguished'. So *The Times* of 30 June 1865 reported. Such was the excitement of the reporter that he described the building as belonging to Messrs. Sotheby, Wilkinson & Co., lithographers, and it was only in a letter from T. Way – a nearby neighbour also affected by the fire who genuinely *was* a lithographic printer – that the mistake was corrected in the paper on the following day. Subsequent investigation revealed that the fire had started in a small yard leading from Savoy Street to the entrance of Sotheby's warehouse, where carpenters at work on the neighbouring premises of John King & Co. had left both timber and shavings lying about after the finish of work at the end of the day, and some tramps had been observed in the area smoking. The damage was cruelly extensive and both Sotheby's and Mr. Way lost the greater part of their stock, their records and equipment and virtually their entire premises.

Another newspaper reported that 'the flames seemed to have visited almost every room in the house, with one or two exceptions, and scarcely a volume of the valuable collections stored there has escaped injury. An eleven day sale of Mr. George Offor's rare biblical library commenced on Tuesday and the whole of that collection was stored in the auction room and others near it. This room has suffered terribly. In some parts the floor has been burned through; the doors and windows are all charred; some of the bookshelves with their contents have been burned to ashes, and though some still stand, the books upon them are all charred on their edges and soaked with water, which continued during the morning to drip from one to the other. Some of the rarest vellum manuscripts were supposed to be lying under a heap of charred paper and wood; and numbers of coverless books were lying scattered loose from their burnt bindings on the blackened floors. The bibliopolists who had come to the office, expecting to buy some of the collection, looked upon the scene with most melancholy faces; and one well-known collector almost shed tears at the sight'.

The report concluded: 'Other valuable collections were on the premises, besides Mr. Offors, but it is impossible to say at present to what extent they are damaged. The account-books of the firm were saved, and the firm was to some extent insured'. The value of the books lost was later reported to have been in excess of £60,000.

One of the firm's partners wrote to Sir Thomas Phillipps on 1 July 1865, 'You have doubtless heard of the astounding calamity that has befallen us, our premises with its valuable contents having been almost totally destroyed by fire. We are much pleased that we have succeeded in saving your purchases of Heraldic Books and MSS. In the fearful confusion we are in we cannot send them today, but we will do so on Monday or Tuesday'.

The Offor Collection was indeed a great loss.[1] The illuminated gospels and other very early printed bibles had fetched the remarkably high total of £1,799 19s. od. on the first day of the eleven-day sale, and £1,102 2s. 6d. on the second. So lament by all the newspapers was indeed appropriate. George Offor – a retired bookseller who had made a fortune – lived in Grove House,

1. In fact, some of the most valuable books from later days of the intended sale survived: a number of the Caxtons and other early printed volumes catalogued for the fourth day were housed in a safe which remained untouched by the fire. Similarly, J. O. Halliwell-Phillipps had certain of the books from the library of Lord Charlemont on loan at his home in Old Brompton, and again these were saved.

Hackney and had assembled a notable series of the works of John Bunyan, largely as an aid to a biography he wrote of the great religious author. A strange reminder of the celebrated fire occurred in 1946 when Sir Leicester Harmsworth's fine Bunyan Library came under the hammer, and many charred fragments from the earlier collection re-appeared in the sale-room, a melancholy reminder of the disaster.

Also awaiting sale on 11 August 1865 were the books and manuscripts of the 2nd Earl of Charlemont (they were, in fact, being sold anonymously), but although many were damaged, the majority were saved and the sale took place on the date originally advertised at 21 Wellington Street instead of at No. 13. Wilkinson and Hodge must have blessed the foresight of their late partner in constructing spacious, additional premises there, for these now became the firm's principal centre of activity while reconstruction of the premises at No. 13 got under way. Probably because of the fire, the sale attracted quite unusual attention, and John Wilkinson wrote in a letter on 14 August, 'The Charlemont Sale went off with great *éclat*, worthy of the most exciting times of bibliomania'.

Another major consignment that was totally destroyed was the personal library of the distinguished Paris bookseller J. Joseph Techener. The heartrending, grief-stricken reaction of the Frenchman, M. Techener, and his family was in stark contrast to the stiff upper-lip behaviour of the British Wilkinson and Hodge. Neither old Techener nor his son could at first believe the news when they received a letter on 1 July from Wellington Street, which began, 'We have the unpleasant duty to inform you that in consequence of a fire which took place yesterday morning, we fear your property has been entirely destroyed'. There were some 40,000 volumes, and they represented two collections, each a lifetime's most careful garnering of particular bibliographic treasures. They were sent to London because the sale season there continued longer into the summer, and because it was thought that the works concerned particularly appealed to the London market. Old Techener hastened to London to verify with his own eyes that the disaster had indeed occurred. The son reports:

My father went to London, there to receive the sad confirmation that the auction house of MM Sotheby had been entirely destroyed! The conflagration, fanned by the wind, had begun by devastating the basement storerooms; the floors of the building, weighed down by books, collapsed one after another as the fire advanced to the upper stories. The huge packing cases containing our books had been stacked in the middle of a large room on the first floor over the second basement. The floor, weakened by the fire, was one of the first to collapse; our packing cases were plunged into the immense furnace below and fed the flames, which then roared up to reach every inch of the worm-eaten panelling on all sides of the antiquated premises. Within a few hours the fire had devoured everything! ... Several days later, the crumbling remains were extracted from the ruins, and cartloads of charred and blackened books were taken out, together with many misshapen volumes, for the water had destroyed everything that the fire had spared.

It was an irreparable loss for Bibliophiles!

As a memorial to what had perished, the Techeners produced a detailed catalogue, painstakingly researched and lovingly annotated, as something akin to a funeral oration. It was a charming gesture towards the great body of book collectors all over the world who could not now share in the distribution of a magnificent library which included innumerable manuscripts, *incunabula* and Aldines, as well as a wide range of works on theology, science and the arts, Belles-lettres, history, bibliography and archaeology.

A curious fate befell another property, victim of the fire, the famous drawings made in 1585–86 at Roanoke Island, Virginia, by Raleigh's companion, John White, which were engraved for de Bry's edition of Hariot's *Virginia*. They were so saturated with water that a collection of offsets was formed on the tissue paper laid between them. Their owner, Henry Stevens of Vermont, sold both the drawings and the offsets to the British Museum in the following year.

Considering the fearsome impact of such a conflagration, the firm rallied remarkably quickly and not much more than the summer recess was allowed to elapse before sales began once more. There were no sales in July, two in August (including that of Lord Charlemont), as advertised, and three in September. The regular rhythm of sales began again on 25 November and does not seem to have faltered thereafter. There was, however, one loss which was totally irreparable. The firm lost all the documentation and records relating to its past and, no doubt disheartened by this privation, neither the partners nor any historically-minded member of the staff ever seriously set about recovering duplicate material of the past, or indeed the methodical storage of current reference material. It is this which has delayed the chronicling of Sotheby's history for so long and has made it so difficult.

5

The Quaritch Era

ONLY three years after the fire the firm reached an unprecedented level of activity. It was a remarkable achievement for John Wilkinson, now aged 65, and still the driving force at Wellington Street. For there was no lack of competition. In the field of what we now call the fine arts Christie's held undisputed sway, with Foster's trailing behind. In the field of books Sotheby's were the undoubted leaders and certainly got most of the plums, though Puttick & Simpson were holding nearly two-thirds as many sales as Sotheby's. Often Christie's would sell the pictures and Sotheby's the books from the same estate, though increasingly Sotheby's made inroads into the antiques market. In 1868 Sotheby's held the first of a long series of sales of the library of the Rev. Thomas Corser (there were eight sales up to 1873), one of the most learned and enthusiastic book collectors of the Victorian era. He had marvellous and sometimes unique editions of the early English poets and dramatists, no fewer than seven Caxtons and unusual items, such as books of emblems, drolleries, jest books and garlands, as well as choice manuscripts. Failing eyesight precluded his further enjoyment of the library and so, exceptionally, it was dispersed during a great collector's lifetime. The whole fetched nearly £20,000.

1868 also saw the sale of the library and those prints which he had not given away, of that great collector and benefactor of the arts, Felix Slade, who founded professorships of Fine Art at Oxford, Cambridge and in London, and bequeathed magnificent collections of glass, coins, Japanese carvings in ivory and metal, engravings and manuscripts to the British Museum; of the library of Edward Hawkins, the Keeper of Antiquities of the British Museum; of Sir Robert Smirke, the architect to the British Museum; and of J. M. W. Johnson, the Radcliffe Observer at Oxford. In the latter sale, which included properties of other anonymous owners, there was one wholly unheralded item which arouses one's most ardent curiosity. This was lot 315. It was simply titled: 'WREN PAPERS: a very large collection of Letters, Papers and other Original Manuscripts, chiefly by Christopher Wren, Esq. [the architect's son], and other Members of the Wren Family, and supplying amongst much that is interesting, some particulars of the Family Estates in Shropshire, Staffordshire, etc. . . . ; Lives of Sir C. and Bp. M. Wren; Verses; Letters, etc. (*a very speculative lot*)'.

While there were 38 book sales that year, the firm staged no fewer than 95 sales altogether. Twenty-three were devoted to prints, and often oil paintings, watercolours and drawings were included in such sales. Five consisted of autograph letters, eleven of collections of ceramics and general antiques (the cataloguing of these was still of the most rudimentary kind when compared with books), nine of coins and medals, two of arms and armour, and one final sale which was entirely devoted to wine.[1] This was an innovation. The catalogue listed some 1,300 dozen Rhine wines, the stock of Mr. E. Scheller, a neighbouring wine merchant in Wellington Street who was retiring from business and returning to his native Germany. No doubt the partners had been sampling Mr. Scheller's wares for years.

As we shall see, though there were to be gruesome periods of economic decline in the next decade, the 1868 pattern more or less repeated itself in the years that followed and one can claim with some justification that the era up to the death of Queen Victoria was one in which Sotheby, Wilkinson and Hodge finally achieved unchallenged supremacy in the realm of book auctioneering.

It is unlikely, however, that this achievement would ever have been attained so strikingly if it had not been for a single antiquarian bookseller of German origin who completely dominated the field in the last thirty years of the century. This was Bernard Quaritch, a compact, broad-shouldered man of immense energy with a large domed forehead and an impressive beard, who became a veritable Napoleon of the auction room and attracted the foremost book collectors from all over the world to his establishment. His background was unusual and it may be useful to consider it in some detail. After an apprenticeship with a bookseller in Nordhausen in Upper Saxony and three years with a Berlin publishing house, Quaritch was anxious to increase his experience outside Germany. At twenty-two he arrived in England with introductions to a number of well-known London booksellers. In 1842 Henry George Bohn gave him employment which lasted for two years. Quaritch then spent two further years in Paris with the noted bookseller Theophile Barrois, and rejoined Bohn in a more responsible capacity for a further period before setting up in business on his own. It is clear from Quaritch's subsequent career that Bohn's influence on him was very strong and that in many ways he became the model that Quaritch emulated, and in some directions eventually completely overshadowed.

Henry George Bohn,[2] born in 1796 and like Quaritch of German descent, set up a lively antiquarian business in the early 1830s, in direct competition with his father who was also a bookseller. He assembled his stock for it from all over Europe at a time when the aftermath of the Napoleonic wars had uprooted many distinguished and long-established libraries, and built up an excellent

1. Quite coincidentally, Sotheby's wine department was revived exactly a century later.
2. Bohn, of course, was a major client of Sotheby's and, indeed, there was a strong family link with the firm – his brother, John was senior book cataloguer there. It is presumably to the latter that we can, for example, attribute the lovingly detailed descriptions of the finest of Felix Slade's bindings and manuscripts in 1868. It was a style that had borrowed something from Libri but retained the ultimate objectivity that was the Wellington Street hallmark.

Another brother, James Stuart Burgess Bohn, a Wykehamist, had set up *his* own bookselling business in 1834 and also published major catalogues, but he gave up bookselling in 1847 after twice failing in business. So many members of one family in the trade was obviously an unending cause of confusion. Understandably, Henry George Bohn still included a note even in his 1847 catalogue in which he said: 'The publisher regrets having again to advert to mistakes which arise from his not being sufficiently distinguished by his correspondents from other members of his family, and respectfully urges the addition of both his Christian name and Address to all communications intended for him'.

reputation among bibliophiles for having out-of-the-way books. As his business grew he took more and more to buying up publishers' stock remainders and in 1841 he published a remarkable catalogue of more than 23,000 items and 1,945 pages (including 152 pages of remainders) which he sold for a mere guinea. It was a landmark in book trade history. Through Bohn's trade in remainders, he acquired an increasing number of copyrights in the titles themselves and began to turn to occasional publishing. Eventually he started a whole series of cheap 'libraries' of standard reprints of well-known books, and after he had taken over a rival firm in the same line of business (by suing them for infringement of a copyright he owned – and bankrupting them), he expanded his list to some 600 titles in various fields.

Henry George Bohn's interests changed completely during the last twenty years of his long life (he died in 1884) and this had far-reaching consequences. One of the many works he had included in his 'Illustrated Library' was the catalogue which Christie's had compiled in 1855 for the sale of the collection of Ralph Bernal, an event that contributed greatly to the shift of interest among collectors from the work of the artist to the product of the craftsman. The original catalogue included European and oriental pottery and porcelain, ornamental metal-work of all kinds, arms and armour, enamelware, glass, French, German and Italian furniture, Renaissance silver and bronzes, clocks and watches, ivories, antique jewellery, heraldic devices, scientific and navigational instruments, old costume and an immense collection of early portraits (acquired largely as documented illustrations of costume), prints and engravings. Bohn added a preface to this, reprinted a lecture on pottery and porcelain, used the original illustrations which he had bought for a trifle, included a detailed list of contents, as well as the names of buyers and the prices they had paid, a list of pottery and porcelain marks taken from Brongniart's and Riocreux's *Musée Ceramique*, and added some of his own comments. He titled the catalogue a *Guide to the Knowledge of Pottery and Porcelain and other Objects of Vertu* – with himself as the author, and found he had published a little classic that reprinted and reprinted and became a favourite *vade mecum* and guide for Victorian collectors of antiques.[1]

During his second stint with Bohn, Quaritch had spent much of his time preparing the second, enlarged edition of the great Guinea catalogue (in which Bohn claimed that he had over 500,000 books in stock). Quaritch was now paid a little more than the 24 shillings a week he had originally earned as a porter in Bohn's shop. He was shrewd enough to supplement his income by making use of his keen interest in English politics by acting as the English correspondent to the *Rheinische Zeitung* of both Marx and Engels. When he had saved up some £100 out of his earnings, he decided that the moment had now come to set up in business. After he had handed in his notice, Bohn asked the younger man

1. In 1864, when it became clear that his sons were not going to follow him into the business, he sold his published stock and copyrights to Bell and Daldy for £40,000, his principal copyrights outside his 'Libraries' to Chatto & Windus for another £20,000, and his bookseller's stock at Sotheby's in 1868 and 1870 (and elsewhere) for a further £13,000.

what he was going to do. Quaritch replied frankly that he meant to set up in opposition to his employer. Bohn, the legend goes, laughed and said 'don't you know that I am the first bookseller in England?' 'Yes,' came the reply, 'but I'm going to be the first bookseller in Europe'.[1]

After something of a false start in an agency partnership off Great Russell Street – which came to a rapid end through a dispute with Bohn – Quaritch opened his own small, bow-fronted book shop at 16 Castle Street, Leicester Square (now part of Charing Cross Road) in October 1847, for a weekly rental of 16 shillings. The shop was ingeniously sited within a few minutes walk of Puttick and Simpson at 47 Leicester Square and Sotheby's in Wellington Street just off the Strand. One of the first customers to enter the shop, who became a lifelong friend, was William Gladstone. Other early patrons were Lord Stanley of Alderley, Lord Lindsay (later 25th Earl of Crawford), Disraeli, Prince Louis Lucien Bonaparte (Napoleon's brother), Lord Dufferin (who became Viceroy of India), Edward Fitzgerald, translator of the *Rubaiyat of Omar Khayyam* which Quaritch published, and several members of the Rothschild family.

In fact, the young man who launched himself on the London book world had such determination, efficiency and eagerness to succeed, and was blessed with such a remarkable memory, flair for books, breadth of knowledge and precocious understanding of business methods that he was bound to make an impact very rapidly. The sales from his shop in that first season amounted to £168 10s. The following year they came to £766 10s., by 1850 they totalled £2,382 14s. 6d. and by 1855 had risen to £6,865 5s. By then it was time to move to a more spacious and impressive establishment. Quaritch took premises at 15 Piccadilly, the site of what is now Swan & Edgar facing Eros in Piccadilly Circus, and there he remained for the rest of his long life. Rarely can a man have built up a business more single-mindedly. He never took holidays though he travelled all over Europe, and occasionally America, in search of books. He soon emulated Bohn in buying up remainders, but concentrated mostly on books on remote academic and scientific subjects and oriental and middle-eastern languages. He also became a publisher of dictionaries and grammars of such languages and of heavily illustrated volumes of learned works. There can never have been any thought of his returning to Germany for he had become a naturalised British subject whilst still working for Bohn. His English, both in written and spoken form, always retained slight idiosyncracies.

In Piccadilly the business continued to expand steadily. By 1866 sales were £23,269; by 1868, when he had certainly become an established and important customer of Sotheby's they were still much the same, but by 1874 they reached £42,643. Another of Quaritch's earliest customers who became a close friend (it was he who advised the move to larger premises in 1860) was the economist, John Ramsay McCulloch, and Quaritch and he had never-ending discussions on the management of money in all its aspects. Where disagreement on the solu-

1. Quoted from F. A. Mumby's *Publishing and Bookselling: a History*, London, 1930, but the story is printed, with variations, in many other places.

tion of contemporary economic problems arose, it appears that Quaritch was often ultimately proved right and the author of *Principles of Political Economy* wrong, though McCulloch certainly formulated one sound economic proposition when he wrote in the foreword to the catalogue of his own library:

> A man acts foolishly, if he spend more money on books or anything else than he can afford; but the folly will be increased, not diminished, by his spending it on mean and common, rather than on fine and uncommon works. The latter when sold will invariably bring a good price, more perhaps than was paid for them, whereas the former either bring nothing or next to nothing.

Quaritch's own lifelong policy was that all spare cash not needed for staff wages, overheads or his own domestic purposes should be at once re-invested in stock, and during his lifetime his stock hardly ever seems to have stopped growing. Another principle was to resist claims for discounts to his customers at a time when they were the accepted norm between tradesman and customer. To one unfortunate clergyman who had deducted 10 per cent from his cheque when ordering a book he had seen in a friend's copy of a Quaritch catalogue, the latter wrote brusquely: 'As you have not before favoured me with any of your orders, you do not know the system upon which I carry on my business. My books are marked *nett*; from these *nett* prices I give no discount whatever; I do not even pay carriage'. Occasionally he made reluctant exceptions for substantial purchasers; on the other hand he expected and received immensely high discounts when he bought from others in the book trade. One can judge from his purchases at Sotheby's and the sales price attached to the identical items in Quaritch's own catalogues, that he added a relatively small amount for overhead and profit; often it does not seem to have come to more than 33⅓ per cent. But if any man crossed him or tried to cheat him, Quaritch could be devastating in response. His surviving letters bear witness to this. To another bookseller, George Willis, in the Strand, he wrote: 'Sir, By some of our actions we protect our interest, by others our dignity; it often happens that what is conductive [*sic*] to the one, is opposed to the other. Where equals meet, no loss of dignity can arise from settling amicably a bone of contention, but when two parties meet, unequal in position, the inferior has all the advantage over his opponent. This I have repeatedly noticed in our small transactions; however profitable amicable settlements between you and me have been, I have lost both in cash and in dignity whenever I have had to deal with Mr. Francis, your "buyer" . . '. There were no further such transactions.

It is remarkable that for a bookseller who probably dealt in larger sums on single titles than anyone before him had done, small items seemed just as important as large ones. Quaritch argued as much about pennies as about pounds, though occasionally even he had to admit defeat. He wrote to one quarrelsome customer, 'You insist upon having a pound of flesh from my body. You evidently have the leisure and the will for legal proceedings. I have neither. My position as a commercial man is such, I must not only be just to my customers, I must also appear so in the eyes of persons blinded by avarice. I therefore send you by bearer . . .'. He was just as fierce with fellow booksellers to whom he sold quantities of the many journals published by learned societies for whom he acted as agent, as well as the books he himself published. Thus he wrote to a bookseller in Nottingham, 'I am extremely sorry you should have backed out of your order of 100 copies of Haite's *Plant Structure*. Your now saying you only ordered Part I is simply childish talk . . .'.

Once a year Quaritch organised a trade sale for all his fellow booksellers where he was the most genial and good-humoured of hosts. In 1885, for example, he produced a special twenty-page catalogue of some 223 titles, and invited them all to the Freemasons' Tavern – 'dinner on the table at 5 o'clock punctually'. There was a multitude of carefully chosen wines and champagne and no fewer than seventeen courses. To give the occasion added spice Quaritch had invited as guest of honour none other than Captain (later Sir) Richard Burton, the great African explorer and translator of the *Arabian Nights*, who read aloud some yet unpublished chapters from a forthcoming book (which Quaritch backed heavily when the author published it privately). At 8.15 the serious part of the evening began. Quaritch proceeded to auction the contents of his catalogue. He put into his performance everything he had learned below the rostrum in the sale-room, particularly one gathers from John Wilkinson, and disposed of the entire contents. The occasion was of vital importance to him. It was one of his principal sources of income.[1]

There can be no doubt that Quaritch was at his happiest buying in the auction room. Here he was totally resolute and on many occasions unashamedly ruthless. A motto he mouthed constantly before important sales was 'L'audace, encore de l'audace et toujours de l'audace'. He frequently bought on commission for Sir Thomas Phillipps though, not surprisingly, the two men fell out from time to time. Rarely can Sir Thomas, who was noted for his devastatingly outspoken letters, have met a correspondent who was so ready to give as good as he got. When after one of the Libri sales Phillipps accused Quaritch of *watching him* which 'showed malice in your heart', Quaritch replied:

> To charge me with 'malice' is the same as if the sportsman charge his game, be it fox or rabbit, with malice, you with your great knowledge (better understood by me than by any other bookseller) and your great wealth were in the position of the sportsman, rifle in hand, I had to defend myself against you and your desperate onslaughts as best I could. You say I watch you; that implies you watch *me* as well. If I had only represented myself at the Libri sale I should have acted differently but I had several extremely high commissions from first class buyers and I, as an honest man, had to endeavour, either to buy the books as cheap as possible or to drop them on my opponents as dear as possible. . . . Mr. Hartland, whom you know well, will bear out that I always act fair towards my customers. My opponents I naturally cripple as much as I can at sales.

Such a competitive and combative spirit cannot have come amiss at Sotheby's. The presence of Quaritch added zest and sparkle to the auction

1. A full description of such a sale is given in an off-print of an article by Karl W. Hiersemann in the *Börsenblatt für den Deutschen Buchhandel*, No. 265, Leipzig, 1885.

room, kept up prices, brought the press to all major sales and thus kept the public eye firmly on Wellington Street. He made no secret of his tactics. A bookseller with whom he had particularly fierce battles in the sale-room over the years was Frederick Ellis,[1] who before the advent of Quaritch had always been considered 'the head of the trade'. Ellis had started as assistant to Thomas Rodd, the official buyer for the British Museum, and took over this post after Rodd retired. Quaritch always felt that the job should have gone to him. He had an uncanny instinct for knowing what the museum authorities were after at any sale and boasted quite truthfully that over the years he had cost the museum £70,000 by bidding against Ellis. Ellis on the other hand always maintained that he made Quaritch pay many inflated prices by bidding him up on books *he* did not particularly want. But there was a happy ending to the many years of altercation and competitive strife between the two men. Ellis had a heart attack and decided to sell his stock – at Sotheby's of course – in 1885, though his business was carried on by his son and a partner as Ellis & White. Quaritch attended the sale and turned what could have been rather a sluggish occasion into a lively and successful sparring match with the rest of the trade, despite the fact that a general depression prevailed at the time. Ellis wrote to express his gratitude in generous terms from Torquay where he had gone to recuperate. In an earlier letter when he had still thought of going on with his business he had written to Quaritch, 'I can only hope that I may always have equally honourable and upright competitors to deal with as yourself'. Now he wrote, 'I sincerely congratulate you on the grand position you have made for yourself. You cannot only say "alone I did it", but also that it was done in spite of adverse circumstances which would have crushed any man of less ability and determination than yourself. You are at the head of your profession . . .'. He could not resist, however, ending on a practical note. 'I see you have got some things very cheaply at the Wodhull Sale – don't sell them too cheaply. . . . I never got anything but DERISION if I sold a book very cheaply.'

Quaritch's reply probably contains the most candid musings about himself which survive. They highlight various aspects of his career. After expressing a hope that Ellis will recover sufficiently in order eventually to re-enter the trade (Ellis had written that he was 'quite unequal to the strain which in so many ways the book business requires'), Quaritch continued:

My dear Ellis,
It is a fearful visitation of providence to receive in the prime of life such a blow, as you have had to endure of late. I sincerely hope you will soon be yourself again. My own career now draws to a close. I have been fifty years at it; I may say, I never had a week's holiday in my life. I long for the mountains. When shall I get

1. Ellis's best customer was the great Huddersfield bibliophile, Sir Thomas Brooke whose library was of considerable importance to Sotheby's. After Brooke's death in 1908 there were major bequests of important MSS to the British Museum, the Society of Antiquities and Henry Yates Thompson. The rest of the library was sold by Sotheby's in a lengthy concatenation of sales under various anonymous headings in 1909, 1913 and 1920, and after Sir Thomas's son had added to the library, further sales took place in 1921 and 1923.

the rest? [Quaritch was 66 at the time and was to remain in business for another 14 years. Ellis outlived him by two years.]

I have still three sections of my catalogue (the last) to complete: 1. Geography, 2. Oriental Literature, 3. Typographic Monuments. After that I shall and must relax. This will be the time for *you* to buy bargains. You see I am so selfish as to wish you well because I know that you can do more for me than anybody else. Without you Ridler & Co. get early printed books for nothing. You know that Ridler [a rival bookseller, who, though successful, always kept out of the limelight] keeps his carriages now and he deserves all his success.

However since poor Bicker's funeral I have suffered from inflammation of my chest and ought to have taken some rest, but my creditors (S.W. & H.) will not allow it, they clamour daily for money——(P. & S. are paid).

As for the forthcoming sales at Sotheby's I view them with horror I am so overstocked that I don't want another book. There will be a great downfall in prices; I *cannot* keep them up any longer.

Mr. Smalley's articles against me [in the *New York Tribune*] are inspired by spite and envy; he is a miserable wretch, but cannot understand men like you and me; he sees in us merely money-grubbing dealers, he cannot conceive that you and I are really the first (if not the only) bibliophiles in England; he does not understand the holy fire which animates our struggles for the best books, because he is a mean spirited reptile.

A London tradesman must accept competition; if he cannot stand it, he must return to the provinces.

Your name and mine will go down together in the Annals of bookselling and I am presumptuous enough to say, our reputation is like Bayard's 'Sans peur et sans reproche'.

However, our biggest struggles are now past, – no more Perkins, Sunderland, Beckford, Thorold sales; the next sales will be interesting but I, for one, shall show not much more of my old spirit.[1]

In the event Quaritch's activities were to remain as electrifying as ever and his greatest asset, his supreme self-confidence, rarely faltered. It was probably the relationship with a single client that had done more to strengthen it in Quaritch's early days of independence than any other single factor. In 1852, five years after he had opened his shop at Castle Street, from which he at once started issuing catalogues, Quaritch received his first order from Lord Lindsay – later 25th Earl of Crawford – and probably the most knowledgeable and outstanding of the many great book collectors of the second half of the nineteenth century.

In the general absence of good reference libraries, particularly in the north of England, Lord Lindsay set about establishing a library which covered all aspects of human knowledge and striving, and quite deliberately avoided buying books merely because they were bibliographical rarities. Quaritch's efficiency, knowledge of the books Lindsay required and his success at finding them at reasonable prices, soon endeared him to Lord Lindsay who was, for many years, Quaritch's most important customer by far. For Quaritch the great advantage of

1. This was not the end of the relationship, for Ellis contributed a number of major articles to Quaritch's *Dictionary of English Book-Collectors*, first published in 1892.

the relationship was that Lord Lindsay always paid his bills with the greatest promptitude and this often enabled Quaritch to speculate over the purchase of books which he thought Lindsay might require later, and this further tended to cement the relationship.

It gave Quaritch the greatest pleasure and satisfaction in his early days of independence to be able to buy important and expensive books on commission when he attended sales, and it might well be said that Quaritch's dominance of the sale-room was achieved on the shoulders of the Crawford family. As we shall see, Quaritch was able to buy so exhaustively because he combined commissions for his increasing number of private clients with those for continental booksellers for whom he acted as agent – notably Louis Damascene Morgand, a leading antiquarian Paris bookseller whose firm was later taken over by his friend, Eduard Rahir – as well as for his own enormous stock at 15 Piccadilly.

The relationship with Sotheby's became the dominant factor in Quaritch's life for the simple reason that the firm granted him the most generous credit facilities. Christie's bluntly refused him any such arrangements whatever, and Puttick & Simpson did what they could, but they certainly could not afford to be as forthcoming as Sotheby's. Usually before a major sale Quaritch called at Wellington Street and discussed his requirements with the partners. Often it was agreed that he should make payments at so much a month over a period of six months after a sale. On other occasions he issued promissory notes which Sotheby's would call in on a monthly basis. He was therefore continuously indebted to Wilkinson and Hodge. This is the fact that he refers to in his letter to Ellis. The arrangement suited both sides. Sotheby's could assure the owners of outstanding properties that they were sure to get a reasonable price for them; and because he knew he had some time to find suitable purchasers, Quaritch could afford to pay more than his competitors for what he regarded as distinguished books. His judgement of prices again seems to have been quite uncanny and it must have been one of the factors which his clients most appreciated, for his advice on what they would have to pay, at least in the London auction rooms where Quaritch knew exactly what the opposition would be, was almost always accurate. In France, Germany and Belgium it was harder for him to give precise forecasts. And lest it be thought that Quaritch was only interested in major events in the sale-room, it should be stressed that his attendance there, particularly at Sotheby's, was absolutely regular and one finds his name as purchaser at most work-a-day sales beside hundreds, if not thousands of books each year where lots fetched as little as 2s., 5s., 10s., 18s. or £1 5s. It was all grist to his mill and represented his principal source of material for the magnificent catalogues of his stock which Quaritch issued regularly. The most important of these (and it represented the culmination of decades of work and, incidentally, the separate issue of many specialist sections) was the catalogue completed in 1888. This contained 38,552 items on 4,066 pages with an index published in 1892 of 427 pages set in triple columns with something over 100,000 entries. Quaritch had a faithful team of cataloguers who tackled this work. The most outstanding, and a vital prop to his business, was the legendary Irishman, Michael Kerney, who, while Quaritch supplied the drive, took the financial risks, devised the systems and bludgeoned his way to fame, set the style of the catalogues, supplied the scholarship and the wide-ranging knowledge of linguistics, wrote the many monographs that appeared over Quaritch's name and turned the catalogues into magnificent selling tools with ingeniously contrived forms of typographical display. Over catalogues linked with particular sales there was close collaboration with Sotheby's, who often supplied Quaritch with early copies of their own, so that he could devise advance prospectuses under his own name which went to his clients all over the world.

In the late 1870s and particularly throughout the 1880s Sotheby's staged a series of sales that might have been specifically designed with Quaritch in mind as principal character in a theatrical setting, and he rose unfailingly and sensationally to each occasion. There was no secrecy about his performances. Quaritch's bidding was clear to everyone present in the auction room, though few, of course, understood the coded messages in his catalogue, nor could they determine what was going on behind his ever impassive mien. Not for him the methods of the elderly Boone who always sat immediately under the rostrum and tapped Wilkinson's heel with a pencil when he was bidding! Nor did Quaritch scorn the 'bundle hunters' who rarely bid above 3s. for any single item and lived in constant hope of uncatalogued treasure in multiple lots. He had found many a valuable item himself in the same way.

A collection sold in the Seventies, in which Quaritch swept the board of almost everything that was bibliographically desirable, was that of a civil engineer, William Bragge, a figure typical of the immensely energetic Victorians whose libraries came Sotheby's way. Bragge had made his fortune by constructing the first railway line in Brazil, as well as carrying out the lighting of the city of Rio de Janeiro with gas. Subsequently he became head of a Sheffield engineering firm and mayor of that city. He was not so successful in developing the sewers of Paris into sources of manure. The scheme proved a flop and the promoters who had employed him went bankrupt. Bragge returned to his native Birmingham and started a large organisation that manufactured watches by machinery of a system then current in America, rather than assembling them by hand in the traditional method. This proved highly successful. Bragge had a great penchant for collecting. One of his interests was anything to do with smoking. He collected no fewer than 13,000 pipes and examples of smoking apparatus from all over the world, as well as samples of several hundred kinds of tobacco. He spent some years in compiling a catalogue, but the collection was sold after his death. His cabinet of gems and precious stones, culled on his travels throughout Europe, was eventually purchased for the Birmingham Art Gallery. He was also keenly interested in books and illuminated manuscripts. His collection of 1,500 works by and about Cervantes was second to none. He presented it to the Birmingham Free Library, but it was destroyed by a fire there in 1879. Towards the end of his life he became almost totally blind and his magnificent collection of manuscripts and books was sold anonymously at

Sotheby's shortly after his death. It was described as the property of a Gentle-man of consummate taste and judgement. 491 lots sold over four days and fetched something under £12,500. Ellis bought a number of the best MSS for his foremost customer, Sir Thomas Brooke.[1] Dr. Thomas Shadford Walker of Liverpool, whose own MSS were to be sold by Sotheby's only ten years later (23 June 1886), bought substantially too; but far and away the biggest buyer was Quaritch. He spent nearly £7,000, £3,700 of which was for stock. One item in particular made the headlines – a set of ninth-century Latin Gospels for a record-breaking £780.

In the year that followed, Quaritch's attention – as well as his financial resources – were taken up with the long drawn-out sales of the Didot Library in Paris; and at about the same time in 1878 a great collector of Italian, Spanish and to a lesser extent French literature, Robert Samuel Turner, sold his French books at the Salle Drouot in Paris where 774 lots realised something over £12,000. This was considered prodigious, and the fact was repeatedly recalled when Sotheby's sold his 3,000 remaining titles for only £14,000 after Turner's death in 1888. The French books had averaged £16 each; the ones sold in London only £4 10s. 1878 was the year too in which 'Young Tom', Edward Grose Hodge's son, joined Sotheby's. The family tradition was thus continued. Finally, it was the year in which Quaritch, and many other London booksellers, noted with regret the passing of Henry Huth, another giant among book collectors – but more of him later on.

Henry Huth's death was not the only piece of bad news that hit the book trade. All had noticed a gradual slowing down of business since 1876 and it soon became clear that this national malaise had fundamental causes which would not go away in a hurry. The first bout of the decline lasted from 1876 to 1879, and there was a second catastrophic period from 1884 to 1886. Altogether this lean period in Britain's history lasted twelve bitter years, and was eventually branded 'The Great Depression'. Victorian prosperity suffered major reverses on two fronts, agriculture and industry. The principal cause of the agricultural decline was to be found in the United States, which had vastly improved its steel manufacture and then its railway system in the 1860s and the early 1870s. In 1873 American farmers benefited beyond anyone's dreams when a self-binder was invented which could be attached to every reaping machine. What this meant in simplified terms was that every prairie farmer could double his crop, and furthermore that this could be moved from producer to consumer much more cheaply. Gradually too steam was displacing sail in trans-Atlantic transport. The cost of sending a ton of grain from Chicago to Liverpool went down from £3 7s. in 1873 to a mere £1 4s. in 1884. Unlike most other European countries, Britain refused to put tariffs on imported wheat. For the farming community the consequences were disastrous. The price of a bushel of wheat fell from 56s. 9d. in 1877 to 31s. in 1886. Our import of cereals increased from 2 per cent in 1840 to 45 per cent in 1880. In addition, there had been unbeliev-ably bad, wet summers from 1875 to 1879; the United Kingdom had its last

1. Six of the major items are now at Keble College, Oxford.

and most devastating outbreak of rinderpest in cattle in 1877, and suffered a major outbreak of liver rot in sheep in 1879 and another of foot and mouth disease in 1883. The result was that land values tumbled and rent bills were decimated. A tremendous drift away from the land led to rapidly increasing urbanisation. Countless bankruptcies and forced sales followed.

Industry had fared little better. The earlier generation of innovators and strongly-muscled captains of industry had been replaced by the limited company, and a second generation that lacked fire in the belly; and following upon the Companies Act of 1862 there had been such a rush of new share issues that it had put a great strain on the capital available. Furthermore, many sectors of British technology and manufacturing machinery had become out-dated. Improvements and replacements were slow. Newly invented technical processes developed in France and Germany brought down prices with a bump. The increased competition not only cut the supremacy of Britain as an exporting nation, but actually brought vastly increased imports into Britain and thus hurt industry both ways. At its zenith in 1870, British foreign trade had exceeded that of France, Germany and Italy put together. This happy state was never to return.

The impact of all this on the auction room was far-reaching. Private collections and libraries quietly accumulated over generations in family houses, both in town and country, came on to the market in ever-increasing numbers. This did not, of course, happen at once, but it gradually led to the heartbreak of the dispersal of historic properties that had come to be regarded as almost inviolable. The process was probably accelerated by legislation culminating in the Settled Land Acts of 1882 and 1884. These permitted the Court of Chancery to authorise the sale by trustees of property passed on as heirlooms, however forcefully the testator might have prescribed preservation by his family (which accounts for the increasing number of 'Heirloom Sales' held both at Sotheby's and Christie's in the forty years that followed). Similarly, the collections assembled more rapidly by the new technocrats often had to be dispersed at short notice. Overall, therefore, Sotheby's had infinitely more to sell but buyers were harder to find and prices fell.

Quaritch struggled mightily to buck the trend, and increasingly he found customers overseas, both in Europe and America, though he was one of the first to realise that this presaged the reversal of something that had gone on uninterruptedly since the era of the Grand Tour. For generations British collectors had imported books and works of art from overseas. Now, as the wealth of Europe and America increased, a massive exodus of such treasure from Britain began. Perspicacious dealers such as Quaritch and later Duveen in London and Seligmann in Paris, began to sell to those very men who had indirectly hastened our own economic decline: the American steel and railroad magnates, French bankers and Ruhr barons. In the late Eighties and the early Nineties, *official* as well as private collectors from overseas began to take advantage of the straitened financial circumstances of the British aristocracy, land owners and industrialists. They sought particularly illuminated manuscripts and Old Master paintings. Wilhelm von Bode, probably the most distinguished of all directors of Berlin's Kaiser Friederich Museum, began to come to London several times a year in order to make important acquisitions at what he considered ridiculously low prices.

In the world of antiquarian books the increasing tempo of sales led to a gradual surfeit of stock. In 1881 Quaritch wrote in a letter to a general in the Indian army who had been a long-standing customer of his:

> I am extremely sorry that you should have been so disappointed with our last transaction, my buying from you for £200 cash, for what you said you paid me £467. The facts of the case are that when you bought these books from me, *book buying* was going on briskly – now book buying has come to a dead standstill: all my best customers are dead. I myself went to realise and not add to my stock.
>
> What I paid you £200 for I may, ere long have to sell at cost price or for less if the present stagnation continues.
>
> There are only *sellers* and no buyers. . . .

Nevertheless, Quaritch bought vigorously at Sotheby's sale of the first portion of the 'Rare Books and Manuscripts relating chiefly to the History and Literature of America'. This was the property of Henry Stevens of Vermont, one of a family of American booksellers who had settled in London and bought on behalf of a substantial American clientele. It is interesting that he decided that London, and Sotheby's in particular, were most suitable for the sale of his private collection, which was adventurous and scholarly, as indeed was the cataloguing of the sale which Stevens had undertaken himself, though it looks as if on occasion he had allowed his enthusiasm to overtake his objectivity! In his introduction he wrote:

> . . . he confesses that the extended notes are in many cases disproportioned to the value of the lots to which they are attached. They are intended to give a bibliographical flavour to the whole, and if possible to lift the catalogue out of the current run, hoping that it may be deemed hereafter of some bibliographical use to librarians and to collectors of this class of Books and Manuscripts. The collections are very miscellaneous, and no attempt has been made to classify them beyond the democratic alphabet [a nice touch], but if the persevering Collector reads to the end he will have noticed nearly all of the great collections of early Voyages and Travels, together with very many of the separate voyages of the earliest English, Dutch, French and Spanish Navigators; books relating to the East and West India Companies, Dutch and English; the English and French Colonies in North America; Canada, New England, New Netherlands, Pennsylvania and Virginia; Brazil, Mexico, Peru and other parts of Spanish America. . . . Besides there will be found many uncommon books relating to the early history of America, the American Revolution and the war of 1812 . . .; also examples of early printing in America, especially New England, and a great variety of miscellaneous American literature, political, historical, geographical, genealogical, local and general.

There was much else besides (the sale lasted five days), including manuscript material among which were eighteen original autograph letters of the

youthful George Washington. Lot 1269 was the *pièce de resistance* in the catalogue and it was offered at the 'upset' price of £7,000 (it was most unusual to
reveal a reserve price in this way). It consisted of 3,000 different manuscripts
and nearly 300 printed books all by or concerning Benjamin Franklin.[1] The full
description covered thirty pages. Stevens began it charmingly thus: 'Sooner or
later everything saleable is believed to turn up in London, the centre of money
and mutability. Here it is said most do congregate historical materials and
historic doubts. At all events the present collection is a sample of what one may
achieve in a single generation in London by good luck, persistence, vigilance
and a dogged weakness for sacrificing other worldly gains to a pet object.
Rightly or wrongly this has been done and the results are here for the first time
summarised and set forth'. There must have been great disappointment when
the lot was withdrawn just before the sale. Stevens's ploy to get a higher price
from outside the sale-room had succeeded. He succumbed to an offer on behalf
of the Library of Congress, and there – very suitably – the collection came to
rest.

Be that as it may, depression or no, here was material too tempting to pass by.
No doubt well armed with commissions from the other side of the Atlantic, the
trade turned up in force and made it a memorable occasion. Quaritch bought
substantially.

In December of that same year, 1881, a much older library began to come
under the hammer which again tempted Quaritch to buy heavily. It had
remained untouched for the best part of 150 years. It had originally been
brought together with great taste and without any regard to cost by Charles
Spencer, 3rd Earl of Sunderland (1674–1722). It was valued at his death at the
remarkable figure of £30,000, and the King of Denmark had been anxious to
buy it at that price from Sunderland's heirs. It later passed by marriage into
the possession of the Marlborough family and was moved to Blenheim in 1749.
The library contained some 20,000 books, a useful sprinkling of manuscripts
and was particularly strong in *incunabula* (a good many printed on vellum), in
fifteenth- and sixteenth-century literature of all kinds, in bibles and, of course,
the classics. An enormous catalogue had been published in a tiny edition by the
Duke of Marlborough in 1872. Early in 1881 the Duke decided to part with the
library and asked Ellis to sell it for him. It was offered as a collection at a price
between £20,000 and £25,000, and was actually being considered by Baron
James de Rothschild of Paris when the latter suddenly died and negotiations
collapsed. It is said that Lord Crawford was tempted for a while to buy it, and
certainly Quaritch had tried to raise the cash in order to buy it for himself, but
failed. The trade generally was concerned that such an enormous influx of books
on the market would further depress prices at what was already a difficult time,
and was worried too that the bindings (mostly in calf) of the books, having
remained untouched for so long, were 'dry' and in poor condition, and indeed
The Times described their condition as 'little less than shocking'. Ultimately

1. Tradition has it that Franklin had been one of Sam Baker's customers for books in the
1740s.

an auction sale in five parts, spread over two years, was organised by Puttick & Simpson. The mystery is why it did not go to Sotheby's. One can only surmise that the now elderly Wilkinson and the more dynamic Hodge must have thought that the sale would not be a success. In the event the 13,856 lots realised £56,581 – a tremendous sum in its day – though if one studies the prices they were, with some exceptions, on the low side. Quaritch had a field day. For once he was able to make long and satisfactory credit arrangements with Puttick & Simpson, and he spent no less than £33,185 out of the total. The trade gasped and spluttered. Quaritch issued special catalogues and his sales in the ensuing years shot up to record levels. It is a strange fact too that the Sunderland catalogue, which received universal acclaim, was compiled by John Lawler, later Sotheby's senior cataloguer for many years and at that time already thought to be employed by Sotheby's. A specially bound edition of the catalogue inscribed by Simpson to Lawler is still at Sotheby's today. *The Times* reported that 'the sale was not allowed to close without an acknowledgement made in a characteristic little speech from Mr. Quaritch who begged as the largest purchaser to say that this was the most wonderful library that had been sold by auction in the present century and the sale had been most satisfactorily conducted. . . . If he had the happiness to reach Heaven he would seek out the Earl of Sunderland, and he should bow down his head before him with the deepest respect and gratitude'.

Quaritch's financial problems were to be stretched even further concurrently with the Sunderland sales by another series of important sales launched by Sotheby's. It may indeed have been the knowledge that these were in the offing which had deterred them from taking on the Sunderland dispersal. The event concerned was the sale of the entire contents of Hamilton Palace, the home of the Dukes of Hamilton. George Redford, *The Times* sale-room correspondent at that period, described the building as 'a sombre, stone-faced edifice of vast size built in the depressed Classic style of the seventeenth century, with parts added at the wings, forming the Beckford Library at one side, and the new state rooms built in 1838 on the other, presenting a front by no means imposing, but rather heavy and gloomy in appearance, with indifferent approaches. Having a *souterain* of vast mineral wealth, it has suffered like many other great residences in the North from the encroaching spread of coal and iron works, and numerous mills and factories, the tall chimneys pouring forth their perpetual fumes of smoke and noxious vapours in every direction, and rendering it every year more and more unsuitable as a residence for a great nobleman'. The sale was one of the many instances of the period where Christie's were the auctioneers of the furnishings and works of art while Sotheby's disposed of the library. The latter was in two quite separate parts: the books which William Beckford had assembled and which had passed by inheritance to his son-in-law, the 10th Duke of Hamilton (who had married Beckford's second daughter Susanna), and the Duke's own library. The two libraries were physically separated by an immense state dining-room.

The whole dispersal had been made possible by the recent parliamentary legislation permitting the sale of heirlooms and was particularly understandable when Redford's description of the palace was taken in conjunction with the 12th Duke's public avowal of the need for money. He had taken great care to nurture and maintain what his grandfather, Alexander, the 10th Duke, had begun and his father, William Alexander, the 11th, had wonderfully supplemented and consolidated. Alexander in particular was a man cast in a heroic mould who devoted much of his life to giving rein to an intense passion for collecting rare works of art of all kinds. His taste was for the ornate tending to the magnificent, which expressed itself in death as well as in life, for he built for himself a sepulchral and massive mausoleum in the Palace grounds where his remains lie to this day in an ancient and valuable Egyptian sarcophagus which he especially imported for this purpose. The sale created an interest unmatched since the Stowe sale in 1848, and both old Mr. Woods of Christie's and Edward Hodge at Sotheby's did their utmost to fuel and to satisfy public curiosity in the event.

Christie's sold the superlative palace contents and works of art in 2213 lots in seventeen days. It constituted 'the finest single collection ever to have come under the hammer'[1] and realised £397,562. It was a total the like of which had never been known before and constituted a record unbroken for generations. It was certainly an achievement which Sotheby's had to work hard to live up to. Their sale of the library opened on 30 June 1882 in Wellington Street, thirteen days after Christie's had started auctioning the contents at King Street. Beckford's books were remarkable for the splendour of their bindings, the beauty of their illustrations and their superb condition.[2] Furthermore, Beckford's taste had been years ahead of his time and was of particular interest to a small but active body of collectors who were buying strongly in the 1880s, and whose number was to grow appreciably in the future. There were many volumes by out-of-the-way authors who appealed to Beckford's brilliance, and he had pencilled what the catalogue described as 'quaint and often sarcastic notes on the fly-leaves of almost the greater portion of his books'. The introduction to the catalogue continued, 'Beckford, who was indefatigable in watching the great sales in London and Paris, eagerly secured copies of works bearing the arms and devices of eminent collectors, such as Francis I, Henry II and Diane of Poitiers, Henry III, Henry IV, Marguerite de Navarre and the later kings and queens of France, as well as royal mistresses and their issue'. Books belonging to eminent Popes and cardinals also fascinated him. He had an immense collection of books on travel, and a fabulous collection of books of engravings in their finest state. Among them was a collection of Van Dyck portraits (including

1. Gerald Reitlinger, *The Economics of Taste*, Vol. I, 1961.
2. 'Even the worthless volumes in Beckford's were in the finest condition which reflects the highest credit, not only on his own taste, but on the carefulness of those who had charge of the books since his death. . . . The collection from Hamilton Palace has come to the hammer as clean and unscathed as if the books had only left the binder's workshop a few months ago.' *The Times* commenting on the whole sale on 26 December 1882.

some twenty of the particularly rare etchings). They were contained in three large folio volumes all mounted on thick paper, bound in 'Russia Extra', with old French tooling. Edward Hodge, who was given to holding little speeches before he started accepting bids for really major items, read out a letter from the rostrum which he had received from an elderly collector who had viewed the sale. The letter referred to a passage in Cyrus Redding's memoirs of Beckford where a friend had visited him in his home in Bath towards the end of the great collector's life, to admire the second library which he had accumulated (the first having been sold at Fonthill in 1823) and had asked him about the three volumes. Beckford explained that they had been bought for him at the sale of Count Fries in Amsterdam for 1,200 Guilders, then about £100. 'These', said Beckford, 'are Vandycks to fall down and worship; such glorious impressions are nowhere to be found.'

Ellis began the bidding for them at £1,000 (an opening bid of this size for a book was virtually unheard of at that time), but the volumes eventually went to the Paris dealer, Thibaudeau, for £2,850.

The first portion of Beckford's library – it consisted of 3,197 lots sold in twelve sale sessions – fetched £31,516. The second portion came under the hammer in December of 1882 and two further portions followed in July and December of 1883. Altogether the four portions realised £73,551 18s. Although Quaritch had said publicly at the Sunderland Sale that in contrast he thought little of Beckford's library and that he could 'form another like it tomorrow', he spent no less than £44,105 on these and the succeeding Hamilton Library volumes, out of a total of £86,444. In fact, he issued a special book plate which was inserted in all the books he acquired from the two libraries.

There were daily accounts in most newspapers of each stage of the sale. Always Quaritch's name occurred prominently as the purchaser of the most important titles and this sale, probably more than any other, established him in the public mind as the hero of the day and the greatest bookseller of all time. The most important fact to emerge from the twin events of the Sunderland and the Beckford/Hamilton sales was that rare books reached an altogether new level of prices which all who pondered about the matter found difficult to explain. The reason was that, despite the financial difficulties of the time, there were now far more collectors of books of this kind all over the world, and the sale had been almost as well publicised in America as in Britain and on the Continent.

It might seem surprising that after all the earlier éclat the Duke of Hamilton's own library only added £13,000 to the total when it reached the sale-room in May 1884. The reason behind this constitutes one of the most extraordinary chapters in Sotheby's history of this period. For it had been decided that the tenth Duke's collection of manuscripts, which was wonderfully rich in bibles and portions of the scriptures, missals, breviaries, antiphonaries and Books of Hours (many of them having been written for Francis I, Charles VI, Charles VII and Louis XII, Kings of France, the German Emperors Maximilian I and Charles V, Pope Leo X and the Duc de Guise), should be sold privately, and if possible, to a single buyer. Sotheby's, as we have already seen, had handled a vast amount of work by the great scribes and illuminators who produced the reading matter that preceded the invention of printing. Indeed it would be interesting to know, though virtually impossible to establish, how many thousands of such works had been catalogued by the firm since the days of Samuel Baker. These several hundred manuscripts – many of them virtually unknown – which had been lovingly assembled by the Duke of Hamilton from sales in Paris, Venice and other parts of the Continent, seem to have exceeded in quality any previous collection that had come on to the market. Under the circumstances it seems less astonishing that the principals of an auction house should have felt impelled to sell the collection as an entity, rather than to scatter it among a multitude of new owners. For many people the most important item was a text of Dante's *Divina Commedia* illustrated with eighty-four large drawings by Sandro Botticelli. All who had studied the manuscript had agreed that Botticelli had here distilled years of artistry devoted to the painting of large scale works on wall and panel into a miniature brilliance, which showed his work in an unusual light and promoted a mere manuscript (as such things were often considered at the time) into a very great and important work of art. The artist's vivid scenes from the Inferno and Purgatorio startled all who were fortunate enough to see them.

In addition to the liturgical works there were a multitude of manuscripts depicting chivalry romances, song books and other texts many of which had particularly lively forms of illuminated illustrations. Anyone who was allowed to spend two or three hours to examine the Duke's collection seems to have experienced a wholly delightful and almost unique excursion into the colourful world of the picture books that artists provided for the delectation of their fellow men from the seventh to the sixteenth century.[1] The man who was most smitten with a burning ambition to possess the collection was Friedrich Lippmann, Director of the Kupferstichkabinett (print room) in Berlin. He came to London accompanied by Wilhelm von Bode and two other experts. A fact which made any negotiations difficult was that the booksellers, Ellis and White, who handled them on behalf of Sotheby's, insisted that it had to be an 'all or nothing' deal. For this reason, despite pressure put on the authorities, and in spite of attempts by the British Museum to move the Treasury, no offer was forthcoming to retain the collection in Britain. Lippmann and his colleagues inspected everything most carefully; their plea to be allowed to buy only part of the collection was rejected; they discussed, they calculated, they negotiated, they consulted other authorities, they wrangled but finally they decided to plunge for the whole lot – for a sum variously estimated at between £70,000 and £100,000. They made the purchase, aided and abetted – it was thought –

---

1. Ruskin had this privilege in 1853, and so did his fellow-guest, Walter Sneyd, another enthusiastic collector of manuscripts (see page 91). In *Phillipps Studies*, Vol. IV, page 96, Munby quotes a letter where Sneyd writes to Robert Curzon (another manuscript collector), 'My only marvel is that *any* individual even with inexhaustible opportunities could have succeeded in getting together such a collection'.

by the Empress Victoria, formerly the Princess Royal of England, and took it with them to Berlin (with the exception of a few works of specifically English interest).

While there was obvious delight in the German press and particular pleasure that here was money being spent on cultural rather than warlike possessions, and congratulations poured in from all over the world, the British press noted the German acquisition with understandable but muted regret and used the opportunity to plead for more museums in provincial cities and more money for the arts generally. 'The regret at this loss', said a leader in *The Times* of 1883, 'will be sharpened by a glance at the enormous sums England is ready to lavish on any object that it deems worthy of public consideration. Think of the Abyssinian war, the Afghan war, the Zulu war, and now this Egyptian business with its long tail of consequences. A single year's interest on the cost of any one of these wars would suffice to turn the scale in favour of high art and public refinement in this country.'

Back in Berlin, gradually and quite unexpectedly, the most fearful bickering broke out among various German museum and library authorities over who should have the privilege of owning various parts of the collection. The question of payment presented particular problems because the sums involved were vastly greater than the annual acquisition grants to the various institutions concerned. A cabinet minister was called in to arbitrate, but even this did not calm the strife. Bismarck himself took a hand in the matter and made it clear that the extra money needed would not come from any of the Imperial treasure chests. In the end, after five years of squabbling and, incidentally, non-payment, and the convenient death of the Emperor, Lippmann, who had almost gone grey in the process, decided with heavy heart that in order to raise the funds to keep at least the Dante/Botticelli MSS and a minority of the others, the remainder would have to be put up for sale again. Some were purchased by the dealers Joseph Baer and J. and S. Goldschmidt in Frankfurt. Another batch, relating mostly to Scottish matters, went quietly to the British Museum. A third and much the best, which included the renowned Latin Gospel on purple vellum in uncial letters of gold, written for Archbishop Wilfred of York between 670 and 680 by an Anglo-Saxon scribe and given to Henry VIII by Pope Leo X when he conferred upon Henry the title 'Defender of the Faith', was sold to Trübner of Strasbourg, who, in his wisdom, decided to sell the MSS once again at Sotheby's. A new catalogue of some 91 items, with a lamely apologetic introduction by 'the Compilers of the Catalogue' (presumably the German museum authorities), stated, 'That the Prussian Government never intended to keep the Hamilton Collection in its entirety is proved by the fact that not one of the MSS now before the public has been stamped. They still bear the numbers of Messrs. Sotheby, Wilkinson & Hodge's Sale Catalogue'. The sale, which the papers described as 'of a very remarkable and, indeed, unprecedented character' and in other glowing terms, was announced for 23 May 1889. But as *The Times* was quick to point out, at least twenty of the 91 lots did not come from the Hamilton collection at all. Nevertheless the sale-room was crowded when

Edward Hodge got into the rostrum at precisely one o'clock on that memorable Thursday. To everyone's disappointment he began the proceedings by announcing that lot 1, the magnificent folio Evangelarium on purple vellum, would be sold at the end of the sale. This was the work which Quaritch wanted above all else and he must have been vexed that his name would not now come first – as it usually did – in press reviews that appeared on the following day as the buyer of the first important item. In fact, his first purchase was lot 6, a twelfth-century *Breviarum Romanum* by a German scribe with 192 initials in gold on coloured ground and 27 full-page illustrations. It moved up rapidly from £50 and went to Quaritch at £205. He also bought the next lot, a beautiful two-volume, thirteenth-century folio bible in French (with 76 miniatures in the early Gothic style, by a French artist, executed in grisaille and vivid colours on a diapered gold ground) for £250. For lot 9, a sumptuous illuminated Italian bible on vellum that had once belonged to the Salviati family, he had to pay £155. He also bought lot 10, a vellum *Roman de la Rose* with 101 delicate miniatures in grisaille, for £325. The sale-room clerk, Mr. Snowdon,[1] who had had the most enormous number of commissions in the earlier Beckford and Hamilton sales, bought lot 11, a Flemish, vellum St. Augustine with over a thousand decorative initials and 23 magnificent paintings, for £520 on behalf of an anonymous client. Goldschmidt of Frankfurt paid £1,700 for a Boccaccio on vellum at more than three times what Quaritch thought it was worth. Ellis got a snip when he only paid £80 for lot 13, a thirteenth-century *Chronicle of France* with many initials. Quaritch paid £200 for lot 14, a French *History of the World* on vellum 'with 63 portrait initials, historiated with miniatures and 410 capital letters'. He also got lot 16 and – after a real scrap – lot 33, a Diodorus Siculus manuscript on vellum, richly ornamented with capital and other decorations in gold and colour and 41 miniatures executed by that great artist, Geoffrey Tory himself. Prefixed to the history was a full-page painting in exquisite detail of King Francis I (who had commissioned the work) surrounded by his three sons listening to a recital with a host of courtiers standing round about. The volume had been produced in about 1530 and was in its original binding. Quaritch started the bidding at £50 and the price gradually rose to £200 when the contest lay between the Fitzwilliam Museum (who bought quite a number of works in the sale), Goldschmidt (thought to be buying on behalf of the Duc d'Aumale) and Quaritch. At £700 the Fitzwilliam dropped out and at £950 Goldschmidt had reached his limit. Quaritch carried the day at £1,000. He was buying on commission for his friend Morgand of Paris.

There was also a bit of a squabble over lot 49. Once again the bidding was only between Quaritch and Goldschmidt. Edward Hodge knocked it down to Quaritch at £124, but Goldschmidt claimed at once that he had bid the same amount. The book was put up again and Quaritch had to pay another £40 for it. Fairfax Murray, of whom we shall hear more later, attended the sale and bought a Cicero on vellum for £20 (lot 52). Lot 58 saw a further animated duel

1. G. S. Snowdon had taken over the post of Senior Sales Clerk from F. G. du Pasquier in 1873. He held the post until 1910 when J. B. Lambert took his place.

between Quaritch and another London dealer called Whitehead for a Book of Hours erroneously thought to have been decorated by Tory. Quaritch had to pay the enormous price of £1,230 for it, but he was buying for Morgand. In contrast, he was practically *given* two Books of Hours (lot 68 and lot 69) at six guineas and £5 respectively; the second, by a German sixteenth-century artist, contained five large initials framing perfectly painted landscapes. He had to pay £495 for lot 70, a French Book of Hours with 1,855 particularly imaginative decorative initials and 29 miniatures. This again was being bought for Morgand.

Lot 88 had caused great interest before the sale and there was spirited bidding for it now. It was a splendid manuscript on particularly fine vellum of a well-known poem written in the fourteenth century in the hand of a German scribe, and had once been owned by the Emperor Maximilian and his wife, Mary of Burgundy. There were 116 miniatures showing scenes of contemporary life (in which the figures were a little stiff). Quaritch eventually bought it for £340. He also bought the last three lots in the sale, when the battle for lot 1, the manuscript on purple vellum, began. The time was four o'clock. It had taken Hodge exactly three hours to sell ninety lots – an unbelievably slow rate of sale by today's standards.

It had only recently been discovered that the remarkable example of palaeography in lot 1 was the work of an Anglo-Saxon scribe. The inscription, arms and ornaments on the scarlet morocco binding was thought to be the work of Hans Holbein. An English bookseller had offered the amazing sum of £5,000 for the acquisition of the manuscript some years earlier after an article on its origin by Professor Wattenbach of Berlin had appeared in a learned journal (the article was quoted at length in the catalogue). All these were points that Mr. Hodge touched upon in a little preamble to putting lot 1 up for offer and he also expressed the pious hope that the manuscript might eventually go to the British Museum, though he feared that the pecuniary means were unlikely to be available at the present time. A point he did not mention (but the catalogue in all honesty did) was that the 'ex-libris' of the Royal Library of Berlin had been removed, according to the rules of that institution, before the sale, thus making palpable nonsense of the assertion that it had not been intended to keep the MS there!

Quaritch again opened the bidding with £500. Goldschmidt countered with £600 and then the bids came excessively slowly until £1,000 was reached. Quaritch came in again at £1,360, was out-bid up to £1,490, but like a cat who has known all along that the mouse has no chance, allowed a long and pregnant pause before bidding £1,500 to win. There was loud applause. He had marked the expected price in his catalogue at £1,555. The total for the sale came to £15,189. Of this Quaritch had contributed £6,774 8s. 6d. for 28 lots. He had spent £3,594 for Morgand, £483 5s. for commissions from other buyers and £2,697 3s. 6d. for his own stock. There was no chance here for any 'returns'. Normally after book sales, Quaritch collated what he had bought with minute care, and a considerable percentage was returned to Sotheby's as imperfect. Often these same items were then re-purchased at much lower prices. In many instances they could be made good from other imperfect copies of the same titles. This was a painstaking procedure which all booksellers practised, but Quaritch was better at it than most and it helped to finance a not inconsiderable part of his annual outlay. Sotheby's hated it, but were used to the practice. The best defence was accurate cataloguing.

There can be no doubt that Quaritch felt great satisfaction over this unexpected postscript to the Hamilton saga, even though the material that had now been sold was only a fraction of what had gone to Berlin originally. The whole book trade had felt cheated in 1882 when this prize of prizes had been snatched from their grasp by Dr. Lippmann. Quaritch could feel pleased too because he had had to pay rather less than he thought likely. In celebration of the event he staged a little exhibition of the purchases made for himself at a *soirée* of Ye Sette of Odd Volumes, a book trade social club over which he presided for many years and in which he took the greatest interest. It was held on 17 June 1889 at Willis's Rooms and a carefully printed catalogue on pink paper produced for the occasion. Quaritch's personal valuations of each of the thirteen works exhibited was included in each entry. In the case of what he now called 'The Golden Gospels of Henry VIII', it had risen to £2,500 from the £1,500 he had paid. Lot 7 had increased from £250 to £500, lot 88 from £340 to £450 and the other increases were correspondingly modest. Quaritch eventually sold the Golden Gospels to America where they were bought by Theodore Irwin of Oswego, and resold in 1900 to Pierpont Morgan.

There was pleasure at the results of the sale at Wellington Street too. The ghost of old John Bohn who had compiled the original 1882 catalogue with scrupulous care and much scholarship must have rejoiced that some of his work was eventually used. John Wilkinson, now long retired from active participation in the business, wrote a charming letter congratulating the Hodges, father and son, on the outcome of the sale.

Let us return, however, to 1884, when the last of the Hamilton Palace Library books had gone from Wellington Street. A mere six months later starting on 12 December and going on for seven days those distinguished auctioneers of Literary Property and Works Illustrative of the Fine Arts, Messrs. SW&H, began yet another epoch-making sale. The reader might well have got tired of such superlatives by now, but their use in this instance is genuinely merited. *The Times* stated categorically that such excitement had never before been witnessed in the famous rooms of Sotheby, Wilkinson and Hodge as at the sale (then just concluded), of a selection only, from the library of the late Sir John Hayford Thorold of Syston Park near Grantham in Lincolnshire, and that the results of the sale completely put in the shade what had been achieved at the Sunderland, Beckford-Hamilton and other recent and well-publicised sales. The occasion did indeed have all the ingredients that make an auction a milestone in sale-room history. The books had been assembled two or three generations earlier; they included not merely the best, but the very best items of their kind, and the first collection had been – like the manuscripts at Hamilton

Palace – sifted and then strengthened by a second collector with as much perception as the first; and the whole had then lain dormant and forgotten for fifty years. The only major snag was that a great number of the books had been cruelly maltreated by a local binder whom the collector had patronised.

Sir John Thorold, born in 1734, the year that Samuel Baker began in business, had succeeded to the baronetcy in 1775 and collected the most magnificent *incunabula* that had come on to the market for forty years. Like Alexander Hamilton, he bought particularly actively at Paris sales where the Parisian booksellers referred to him as the 'Chevalier Thorold'. His son, Sir John Hayford Thorold, sold the duplicates after his father's death in 1815 and added books of equal merit (including a fine collection of Aldines and Elzeviers) for fifteen years from the great sales of his time, before he himself died. When Sotheby's catalogued the library it contained a particularly beautiful copy of the Gutenberg Bible (then always referred to as the 'Mazarin' Bible since the discovery of a copy in the library of Cardinal Mazarin); the even rarer Mainz Psalter of 1459 printed by Fust and Schöffer; the Latin bible on vellum printed by the same printers in 1462; one of the earliest of the block-books, the *Apocalypse*; the Polyglot Bible of Cardinal Ximenes; the four Shakespeare Folios; and a number of Caxtons. It was enough to make collectors of such desiderata all over the world look at their bank accounts and send commissions to London in spite of what they might already have purchased in the preceding years.

The first day of the sale produced no great excitement. The second was quite different. Quaritch bought the Polyglot Bible for £176; the Sunderland copy had fetched £195. The Latin Bible brought £1,000. The Gutenberg Bible was lot 284. Sotheby's had a reserve price for it of £1,200. The last copy previously to have come up for sale was one for which Quaritch had paid £2,690 in the Perkins Sale (not staged by Sotheby's), but that had been twenty-five years earlier and it had been bought from Quaritch at once by Henry Huth. *The Times* explained to its readers what had happened to earlier copies and that this was 'the earliest book printed with metal types by the inventors of printing. It is a superb work printed on paper as thick and rich in tone as vellum with glossy ink, intensely black and very uniform in impression;[1] the letters large and similar to those written by the scribes of the Church missals and choral books. After a preliminary buzz of excitement as the wonderful book was passed with great solemnity and admiration up and down before the two rows of professional and amateur bibliophiles seated in front of the rostrum, the first bid of £500 was made and immediately met with one of £1,000 from Mr. Quaritch, who had to advance against the biddings on commission made by the auctioneers' clerk, Mr. Snowdon; and so the contest went on by bids of £50, the excitement rising higher and higher as £3,000 was called for by Mr. Quaritch, followed by

1. 'In contemplating the splendid workmanship', said Sotheby's note in the catalogue, 'it seems marvellous that the Inventors of Printing should by a single effort have exhibited the perfection of their art.' In fact, there is now reason to believe that Gutenberg had printed other works before the great 42-line Bible.

£3,100 from his opponent, while each seemed to get fresher with the fight up to the fifty-seventh round when at £3,650 the commission was exhausted and at Mr. Quaritch's bid of £3,700 everyone expected the hammer must fall, but here Mr. Ellis, who had hitherto only watched the contest, joined issue with two or three spirited bids, and a last one of £3,850, leaving it to Mr. Quaritch to possess this splendid Mazarin Bible at the enormous price of £3,900. There was a round of applause given as the hammer fell and it was some minutes before the excitement subsided'.

We must remember that this was in an era in which a farmworker took home 12s. 6d. at the end of the week and that the skilled compositor who had set up the piece in *The Times* just quoted received perhaps 32s. for a week's work, in order to get an impression of what this highest price ever paid for a book represented. The same bible (which Quaritch in fact sold to America) came up for sale again in the Makellar Sale where Quaritch bought it back for only £2,950 and then sold it to the General Theological Seminary, New York. When that institution put up the bible for sale by Christie's in New York in 1978, it fetched another world record, £1,176,000 ($2,200,000). The point needs to be stressed that the world was probably much more astonished by the price of £3,900 in 1884 than it was by the figure of more than £1,000,000 in 1978. It was an extraordinary coincidence that two further Gutenberg Bibles, of the forty-eight known to exist, changed hands after the first in 1978. One was sold by H. P. Kraus of New York to the Gutenberg Museum at Mainz for $1,800,000. The second, which belonged to the Pforzheimer Foundation in New York, was sold to the University of Texas for $2,400,000, and who were the booksellers who handled this deal? None other than Bernard Quaritch Limited, still going strong in London 131 years after their foundation.

The founder himself had more business to transact at the Thorold Sale. The climax came on the seventh day. As usual, when it came to a great book, Edward Hodge uttered a brief eulogy on lot 1650 before starting to sell the *Psalmorum Codex*. Copies sold previously had all been faulty. This perfect copy on vellum was, in fact, the second edition of 1459 (the first had appeared in 1457) printed by Fust and Schöffer. It was only the second printed book to include a date of publication, and contained the Athanasian Creed printed for the first time. *The Times* devoted almost an entire column to the sale of this single item. No one had expected it to produce a great battle. Indeed, the sale-room was only half full when it started. Once again the contenders were Snowdon, Ellis and Quaritch. The price moved up slowly from £500, while the audience looked on totally spellbound, to £4,850. After agonising minutes of silence Ellis bid £4,900. Quaritch at once countered with £4,950, 'at which, after calling this enormous price three times, Mr. Hodge raised his hammer for the last time and sealed the purchase of the famous Codex to Mr. Quaritch at this unprecedented price amid the loudest applause ever heard in this room'. It was clear that no one at Wellington Street had anticipated anything like such a price, for Hodge had one bid written into his catalogue at £325, and if the truth were to be told, a reserve of no more than £100. His normally rock-like hand must have shaken as he entered the figure into his catalogue, for the numerals have been gone over twice.

The total for the sale after the final session on the following day, the eighth, came to £28,001 15s. 6d. of which Quaritch had paid more than £20,000. As if this was not excitement enough, Hodge used the opportunity of the end of the sale to announce that the next great private library which would be offered at auction by Sotheby's would be that belonging to the Earl of Jersey, long preserved as Osterley Park and assembled by his ancestor, Bryan Fairfax, who had died as long ago as 1747. It would contain, said Hodge, not only some very rare manuscripts but no less than eleven books printed by Caxton.

So once again, in the following year, Quaritch plunged heavily. He bought nine of the eleven Caxtons and spent more than £10,000 out of a total of £13,000. Like all the really great dealers of their time – one also thinks of H. P. Kraus in the post-Second World War period – Quaritch realised that even among the flood of great libraries coming on to the market in the 1880s those from Syston Park and Osterley Park represented pinnacles, and felt compelled to buy the rarest books even though – unlike his principal rival, Ellis – he did not always have immediate customers in mind for them. No doubt this necessitated long discussions about credit arrangements with Edward and Tom Hodge before each sale. In the course of time Quaritch helped to build up the libraries of many of the greatest collectors of the era, such as Lord Amherst of Hackney, Lord Carysfort, the Earl of Rosebery, William Morris, H. H. Gibbs, Lord Peckover of Wisbech, the first Lord Aldenham, Samuel Sandars and, in a different capacity, Henry Bradshaw, the scholarly and magnificently acquisitive librarian of the Cambridge University Library.

The Great Depression continued to take its toll. In 1887 (and 1889) Lord (Ludovic) Crawford was forced to sell a part of the great library at Haigh Hall. In the adverse conditions which then prevailed, long-standing mortgages on his estate were suddenly called in, and as he wrote much later,[1] 'I was forced to realise as best as I could; my only available resource being the library'. When Quaritch heard of Crawford's predicament he offered to select books from the library in order to raise the needed sum, but the owner remained obdurate about arranging a sale. Sotheby's reduced their commission from 12½ per cent to 10 per cent because he had written the descriptions of most of the books himself. The first sale brought only £19,000. Many of its greatest prizes went for paltry sums. Quaritch again bought the lion's share then and at the second Crawford sale in 1889, when the outcome was no happier.

The Sotheby–Quaritch epic continued uninterruptedly until 1899. After the Ellis stock sale in 1885, the roll-call continued with books from Michael Wodhull (1886), Baron Seillière (1887), J. T. Gibson Craig (1887–9), R. S. Turner (1888), the Earl of Hopetoun 1889, the Duke of Buccleuch (1889), Frederick Perkins (1889), Thomas Gaisford (1890), Sir E. Sullivan (1890), William Horatio Crawford (no relation of the Earl – 1891), Count Louis Apponyi (1892),

1. In 1910, in the introduction to the first volume of the great eight-volume catalogue of the *Bibliotheca Lindesiana*.

the Bateman Heirlooms (1893), the Rev. W. E. Buckley (1893-4), the Rev. W. Makellar (1898) and William Morris (1898).

Quaritch fought hard to stem the tide of declining prices, and very frequently got condemned for his pains, particularly in the American press. When eventually he died at the ripe old age of eighty he had, says de Ricci, 'hardly a penny to his name, but he owned the finest stock in the world'. The relaxation he craved never materialised and the end had come with great suddenness. He had been in the office right through Sotheby's December sales in 1899. On 16 December he had gone into 15 Piccadilly, despite a severe bronchial cold, and the next day was dead of pneumonia. The world mourned his loss with genuine grief. An obituarist in the *Daily Telegraph* wrote of him as 'the king of Booksellers, incomparably the greatest, wisest, best informed, most liberal and munificent bookseller of his or any age. A perfect judge of books, a princely purchaser, described at sales as the Napoleon of the Sale Room. Good old, wise old, wonderful old, Bernard Quaritch'.

No place can have mourned his passing more than Wellington Street. Hodge, father and son, must have felt more than a tremor of uncertainty passing through their minds. Quaritch had set the pace and Quaritch had set the standards. He had constituted the present for Sotheby's for so long. It was not at all clear what would happen now that he was no more. Certainly nobody could have guessed with assurance at that stage that the many libraries he had helped to create would ultimately constitute some of the greatest sales at Sotheby's in years to come. It was only the ghost of Samuel Leigh Sotheby who knew for certain that 'most of what we sell comes back to us in the end'. In particular Quaritch's achievement was that he had given the world an awareness of the significance and the beauty of early printed books and the manuscripts that had preceded them.

PART TWO

Enter Barlow, Hobson and Warre

CATALOGUE

OF SUPERB

PRINTS, DRAWINGS, PICTURES, AND ARMOUR

FROM

The Historical Collections

AT

WILTON HOUSE, SALISBURY,

THE PROPERTY OF THE .

Rt. Hon. The EARL OF PEMBROKE & MONTGOMERY

WHICH WILL BE SOLD BY AUCTION.

BY MESSRS.

SOTHEBY, WILKINSON & HODGE

Auctioneers of Literary Property and Works illustrative of the Fine Arts,

AT THEIR HOUSE, 34 & 35, NEW BOND STREET,

On THURSDAY and FRIDAY, JULY 5th and 6th, 1917,

AND

MONDAY and TUESDAY, JULY 9th and 10th, 1917,

AT ONE O'CLOCK PRECISELY.

May be viewed: MONDAY, TUESDAY and WEDNESDAY, July 2nd, 3rd and 4th.

LONDON: WILLIAM CLOWES AND SONS, LIMITED, DUKE STREET, STAMFORD STREET, S.E.1.

The first major sale after the firm's move to Bond Street. It heralded a determined effort to break into the world of fine art auctioneering after decades of concentrating mainly on books.

6

The Final Years at Wellington Street

THE final years of the nineteenth century saw a number of changes in both the direction of the business and in the staff. There was a slow and tentative diversification into other fields, though it is difficult to fathom whether or not this was the result of a conscious decision. The firm never hesitated to tackle something different when the occasion arose, as in 1882, when they found themselves selling the Walker Collection. Fans were one of the favourite objects which Victorian ladies collected, and when Robert Walker of Uffington put up his immense collection of fans of all ages and from all over the world for sale in 1882, the illustrated edition of the catalogue contained such valuable and detailed information that it became one of the few standard works of reference on the subject for years. It had been compiled by the collector, at Sotheby's suggestion, an idea which clearly appealed to him.

> I do not pretend to infallibility, but in the following compilation, I believe most of the descriptions are accurate. . . . In cases of 'difference of opinion' I must shelter myself under the auctioneer's fifth condition of sale [this related to non-responsibility for errors of description]. I part with the collection with regret; it having been a source of much pleasure in hours of relaxation. It has now, however, outgrown the accommodation of my Berkshire cottage home.

The collection was first offered as a whole in one lot, because Walker hoped that it would be bought for a museum. As no buyer came forward it was – stated the catalogue – with the exception of about half a dozen lots, sold without reserve. The 460 fans fetched £1,708 9s., and some examples with strong historic associations or designs by well-known artists fetched good prices. An eighteenth-century French marriage fan which sold for £23 in 1882 re-appeared in the sale-room in 1974 (it was clearly recognisable from the original catalogue illustration) and then fetched £485.

A much more important area of sales, where the firm seemed to lead the field, was that of coins. There were sixteen coin sales in the year of Quaritch's death and eighteen in the first year of the new century, 1900. The most important such sale the firm had tackled for many years began in November 1895 and continued at intervals in eight parts over two years.[1] Hyman Montague was a brilliant barrister who loved collecting as a foil to his legal work. Even as a schoolboy he had assembled a distinguished collection of beetles, and, as the long and detailed introduction to the first of his sales recounted, 'What Mr. Montague undertook, it was always his endeavour to accomplish thoroughly,

1. There had been three earlier sales in 1886, 1888 and 1892.

and this dominant feature in his character was the keynote to his success'. At first Montague concentrated on English coins from Ancient British and Anglo-Saxon times onwards. In the beginning he bought cautiously but as he became more knowledgeable and experienced in the field he bought entire collections. After a few years he had acquired, with such additions, the most complete collection of British coins outside the British Museum and there was little left for him to buy. It normally took Sotheby's a single day to sell a good and reasonably complete collection of Ancient British and Anglo-Saxon coins. In Montague's case they extended to six days and were still far from exhausted. He sold the later British coins (from George I to Victoria) to Spink's, and started to form a Greek and Roman cabinet. He amassed, for example, no fewer than 1,300 specimens of Roman gold coins, the largest series ever brought together by a private collector, and his Greek collection was just as enormous. Later on he turned to English medals and soon owned 3,000 particularly fine examples. He was a long-serving Vice President of the Numismatic Society and published thirty papers in thirteen years in its journal. He had further great plans for the compilation of numismatic works of reference when he died quite unexpectedly at fifty, and because no individual or institution could be found to buy the collection, or even part of the collection, it was put up for sale by auction. The Roman coins were thought by his executors to appeal more to the Continental market and were placed for sale in Paris with Rollin and Feuardent. Sotheby's sold the remainder for £48,860 (in a total of 55 days, between 1886 and 1897). The principal purchaser by far was John G. Murdoch who was fired with the same ambition as Hyman Montague, to own the best coin collection (in this case, only of British coins) of all time. To a large measure he succeeded, and after *his* death the collection came to Sotheby's again, where it was dispersed under the terms of Murdoch's will in a series of six sales beginning in February 1903, when it realised a total of £38,620. As it happened, a major purchaser on this occasion, of the principal patterns and proofs (which stemmed originally from Montague), was an eccentric Italian collector, Count P. Ferrari. His executors decided in 1922 that London should be the venue for a sale of a part of his numismatic collection, and the often referred-to 'mystery sale' in March of that year, catalogued as 'the Famous and Remarkable Collection of British and Colonial Coins, Patterns and Proofs, formed by a Nobleman recently deceased', was indeed Ferrari's. That fact became known at what was probably only the fourth sale of such quality, that of the Douglas–Morris Collection of gold coins sold at Bond Street in November 1974 which fetched the truly remarkable total of £569,390 for only 237 lots. Quite a number of the coins were, in fact, the identical specimens that had been owned in turn by Montague, Murdoch and Ferrari.

Tom Hodge

Although still nominally in charge of the firm, Edward Hodge had gradually withdrawn from active involvement and Tom had become head of the business in all but name. He was a gentler man than his father and had reduced the manner of auctioneering to a precision and economy that endeared him to the trade. His knowledge too was much wider than his father's. He knew a great deal, not only about books but also about mezzotints, etchings and engravings, about coins, porcelain and antiques of all kinds.

The more one studies the man, the more impressive a personality he turns out to be. With the help of a minute but highly proficient staff he carried on single-handed a complex, specialist and often difficult business. From contemporary reports it appears that Wellington Street – except during major sales – was a very calm and unruffled place; and to a large extent this apparently placid atmosphere was due to Tom's extreme efficiency and hard work. Certainly he had habits that would make any office manager today shudder. He went through the post each morning with his confidential clerk, de Courville. Any letter that was interesting was put in one pile for answer, but any letter offering something that he did not consider worth including in a sale was termed 'N.S.V.', variously transcribed as of 'No Sales Value' or 'Not Sufficient Value', and went straight into the waste-paper basket. Many important matters he answered himself in his own very rapid and illegible hand. He kept no copies, though in the case of really vital letters he wrote out the odd draft. Filing was kept to an absolute minimum, and was mostly done in old envelopes and kept on window-sills. On the other hand the proprietors' ledgers and account books were kept with meticulous care and the business with its price estimates, pre-sale reserves, varying commissions and multitude of special arrangements, such as the credit for returned books, was a model of good communication between the firm and its clients, both sellers and buyers. Administration too was excellent. The opportunities for confusing ownership of property and losing books were immense, but such things hardly ever occurred.

Hodge kept most figures in his head and his reluctance to look anything up in old records became legendary. He regarded doing so as a profligate misuse of time that could be devoted to obtaining and organising new business. Like many men who have worked in their father's shadow for a long time, it was not generally recognised what a strong and occasionally stubborn character he had of his own, though the trade certainly loved and respected him and the anti-quarian booksellers of the day – men like the younger Quaritch, Maggs, Spencer and Tregaskis – were tough, shrewd operators to whom respect did not come lightly. They enjoyed Tom Hodge in the rostrum and respected his fairness, his remarkable astuteness and his way with collectors. They admired his appearance. He was a tall, elegant man with white hair and a white moustache and brilliant blue eyes, almost always dressed in a dark blue suit. They admired his very wide knowledge of everything the firm dealt in, whether it was books, manuscripts, prints, coins or works of art. They forgave the frequently pedantic tone of his letters particularly when they were late with payments, and they blessed him for his sense of humour.

Tim Wilder[1] tells a story of a particular auction at the turn of the century

1. The oldest surviving member of Sotheby's staff (see page 109).

when shilling bids were still taken and sales were held on Saturday afternoons. Several lots had gone for trifling sums when a valuable illuminated manuscript was reached in the sale. Little Bertram Dobell, bookseller and poet, eyebrows rising into his forehead, but without looking up from his catalogue, thought to introduce some comedy into the proceedings. 'A shilling, Sir', he said. Tom Hodge paused and said, 'Come, come, Mr. Dobell, you ought to know better than that'. 'I'll give a shilling for any lot, Sir', said Dobell without looking up. Tom Hodge made no further comment, but proceeded with selling the manuscript for a large sum, in those days, of several hundred pounds. A few lots later a bundle of books came up for which there was no bid. Rapping with his gavel, Hodge said: 'A shilling to Mr. Dobell'. Startled at last into raising his head, the astonished Dobell said 'I didn't bid, Sir'. Laying down the gavel and leaning back in his chair, Hodge replied: 'Mr. Dobell, just now you said you would give a shilling for any lot'.

And that was that. For the rest of the sale, when there was no bid, instead of the usual 'Passed' the appreciative company heard, 'A shilling to Mr. Dobell'. Ruefully, at the end, the would-be comedian contemplated a vast quantity of worthless volumes, left for him to clear.

Hodge was a man of great courtesy and for one with so much authority he was remarkably complaisant. He was also staunchly conservative: so much so that he did not allow either telephones or typewriters into the office until long after these had been introduced into other businesses. Beneath the calm exterior, he was highly strung, and the constant stress of his job led to various physical complaints, including lumbago. It was for this reason that he was always visiting spas to seek relief from these ailments during the intervals between sales. He was also a great solver of other people's problems and arbitrator in trade disputes. He really was 'king' in that small, select, but well-chronicled world of people who bought and sold old books.

In the event he, and his father, need not have worried unduly about the death of Quaritch. For some years the old man had been inducting his son, Bernard Alfred Quaritch, into the business. 'Alfred', as he was always known, was plump, round-faced with a pointed waxed moustache, every inch a ladies' man. He had ability and drive and was generally much more profit-orientated than his father, and he very quickly got the business at Piccadilly on to a much sounder financial footing. He had been sent to America on a selling trip at the age of only nineteen, and it was clear to him forever after that the United States was where the firm's principal customers would be found in the new century. The relationship between Edward Grose Hodge and Bernard Quaritch had been very Victorian: business-like, efficient, respectful but never intimate. 'Young Tom' and Alfred seem to have been closer. They were constantly in touch over some of the major sales just before and after 1900. An interesting example of their collaboration was a pamphlet put out by Quaritch in March 1897 announcing the sale of the first part of the Earl of Ashburnham's great library. The elder Quaritch had already bought one Gutenberg Bible from Lord Ashburnham privately for £4,000. The projected sale included another copy printed on vellum. Quaritch announced at the same time that he was authorised to offer the remaining Ashburnham manuscripts for sale[1] *en bloc*, and further the 'Library of Splendid Illuminated Manuscripts and early printed Woodcuts' collected by the late William Morris – at a price fixed by Mr. Morris's executors. 'Intending buyers should telegraph to me to ascertain the exact amount. A small list prepared by me containing brief titles and particulars of all the more beautiful and desirable articles among the printed books as well as the manuscripts, accompanies the present circular. If no buyer of the library *en bloc* is found, this season, it will be sold by public auction at Sotheby's.'[2]

The Ashburnham sales continued among much publicity after Bernard's death. Alfred bought as heavily as had his father. In the same way young Tom and Alfred saw a good deal of each other over some of the sales that were to form the longest and probably the most important in Sotheby's history – those of the manuscripts and books of Sir Thomas Phillipps. It has been calculated[3] that during his long life Sir Thomas collected about 60,000 manuscripts, 50,000 books and 50,000 charters. He had devoted much ingenuity to devising a means of keeping the collection intact after his death. The British Museum and Oxford University had both been considered as possible recipients, but Phillipps invariably stipulated conditions that made any such proposition impracticable. He constantly re-drafted his will – for the last time only five days before his death in February 1872. His principal objective towards the end had been to make certain that his detested son-in-law, James Orchard Halliwell, should have nothing to do with the collection, and thus, says Munby, 'it was that Phillipps' second daughter Katharine and her husband, John Fenwick, received a bequest of an acutely embarrassing kind, the life-tenancy of a vast entailed house and library with an endowment totally inadequate for its upkeep. Reforming legislation enabled the Court of Chancery in 1885 to rescue the Fenwicks from their predicament; and a year later began the series of sales of manuscripts and printed books with which the name of Phillipps and Sotheby will always be associated'. The first sale of books took place on 3 August 1886 and fetched £2,215. Sixteen sales (of which only three were of books, and the remainder consisted entirely of manuscripts) had taken place by 1913 and realised £71,272 3s. 6d.

The twelfth Phillipps sale occurred in the same year as another sale of a great manuscript collection. This time of Walter Sneyd, in December 1903. Sneyd, a close friend of Robert Curzon, was one of the most active later Victorian collectors of manuscripts from the Middle Ages. The most valuable item in his sale was lot 513, a thirteenth-century text of the Song of Songs, Proverbs and Ecclesiastes with 267 miniatures by a French artist, 45 of them full-page. It had been given to Sneyd by the 11th Duke of Hamilton during a visit to Hamilton

1. See page 186.
2. As we shall see later, it was in fact bought privately by Richard Bennett, who kept the best for himself and put the rest up for sale at Sotheby's.
3. By Dr. A. N. L. Munby in 'Sir Thomas Phillipps: a Centenary Tribute', *Art at Auction*, 1971–72.

Palace in 1856.[1] Alfred Quaritch paid £2,500 for it, twice as much as any other item in the sale, and sold it to the French Rothschilds. The other major purchaser at the sale was Charles Fairfax Murray who founded his own collection of manuscripts with a nucleus from Sneyd's. These in turn passed to C. W. Dyson Perrins,[2] and three manuscripts in particular, for which he paid £1,250 in 1903, realised £30,000 at the Dyson Perrins sale held at Sotheby's nearly fifty years later.

Another sale of this period which caused something of a stir was when the library of the American, William C. Van Antwerp, actually came to London to be dispersed. The sale was held on 23 March 1907 at 1.00 p.m. sharp. Attending it was a book collector on a visit to London, who wrote a detailed account of the event. This was Sir William Osler, a great surgeon, teacher of medicine and collector of medical books. He was particularly impressed by the matter-of-factness of the occasion and the apparent lack of tension. He found book sales at Sotheby's wholly fascinating and a startling contrast to similar events at the Hôtel des Commissaires Priseurs, the Hôtel Drouot in Paris, where prices seemed much lower. He wrote:

> One was impressed by the extremely decorous character of the proceedings, without the slightest noise or bluster such as one is accustomed to think of in connexion with sales. The auctioneer, Mr. Tom Hodge, presided at a raised desk at the end of an oblong table about which were seated some twenty buyers, the principals or the representatives of the leading English booksellers. Around the room were twenty-five or thirty onlookers, mostly seated, a few standing about. Bids were offered only by the dealers and by a man who held a catalogue marked with the bids sent directly to the firm. The auctioneer, with a soft voice and a good-natured manner, called out the numbers and, as a rule, offered no comments upon the books; in fact, he did not often have to ask for a bid, which was started spontaneously. Occasionally, of course, he could not resist a remark or two. Sometimes he would suggest a bid. It was astonishing with what rapidity the different items were sold. Evidently the dealers knew just what they wanted and what they were willing to pay, and in many cases one could easily see that they had been given a limit by those who had sent the orders.
>
> The first work of special interest sold was the 1817 edition of poems of Keats, a presentation copy, with an inscription by the author. Starting at £20 it rose quickly to £70 and £80 and in less than a minute was knocked down to Quaritch at £90. I say knocked down, but the process was altogether too dignified for such an expression, and no final rap was ever given. The catalogue of the Rowfant Library brought £7. Two books of Richard Pynson's press brought high figures. It was remarkable, also, to see a ragged rough-looking, unbound, but uncut play of Philip Massinger knocked down to Stevens at £48. Bidding upon the copy of 'Comus', one of the rarest of Milton's works, was started by Quaritch at £50 and ran up pound by pound with the greatest rapidity to £100, and finally to £162. Nothing was heard but the monotonous repetition of the figures by the auctioneer, who simply watched the nodding heads of Mr. Quaritch, and his rival, Ellis of Bond Street. The 'Paradise Regained', an uncut copy and a great rarity in this state – so much so that the auctioneer remarked, 'Uncut, and need I

1. See page 76n.   2. See pages 123 and 189.

say more? All you can ask!' – was secured at £94 by Maggs. Three beautiful first editions of some of Pope's works did not bring very high prices, though the 'Windsor Forest', in sheets loosely stitched together, entirely uncut, brought £48. One of the finest sets of the collection was 'Purchas his Pilgrimes, in five Books'. As the auctioneer remarked, 'It is one of the finest copies ever sold and Mr. Van Antwerp had had a most detailed and complete collation made'. The volumes were in the original vellum, absolutely perfect. Starting at £50, the fifth bid reached £100, and the set was knocked down to Maggs at £170 against Quaritch – one of the few instances in which Mr. Quaritch gave up. . . .

Then, after the sale of lot 189, came the remarkable set of original Shakespeare folios. Just as a foil, it seemed, and to show the contrast between the new and the old, Sidney Lee's facsimile reprint of the first folio, issued by the Clarendon Press in 1902, was put up (£2 12s.). When lot 191 was called out, there was a stir among the auditors, not such as you could hear, but it could be felt, as the famous first folio of 'Mr. William Shakespeares Comedies, Histories, and Tragedies' was offered. It was in a superb red morocco binding by Bedford and enclosed in a new crushed red morocco slip case by Bradstreet. . . .

'Language fails me, Sirs,' the auctioneer said, 'I can only ask you to look at the book and give your bids.' Special interest existed as to whether the record price of £3,000, paid by the Bodleian, would be exceeded, but the circumstances were then exceptional, as that copy had originally been in the Bodleian. . . . Previously as much as £1,720 had been paid for the first folio, and £3,000 was thought to be a fabulously extravagant price. . . . It cheered the book-lover's heart to hear Quaritch lead off with a bid of £1,000, followed immediately by the representative of Stevens with £1,500, and then the figures ran £1,800, £1,900, £2,000, £2,400, £2,800, and at the £3,000 there was a pause. Stevens, thereupon, said 'Fifty' and the previous record price was passed, then £3,200. At £3,500 Stevens stopped, and a record – long, let us hope, to remain such – was made when Quaritch secured it as £3,600. Everyone in the room applauded his victory.

The second folio brought only £210 (Stevens). The third folio brought £650, and the fourth £75. The quarto copies of the individual plays did not bring such very high prices as were realized the previous year. Sidney's 'Arcadia' brought £315. When Swift's 'Gulliver's Travels' was offered it was stated that the signature of Oliver Goldsmith, 1766, was on the Lilliput title. Leighton spoke up and said that Goldsmith's name was not written in this copy when he had it, and he asked why it should be mentioned in the catalogue: to which the auctioneer replied, 'In order to make a proper copy of it'. It came from the Rowfant Library, and Leighton added 'I should know, as I sold it to Mr. Locker-Lampson'. There was much fun over this incident, but it did not diminish the liveliness of the bidding, which was started at £50, and the treasure was secured at £132 by Stevens.

When lot 235 was called, a man inside the arena held up a small octavo in its original sheep jacket – as Locker-Lampson says, a most commonplace, ordinary little book, but one of the great treasures of English literature and one that brings the highest price known in the auction room with the exception of the Shakespeare folio – 'WALTON (IZAAC) THE COMPLEAT ANGLER, or the CONTEMPLATIVE MAN'S RECREATION; being a Discourse of Fish and Fishing, not unworthy the perusal of most Anglers. Simon Peter said, I go a fishing; and they said, We also will go with thee (*John* xxi, 3), FIRST EDITION. sm. 8vo. Printed by T. Maxey for Rich.

Marriot in S. Dunstan's Church-yard, Fleetstreet, 1653 . . . This copy has always been spoken of as one of the finest, if not the finest copy known. It is quite perfect and in the original state as issued. The late owner, Frederick Locker, has written a note or two in the fly-leaves.' The auctioneer remarked, 'It is impossible to over-estimate this copy, an absolutely unique and perfect specimen in the original binding. Not a copy like this has been in the sale room for many years.' Amid suppressed excitement the bidding began. Quaritch started at £200, and it ran to 500, 600, 700, 750, and £800. Then began a most interesting duel between Quaritch and the representative of Pickering and Chatto, and after a little while nothing was heard but the counting, which ran up the bids (I took them down verbatim) as follows: 30, 50, 60, 70, 80, 90, £900; 20, 30, 40, 50, 60, 70, 80, 90, £1,000; 10, 20, 30, 50, 60, 70, 80, 90, £1,100; 10, 20, 30, 40, 50, 60, 70, 80, 90, £1,200. Here there was a halt, but Mr. Massey started bravely and 10, 20, 30 was reached, whereupon, to the auctioneer's sorrow, all stopped, and he said, 'Dear me! Dear me, Mr. Massey!', which encouraged him to go on – 40, 50, 60, 70, 80. When £1,290 was reached by Mr. Quaritch, the auctioneer said interrogatively, 'Come, Mr. Massey, £1,290?', and again, '£1,290?'; and when there was no reply, he simply said '£1,290, Mr. Quaritch', adding in a quiet voice, 'This is one of the numerous records we are making every day'. It was a remarkable increase over the £415 paid in 1896,[1] which had hitherto held the record.[2]

A Death in the Family

On 18 May 1907 Edward Grose Hodge ('Old' Mr. Hodge) died. It was now more than thirty years since Tom, his second son, had joined him in the business. *The Times* wrote, 'For over forty years [old] Mr. Hodge was a most familiar figure to collectors. All lovers of books and works of art knew him and delighted in a chat with him in the familiar rooms in Wellington Street, for Mr. Hodge was far from being merely a business-man. He was essentially a personality which, with a peculiar charm of manner, was the secret of his success'. 'Young' Tom had become a partner in 1896 and had run the business single-handed since his father had been overtaken by ill health and had virtually retired long before the death of Bernard Quaritch.

Like the younger Quaritch, the younger Hodge was a better businessman than his father. In the first year in which the firm was under his control (1895) it had made a net profit of £6,076. The figure increased thereafter steadily almost every year until 1907 when it reached just short of £17,000. The gross commission income – on which, of course, the profit depended – had climbed from £10,719 in 1897 (the first year for which we have records) to £28,287 in 1907. By then the annual sales turnover was £242,678.

One would have expected Tom to welcome the sole responsibility after waiting for it so long, but in fact there were complications. For one thing, father and son had been very close and the bond between them had lent the son more strength than people had appreciated. For another, the older man had

1. See also page 51.
2. Taken from *Bibliotheca Osleriana*, Appendix I, 'A Record Day at Sotheby's', Montreal, 1969.

died without leaving a will: a curious omission when one considers that he had spent most of his life disposing of other people's estates under the hammer. But certainly he had made no definite provision for his three sons and two daughters, and Sotheby's was the major item of their inheritance.

'Young' Tom was deluged with letters of condolence. His reply to one of them is of particular interest. He wrote to a fellow book auctioneer, John Edmund Hodgson, as follows, 'Many thanks for your kind sympathy. I have suffered a severe loss, for such men as my father leave voids behind them, which not even time can fill, and to me he was father, friend and only partner. Your firm and mine had many friendly transactions and it is pleasant to know that you feel for me in a private matter. Please give my kindest regards to your father who I hope is well.'

Although John Edmund's brother, Sydney, was also in the business, his own situation was not unlike that of Tom Hodge in that the brothers' father, Henry Hill Hodgson, had retired from active control seven years earlier, but was still a dominant figure in the background. Perhaps it was this fact which Hodge remembered when he wrote to J. E. Hodgson again 'as from the Constitutional Club in Northumberland Avenue', a little later, 'Dear Mr. Hodgson, When can you find it convenient to see me on a matter of business, the sooner the better? Or I shall be much more pleased if you will dine here with me on Monday evening at 7.30 or later if more convenient to you. We should be quite undisturbed here but at Wellington Street it is difficult for me to get ten minutes without interruption.'

In his reply Hodgson already adopted the rather timorous stance which was to characterise the protracted correspondence between the two men. 'I shall be pleased to dine with you at your Club on Monday evening next at half past seven. I may perhaps take this opportunity of adding that I am the more glad to take advantage of being able to have a little chat with you, as there are one or two matters – personal and otherwise – which have been on my mind for some time past on which I should like to speak to you, but I have not liked to encroach on your time knowing that it is always so very fully occupied.' Hodge's avuncular reply read: 'I am very glad you can give me tomorrow evening. If you will ask for me in the hall one of the messengers will find me. It will be a pleasure to me to consider any points you may have in mind. Believe me, Yours sincerely.'

A Possible Merger

No record of what passed between Hodge and Hodgson has come down to us, but it would not be unfair to assume (from what occurred subsequently) that Hodge was cautiously sounding out young Hodgson about the possibility of a merger, or even a sale, of Sotheby's to Hodgson's. Although he was only forty-seven, Hodge was not at this stage in good health. We also know that his siblings wanted part of their inheritance in material form, that is in cash. Hodge needed a buyer for Sotheby's who would come up with a capital sum that would fairly reflect the worth of the business as the leading firm of book auctioneers in the world. But it was also clear to Hodge that as sole partner and sole practising auctioneer, he could not sell the business *and retire* from it, unless he could find another competent auctioneer to take it over. That first dinner must have gone reasonably well, for five weeks later Hodge issued an invitation to another dinner, but so little impact had John Edmund made on Hodge that he addressed the letter to the wrong brother!

Further meetings between the two men took place during the autumn. There is a delightful exchange of correspondence when young Hodgson asked Hodge what he should do about attending a trade dinner of the Second-Hand Booksellers Association organised by its secretary, Frank Karslake.

> The confidence you have shown in me must be my excuse for asking your advice in a small matter in which I understand you are also interested . . . my first inclination is to refuse and yet I do not wish to appear discourteous to those members of the Trade who form the Society. Still less should I wish to appear to differ from you as Head of the Book Auctioneers in London.

That Head thunders back:

> I too have received an invitation to the dinner but I shall certainly not accept it for three reasons. First I consider it is entirely a mistake and altogether inadvisable for Auctioneers to be looked upon & ranked as one of the trade; secondly the Association is far too closely identified with its founder [Karslake]; thirdly I am not going anywhere just yet on account of my father's death.
>
> The Association, started by the Secretary, is an obvious attempt to reinstate himself in the good opinion of second-hand booksellers but until the Association absolutely eject him I do not see how it can ever get a good reputation & when he is gone the Association falls in pieces. I very much regret that many ever honest men have in any way allowed themselves to be coupled with Mr. Karslake.
>
> I do not think you & I need care two pins about it beyond being careful to keep clear of it. We are not of, nor in the trade & booksellers must be made to remember this.
>
> I have not yet thanked you for the charming copy of *A Hundred Years of Book Auctions* which you were so good as to send me nor for the generous & handsome reference which your good father made to my firm at the dinner.[1] But I deeply appreciate your kindness, & press of work, an excuse which you will hold valid, is my excuse.
>
> I hope after Christmas to resume negotiations with you. A great season is before me & it is at such a time that the change should come.
>
> Ever yours sincerely,
TOM HODGE

Frank Karslake was the editor of *Book Auction Records* – an invaluable book trade manual – which he had started in 1902 and which came out in quarterly parts. He had an astounding memory and was something of a self-publicist. This quality evidently did not endear him to Tom Hodge, though in 1909 Karslake published his *Notes from Sotheby's* which he must have done with the

1. Hodgson Senior was Master of the Stationers Company, one of the best known of the City of London Guilds, in 1907.

firm's consent. In a leaflet publicising the book to the book trade he says: '... the work was a labour of love, done because I saw that it *ought* to be done and not caring very much whether it paid or not, but because my experience in bookselling showed me that Sotheby's catalogues contained a mine of hidden wealth which only required digging out for it to be of immense service to every seller of books'. The volume consisted of particularly detailed descriptions of some two thousand major books and manuscripts sold by the firm between 1885 and 1909.

One Hundred Years of Book Auctions was a brief history of Hodgson's written by Sydney Hodgson to commemorate the centenary of the firm. It also contained a delightfully disingenuous puff on the virtues of book auctions intended, one assumes, largely for executors of estates which included a library.

Tom Hodge's busy season on either side of Christmas 1907 was indeed remarkable. He was in the rostrum for seventeen days in December up to the Christmas break. On 5 December there was an anonymous sale of early printed books, magnificent *incunabula* innocently billed as 'chiefly the production of the Continental Presses of the fifteenth Century': 275 lots of mouth-watering bibliographic treasures catalogued in great detail which sold for the seemingly ridiculous total of £1,284 14s. 6d. On 9 and 10 December very fine Egyptian antiquities, the second portion of the collection of Robert de Rustafjaell, fetched £308 12s. Egyptian antiquities were still regarded as being very much in the nature of archaeological artifacts of only specialist interest and were not to come into their own until the early Twenties. On 12 December and the two following days there were 'Valuable Printed Books, Illuminated manuscripts and Autograph letters' but there was trouble over the last and probably most important lot in the sale, No. 624, the property of Shrewsbury School, sold by order of the governing body: it was John Gower's *Confessio Amantis* printed by Caxton. It was the first edition: a nearly perfect copy, described in the catalogue as 'probably the finest copy that has ever occurred for sale': a gift to the school library in the eighteenth century by Mr. Watkis, its own regular bookseller. It was withdrawn at the last moment. It was a great disappointment. No reason has ever been discovered for the withdrawal. On 16 December, Hodge started the first portion of the sale of the English, Scottish and Irish coin collection of H. Osborne O'Hagan. It lasted five days. In all, this collection was dispersed over twenty-four days by July 1908 and raised £15,486. 1907 was a year when coin sales at Wellington Street were becoming very frequent. It was an area where Sotheby's still held complete supremacy. There were no fewer than twenty during that year.

The final pre-Christmas sale on 21 December was again the cause of excitement. It consisted of a valuable collection of early editions of the works of Shakespeare belonging to the Right Honorable Richard George Penn, Earl Howe, but although quite a number of particularly valuable items were withdrawn from the sale, including a second quarto of *Hamlet*, the day's takings amounted to £5,835 5s. 6d., an unusually high total. A great many of the finest lots were bought by Sotheran, presumably acting on behalf of the Rylands

Library in Manchester, and it emerged later that the items withdrawn were, in fact, sold privately to H. C. Folger, the great collector of Shakespeariana.

Following the Christmas break the season started again on 15 January with a three-day sale of books and manuscripts (1,003 lots sold for £1,066 19s.). The highlight of the first three months of 1908 was the valuable library of Bishop Gott which raised £12,831 in two days. Apart from that Tom Hodge took thirty-seven sales in that first quarter. It was not surprising that he was anxious to seek relief from such pressure.

The negotiations with the Hodgsons took a new turn on 17 February 1908. Hodge wrote to John Edmund Hodgson from Wellington Street: 'The bearer is Mr. Knight of Knight, Frank & Rutley who are the firm in negotiation with us for the purchase of this business. He is desirous of approaching you as to joining them as a partner and for that purpose is now calling on you. I am sure you will regard this letter as strictly confidential. If you would like to see me I shall be here every day between 11 & 1 and 3 & 6.'

Hodgson noted on the letter two days later: 'Called on Mr. Knight on Wednesday 19th & had about an hour's conversation with him, Mr. Frank and

consisting of book debts

With regard to the capital, I presume that the continuance

for a period of say 10 years

of this capital in the business can be arranged to an substan-

the
tial extent. of say £50,000

with regard to the latter

(aware)
As I understand I am aware of course that you

but
have been negotiating with Mr. Frank, though I am not quite

clear how far the negotiations have gone.

now
I mention these matters in particular because they have

although they belong more properly to a deed of partnership,
they have an important bearing on the financial aspects of the case.

the same time I feel strongly (as indeed I have done ever

since you first wrote to me 18 months ago) that there are

+ other factors in the career (that is my brother & myself)

other aspects of which we may justly lay stress on.

To put the position briefly; and in purely commercial

language, I regard the matter in this way; You are in a posi-

desire
tion and wish for one reason and another, to sell a 1/3

share in your business, and you are naturally desirous of

(at the same time to
obtaining a partner or partners who have practical experience

the
and knowledge of that branch of your business on which its

prestige largely depends. On the other hand We

my brother and myself should be glad to avail ourselves of

an honorable
this opportunity of becoming associated with a house that we

firm whose methods are so much akin to our own, & with whom relations have always been friendly

but having regard to the practical knowledge and experience

for this
and are we me quite prepared to pay a
fair & reasonable price

(4)

Not that I would have you think that the financial aspect is the only one on the contrary

Not in

In 1908, Tom Hodge, sole proprietor of Sotheby's, set about selling the business. He offered it to Hodgson's of Chancery Lane, a rival firm of book auctioneers. Hodge had a brilliant mind but his handwriting left much to be desired. Opposite is a typically illegible reaction to an offer from the Hodgsons that Hodge did not much care for. Deciphering it caused agonies at Chancery Lane. The Hodgsons' approach to the negotiations was infinitely circumspect. Above is one of their extensively corrected draft replies to Hodge, in which at least four people had had a hand.

Mr. Rutley being also present. Arrived at a point at which the amalgamation of Hodgson & Co. with Knight, Frank & Rutley, and Sotheby's, Wilkinson and Hodge was suggested and left open for further consideration'. However, a week later Hodgson wrote to Knight, Frank & Rutley in the most courteous terms to say that from his own firm's point of view 'it would not be advisable at the present juncture to enter into the proposal'.

There the matter must have rested until 28 July 1908 when Tom Hodge tried again. He wrote 'if you are inclined still to consider the matter I was discussing with you this time last year, will you give me a call one morning between 11.30 and 12.30. I have two sales every day this week . . .'.

Perhaps it should be said that all Tom Hodge's letters were written by hand in a hasty and highly illegible scrawl on black-bordered notepaper. Once again he made no drafts and kept no copies. The Hodgsons on the other hand drafted (and re-drafted) their letters by hand and usually sent away typed versions of which they kept one or more copies. Usefully from our point of view, their draft replies were often pencilled on the blank spaces of Tom Hodge's letters.

In this instance Tom Hodge must have worked minor miracles of persuasion in the background, because the tripartite negotiations began again in August. There was a flurry of correspondence between Chancery Lane and Wellington Street, sometimes twice daily, and both sides now brought in their advisers. Then, even as now, the summer holidays were something of a bugbear in the negotiations and certainly in young Hodgson's case, replies to his queries always came back from Lowestoft, Torquay and other resorts, usually too late and *after* he had had to take his own decisions in their absence, but at least there were now concrete discussions about cash. Tom Hodge wanted £10,000 (£6,000 at once and £4,000 later) from the Hodgsons for a one-third share in Sotheby, Wilkinson & Hodge. Knight, Frank & Rutley had apparently agreed to pay their third share in cash on the nail.

Still the Hodgsons hesitated. They were provided with the figures by Sotheby's accountants, Messrs. Cates, Brown & Harding, and good, respectable results were put before them. The purchase price was based on the average profits over the previous few years, but the profit for 1906–7 at nearly £17,000 – the first year to be included – was so much better than any other year in the preceding twelve that some member of the Hodgson family, probably the father, took objection to this, wanted it pointed out to Tom Hodge and subsequently to have the price reduced. Young Hodgson's letters became longer and longer. Clearly he was embarrassed by his family's pernickety attitude. In one letter he writes to Hodge: 'I will only add that I fully appreciate your desire to act with all fairness. For my part I am reminded at the moment of the generous words used by Steele – I daresay you know them – when he called in Addison to aid him in conducting the *Tatler*. Even if I cannot hope that you will ever be able to use those words of me in any modified sense, I may still hope, if an opportunity is afforded me, to show you that I am capable of strenuous and loyal service'.

However, this charming declaration of intent fell flat, for Hodge replied:

'Alas, I do not remember Steele's words, but yours are more important to me now'. Though he added 'I unreservedly believe your expression of good will, kindness, loyalty and strenuousness & had I not felt the same esteem and regard for you and your father I should never have approached you'.

In the meantime, it must have become clear at Chancery Lane that speed and initiative were becoming vital if a unique opportunity was not to slip from their grasp. The Hodgson family clearly did not like the thought of an association with Knight, Frank & Rutley and their advisers were instructed to consider the financial implications of a straight merger between Chancery Lane and Wellington Street. Matters were complicated in September when the new car bought by young Hodgson came off the road in a violent manner. Tom Hodge wrote on 24 September:

the motor accident does not surprise me for a skid is an act of spite and mischief common at any moment to any car & even the most experienced drivers may meet with disaster from it. I am only astonished that you have already driven so much with so little trouble: those telegraph posts are very dangerous things & you should really be thankful that neither you nor your father are hurt. My personal car is a bad skidder but I find the Kempshall tyres very effective.

Do not hurry over our business negotiations, but I would like your answers as soon as may be for until I have it it I can do nothing elsewhere.

I have now filled the first six weeks with sales every day and on Monday I leave for Llandridod Wells to undergo the cure, but this will not affect our negotiations for all letters are sent on to me and I shall be glad to write to you.

By 7 October the accountants had done all their sums and Hodgson now wrote formally to Tom Hodge. It was back to the tripartite agreement and he wanted the value of the third share reduced from £10,000 to £9,000. For once Hodgson summarised the position with total clarity:

You desire for one reason and another, to sell a third share in your business, and at the same time to obtain a partner or partners who have practical experience and knowledge of that branch of the business on which its prestige largely depends. We on the other hand should be glad to avail ourselves of an honourable opportunity of becoming associated with a firm whose methods are so much akin to our own and with whom our relations have always been friendly. For this we are quite prepared to pay a fair and reasonable price, but having regard to the practical knowledge and experience which we have of this particular branch of our profession, one practised by very few, and in which experience is a most essential qualification – we feel, naturally, and I think properly, that we too have, on that account, something to offer, and are justified in placing a due value thereon.

The correspondence and the negotiations dithered on till mid-December. Although he was remarkably patient with a host of timorous quibbles that came his way from Chancery Lane, Tom Hodge was not an easy man with whom to negotiate. He was something of a rumbling volcano and some of his seemingly careless asides caused the Hodgson hours of anguished discussion. He did not always get his sums right. Often he could not remember what he said from one letter to the next, and his handwriting was so atrociously illegible that the

Hodgsons frequently could not make out what he wanted. But he was always direct and his meaning was usually clear, while they were still infinitely cautious and often rather opaque. In the end, while both parties had become utterly weary of the correspondence, matters seemed too delicate actually to discuss them face to face. To a third party it seems clear that towards the end Tom Hodge had found other fish to fry, which was indeed the case. One can only wonder why the Hodgsons hesitated so long over what for them would have been a unique opportunity totally to dominate the book market. At one stage all that was needed was £6,500 down with a second payment of £3,500 within two years, and a guarantee to buy a second one-third share over a period of five years thereafter. Against this outlay a sum would be deducted representing a proportion of the worth of the Chancery Lane business. The stumbling-block for a long time was that Hodge wanted to retain effective control until the second one-third share was being paid for. He was not without a sense of humour. He began the longest letter in the correspondence to J. E. Hodgson: 'Your letter fills me with admiration. I don't think a combination of the intellects of a lawyer *and* an accountant could do better, do you?', and finished 'Your power of driving a bargain makes me respect you more than ever'. Young Hodgson had to admit in his reply that he had had more than his fair share of professional advice!

The correspondence continued to be punctuated with interesting asides. Tom Hodge: 'My temper is bad today for the Renault has to go into dock today for repairs'. Hodgson: 'Many thanks for the Amherst catalogue . . . I hope the sale will prove as successful as the catalogue is beautiful . . .'. Hodge: 'I am most pleased that the Amherst catalogue meets with your approval; as to the result of the sale I have most grave fears. The Press and the noble owner between them have done their best to ruin it'. Eventually, however, Tom Hodge writes on 8 December 'This correspondence is harder work than business, so please try and bring it to a close. I cannot write again until I know your propositions as to agreeing with or differing from mine'. Neither man seemed willing to launch a properly drawn-up Deed of Partnership, the legal document without which there could be no agreement – and it was this finally that brought to an end the possible merger of Hodgson's and Sotheby's.

The Alternative Solution

It must have been clear to Tom Hodge long before these discussions petered out that he himself would never be comfortable with new personalities to carry on Sotheby's business whom he could not respect. An acquaintance for whom he did have the greatest respect was a barrister, specialising in the Ecclesiastical Courts, called Montague Barlow, whom he had known since boyhood. Tom's father had been churchwarden of St. Mary's, Islington, when Barlow's father was vicar there. Barlow senior had gone on to become Dean of Peterborough and there had been a parting of the ways. But Hodge was a great sportsman who loved his golf, his fishing and his shooting. On joining a new shooting syndicate, he discovered that Barlow was a fellow member. After some preamble Hodge consulted Barlow professionally about helping him to find possible purchasers for the firm.

Barlow was a man of remarkable brilliance. He had been head boy at Repton and had got a First in law at Cambridge. He had been called to the Bar in 1895 and practiced mainly in educational and charity cases. He was also at that time a prominent member of London County Council and was to go into Parliament for the first time in 1910, elected as Conservative Member for South Salford. He lectured at the London School of Economics and was examiner in law to London University. People who knew him remember him for his enormous energy, for his efficiency as an administrator, for his integrity, for his continuing devotion to the Church of England, for his progressive ideas relating particularly to conditions of employment and, ultimately, for his sense of vision. He was an outstanding personality and one who made a deep impression on Tom Hodge. Two qualities came to light later: although incisive, Barlow was a very cautious man; and again, although he was an excellent speaker he could be stilted and ambiguous on paper. After some discussion he agreed to look round for purchasers or suitable partners for Hodge.

In due course he reported success in the foray and came to present the three possible contenders to Hodge at Wellington Street. He introduced two much younger men, Felix Warre and Geoffrey Hobson, to the auctioneer. 'Well, now', Hodge is reputed to have said, 'we have here two prospective partners. Where is the third?' 'I am the third', Barlow replied. Hodge was completely taken aback for he had thought of Barlow merely as an intermediary, but clearly the idea of Barlow as a colleague appealed to him. Matters took some months to arrange and an announcement was made to the press on 2 October 1909. The announcement mentioned that interests in the business had been acquired by Warre and Hobson, who were to assist Hodge. It made no mention of Barlow.

The reasons for this were to be found in Barlow's family background. His upbringing had been rigidly evangelical. The Dean of Peterborough was very particular about the profession his son should follow. He was given the choice of either medicine or the law, and he chose law. Any involvement with commercial activity was regarded as out of the question. But the family was not well off and Barlow did not find it easy to make money in his chosen profession. When his father died at this time therefore, Barlow felt free to make a change of career, and it must have required courage and determination to leave the legal profession and to enter what was clearly regarded as a 'trade' at the age of forty-one. Barlow's vision was of a very practical kind: he was by nature a planner. His immediate objective was to enter Parliament. Sotheby's was to be the vehicle to enable him to enter the career of public service that he sought above all else. His hope was that it would eventually give him complete financial independence, as indeed it did, for he departed with a consummate sense of timing.

He decided to continue his legal practice on a declining basis while he became familiar with the running of Sotheby's. Nothing would be said officially of this change for the time being, though he told his more intimate friends that he was resolved to make auctioneering socially acceptable. His widow has put it charmingly: 'He was determined to make the art auctioneering business in London a gentleman's business for gentlemen, you know. He had the vision of putting it on to an entirely different social status because I remember one of his friends in Society saying, "Oh, *he*'s an auctioneer." He was resolved to remove the slur of the auctioneer business and to bring it on to a higher level.'[1]

He had certainly chosen his fellow partners with this very much in mind. Felix Walter Warre, born in 1879, was the fifth son of Dr. Edmund Warre, a famous and particularly distinguished Head Master of Eton, who was himself the fifth son of his father who was, in turn, another fifth son, and the family had already lived in Somerset for seven generations before their ancestor, Sir Richard Warre of Hestercombe, had been knighted in 1501. Warre had been educated at Eton and Balliol. He was a great oarsman and had won almost every honour in rowing that was possible, both at Eton and Oxford. He was a man of commanding presence, had wonderful shoulders and was known by his contemporaries as 'Bear'. Before going to Sotheby's he had been in the banking business in Hong Kong for six years.

The youngest member of the new triumvirate, Geoffrey Dudley Hobson, was born in 1882. In the long term he was to turn out the most brilliant of the 'new men', and was certainly one of the three or four most remarkable figures in Sotheby's long history. He was the fourth son of Richard Hobson, a wealthy Cheshire cotton broker. He had been educated at Harrow and University College, Oxford, where he obtained a First in modern history in 1903. Subsequently he passed the Foreign Office examination with distinction *and* was called to the Bar. But he was at this time smitten with what today we would regard as a relatively minor ear affliction which left him permanently deaf. He was thus unable to enter either the Foreign Service or to practise at the Bar, and he travelled on the Continent for some time instead. Sotheby's was to benefit immeasurably by having within its top management a man with a fine brain who was not as involved with the daily routine as his partners because he was unable to conduct sales in the rostrum an account of his deafness. He was nevertheless a shrewd businessman, of indefatigable industry and was, in due course, to become a renowned authority in the field of rare books, specialising particularly in book bindings. He was also a very good classical scholar and a fine linguist, with fluent command of French, German and Italian and, in addition, he could read and speak Spanish, Portuguese, Dutch and some of the Scandinavian languages.

Legal agreement between Tom Hodge and the new owners was not finally consummated until 9 June 1910, in a mammoth and immensely complicated twenty-four page document. One assumes that this was initiated by Montague Barlow and that he brought all his experience as a legal man to bear on it. Yet it demonstrates clearly that, despite his dislike of anything that was not simple

1. Lady Montague-Barlow in a recorded interview with the author in July 1976.

and completely straightforward, Hodge was extremely subtle as a negotiator and had clearly been at least a match for Barlow.

It is interesting that while this final agreement included Barlow and Hobson as principal purchasers, Warre had been brought in as a subsequent co-purchaser, though an earlier provisional agreement of 28 May 1909 had allowed Hobson and Warre to enter the business forthwith and to take an active share in the running of it.

The purchase price was £25,000 for the goodwill of the firm. £60,000 of capital invested in the business was to be withdrawn and repaid to Hodge over a period of five years. Interest of 4 per cent on the capital remaining until that time was to be paid to Tom Hodge who agreed to remain in the business without pay for two years from 30 September 1909 and to assist the new purchasers. In the event Barlow thought this arrangement was unreasonable, and Hodge received exactly the same salary as the new partners. He was to work only four days a week; he could go home at 4.30 on those days and he was entitled to three months holiday a year. He was to have an equal voice with the purchasers in the management of the business, although he was not *de facto* a partner. Hodge rather ingeniously retained the lease of the property in Wellington Street as security against the ultimate repayment of the capital and thus kept effective control. It was further agreed that he could stay in the business after the initial two years were up if he wanted to (though still officially without remuneration), but that once he had left he would not be permitted to engage in any business of a like character in the U.K., America, Canada, France or Germany for a period of at least ten years. Clearly he was regarded as too formidable a potential competitor elsewhere.

Tom had clinched the initial transaction on 28 May 1909, more than a year before this final agreement, with a typically vague letter to Barlow. He had written 'My dear Clem, I am sorry it is really impossible for me to answer even the majority of your questions definitely . . . some could not be answered without the better part of a day's work among the accounts of past seasons and just now I am really too busy attending to the present and the future to have time for the past'.

He went on to say that he did not know exact figures; that the accountants could establish these later and 'any difference can without doubt be adjusted'. The letter clearly implies that at that stage Barlow was still acting as an intermediary and that Hodge had no inkling then that Barlow might be involved as a purchaser. 'Let your people examine my books by their accountants. . . . I will give *them* two years service', though he emphasised that he did not want to work at his old killing pace in the future. 'As to insurance, I have not the least idea as to the amount we pay on, but it must vary very much; the Law Fire is our only office. Friday will suit me very well to see you all, 12 o'clock; tomorrow I shall be glad to see you but please come before 12.45 as I have a rather important sale of MSS. . . . Ever yours, Tom.'

Probably, the second, much more detailed contract had been considered necessary because Hodge had under-estimated the amount of money tied up in the business by no less than 20 per cent. His guess of £60,000 turned out to be an actual £72,500. All the assets that were to be transferred to the purchasers were carefully listed. The only items that Hodge wanted to retain were 'an old inlaid mahogany table, two old chairs, presentation books and portraits'. One might have expected rather more detailed descriptions from London's leading auctioneer! There were innumerable detailed clauses enjoining the new owners to run the business properly: if they did not, Hodge was to get additional payments.

It seems that another – if not the principal – reason for Barlow's belated entry was that he had had some difficulty in raising the necessary capital. In the event Hobson started off as a major shareholder with £36,000 invested in the business; then came Warre with £17,000 and finally Barlow with £16,000.

Barlow's participation in Sotheby's was not announced publicly until 10 January 1911. By this time he had already begun to make his name as an M.P. The *Daily Graphic* commented 'his ambitions apparently stretch as widely into the world of art as they do into that of politics'. This was certainly true, for as soon as he began to see that the future of Hobson, Warre and himself looked good he began to plan ahead for expansion and indeed for a move of premises, as the lease of the three houses in Wellington Street would run out in 1917.

Reorganisation

Tom Hodge had been in charge of Wellington Street for so long that the business virtually ran itself under his benevolent autocracy. But with four partners a different type of organisation was called for. A partners' meeting on Monday mornings was instituted to discuss any outstanding problems and to work out a roster of who was to take the sales during the ensuing week. The morning's mail was divided among the directors according to their responsibilities and each would then discuss matters with his own departmental experts and cataloguers. All book cataloguing was, of course, done inside the firm but more specialist items including autographs, arms and armour, prints and coins were catalogued by outside firms such as Spinks and Baldwins in the case of coins; W. V. Daniell and his assistant Frederick Nield in the case of autograph letters; prints were initially tackled by F. B. Daniell & Son (W. V. Daniell's brother and nephew) and later by Herbert Breun.

At the outset Barlow made himself responsible for administration, staff and the getting of new business. He was also personally responsible for some of the books,[1] and the department that dealt with drawings, etchings and engravings and, later, with pictures. He was enthusiastic enough about etchings to want to master the technique himself and, when time permitted, he attended classes on etching in South Kensington. He was, of course, much older than the other students and, to protect his clothing between the office and the House of Commons, he would put on dungarees. The other students dubbed him

1. The partners divided the correspondence on the subject of books: each took one-third of the alphabet.

'Dungaree Charlie', and this also became his nickname among the lower echelons of the Sotheby staff.

His experience as counsel in cross-examination stood him in good stead in the rostrum. The trade took to him surprisingly well, as indeed they did to the other new partners. When there was too much noise in the sale-room, Barlow got in the habit of saying 'I must have a little more silence'. Or if this had no effect, 'if I don't have a little more silence I shall have to name someone'. That always did the trick.

Felix Warre took charge of the Coin and Antiquities departments, and because he proved to be a particularly good auctioneer, he took more sales in the rostrum than any other partner. While he lacked the brilliance of either Barlow or Hobson, his charming manners and total integrity endeared him to dealers and collectors alike. However, the partners became involved in one error of judgement early in their career which cost the firm dear in the long run. Hobson objected to the amount of time J. B. Caldecott, the firm's expert on many forms of antiques and particularly coins, spent attending monthly meetings of the Numismatic Society and the fact that Sotheby's should pay Caldecott's annual subscription to the Society. This mean streak led to friction, and Warre decided to attend these meetings himself, though rather reluctantly, for they clashed with rehearsals of the Bach Choir of which he was an enthusiastic member. His lack of knowledge about coins did not cut much ice with collectors and the numismatic business coming Sotheby's way soon began to decline, particularly when it was decided that the cataloguing would be done in the house. A lot of business went initially to Switzerland, because the Swiss had begun to illustrate every single coin they catalogued and this appealed to collectors. Later, Douglas Glendining set up his own firm of specialist auctioneers in coins and medals and a lot of the business began to drift to him, particularly as he competed fiercely by cutting commissions. It was to be nearly fifty years before Sotheby's recovered their status in this market (under Derrick Crowther and Michael Naxton).

Geoffrey Hobson took on the department that concerned itself with works of art – that is, porcelain, pottery, glass, arms and armour, oriental and European *objets d'art* – and in conjunction with Tom Hodge he looked after books, autograph material and manuscripts. In general, he was also responsible for the preparation and presentation of catalogues and, in part, for the firm's publicity, though Barlow was an active publicist too.

The old Wellington Street premises faced the new wing of Somerset House and consisted of two unobtrusive houses joined together (a third adjoining house was leased later). There were three doors at street level: the central one gave on to a hall and a staircase which led up to the sale-rooms on the first floor; the right-hand door opened into the Counting House and the left-hand one was used as a goods entrance. Books were stored in the main Book-room behind the Counting House. This was lit by a small glass dome. Two book cataloguers worked here and to their left were further, smaller rooms lined with shelves where the other cataloguers worked. The first floor contained a large sale-room, and a smaller one, again lined with shelves. This was the one most frequently used for book sales. Both sales' galleries had skylights overhead. The Partners' Room, the hub of the business, was behind the sale-rooms. At the front of the building on this first floor was a long, narrow room where special items could be displayed before sales. It was here, for example, that the Chibcha gold ornaments dredged from the sacred lake Guatavita in the High Andes of Columbia were displayed in glass cases. Their history was interesting. According to the accounts of ancient historians, the Chibchas were wont at the bidding of their high priest to throw into the lake on the occasion of great religious festivities, gold ornaments and precious stones, so that in the course of time a vast amount of treasure accumulated beneath the waves of Guatavita. A consortium of adventurers, which called itself 'Contractors Limited', had drained the lake and, despite great hazards, had extracted golden breastplates, gold and jewelled ornaments, sceptre heads, a gold figure of a goddess and an unusual form of pottery. Sixty-two of these items were sold on 11 December 1911, and most of them went to ethnographical museums in the UK. From this long gallery an iron spiral staircase led to two tiny rooms in the mansard roof, where Will Edmunds, popularly known as 'Hiroshige', catalogued the Japanese prints.

The steep slope of Savoy Hill at the back of the building (which has long been demolished) allowed space for a double basement – and for the inconspicuous back entrance through which thirsty porters disappeared pubwards in the afternoon. The upper basement was the vital storage space that any auction house needs for continuous sales (it was also here that the foreman porter brewed his tea); the lower consisted of cellarage to house the coal for the open fires which heated every part of the building, including the two sale-rooms, although the larger of these also had a ring of gas jets under the skylight. One evening during the First World War, someone pulled the blackout blind while the gas was still alight, and for a few ghastly moments the staff were reminded of the great Sotheby fire of 1865! However, even this heating was not adequate for cold winter weather and both staff and dealers complained that 'their feet got frozen insensible, sitting through three or four hour sales'. It called for a high turnover of lots per hour.

By today's standards the staff was tiny. It was divided between sale-room staff, which included clerical and accounts work, cataloguers or experts, and the porters. It is easy to forget in our relatively relaxed times how strict conditions of employment were early in the century. The hours of work were from 9.30 to 7 p.m. (the porters started at 8.30), and as there were frequent Saturday sales, work on that day very rarely stopped at one o'clock as it was supposed to. Time keeping was regarded of the utmost importance and any small misdemeanour could lead (though this happened very rarely) to dismissal. It was not long before Barlow made a number of moves to improve the working conditions.

In 1910 there were seven or eight porters, under James Hayman, the foreman. These were strong, skilful men capable of moving the goods in and out of the premises, and they often had a good understanding of what they were handling.

Many was the additional item which was put up for sale because a porter had spotted and identified it for the owner while visiting a house from which property was being moved to Wellington Street.

In the Counting House the chief cashier was old Mr. Douglas King whose exquisite handwriting is at once distinguishable in proprietors' ledgers and invoices of that era. He was a most efficient man whose memory stretched back to the middle of the last century. He was assisted by Mr. Clinton, who worked in a little separate, glass-partitioned space and had the official title of Book Keeper. He was slim and erect, a little bit above average height with iron-grey hair and had lived in Germany for some years. He spoke German fluently, and trained the ends of his moustache fiercely upwards, not unlike the Kaiser. He was, however, intensely patriotic and claimed relationship to Earl Clinton. Edward de Courville was dark, of sturdy build and suffered from asthma. He was a half-brother of Alfred de Courville, the famous Revue producer, spoke fluent French and Italian and acted as Tom Hodge's personal clerk. He sat beside Mr. King at a long desk and his duties included attending to clients, entering reserves and commissions and writing letters that Tom Hodge dictated. He was blessed with a superb memory and was incredibly quick at mental arithmetic. He was particularly good at working out silver prices. Silver in those days was still sold by the ounce. As a piece of private enterprise he compiled, edited and published an annual record of the price of autograph letters at auction called *Autograph Prices Current*. During the First World War he took a number of sales.

A coveted and important post was that of auctioneer's clerk, the man who sat beside the auctioneer's rostrum keeping final records of successful bids. Above all, it was the sales clerk who had to know the buyers. The post was held by J. B. Lambert at this time and his assistant was Henry Rham who later succeeded Mr. King as cashier, and later still achieved fame as Dr. Rosenbach's official contact man inside Sotheby's, when 'the Doctor' was buying on an immense scale from Philadelphia.

When Barlow became a partner officially in 1911, he took on as junior clerk a lad called Tim Wilder who found himself ensconced in a little alcove off the main book room, with the only typewriter, a small telephone exchange with three or four extensions, an arrival book in which to enter properties coming into Sotheby's for sale, and always more letters to type than he had time for. Under the terms of his engagement he was employed partly by the firm and for the rest as a personal clerk to Montague Barlow. In the mornings he would go to the Whitehall Club where Barlow, a bachelor, lived and in the evenings to Barlow's room in the House of Commons. Clearing up his legal practice and nursing his constituency in South Salford, as well as dealing with his new vocation, involved Barlow in an enormous amount of correspondence. Tim Wilder was to become one of Sotheby's foremost print experts, and continued to work for the firm until 1978 – sixty-seven years after he joined; then he set up in partnership as a print and picture dealer with another former member of the staff in an office next door to Sotheby's. Without his astonishingly clear memory, we would know a great deal less about those far off days of the firm's history.

The cataloguing staff was in many ways a world apart. Chief among them was John Lawler, the senior book cataloguer in the house and the man who had catalogued the Sunderland Library. Again, his was a post much coveted in the book trade. He was author of *Book Auctions in England in the Seventeenth Century*, and at this time he was getting on in years and very much a law unto himself. A small man with twinkling eyes under bushy eyebrows, he used to scandalise some of the staff (and Mr. King in particular) by walking through the Counting House mouthing Shakespearian obscenities, of which 'the devil damn thee black, thou cream-faced loon' was among the mildest. A fellow cataloguer[1] remembers his 'devastating tongue, which he used on both partners and colleagues. Partners put up with it on account of his age and his excellent work . . . so what with one thing and another Mr. Lawler did as he liked and not what Mr. Barlow and Mr. Hobson liked'. Lawler's son also worked in the firm as a book cataloguer, but seems to have left under something of a cloud. There were two other elderly cataloguers: a charming, rather retiring man, Mr. Palmer, who died during the course of the war, and Mr. Wilson, then in his eighties, with a large, square-cut, snowy-white beard, who could remember the days when Sotheby's had previously sold pictures. He was fond of giving an imitation of John Wilkinson of fame, stooping down, holding his pince-nez on his nose, and intoning '*A Landscape with Cattle in Foreground*. What am I offered?'.

Finally, there was 'Hiroshige', already mentioned, a great character who catalogued Japanese prints, netsuke and other oriental works of art. His real name was Will H. Edmunds. He had formerly been a journalist; he was also something of a poet and author of *Pointers and Clues to the Subjects of Chinese and Japanese Art* (1934). He was a small man given to wearing enormous broad-rimmed felt hats in winter and straw hats in summer, and lived to a great age. There was then a very lively interest in the Japanese colour prints of the eighteenth and early nineteenth centuries, but to some extent this diminished after 1921 when the market became flooded with so many reprints and good imitations that it was difficult for collectors to find their way about the subject with confidence. Edmunds had come to Sotheby's just *after* one of their greatest sales of this kind: the collection of John Stewart Happer of New York, a four-day sale starting on 26 April 1909 (though even this did not measure up to the recent and celebrated Vever sales). Edmunds had his work cut out soon after he arrived because, although Paris had always been the centre of interest in things Japanese, the Happer sale attracted other collectors to London and Sotheby's made something of a corner in that market for itself. There were at least ten magnificent sales of Japanese prints between 1910 and the beginning of the First World War.

Tom Hodge was well aware that his book cataloguers had become elderly and advised that replacements should be found in some instances. Lawler's experience, however, made him difficult to replace at short notice, and fortunately he

1. Millicent Sowerby. See page 149 ff.

made it clear that despite his advanced age he would see the new owners comfortably established – though they had to give him a swingeing increase in salary. In the spring of 1913, A. G. E. Phillips was taken on as his successor-designate. Phillips had started working in the library of the Earl of Crawford and Balcarres at Haigh Hall, Wigan, in 1896 and had become librarian in 1904, succeeding the formidable J. P. Edmond.

The 26th Earl, a great book collector like his father before him, had died in January 1913, but his eldest son who succeeded him decided that he could not

TELEGRAMS:
HAIGH.
TELEPHONE:
HAIGH, No 5.

HAIGH HALL,
WIGAN.

19th. March 1913.

Dear Mr. Hodge,

Many thanks for your kind letter of yesterday's date. I understand that your convenience will be suited by my commencing my provisional engagement on April 7th. next.

I have carefully studied the forms and styles of various entries in your catalogues, and I imagine I have got the 'hang' of the work. But I should like to know if you have any defined rules which govern the treatment of certain lots, and to this end, I beg to enclose a few queries.

Yours very truly,

A. G. E. Phillips

A. G. E. Phillips came to Sotheby's as senior cataloguer from the Earl of Crawford's Library at Haig Hall. His queries about consistency in the style of cataloguing were dismissed rather brusquely.

continue to maintain a library staff of seven. In fact, he decided to close the library, and Phillips found himself with the prospect of looking for a new post and was delighted and relieved to go to Sotheby's (though at a lower salary). He spotted and pointed out even before he came to Wellington Street how inconsistent the firm's cataloguing was. He wrote to Hodge, 'I should like to know if you have any definite rules which govern the treatment of certain lots and to this end I beg to enclose a few queries'. He was told that he could sort this out when he arrived. It is of interest that he came for a trial period at £275 per annum. He turned out, in fact, to be an excellent cataloguer but was soon found to have an incurable disease and died, still tragically young, in the early 1920s.

Later there were many changes of staff, but in 1911 the total annual bill for salaries, excluding the partners, came to only £3,457. In 1912 it was £3,399, and £3,898 in 1913.[1] The steep rise was largely due to Lawler's sizeable salary increase. The second most expensive item in that last year (1913) was £2,914 for printing catalogues for the 113 sales that had taken place. Consultation of outside experts, who also prepared catalogues for the non-book sales, came to £2,089, and rent, rates and taxes to £1,116. This euphoric position, as far as tax was concerned at any rate, was to change very rapidly during the First World War. All this (in 1913) related to a total turnover of £309,061, and left the partners a near record profit of £20,570. The basic salary they paid themselves – and this included Tom Hodge – was only £700 each, but they drew further remuneration under the headings of interest (on the capital they had put into the business), bonuses, accumulated profits and additional accumulated profits. Income tax fluctuated around one shilling in the pound. The number of selling days increased as the new partners got into their stride. It had risen from 193 in 1912 to 229 in 1913. This helped to spread the overheads and the expenses per day's sale were reduced from £70 17s. 3d. to £61 13s. 10d. It was a very satisfactory achievement.

---

1. For comparison, this was slightly more than the cost of the *entire* staff at the National Portrait Gallery in the same year at £3,051. The salaries and wages bill at the National Gallery amounted to £7,719. At the much larger Victoria & Albert Museum they totalled £49,974 and at the British Museum £61,526. The annual cost of producing the British Museum catalogues came to £8,067.

7

The Huth Sales

WHEN Tom Hodge was in the process of selling Sotheby's he could rightly say that the new owners would be assured of a steady and continuing stream of material that would pass through the book room. The ace up his sleeve was the knowledge that the firm would in all probability be dealing soon with what De Ricci has described as 'one of the most striking events in the history of the English sale rooms'. This was the dispersal of the Huth Library. It had been built up over half a century by a father and his son and its origins were inextricably linked with earlier Sotheby sales.

Henry Huth (1815–1878) was in every sense a personification of the book collector's ideal. At the prime of life he looked the very epitome of Victorian distinction, with his full, grey beard; deep-set, intelligent, slightly melancholy eyes; and a balding, domed forehead. He never bargained about a price or spoke an ill word of any acquaintance. He was never ruffled and quality was his watchword. He had a fine brain and a lot of money, and while his contemporaries thought he was paying outrageous prices for unique items, the passage of time proved him one of the shrewdest collectors of rare books in the nineteenth century.

He was born in London of a German father and a Spanish mother. It was originally intended that he should enter the Indian Civil Service so he set about learning Hindustani, Arabic and Persian in preparation; this on top of a sound knowledge of the classics and fluent French, German and Spanish. But when the East India Company lost their Charter in 1833, he went into his father's merchant banking business instead.

He worked so hard that his health failed and he was sent abroad to travel, which he did extensively all over the world, re-joining the family firm in 1849. Under his eventual direction, the firm became one of London's leading finance houses. When asked to explain its phenomenal success he used to say: 'We don't profess to be cleverer than other folks, but we get up earlier in the morning'. Already as a boy he had begun to form a library and increased it everywhere he travelled. He began to take book collecting really seriously after 1850. 'He gave commissions at most of the important book sales, and called daily at all the principal antiquarian book sellers on his way back from the City, a habit which he continued up to the day of his death.'[1] He formed a particularly close link with Joseph Lilly, who had a small book shop in Pall Mall, and is said to have spent more than £40,000 with him over the years. Although Lilly had a reputation of being brusque, aggressive and mean, he had an

---

1. W. Y. Fletcher, *English Book Collectors*, 1902.

excellent knowledge of English books and served Huth extraordinarily well, and although they were markedly different in personality, the two men became firm friends.

Huth always bought on his own judgement and never purchased a book that was not in perfect condition. An annotated list of his acquisitions has survived, which enables one to follow his activity in detail until the eve of his death. De Ricci said 'his aim was to build up a general library of rare books and he seems to have been a most generous and methodical buyer. He collected fine illuminated manuscripts, *incunabula*, including Caxtons [of which he had twelve] and *editiones principes* of the classics, early Italian, Spanish and French literature and early books on travel and America in every language. His English books were the best after those at Britwell,[1] and were remarkable, as all the other sections of the Huth Library were, for the choice selection of the editions represented, and the beauty of the copies, chiefly bound by Francis Bedford.[2] The poetry and drama sections were as complete as any man could make them, especially for the earlier periods'.

He had bought substantially at the Wellington Street sales of George Daniel (1789–1864) whose library of Elizabethan and Shakespearian plays, as has been seen,[3] was one of the choicest in private hands. As we know, it fetched no less than £15,865 in July 1864. Huth also made extensive purchases at the eight Sotheby sales of the library of the Rev. Thomas Corser (1793–1876), who had another especially fine collection of early English literature. These sales took place between July 1868 and June 1873. His dependence on Sotheby's as a source of supply was further demonstrated by the fact that he made purchases at the sales of Utterson (one of the last survivors of the Roxburghe sale) in 1852 and 1857, Hawtrey (July 1853 and the sixteen-day sale in June and July of 1862), John Dunn Gardener (July 1854 and November 1875), George Smith (in July and August 1867) and Felix Slade (August 1868). Through Quaritch he bought a number of *incunabula* and block-books from the Yeminez Library which was sold in Paris in 1867, and from Colnaghi's he bought an incomparable series of Dürer engravings in two large folio volumes. He bought Americana from Henry Stevens of Vermont; French books from Gancia and Tross; miscellaneous rare items from J. O. Halliwell and from the bibliographer, William Carew Hazlitt, from Boone, Hatchard and F. S. Ellis. In fact *The Times* was constrained to comment at the end of the first day's sale of the library proper on 16 November 1911, 'Since all great libraries are built on the debris of others, it is interesting to mention that the first two days alone of the present portion include books which have been traced back to nearly thirty other fine collections'.

In 1868 Huth felt that his library needed a catalogue and started to work on this. It was to be a magnificent, painstaking labour, though because of his

1. See page 196 ff.
2. An English bookbinder (1799–1883) much used by the great book collectors of the nineteenth century.
3. See page 50.

premature death, it had to be completed by his son, Alfred Henry Huth (1850–1910), and finally appeared in five volumes in 1880. Its publication brought about a substantial advance in bibliographical method, for Huth Senior insisted that F. S. Ellis and W. C. Hazlitt, who helped with its compilation, should include the *complete titles* as they appeared on the title page, and the full collation, of every work listed. These were innovations of great bibliographical significance which set a precedent for future collectors and, indeed, for auctioneers' catalogues.

Huth's son not only completed the catalogue begun by his father; he also augmented the library wherever he detected gaps, adding, for instance, a nearly complete series of Restoration plays and many valuable items of seventeenth-century English literature. When the younger Huth died without issue, 'he bequeathed to the British Museum fifty items which were to be selected from the Library, a most generous thought which enabled the British Museum to secure a certain number of highly important books (such as some Shakespearian Quartos) which it was the last opportunity ever to obtain'.[1]

The remainder of the books were to be sold by Sotheby's in no fewer than twelve sales between 1911 and 1922.[2] It was a veritable vein of gold for the new partners which over the years netted a total of well over £300,000. Again *The Times* had the last word. Its correspondent wrote: 'The Duke of Roxburghe's sale in 1812 created an epoch in the annals of book collecting and book prices, and the Huth sale, when the last volume is claimed by its new owner, may be fittingly regarded as closing the great sales of the last hundred years'.

Tom Hodge had managed to effect a private sale of some 43 items catalogued at the end of the first portion (lots 1187–1228) comprising the four Shakespearian Folios and 39 Quartos. This transaction had been initiated by Alfred Quaritch and the collection was bought by Alexander Smith Cochran, an eccentric young American millionaire who led a rather unhappy life in Paris. It had caused Tom Hodge no little problem with Huth's executors, who had refused Quaritch's first offer, but they finally accepted a sum of £31,500, only just before the auction was due to take place. Hodge refused to reveal the anonymous buyer to the press, but with the new owner's consent, Quaritch made a statement a few days later that Mr. Cochran had donated his purchase to the Elizabethan Club at Yale. One newspaper report quoted Quaritch as saying: 'You see, Mr. Cochran was at Yale and he does this sort of thing', and commented 'Every alumnus of Yale will hail this as an unconsciously beautiful summing-up of a pious act'.

As usual, Alfred Quaritch dominated the first few Huth sales where he had an immense number of clients for whom he was bidding on commission. They included the British Museum (both the departments of books and manuscripts), the Bibliothèque Royale in Brussels, Harvard University, the Bodleian Library at Oxford, University College of London, and private clients from America

1. De Ricci, *op. cit.*, page 151.
2. A sale of duplicates had already taken place at Sotheby's on 27 March 1906.

such as Pierpont Morgan, H. C. Folger, Beverley Chew,[1] H. E. Huntington (direct – not through G. D. Smith), W. A. White (who agreed to give the British Museum first choice of anything they wanted which coincided with his own *desiderata*), Henry Widener (who had written 'things are not very cheerful here at present and the outlook for my getting any of the more expensive items at the Huth sale is very dull'), and Alexander Turnbull; Dr. Backer of Brussels, C. W. Dyson Perrins, C. F. G. R. Schwerdt (the great collector of books on Sports and Hunting), W. A. Cadbury of Bournville (who never allowed Quaritch to bid a shilling more than the limits he had set), and, finally, from a number of overseas dealers in books, the foremost of whom was Dr. Rosenbach of Philadelphia.

No wonder the sales went with a swing and no wonder either that when Quaritch paid £1,950 for a small octavo volume containing the first edition of *Bacon's Essays* (which cost Huth £13 5s. od. in 1870) the press went wild. Even the popular *Daily Globe* sent its reporter along to Wellington Street and he recorded the bidding verbatim:

... 'A thousand pounds!' called Mr. Hodge, but there was never an instant's pause. Up and up went the bidding. It was a battle of giants, waged in nods and whispers. Then at last the pace began to slacken. Only three champions were left. The auctioneer applied a gentle spur. 'Now Mr. Pickering, come! It's against you, sir! Come, Mr. Maggs, you may never get another chance! Nineteen hundred?' Mr. Quaritch looked along the row of impassive faces with a gleeful glint in his eye. 'Fifty!' he said, and the book was his. 'Deliver this one!' he called and he took it from the porter's hand and dropped it into the breast pocket of his well-worn jacket like a packet of sandwiches....

The headline to this piece, and to many others appearing on that day in a similar vein, was '£1,000 an Ounce!'.

A new factor that became evident during the first few Huth sales was the much stronger buying by American dealers. Enthusiasm for book collecting had increased enormously on the other side of the Atlantic. Interest there at this stage was particularly strong in early English literature, and the longer purses of American collectors soon began to make themselves felt in London. The mere trickle of rare books that had left the capital now became something of a torrent. At the head of a host of great collector names were three giants: Henry Clay Folger, Pierpont Morgan and Henry E. Huntington. Folger was interested in anything and everything to do with Shakespeare; Morgan sought examples of early printing and illuminated manuscripts, and Huntington set himself the most ambitious task, of providing the Pacific coast with a library which would 'not only rival the riches of the older institutions of the eastern seaboard but should put San Marino in the same class as London, Oxford and Cambridge'.[2]

1. Who had written to Quaritch 'I take it for granted that the London market will retain its sanity and that there will be no repetition of the foolish extravagance that characterised the Hoe sale'.
2. John Carter, *Taste and Technique in Book Collecting*, 1948.

The activities of all three collectors were to be of vital importance to Sotheby's. The most immediately significant personality in this connection was the New York bookseller, George D. Smith, a poker-faced, horse racing enthusiast, who acted as Huntington's agent, and reflected his client's enormous energy and was backed by his well-nigh inexhaustible funds. The first indication of this new demand had become evident at the Robert Hoe Sale which had started in New York on 24 April 1911, only six weeks before the Huth sales began in London. Hoe and Huth had collected more or less simultaneously and along parallel lines. Both bought enthusiastically 'not only *incunabula* and Caxtons, but also first and early editions of English literature from Chaucer to Shelley; and if Huth's collection of Americana was remarkable for an Englishman so for an American was Hoe's for French literature and illustrated books'.[1] Both libraries represented the grand manner in book collecting. Hoe, a manufacturer of printing machinery, had produced a sixteen-volume catalogue of his library, and the four sales (the last three took place in January and April 1912 and in November 1914) produced about £400,000, a truly phenomenal sum for its day.

The first Hoe sale created a level of excitement that was altogether new in the rare book world. 'From the outset it was apparent that it was a battle of Titans; mere demi-gods and heroes were outclassed. Thousand dollar bids were piled up like Ossa on Pelion. Huntington took the Gutenberg Bible on vellum away from P. A. B. Widener at the record price of $50,000. At $42,800 Pierpont Morgan beat Huntington for the excessively rare first printing by Caxton of Malory's *Morte d'Arthur* . . .'[2] When the sale was totalled up it was found that George D. Smith had spent for Huntington over half the total of the $1,000,000 which the sale had realised. It was a useful portent for Sotheby's.

The preparation for the sale of even the first few parts of the Huth Library had involved a great deal of work at Wellington Street. Most of the cataloguing was done by John Lawler, but the staff had been stretched to the utmost and it was quite clear that it would have to be strengthened if the business was going to grow as the partners hoped. For Hobson the Huth Library must have been something of a revelation for it contained a magnificent range of splendid book bindings adorned with the arms of the noble owners to whom the volumes had formerly belonged: Grolier, Maioli, Canevari, Diane de Poitiers, Henri IV of France, de Thou, Count Mansfield, Louis XIII and the Dukes of Burgundy. Many of them were later to become the subjects of Hobson's scholarly researches.

The last of the Huth sales (lots 7843–8357) took place in June 1920, nearly a decade after the first.[3] The whole pattern of collecting had changed during that time. Fashions had been created and destroyed. Innumerable price records were

---

1. John Carter, *op. cit.*
2. Edwin Wolf with John Fleming, *Rosenbach*, 1960.
3. The book sales as compared to the sales of autograph letters, engravings and woodcuts, and imperfect copies, had been unusual in that all nine of them were catalogued in one continuous alphabetical series.

broken and yet there were inexplicable disappointments. Lots 2096–2187, for example, the works of Daniel Defoe in the original editions, seemed extraordinarily cheap at about £1 each. Quaritch bought most of these for an interested client. Both were delighted by such a string of bargains. Booksellers both from home and abroad (wartime conditions permitting) bought stock that was to last them for years ahead: many too bought back items they had sold to Huth, now paying vastly greater prices, and their shelves were filled with works which had been unobtainable for generations.

The press reported euphorically on each sale. But among all the glib comments on the extent and completeness of the Huth Library, it is easy to overlook how much learning, connoisseurship and sheer hard work had gone into assembling it. Huth was not only an outstanding collector but also a great reader of books and many of the most important works in his library were in the classics or in foreign languages which he could enjoy in the original. The whole collection demonstrated superbly the gradual emergence of knowledge and literature following upon the invention of printing.

Chatsworth Library.

KEMBLE-DEVONSHIRE COLLECTION
OF
ENGLISH PLAYS & PLAY-BILLS

CONSISTING MAINLY OF

PLAYS, &c. PRIOR TO 1640.

———

PREFATORY NOTE ON THE HISTORY & CHIEF FEATURES
OF THIS SUPERB COLLECTION.

TOGETHER WITH

A FULL CATALOGUE OF THE PORTION CONTAINING
THE SHAKESPEARE FOLIOS AND QUARTOS,

COMPRISING

THE FOUR FOLIOS & FIFTY-SEVEN OF THE QUARTOS.

———

[COPYRIGHT]

SOTHEBY, WILKINSON & HODGE,
13, WELLINGTON STREET, STRAND,
LONDON, W.C.

Chatsworth Library.

KEMBLE-DEVONSHIRE COLLECTION OF
ENGLISH PLAYS AND PLAY-BILLS

CONSISTING MAINLY OF

PLAYS, &c. PRIOR TO 1640.

———

The Four Shakespeare Folios.

No. 1.

 HAKESPEARE. [FIRST FOLIO, 1623]. Mr. WILLIAM/ SHAKESPEARES./ COMEDIES,/ HISTORIES, &/ TRAGEDIES./ Published according to the True Originall Copies./ portrait by Droeshout with verses opposite, inner plain margin of the verses renewed and small holes repaired, not injuring the text, as is also the case with the title, not injuring the portrait ; lower outside corner of 11 in Henry VI mended, injuring three words ; 3½ inches of the top outer margin of 11 in the same play mended, and the missing letters supplied in MS.; lower plain margins of aa 4, 5, 6 and 11·4 renewed, old calf, line tooled, blue edges folio. Printed by Isaac Jaggard and Ed. Blount. 1623. [Colophon] Printed at the Charges of W. Jaggard, Ed. Blount, I. Smithweeke and W. Aspley 1623

** A PERFECT COPY OF THE FIRST FOLIO, APART FROM THE SLIGHT DEFECTS NOTED ABOVE; GENUINE AND CLEAN THROUGHOUT, measuring 13 by 8 in. Lowndes mentions a copy in the possession of Messrs. Longman, in which at the head of p. 333 in Othello were the words "and hell know his bones" before Rodrigo's speech. This copy has the same reading.

Pages from one of the two special catalogues which Sir Montague Barlow had prepared in order to publicise parts of the Chatsworth Library in America. He sold the books concerned privately to Henry Huntington.

8

Private Sales

IT is difficult to believe how international the rare book business already was before the First World War. When someone like Quaritch came to an important, well-publicised sale, he would have commissions neatly penned into his catalogue from the United States, South America, France, Belgium, Germany, Spain, Italy and other countries. Hodge too knew most of the dealers and collectors of those overseas areas.

This widespread network of contacts enabled Hodge to develop and master another side of the business (though it was a wonder how he found the time), which had been initiated to a much lesser extent by his father: the private sale. It usually involved some major property which the owner wanted to sell without the publicity attendant upon a public auction but under the auspices of a firm with the reputation for integrity which Sotheby's enjoyed. It worked in two ways, because not only were there vendors looking for buyers but there were also collectors who asked Hodge to approach owners of outstanding libraries and collections that might not yet have come on to the market.

Old Hodge's greatest coup in this direction was when he had been instrumental in selling to Mrs. John Rylands one of the most magnificent libraries of all time, that of the 2nd Earl Spencer (of Roxburghe Sale fame). He gave her agent, A. B. R. Railton, the manager of the long established booksellers, Henry Sotheran & Co., a week's option on the Spencer Library at £220,000. Mrs Rylands to her eternal credit countered with an immediate offer of £210,000, which was accepted, and she thus probably got for the library she was establishing in Manchester one of the greatest bargains in the history of major book sales. This was in 1892.[1]

The particular catalyst that stimulated Hodge to quite remarkable but little-known achievements in the area of private sales was Pierpont Morgan. Morgan admired Sotheby's. He respected their long tradition, their honesty and expertise, and the force and speed with which they could move. His own major acquisitions of rare book and manuscript material were made in the relatively short period between 1895 and 1910. Tom's first major sale to Morgan was the library of Richard Bennett, an eccentric Manchester businessman whose special interests were *incunabula* and illuminated manuscripts on vellum. Bennett had bought substantially at the Ashburnham sale and after William Morris's death in 1896, he acquired the latter's fine and extensive medieval library for £18,000. Bennett selected the best for himself and re-sold the rest at Sotheby's on

1. In 1900 Mrs. Rylands struck again. Railton bought the Crawford Collection of manuscripts on her behalf, with the exception of the material relating to the French Revolution (see page 245) for some £155,000. He dealt with Lord Crawford direct; Sotheby's were not involved on this occasion. It was, if anything, an even more astonishing purchase.

5 December 1898, where it fetched nearly £11,000. He had an inexplicable antipathy towards folio-sized volumes and although he was a passionate collector of Caxtons he never bought Caxton's *Golden Legend* because its height exceeded his personal limit of thirteen inches. For the same reason he sold all Morris's magnificent folios.

He had done much of his buying through the old-established firm of Pickering and Chatto. In 1902 he asked them to dispose of his library, having printed a private catalogue two years earlier with a sale in mind, but the asking price was £100,000 and Thomas Chatto failed to find a customer at such a price. He therefore turned to Hodge. The proposal was that anything Sotheby's could get over and above £100,000 would be theirs to keep. If no private sale was concluded the library would be put up for auction.

Hodge made a personal revaluation of the collection, which consisted of 559 *incunabula* and 107 manuscripts all on vellum and nearly all illuminated. He then approached Morgan. The asking price was £140,000. Morgan liked to have an asking price stated to him against which he could then make an offer. This was his buying policy and he made no bones about stating it boldly in a letter to Hodge. The great financier was 65 at this time and reputed to have a fortune in excess of $100,000,000. But even though he bought on a mammoth scale he was most particular about the prices he paid. In this instance he was certainly getting good value. Among the *incunabula*, for example, were thirty-two Caxtons, the fourth largest collection in existence. Morgan for once was clearly excited by the prospect of such an acquisition and cabled back an offer of £130,000 (then $600,000). Tom accepted it at once. In case anyone today should think that this was chickenfeed, it should be said that it was the largest single purchase ever made for Morgan's library.

It netted Hodge a profit vastly greater than any previous whole year's auction activity on the part of Sotheby, Wilkinson and Hodge, and no coup quite like it was brought off again for many years. The Bennett library sale was treated as a separate item in Sotheby's accounts for years to come. Thus Charles Brown, of Cates, Brown and Harding, Sotheby's auditors, writing to Hodge on 17 March 1909, said: '. . . the total profits for the eleven years ending 30 September 1908 have amounted to £126,221 2s. 3d. or an annual average profit of £11,474 13s. 0d. This does not include the *special* profit of £24,700 made in 1902-1903, of which you are aware'. Understandably, no mention of it had been made in all the figures revealed to Hodgson's at the time of the proposed merger.

When agreement had been reached (in mid-April 1902), Morgan, who spent much of his time in London at his magnificent house at 13 Princes Gate, wrote to Hodge to say 'My custom in making purchases is to make payment during the current year, which I have no doubt will be agreeable to you as it is to everyone else'. Hodge thereupon sent an invoice which elicited this reply: 'I hereby agree that the sum shall be paid on or before 31st December next. Should for any reason Mr. Bennett desire part payment at any particular time, I will do my best to arrange it for him, but I do not wish to make any absolute commitments in advance – this being the basis upon which my purchases of

J.S. MORGAN & Cº
22, Old Broad Street,
London.

Telegraphic Address:
"MORGAN, LONDON."

London, 15th April 1902
E.C.

Messrs Sotheby Wilkinson & Hodge
13 Wellington Street
Strand. W.C.

Dear Sir,

I have received your note, and assume the purchase of the library from Mr Bennett on the terms you mention, and also confirm the delivery to Mr Quaritch.

As regards the purchase-money, as I explained to Mr Junius Morgan, and as, I suppose, he has communicated to you, I would say that my custom in purchases is to make payment during the current year, which I have no doubt will be agreeable to you as it is to everyone else.

Yours truly,
J Pierpont Morgan

Pierpont Morgan was one of Sotheby's most important clients at the turn of the century. He preferred to buy privately before a collection actually came up at auction. The sale to Morgan of Bennett's Library in 1902 was one of Tom Hodge's major coups. Morgan was never invoiced. He stated his terms of payment and paid on the nail without reminders. *Below* – a typical cable from Morgan.

J.S. MORGAN & Cº
22, Old Broad Street,
London.

Telegraphic Address:
"MORGAN, LONDON."

London, 30 June 1902
E.C.

Mess. Sotheby Wilkinson Hodge
9 Wellington St. W.C.

Gentlemen,

At the request & for account of Mr J Pierpont Morgan we enclose cheque £ 60000 (Sixty Thousand pounds) receipt of which please acknowledge.

Yours faithfully,
J Morgan & Co

The Anglo-American Telegraph Company,
LIMITED
ESTABLISHED 1866
FOUR CABLES TO AMERICA
AUTOMATIC DUPLEX SYSTEM

IN DIRECT TELEGRAPHIC COMMUNICATION WITH.

"Via ANGLO."

From New York

TO Sotheby London

Will give Six thousand for Dalhousie Burns reply

Morgan

PLEASE HAND YOUR REPLY DIRECT TO THIS OFFICE.
ONLY DIRECT ROUTE TO NEWFOUNDLAND.

books, bric-a-brac, and other works of art are made, and which I have no doubt will be satisfactory to Mr. Bennett'.

Tom was not quite happy about this. He wrote to Morgan to ask for £60,000 before 30 June. 'Left to ourselves we should not trouble you with this letter, but you will understand we are merely acting for a client.' The figure he initially wrote down was £50,000. One might have thought that the change to £60,000 had been prompted by consideration of his own work in the deal, but in fact, the entire sum was handed over to Bennett, after Morgan had paid it exactly on the date as asked. The further £70,000 arrived unprompted at the end of December.

It was a most satisfactory transaction and everyone – Bennett, Chatto and Tom Hodge - were pleased with its success. But though this remarkable client kept asking for more, not every prospective sale came off. There was the rather unfortunate case of a collection of Shakespeare material which J. Pearson (another dealer in rare books, whose stock Sotheby's was to sell later) asked Tom to bring to Morgan's attention. Tom's first letter was lost. Subsequently Morgan discovered that the item had appeared in a Pearson catalogue at a lower price than was now being asked. The correspondence meandered on but the collection did not go to Morgan. In the final letter about it Junius Morgan, the financier's nephew, and a passionate connoisseur of books, prints and engravings in his own right, who often acted on his uncle's behalf, wrote to Tom: 'I think you were rather shabbily treated by the owner of the Shakespeare collection and I do not wonder that you have decided to take no further steps in the matter. I would be very glad if you could keep us posted in regard to Mrs. Morrison's collection.'

And thereby hangs an interesting tale. The collection of autographs assembled by Alfred Morrison and his wife was probably the greatest of its kind. Its fame was world-wide and its catalogues were in every major library. Though Alfred Morrison had died in 1892, his widow had continued to add to the collection. Pierpont Morgan became keenly interested in buying the Morrison collection but found it difficult to approach Mrs. Morrison who was a formidable lady. He asked Hodge to make enquiries about the matter. Tom wrote to Mrs. Morrison at Fonthill where she lived. His letter elicited a starchy, negative couched in the third person and penned in a most unusually florid hand. Very often there were only six or eight words on a page. 'Mrs. Morrison presents her compliments to Messrs. Sotheby, Wilkinson and Hodge and would have answered their letter before but she has been ill with influenza. She is much obliged to them for their communication about the autographs but they must inform their client that they are *not* for sale.'

Tom Hodge, however, did not give up so easily. He wrote in a further letter that his client 'was extraordinarily anxious to possess' the collection and was there *no* sum that would obtain it for him? A hint of a positive reaction led him to discuss the matter at length with Pierpont Morgan's nephew and they agreed that it would be advisable to make an actual offer. The sum involved, with Pierpont's blessing, was a cool £200,000. Mrs. Morrison did not have a reputation of being formidable without good reason, and she countered with an asking price of £250,000, this figure to be exclusive of Sotheby's commission as their approach had been totally unsolicited. In the interim Morgan had bought another smaller collection of manuscript material and was on his usual wanderings around the world. Ironically, after five further letters and a lapse of two months, Mrs. Morrison agreed to the precise terms initially suggested though the matter petered out thereafter, but as we shall see, it cemented a relationship between Sotheby's and Mrs. Morrison which resulted in one of the most important series of sales the firm held during the First World War.

Almost simultaneously, Tom was approached to see if he could sell the autograph material of R. D. Blackmore's *Lorna Doone* by a private treaty. 'Any money you may be able to obtain beyond £1,000 will be your property' wrote the owner.[1] Tom cabled Morgan, knowing the latter's *penchant* for literary manuscripts. Morgan cabled back, 'Think price for manuscript excessive', and it finished up instead in H. E. Huntington's library.

In 1905 Morgan bought a collection of Burns's letters and manuscript material for £6,000 from Sotheby's and there were other unidentified items that continued to tempt him. He sent the most courteous expressions of gratitude for Tom's labours on his behalf. 'In any event I should like to talk the matter over with you whether I do anything or not' (16 February 1905); 'I am greatly obliged for the interest you have taken in this matter for me, which I shall endeavour in some way to make good' (24 March 1905); and 'I am deeply grateful to you for calling my attention to them [a series of musical autographs which he turned down]. I hope you will do this with anything you may have in the future' (24 January 1907).

The rejected musical autographs had been returned to Sotheby's with a letter signed by a new personality in the Morgan entourage. This was Belle da Costa Green who was engaged as Morgan's librarian and confidential art secretary in 1905. Later she was to become the first director of the Morgan Library and one of the great figures in the American art and bibliophile world, adding lavishly to the initial collections under the aegis of Pierpont Morgan's son and the trustees of the Collection. It was reported to be Miss Green who had pointed out to Morgan the importance of a collection of fifteen Caxtons which was to be included at the end of the sale of the library of Lord Amherst of Hackney in December 1908, and once again they passed to Morgan by way of a private sale arranged by Hodge, for a sum reputed to be £25,000. Although there was some public reaction to this sale, the introduction to the catalogue had stated quite clearly that Lord Amherst had authorised Sotheby's to make private sales if the right offer came along.

In 1906, however, another formidable collector had appeared on the horizon who liked the offer of *en bloc* collections on the same basis. This was the wealthy Worcester Sauce manufacturer, C. W. Dyson Perrins, who was very ardent collector of illuminated manuscripts and *incunabula*. His first accession in this manner from Sotheby's was the entire collection of early Italian, German and

1. Eva Pinto Leite.

French woodcut books formed by Richard Fisher and his son, R. C. Fisher, to illustrate the development and history of the art of engraving. It contained all the most celebrated early printed editions of Aesop's *Fables* of 1485, 1493, 1501 and 1510; an *Apocalypse* of 1515; the Dante of 1491; the Ovid of 1497; the Petrarch of 1500; a superb series of French Books of Hours and a most celebrated set of German block-books and bibles. Dyson Perrins paid £10,300 for the whole collection which he bought from Sotheby's through the agency of J. & J. Leighton, a firm of booksellers and binders. R. C. Fisher bombarded Tom with anxious letters both before and after the sale: before, because he was worried that it would not go through on a private basis, and a public auction – which he wanted to avoid at all costs – might be needed; and after because he felt that Hodge had kept too large a commission. Tom handled him with his usual flair and left Fisher, who died very shortly after the sale, a contented client.

In January 1907 Dyson Perrins also bought privately a large collection of illuminated manuscripts belonging to Fairfax Murray for £25,000. Hodge had been asked to sell this by Agnew's, the art dealers. It was an unusually profitable transaction because, as on previous occasions, Hodge had been given a fixed sales price of £15,000 with authority to keep any additional sum he might obtain.

It was quite clear that Barlow was very impressed by Tom's skill in this unexpected and little known side of the business and he made a particular study of it. In the early days after the purchase of the business Barlow shared the partners' room with Tom Hodge. They sat side by side so that Barlow could see everything that passed across Hodge's desk. Warre and Hobson had separate offices downstairs, partitioned off from the general working area on the ground floor. Tom had generally been approached about private sales by members of the trade who wanted help with placing particularly costly collections, but Barlow soon found that his political and parliamentary contacts would yield useful results in the same way. He was also shrewd enough to see that the continual withdrawal of major items or sections *en bloc* from catalogues already printed and circulated was going to prove very unpopular. He therefore changed tactics and produced abbreviated prospectuses specifically for possible private sales. His greatest success with such material was on behalf of the Duke of Devonshire. It was achieved in close collaboration with Hodge. As we have seen, Tom on his own was formidable, and Barlow was an altogether new sort of phenomenon in the rare book world. Together they proved a combination quite as successful, in their own way, as Duveen in the world of Old Master paintings, though in contrast to that master salesman they worked very quietly, shunning all publicity. Unfortunately, this very close partnership was only of short duration.

In November 1913 Barlow was asked to Chatsworth, the palatial Derbyshire home of the Dukes of Devonshire. The Duchess and the Librarian showed him around. It was impressed upon Barlow that some sort of sale was a matter of urgency, and he advised on what was most saleable. On his return to London he wrote a four-page memorandum on what was to be done. He was planning a visit to the United States at Christmas and it was decided that he should endeavour to make arrangements for a private sale of some sort while he was there.

A number of the Dukes of Devonshire had been really great book collectors. The most outstanding was William Cavendish, the 6th Duke (1790–1858) who, like the Americans at the beginning of the twentieth century, had bought whole libraries early in the nineteenth century. He succeeded to the Dukedom at the age of twenty-one and was one of the major purchasers at the Roxburghe Sale in 1812, where he bought a copy of Caxton's *Recuyell of the Historyes of Troye* – the first book printed in the English language – for the then record price of £1,060 10s. 0d. This same copy had once belonged to Elizabeth Grey, wife of Edward IV. In 1821 he purchased for £2,000 the magnificent collection of English plays belonging to John Philip Kemble, the great Shakespearian actor and brother of the famous Mrs. Siddons. The Duke added a lot of material to Kemble's very scholarly collection. The most notable addition was what was then regarded as the only copy extant of the 1603 edition of *Hamlet*.

It was the collection of twenty-five Caxtons and the Kemble–Devonshire Collection of English Plays and Playbills that were finally singled out as the items Barlow was to sell when he got to New York and special, though brief, catalogues were hurriedly prepared for each. The Caxtons included the first and second (illustrated) edition of *The Game and Playe of the Chesse*, *Vocabulary in French and English*, the first edition of *The Chronicles of England*, Higden's *Polycronicon*, the *Historyes of Troye* from the Roxburghe Sale, the first and second editions of *Mirrour of the Worlde*, two editions of *The Golden Legend* and an uncut copy of the *Dictes and Notable Wyse Sayenges of the Phylosophers*.

The catalogue of the play collection only listed the four Shakespeare Folios and fifty-seven of the Quartos, though there were more than 7,500 plays in all.

Barlow wrote to Chatsworth: 'If no private sale can be arranged within a reasonable time then it is understood there will be no objection to a sale of any of the above items taking place by auction. No offer for private sale of the books . . . will be concluded without consultation with and approval by the Duke, if necessary by cable. Probably it will be desirable to agree on the use of a Code Book before I go to America'.

After various mundane details about packing and insurance he added: 'As in the case of the Huth Library Sale, commission will be the same whether the library is sold privately or publicly . . . and as I explained in conversation with regard to the furniture it is most unsatisfactory and leads to confusion and almost always spoils the chance of a good private sale if negotiations proceed at the same time through more than one person. I therefore assume that for the present and for a reasonable period after my return from America the matter of any negotiation for a private sale . . . will be left in my hands'.

Once he got to New York Barlow contacted his friend, G. D. Smith, who realised at once that here was something that would appeal to H. E. Huntington. One must admire the speed with which such Titans made up their minds.

Huntington did not quibble. He agreed to pay the enormous sum of $750,000 for both the Caxtons and the plays, *sight unseen*, for they were still at Sotheby's packed in some twenty-seven large packing cases, awaiting shipment to New York. A contract was drawn up and signed at Huntington's residence at 2 East 57th Street on 19 January 1914. He gave Barlow a cheque for $150,000 and three promissory notes for $200,000 each to mature in four, eight and twelve months. The shipments were to go to New York, batch by batch, following these payments.

Barlow returned to London well pleased. The whole trip to the States – including his passage there and back, hotel charges for a month and innumerable cables – had cost the firm a mere £235, and he had brought about another private sale that more than matched the firm's previous record. There was pleasure too at Chatsworth: it was now unnecessary to make any further sales.[1] His Grace's auditors, Messrs. Price, Waterhouse, checked the final accounts and found an over-payment by Sotheby's of £371 os. 11d. They sent a cheque on behalf of the Duke of Devonshire and asked for a receipt. There must have been red faces all round when it was discovered that a clerk at Wellington Street had made this out to the wrong duke, the Duke of Westminster!

Interesting too that even then there were constant fluctuations in the rate of exchange, which had to be watched with care. There had been a fall in the rate of exchange between dollars and pounds sterling. Initially this had been calculated at five dollars to the pound. By the time the second payment was made the pound had improved to $4.8825. It made a difference of £4,200 on the total sum paid.

George D. Smith

Probably the person most satisfied by this particular sale was George Smith. He cleared $100,000 on the deal. Huntington was aware of this and seemed quite contented. In fact, after the Devonshire acquisition, the pace of Smith's purchases for Huntington quickened, both in the States and in Europe. He was to undertake at least two more major transactions with Barlow. One was to buy *en bloc* the 346 lots of Americana from the first of the Britwell Sales in August 1916. These were described in the catalogue as 'being the finest collection of Americana ever offered for Sale by Auction in this Country'. The sum paid for it was £25,000.[2] The second major sale to Smith took place in 1917 when Barlow sold him the Earl of Ellesmere's Bridgewater House Library. This had been formed by Sir Thomas Egerton, Queen Elizabeth I's Lord Keeper and James I's Lord Chancellor. It was extraordinarily rich in English books of the sixteenth and seventeenth centuries. But it also included some 12,000 manuscripts of which the most famous was the illuminated Ellesmere Chaucer, and the great masses of manuscript plays accumulated by John Larpent, the Lord Chamberlain's censor from 1778 to 1824.

1. Though the Duke sold the Playbills in a sale at Sotheby's ten years later (10 April 1924) when they were bought by Dr. Rosenbach.
2. Various other sums have been quoted in print in the past.

Smith continued to be of vital importance to Sotheby's, right up to his sudden and unexpected death in 1920, but it was much more as a figure in the public gaze, buying stolidly and sometimes sensationally at auction, so that the need for increasing revenue by private sales grew less pressing. Smith was a man whose stature has not always been given the credit it deserves. A. E. Newton, a great book collector in his own right,[1] and leading American author on the whole sport of bibliophily, wrote of Smith: 'he was a many-sided man, a man of nerve and daring, and he had that pre-requisite for distinction in his field – a wonderful memory. Perhaps I should say he was born without any forgetting apparatus. He never forgot the date of a book or a point or a price or a name or a face' (or, where his other great passion was concerned, the per-formance of a horse). Newton went on to say: 'George was in a class by himself. He had his own methods and no operator in Wall Street was quicker at making decisions or at putting his decisions into effect. He bewildered his rivals, and they were many. He was the mainstay of the book auction room . . . but it would have made no difference in what direction George Smith would have elected to make a living, he, starting penniless, would have risen to the top'.

He certainly caused more than his fair share of bewilderment in the London book trade, by disrupting the comfortable groove in which the leading practitioners were used to working. One of his keenest critics was E. H. Dring of Quaritch, though he was not the only bookseller by any means who played the game of 'trotting' the American, that is of bidding him up and up on a lot and then stopping at the last possible, psychological moment. Yet there was genuine universal sadness when Smith died. It might have been a great blow for Sotheby's, but another personality had reached the precise moment where he could step into the breach, even to the point of acquiring Huntington as his principal customer. If Tom Hodge, Barlow, Hobson and Warre had sat down to *invent* him they could not have improved much on the real-life figure that now began to dominate the rare book world. This was the mercurial Dr. Rosenbach, known affectionately to his friends as 'Rosie' and to the trade as 'the Doctor'. The doctorate was awarded in 1900 by the University of Pennsylvania for his thesis on 'The Influence of Spanish Literature in the Elizabethan and Stuart Drama'. Rosenbach's encyclopaedic knowledge of Elizabethan drama and literature was the foundation of a career in antiquarian bookselling that made him the most celebrated figure in that field which America had ever had. 'His name became synonymous with great books at great prices. It was not just that he paid more money for books than anyone before, but that his buying and selling were the manifestations of a faith in the greatness of great books that he persuaded other men to share.'[2] Sotheby's was the setting of many of his greatest triumphs.

1. His library was sold after his death in three great sales at Parke-Bernet in New York in 1941.
2. Quoted from *Rosenbach, a Biography*, by Edwin Wolf with John Fleming, 1960, a detailed and marvellously lively, blow-by-blow account of the Doctor's career. For another portrait of the Doctor, see also E. Millicent Sowerby's *Rare People and Rare Books*, 1967.

9

'The best is yet to be':
The Browning Sale

LET us go back to the moment when Barlow began to devote himself particularly to private sales. At that time the firm was given the opportunity for the arrangement of a sale that marvellously suited Geoffrey Hobson's combination of talents. The painter, Robert Wiedemann Barrett Browning ('Pen'), died intestate that year in Italy. He had made little impact on his contemporaries as an artist but all the world knew of him as the offspring of the most famous romance of the mid-nineteenth century, the marriage between the poets Robert Browning and Elizabeth Barrett (of Wimpole Street). Because there was no will and rather more than twenty heirs, everything that Barrett Browning had owned had to be sold. And that included all his parents' books, pictures, furniture and, above all, their letters and manuscripts. Among the letters were the incomparable love letters from Robert and Elizabeth, written to each other during their courtship. These had, in fact, been published in 1899 under the editorship of Sir Frederic Kenyon, but the outcry that went up in the correspondence columns of the press when it was learned that they were to be sold by auction was described by *The Times* as 'a bludgeoning controversy, for it is one of the ironies of human nature that disputes on delicate matters of taste provoke access to the heaviest weapons'.

The property was scattered among four houses in Italy. The Brownings had lived permanently in that country until the time of Elizabeth's death in 1861 and Robert had died there too in 1889. Their principal residence was the magnificent Ca' Rezzonico in Venice. Then there were two villas in Asolo and another on the outskirts of Florence. Hobson set off to Italy in the summer of 1912 to survey and select the material and to organise its packing and return to England.

After Tennyson, Browning had probably been the most widely appreciated English poet of his time. While the young in 1912 might have felt rather less enthusiastic about his work, many members of an older generation still thought of it as the height of poetic achievement. Hobson went to Italy steeped in Browning and all his works.[1] The poet's public image was based very much on the portrait of the bearded da Vinci-like figure, painted by his son (lot No. 62 in the sale), and Bagehot's 'He is great not in mere accomplishment, but in himself', though Henry James had dared to call him 'a poet without a lyre' a few years earlier.

1. His annotated copy of *The Life of Robert Browning* by W. Hall Griffin and H. C. Minchin (Methuen, 1911) survives at Sotheby's to this day.

A splendid incident occurred on Hobson's final journey back from Italy after many months of preparatory work there for the sale. For ultimate safety he carried the most precious items in his hand luggage. These were the love letters and Browning's death mask. He was in a crowded compartment of the Simplon Express when the train stopped at the frontier and customs officers came round to examine the passengers' baggage. When asked what he had in the hat box on the rack above his head, he could not recall the Italian word for a death mask. Improvising, he enunciated very slowly and in sonorous tones, 'I have up there the head of a dead man'. The bewildered customs officers gave him a strange look and all the passengers in the compartment melted away to other parts of the train. He travelled the rest of the journey in comfortable solitude.

The catalogue that he produced for the six-day sale in May 1913 was in every sense a labour of love. It was learned. It was discreet. It contained much that was new, unknown and important about Robert Browning himself, his remarkable father and Robert's uniquely talented wife. It read like a voyage of discovery through the poets' lives and all who mattered to them, and with its tracery of personal detail it was infinitely more evocative than any straightforward biography. Issued some time before the sale, the press lapped it up. 'The sale is a deep mine of literary and artistic association. Whichever way one turns some lode is struck.' 'In the masterly catalogue issued by Messrs. Sotheby suitable reticence and restraint are shown.' Discussing the love letters in particular, the *Telegraph* wrote:

> Neither the poet nor his son apparently dared to destroy the literary expressions of a love which, in its ardent constancy and scorching self-sacrifice, remains a world example in the high chivalry of devotion. No man has a soul so dead that he can arise from a reading of these peerless communings of two faithful hearts without feeling that the world would have lost a priceless message if the letters had gone to the fire that burns. . . . To one holding these views the appearance of the wondrous originals at auction on May 2 causes no forebodings. There cannot be any unworthy end to the seemingly prosaic act. The possession of the letters will transcend any possible ownership.

Much of the newspaper comment was written in such purple prose. Yet it seems entirely appropriate. The Brownings represented a pinnacle of sentiment. Even today one cannot read the catalogue[1] without some stirrings of the romantic.

In the catalogue, the entry for the most disputed item read:

Lot 166 BROWNING (Robert and Elizabeth Barrett)
THE LOVE LETTERS, a series of Two Hundred and Eighty-four from Robert and Two Hundred and Eighty-seven from Elizabeth Barrett Browning, *in the original cases where they were always kept until sent for publication, her letters being kept by him in a marqueterie box, and his by her in a collapsible gold tooled leather case.*

1. It was re-published under the general editorship of A. N. L. Munby in Volume 6 of *Sale Catalogues of Libraries of Eminent Persons*, with an introduction by John Woolford (Mansell, 1972).

*_** It is impossible to exaggerate the importance of this, probably the most famous series of letters in the world. We may, however, point out that it is unique in a double sense, for not only are these the only love letters which have passed between two great poets, but also they are the only letters which passed between Browning and his wife, for after their marriage they were never separated for a day. We reproduce the first and last of the series.

The first letter began: 'I love your verses with all my heart, dear Miss Barrett – and this is no off-hand complimentary letter that I shall write, whatever else – no prompt matter-of-course recognition of your genius, and there's a graceful and natural end of the thing . . . I do, as I say, love these books with all my heart – and I love you too. . . .' And the correspondence ends with Elizabeth's 'By tomorrow at this time I shall have you only to love me, my beloved. You only – as if one said God only. And we shall have Him besides, I pray of Him'.

In lot 228 the delightful but formidable Mrs. Anna Jameson, high priestess of artistic commentary to a whole Victorian generation, writes of her travels through Italy with the Brownings only a few weeks after their marriage. 'He is full of good spirit and good humour, and his unselfishness and his turn for making the best of everything . . . render him the very prince of travelling companions, *but* (always BUTS ! !) he is in all the common things of life the most unpractical of men, and the most uncalculating, rash – in short the worst *manager* I ever met with. . . .' She expresses grave misgivings about the success of the marriage and 'doubts the poetic temperament as a means of permanent happiness'.

Carlyle, on the other hand, wrote in a remarkable letter (lot 205) 'If ever there was a union indicated by the finger of heaven itself, and sanctioned and prescribed by the Eternal Laws under which poor transitory Sons of Adam live, it seemed to me . . . to be this!'

The battle for the principal items evoked such headlines as 'Extraordinary Bidding at Sotheby's', 'The Browning Love Letters: Remarkable Prices' and 'Love Letters at £11 9s. Each'. Felix Warre conducted the sale on that second of May with his usual, quiet panache. The room was packed. The dealers were there in force, but so were Browning lovers, and literary figures, and droves of Browning relatives and a great multitude of those who were simply curious to see what they guessed would be an epic sale. The *Telegraph* had expected some public protest at the last moment, but there was none. 'Mr. Warre, the auctioneer (and son of the Provost of Eton)', it wrote, 'was not challenged in the conduct of his business by even the mildest of expostulations. To kick against the pricks of auction is a hapless task indeed. . . .'

'There was a buzz of excitement', said the *Mail* 'when lot 166 was announced.' 'For rarely', continued the *Globe* 'has Sotheby's been patronised by so many ladies drawn thither by the irresistible collection of the famous love letters.' The opening bid for them came from Frank Sabin, far and away the most active buyer at the whole sale. Alfred Quaritch topped it by £50. Near him sat Mrs. Alice Meynell, the poetess. Opposite, close to Sabin, sat Mrs. Florence Barclay, a well-known novelist of her time, in purple hood, nervously toying with a rosary. After a few intervening bids Sabin and Quaritch fought out the duel between them with quick professional nods. The whole thing took barely two minutes. Quaritch agreed to a figure of £6,500. Sabin capped it with another £50. The sale-room held its breath. Quaritch slowly shook his head. The letters had gone to Sabin. He was 'immediately assailed by questioners' (for had he not also purchased Nelson's famous last letter to Emma for a record price at Sotheby's in 1904), but he only replied curtly 'I have bought the letters for myself'.[1]

In contrast, Mrs. Jameson's letters fetched a mere trifle at £15 10s. od., and went to Tregaskis. Sabin again bid £57 for Carlyle's letter. Prices generally for anything in the hand of either of the Brownings – both literary compositions and letters – went for record sums. Lot 152 also caused much excitement. This was the manuscript of 43 of the 44 *Sonnets from the Portuguese*. These represented in literary form the gist of Mrs. Browning's love letters. They had been included in her *Collected Poems* of 1850 and this was the very manuscript used by the printers. The Sonnets were bought by Quaritch after a brief battle for them between himself, Frank Sabin and Mr. Brown (acting on behalf of an American buyer). It was one of the last public appearances of the indomitable Alfred Quaritch; he died later that year at the early age of forty-two after contracting influenza at the Hoe Sales in New York in the previous year, from which he never fully recovered. A silent but tense spectator at that part of the sale must have been the 'great' bibliophile, Thomas J. Wise. It was he who had put about the romantic story of an earlier publication of the *Sonnets* in 1847 to cover his own forgery of a *whole edition* of these poems. But no one knew or even suspected this in 1913, and Wise, as we shall see, who was a constant attendant at Sotheby's sales and a close friend of Tom Hodge, was not finally unmasked as the perpetrator of these fraudulent activities until 1934.

Poor Barrett Browning's pictures on the first day of the sale were not appreciated at all and fetched undeservedly paltry prices. Indeed his largest composition, *Heresy*, of a monk remonstrating before a heretic lying on a dungeon floor found no buyer at all even though it had been exhibited at the Royal Academy in 1881. The portraits of his parents fared somewhat better. In general the Italian Primitive paintings so lovingly collected by the poets proved unpopular, though Dowdeswell paid £500 for Antonio Pollaiuolo's *Christ at the Column*[2] which had inspired part of Stanza XXVIII in Browning's *Old Pictures in Florence*:

---

1. Sabin retained the letters in his stock for sixteen years and eventually sold them to the American dealer, Gabriel Wells. They were bought from him by E. D. North for a sum in excess of $75,000 and were finally purchased from him for $80,000 by Miss Caroline Hazard for presentation to the English Poetry Collection at Wellesley College Library in Massachusetts in 1930.

2. He never sold it. It was included in a sale at Christie's in 1916 of the whole of the dealer's stock, where it fetched £800.

> Could not the ghost with the close red cap,
> My Pollajolo, the twice a craftsman,
> Save me a sample, give me a hap
> Of a muscular Christ that shows the draughtsman?

Lot 11 on the first day also caused a great stir. It was a delightful record of a memorable literary meeting in 1855 when Tennyson had read his long, newly completed poem *Maud* to Robert and Elizabeth Browning in the presence of Dante Gabriel Rossetti. Elizabeth had described the occasion in a letter to her friend Miss Mitford. 'One of the pleasantest things which has happened to us here is the coming down on us of the Laureate, who, being in London for three or four days from the Isle of Wight, spent two of them with us, dined with us, smoked with us, opened his heart to us (and the second bottle of port), and ended by reading "Maud" through from end to end, and going away at half-past two in the morning. If I had had a heart to spare, certainly he would have won mine. He is captivating with his frankness, confidingness, and unexampled *naïveté*! Think of him stopping in "Maud" every now and then – "There's a wonderful touch! That's very tender. How beautiful that is!" Yes, and it *was* wonderful, tender, beautiful, and he read exquisitely in a voice like an organ, rather music than speech'.

Rossetti had sketched Tennyson half kneeling on the sofa, declaiming, and had written across the top of the drawing the opening line of the poem, 'I hate the dreadful hollow behind the little wood'. Frank Sabin acquired that sketch for £225.

The very letter that described the occasion was probably included in lot 130 – a packet of between three- and four-hundred letters (of which only forty-nine had been published) – which Elizabeth had written to Miss Mitford, the author of *Our Village*, between 1836 and 1855. Sabin bought that lot too, for £245.

One of the most touching items sold was lot 144 which included a photograph of Mrs. Browning presented to her husband. The catalogue described it as stained and dirty, and it was inscribed 'Elizabeth Barrett Browning – for R. B. only – with all her love and very little likeness. Sept. 17, 1858.' It was thought never to have been reproduced. Mrs. Meynell, the poetess, bought it for the enormous sum of £54 0s. 0d.

The last day (the sixth, after the poets' books had been sold on the third, fourth and fifth) included the more valuable of the Brownings' personal possessions and household effects: the silver and plate, the china and pottery, the bronzes and busts; furniture, including his writing desk (bought for £12 10s. 0d. by Bagot), the personal jewellery (lot 1366 – a pair of oval gold cuff links, engraved with the initials R. B., worn by the poet and his father: they had fetched £5); even the poet's robe, as Doctor of Civil Law, which he had worn when he received an Honorary Degree from Oxford University on his seventieth birthday. It fetched £5 and was the last lot (1407) in a sale which totalled £27,934 5s. 0d., vastly more than anyone had expected. Only the death mask had been withdrawn at the last moment. (The poets' church marriage certificate had also been excluded from the catalogue at the eleventh hour.)

The Times commented: 'There was an ardent display of devotion up to the last, matching any exhibition of hero worship either in the Dickens Sale of 1870 or in the Irving Sale of 1905 . . . Sentiment and emotion swayed over the auction arithmetic yesterday and duels between Browning lovers for the possession of some coveted prize were frequent.'

The Browning Sale was important beyond the unexpectedly high turnover it produced in an auction house. The great publicity it attracted redounded very much to Sotheby's credit, but of more lasting significance was the fact that it brought about an awareness once more among an enormous audience of the interest and fun in collecting old letters. The appeal of the Browning letters was strangely universal. It crystallised the fascination that two brilliant writers with a heightened awareness could give to relatively mundane events.

As is so often the case, there was to be an important sequel to the first disposal of Browning relics. On 7 June 1937, Sotheby's held the sale of another substantial collection of Browning letters. One-hundred-and-eleven were from Elizabeth to her favourite sister Arabel Barrett who had remained at home to look after her father in Wimpole Street; fifty-seven were to her brother George Barrett, and one-hundred-and-twenty-six were to her friend, Mrs. Sophia May Eckley. The sale was brilliantly catalogued by John Taylor under Hobson's aegis. It consisted of only fifty lots, but they grouped the letters in such a way as to give each of the prospective owners a biographical entity and, if anything, this catalogue makes even more lively reading than the 1913 one. Elizabeth unburdened herself to her sister with wit and sparkle, and a directness which the subtlety of the love letters had lacked. She wrote from Florence in August 1854: '. . . in profound confidence I will tell you what has complicated our pecuniary vexation. Dear Mr. Kenyon forgot to pay the £50 [he gave the Brownings an allowance of £100 a year – their principal source of income]. People must live upon pence - air won't do altogether – not even Florence air – I dare say we are not miraculous oeconomists – but I am quite sure that not a single person with whom we are in association has an idea of the smallness of our actual income – While I write, Chapman & Hall's [the Brownings' publishers] account arrives . . . there's not much for us . . .'.

In January 1855, describing how Christmas was spent at Casa Guidi: 'Robert and I do work every day – he has a large volume of short poems which will be completed by the spring [*Men and Women*] – and I have some four thousand-five hundred lines towards my own – I am afraid that six thousand lines will not finish it [*Aurora Leigh*] . . .', and in May 1855, when her portrait was being painted by the American artist, Latilla: 'you never saw such a vision of a dishevelled nun, the hair nearly down to the waist in expectation of the fatal shears, the countenance in profound melancholy and the mouth full of sugar plums . . . administered in the way of comfort by the lady abbess! And that's ME, and so I am to float through the Union . . .'. In June 1855, the Brownings had an adventurous journey from Florence to Paris. Some of their luggage was lost at Marseilles. '. . . our box containing all my Penini's [the son's] pretty dresses, embroidered trousers, collars, everything I had been collecting to make him look nice in . . . isn't it horrible?' The same box also contained the manuscript of the newly completed *Aurora Leigh* but this, being of less importance to Elizabeth, is not even mentioned – though it was a great grief to Robert. However, both clothing and manuscript were eventually recovered.

In this sale Maggs and Quaritch took most of the major Browning items, though a new name that was becoming increasingly important in the rare book world, Elkin Mathews, paid high prices for some of Elizabeth's manuscripts of early creative work. Dr. Rosenbach took home the most outstanding non-Browning item for £950 – the last sixty lines of John Keats' autograph manuscript of 'I stood tip-toe upon a little hill'. Keats had given this to B. R. Haydon, the painter, who in turn had presented it to Mrs. Browning in 1842.

10

First Thoughts
of Bond Street

1913 had been an altogether remarkable year. The 'new men', as they had become known, had served their apprenticeship; they were now 'old hands'. They took a number of far-reaching decisions which were to broaden the base of the business. The boldest of these by far was to purchase new premises if any could be found that seemed right, even though they would not be wanted for some years. For, as we have seen already, the lease at Wellington Street would run out in 1917. The partners' rapid successes under Tom Hodge's tutorship had brought in a great deal of money and vastly improved the cash situation. There had been thoughts of another merger in the summer of 1912. Sir Howard Frank of Knight, Frank & Rutley, whom we have already encountered during the negotiations between Tom Hodge and Hodgson's, was now introduced to Montague Barlow by Hodge. It seems that relations between Frank and his partner, Knight, had become somewhat strained and Frank wanted to explore the possibility of allying himself to another business without a total amalgamation. The advantage from Sotheby's point of view was that this would have enabled them to move into new premises at a low rental for a long term without tying up any more capital. The partners studied the available space in Knight, Frank & Rutley's elegant offices in Hanover Square and worked out how their staff could be accommodated. It seemed possible. But Barlow didn't want to sell any shares in Sotheby's and Frank would only consent to a pooling of interests – such as making over his 'chattel sales' to Sotheby's – in exchange for shares, so the discussions came to a halt in July 1912. Frank said in his final letter to Barlow: 'I am sorry to think we have spent so much time to no purpose but I shall arrange *something* with you one of these days'.

He did. The partners had decided that Sotheby's new home should be in the West End. This was where the book and art trades increasingly found most of their customers. The Wellington Street end of the Strand was no longer the quiet, bookish backwater it had been in the days when Samuel Sotheby had moved there, and Charles Lamb could write of 'the print shops, the old book stalls, parsons cheap'ning books . . . Jeremy Taylor's, Burton's on Melancholy and Religio Medici's on every stall'. Traffic poured across Waterloo Bridge in an ever-increasing stream. Somerset House – where the Royal Academy held its exhibitions until 1836, the Society of Antiquaries met till 1872 and the Naval Museum was housed till 1874 – was now the office of the Board of Inland Revenue. Holywell Street – or Booksellers' Row – was long demolished, and the widening of the Strand from the Law Courts to Wellington Street between 1900 and 1905 had been the biggest London road widening scheme and improvement since the grand design for Regent Street by Nash in 1820.

Howard Frank located new premises for Barlow which seemed to have all the necessary requirements; a good address, a pleasing appearance, capacious cellars for storage, and well-lit galleries that would make good sale-rooms. There was also a welter of small offices and labyrinthine staircases that seemed delightfully reminiscent of Wellington Street. The property had a long lease (thought to be eighty years at that particular stage) and the price seemed reasonable. The partners started negotiations for the purchase and set about finding a mortgage on favourable terms. The new address was to be 34 and 35 New Bond Street.

Centuries earlier this had been the site of an ancient hostelry named The Black Horse. Part of the underground storage rooms were now being used as the cellars of a firm of wine merchants called Basil Woodd & Co. Their monogram can still be seen today on some of the iron supporting pillars, where these have not been cased in, and when Barlow took an advance party round the empty premises on a tour of inspection just before the firm moved in they remarked on the old, purple glass windows with clusters of grapes, which were only gradually replaced. There was also a useful drive-in for the wine merchant's horse vans. Another part of the downstairs premises was occupied by a firm of wholesale bookbinders called Birdsall & Son.

The most interesting tenant was the Doré Gallery, a well-known feature of the London art world since Victorian times. The gallery was owned by two art dealers called Fairlees and Beeforth who had made an exclusive arrangement with the celebrated French illustrator and painter, Paul Gustave Doré, to market both his paintings and engravings in London. For many years the firm flourished and Doré's rather maudlin religious subjects became almost as popular as the stag in Landseer's *Monarch of the Glen* on late-Victorian parlour walls. But after Fairlees died in Cairo in 1891, the business began to languish and Beeforth sold the stock of pictures and engravings to D. H. Evans, the department store, some years later, for £10,000. By the terms of their contract with the gallery D. H. Evans were not allowed to dispose of Doré's work below its original advertised prices, but the fashion for it had passed and their sales of it were disastrous. After three years only a handful of engravings had been sold. Despite the pleas of D. H. Evans's manager to relax the restrictive covenants concerned, Beeforth remained adamant about enforcing them and not allowing any sales at reduced prices within the UK. So D. H. Evans eventually had to ship their entire stock of Dorés to Australia and South Africa and sell it there at what it would fetch.

For the frequent exhibitions of the work of Doré and other artists after the Doré sale, Fairlees and Beeforth had built special galleries with top lighting, but Barlow thought these were still not adequate for Sotheby's needs and a considerable volume of reconstruction and enlargement was to take place before the Bond Street premises would be ready for their new occupants.

In the meantime, however, the partners decided to keep their plans strictly to themselves and to sit tight. For though they had been through four golden years, the Balkan wars had brought about a general unsettlement in Europe and the future looked far less assuredly golden than it had at any time for almost three decades.

Pictures, Publicity and Broken Pots

All the more reason then, thought Barlow, for enlarging the business while the going was good. It was in 1913 that he is credited with taking the momentous decision that Sotheby's should go back into the picture business, which it had virtually abandoned half a century earlier, though even then it had not been a really important part of the turnover. Since that time all pictures of any quality had been passed on to Christie's, who had on a tit-for-tat basis passed most of the books they received on to Sotheby's. There really was not the space at Wellington Street to handle such bulky items as furniture, carpets and pictures, but there would be at Bond Street, and the partners felt it would be a good plan to start building up that side of the business in the expectation of a move.

What happened was that Barlow literally stumbled across some pictures stacked up in a half-lit corridor. They had been sent to Wellington Street apparently in error. Instead of cursing their presence – and his bruises – he asked what they were. He discovered that they included quite a number of saleable items. Strenuous efforts were now made to find more. Cataloguers were soon located and Sotheby's was back in the picture business.

At first this resulted in a mere two sales a year, and even these were tacked on to what were essentially print and drawing sales, but in the summer of 1913 a Frans Hals portrait belonging to Lord Glanusk, for whom Sotheby's had sold a Shakespeare First Folio that January, arrived at Wellington Street. This was a much more important picture than the firm had sold for many years, and it was duly catalogued for inclusion in a mixed drawing, etching and picture sale, for 20 June 1913. Quite coincidentally it turned into something of a watershed in Sotheby's history, for two other Frans Hals portraits appeared at Christie's on the same day. This was the period when the Dutch were beginning to want their old masters back again, and several dealers from Holland had come to London for the two sales. There was brisk bidding for the Glanusk portrait at Sotheby's, which was the best of the three (and the first to be sold), and for the two other Hals portraits at Christie's. In fact, the interested dealers had to dash speedily from one auction room to the other in mid-sale.

The Sotheby portrait was described as of a man, 'full-face, life-size, half-length in black dress with white collar and tassels, wearing a hat and with his right hand across the breast, holding gloves, a characteristic Hals subject'. It had been bought by the first Lord Glanusk, then Sir Russell Bailey, in the William Russell sale at Christie's in December 1884. Someone now remembered that the portrait had at that time just been cleaned to reveal its quality, and yet, together with an anonymous Flemish still-life thrown in for good measure, it had fetched only five guineas. The bidding at Sotheby's started high: at £1,000, and moved up briskly to £7,500. It finished, in the sort of battle beloved by sale-room correspondents, between the famous collector and *marchand amateur*, Sir Hugh Lane, and Messrs. Tooth, who were known to be acting on behalf of a dealer from The Hague, Mr. A. Preyer. Sir Hugh took the price up to £8,500 but Mr. Preyer's agents secured the prize at £9,000. A. C. R. Carter called it the 'most piquant Sale Romance of the year' in the 1914 edition of *The Year's Art*, which he edited. Altogether the affair had been a revelation to the partners, though it was to be many years before they were able to establish regular sales of Old Masters of real quality.

Certainly it was not for lack of trying. Montague Barlow was an able publicist when he chose to become involved in that side of the business. One finds fairly frequent, shrewdly timed letters from him to the sale-room correspondents of the major dailies, such as A. C. R. Carter of the *Daily Telegraph* (who was the doyen of them all), William Roberts of *The Times* and Tom Greig of the *Morning Post*, asking that they should give particular attention to this or that sale, and usually they did, for there was a long tradition of detailed pre- and post-sale reporting. The space devoted to such pieces in these papers was infinitely greater than it is today. The much smaller scale of the auction world and the much more limited number of dealers involved meant that the constant colourful reporting of their activities gave the more outstanding among them a close personal following among the readers of each paper that any television personality of today might envy.

As a result of this much increased publicity Sotheby's began to make its presence felt to an increasing extent as a competitor to Christie's, though for many years to come their great King Street rivals dominated the works of art market, and particularly the picture market, to a degree that must have some-times made Barlow, Hobson and Warre despair.

An interesting example of Barlow's efforts to publicize a sale is the following letter to Carter on 21 June 1918:

> My dear Carter,
>   I am enclosing you herewith a very interesting catalogue; it is to be released for the Press for Monday. You will note the fine pastels of the late Mr. Stott which form the second day, and which will make a very fine sale. There are also some other very interesting items in the first day including a superb Van Goyen sketch book, Lot 124, which is fully described by Campbell Dodgson in this month's Burlington.
>   I hope you can give a good notice of the sale in Monday's issue.

Carter took the hint and complied. It was, in fact, a sale which lent itself to easy 'copy'; the sort of thing which Carter enjoyed writing up. Stott was a sentimental, almost forgotten, star-pupil of Cabanet at the Ecole des Beaux-Arts in Paris, who had laboured quietly and not very successfully at Amberley in Surrey for the rest of his life. Thanks to the efforts of one particularly enthusiastic collector, W. W. Sampson, who was usually referred to in the press as 'the professional champion of British Art in the Sale Room',[1] a number of the pastels and drawings fetched high prices. Carter wrote: 'these exquisite sketches palpitated with love and worship of simple truth and beauty, and seemed to bring the pure air of the pastoral to town'. The painter had left the proceeds of this studio sale to his 'faithful friend and helper, Miss Annie Dinnage'. She got £3,195 for some 150 drawings, but more remarkably Carter reported that Stott had left the bulk of his savings to the Royal Academy 'which never bought one of his inspired achievements for the Chantrey, to aid and cheer artists prepared to struggle and win, like himself'.

What Barlow had not mentioned, and Carter did not either, was that the sale also contained some very fine Old Masters that belonged to Felix Warre's father, the Provost of Eton. They included a Honthorst, a Taddeo Zucchero, a Mabuse School *Madonna and Child* of great beauty, which had been exhibited in the Royal Academy Winter Exhibition of 1907, a Jan van Scorel replica of a portrait of a Flemish lady in the Rijksmuseum, a Pinturicchio *Flight into Egypt*. But they were not well catalogued and regrettably fetched mediocre prices.

The most interesting lot in the sale was the 'sketch book of a Dutch Master, attributed to Paul Potter, but more probably the work of Jan van Goyen'. It contained over 200 drawings, some of great charm, and had been written up at length by Campbell Dodgson of the British Museum in the *Burlington Magazine* for June 1918. Hofstede de Groot had examined it, the catalogue entry reported, but it failed to include his comments. Certainly the eight sketches reproduced were of high quality. It fetched £610 and was bought by Colnaghi's. Everyone involved took it in their stride. Today the sketch-book would be a major sale sensation.

In fact, an intriguing postscript to that sale occurred on 21 March 1977 when three leaves from the same sketch-book[2] came up for sale at Sotheby Mak van Waay, the major Amsterdam fine art auction house which Sotheby's had acquired in 1974. By this time the sketches were known to have changed hands at least six times, and they had been written up in eight further publications since Campbell Dodgson's article in 1918. The sketch-book was now definitely attributed to Van Goyen and was known to be the record of a trip by the artist along the Rhine to Amsterdam and Haarlem in 1650–51. Almost every view had been identified and there had been some speculation about the date when the sketch-book had been broken up. The three lots fetched £3,250, £2,750 and £2,000 respectively. On that basis the whole sketch-book some sixty years after its first Sotheby sale could be valued at about £350,000. It is an illuminating instance of values prevailing then and now.

1. He was, in fact, a dealer with a shop in the Haymarket and was widely known in the sale-room circuit as head of the modern (i.e. Victorian and Edwardian) picture Ring. He had an arrangement with at least one living artist to take the whole of his output. He was credited with supplying a large amount of material for Christie's Monday Sales at a time when they held two sales a week of modern and old pictures and drawings.
2. Lots 66, 67 and 68.

Barlow summarised all the events of 1912 and 1913 in a long document for the partners, analysing their financial achievements so far and highlighting the way ahead. Once again one marvels (with hindsight) at his sense of timing. There were a number of minor features, as well as major sales, that had helped to make the business more profitable. It had, for instance, been decided that year to charge clients for the inclusion of illustrations in catalogues. This had meant more impressive catalogues at lower cost. Obviously there had been some doubt whether the clients would accept this additional burden, but they did. To get the extra business in the pictures and works of art departments in competition with Christie's, the commission was pitched at only 7½ per cent, much less than the standard for books, coins and engravings. This increased turnover but did not bring about a proportionate increase in profitability. Insurance, always a vital factor in an auction house, was costing less. This was not unconnected with the fact that Barlow had become Deputy Chairman of the Agricultural & General Co-operative Insurance Society, and a lot of Sotheby's business was now being placed there. It was also decided to establish a policy of ploughing back some of the profit in more prominent advertisements of important sales in *The Times* and elsewhere 'in a bold and arresting way . . . plenty of space being left blank so as to draw attention to the printed matter'.

However, the ventures into new areas meant that occasionally the partners were led into serious errors of judgement. This happened spectacularly with a pair of Italian gentlemen, resplendently titled Signor Avvocato Marcioni and Cavaliere Capitano Lucatelli. They had brought with them samples of a formidable collection of very early Italian majolica. What the partners did not know at this stage was that it had been hawked all round Europe and universally rejected because so much of the material was damaged and badly repaired, but this was for a good reason. The introduction to the catalogue explains: 'The missing chapter . . . in the history of Italian ceramics . . . may now be bridged over . . . thanks mainly to the peculiar situation of the ancient city of Orvieto. Perched on a huge rock with precipitous sides, accessible from the plain at one point only, the lofty position of the city necessitated the construction of cellars and receptacles for rubbish in the solid rock. Some of these evidently existed from a very early period, but their use became obligatory under a law passed in the year 1324, by which the owner or occupier of every house had to construct a deep well for the purpose of receiving the household refuse. It is from these receptacles (*pozzi*) recently explored that have been derived numerous more or less fragmentary specimens, from which it is possible to construct a fairly complete series, showing the development and the chronology of Italian domestic vessels, their forms and decoration. In Orvieto, Signor Avvocato Marcioni and Cavaliere Capitano Lucatelli were among the first to appreciate the importance of the discoveries, and their two collections, now brought together, contain the major portion of the pieces which have been unearthed. Some of the chief museums have acquired a few examples of this very interesting ware, but it is unrepresented in most collections. With the attention now given to the subject, it is evident that, in future, pieces will be difficult to obtain. The excavations have been practically exhaustive, and it is unlikely that many more specimens will be available. These facts make even very imperfect pieces desirable. Though, as might be expected, very few vessels retrieved from the *pozzi* are complete, the two collections combined are rich in characteristic designs from the eleventh to the sixteenth centuries, and some of the examples are of great rarity and importance.'

The London trade did not share the combined enthusiasm of Sotheby's and Messrs. Marcioni and Lucatelli and the two-day sale, starting on 16 February 1914, was an almighty flop. Including a great mass of decorated fragments as well as relatively undamaged pieces, there were no fewer than 1,237 items included in more than 350 lots: it represented a nightmare of packing and subsequent identification. Bids, however, were in shillings rather than in pounds. Most items were regarded as of archaeological rather than of commercial interest. In the event, the total realised for the sale was only £777 12s. od., and a great deal had to be bought in. Apparently, the partners had been so persuaded of the value of the collection that they had advanced a large sum to the owners that was not returnable. Their loss on the transaction exceeded £3,000. They accepted it philosophically. It was the price of progress.

The Star-spangled Summer

Despite what Barlow always called the *disastrous* Marcioni and Lucatelli transaction, 1914 too looked like being a very good year. Huth continued on its profitable way. So did the extensive library of George Dunn, which was particularly strong in books and manuscripts relating to English law. The first portion of this had been sold in February 1913. The second was sold in a five-day sale in February 1914. January had seen the first sale of the stock of the bookseller, John Pearson, a Sotheby client for many years, now being dispersed 'in consequence of declining health'. Booksellers' stock sales were always useful grist to Sotheby's mill, though prices rarely reached the heights they did when identical items from a privately owned library were being sold.

For sixteen days in late April and most of May there was a sale of the property of John Eliot Hodgkin, F.S.A., who had died recently. Hodgkin had been an omnivorous collector in the old tradition, an antiquary in the finest sense of the word, who had amassed a vast quantity of out-of-the-way curiosities in many fields. In some -- such as printed ephemera, early children's books and books of science -- he was generations ahead of his time. The collections were widely known because Hodgkin had published a three-volume catalogue in 1903 called *RARIORA: being Notes on some of the Printed Works, Manuscripts, Historical Documents, Medals, Pottery, Engravings, etc., etc., collected between 1858 and 1900*. The work had received a rapturous review in the *Connoisseur* under the heading of 'An Ideal Collector'. 'There are many collectors, many eager connoisseurs, who have experienced what Mr. Hodgkin eloquently calls "the insidious, enthralling, indomitable joy of collecting", but few indeed of that ever increasing guild share his generous desire to impart that joy to others.'

The first two days of the sale were devoted to Hodgkin's works of art collections. These included fairly conventional items of pottery and glass, pewter and fans, but there was interesting tapestry and stump work, various royal relics, an altogether outstanding collection of netsuke (by no means the first that Sotheby's had sold), some fine cameos and a most unusual collection strongly reminiscent of a seventeenth-century collector's 'Cabinet of Curiosities' – exceptionally illustrated in colour – of *Lusus Naturae*, precious stones that nature had, through some accidental geomorphic quirk, formed in the shape of portrait heads or in the form of animals and birds. Most of these were mounted in gold or silver, and they were contained in a polished mahogany cabinet with fine silk plush-lined trays, that had once belonged to Queen Victoria. Then there were innumerable items carved in horn, and an unusual assemblage of portable sundials. By and large it was all rather strange to see such things at Wellington Street.

This was followed by a two-day sale of very fine commemorative medals and an *immense* number of seventeenth-century trade tokens (which have today virtually disappeared from the scene). The sale of the autograph letters and historical documents included a great many letters from and to English monarchs and many of their most devoted servants like Lord Burleigh, Lord Leicester and Samuel Pepys. A contemporary copy of the Magna Carta with a considerable number of textual variants from the copy in Lincoln Cathedral went for a mere £50, but a letter from Lucrezia Borgia to her brother-in-law, Cardinal d'Este of 14 January 1502, thanking him for his advice and for a necklace he had sent her which 'happened to arrive at a most opportune and necessary moment', and which bore her signature and her seal, changed hands at a record £245. There was lively interest in a substantial collection of letters and documents concerning the Pretenders and their adherents; in a long document on vellum of 5 December 1610 relating to the foundation of the Virginia Company; and in a lot containing five bills for sending Con O'Neill, grandson of the famous Earl of Tyrone, to Eton College. From them, and they were the earliest bills then known, it emerged that the tuition fee at Eton in 1615 was only £1 per term.

One of Hodgkin's favourite pursuits had been collecting letters and documents connected with the Chevalier D'Eon, who puzzled his eighteenth-century contemporaries and historians subsequently by posing alternatively as a man and a woman.[1] This was one of the last items in that portion of the sale. There were some 3,500 pages of material contained in 62 volumes as well as several large boxes of documentation in a single lot. It was a 'snip' for Maggs at a paltry £170.

Hodgkin's marvellous sense of history came to the fore in the disposal of the trade cards, book plates, papal indulgences, news sheets and early newspapers. It seemed that every major event in England since Elizabeth I was chronicled here in one form or another; and the seventeenth century in particular was represented in great strength. The trade cards covered every conceivable

1. Leigh and Sotheby had sold the Library of Mademoiselle *La Chevalière* D'Eon in 1793.

occupation from bookseller to brick-moulder, from floor cloth maker to glass cutter, from Indigo dealer to money changer, from profile painter to sago powder maker, from tallow chandler to whip maker – and all 375 lots of riveting social history went for a mere £1,630 in the two days. Another two-day sale of engravings covered the same historical ground in visual form, and finally there were six long days in which Hodgkin's magnificently eclectic library was dispersed in 1,622 lots to a multitude of specialists for some £4,201. The Hodgkin sale was not a great success in terms of money taken but its memory lingered on for many years, for nothing quite like it came on to the market afterwards, and the material scattered among the London trade fed a host of interested collectors for several decades to come.

It was merely the longest session in a season memorable for autograph material. How Tom Hodge must have revelled in this burgeoning of a Sotheby tradition. There were important Thackeray manuscripts, and later a selection of Brontë material from Haworth (some of it went back there). There was a special, brief sale wholly devoted to items important in Australasian history, which included four letters from Captain Cook. One dated 13 September 1771 gave a long account of Cook's first voyage in the *Endeavour* when he determined that New Zealand was not joined to the mainland of Australia, then called New Holland, and gave the eastern portion of that continent the name of New South Wales. The other three letters were all concerned with Cook's second voyage in the *Endeavour* and written between 1772 and 1775. Maggs bought all four items for £540. The other principal lot in the same sale consisted of a diary and letter book kept by Lieutenant Ralph Clark on his journey to Botany Bay and his subsequent stay in Australia and on Norfolk Island. Some volumes of his diary had been lost in a shipwreck and were not included, but those sold covered the period 1787 to 1791 and fetched £520.

Eight letters from Charles Lamb to his close friend Thomas Manning made £420 on 21 July, although the majority had already been published, and various Robert Burns letters fetched high prices on the same day. Two days later a whole lot of items and letters relating to Robert Louis Stevenson which had belonged to his stepson, Lloyd Osbourne, also did remarkably well, and, astonishingly, *Alice in Wonderland* – admittedly in the first (withdrawn) edition, and enhanced by the inclusion of an autograph letter from the author and another from Sir John Tenniel – made the unheard of price of £200. This was a portent of things to come. Another one had been the sale of a *Collection of all the Dramatic Pieces published in the reign of King George III* in 57 volumes. Together with a volume entitled *Prologues* this collection had been assembled by Horace Walpole, and all but four of the volumes bound in old calf, displayed the Walpole Arms in gold on the front board and the name and crest of Horace Walpole were on the remainder. The collection was sold in one lot and fetched £210 and had been sent into Sotheby's by one Mr. Christie-Miller of Britwell Court, Burnham, Buckinghamshire, of whom we shall hear a good deal more.

The best has yet to be told. For 'The great event of the month', wrote the *Connoisseur*, 'and so far of the season, was the sale of the famous Pembroke

Library, most of which was acquired by Thomas Herbert, 8th Earl of Pembroke (1656–1733), a distinguished politician and enlightened collector and patron of learning. His judgement as a bibliophile has been confirmed by posterity, for the collection when dispersed by Messrs. Sotheby on June 25th and 26th realised £38,936 for 211 lots, the largest amount ever made in a two days book sale in Wellington Street. The previous record for a single day was attained in the fourth day of the first Huth Sale, on 20 November 1911, when 150 lots brought £17,187. This record was surpassed on both days of the Pembroke Sale, £20,409 being made on the first and £18,527 on the second.' This was just as well, for the reserves recommended by the Earl of Pembroke's advisers on some of the major items had been very high.

Before the sale George Smith had approached Barlow about another *en bloc* purchase. 'I saw G. D. Smith, who was here a long time yesterday', Barlow had written in a note to Tom Hodge. 'He is so far fairly tame for him. He talks of buying Pembroke en bloc – but only for himself. This is no use so far as we are concerned. He had much better buy at the sale. . . . I promised Pembroke I would sell one day of the sale myself. Will you let me know which day you would rather take?' But Barlow could hardly blame Smith for wanting to buy *en bloc*: there was an open invitation to do so in the preface of the catalogue.[1] Unusually, it listed all the items included in this sale in an index sub-divided into the countries from which the books originated. There were five blockbooks; ten titles from the early German presses; 173 from Italy – again these were subdivided into the towns of origin such as Subiaco, Rome, Venice, Florence, Milan, Verona, Vicenza, etc. No fewer than twenty-one titles were printed by two of the very earliest printers, Sweynheim and Pannartz; there was one from Switzerland; four from France; two from Holland; four from Belgium and – listed discreetly at the end – six Caxtons, one excessively rare book printed by a near contemporary of Caxton's, the anonymous St. Albans schoolmaster printer, and one printed by Theodoric Rood, the first university printer at Oxford. The author of the preface was quite justified in claiming that 'where every book is a masterpiece, it is difficult to select any for special mention'.

Smith bought heavily, 97 lots out of 211. Quaritch bought 41, but probably paid not much less in total, having purchased some of the most expensive items, such as the superb block-book of 1460 of the *Apocalypse* for £2,120 (lot 5) (though curiously, the Amherst copy a few years earlier had been bought in at £2,000); the Caxton *The Game and Playe of the Chesse* for £1,800 (lot 49); Nicolas Jenson's 1472 edition on vellum with beautifully illustrated decorative borders and miniatures of *Macrobius: Expositio in Somnium Scipionis M.T. Ciceronis* for £1,600 (lot 135); this volume changed hands again twice before the end of 1921 at *lower* prices.

1. What Barlow does not mention in this letter is that Tom Hodge and he had already been involved in an earlier offer from the German government to buy the collection *en bloc*. They had dissuaded the Earl of Pembroke from accepting this and events had proved them right for the total received at auction vastly exceeded the German offer.

Smith took to America lot 13, the fifteenth-century block-book of *Ars Moriendi*. It cost him £500. He bought the St. Albans schoolmaster's book on Hawking and Hunting for £1,800 (lot 26); he bought the *Biblia Pauperum* (lot 30) – another fifteenth-century block-book – for £780, and the *Treatises of Cicero* printed by Caxton in 1481 (lot 68) for £1,050. This copy had the added attraction that it had once belonged to, and contained the autograph signature of, Thomas Culpeper, the great herbalist. Another high price he paid was £1,200 for lot 184, *Speculum Humanae Salvationis*, a very fine Dutch block-book of 1471. He must have been pleased when he only had to pay £600 for lot 109, a particularly exquisite fifteenth-century Book of Hours. It was principally French with nine full-page illuminations and thirty-seven miniatures; but it also contained nine full-page Flemish illuminations of the same period, which had been added later.

At the end of the first day Sotheby's had put up for sale two illuminated manuscripts which were the property of Henry Yates Thompson, probably the foremost British collector of such items. Further important sales from his collection were to take place in 1919, 1920 and 1921. By now Barlow must have become something of an authority on Caxtons. Certainly Hobson knew a great deal about them, for Sotheby's had handled rather more than fifty books by the great printer since Tom Hodge had sold the firm to the new partners.

The most remarkable event in the four-day Huth Sale in July occurred on the third day when the sale of a small quarto volume which contained *The True Chronicle History of King Leir*, of 1605, a first edition of the play from which Shakespeare is supposed to have taken the outline and some of the incidents for his own *King Lear*, fetched £2,470. The very same copy had been sold for £210 at the Halliwell Sale in 1865, and another copy, admittedly rather cropped, had fetched only £480 at Wellington Street in 1905. Both are now in the British Museum. This price was due to another duel between George Smith and Quaritch, though in this instance Quaritch won. In general the two dealers dominated the whole sale, and the prices they paid were regarded as phenomenal in their day.

The Realities of War

WHEN the gavel came down for the last time at the end of the 1914 summer season, the partners must have felt a great sense of achievement. The hard work had paid off and the financial yield had been substantial. For a firm so small, the gain in public stature had been far-reaching. Among those who mattered, the name 'Sotheby's' now meant as much in New York as it did in London. But during that very week when the sales had finished in Wellington Street, and during which the clerks there had been adding up and checking a record season's totals, the clouds over Europe had darkened. At the end of June the Archduke Francis Ferdinand of Austria and his wife had been assassinated at Sarajevo by a Bosnian revolutionary. On 20 July the French President had paid a panic visit to Russia. On the 23rd there came the Austro-Hungarian ultimatum to Serbia. The next day Sir Edward Grey had proposed four-power mediations on the Balkan Crisis, but nothing came of it. On the 26th the Austrians mobilised along the Russian frontier (and there was the threat of an Irish rising in Dublin). On the 28th Austro-Hungary declared war on Serbia. On 1 August Germany declared war on Russia, the French mobilised and Italy announced her neutrality. On 2 August Germany occupied Luxembourg and sent an ultimatum to the Belgians to allow the passage of troops through their country – *and* the Russians invaded East Prussia. On 3 August Germany declared war on France and invaded Belgium. On 4 August Britain declared war on Germany – and the United States declared her neutrality. Four days later British troops landed in France. For the time being rare books were of secondary interest. The golden glow was over.

Barlow had spent much of this critical period in the House of Commons. He had to take most of the important decisions affecting Sotheby's there, and to communicate with his partners by note. Once war was declared his first duty was to his constituents. He rushed up to Salford. There, as in the country generally, the primary need was for more men to strengthen the army. Barlow became chairman of the committee controlling the Salford Battalion, and here for the time being he exchanged the sound of the falling hammer for the rhythmic tramp of marching feet.

He was in his element in the pressures and crises of wartime conditions. A glutton for hard work at the best of times, he now worked indefatigably round the clock, taking on additional duties. His love of organisation was stretched to the full. At Westminster he had politics, he felt close to the seat of power, and his competence was recognised as he slowly moved towards the Cabinet. At Wellington Street he found himself presiding more frequently at sales; he planned the move to Bond Street and superintended all the reconstruction work necessary. At Salford he spent his time recruiting, equipping, improvising, and building barracks – a highly intelligent amateur helping to create a professional army.

The staff at Wellington Street was quickly depleted as able-bodied men volunteered and disappeared into the armed services. Of the partners, Warre soon joined the King's Royal Rifle Corps. He spent some time at the front in France, was wounded in 1915 after winning a Military Cross, and was then transferred to administration and intelligence duties at the War Office. Later, he returned to France, served at General H.Q., was mentioned in despatches twice, received the O.B.E. and retired as a Major in 1919. Coins and the occasional antiquities that came in, were kept for Warre to attend to when he came into his office on his occasional periods of leave from France. One gets the impression that such sales were only held between battles.

There is a marvellous story told by Tim Wilder of a war-time meeting between Warre and a small, rotund Sotheby porter called Bill Addison, a natural comic, who had been called up and sent to France in the Pioneers. Digging trenches beside a road one day he looked up to see a company of infantry approaching, an officer leading, mounted on his horse, Captain Warre – his old guv'nor! Forgetting all his military training Addison scrambled out from his trench, waved his arms frantically and shouted 'Aye-aye, sir; aye-aye, sir!' Crestfallen, he saw his old guv'nor calmly riding away, taking no notice whatever. A long time later, back in 'civvies', after hostilities had ceased, *Major* Warre one day stopped Addison who had survived the holocaust in France, in the sale-room. 'Oh, by the way, Addison', he said, 'the correct thing to do in the Army when you see an officer passing at the head of a company, is to stand to attention and salute – *not* to jump up and down shouting "Aye-aye, sir".' The story epitomised all the attitudes of its day.

At first Hobson, alone of the three partners, remained in the office full-time and in a letter to Barlow he offered to 'mind the shop for the duration', if Warre and Barlow were going to be involved exclusively in military duties. In the event the Foreign Office sought out his services and for the rest of the war he divided his time between Sotheby's and working there. One of his final, official duties was the preparation of briefs for eventual peace negotiations.

Following the outbreak of war, sales were abandoned altogether for the rest of 1914. For longer than anyone could remember, a whole autumn season passed without a single bid being recorded at Wellington Street. Tom Hodge was mostly left in charge to hold the reins. Late in September of 1914 Barlow wrote to him from the Salford Battalion Headquarters at the Pendleton Town Hall: '*Re War*: I have a big job on hand with the Battalion. I am now under orders from the War Office to build them a camp.' He expressed the view that it would be impossible to have sales again until the spring, or perhaps not even until the autumn, of the following year. Many booksellers still had extended credit, but with the foreign exchanges mostly closed Barlow feared that 'our booksellers have practically no market for their goods at all'. It was a bleak outlook.

By February of 1915 Barlow's letters showed that there were first two, then three Salford Battalions, and later their number was to rise to five. On 22 March 1915 he again wrote to Tom Hodge:

> I am very much rushed this week but I must get to town somehow, and it will probably be Thursday arriving at about 1.15. I have to get 700 or so of my third Battalion off to Penmaen-mawr on Saturday. The Kitchener Review yesterday was a great show I am glad to say. Being clearly quite impartial I can say that the Salfords were *splendid*!
>
> I wrote to Hobson to ask if there was any news of the Graham or Huntington payments? If not, Brown Bros. [Sotheby's New York agents] should be wired to see how matters stand.
>
> K [Lord Kitchener][1] was very complimentary yesterday but said I must go on and raise another Battalion and so complete the *BRIGADE*!
>
> I much doubt if I can get to you at Easter: many thanks all the same.

Barlow continued to spend a good deal of time at Salford throughout 1915 and 1916, though progressively less than in those first frantic months. He succeeded eventually in building a great hutment for the Brigade of five Battalions of Lancashire Fusiliers that had been raised, clothed and equipped under his personal aegis. He was knighted in 1918 specifically for this achievement.

Women at Sotheby's

As Barlow had predicted, sales did not start again until the spring of 1915, and there were precious few of them: one at the end of February, one in March, one in April and one in May. There were six in June and seven in July, one in October, none in November and ten in December. Twenty-eight in all, compared with 108 in the last full year of 1913. Quite a number of them were executors' sales that had to take place in order to wind up estates. A surprisingly high proportion were sales of works of art. By today's standards these included very acceptable collections of English glass, pottery, porcelain, needlework, silver, Japanese prints and netsuke, minor Old Masters, oriental porcelain, and antiquities from Egypt, Rome, Greece and Persia. The prices realised at this time were miserable, judged by any criteria, as indeed they were for books and manuscripts. All in all, 1915 was sheer, unmitigated disaster, and if it had not been for the staggered payments for private sales still coming in, the outlook for the future would have been very gloomy indeed. This state of affairs, of course, did not apply to Sotheby's alone. It was equally true of the whole of the art and antique trade, as well as of booksellers, but it seems to have been some sort of rallying point for Tom Hodge. He had been through such crises before. He set about rebuilding confidence and regenerating business. He helped booksellers to dispose of stock as far as this was possible for him through his contacts with

1. Field-Marshal Kitchener had become Secretary of State for War in 1914. He was almost alone in envisaging a long war, and succeeded in increasing the British Army from six regular and fourteen territorial divisions to seventy divisions – nearly 3,000,000 men having voluntarily joined the colours between 1914 and 1916. He it was in the famous poster balefully pointing his finger from every wall, saying 'Your Country needs YOU!'

collectors both in England and America, and he patiently gathered in the large amounts of money that were owed to Sotheby's. He began to prepare the ground for an improved 1916, but there was one inescapable factor of wartime conditions which he found it almost impossible to accept – and this was that women had to be engaged in increasing numbers to replace some of the men who had joined up.

In 1915 Barlow had taken on two young female secretaries for himself and for Geoffrey Hobson, Adriana Lachlan and Edith Bourne, though he insisted that they should wear dark blue overalls in order to make themselves as inconspicuous as possible. They were both lively and pretty girls and their arrival caused something of a stir in that all-male world, where no woman had ever previously been seen, the porters having always undertaken even such apparently feminine chores as cleaning and dusting. In 1916 Barlow took things even further: he employed a female book cataloguer, an altogether exceptional young woman of 33 who was to rise to dizzy heights in the rare book world by the end of her long career. Emily Millicent Sowerby had been to Girton College in Cambridge, had got a good degree, had spent eighteen months working for that legendary antiquarian bookseller of Polish origin, Wilfred Voynich, who ran a book shop in Shaftsbury Avenue, and finally she had worked for MI5 in Paris for many months under Sir Denison Ross. Barlow made the minutest enquiries about the background of new staff whom he employed. He wrote off for as many references as he could obtain and there were generally one, if not two, gruelling interviews with the prospective candidates. In this case, Barlow again impressed upon Miss Sowerby the need for the dark blue overall so that she would remain as inconspicuous as possible, and, most important, that never, but never, was she to catch a man's eye in the sale-room.

The new cataloguer thoroughly enjoyed her work. 'It is the most stimulating and educating experience it is possible to have. Every kind of book or manuscript, in every possible language, that is ever collected by anyone comes through his hands', she wrote.[1] And she loved Sotheby's. 'Sotheby's was a most remarkable firm. I was too inexperienced at that time to realise its unusual character but life has taught me many things since and I take my hat off to it with a low bow whenever I think of it. The two most outstanding characteristics of the firm which have never ceased to impress me, as I have never met anything like it in my later experience,[2] were its absolute honesty – it bent completely backwards in its consideration of its clients – and, secondly, its treatment of its employees, which was most extraordinarily in advance of the time and, as far as I know, still is at the present day. The dignity of the firm was upheld by the fact that the partners themselves were the auctioneers and conducted the sales.'

She plunged into her work without any break, immediately after her return

1. In her light-hearted and altogether delightful memoirs, *Rare People and Rare Books* (London, 1967).
2. She moved to America working first at the New York Public Library, then for many years for Dr. Rosenbach, and eventually in the Library of Congress.

from Paris, and although she writes that soon after, 'I had extremely bad news from the front and was suffering from shock and only wanted to bury myself in work so as not to have time to think', Barlow insisted that it was not possible for *any* human being to do proper work without a break and a change, and that she should take at once at least ten days of her three weeks paid annual holiday. She also recalls that at Whitsuntide the staff 'was always given a full week off to relax after the hard work of the winter and to collect their strength for the forthcoming season'. There was a host of other ways in which Barlow showed consideration for the welfare of the staff that was decades ahead of its time, and which stood him in good stead when he became Minister of Labour.

She soon realised that book cataloguers needed to be not only accurate and objective but also to have a finely developed sense of commercial values. It was cataloguers who fixed reserves, and reserves were essential to protect clients' interests against dealers who worked in 'rings' and who took part in the 'knock-out'. These activities are the scourge of reputable auctioneering and were then widely practised, though to a greater extent in provincial and country sales than in London. The first stage of 'knock-out' was an arrangement made by a group of dealers not to bid against each other so that lots would be knocked down far below their true value. After the sale the dealers involved – the 'ring' – would retire to the nearest pub and hold an entirely unlicensed auction of their own of the goods they had just bought, buying them from each other at their proper value and then sharing out the proceeds among themselves.

Miss Sowerby thoroughly enjoyed pitting her wits against the more seamy side of the book trade. Another unscrupulous practice by certain dealers was to make nonsense of the spirit of the ruling that went right back to the first book auctions, that if a book was imperfect and not as catalogued, the buyer could return it and get his money back. As we have seen, no conditions of sale appeared in Samuel Baker's first catalogues, and it was the more cautious George Leigh who insisted on their inclusion. By the 1770s five standard conditions of sale were included in every catalogue. The third of these read: 'The books are presumed to be perfect unless otherwise expressed; but if upon collating at the Place of Sale, any should prove imperfect, the Purchaser will be at Liberty to take or reject them', and with minor variations over two whole centuries the same condition applies to this very day, except that the period allowed for making returns increased first to a week, then to ten days, later a fortnight and today it stands at three weeks. Time in an auction house, of course, is money; complete collation takes time[1] so it was clearly impossible to check every page of every title and occasionally books *did* slip through in an imperfect state, though these were usually the less valuable titles. Lots so returned were included in later sales and sold 'with all faults' and usually without reserve. There were dealers who were quite prepared to bid a book up to some vastly inflated price in order to have this figure included in *Book Prices*

1. One of the most reliable collators at Sotheby's was the first tea-lady Barlow took on during the First World War, who did this work in between making tea for the staff in mid-morning and mid-afternoon!

Current or *Book Auction Records*, in the knowledge that they were going to return it. This inflated price could then be quoted to gullible customers who came along later. Miss Sowerby's defensive dexterity in these matters was clearly recognised by Geoffrey Hobson – whom she much admired, though she was a little over-awed by him – and he put her in charge of examining books returned as imperfect by purchasers. Her greatest joy was to tell them that they had made a mistake and that the book was quite perfect. 'How well I got to know every means of making a book temporarily imperfect', she wrote, 'in such a way that its original perfect condition could be quickly restored, or, alternatively, of creating a negligible imperfection, but one that according to the extremely high standards of Sotheby's would make the book returnable should the purchaser wish! I soon got to know the dealers in both classes, and knew what to expect when any lot was knocked down for more than its value. One dealer was considered to have the finest set of tools for making worm holes of anyone in the trade!'

Other dealers tore off tiny corners of a leaf in valuable manuscripts or *incunabula* that could be easily patched back. Another was an artist at removing whole plates with a wet piece of string. On one occasion a dealer insisted on returning a book described as water-stained on the grounds that the stains were made not by water but by beer. Her most memorable battle was over an edition of Goya's *Los Caprichos* returned by a dealer who had paid £300 for a book considered then to be worth £15. The reason was that the volume lacked a title page. After consulting no less an authority than Campbell Dodgson at the British Museum it was discovered that this particular edition *had* no title page. To his chagrin the dealer had to keep it. This incident caused great jubilation within the book department because the book had belonged to an impoverished old lady who had been delighted to get so much more for it than she had expected.

Wartime conditions, the arrival of an increasing number of women, not only as secretaries and an 'expert' but also as clerks and charladies, in fact change all around him in every way, finally precipitated a crisis between Tom Hodge and the other partners. Although he continued to take sales right up to the end, both Millicent Sowerby and Edith Bourne remember him as an uncompromising Victorian who could not adapt to a changing world and kept himself entirely aloof from the rest of the staff. He disappeared without as much as a by-your-leave or goodbye at the end of 1916. The parting when it came was marred by a piece of ineptitude on Barlow's part. He insisted on advertising in the press that Hodge was no longer associated with Sotheby's. Although this was legally justified, one cannot be surprised that Hodge took it as a slight that he never forgot,[1] and as is so often the case, once he had left the business which he had fostered for so long – victim of the change he himself had brought about – his

---

1. He did, however, forgive. Barlow realised that he had been highly insensitive and after various gestures on his part, cordial relations between the two men were finally restored at the time of Barlow's own retirement from the firm in 1929 (see page 255).

life lost its *raison d'être*. He retired to a long life of bee-keeping at his house in Sussex, acting as magistrate, and gentle peregrinations to his beloved Harrogate and Torquay. His friends in the press briefly mourned his departure – they had little enough information to go on. 'He can claim to have obtained record prices for notable books,' wrote one, 'and had few, if any, equals in the charming way in which he induced bidders to go much above the prices they had originally fixed as their limit . . . the fortunes of the firm will always be largely identified with the two Hodges, father and son.'

To take Tom's place Barlow brought in his sister, Evelyn, a highly competent, gracious and unassuming woman, who had acted as secretary to her father, the Dean of Peterborough, and had travelled with him all over the world, including long journeys to India, Egypt, Palestine (as it then was), Russia and Canada. She had had some training as a public speaker and addressed innumerable meetings of women all over India on the subject of educational reform. Her principal task at Sotheby's was to look after the increasing number of girls on the staff, but after a few months within the firm she began to take sales and soon became quite capable in the rostrum. She was at that time the only woman to hold a licence as a 'chattel auctioneer' and was much interviewed in consequence. In fact, her specific responsibility was the Pictures and Prints Department, but she also took sales of coins and Japanese art, and developed a particular penchant for dealing with the idiosyncrasies of oriental buyers.

In her time she became a leading Soroptimist [the rather gentler predecessor of 'women's lib') and lectured widely on the subject. She was always encouraging girls to go into the auction business as a career. She maintained that women had as good, if not better, a sense of values than men; and often they had more taste, which was of particular importance in art auctioneering. It is said that the Institute of Auctioneers opened their qualifying examination to women largely through her indirect insistence. She was never a dominant figure, though, like her brother, she did not suffer fools gladly. She became a full partner with a sizeable holding of shares soon after the war and after fifteen years retired in 1933 at the height of the slump. Her sister Margaret also came to work at Sotheby's a little later. She seems to have been largely concerned with the plans for the move to Bond Street, but she was not a success and did not stay very long.

12

The Move and After

1916 saw the gradual re-establishment of a proper and profitable sales pattern, especially as far as books and manuscript material was concerned and 1917 started off unexpectedly strongly with various medium-sized libraries, such as those of Victor van de Weyer, the Earl of Mexborough and Colonel W. F. Prideaux. There were some good print sales, and among the autographs sold in March were the famous *Napier Papers* dating from 1456 to 1857, which belonged to the Dowager Lady Napier. There were also Major R. W. Duff's *Abercromby Papers*, which consisted of that British Commander's correspondence in America between March and November 1758 and which were sold as one lot for the high price of £1,300. The spring season, as was always the case during each of the war years, was dominated by the gigantic Red Cross Sale at Christie's which in some years lasted as long as three weeks. All the objects were donated and they were often of superb quality; many were put up for a second sale by the first purchaser in order to raise more money.

The most exciting spring sale at Wellington Street was of the Watts-Dunton Library between 13 and 16 March. Theodore Watts-Dunton was the former solicitor and literary critic who rescued Algernon Charles Swinburne when he was *in extremis* and housed the poet for nearly thirty years. Watts-Dunton's beautiful young widow with her long, red hair frequently came to Wellington Street to help in the arrangement of the sale of the Swinburne relics and regaled the staff with long accounts of life with her husband and Swinburne at their Putney home, 'The Pines'. Thomas J. Wise, however, had bullied Watts-Dunton into selling him the best of Swinburne's autographs and books immediately after the poet's death in 1909, and despite the publicity for the sale, the 1,204 lots only fetched £2,761.

The partners now decided that, despite the uncertainties of the times and the gloom of war, it would be impolitic to delay the move from Wellington Street any longer. In any case, the leases there were due to run out that year, and another factor that confirmed their decision was that even a temporary renewal of the leases would be unwise because the old premises were to be demolished in a London County Council scheme to widen Waterloo Bridge and the access roads to it. The reconstruction of the Bond Street premises therefore was set in motion, under the aegis of the architect J. S. Gibson with Dove Brothers of Islington as builders, and proceeded reasonably well despite the wartime shortages of materials. Things were made easier by the fact that the greater part of the new premises was empty: the Doré Gallery having closed down at the beginning of the war. What Doré paintings were left at the time were shipped to America. For many years they were thought to have been torpedoed and sunk, but they were eventually found, returned to England, and – with a touch of irony – sold at Christie's in 1964. The largest ones had suffered badly from being cut from their stretchers and rolled.

The date fixed for the move was midsummer 1917. A few weeks beforehand the first bombing of London took place from Zeppelins which came over at night, and the Strand area suffered. There was relatively little damage but a lot of broken glass in the streets. Sotheby's itself suffered no damage beyond broken glass from a falling shell. A few bomb fragments were found and treasured for a while. They were somehow symbolic of the end of an era.

So were two regular visitors to the sale-room who were soon to disappear. The first was Lord Stamfordham, formerly Queen Victoria's secretary and later private secretary to King George V, whose duty it was to keep a watchful eye on all manuscripts concerning Crown and State which might appear in a sale. He was a tall, upright, venerable figure with a courtly dignity and the most delightful old-world manners. On one occasion before the move he spotted a collection of private and political papers found in the house of a long-dead Foreign Minister, that had been entrusted to Sotheby's for sale by his descendants. The sale was stopped and the papers removed to the Foreign Office, even though the war which they concerned had taken place a hundred years earlier at the time of Napoleon I.[1] If, in contrast, Sotheby's was selling modern books of which the copyright had not expired, during the three days when they were on view before the sale they would be scrutinised by inspectors whose job it was to make certain that there were no illegal Mosher imprints among them. Mr. Mosher, a printer in the United States, was at that time making himself a nice profit by printing editions of English books copyrighted in England but not in the United States, so that although he was breaking no law in his own country, he was depriving the authors and copyright owners of their rightful dues. Mosher imprints were illegal in England at that time and could not be sold at auction. This form of piracy stopped when the copyright law was changed.

The installation of the famous black, lion-headed goddess Sekmet, from Egypt over the front entrance at Bond Street from a similar position at Wellington Street, heralded the beginning of the actual move. It was a long operation. After nearly a century in the same premises at Wellington Street the quantity of unlabelled detritus was immense. All this had to be inspected and sorted. In the end, for example, it was decided to remove to Bond Street a vast quantity of unclaimed items that had not been sold or were considered of 'No Sales Value' because the owners might mount sizeable claims against the firm, even though the items had seemed unwanted for years. Thus one lady, after a complete

1. A similar event occurred in July 1935 when the Foreign Office caused the postponement of the sale of the papers belonging to Lord Stuart de Rothesay, who had been British Ambassador at the time of Waterloo. There were other such hazards: also in 1935 the Central Chancery of the order of Knighthood at St. James's Palace intervened in a sale of regalia of the Orders of the Garter and the Bath, the property of Princess Brassow, widow of the Grand Duke Michael Alexandrovich, brother of the last Tzar.

silence of four years, accused Sotheby's of losing her 'Michelangelo' and was about to sue the firm for £10,000, when the picture was found at the last moment. She had not even put her name and address on it, but had told a porter that she would be back for it in an hour.

All the planning of the move took place with military precision under Barlow's personal supervision. His meticulous preparations resulted in a very smooth changeover and everything fitted neatly into its new place at Bond Street. This, of course, was an occasion when the skill of the porters came into its own, and the training of generations paid off handsomely. James Hayman, foreman porter, whose father had had the same job before him, his brother Arthur and the other porters worked minor miracles of dismantlement and re-erection.

An advertising campaign was launched in the spring to announce the move. Thus the May issue of the *Connoisseur* carried a full page stating that 'Messrs. Sotheby, Wilkinson & Hodge will, after Whitsuntide, be leaving their premises at 13 Wellington Street, Strand, W.C., where they have been established since 1819, for new and more commodious premises at 34 and 35 New Bond Street. Several important sales have already been arranged to take place in the new premises'. Among them was a fine engravings sale which included 'a superb set of Turner's *Liber studiorum* from the collection of the late T. J. Barrett, Esq., of Hampstead' on 23 and 24 July; a very good autograph and manuscript sale on 2 and 4 July; the sixth portion of the Huth Library consisting of the letters N to P, and including 'Illuminated Psalters and Manuscripts...' on 11 to 13 and 16 to 18 July; and, finally, and this was the real coup, 'Superb prints and drawings, with two fine pictures and two magnificent suits of armour from Wilton House, near Salisbury, the property of the Right Honble. the Earl of Pembroke and Montgomery...'. Illustrations of the two famous suits of armour flanked the advertisement like steel pillars. But more of that sale anon.

The final sale at Wellington Street took place on 25 May 1917. The *Daily Telegraph* wrote: 'the last day in the old "Mecca of Booklovers" was celebrated by an address from Mr. Barlow, the senior partner in the firm, and by various speeches from enthusiastic patrons of an establishment which has always been conducted on high lines of policy... in its history dating back over 170 years.... To move as far as New Bond Street is a positive migration.... The last day of sale produced as its main features the disposal of a 1667 first edition of Milton's *Paradise Lost* for the sum of £164 and the purchase of a first edition of Thackeray's *Vanity Fair*, in twenty parts, with the original wrappers, for £80.' The article continued not only with an outline of famous Sotheby sales but also stressed the extraordinary difficulties of the book trade in 1917 with desperate shortages of paper and strawboards for binding. It lamented prophetically 'that if the present stringency continues we shall see most of our novels appearing in paper covers'. It complained that it was an unhappy time for lovers of *modern* books when prices were rising so fast, but 'to collect old books is to be released... from restrictions of time and space. The booklover who frequents the auctions of Messrs. Sotheby and acquires the prize on which he has set his heart lives in a world remote from all the mundane troubles of paper shortage and absence of labour, and immune from the barbarous penalties of a European war'.

Other journals, including the *Connoisseur*, were at the same time complaining about the total call-up of all able-bodied members of the antique trade because 'of the prevalent idea that their occupation is without utility and can be completely dispensed with without loss to the country'. The point was made forcefully that theirs was a knowledge acquired only after years of practical experience. The *Connoisseur* explained that high taxation was forcing massive sales of such things as antiques and that most of these were going to America and 'unless we retain experts to handle the matter, American collectors are likely to secure bargains that the country can ill afford to part with'. Military selection tribunals were asked to take note, and one gathers that to a limited extent the point was heeded.

The cataloguing staff had been given a few days leave of absence and sales were suspended during the whole of June while the disruption was at its height. The staff re-assembled in time for what Millicent Sowerby describes as a 'magnificent house-warming'. 'This', she wrote, 'took the form of a grand exhibition of the work done by the wounded and invalided Servicemen in the Lord Roberts's workshops. Each member of the staff was assigned special duties, and a list posted so that we should all know where we belonged and what to do during the period of the exhibition.' It was organised by Sir Algernon Tudor-Craig, the great heraldic expert. Both he, and later his son, advised Sotheby's in the field of armorial matters. Miss Sowerby describes how for once she was allowed to discard the unspeakable dark blue overall and to don her very best Paris dress. She was posted at the entrance to warn the partners of the arrival of Queen Mary who had promised to attend the opening ceremony after the speech of welcome by Lord Lansdowne was over. But his Lordship's address was so protracted that Barlow could not get away in time, and the Queen very nearly had to make an unaccompanied entry. However, Miss Sowerby curtsied low and long – 'Never was seen such a profound curtsey as I made that day' – and Barlow arrived in the nick of time to show the Queen around the premises. Later she became a frequent visitor and a great personal friend of one of the partners.

Geoffrey Hobson had a fine sense of the historic and decided that the occasion of the move was a good opportunity for the publication of a brief history of the firm. Christie's had the monumental, if boring, *Memorials of Christie's* by *The Times* sale-room correspondent, William Roberts,[1] to recommend to those of its clients who wanted to know more of the firm's antecedents. Sotheby's had

1. With whom Sotheby's quarrelled viciously in late 1922, when he published a scoop in *The Times* based on the Burdett-Coutts sale. *All* the sale-room correspondents knew the story concerned, but to a man they volunteered to suppress it out of respect for the dying head cataloguer – A. G. E. Phillips. Afterwards the staff at Bond Street cut Roberts dead, and Roberts almost invariably panned Sotheby's.

nothing. *Notes on the History of Sotheby's* was the result and appeared in October of that year. It was regrettably brief. There were twenty pages of text and one appendix listing the 310 most important sales since the firm's foundation in 1744 and a second appendix which contained an analysis of the most important recent sales, such as the library of Sir Thomas Phillipps (sixteen parts); the coin collection of H. Montague (eleven parts); the coins, manuscripts and books of the Earl of Ashburnham (seven parts); the immense coin collection of J. G. Murdoch (nine parts); and finally, the eight sales that had taken place up to the end of 1917 of the Huth Library. There was a charmingly understated footnote on the *Bibliotheca Phillippica*: 'A considerable portion of the collection is still unsold'. By 1979 the number of sales from this greatest of all libraries had exceeded sixty, and still it was not exhausted.

Hobson mentioned some of the firm's near neighbours in Bond Street such as the old-established bookseller, F. S. Ellis (the friend of William Morris and the Pre-Raphaelites). He also referred to Frank T. Sabin at 172 New Bond Street, and Bernard Quaritch at 11 Grafton Street. He might have mentioned further that Colnaghi's had been just down the road at 144/6 Old Bond Street since 1912; that Agnew's had been at No. 39 (now 43) Old Bond Street since 1875, and that another well-known firm of fine art dealers, Vicars Bros., had been at No. 12 Old Bond Street for many years. Sotheby's new next-door neighbours were Mademoiselle Elsie, Court Milliner, and Alfred Clark (silversmith to every conceivable sort of royalty), at No. 33, and Madame M. Henry, Court Dressmaker, and Arthur & Co., another silversmith, at No. 36.

Millicent Sowerby regarded the cataloguers' new quarters as 'very comfortable', and Mr. Wilder charmingly describes Barlow's pride in the firm's new home. The chairman enjoyed showing important visitors round the building and pointing out the improvements. Smoking was, of course, forbidden, and on one of his tours of inspection Barlow saw a large man smoking a cigarette. To the porter on duty he said 'Haven't you told that man to put his cigarette out?' 'I have told him twice, sir, but he takes no notice.' Approaching the man, Barlow, who was only 5ft. 4in., looked up and said, 'I understand my porter has twice asked you to put your cigarette out'. With that, he snatched it from the man's mouth, ground it under foot and ordered the offender from the place. The 'No Smoking' rule was not, of course, an innovation. Tom Hodge had been known to say pointedly during a sale, to the foreman, 'James, either that cigar goes out or the smoker does!'

With the removal to Bond Street, Sotheby's truly entered a new era, and the partners' firm decision to widen the scope of what was sold proved wise in the extreme. For it was not long before the turnover of the works of art department began to outstrip the sales of books and literary property that had been the firm's speciality for so long.

13

The Wilton Controversy

IT must have seemed to the staff that they had barely settled down after all the disruption of the move when one of the most important non-book sales since the new partners had taken over was upon them in July.

For months there had been protracted negotiations over this with the Pembroke family, who had already sold their library so successfully in July 1914. Now other treasures were to come under the hammer to raise more money for death duties. Many of these were entailed as heirlooms to Wilton House, the family's ancestral home since the sixteenth century, and permission had to be obtained by the Trustees from the Court of Chancery to dispose of this property under the terms of the Settled Land Acts of 1882 and 1884. Apparently the Court was in a position to fix minimum valuations below which the items concerned could not be sold, and these were immensely high by the standards ruling at the time.

Montague Barlow had sounded out the sales possibilities in America. Twice he had risked the dangers of a wartime trans-Atlantic crossing to publicise the event. Joseph Duveen responded cautiously. The Metropolitan Museum seemed enthusiastic. There were other dealers with interested clients. A note in the sale catalogue issued later made it quite clear that on instructions from the Earl of Pembroke, Sotheby's had the right to dispose of items before the sale by private treaty if opportunity offered.

What was it that aroused all this excitement? William Herbert, brother-in-law of King Henry VIII, was created the 1st Earl of Pembroke in 1557. He had been given the abbey and lands at Wilton following the dissolution of the monasteries by the King in 1554, and had straightaway built a house, worthy of his position, upon it. Sotheby's were dealing with the 15th Earl who had only recently inherited the title. Many of the intervening earls had been ardent collectors and patrons of the arts: but the 8th Earl, Thomas, was particularly outstanding in this respect. In addition there had been ceaseless additions of artistic property through marriages, spoils of war and travel. The Trustees decided that some prints and drawings should be sold; a tapestry or two; a few of the great paintings and – most important of all – two famous suits of armour that had been at Wilton since late in the sixteenth century.

Wilton was unbelievably rich in armour. There are various historic accounts of this. The earliest of these, dating from 1635, is one in which a 'Captain of the Trained Bands' tells the story of his visit to Wilton with two friends. He describes some of the very fine suits of armour he saw there, both of English and foreign origin, and estimated that there was enough armour altogether 'to furnish completely and set out 1,000 foote and horse'. Other families had collected armour out of historic interest or curiosity: the Pembrokes had acquired it for purely practical purposes, and had simply hung on to it. From an early guide book to Wilton (the first was published in 1737) we know that the finest suits of armour were located in special niches created for them when the first house was re-built by Inigo Jones after its destruction by fire in 1647. Later on, breastplates and helmets, and other bits and pieces, were hung all over the house as decorations, but the bulk of the armour was stored in a huge barn on the estate. In the early part of the present century an old servant at Wilton remembered that the harvest wagons passed over it, crushing it beneath their wheels, and that, in order to get rid of it, a considerable amount of it was buried in the garden in the middle of the nineteenth century.[1]

So Sotheby's proudly announced many weeks before the sale was due to take place, that the celebrated Armour of the Constable of France, Anne de Montmorency (1492–1567), worn by him when he was wounded and taken prisoner at the Battle of St. Quentin in August 1557, as well as that of Louis de Bourbon, Duc de Montpensier (1513–82), taken prisoner with Anne de Montmorency at St. Quentin, was to be sold at their new premises, 34 and 35 New Bond Street, on 10 July. 'These two magnificent suits', the catalogue said, 'are among the greatest treasures of the armoury at Wilton House. It may indeed be questioned whether any suits of armour in the hands of other private owners can rival their combination of historic interest with beauty of design and craftsmanship; none perhaps can show an unbroken descent in the same home and the same family for over 350 years.'

The provenance seemed unimpeachable. The suits had been described thus in print since early in the eighteenth century, and they had been one of the star attractions at the Tudor Exhibition held in London as recently as 1890. A. C. R. Carter wrote them up in glowing terms on 23 May 1917 in the *Daily Telegraph*. Geoffrey Hobson was delighted and wrote to Carter at length to thank him for the useful publicity. 'A word of congratulation and appreciation on your admirable article in to-day's paper. You have taught me to expect much from you, but I was surprised both by the matter and the manner of your notice of the Wilton treasures. The information about Montmorency himself and recent sales of armour, was extraordinarily interesting, and selected with your unerring eye for the picturesque and opportune. The "Telegraph" should be proud of having such a contributor, and you yourself, if I may say so, should be proud of a paper which will publish such an article at a time like this, and help to keep alive an interest in art and literature.'

A week later More Adey, editor of the *Burlington Magazine*, telephoned Hobson and then wrote to confirm his request that Mr. Charles ffoulkes and Lord Dillon should come to Bond Street to examine the armour in detail so that they could write it up in the 'Forthcoming Sales' column of the magazine. Ffoulkes was Keeper of the Armoury of the Tower, and later that year was to become the first Curator of the Imperial War Museum (which post he held until 1933), and Lord Dillon had been the first Curator of the Armoury of the Tower from 1892 to 1913. Both men were thus formidable experts on armour,

1. A later attempt to dig it up failed to find the hoard.

and naturally Hobson and Barlow were delighted that the *Burlington* was taking the sale so seriously.

In the meantime requests for pre-auction sales were coming in thick and fast. It was public knowledge that the late Duc d'Aumale had offered the Pembrokes a vast price for both suits of armour in order to restore to France such important historic items: in fact, a note in the sale catalogue made reference to this. The Duke's agent in the matter now tried again.

Another major item in the sale was a picture by Andrea Mantegna of *Judith and Holofernes*, a tiny panel measuring only 12in. by 7in. It had the most impeccable antecedents. It had been given to Philip, the 4th Earl of Pembroke, by no less a personage than Charles I in exchange for a portrait of a young woman by Bellini and a picture by Parmigiano.[1] In Charles's day the picture was ascribed to Raphael, even though Mantegna's name appeared at the back of the panel. For some reason the attribution to Mantegna had recently been challenged.

Then there was a marvellous portrait by Rembrandt of his aged mother. It showed her reading a book through a pair of gold-rimmed glasses which were perched right on the end of her nose. This painting had been bought by Thomas, the Collector Earl, in Holland about 1685. In addition, among the drawings were what today we would regard as unbelievably important items by Dürer, Filippino Lippi, Correggio, Antonio del Pollaiuolo, Cosimo Rosselli, Veronese, Leonardo and Van Dyck.

Lord Pembroke himself was on active service in France so Barlow's contacts with the family were mostly with the Countess of Pembroke, the Earl's wife. Her telegraphic replies to Barlow's letters were delightfully succinct. When first informed that Duveen wanted to buy a tapestry (not eventually included in the catalogue), she cabled back: 'Owner dislikes dealer. Will give permission to inspect if offer is firm'. When Barlow made various complicated suggestions about a price she simply cabled back: '£8,000 clear. Lady Pembroke.' Duveen also wanted the Mantegna of *Judith and Holofernes*. Lord Pembroke himself had initially thought in terms of £35,000, a vast sum for those days, and the press was discussing this sale before the auction at a price of around £40,000. But the carping about the correctness of its attribution must have affected the issue because Duveen eventually clinched the sale with Barlow at £12,000 on the day before the picture was due to come up at auction. Duveen was very proud of this purchase, with its provenance going back to Charles I. Berenson wrote it up as an important new arrival to the States in the following year, and the picture was sold to Joseph Widener shortly afterwards. It is now in the National Gallery in Washington, catalogued as a Mantegna.

Another collector who was very anxious to acquire a number of prints and drawings from the sale was the young Lord Lascelles. Like Lord Pembroke he was serving in the trenches in France. His adviser and agent was the Finnish art historian, Tancred Borenius, but between them they underestimated the

1. We have the authority of Abraham van der Doort, who prepared an inventory of Charles I's paintings, for this fact.

competition there would be at the sale and the limits they agreed on were totally inadequate in the event. Lord Lascelles was particularly anxious to acquire a Veronese drawing of *Venice Crowned by Fame*. Although Borenius bid up to £1,600 (in place of the 500 guineas agreed, because he had failed to buy any of the other lots Lord Lascelles had selected) he got pipped at the post by a bid of £1,650 from Agnew's. When he got this news Lord Lascelles pencilled a note from France in which he wrote:

> Of course I am disappointed at not getting any of the drawings. But I expect you were quite right to stop the bidding for the Veronese at £1,600. It becomes a question whether or not I shall offer Agnew a profit of 10% on his bargain at once. I am inclined to do this – but I should like to know what you advise. It seems to me to be the only one I need really regret and which is worth running after. . . .
>
> I have had a bad time lately – for 36 hours they never stopped shelling my headquarters excepting once for two hours. They fell as fast as 72 per minute at one time and varied from that rate to about 1 in five minutes – but never a rest. In the middle the enemy tried to attack! but he never got as far as our wire opposite me, I am thankful to say.

It was remarkable that anyone could concern himself with building up a collection of Italian art under such circumstances.

The four-day sale started placidly enough on the Thursday at one o'clock. Prices only moved into higher gear when it came to a series of Dürer engravings: a slightly stained early impression of *Adam and Eve* went for £88; *Saint Jerome in his Cell* for £82; a portrait of *Erasmus* for £52; *two* copies of Lucas van Leyden's rare and beautiful *Bagpipe Players* fetched £56 for the two; *The Gladiators* by Pollaiuolo went for £90, and a Van Dyck of *Philip le Roy* for £130. The total for the 154 lots was £2,000 4s. od.

The second day continued the sale of engravings and the mezzotints. The latter were still very fashionable – they were to remain so for another six or seven years – and the rather murky *Great Executioner* by Prince Rupert[1] after Spagnoletto sold for the astonishing sum of £1,300. Soon after came lot 298, eight drawings by Dürer dated 1521 and spread over two pages of a sketch-book. They consisted of two landscapes and six studies of animals, including a large monkey and three lions.

Mr. F. B. Daniell, a dealer in prints who usually did the print cataloguing for Sotheby's, had miraculously spotted the sheet stuck to the back of an engraving by Raphael. It only came to light when he grew suspicious about the thickness of the engraving which had been pasted on to a mount. The drawing was now bought by Colnaghi and Obach for £1,000. Today it would certainly fetch not much less than £250,000. The total for the second day was £4,027 12s. od.

---

1. The prince invented the handrocker (a toothed chisel, rounded at the end) which made the mezzotint technique a feasible proposition. The process had been developed by Ludwig von Siegen in Amsterdam in the 1640s.

But when Hobson and Barlow came out of the sale-room that afternoon a shock awaited them. The July issue of the *Burlington Magazine* containing Charles ffoulkes's assessment of the two suits of Wilton armour, to be sold on the following Tuesday, had just been published. Ffoulkes's message was clear: they were nice suits of armour, but by no stretch of the imagination could they be old enough to have the provenance the family had so long attributed to them.

The partners held an agonising meeting. Such condemnation just before the sale was very damaging and could not be ignored. They contacted Lord Pembroke and it was decided to insert a letter, signed by him, in the form of an advertisement to appear on the front page of *The Times* and the *Morning Post* on the day of the sale in order to mitigate the blow. The letter was to protest at such criticism coming only hours before the sale, and to re-emphasize the strength of the arguments in favour of the provenance from other experts.

Barlow's legally trained mind and Hobson's scholarship worked marvellously in harness. Each man analysed ffoulkes's assessment in the minutest detail to find the weakest parts of it. For once there is a record of what passed through Geoffrey Hobson's mind at the time because a long, pencilled memorandum from him to Barlow, written at 5.30 a.m. on the Monday morning, survives. He admits that it had never occurred to him in this instance to doubt the traditional attribution.[1] In any case, this had been confirmed before the sale was contemplated by another world-famous authority on weapons and armour, Baron C. A. de Cosson. But when Hobson checked the various assertions of doubt made by ffoulkes, he realised that some of them were not unreasonable. What irked him was that neither ffoulkes nor Lord Dillon had given the slightest hint of their feelings when they had inspected the armour in Sotheby's galleries three weeks before the sale was due to take place.

Hobson thought of withdrawing the armour from the sale, a course of action which Lord Pembroke (for what reason we do not know) had himself considered only a few days previously. 'Anybody may make a mistake', Hobson had written in his note to Barlow. 'There is no discredit in it, and the error is certainly not a flagrant or a stupid one. But no-one need or should attempt to defend a mistake, once he recognises it.' He had then gone off to the British Museum to check the facts yet again, leaving Barlow to study his lengthy memorandum and to weigh up the pros and cons of the situation and to decide on a course of action.

He decided that it would be wrong to back down and that a strong line was called for. The plan was to allow the armour to come up for sale after publishing Lord Pembroke's letter, to see how the market reacted and to buy it in after the final bid from the floor, unless the prices attained passed the enormously high reserves placed on the two suits by the Court of Chancery, by a very wide margin. This policy would, in any case, demonstrate whether ffoulkes had destroyed credibility in the armour for all time.

1. There had after all been at least eight earlier Arms and Armour sales at Sotheby's since the turn of the century, so they were not novices in the field.

In the event the sale-room on that fourth and last day was packed to capacity with an unusually distinguished audience after the controversy had been high-lighted by the Earl of Pembroke's letter. No doubt the whole art trade too had been stirred by the stinging final paragraph, digested between breakfast and the start of the sale at one o'clock. The paragraph in question read: 'Finally, I should like to add that, in the view of all reasonable persons, it must be most unsatisfactory that statements of this kind attempting to throw doubt on the hitherto admitted authenticity of great works of art of world wide interest should be made on such unsubstantial evidence as in the present case; and, further, that they should be made in this way at the last minute, when practically no time is left for reply.'

The atmosphere in the sale-room was as tense as the partners had ever known it. Barlow had to auction over a hundred individual drawings, some of spec-tacular quality, before reaching the armour almost at the end of the sale. The bidding for it moved very slowly and deliberately at first. Eventually, F. G. Fenton, a leading arms and armour dealer, acting for an American buyer, made a final bid for the Constable of France's suit. It was no less than £14,000. Another overseas bidder reached £10,000 for the Duc de Montpensier's armour. Both suits were bought in at £500 more. These sums were way above any price that had been paid for armour at auction previously, and shows how right Barlow's strategy had been. In the sales of such famous armour collections as those of Richards, Londesborough, De Cosson, Brett and even Spitzer in the previous few years, very few lots had reached four figures, and a price of £400–£500 was quite usual for even a very good suit in a reasonably original condition. In fact, a number of major items in the Brett collection sold at Christie's had been bought in.

There was lack of enthusiasm for the Rembrandt portrait. It too had to be bought in at £11,500, well below the reserve, and it is still at Wilton today. A number of the drawings fetched excellent prices. The three major bidders were Colnaghi and Obach, who bought the Filippino Lippi *Pietà* for £640, a study group for an engraving of the *Combat of Hercules* by Pollaiuolo for £920, and the reputed Leonardo drawing, partly in silver point, of a man seated on a galloping horse (from the collection of Sir Peter Lely) for £300; Agnew's, who purchased a sketch of Venice by Veronese for £1,650, an elaborate study for a *Nativity* by Correggio for £750, a sketch of the *Virgin and St. Joseph* attributed to Fra Bartolommeo for £130; and Langton Douglas[1] who acquired a pen drawing of a horse with anatomical measurements by Verrochio for £100, a Correggio *Adoration of the Kings* for £250, another Correggio *Annunciation* for £380, and a Leonardo *Female Head in Profile* for £280.

The total for the sale was a nominal £52,819, but if we take away the two suits of armour and the Rembrandt which were bought in, this virtually halves

1. Langton Douglas was a remarkable figure who was, during a long and varied career, clergy-man, lecturer, writer, art critic, museum director and picture dealer. At the Pembroke sale he was buying on behalf of the Metropolitan Museum, New York, whose agent he was at that time.

the total. Like some later Sotheby sales which became *causes célèbres*, this sale had not been a success in financial terms. No wonder Montague Barlow had to start a letter to Lady Pembroke 'This must be a business letter'. For not only had the costs been heavy when one considers the trips to America and the unusually elaborate catalogue,[1] but the buying-in commissions were kept especially low and a lot of the business initiated by Barlow on behalf of the Pembroke family in New York looked as if it might by-pass Sotheby's. On the other hand, the sale released a lot of material from other sources that now came to Sotheby's and certainly achieved its purpose in establishing Bond Street as the alternative sale-room for works of art and pictures.

There were further sales of armour from Wilton on 23 June 1921, on 3 March 1922 and 14 June 1923 – over 300 lots in all, though some came up twice after being bought in. This shows how extensive the armour at Wilton had been. The most famous suit of all, made by Jacob the Armourer, was sold in the second sale for some £25,000, and another magnificent suit with matching armour for a horse went for £9,200.

The Montmorency suit finished up in the Metropolitan Museum after all, and many other pieces eventually came to rest in both British and American museums, but the initial controversy about its authenticity raged on for many years. Because of the wide interest it aroused Sotheby's published all the related documents in the case in 1918 in a specially produced pamphlet. Although the arguments were highly technical they fascinated a great number of people, probably because they were based on pure historical research and discovery. The terminology alone was intriguing and delightfully remote. The handful of armour specialists suddenly had to explain to a much bigger audience what exactly it was that they meant by salades, paldrons, cuisses, sollerets, morions, cabassets, poldermittens, animes, gorgets, cops and vanbraces.

While the crux of the problem always remained the precise dating and origin of the armour, the amount of research generated by the controversy gave a great fillip to scholarship in the whole field of armour. A 'Sur-rebutter' on what had become known as the *Wilton Controversy* was published by F. H. Cripps-Day as late as 1944.

In this particular history it is only fair to state that Geoffrey Hobson felt to the end of his days that Charles ffoulkes had had Christie's well-being very much at heart when he wrote his original piece in the *Burlington*, because the Wilton Sale had been the most important effort by the new management at Sotheby's to get away from being simply 'auctioneers of literary property', and to enter the art market in the West End with a fanfare of trumpets against their great traditional rivals. They thus learned early that, while it was fun and while it could be immensely profitable, there were more pitfalls than they had ever contemplated.

There was an amusing footnote to the Wilton armour sales as recently as the mid-Fifties. Tim Clarke, Sotheby's porcelain director, was looking for some old

1. In fact, we learn from Barlow that there had been an earlier special catalogue of the draw-ings largely for American consumption, which must have been destroyed before issue.

catalogues in the firm's basement. When he unwrapped a package in which these were thought to be, there came to light a magnificent breastplate which must have been bought in during the final armour sale. It was duly returned to Wilton House after nearly forty years.

14

*The Morrison
Autograph Collection*

BY tradition, the selling season in the autumn was quite short. It started at the end of October and any particularly important sale of more than a single day's duration was fitted into the fortnight preceding Christmas. This gave the auction houses two peak periods in the year: in July and December. The bleak war year of 1917 was to be no exception. In the summer there had been general astonishment at the quality of sales; now the same story was about to be repeated. On Monday, 10 December, Christie's began to sell the remarkably fine German *incunabula* and block-books of Charles Fairfax Murray, one of the most forceful collector-cum-dealers of his time. It was one of those sales with an unknown drama behind it, for Fairfax Murray was a friend of Montague Barlow's, and Barlow had given Murray very considerable financial support since the beginning of the war, implicitly in the expectation of handling these sales for him. At the last possible moment Fairfax Murray went to the opposition. Barlow was livid when he heard the news and wrote to Murray, more in sorrow than in anger, though still in such scathing terms that the latter must have felt very uncomfortable indeed. Even so, Christie's had a second sale of Murray's property – his French books – on 18 March 1918. A possible explanation may be that Fairfax Murray had long advised Agnew's and Agnew's had always been closely linked with Christie's. In any case, shortly afterwards Murray suffered two strokes in rapid succession and died at the end of the year. His first posthumous sale was held at Bond Street in July 1918 and his executors continued to sell his property there for a good many years. Foster's too had an unusually good sale at this time: they were dispersing the English portraits from the superb collection of paintings at Drayton Manor, the former home of Sir Robert Peel, the prime minister. Peel had been a great collector of old masters and the best of his very fine Dutch pictures had been bought by the National Gallery in 1871 at the bargain price of £75,000.

Sotheby's contribution on that 10 December 1917 was the start of a five-day sale of autograph material – letters, manuscripts and historical documents – the like of which had never occurred before and is unlikely ever to occur again. The title page of the catalogue stated conventionally enough that this was the renowned collection formed by the late Alfred Morrison, Esq., of Fonthill, and now the property of Mrs. Alfred Morrison – the same collection, of course, which Pierpont Morgan had been so anxious to acquire.

As is so often the case, the ways in which the collection had been got together concealed a magical saga. For if one were to choose a single husband and wife to represent what was best and most interesting in the second half of nineteenth-century England, one would find it difficult to surpass Alfred and Mabel Morrison. Both had remarkable family backgrounds. Born in 1821, Alfred was the second of the five sons of James Morrison, an extremely prosperous London draper and vigorous M.P. Morrison Senior was one of the first English traders to depend for his success on the lowest remunerative scale of profit. His motto was the original 'small profits and quick returns'. It is said that his fortune was greatly enhanced by astutely cornering the market in black-bordered handkerchiefs when the Prince Consort lay on his death bed. He was also a perspicacious collector of paintings – Waagen admired and described them in fulsome terms – and he formed a very large library. When he died his fortune exceeded £5,000,000 in the UK and the US, and all his children benefited accordingly.

Alfred, James's son, though a man of a much more quiet and retiring disposition, liked to live with verve and style. He started collecting Old Master paintings, miniatures, Persian carpets, Chinese porcelain, Greek gems and gold work from an early age and gave active encouragement and patronage to such specialist crafts as cameo-cutting, glass enamelling, the inlaying of metals and embroidery. With fastidious taste and immense learning he filled both his London house at 16 Carlton House Terrace and, later, Fonthill in Wiltshire which he inherited from his father, with works of art and countless books. He was a great reader, though he had a curious habit of not opening the many parcels of books delivered to him for months on end, and they remained on the floor with a path kept clear between them from the door to his chair. William Morris was once moved to say, 'Mr. Morrison is the only man I know who keeps his books on the floor and his carpets on the wall'.

Fonthill had, of course, once been the property of William Beckford, the great recluse-collector and author of *Vathek*, but the Morrison establishment was not the same magnificent folly which had fallen down in 1807. It was a much smaller house that had at one time been the servants' wing of the Beckford Mansion and was now called the Pavilion. Morrison eventually added to it three rather ugly galleries to house his vast collections.

Eleven years after his father's death in 1866, Alfred married a girl of rare beauty and driving energy called Mabel Chermside. She was only nineteen at the time and he was twenty-five years her senior. She was already an exceptional and tremendously lively personality. Her upbringing had been a mixture of the utterly sophisticated and the almost feudally rural. Her father was rector at Wilton and her grandfather was doctor to the British Embassy in Paris, having been brought there by Lord Hertford (principal founder of the Wallace Collection). As a child she travelled a good deal round Europe with her parents and spent long periods with her grandparents both in Paris and on a Normandy farm. The mixed *milieus* of great houses, superb collections and grand manners on the one hand, and of the simple agricultural life in France and England on the other, were to be ideal for her long partnership with Alfred. Her hatred of convention and the fact that her outlook on life was years ahead of her time were to label her later as something of an eccentric, and this was heightened by

Mrs. Morrison's florid hand became very familiar to Sotheby partners. In 1903 she rejected the offer they submitted on behalf of Pierpont Morgan for her unrivalled collection of autographs and historic documents. She sold them at auction some years later though she only received a fraction of the original offer price.

her unusual style of dress. From her travels, 'she brought back strange head dresses, shawls and jewels, to add foreign flavour to her own lavish movements, to the beauty of her face and to the brilliancy of her speech . . . to the end of her life she was something like a bird of paradise in the Wiltshire scene'.[1]

Despite their difference in age, she and Alfred were supremely happy. She bore him five children in the first eight years of their marriage, and during this time they also laid the foundation of their great autograph collection. Alfred fostered her taste, her craving for knowledge and allowed her to give free rein to an extraordinary generosity. There is a marvellous story of a friend in straitened circumstances who inherited a large, empty house on the Berkshire Downs. When Mrs. Morrison heard about this she at once despatched there two large pantechnicons filled with very valuable and beautiful eighteenth-century furniture. They arrived like that, quite unexpectedly, without any fuss or ado. On the next morning the friend received a further parcel from Fonthill in the

1. From Edith Olivier's *Four Victorian Ladies of Wiltshire*, 1945, which presents a delightful portrait of Mabel Morrison.

post. It contained what appeared to be the most ragged undergarments – long vest sleeves without vests! They had been considerably darned and mended but would still keep the arms warm. Mrs. Morrison had again bethought herself of that cold house on the wintry Downs and had raided her own drawers without delay. To her this second gift was quite as important as the priceless furniture sent on the previous day, though this was not to say that she did not have an excellent sense of values where purely financial matters were concerned.

The enormous energy she expended in the early years of her marriage led to a chronic illness which made her an invalid for nearly twelve years. Alfred built her a wooden summer house with a lovely view over the Wiltshire countryside, and here they continued to pursue their discussions on enlarging their autograph collections. Alfred was activated by the true collector's zest in the pursuit of a rare thing for rarity's sake, but while Mabel shared his taste, she was driven by a deeper purpose which helped to give their collection its unique quality: she had what almost amounted to a craving for an unravelling of historical facts. She was not interested in other historians' interpretations or commentary. She wanted to seek out and savour the bedrock material of history in its purest form. Nothing could satisfy that craving better than letters and documents in their own hand by those men and women who had been in a position to make a contribution to history, and which expressed their most intimate thoughts and emotions. Thus, together with many other such correspondences, the Morrisons eventually possessed, for instance, practically the whole of the Hamilton and Nelson papers, and Mabel's mind was literally saturated with the story of the relationship between Lord Nelson, Sir William and Lady Hamilton and Charles Greville.

Recognition of the importance of what Alfred and Mabel were doing came from an unexpected quarter. The Morrisons' was one of the few private collections of autograph material accumulated in recent times which was the subject of a report in 1884 by the Royal Commission on Historical Manuscripts. This report by as sober a body of judges as the country could find was, as A. N. L. Munby wrote, 'in a vein which does not often appear in official publications'.[1]

To call it a magnificent accumulation of autographs, without at the same time calling attention to the unusual historic worth of the majority and the singular interest of a minority of the writings, would convey no adequate notion of the merits of a collection, which in comprehensiveness and general excellence, as well as in the high importance of its most remarkable matters, differs from all collections of its kind heretofore formed in this country. . . . The Dillon Manuscripts,[2] the Donnadieu collection, the Rupert and Fairfax Correspondence,[3] the collections of Mr. Robert Cole, F.S.A., Sir William Tite, Baron

1. In *The Cult of the Autograph Letter in England*, 1962.
2. John Dillon's collection was sold at Sotheby's on 10 June 1869.
3. Sold at Sotheby's on 14 June 1852, at that time the property of the publisher, Richard Bentley. The Fairfax correspondence came from the same source as the 'Leeds Papers', see below.

Heath,[1] Mr. Joseph Ridgeway,[2] Mr. George Manners,[3] and the 'Leeds Papers',[4] are some of upwards of sixty different collections from which Mr. Morrison has during the course of years drawn to his hands the larger part of his exemplary epistles. During the same considerable time letters and other documents have come to him in a steady stream from the muniment-rooms of France, Germany, Spain and Italy. It can therefore be readily believed that the Mss., gathered together from so many different sources by a connoisseur, whose enthusiasm in his peculiar department of literary service has never been unattended by critical caution and nice discrimination, may be described in the language of moderation as the most remarkable gathering of historical autographs ever formed by a single private collector in Great Britain.

The writer of an article in the *Dictionary of National Biography*[5] on Morrison, having already commented on the uniqueness of the collection, said that 'it contains every kind of epistolary document dealing with politics, administration, art, science and literature, ranging from the fifteenth to the nineteenth centuries, and especially relating to the public and private life of monarchs, statesmen and other persons of mark of all European countries, particularly Great Britain, France and Italy'. Small wonder that Pierpont Morgan had been so keen to buy it *en bloc*.

Alfred Morrison arranged for the publication of two immensely detailed multi-volume catalogues of the collection. These were edited by A. W. Thibaudeau, an archivist and palaeographer, of Green Street, Leicester Square, who had also taken an active part in advising on the formation and particularly on the arrangement of the collection. Morrison also published separate selections of the Hamilton and Nelson papers and of the Bulstrode papers, an important series of late seventeenth-century news-letters. All these were a magnificent monument to Victorian leisure and amateur effort in the best sense. One also has the feeling that the Morrisons took particular pleasure in the study of other people's letters at a time when the art of English letter writing had reached a zenith from which it has steadily declined during the last fifty years.

Some time after Alfred's death in 1892, Mrs. Morrison moved to Shawford near Winchester, where she added a wing to a beautiful, late seventeenth-century manor house. After Morgan's unexpected but tempting offer had lapsed she must eventually have concluded that she could no longer deal with the great collection of material on her own and that it should be re-circulated among other collectors of autographs.

1. John Benjamin Charles, Baron Heath (1790–1879) F.R.S., F.S.A., Italian Consul-General: his collection was sold at Sotheby's on 24 April 1879; though it contained some forgeries.
2. Sold at Sotheby's on 30 June 1879.
3. George Manners, F.S.A., the owner of a large general collection sold at Sotheby's in four parts, 14 June 1870, 8 July 1878, 20 May 1880 and 27 November 1890.
4. Manuscripts sold with the library of Leeds Castle, Kent, by Christie's on 10 January 1831, being the papers of the Fairfax family and of David Wilkins (1685–1745), editor of *Concilia Magnae Britanniae*.
5. 1909 edition.

After it came to Sotheby's it was decided to dispose of the material in a four-part sale spread over two years. This comprised 3,335 lots and took a total of eighteen days in the sale-room (10–14 December 1917; 15–19 April 1918; 9–13 December 1918; 5–7 May 1919). Despite wartime difficulties the catalogues were well produced and spaciously laid out with a good many illustrations, though one could have wished for even more detail. The total sum realised was £53,151 – a long way below Pierpont Morgan's offer – but as both de Ricci and Munby say 'it must be remembered that the sale took place before the very substantial increase in values which characterised the middle Twenties, and that only ten years later the total might well have been three times this figure'. The purchasers were relatively limited in numbers but included all the famous antiquarian book trade names – Maggs, Quaritch, Sotheran, Tregaskis, Francis Edwards, Pearson and Dobell. The principal purchaser by far was Charles Maggs, and an interesting postscript to the sale is that as recently as 1968, Maggs commented on their vast stock purchases at the Morrison sale in their *Catalogue of Catalogues* and stated that these had only recently become exhausted.

The sale catalogue was based on an earlier six-volume printed one prepared for the collection, and it gives a marvellous insight into the wealth of the material. Its alphabetical listing displayed a delightful jostling of historical characters, cheek by jowl. Thus, three humorous letters by Beethoven, 'signed with fantastical notes and initials' are sandwiched between letters from William Beckford, father of the author of *Vathek*, the original builder of Fonthill and one time Lord Mayor of London, and Bembo, Cardinal Pietro, whose poems have come down to us in the beautiful cursive script of his time; the Buonapartes share a page with the Borgias, and James Boswell another with Robert Boyle: and on the very next page three letters from Buonarotti (Michelangelo) contain instructions from him to pay a mason for a job completed and to Raffaelo de Montelupo the balance for three statues on a papal tomb. In the third letter Michelangelo gives his opinions upon the plans of his predecessors in the construction of the new St. Peter's in Rome. He defends the original plan of Bramante against the alterations introduced by Sangallo.

In the second day's sale the B's end and the C's begin. Cranach is followed by Cranmer, Thomas, Archbishop of Canterbury, and he by Oliver Cromwell. By the fourth day we have reached Dr. Johnson writing in August 1782 (lot 555) 'I was so exhausted by loss of blood and by excessive disorders in the beginning of this year that I am afraid the remaining part will hardly restore me. I have indeed rather indulged myself too much, and think to begin a stricter regimen', and two years later (lot 559) the learned doctor writes to a Mr. Ryland who is to mind his affairs after his death: 'to have a friend, and a friend like you, may be numbered amongst the first felicities of life; at a time when weakness, either of body or mind, loses the pride and the confidence of self sufficiency, and looks round for that help, which, perhaps, human kindness cannot give'.

There were many Byron letters in the collection. In 1811 after two years' absence from home the poet had written (lot 763): 'You will either see or hear from me soon after the receipt of this as I pass through town to repair my irreparable affairs, and thence I must go to Notts and raise rents, and to Lancs to sell collieries, and back to London and pay debts, for it seems I shall neither have coals or comfort until I go down to Rochdale in person . . .'. In another letter written from Ravenna in 1819 about the Countess Guiccioli he added in a postscript: 'If anything happens to my present Amica – I have done with the passion forever – it is my last love – as to Libertinism – I have sickened myself of that as was natural in the way I went on – and I have at least derived that advance from the Vice – to *Love* in the better sense of the word – this will be my last adventure. I can hope no more to inspire attachment – and I trust never again to feel it'. The final Byron autograph (lot 769) was a letter from his valet, William Fletcher, to Byron's sister, describing the course of his master's last illness and the death-bed scene. Mabel Morrison had taken a particular interest in Byron, for both as a very young girl and quite late in her life she stayed at Newstead Abbey, at one time the home of the poet and the scene of some of his wilder antics. Mabel's uncle, General Sir Herbert Chermside, who had entertained her at Newstead Abbey, stimulated no doubt by the interest created by the Byron material in the first Morrison sale, sold his many Byron autograph manuscripts and some association copies of the poet's books at Bond Street on 3 June 1918 in an autograph sale of mixed properties, and these fetched quite handsome prices. Sotheby's joined the Chermside items with more Byron material – a miniature portrait of the poet as a boy, his first gold watch and some crimson curtain material, together with descriptive documents and photographs relating to 'a very curious episode in his early married life', all formerly belonging to a Colonel Alexander Ewing of Tartowie, Aberdeen.

The greatest sale-room interest was, of course, engendered in the correspondence between Lord Nelson and Emma Hamilton which Munby described as one of the most romantic and evocative series of letters ever to have come to the market. It was contained in twelve bound volumes and two portfolios, and consisted of rather more than 1,050 letters and documents dating from 1756 to 1829. The majority of these came from the papers of Sir William Hamilton, which Sotheby's had sold in 1886, and from the collection formed by Thomas Joseph Pettigrew for his life of Nelson of 1849 and again sold by Sotheby's in 1887. The catalogue is unusually lyrical, for its time, in its description of the material and contains some nice human touches:

> The letters which passed between Greville and Sir William Hamilton during the latter's ministry at Naples are of no little interest: Greville tells his friend the news of the town, and Hamilton replies with the latest Court scandal of Naples, and the latest find of Greek vases. In 1785 we come across curious and rather sordid details of the transfer of Emma from one to the other, while later letters deal at length with financial questions and arrangements for the sale of Sir William's collections. There are also many letters from Sir William to Nelson, the earlier chiefly on political questions, the later about domestic arrangements, the last of all being a rather pitiful protest against the position Sir William was made to occupy in his own house.

The most remarkable of Emma's letters are those addressed to Greville, the earliest being written in 1782. They are full of ill-spelt complaints of ill-requited love, and ungrammatical assurances of undying constancy; later on spelling and grammar improve, bearing witness to Emma's docility and Greville's patient tuition, but the sentiments remain much the same till she becomes Lady Hamilton, when they assume the decorum befitting a lady of title. Nelson's Letters to her are extraordinary, and show in almost every line the depth and intensity of his passion.

In the printed price list the single lot is down as being sold to Peterson for £2,500, but Peterson was a name used not infrequently for lots bought in. This is confirmed when we see that the correspondence re-appears as 188 separate lots at the very end of the fourth sale. Here it fetched no more, but it was certainly sold. However, the re-cataloguing gives one the opportunity to see more detail of the letters that came under the hammer. These are worthy of quotation to show their historic importance. The cataloguer describes lot 3228 from Lord Nelson to Lady Hamilton, dated 1 March 1801, *A Very Remarkable Letter*. It begins: 'Now my own dear wife, for such you are in my eyes and in the face of heaven, I can give full scope of my feelings. . . . You know my dearest Emma, that there is nothing in the world I would not do for us to live together, and to have our dear little child with us. . . . I love, I never did love anyone else. . . . I burn all your dear letters, because it is right for your sake, and I wish you would burn all mine – they can do no good, and will do us both harm if any seizure of them, or the dropping even of them, would fill the mouths of the world sooner than we intended.' And the very next lot dated the following day, again from Nelson to Emma: 'This moment received your letter from Trowbridge, my heart bleeds for you, but I shall soon, very soon, return. Damn all those that would make you false.' And again a few days later, '. . . all of yesterday I was employed about a very necessary thing; and I assure you it gave me great pleasure, instead of pain, the reflection that I was providing for a very dear friend. I have given you by will £3,000 and three diamond boxes, and the King of Naples' picture on trust . . . be assured I am for ever, ever, ever, your, your, your, more than ever yours, yours, your own, only your Nelson and Bronte.'

The penultimate lot (3312) consists of a letter from Lady Hamilton to Horatia, her daughter by Nelson. It has an almost Lear-like pathos about it and clearly shows the unhappy ending of the famous liaison.

Horatia, – Your conduct is so bad, your falsehoods so dreadfull, your cruel treatment to me such that I cannot live under these afflicting circumstances; my poor heart is broken. If my poor mother was living to take my part, broken as I am with grief and ill-health, I should be happy to breathe my last in her arms. I thank you for what you have done to-day. You have helped me on nearer to God, and may God forgive you.

Towards the very end of her life Mabel Morrison began to feel an urge that she too should leave behind a record of her manifold activities. She planned to write a book which was to contain her philosophy of life – a summing up of all she had learned from her reading, studying, travel, thought and prayer. But she began too late (in her eighties) and time was against her. At her death the book was nowhere near completion. What she left behind were two desks crammed with scraps of paper, postcards, exercise books and notebooks all covered in her florid, characterful, pencilled hand, but it was purely random material, which no one but she could have linked up into book form. Perhaps one day it will finish up in another great autograph collection.

15

The Advent
of Charles Bell

THE second Morrison Autograph Sale in mid-April 1918 followed hard on the heels of a five-day sale of the library of H. B. Wheatley, the editor of what was for many years the definitive edition of the Diaries of Samuel Pepys, and it had included many rare bindings and important original Pepys autograph documents and manuscripts.[1] Then on 24 and 25 April there took place another sale which was to be notable in its own way.

Subscribers soon realised when they received their catalogue that this was something of unusual quality. It looked ordinary enough. It was not even bound in the embossed, grey board cover that Sotheby's reserved for important catalogues of drawings and paintings at that time. But it read differently. It began with a learned but lucid disquisition on the great collectors of Old Master drawings in England since the days of Sir Peter Lely. In 1918 information on this subject was hardly known at all and reflected the fruits of considerable research. Such an introduction was not intended merely as a parade of scholarship. It made clear the magnificent antecedents and the importance of the 305 items that were included in a sale of drawings that belonged to Sir Edward Poynter, the President of the Royal Academy. The collection had been formed in part by, and had subsequently passed through the hands of Sir Peter Lely himself, Lord Somers, Jonathan Richardson the Elder, Thomas Hudson (Richardson's portrait-painter son-in-law), Sir Joseph Reynolds and Thomas Banks, the sculptor. It had at one stage only just escaped the clutches of Sir Thomas Lawrence, the greatest and most acquisitive collector of Old Master drawings of all time, before Poynter's grandmother inherited it. Certainly the press noticed at once that it was going to be an altogether unusual sale. *The Times* actually commented on 'an excellent sales catalogue . . . of a collection of exceptional interest', and like the *Morning Post* and the *Daily Telegraph* wrote it up in glowing terms.

Sir Edward, who was already in his eighties, decided to entrust the negotiations for the sale of this collection to his nephew, C. F. Bell, who, as keeper of the Department of Fine Arts at the Ashmolean Museum, Oxford, since 1908, was uniquely qualified for the task. Bell prepared a detailed catalogue and had the drawings photographed. The subject of each drawing was described simply and objectively; the technique and dimensions were given in each case; full details of previous ownership and all literary references were included. Above all, there was a detailed attribution to an artist whenever this was known or deducible. Where it was not, the catalogue said so explicitly. With one of the greatest collections of drawings in the world at his personal disposal within the confines of the Ashmolean Museum, it was not surprising that Bell had ample opportunity to catalogue accurately. The material he compiled had originally been sent to America where it was thought there would be the most interest and probably an immediate sale, but none materialised.

Not long afterwards the Wilton drawings were sold at Sotheby's and Bell, impressed by the skilful publicity with which the sale was promoted, wrote to Bond Street and asked for a priced copy of the Wilton catalogue. He and his uncle studied it closely. As a piece of cataloguing it seemed to them disappointing. Bell communicated with Bond Street, nevertheless, and asked for an appointment – 'I should be greatly obliged if you would give me an opportunity of consulting you about the sale of a rather well-known collection of Old Master Drawings belonging to a near relation of mine.' Barlow scented a catch and saw Bell himself. The two men, who were almost of an age, got on remarkably well. Barlow advised on a sale, an immediate sale, using an enlarged version of Bell's prepared catalogue and giving it maximum pre-sale publicity in the United States. He felt sure enough of himself to pooh-pooh Sir Edward Poynter's fears that there might have to be a lot of buying in.

As drawings sales went it was a success. Many items were sketches for known paintings; others – particularly a group of Claudes – were trial compositions; a few were animated doodles by great artists. Prices fluctuated a good deal. Thus an informal, very appealing *Seated Madonna with an infant Christ on her knee, climbing up to embrace her* by Fra Bartolommeo, made £260. This had come from the collection of William Mayor, a friend and admirer of Sir Thomas Lawrence. *A Religious Procession* by Vittore Carpaccio probably fetched £360 because of its splendid provenance. It came from the famous Milanese Collection of Padre Sebastiano Resta which John Talman had imported into England in 1709 and sold in part to Lord Somers and in part to the Dean of Christchurch at Oxford. It had come down to Poynter via Thomas Hudson who bought it at a sale of Lord Somers's Collection, then Sir Joshua Reynolds and finally Thomas Banks. The latter was, in fact, Charles Bell's own great great grandfather.

Annibale Carracci, one of the most popular painters of his period among English collectors, was clearly out of favour on this occasion. His five drawings averaged only £2 10s. od. each. On the other hand, a large *Head and Arms of a female figure* by his cousin, Lodovico Carracci, fetched £125. A sketch for a portrait of a man in a hat by Lorenzi di Credi was sold for £290, but a nude female figure by another one-time favourite, Guido Reni, went for only £56, even though a former owner – the famous eighteenth-century collector, Thomas Udney – had written on the back 'this elegant and beautiful study by Guido is the original study for his fine figure of Liberality in Lord Spencer's picture of Modesty and Liberality, but is far superior to the picture or the fine engraving which Mr. Strange has made from it'.

Even though Bell had drawn careful attention to the difference between Michelangelo Buonarotti, School of Michelangelo Buonarotti and definite copies after the master, the trade felt uncertain about the three definite attributions: one fetched £4; another ten guineas and a third £96. But no one doubted two of the three drawings by Albrecht Dürer and they went for record sums of £1,580 for *A Study of Apollo* and £1,100 for a very typical *Woman in the Costume of the Period*. The five pocket-sized Claudes – characteristic landscapes with classical figures -- fetched high prices, though poor old Nicolas Poussin, represented by eight drawings, had a very bad day.

There were no fewer than twelve drawings catalogued as from the hand of Rembrandt van Rijn. The highest price was £330 for *A subject from the story of Job or of Tobit*. A poignant *Sketch of a crippled boy selling matches* from the collection of William Graham was a bargain at £110. The total for the two-day sale was £12,093, and both Poynter and Bell were evidently pleased with the result.

Despite Barlow's ambition to make a more assertive entry into the picture market, he found progress slow. One of the difficulties was finding a competent and willing outside cataloguer. The authoritative identification of Old Masters is notoriously difficult. In the trade the diffusion of lore was a good deal more extensive than that of genuine expertise. Most knowledgeable dealers guarded their connoisseurship jealously. The temptation was to use attributions suggested by the owner, or to lean heavily on provenance if it happened to be known, or if it could be deduced from old labels that were clearly discernible on the backs of frames. For some years after the partners' decision to sell paintings, Sotheby's catalogues were prepared by William Mason of Mason and Philips. Old Mr. Mason was really a valuer; he was not very prompt; he tended to make major howlers; he always felt he was not being paid enough; he was overawed by Montague Barlow and he could not get on with Evelyn Barlow. Yet many of his catalogue entries are written – presumably unwittingly – in a delightfully rhythmic style that often resembles blank verse. After years of acrimonious correspondence and a final occasion when Mason had *overlooked* the four most important paintings in a sizeable collection, Barlow was relieved to be able to give him three months notice and to transfer his allegiance elsewhere. He made arrangements for Max Morris of Colnaghi's to do the work. Although the proximity of Colnaghi's farther down Bond Street was a great advantage, the new plan did not work too well either, because Morris clearly had to avoid any situation where there could be a conflict of interest with his own firm.

Eventually Barlow thought of Bell. He was in every sense a true scholar – he was scrupulous to a fault – and had shown an impressive level of efficiency where his uncle's collection was concerned. As always, Barlow made searching enquiries. He discovered that Charles Bell was the fourth son of a successful banker and had been brought up in a home where music and the arts played an important role. A close friend of the family was Charles Drury Fortnum, who had made a great deal of money in Australia and had then become an enthusiastic art collector. He intended to donate his great collection of Renaissance art to the Ashmolean and to endow it with sufficient funds to reconstruct the Museum. In 1896 he recommended Bell to Sir Arthur Evans, the famous

ASHMOLEAN MUSEUM
OXFORD
DEPARTMENT OF FINE ART
TELEPHONE № 522

February 4 1920

Dear Barlow

I have been thinking over the suggestion
which you kindly made and now write to say that I should be
very glad to fall in with it and I think I may flatter
myself that the sort of wide, if not anywhere deep, knowledge
and experience which I could bring to the work may very
probably prove of real use in the business.

As long as the work is, as you said it would be,
confined to London, I do not think that I need have any
difficulty in dealing with it nor any hesitation about
undertaking it. But I am afraid that I could not, excepting
possibly upon some very special occasion, undertake to make
any journeys for the firm as, for example, when sales have
been decided upon in general, for the purpose of selecting
what it is desirable to remove to London for the purpose.
This would take more time than I should be justified in
giving. Also I am a very bad traveller. It is this, and
a firm resolve, which I shall always adhere to, never to appear
as an expert witness in any legal dispute concerned with

The letter from C. F. Bell of the Ashmolean Museum accepting the post of picture adviser at Sotheby's, framed in the draft reply from Sir Montague Barlow, then Chairman of the firm.

archaeologist and then Keeper of the Ashmolean Museum, as a suitable assistant. Shortly afterwards Fortnum died and Bell spent many years in transforming the Museum's rather austere department of Western art into one of the most attractively arranged in England. In 1908, after the position had been newly created, he became the first Keeper of the department. His official stipend was only £600, though he certainly had private means and frequently eked out the museum's slender reserves from his own pocket. But once he had brought about the total reorganisation of the museum's fine paintings and its display of the decorative arts, he had relatively little to do. He wrote to Barlow in February 1920, 'I have been thinking over the suggestion which you kindly made and now wish to say that I should be very glad to fall in with it and I think I may flatter myself that the sort of wide, if not anywhere deep, knowledge and experience which I could bring to the work may very probably prove of real use in the business'. He stipulated that his activities should be confined to London. 'I am a very bad traveller. It is this, and a firm resolve, which I shall always adhere to, never to appear as an expert witness in any legal dispute concerned with works of art, which has deterred me from accepting somewhat similar offers which have been made to me before. From your experience of my work on a former occasion you will, I believe, give me credit for being punctual and methodical in detail.'

Thereafter Bell came to London from Oxford every Wednesday. He was happy to be paid a guinea for travelling expenses and a small commission on what he catalogued. He was related to the great and famous, such as Stanley Baldwin, Rudyard Kipling and Sir Edward Burne-Jones, and had the *entrée* to famous collections everywhere. He also introduced other scholars, some from Oxford, to the firm when their experience was needed for specialist sales, such as Sir John Beazley, the world's greatest expert on Greek vases, Howard Carter, the Egyptologist who had discovered Tutankhamen, and the archaeologists, Professor Bernard Ashmole and Sir Edgar John Forsdyke (who was eventually to become Director of the British Museum).

Bell was a precise, bird-like little man, slightly hump-backed and very short-sighted. Generally unassuming, he could be impatient and ill-tempered, although his all-round knowledge made a deep impression on those who worked with him. It was probably his understanding of English drawings, watercolours and paintings which was most immediately useful at Bond Street, though at a time when thirteen drawings by John Constable and engraved versions of two of them could be lumped together to sell at £245, it was only an exceptionally well-known drawing that would fetch an appreciable figure. It was still a marvellous time for the bargain hunters.

The first major sale for which Bell was responsible was in March 1920, when a collection of Old Master drawings belonging to the Marquess of Lansdowne was combined with a selection of English ones, the property of J. P. Heseltine. The latter was one of the foremost collectors of drawings in England, who in 1912 had already sold the major portion of his vast collection to the banker, Harry Oppenheimer, for £32,000,[1] and it was an indication of Charles Bell's standing that the remainder should now come to Sotheby's rather than to Christie's. Lord Lansdowne's drawings were almost entirely unknown. As Bell stated in his introduction to the catalogue, even the assiduous Dr. Waagen had missed them when he looked round Lansdowne House and described the contents in his encyclopaedic conspectus of private collections in England in 1835.[2] The

1. Oppenheimer sold his formidable collection at Christie's in 1936: it was certainly the most important sale of its kind to take place between the wars.
2. For full details of Dr. Waagen's works, see the author's *The English as Collectors*, London, 1973, p. 146 *et seq.*

joint Lansdowne–Heseltine catalogue was the most extensively illustrated Sotheby's had produced so far. The Lansdowne collection was strong in works by French, German, Italian and Dutch masters. There were nine Bouchers, two Canalettos, three drawings attributed to Correggio, three Francesco Guardis, two studies of heads by Hans Holbein, an enchantingly picturesque river scene by Claude Lorrain, an exquisite drawing of a woman carrying one child and walking beside another by Bernardino Luini, which was signed and fetched £410, a Simone Martini, two Adriaen van Ostades, a most attractive sketch by himself of Parmigiano and his mistress, that stemmed from the collections of William Young Ottley and Sir Thomas Lawrence (fortunate purchaser at £50!), a Rembrandt study of a bearded man for a staggering £3,300 (there were four Rembrandt drawings in all), a lovely *Head of a Young Woman* by Rubens at £330 and another of a bearded man at £55.

Among the Heseltine drawings there were four charming sketches by Bonington, no fewer than twenty-three by Constable (though in some instances two or three were stuck on to a single mount) some of which had belonged to the Constable family, a very typical Etty of two nude women, three Flaxmans (two at a mere two guineas and one 'passed'), a pencil sketch of *Card Players* by Hogarth, two Turner drawings (one a seascape; one a harvest scene, at £98 and £100), a Whistler self-portrait (at £96), and an Italian view by Richard Wilson which had belonged to his fellow artist, Paul Sandby (for £4!). The grand total of 14s. less than £14,000 was generally regarded as amazing.

A steady stream of passable collections followed. Often they came from houses of which the libraries had been sold at Bond Street. Occasionally there were highlights: an impressive one was the sale of a mere ten drawings, 'the Property of a Gentleman', for £7,120. There had never been anything like it: it was a mini-Goldschmidt Sale[1] forty years ahead of its time. Two Hubert Roberts, three subjects jointly and separately by the brothers Gabriel and Augustin de Saint-Aubin (at £1,700, £1,000 and £700), a Boucher, a Lancret and two Francesco Guardis of Venice – all with impeccable provenances.

There was a constant progression of pen sketches supposedly by Rembrandt. Bell must have had his work cut out deciding which were genuine. Very often the trade backed his judgement: sometimes it thought he was wrong. In the sale of the collection of John, Lord Northwick, on 5 and 6 July 1921, no fewer than fourteen sketches were at least linked with Rembrandt. None was given a full attribution which was indicated by including both the artist's Christian and surname. Only two were sold for three-figure sums. Altogether there were some marvellous bargains for any collector with a perceptive eye. The 258 lots on that occasion fetched £5,324 10s.

Gradually an increasing number of English eighteenth-century portraits which one would normally have associated almost automatically with Christie's now came into Bond Street, for Bell's knowledge of portraiture was widely appreciated. Raeburns, Romneys, Beecheys and Reynolds's appeared more

1. See page 369ff.

frequently. Occasionally there were earlier ones as well. In June 1920 a magnificent contemporary portrait of Queen Elizabeth I, another of Catherine Carey, Countess of Nottingham and a third of Lady Elizabeth Howard, all by Marcus Gheeraerts the Younger fetched £2,950, £500 and £500 respectively. A further portrait of Lady Howard by Paul van Somer fetched only £210. All four portraits were the property of Lord Willoughby de Broke, and although the arrival of this quartet represented something of a landmark, the cataloguing had been unusually taxing for Bell because he had had to identify the sitters from an inaccurate family genealogy.

Another drawings sale which must have given him great pleasure was that of the collection of Max J. Bonn on 15 February 1922. Bell was consistently un-pretentious and austere in his catalogue presentation, but in this instance he was moved to say on the title page that it was a *very important collection* comprising *choice examples* by members of the Italian, French, English, German, Dutch and Flemish School, including Dürer's *Dead Duck* of 1515, a *superb* sheet of negro heads by Watteau and a *series of magnificent Rembrandts* (in bold Gothic type). The Dürer *Duck* was almost on a par with the same artist's famous crouching hare; it was signed and dated; it had belonged to Sir Thomas Lawrence (the two previous owners were known as well); it had been published by the Vasari Society and exhibited at the Burlington Fine Arts Club. It fetched a remark-able £2,100. There was a haunting *Portrait of a Young Leper* by Hans Holbein the Younger, which brought £600. A marvellously precise drawing of St. Nicholas by Hans von Kulmbach, another fifteenth-century German artist, went for £210. A very simple sketch of *A youth standing, seen from behind, his head in profile*, was attributed to the school of Raphael and fetched £250. The Rembrandts consisted of two distant views, two sepia wash drawings of *A Nude Male Model* and a rather evocative *Woman Looking out of a Window* with a cast iron provenance not often seen in the auction room – the Marquis de Vendé, Joseph Dimsdale, Sir Thomas Lawrence, W. Esdaile, C. S. Bale and H. P. Heseltine. It had been frequently reproduced and fetched a record £1,550. The three studies of a young negro's head by Watteau were sold for £3,200, one of the highest prices ever paid for a drawing at that time. Despite the prevailing depressed economic circumstances, the sale raised a total of £13,010 for 66 lots.

Following immediately after the Max Bonn Collection, the firm sold two bound quarto volumes bound in gilt, crimson morocco which contained 55 sketches for portraits by John Downham, A.R.A. (1750–1824), with hand-written notes by the artist identifying the sitters and giving brief notes about the portraits finally produced in oils. That this was a valuable social document, the artist had himself realised for he had said in a hand-written preface: 'In these volumes are a great part of my pleasant Employment of many Years; and in this assemblage of Portraits, you will see how much different Fashions change the appearance of Persons almost as much as putting a Judge's Wig on an infant.... I perfectly accord with Mr. Horace Walpole that Costume in Por-traits should always be preserved for Truth and obvious reasons.' The two volumes fetched some £3,100 between them. They had been the property of the late Sir Edward F. Coates, Bt., M.P.

Helping Bell on his London visits was Tim Wilder, now with the firm for almost a decade and thoroughly immersed in every aspect of etching and engraving, and particularly expert on English sporting prints. He had first worked alongside F. B. Daniell, and as the latter's business expanded, under Herbert Breun who gradually took over the bulk of the outside cataloguing for Sotheby's in this area. Breun, an intriguing character, was descended from the Duc de Vitié who had fled to England at the time of the French Revolution. He had a shop with a Dickensian bow front in Greek Street and dealt exclusively in portraits for which he had an almost photographic memory: altogether a marvellous tutor for an enthusiastic young man, such as Wilder, who wanted to graduate from the clerical to the expert staff. Charles Bell, with his particular penchant for things English up to about 1820, took a considerable interest in extending his 'assistant's' education and often brought reference books for him from Oxford to do so.

After a few years, however, Bell found himself irritated more and more by Evelyn Barlow – nominally still the head of the Print and Picture Department – and her occasional, ignorant, bossy eruptions. By 1924 he had had enough. He waited until things had settled down after the general election at the end of the year and until Barlow was back in the office, before writing to resign. The withdrawal was accomplished in the most gentlemanly and friendly fashion.

'It has been borne in upon me more and more clearly', he wrote, 'that almost all the firm needs to accomplish the last stages of capturing the biggest picture business is a thoroughly first class whole-time man such as it is impossible for me to become. In fact, I feel that I have been standing in the way. I believe you were so generous as to hope at one time that this sort of man is what I might have become – but I know I am not up to it.'

Bell went back to nursing his perpetual ill-health at the Ashmolean. It was at about this time that he became mentor to a brilliant young man who was eager to learn from him. His name was Kenneth Clark. And although there had never been the slightest thought of this at their first acquaintance, in the very early Thirties Clark took over from Bell the keepership of the Department of Fine Arts at the Ashmolean. At first all went well, but then Clark re-hung all the pictures and changed around the entire museum display – in which Bell had always taken particular pride – while the latter was on a long sojourn in Italy. When Bell returned from his travels and saw the result he was so incensed that he never entered the portals of the Museum again during the rest of his long life, for he only died in 1966 at the advanced age of ninety-five. Bell deserves a special niche in the story of Sotheby's evolution because he brought to drawings and paintings the flair and scholarship that the firm had evolved after generations of experience in the field of antiquarian books, and it was on this slender foundation that Sotheby's eventually soared ahead to become a world leader in fine art auctioneering.

24. With the firm's move to the West End a considerable effort was made to expand sales of works of art and paintings. The magnificent armour and other treasures from Wilton were a great magnet in the opening season. The illustration shows a full-page advertisement in *The Connoisseur*.

25. Included in the Wilton Sale were these pages from a sketch-book by Dürer. They had been discovered by accident by an outside cataloguer who noticed a slight bulge under an engraving pasted into a portfolio. The drawings were bought by Colnaghi for £1,000.

26. The first major painting which Sotheby's sold after the firm's decision to compete with Christie's in this field was Lord Glanusk's *Portrait of a Man* by Frans Hals. It fetched a record price of £9,000 in June 1913, the highest auction price that year.

27. The man responsible for Sotheby's expansion after 1909 and its move to Bond Street was Sir Montague Barlow, a former ecclesiastical lawyer, one of the three partners who bought the business from Tom Hodge. Barlow was also an ambitious politician and served as Minister of Labour in two post-war Conservative administrations under Bonar Law and Baldwin.

28. Felix Warre joined with Barlow in the acquisition of Sotheby's in 1909, after a short career in banking in the Far East. He became the firm's principal auctioneer and chairman after Barlow's retirement in 1928.

29. Montague Barlow's sister Evelyn joined Sotheby's during the First World War. She looked after administration and was also responsible for the sale of pictures and drawings. She was probably the first woman to take auctions at Sotheby's.

30. Geoffrey Hobson was the third member of the triumvirate who bought Sotheby's. A slight deafness precluded him from taking sales. He concentrated on the book department and became a great authority on bindings.

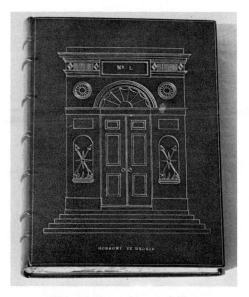

31. Hobson was a man of some means and lived in stylish splendour at No. 1 Bedford Square.

32. This binding of one of his own scholarly works on the subject of bindings is decorated with an impression of the entrance to No. 1 Bedford Square.

33. Hobson also had a strong predilection for antiques of all kinds and did much to build up Sotheby's works of art department between the wars. The drawing-room at Bedford Square reflects his own remarkable taste.

34 & 35. Two views of the principal auction gallery at Bond Street which show the extent to which Hobson and his partners were attracting pictures to Sotheby's between the wars.

36. Charles des Graz conducting one of the Britwell sales in the 1920s. The seated figure in glasses looking at the book held by the porter is Dr. Rosenbach, one of the firm's most important transatlantic clients for many years.

37. Felix Warre taking the Powis Sale on 19 March 1923. Des Graz is standing on his right. The porter in the ring is Addison. Dr. Rosenbach is in his usual place (seated immediately to the right of the rostrum) and next to him is Seymour de Ricci.

38. One of the highlights of the inter-war period was the sale of the manuscript of *Alice in Wonderland* in April 1928. Dr. Rosenbach bought it for the then record price of £15,400. He subsequently played a considerable role in its return to Britain as a gift to the British Museum.

39. The sale of a wonderful diamond necklace, once the property of Marie Antoinette, on 1 July 1937. It was bought for £15,000 by an Indian maharaja (possibly the seated figure to the right of the porter) who had come to London for the Coronation of King George VI.

40. Tancred Borenius, Sotheby's adviser on paintings from 1924 to 1945, studying a Lorenzo Lotto which he had 'rediscovered' in 1934.

41. A portrait of Borenius taken some years later. He was born in Finland, remained an ardent Finnish patriot all his life and acted as Finnish consul in London for long periods.

42. H. C. Rham looked after the firm's finances for many years in a number of roles. He also acted as London liaison with Dr. Rosenbach and assisted in the first ever broadcast commentary by the BBC on an art auction at the time of the Rothschild Sale.

16

Manuscript Milestone

IT did not take long for Barlow's dream of expansion to materialise after the move to Bond Street. The departure of Tom Hodge had not ultimately detracted from the firm's reputation as some had feared. Following the Poynter Sale, 1918 continued to be a good year, and in June a selection of books from the library of Sudbury Hall, Derbyshire, totalled over £20,000 in a three-day sale. They were being sold by Lieutenant Lord Vernon, R.N., a descendant of the 5th Baron Vernon (1803–66), who had been a famous Dante scholar and had added some fine early French and Italian books and manuscripts to a long established family library.[1]

Among the Vernon books was a richly illuminated manuscript on vellum of *Le Roman de la Rose*. The 104 miniatures by sixteenth-century French artists represented an almost complete repertory of French costume of the time of Francis I. It was a superb manuscript of its kind, and G. D. Smith had left a bid for it with Sir Montague of £2,000, but the volume was bought by B. F. Stevens, who also generally bought for the American market, for a mere £100 more. Stevens further bought lot 358, a beautifully illuminated missal printed on vellum in Paris about 1520 for £760, with Quaritch as the underbidder. This must have been something of a surprise for Barlow because the reserve was only £40. But Quaritch had his revenge when he bought a Shakespeare First Folio for £2,100, beating both Stevens's and G. D. Smith's bid of £1,100 left with Barlow. Smith, however, did get a Shakespeare Second Folio for £240, £160 cheaper than he had anticipated. But after that Quaritch capped all Smith's bids for other rare Shakespeare items. Smith also failed to buy another lot he wanted, one of the most interesting in the sale, a copy of Dibdin's *Bibliographical Decameron*, or 'Ten Days Pleasant Discourse upon Illuminated Manuscripts and subjects connected with early Engravings, Typography and Bibliography'. An earlier owner of the book (G. H. Freeling, an eminent collector and postal reformer) had expanded the original three volumes to no less than twelve by adding proof plates for the book which were not subsequently published, other material written by Dibdin, several hundred drawings and tracings from *incunabula*, and over five hundred 'other items of miscellaneous character, including views, woodcuts, printers' devices, title-pages, alphabets, initials cut from illuminated MSS, leaves cut from missals printed on vellum by Vérard and Pigouchet . . . and fifty-two autograph letters from eminent Book Collectors, publishers, printers, etc.' Bumpus bought this magnificent rag-bag, any

1. It was from this almost unknown library that years before Robert Staynor Holford had bought many of his finest books, which were to make a great mark when Dr. Rosenbach acquired some of them from Holford's son, Sir George Holford (whose interest ran more towards orchids than books), in 1925, and when the rest were sold at Bond Street two years later.

bibliographical scholar's dream, for £220. It is now in the Grolier Club in New York.

It was this same item (for which the reserve was only £50) that precipitated a major altercation among the members of the Roxburghe Club, the most select society of bibliophiles in the world. The Club secretary, John Murray, the publisher, suggested to Sydney Cockerell, the Director of the Fitzwilliam Museum in Cambridge,[1] that he should inspect it to see if it would be a useful purchase for the Club. Cockerell replied in his usual forthright manner: 'I went up to see the Dibdin yesterday. It is certainly a thorough and very interesting piece of grangerising, and if the Roxburghe Club were what it ought to be, a club of book collectors and connoisseurs – instead of consisting largely of distinguished personages with little or no real interest in the subject – and if it had any life in it and held meetings of a reasonable kind for the discussion and exhibition of rare and valuable books – I should say that these volumes would be quite worth bidding for. But in the circumstances I think the money would be thrown away'.[2]

This certainly seems to have made its mark, and it was another Club member, with a similar reputation for outspokenness, Henry Yates Thompson, who eventually congratulated Cockerell on his courage in thus bringing about a reshuffle of the Club's officers and in jolting it back towards the objectives originally laid down by its founders a century previously.

That same Yates Thompson was the unexpected purchaser of lot 518 in the Vernon sale, a fifteen-century Italian illuminated manuscript on vellum of the works of Virgil. Half the trade had wanted it and there was fierce bidding, but Yates Thompson had left an enormously high bid for it with Barlow which was almost ten times as great as the owner's reserve, and this secured him the book. This acquisition was to be a link in a memorable chain of events.

Yates Thompson was probably the greatest collector of illuminated manuscripts of his era. At the time of the Vernon sale he was already eighty years old and had led a particularly interesting life. His father had been partner in a Liverpool bank, and his mother, a woman of exceptional ability, was the daughter of a great merchant, philanthropist and book collector. First educated privately, Thompson was then sent to Harrow where he became Head of the School. He won the Porson prize for Greek verse at Cambridge. Having turned his back on careers in schoolmastering and at the Bar, he decided to devote himself to travel and went to Egypt, the Holy Land, India, the West Indies and spent some time in America. He arrived there at the time of the sternest phase of the American Civil War and witnessed some of its fiercest battles. On his return he stood unsuccessfully for Parliament in several elections as a Liberal candidate. He was much too blunt a speaker to make a politician, and eventually became private secretary for six years to Lord Spencer, the Viceroy of Ireland. After further travel he married in 1878 Elizabeth, the eldest daughter of George Smith, a distinguished publisher and owner of the *Dictionary of National*

1. He was Charles Bell's opposite number in Cambridge.
2. Quoted in *Cockerell*, by Wilfrid Blunt, London, 1964.

Biography and the *Pall Mall Gazette*. Sixteen years younger than her husband, Mrs. Thompson was a charming, highly intelligent, commanding personality, who could 'soften his disconcerting bluntness by an unfailing tact. Her light explanatory interpolations were as spontaneous as they were intuitive. Her celebrated dinner table often included the best minds of all countries and her serene temper, her lightness of touch, her fresh gaiety were never more in evidence than when her husband had brought together, with no forewarning to her, the most apparently uncongenial and incongruous elements'.[1]

Towards the end of his life Yates Thompson looked for all the world like a retired sea-dog with his full, white beard, his unusually slit-like eyes, his highly polished boots and his peppery temperament. He had a marvellous sense of humour, loved teasing his friends and was quite happy to be nick-named 'the Pound of Tea'. *The Times*, in a long obituary, described him thus:

First impressions of the large head, short, compact build, square, broad shoulders, the direct glance, shrewd and penetrating under the heavy brows, the sudden glint of laughter lighting up the grim, bearded countenance, the gruff voice and the bluntness, almost rudeness, of address soon yielded to recognition of the breadth of his interests and the richness of his experience. Further knowledge revealed a man of great strength of will, indifferent to the opinion of the multitude, at once reserved and outspoken, whimsical and generous, humorous and austere. To his friends, and they were many, no substitute can be found for that ample, genial presence, with the sharp yet kindly glance, the open mind, keen and humane, and the large heart.

Thompson eventually managed the *Pall Mall Gazette* for some years, changing its political bias from Conservative to strongly Liberal, and employed such editors as John Morley and the brilliant W. T. Stead, who virtually invented the journalistic interview. But the work exhausted him both physically and financially, and he finally sold the paper to the first Lord Astor. Thereafter he was free to indulge his taste for rare books, and particularly for illuminated manuscripts. He had already inherited a number from his mother's father, Joseph Brooks Yates. Some of these he sold and then determined to set about acquiring a collection limited to one hundred in number of the finest manuscripts money could buy. He started to do so at what was in many ways an ideal moment; for the greatest collector and most rapacious purchaser of manuscripts of all times, Sir Thomas Phillipps, had died in 1872 and no one had quite taken his place. There was nothing new about appreciating the work of the scribes and illuminators who had preceded the invention of printing. Sotheby's had been selling missals and decorated manuscripts since the days of Samuel Baker. But an awareness that these superb relics of five, six, seven and eight centuries ago were not just pretty picture books but the contemporary equivalent of later easel paintings had only recently dawned. Not many collectors as yet appreciated the artistic achievement of the early illuminators, and relatively low prices

1. *The Times*, 10 July 1928.

for their work reflected this lack of wider interest. One could not display manuscripts in magnificent frames on the walls of sumptuous houses: they were a much more private form of acquisition. As much as any single man could, Pierpont Morgan had towards the end of his life, precipitated a change of attitude towards them but Yates Thompson's interest preceded his by several years and he did his buying very quietly.

An important aspect of book collecting, as we have seen already, is the continuous re-circulation of the same major items, as often as not through the auction room. Yates Thompson's quickened pace of collecting coincided with a number of dispersals of other great collections. He bought some of his finest items at that most curious of Sotheby sales in 1889 when the Prussian Government was forced to dispose of its resplendent private purchase from the Hamilton Palace Library.[1] He acquired individual items at general book and manuscript sales throughout the Eighties and Nineties. He purchased several of the best manuscripts at the John Ruskin sale at Sotheby's in 1902. He bought from the Ambroise Firmin-Didot Collection and N. S. Bing in Paris, and from Dr. Baer in Frankfurt, and elsewhere in Europe. Above all he had the courage to lay out the seemingly enormous sum of £30,000 – and he was certainly not in the Morgan class of millionaire – in May 1897, for what was known as the 'Ashburnham Appendix'. Bertram, 4th Earl of Ashburnham (1797–1878) was, as we have seen, an avid collector of books *and* manuscripts. By the bulk-purchases of three great collections, those of Libri, Barrois and Stowe, in a period of only two years, between 1847 and 1849, he had acquired 3,600 manuscripts for an outlay of £22,000. Other manuscripts which he purchased singly over a much longer period, from 1844 to 1877, were collectively termed the 'Appendix'. Among them were the Lindau Gospels, a ninth-century manuscript in a contemporary jewelled binding, the St. Omer Psalter, a famous cycle of York Miracle Plays, a host of important early Italian manuscripts and a tenth-century Spanish text of *Beatus Super Apocalypsum*: some two hundred and fifty manuscripts in all. For various reasons the 5th Earl decided to sell much of his father's library in the 1890s. The Lindau Gospels went to Pierpont Morgan for £10,000. Yates Thompson bought the rest.

He rapidly disposed of four-fifths of this purchase. The English Biblical manuscripts went to the John Rylands Library in Manchester and two hundred volumes were sold at Sotheby's in a first sale on 1 May 1899 (177 lots) and in a second on 11 May 1901 (19 lots). Altogether he had disposed of manuscripts and books there in nine sales by 1914, so that by that time he was well-known to the firm. He asked the most notable scholars and experts to help him in the cataloguing of what he retained. These included Dr. M. R. James, the famous writer of ghost stories and Provost of Eton, Sir Sydney Cockerell, Sir George Warner (Keeper of MSS at the British Museum) and Sir Edward Maunde Thompson, a great palaeographer and Director of the British Museum. Their work was published in a whole series of catalogues which Yates Thompson

<hr />

1. *See* page 75ff.

produced privately over a period of many years. In the last volume of all he added a postscript, which proved to be something of a bombshell. It read:

Now that I have done all I can by way of description and reproduction of these fascinating works of art, the question arises as to how the Hundred Illuminated Manuscripts shall be finally disposed of. After consideration, I have decided that the best course for me, in all the circumstances, is, with three or four exceptions, to sell the whole collection by auction.

I am aware that some would prefer that I should make an arrangement by which the collection might be permanently kept together. In the case, however, of a small group of books, in which each individual is so important as to be well qualified to stand by itself, I prefer that the volumes should be in private hands, rather than be merged in any public collection.

I have decided, therefore, that these precious manuscripts which have been to me of such absorbing interest shall go, in the language of Edmond de Goncourt's will, 'aux héritiers de mes goûts'.

Unless I am over tempted by some previous private offer the sale of the first portion of the manuscripts will probably be announced at no distant date; and I can only hope that future possessors will obtain from them as much pleasure as they have given me.

Yates Thompson must have realised that there would be a reaction to this announcement but the fervour of it took even him by surprise. Long before the postscript saw the light of day Sydney Cockerell had written to him: 'Since I saw you and last heard from you, what you have told me of your intention to sell your manuscripts has been a constant weight and dragging oppression on my mind – a sort of wound of which I am almost never unconscious. . . . Your collection as it stands, gathered together with rare taste and judgement during a quarter of a century which has been rich in opportunities, is now splendidly complete. In its way it is quite without rival. Kept together it is one of the great artistic and spiritual assets of England. That you should be willing to scatter it, unless for good reasons that you have not disclosed, seems to me – and would seem to others, were I at liberty to speak of it – lamentable in the extreme'.

He went on to outline in detail every manuscript which he had helped Yates Thompson to buy, and concluded: 'If you will give me a chance and a time limit I will at least try my utmost to save them from the hands of ignorant millionaires who do not know how to handle or appreciate such inestimable treasures'. As Cockerell was one of the most successful museum directors ever to coax benefactions out of the wealthy, this was no idle boast.

M. R. James was even blunter: 'This is too bad. Cockerell has told me now the dreadful news that you mean to sell your books. I cannot say what a grief this is to me. I did think they were at least safe for England and were not, once gathered, to be dispersed again among Boches, Jews and Transatlantics. If I were by you I would go down on my knees to beseech you to give up the idea.'

These pleas did not fall entirely on stony ground. Yates Thompson gave the fourteenth-century Psalter of the St. Omer family of Norwich to the British

Museum. The famous Metz Pontifical he proposed to donate to the Fitzwilliam Museum[1] and the 'Friends of the Fitzwilliam' were able to purchase his Psalter of Isabella of France. To Cockerell, Thompson replied sternly although mentioning his intended gift; to what he called James's 'most pathetic appeal' he responded rather more gently and apologetically, though he concluded 'my will is that the MSS should go into private hands. Personally, I have greatly enjoyed their possession because they were mine and because I could handle them whenever I wanted. . . . I may also add for your special information that having expended in this collection a sum of money decidedly larger than I had any business to expend on a private whim, I am not inclined to make a considerable sacrifice to accomplish an end which I do not cordially and completely care for.'

Cockerell accepted the gift with a good grace, but made one more effort through Mrs. Thompson to prevail upon her husband to change his mind. Unfortunately he was excessively brusque even by his own unfettered standards and there were dire consequences. Having been a regular guest there for many years he was never asked to the Thompsons' house at 19 Portman Square again, and Mrs. Thompson determined thereafter – as we shall see – to take a hand herself in making arrangements for the ultimate distribution of some of her husband's most precious manuscripts.

In the meantime the postscript had been drawn to Barlow's attention and he had not been slow to respond. No one appreciated more clearly than he how important the disposal of the Yates Thompson Collection would be to Sotheby's. He and the collector met to discuss the sale in the summer of 1918 following Thompson's purchase in the Vernon sale, and in September Barlow suggested the possibility of arranging a private sale while he was in America, where he expected to be not only on the firm's, but also on government business. But despite the suggestion in the postscript that he might just be tempted, Yates Thompson said no. With his knowledge of the other collectors in the field he would have no difficulty in arranging a private sale himself if he wanted it. Barlow concurred that auction was probably the best means of disposal: 'Your wonderful collection must be worth such a very large figure that the number of buyers is probably a limited one'. He suggested another meeting and this took place towards the end of October when the terms for a first sale of thirty major items were agreed. Most unusually, Yates Thompson was to undertake the cataloguing himself and to choose and to pay for the illustrations. In consideration of this and 'in view of your long and friendly association with us', Barlow agreed to sell the collection for half the normal commission, 5 per cent. Despite Yates Thompson's occasional fears of a post-war slump in prices,

1. It should be pointed out that, together with his wife, Yates Thompson was a remarkably generous public benefactor: to the Louvre he gave a manuscript with miniatures by Jean Fouquet; he supported the London Library in a multitude of ways; to Harrow he gave an art school; to Newnham College in Cambridge a library; to the city of Liverpool a great public park; to the Lancashire & Yorkshire railway two complete hospitals; to the Picture Gallery at Dulwich three new rooms and some pictures, and much more besides.

Barlow must have anticipated record results. But although he kept pressing for an immediate sale, Yates Thompson still hesitated about fixing a final date.

Matters were complicated when that other great English collector of manuscripts C. W. Dyson Perrins, offered Yates Thompson £100,000 for the entire collection in November, even though he did not know all it contained, and asked for an opportunity to examine it in detail. Nothing came of this, though Dyson Perrins was to play a considerable, though unpublicised, part in the auction sale later. Two Paris dealers also approached Yates Thompson unsuccessfully. A third collector, Chester Beatty, however, did buy a *Book of Hours* from Thompson for some £4,000 before the sale, and the British Museum bought the St. Louis Psalter from him privately for the same sum.

Barlow's preliminary promotion in America must have prompted an animated response, and after a number of cables he finally persuaded Yates Thompson to agree to a first sale on 3 June 1919. The preparation of the catalogue was put in hand and it appeared in unusually good time before the sale. It was profusely illustrated, though in a somewhat clumsy way, because the illustrations had been reprinted mostly without alteration from Yates Thompson's earlier private catalogues. A prefatory note by Sotheby's explained that 'in the case of this superb and unique collection we have been glad to accept the suggestion of the learned owner that he should himself prepare the catalogue. This, in consequence, has the advantage not only of the owner's scholarly knowledge, but of many interesting personal touches which would otherwise be lacking'.

One cannot but smile at this diplomatic defence of many of Yates Thompson's rather unsalesmanlike comments on some of the items, both in the first and the subsequent sales. One newspaper described them as 'refreshingly unconventional'. A delightfully human touch in the description of lot 30, the last item in the first sale summed up the collector's feelings: 'in the composition of this sales catalogue my continual difficulty has been to avoid superlatives. The sale catalogue is a sort of funeral of my MSS and my endeavour has been to avoid excessive praise, which is the bane of funeral orations.'

As was only to be expected, the prospect of the first sale caused great excitement, even though it was clear that very few contenders would be able to afford the prices of the manuscripts. As Edmund Dring of Quaritch explained to Belle da Costa Greene, the librarian of the Pierpont Morgan Library, in a long letter: 'You ask me if there are any collectors in England except Dyson Perrins. Well really he is the only man who could spend £15,000 to £20,000 on a sale, but there are at least half a dozen people who would be quite willing to buy one fine manuscript at a cost of, say, two or three thousand pounds just for the sake of possessing one really good specimen of early art, and that will be my difficulty in regard to the sale.' He then goes on to make this remarkable comment, 'in fact, one man, a Roumanian, came to ask my opinion on some of the lots, and he said he only wanted one or two really good specimens, but he did not mind, if I advised him, going up to £6,000 or £7,000 for each item. I am afraid I gave him the cold shoulder, because he is not a man I like.' The man concerned did ultimately buy two lots in the first sale through a Paris dealer, at a total cost of only £1,620, and the two most outstanding lots in the second sale, and one wonders whether Dring was wise to reject him as a client. His name was Calouste Gulbenkian.

However, in every other way, Dring was the unsung hero of the sale. He acquired twenty-one out of the thirty lots for his customers in the first sale, and twenty out of thirty-four in the second. In financial terms he subscribed probably two-thirds of the total raised. But he did have remarkable customers, and he certainly deserved them, for his assessment of the sale prospects was extraordinarily shrewd. His clients included Chester Beatty, Dyson Perrins, Dr. Rosenbach, Miss Greene, the British Museum and the Bibliothèque Nationale. Each had written to him for advice on the condition and probable prices of the manuscripts they considered bidding for.

Sir Montague Barlow took the rostrum on what the *Morning Post* described as 'the most important day's sale in the history of the Sotheby firm'. The room was crowded with *cognoscenti*: the Director of the British Museum, the Keeper of Manuscripts there, Sir George Warner, St. John Hornby – Chairman of W. H. Smith and owner of the Ashendene Press, Sydney Cockerell, Seymour de Ricci, but above all, Yates Thompson was there too. 'It is an open secret,' wrote the *Daily Telegraph*, 'that he who has had many a collector's joy in amassing his treasures, determined on an open sale not only because failing eyesight was robbing him of the full delights of contemplation, but because he wished to enjoy the thrill of hearing the progressive bidding in the auction room testifying the approval of the world's collectors. Yet he sat like a sphynx as Mr. Edmund Dring of Quaritch and Dr. Hagberg Wright of the London Library fought for lot 5, the beautiful *Book of Hours* of Jeanne II, Queen of Navarre, of circa 1334, with 108 miniatures.' The bidding started at £2,000, and Dring took it to the unheard of, unprecedented sum of £11,800. Yates Thompson had acquired this for a modest £300[1] from the Earl of Ashburnham. A great deal of public guesswork went into the possible identity of the ultimate purchaser. Dring wrote to him immediately after the sale: 'I was successful in buying for you both lots you wanted, but for lot 5, for which you gave me a commission of £12,000 I had to pay £11,800. The person who rang me up was Dr. Hagberg Wright[2] of the London Library in St. James's Square, but I have not the slightest idea for whom he was acting. I was, however, more fortunate in regard to lot 23, the Oriental Manuscript [a Persian manuscript from Samarkand of 1410 which included a miniature of a polo match in which a Roman emperor was one of the players] for which you gave me a commission of £9,000. This I bought for £5,000.' They were the two most expensive items in the sale and the purchaser was Baron Edmond de Rothschild.

Dring bought seven lots for the Pierpont Morgan Library. By and large they

1. The code Yates Thompson used to record prices in his manuscripts was based on the word BRYANSTONE, where B = 1, R = 2, Y = 3, etc.
2. The Yates Thompsons were on very friendly terms with Hagberg Wright and greatly admired his bibliographical scholarship.

cost him much less than he had estimated before the sale and Belle da Costa Greene thought she had got some great bargains. She was ecstatically proud of her purchase of lot 30. Dring had paid £2,900 for what Yates Thompson described as 'the most magnificent book in the world' (printed in Venice in 1483 by Andreas de Asolo on vellum with thirty historiated initial ornaments and two wonderful full page miniatures by a painter of the Ferrarese School, the two volumes weighing no less than 33 pounds).

It had taken Barlow one-and-a-half hours to sell the thirty items and in that time he had established a record figure for a single sale session of £52,360. The papers cried 'amazing', and clearly Yates Thompson was pleased, for a second sale was soon agreed upon, though there were complications over payment for the first. Not all collectors were Rothschilds or Dyson Perrins who settled their bills with despatch. Barlow was exasperated by the endless delays over settlement but not half as exasperated as Yates Thompson. He did not get the full amount due to him for several months, which was certainly much longer than he had been led to believe would be the case. But because Barlow had undertaken the sale for an unusually low commission rate, he could not afford to borrow money from the bank as a bridging loan. He had, in consequence, to face a continuous barrage of irate letters from Yates Thompson.

For the next sale a 5 per cent commission on manuscripts and $7\frac{1}{2}$ per cent on printed books was agreed, and Sotheby's undertook the cataloguing of the latter. The date fixed for it was 23 March 1920. The most outstanding items were to be a series of fourteen early English manuscripts, three French MSS that had once been in the library of the famous fourteenth-century book collector the Duc de Berry, and a Boccaccio *Des Cleres et Nobles Femmes* of 1410. This last was a large folio volume with forty-eight miniatures, but it lacked eighty leaves of the original 270. Fifty-seven of the missing leaves contained pictures. Sydney Cockerell had written nevertheless: 'the MS remains a priceless one, and the width of the margins, its almost immaculate condition and the brilliant splendour of the surviving miniatures make one utterly forgetful of the defects.'

Barlow took the sale once more; Yates Thompson again sat in attendance. Dring of Quaritch returned with a new notebook full of commissions. Belle da Costa Greene attended the sale in person this time, having made a special trip from New York. Many other American collectors were present on this occasion, for post-war travel conditions had become easier in the intervening nine months. Gulbenkian had learned a good deal from the first sale. His representative, S. Devgantz, was more fully briefed and with much higher limits. The palaeographical intelligentsia was there in force: so were the collectors, Chester Beatty, Dyson Perrins, Cortland F. Bishop and a little-known dealer, Hugh Blaker, who was advising those generous patrons of the arts, the Misses Gwendoline and Margaret Davies of Gregynog in Wales; so was the trade, the press and the curious public. The main gallery at Bond Street was jam-packed.

In the event the results of this second sale were even more sensational than the first. This was all the more surprising in a period of general economic uncertainty. Quaritch bought twenty lots for £42,000 out of a total of £78,000.

Devgantz bought four items for Gulbenkian for £20,400; Hugh Blaker bought two manuscripts for the Misses Davies;[1] Tregaskis bought three and Maggs bought a couple.

The catalogue numbering continued from the first sale: lots 31 to 44 consisted of the manuscripts of English origin; lots 45 to 52 were illuminated and illustrated *incunabula*, and lots 53 to 64 French and Italian manuscripts. The combination of early printed books and manuscripts in this sale demonstrated particularly well that the illuminator's art did not die with the invention of movable types but continued for many years to be employed in decorating printed books, in an attempt to make these novelties no less acceptable to prospective owners than the traditional, hand-written models had been. The English manuscripts varied a good deal in quality but were an astonishing assemblage from the infancy of creative artistic effort in our history. The binding alone of lot 31[2] was a uniquely magnificent piece of craftsmanship. And when one considered that it had survived almost eight hundred years of use virtually intact, one could only marvel, as must have done two of its earlier owners, Sir Thomas Phillipps and William Morris.

Yates Thompson's description of the *Life of St. Cuthbert* by the Venerable Bede, written on vellum at Durham about the year 1180, contains the bland comment that it was lent from the Cathedral Library to the Archbishop of York, Richard Le Scrope, who was beheaded in 1405: 'He completed the building of the Choir of York Minster and may have borrowed this volume when the Cuthbert Window was in contemplation, and failed to return it, owing to his execution'. This was to explain its disappearance for nearly five hundred years until it had turned up for sale at Sotheby's in 1906 where Yates Thompson bought it for £1,500. It was now bought by Dring of Quaritch for the British Museum for £5,000.

Lot 37 fetched the highest price so far in the second sale. Devgantz bought it for Gulbenkian for £5,800. It was a profusely illustrated *Apocalypse* produced separately from the Bible in the thirteenth century. Yates Thompson wrote in the catalogue, 'I imagine it to have provided the light reading of the period – a romantic story filled with monsters and miracles, the wonders of Heaven and the horrors of Hell, all very theatrically displayed by the best artists'. He went on to describe 'the tale of my pursuit and final capture of this treasure, the chase having lasted three years, from the first sight of some photographed pages to the final purchase at a Palazzo at Rimini'.

The brilliance of the occasion and its financial success were only marred by one subsequent incident. Dring returned the last item in the sale, a late Italian *Book of Hours*, as imperfect. He had bought it for £2,700 for Chester Beatty, and now claimed that some of its pages were modern fakes. Yates Thompson consulted Sydney Cockerell whose Delphic response persuaded him to accept

1. Lot 36, a fourteenth-century English missal, one of the earliest of its school to have survived, which had at one time been the property of the Sherbrooke Family (£860), and lot 42, a fifteenth-century Book of Hours known as the 'De Grey Horae' (£1,270).
2. A Winchester binding, later owned by Dyson Perrins.

the return. This still left the total sum realised for the sale at over £75,000, another all-time record, and a third sale was planned for the following year.

The usual delays over payment caused that sale to be postponed until 22 June 1921. Another stately catalogue was published for the event and Yates Thompson summarised the arithmetic of the dispersal of his Hundred Best Manuscripts in the introduction: fifty-two titles had been sold by auction, two in private sales and four had been given away. Of the remaining forty-two, he now offered the public a further fifteen.

In the meantime the British economy had suffered severe reverses with a crippling miners' strike and increased unemployment, and the appetite of the few collectors of this type of rarity had been sated to a large extent in the first two sales. Yates Thompson himself was less convinced about the need for the third sale as, owing to an operation, his sight had begun to improve. He was, therefore, very disappointed when the third sale realised only £18,000. The fifteen early printed books he had included in it fetched particularly miserable prices, only about £1,800 in all, and in a number of instances he allowed them to be sold well below the reserves agreed before the sale.

Although Dring supported the sale with five of the most expensive purchases, Edmond de Rothschild did not seem to be buying on this occasion, though the dealer was still acting for Dyson Perrins, Chester Beatty and the American collector, Cortland F. Bishop. With an almost uncanny instinct Dring paid only a fraction more than the reserve price in each case. Six major items had to be bought in. The star turn of the sale was lot 69 – a superb fifteenth-century French manuscript in three volumes devoted to the adventures of Lancelot du Lac in the quest of the San Graal. Twenty years earlier when this had come up at Sotheby's in the Barrois portion of the Ashburnham manuscripts, it was bought for the then great sum of £1,800 by Charles Fairfax Murray, and Tom Hodge had commented publicly that the purchaser was 'just beginning to form a collection'. Yates Thompson bought it from Fairfax Murray, and Dring now bought it for Cortland Bishop for £3,500.[1] The Louvre bought the last item in the sale, a magnificently detailed fifteenth-century drawing attributed to Jean Fouquet, showing a scene in the Battle of Cannae.

Yates Thompson's disappointment over the poor result, and the fact that he had had to buy in four of the manuscripts and two of the earlier printed books, was exacerbated by increasing irritation with Sotheby's over the even slower than usual rate of payment of what was due to him. Barlow had sent him a cheque for £3,800 a month after the sale, but Yates Thompson was less than sympathetic about Barlow's pleas that Quaritch was having problems in collecting the money due to *him* from America. He was also resentful of the fact that the improvement in his sight might have meant that he could have arranged the sale later.

When no further money had reached him by the middle of October he took himself to Bond Street unannounced and, finding Sir Montague out, discussed the matter with Evelyn Barlow instead. Sir Montague thereupon sent him a

1. When *his* collection was sold in 1938 the same book fetched $16,500.

further cheque for £5,000, noting wistfully that this was much more than the firm had received for the sale so far. Yates Thompson then heard nothing further for six weeks. By early December he was seething with rage at this lack of communication and stomped into Bond Street once again and blasted poor Evelyn Barlow. A couple of days later he drafted a rather more temperate note to the firm, which he showed to his solicitor for approval before it was sent off. But by now Barlow's hackles were up too. He wrote to Yates Thompson: 'I was very surprised to hear that when you called . . . you had again brought up the question of finance with Miss Barlow. I was still more surprised by the way you behaved. You had no grounds whatever for the statements you made, and still less, if I may say so, for the manner in which you made them'. Yates Thompson realised that he had transgressed even his own inimitable standards of discourtesy and sent a handsome apology in reply. Even so, matters dragged on until the following April before final settlement was made, and not before there had been threats of litigation. This problem of inertia over payments by the major booksellers and the consequent delay in settling up with proprietors was to bedevil the business throughout the Twenties and Thirties. Barlow frequently commented to his younger colleagues when their discussions at meetings veered round to the painfully long credit that was expected by booksellers: 'the book trade is our life blood. Sotheby's has been financing it for generations. We cannot stop doing so now'.

Despite these irritations Yates Thompson had done exceedingly well, and the £150,000 resulting from the three sales showed him a very handsome profit indeed over his original outlay for the collection, and he still retained a considerable number of valuable books and manuscripts. He now devoted himself to the compilation and printing of a catalogue of the pictures, portraits and miniatures in his house at 19 Portman Square. While visitors always commented on the crowded, very Victorian interior, there were some fine things among the bric-a-brac. The very personal collection of pictures which Yates Thompson had bought during his long life (often for very small sums indeed) included a fine Greuze portrait, a Richard Wilson, two Michael Marieschis of Venice, two Guardis of the Doge's Palace in Venice, a Canaletto ('a very lively and gorgeous scene of gay Venetian life which seemed to me so well suited for public exhibition that I gave it to the Dulwich Gallery'), a Turner, a Constable, Dutch and Flemish pictures and family portraits. He modelled the catalogue on the format of those which had been produced for the Dulwich Gallery while he was a Governor of the College and Chairman of the Gallery Committee.

Henry Yates Thompson died in 1928 in his ninetieth year and his wife, Elizabeth, who had spent an increasing part of her life in their country house at Oving in Buckinghamshire, survived him until 1941, twenty years after the final sale. Her interest and knowledge of the manuscripts almost equalled her husband's, and it gradually became clear to her friends that she had not liked the long dispersal at all. In fact, unbeknownst to her husband, she had bought several items in the final sale. The Yates Thompsons had no children and her generosity in widowhood was truly remarkable. She bequeathed some forty-six important manuscripts – mostly Italian ones of the fifteenth and sixteenth centuries – to the British Museum, to the great delight of all those palaeographers who had helped Yates Thompson to establish his collection and who were still alive. It was the greatest benefaction of its kind the Museum ever received. She also donated to the British Museum a collection of Brontë manuscripts, which she had inherited from her father (who had been the Brontë's publisher). Finally, having inherited the *Dictionary of National Biography* also, she gave this to the University of Oxford, who she felt sure would continue to up-date it and keep it in print in the spirit which her father had intended.

The Yates Thompson saga came to an end when in the hot, sticky summer of 1941, Sotheby's was asked to put up for sale the contents of the household in Portman Square and what remained of the library. Wartime conditions were not propitious for either dispersal and yet, such was the magic clinging to the famous name, that both sales caused a fine swell of optimism in a generally depressed atmosphere.

For many years the Yates Thompsons' next-door neighbour at 20 Portman Square had been none other than Samuel Courtauld, the uniquely successful manufacturer of synthetic textiles and a most enterprising and relatively very early collector of French Impressionist paintings. In 1932 the collector's house became the home of the Courtauld Institute which he had endowed for the study of the history of art. Later on, through a nice quirk of fate, the Yates Thompsons' house was added to the Courtauld Institute.

17
Britwell

FOR nearly forty years the most important series of sales at Bond Street was summed up in the one word, Britwell. It was the most gigantic library that passed through Sotheby's in the present century. The bulk of it had been got together by a Scottish bachelor called William Henry Miller (1789–1848). He worked in Edinburgh as a solicitor and became an M.P. in 1830, having two long spells in Parliament for different constituencies. He moved to England towards the end of his life and settled at Britwell Court near Burnham in Buckinghamshire. He began book collecting in earnest around 1825, and because 'he was very particular about the condition and size of the volumes he purchased, and from his habit of carrying a foot rule about with him for the purpose of ascertaining their dimensions, he became known as "Measure Miller" '.[1] He seems to have led a very quiet life, spending most of his time in bookshops and sale-rooms. He bought enthusiastically and very extensively from the dispersal – largely, but not exclusively, by Sotheby's – between 1834 and 1837 of the enormous library of Richard Heber (1773–1833), 'a biblio-maniac if ever there was one. 'No gentleman', Heber used to say, 'can be without three copies of a book; one for show, one for use and one for borrowers',[2] and he had filled eight or nine entire houses with them, some in England and some on the Continent. Between Measure Miller's death and the early 1900s, the Library passed through the hands of various descendants who all added to it, some quite extensively (the Christie-Millers were enormously wealthy hat manufacturers). The most important accretion by far was the purchase by Wakefield Christie-Miller in 1893 of the Elizabethan books from Lamport Hall – which had remained in the hands of the Isham family since the seventeenth century – when the books were found in an otherwise empty garret where they had lain undisturbed for many generations.

A few duplicates from Britwell Court had already been discarded at Sotheby's in 1908 and 1910, and in the summer of 1916 Mr. Sydney Richard-son Christie-Miller decided to sell another portion of the Library, the Americana. As we have already seen, this was bought *in toto* by George D. Smith for Huntington. Cheered, no doubt, by the success of this transaction, Mr. Christie-Miller decided to part with the rest of the library by degrees. In the end there were twenty-one sales between 1916 and the final dispersal in 1927. Henry Huntington in particular realised that this great release of wholly exceptional books on to the market presented an opportunity that would not recur for enriching his library in California. It was the Heber story all over again, ninety years later. This must have been hunch on Huntington's part rather than factual knowledge, for up to the end of the First World War the Britwell Library was

1. W. Y. Fletcher, *op. cit.*   2. Seymour de Ricci, *op. cit.*

renowned principally for its total inaccessibility[1] even to famous scholars, and there was no printed catalogue. Its extraordinary riches were only revealed as catalogue after catalogue was issued from Bond Street. The logistics alone in selecting works for each sale and transporting them to London was fraught with difficulties, and although the sale was ultimately a resounding success it posed great problems at Sotheby's. *The Times* said at the beginning of the Britwell dispersal that 'it is almost like an empire falling', and at the end that 'the sale of the Library has been a continuous story of high prices and large profits – profits which have scarcely any parallel in fact or fiction', for Measure Miller had bought very cheaply at the Heber sales because they had taken place at a time when one generation of great bibliophiles was dying out and the next had not yet come into being. He was said to have spent less than £50,000 for all his book purchases.

The resulting total after the last sale in July 1927 for the concatenation of twenty-one sales at Bond Street was £605,000 – more than any library had ever fetched at auction, and twice as much as the Huth Sales had brought. But it was obvious that one man was largely responsible for this – Henry E. Huntington. First Smith, and after his death, Rosenbach, had completely dominated the sales on his behalf. The two dealers between them had spent £485,000 on Britwell books, nearly 80 per cent of the total. The other major buyer had been Sir R. Leicester Harmsworth, who had purchased privately the first portion of the large theological library which was to have been sold on 31 January 1921, in order to supplement his own great collection of books by John Bunyan.

It would not be difficult to write a whole book on the Britwell Library and its dispersal. Seymour de Ricci devoted more space to it than any other library in England. He took pains to point out its extraordinary importance 'as a collection of old English books, the greatest ever brought together by a private individual. In many respects it rivalled, or even surpassed, the British Museum. It was extremely catholic, covering every branch of book, from theology to law, science, travel, history and literature. In poetry it was wonderfully complete and the successive owners deserved great credit for the minute care with which they gathered and preserved minor seventeenth- and eighteenth-century poems, in days when they were worth as many shillings (or even pence) as they now cost pounds'.

Matters were complicated when Mr. Christie-Miller moved from Britwell to Clarendon Park, near Salisbury, early in the Twenties and also changed his London residence during the long drawn-out period of his sales. In fact, the Britwell Librarian, Major Herbert Collmann, spent so much of his time at Bond Street that some thought he was a resident member of the staff there. Despite this, it has never been made clear before in what a muddle the books were before they were moved to Sotheby's, and for years the sales were dogged by losses which only came to light often when it was too late to do much to

1. 'It was to most people, as difficult of access as the Harem of an Oriental potentate', said *The Times.*

retrieve them. Matters were not made any easier by a kleptomaniac book porter who, when confronted by such *mountains* of shabby, leather-bound volumes which he had to move around, thought that a few would not be missed, and took them a few at a time to Hodgson's in Chancery Lane who sold them as anonymous property. It took Barlow years of correspondence, litigation and a great deal of the firm's money to recover them.

The matter came to light in a way that must have abashed even the composure of the unflappable Barlow. A member of the book trade commented in confidence to Rham, who was the firm's chief cashier at the time, that he thought it was 'a bit off' that Mr. Christie-Miller should be selling some of his books at Hodgson's at the same time as he was selling others at Sotheby's. Rham felt it his duty to report the matter to Barlow. Barlow – always a man to react quickly – sat down and dictated a frosty letter to Christie-Miller complaining about the simultaneous disposal of books at Chancery Lane as well as at Bond Street. After that the fat really was in the fire. A full scale investigation aided by Scotland Yard soon revealed what had happened, though it was Barlow himself who finally pinpointed the culprit. He felt bitter not only because Hodgson's had sold the books without making any detailed enquiries into their ultimate origin, but also because the thief had been rather a pathetic man in whom Barlow had taken a great personal interest and whom he had gone out of his way to help. The partners held meeting after meeting on the matter. Barlow cancelled his much-needed holiday in order to have time to resolve matters. In the end it was Jim Kiddell, who had been in the firm for only a matter of months, who volunteered to explain that the cause of all the trouble was a man who, unbeknownst to Sotheby's, suffered severely from epilepsy which had been exacerbated by gassing and shell-shock during the war. This explanation totally defused the anticipated explosion from Mr. Christie-Miller, a retired officer who had had experience of similar cases, and the matter was resolved amicably, though things did not rest there. The insurance company met the initial claims even though there was a loophole in the policy which could have precluded restitution, but further claims continued for such a long time that litigation eventually ensued and was only settled years later.

After the unexpected private sale of the Americana in August 1916, the next sale was, curiously enough, described only as 'the Property of a Gentleman'. It took place at Bond Street – soon after the move there – on 31 July 1917, and consisted largely of *incunabula*. Then there was a long gap until 30 June 1919 when 897 lots of books on voyages and foreign history were sold. The November sale was postponed because a postal strike had delayed the distribution of the catalogues, so there were two memorable sessions on successive days, on 15 and 16 December 1919. The 15 December sale was devoted to early English music; the next day was to consist of only 108 lots of books of early English literature. (It was the most important peace-time sale up to that moment.) During its lengthy preparation the code name aptly used for the sale in correspondence between the owner and the partners was 'PLUMS'.

A few days before the great day, George D. Smith made another offer for a private *en bloc* purchase. Mr. Christie-Miller came up to London to discuss the matter with Geoffrey Hobson. Hobson felt in duty bound to report the offer and could not advise the owner to refuse it point blank, though he hinted that his own view would be to let the auction take its course. Christie-Miller put on his hat and walked around the block. He came back a few minutes later and told Hobson to go ahead with the sale.

At Bond Street it was anticipated to be of such importance that the iron rule of those days that book cataloguers could not attend sales was broken at Geoffrey Hobson's behest, and all the cataloguers piled into the sale-room. By all accounts it was crowded more densely than anyone could ever remember: 'it would have been impossible to force a pin between the standees, so closely were they packed', Millicent Sowerby remembered. At precisely one o'clock, the usual hour when sales started at that time, Barlow, a small, dapper, lithe figure bounded into the rostrum. His face was tense and so pale that his complexion matched the white carnation in his buttonhole. This was going to be the make-or-break sale of the new post-war era.

The catalogue that everyone held in his hand must have been a joy to prepare. Over and over again the cataloguer had been able to add such comments as *the only copy known; only one other copy known; of the greatest rarity; probably not more than two copies in existence; the only copy now extant; probably the only copy in existence; an edition of the greatest rarity; only two other copies known; this little work . . . is probably unique; this appears to be the only copy known; believed to be the only copy of this edition in existence*, and a great many other variations on the same theme. If there was one thing that tempted Huntington it was a book thought to be unique. He and Smith conferred at length, and Smith went to London with virtually unlimited reserves for the sale. He and Edmund Dring of Quaritch sat facing each other unusually grimly, for Dring too had hefty commissions from his clients and it would not be good for his business if he could not take at least *some* of them out of the sale-room under the Quaritch banner.

He won round one of the contest: he bought lot 1 for £1,700, *A Treatise on Fysshinge* by Wynkyn de Worde, and described as the first separate edition and *the only copy known*. It must have been a jolt for Barlow, for the reserve on the book was only £600. It also stirred George Smith into action. Dring registered his bids with a nod of the head; Smith with a flick of his fingers. From now on the fingers never stopped flicking. Smith took lot 2; Dring lot 3. Then Smith bought fourteen lots in a row, including a collection of eighty-eight virtually unknown Elizabethan Broadsides and Ballads with a superb provenance going back to the Ipswich Postmaster (William Fitch). Smith paid £6,400 for them. Barlow's reserve was £2,000. And so it continued. There was yet another multitude of Caxtons. They fetched higher prices than ever before. Over and over again the reserves were completely out-distanced by the actual prices.

The atmosphere had reached fever pitch by the time the sale reached lot 85. This consisted of a small, shabby volume from Lamport Hall. It contained the 1599 edition (the fourth) of Shakespeare's first great work, *Venus and Adonis*, of

8

which no other copy was known; Shakespeare's *Passionate Pilgrim* of which two other copies were extant and one was already in America; and *Epigrammes and Elegies* by Christopher Marlowe and Sir John Davies. Barlow had a reserve of £12,000 written into his catalogue; it was a very ambitious figure. At once there was bidding from all over the floor. Then, inevitably, it became another duel between Dring of Quaritch and George Smith. £100 by £100 the bidding passed £12,000 and reached £14,000. Quaritch kept nodding up to £15,000. Smith flicked his fingers at £15,100. Dring – the whole room staring at him – sat tight and never moved a muscle. He had reached his limit and lost. Barlow patiently invited other bids, but there was only silence, and the hammer came down at £15,100 for Smith. It was the highest price ever given for a printed book. The whole room cheered. Cheering had been known at Christie's for record picture prices but never at Sotheby's. Barlow relaxed and smiled. No doubt he was reflecting on one line from the precious volume he had just sold: 'Gold that's put to use more gold begets'. With twenty-three lots to go the total for the sale had already reached £91,375. The next few minutes brought it up to £110,356 – the highest sum ever achieved in a single day, more than four times the record total achieved on a single day at the Pembroke Library sale in 1914. It was a new record that was to stand for many years. It indicated a post-war boom. Certainly it had been led by George Smith who had bought eighty lots out of the 108; Quaritch had bought nineteen and Maggs two.

Naturally, the sale made headlines all over the world, and subsequently Bond Street was besieged with letters that started: 'I have a copy of Venus and Adonis . . .'. But there was one incident which followed the sale that was much more akin to fiction than to fact. Two young men were practising archery one summer afternoon at their home on an estate in Shropshire, called Longner Hall. They needed a target, went upstairs to the library and chose an old book with a vellum binding because it was white and easily visible at a distance. One of the boys looked at it and saw that it was a copy of *Venus and Adonis*. He remembered reading about the sale of a copy at £15,000 not long previously. The target as a target was put aside and the family communicated with Sotheby's. It really was another 1599 edition. The excitement about the dis-covery was immense, and *The Times Literary Supplement* devoted a good deal of space to the new find.

Eventually a sale was fixed for it on a date which would suit Mr. Smith because, of course, Mr. Huntington wanted this copy too. Smith was about to leave for Europe for the sale and was actually sitting in his office waiting for a car to take him to board the liner in which he was to sail. A letter was handed to him but it dropped to the floor. He bent down to pick it up, but never rose again. He died instantly of a heart attack. The shock in the book world was so great that the sale was cancelled. The second copy was eventually sold privately[1] to Quaritch for £10,000 and finished up, as one might have expected, in Henry Huntington's library.

1. On 22 March 1920. The intention had been to sell it at the conclusion of the second Yates Thompson manuscript sale but it was withdrawn at the last moment.

We have already seen how highly A. E. Newton thought of George Smith. 'The book business will go on without him, so much is certain. But unless it be Dr. Rosenbach of Philadelphia, who is a scholar as well as a bookseller, there is no one to rank with *him* who has just been taken from us', he now wrote. This fact seemed to become more firmly established in people's minds on both sides of the Atlantic, and Dr. Rosenbach lost no time at all in introducing himself to Smith's major customers, such as Folger and Huntington. Only a few months later the following unsolicited eulogy which appeared in the American book trade journal, *Publishers Weekly*, must have helped to sway those who might still have doubted the Doctor's pre-eminence:

The fact is now getting to be pretty well recognised that Dr. Rosenbach is one of the most original, resourceful and dominating figures that have appeared in our rare book field. He attracted attention from the beginning but his successes were won so quietly, easily and as a matter of course, that they caused little comment. . . . It is perfectly clear that Dr. Rosenbach knows exactly what he wants. His education, taste and ambition lead him exclusively to the great rarities. His skill, courage and resources in gathering stock finds its counterpart in his knowledge of collectors and his ability to pick customers.

Publishers Weekly had been particularly impressed by the Doctor's recent new catalogue, which listed items worth well in excess of $1,000,000, and by his flair for personal publicity. He had, in fact, bought at Sotheby's in person as early as 1907, but made his first impact at Bond Street in March 1921, when he bought 207 out of 321 lots in the tenth Britwell Sale at a cost of £40,584 out of a sale total of £48,552. His was a much more flamboyant personality than Smith's, and the press turned the full glare of attention on to him, though he was often referred to as 'the wealthy American *collector*' rather than *dealer*. In the history of Sotheby's Dr. Rosenbach was important because he provided competition to the London rare book dealers. In the 1919/20 season the firm of Quaritch spent a record figure of £166,172 at Sotheby's. In 1920/21 they spent £66,886 against Dr. Rosenbach's £42,089. In 1921/22 the Doctor shot ahead to £91,304 and Quaritch dropped to £29,232. By 1925/26 Quaritch were lapping the Doctor again at £46,220 against his £44,464. In the interim he had led with more than double their total. In 1926/27/28 the London firm remained solidly in the lead. They continued to do so right through the slump when the Doctor entered a period of quiescence, though their greatest London competitor, Maggs, who had been a very respectable third previously, overtook them both from 1932 onwards and remained consistently ahead for twenty years or more.

In one respect Dr. Rosenbach was not quite the model buyer that Smith had been. He was a slow payer. He was also a great man for returns and for claiming reductions in payment for the most trivial imperfections. But Sotheby's learned to live with this. What was much harder to bear initially was that the immediate consequence of Smith's sudden death was a freezing of all his assets. It took months of patient, and ultimately quite bellicose negotiations, with the administrators of his estate to get payments released. Not surprisingly, Mr.

Christie-Miller was anxious to get the very large sums due to him but Barlow was concerned about avoiding the dissipation of the firm's profits by borrowing money for long periods at the then relatively high interest rates of 7 to 8 per cent. One way or another Barlow became more involved with the Britwell Sale than any other major event at a time when he was reaching the climax of his own political career. Certainly the fact that he was at first a junior and later a full cabinet minister made a deep impression on all with whom he came into contact in the auction world.

After the Britwell Sale in December 1919, it became clear to Barlow and to Hobson that they needed an additional partner for the book side. The business was growing and Barlow knew that his political career was going to take up a good deal more time than previously. In fact, he became Parliamentary Secretary to the Minister of Labour in the spring of 1920. The partners put about the word that a *very* bright young man was needed and they began to scrutinise possible candidates.

PART THREE

From One War
to the Next

Messrs. SOTHEBY & CO. beg to announce that their charges for offering the following categories of property for sale are in general 7½ %

> *Pictures, Modern Drawings and all other Works of Art, including Armour and Bronzes, Ceramics and Glass, Objects of Vertu, Furniture, Silver, Jewellery, Miniatures, Tapestries, Rugs and other Textiles.*

A commission of 10 % is charged on every lot of the above which does not realize £100.

12½ % is charged for offering the following:—

> *Antiquities, Autograph letters, Books and Manuscripts, Book-plates, Coins and Medals, Engravings, Etchings and Old Drawings, Japanese colour prints, and Japanese Works of Art, Persian and Indian Miniatures.*

All the above charges include cataloguing, advertising and all other expenses of the sale after the property is received, except insurance and illustrations in catalogues should such be desired.

In the case of lots which are not sold, a reduced commission is charged on the amount actually bid at the Sale.

Messrs. SOTHEBY & CO. receive and inspect Property without charge at Owners' risk. Large consignments by case or van can be received at their Goods Entrance, 5, George Street, Hanover Square, W.1, and addressed labels can be obtained on application. No responsibility can be undertaken for the return of packing cases unless special arrangements are made beforehand in writing.

A page from a prospectus put out by the firm in the early 1930s to advertise their services. The 7½% commission was lower than that of rivals.

18

The Book Department: New Phase, New Faces

T HE general relief at the end of hostilities after four years of slaughter of the young and the able on a scale never previously known in history is difficult to imagine sixty years later. There were virtually no families who had not suffered some loss during the war. So obviously there were gaps among those who reassembled for a great Victory Dinner which Barlow organised for Sotheby's staff in June 1919. It was also to be a belated celebration of the successful move from Wellington Street to Bond Street. The occasion offered Barlow a splendid opportunity to announce a newly created Staff Bonus Scheme under the terms of which the firm would give every employee a capital sum equal to 20 per cent of his or her annual salary in their second twelve months of service. In the third year and thereafter they would be given a sum equivalent to between 15 and 25 per cent of their salary, depending on length of service. In addition, interest would be payable to staff on the capital accrued. The scheme was as generous as it was novel, and some of the more cynical doubted whether it would ever come into being. But it did, in December 1919, though it had one consequence which Barlow and his fellow partners had not foreseen. It provided such excellent nest-eggs for female employees that it led to a spate of early marriages and, similarly, it could be used by ambitious young men to launch small businesses of their own. For this reason, more than any other, it was modified in 1923 and again in 1928. It had to be abandoned altogether in the disastrous economic collapse of the Great Slump. But it was a marvellous fillip to effort at a time of great expansion and must have been one of the earliest profit-sharing schemes of its kind.

Charles des Graz joins Sotheby's

After the war the amount of material coming into Bond Street increased by leaps and bounds and the number of sales went up accordingly.[1] Many people needed to sell; many more wanted to buy. In particular, the interest from America made itself felt much more strongly. Lloyd George's policy of increasing death duties was a major factor in releasing property on to the market. If some cast him as chief of the Forty Thieves, Sir Montague Barlow could well have been Ali Baba, determined to get for Sotheby's a share of the fabulous things from the treasure caves of the aristocracy and the landed gentry.

A number of those members of the staff who had remained with the firm during the war beyond the normal age of retirement now wanted a gentler pace

1. In 1917 there were 49, in 1918 64, in 1919 95 and in 1920 114.

of life. The first major changes took place in the book department. They started at the top, for as we have seen, Barlow and Hobson had recognised the need for more strength on the management side. Barlow thought he knew just the man for the job and the search for such a new, younger partner soon narrowed down to a single name which had been recommended from a great many directions: as it happened, this was the same as Barlow's initial choice – Charles des Graz.

The young man in question had been Captain of the Oppidans at Eton. After three years as a scholar of Trinity College, Cambridge, he had had an impressive career during the First World War in the Censorship Department of the War Office. Afterwards he had been appointed Director of the British Library of Information in the United States. All the reports indicated to Barlow that here was a very brilliant young man, who was not entirely happy with his job in America. As was so often the case in those days, the first discreet approach was made to the candidate's father. The young man's much respected, former house master at Eton, Ernest Churchill, was asked to write to des Graz Senior, a former British Ambassador to Vienna, who lived in Ireland.

> I am writing to you to know whether you regard Charlie's present occupation as likely to lead to anything permanent, or whether you would agree to consider an offer which I think I could get made to him. When I saw him before he went out to America it appeared to me that he was afraid that his present work was rather a blind alley.
>
> The offer alluded to is that he should go into what could not help being a very interesting business connected with books and artistic matters of all kinds. . . .

Mr. Churchill then outlined details of salary (starting at £600 or £700 a year) and the solid prospects of a partnership in three or four years, if Mr. des Graz could eventually find a capital sum of between £10,000 and £20,000 to put into the business. He continued:

> As regards the work, it will take up all Charlie's time except that he will get three out of four Saturdays off. It is a kind of business that will mean working mainly in London with occasional trips to other parts of the world. All these partners are Varsity men. The one thing you may regard as a drawback is that all the partners must do their share of selling by auction. I feel quite confident that if Charlie cared for such a position he would be just the right man for the job and I should think that with his tastes the job would suit him. I am not at liberty to tell you more and if you guess by any chance what the business is you had better not let me know that you have done so. But supposing you think, and Charlie thinks, that he would like to try it, I will put you in communication with the man who approached me about it. . . .

There was no immediate response and Barlow, impatient as ever, cabled Charles des Graz in America to say that the offer had come from him and followed it up with a five-page letter outlining the initial salary proposed, the terms and prospects for a partnership and the likely financial profits accruing from it. Barlow put a lot of thought into the letter. He very much wanted des Graz to join the business and he knew that the job would have to seem tempting. But this letter was also something of a chairman's progress report and a statement of personal philosophy. Des Graz clearly regarded it in this light for he kept it in his desk until the time of his sudden death thirty-three years later. It is the only written evidence we have of what the principal architect of the modern Sotheby's felt about the firm. As such, it is perhaps permissible to quote from it at length.

PRIVATE AND CONFIDENTIAL   22 April 1920

My dear des Graz,

You will have received a letter from Ernest Churchill to your father forwarded on to you in Washington relating to a business opening; this was in quite general terms, but after consulting my partners (G. D. Hobson, Esq., whose brother Aylwyn I believe you knew well, and Major Felix Warre, son of the old Provost) I cabled you saying that the proposal related to our Firm. I gather your father sent the letter on with provisional approval, and that you are probably now considering the matter; I expect that you will be consulting the Foreign Office authorities with a view to seeing what they propose to offer you. May I, on our side, tell you what we want, and what we could hold out to a good man like yourself?

The pure business proposition would be as follows:

(a) We want more help in the business especially now I have accepted a position as Parliamentary Secretary to the Ministry of Labour in the Government. We should be prepared to offer to start with six or seven hundred a year to a really good man, rising annually by a substantial amount, say fifty to a hundred a year up till 1923. The first six months would probably have to be more or less on trial on both sides.

(b) In 1923, three years from now, our partnership will be re-adjusted and we could then offer to you or anyone in your position a junior partnership of one-ninth share conditional on one-ninth of the capital required in the business being brought in. This, on present capitalization, would be £15,000. . . .

(c) This re-arrangement of partnership would go on for five years only, I and my two present partners remaining in the Firm during that period, i.e. till 1928, together with the new junior and probably my sister who has done yeomen service in the Firm for the last five years and looks after our large female staff. At the end of the five years the junior would become a full partner. . . .

. . . in the last three or four years since we have moved up to Bond Street, the business has developed very much in every direction; we have already had to take on some new premises and the possibilities of expansion still continue if only we can get more expert help. . . .

But now I should like to say a word or two about the general position; in the first place, it is absolutely a gentleman's business; we are all on very friendly terms with one another; I personally should enjoy having you with us, and I think you would be happy with my two partners. Of course we are Auctioneers, and it is necessary that the partners should be prepared actually to sell in the rostrum, as I do myself. But I find the auctioneering itself of great interest and the business which deals all the time with fine books, fine pictures, fine prints, furniture, coins, etc., is absorbingly attractive, and I think it would appeal to you tremendously; we want badly a partner who would take up and be really expert in the *book* department: the backbone of the business is fine books, especially the early books and manuscripts, and this is a department which you, with your literary interests, and great knowledge of languages, would be peculiarly fitted for.

I think at the end of the five years period, i.e. in 1928, probably two of the present partners would go out, and any junior who comes in now would really have a very influential position in the Firm provided he is a man of real energy and intellectual ability; and if he chose to then stay with the Firm say for another five years, or thirteen years from the date of joining, he ought to be able to begin to build up for himself a decent little fortune. I do not know whether you have ambitions in Public life or not, but if you have you will find a leading position in Sotheby's (judging by my own experience) of distinct use. I deliberately went into the business with a view to secure a reasonable financial position so that I could take up Public life properly: no man should go into the House of Commons unless he has at least £2,000 or £3,000 at his back. But, in addition to that, work at Sotheby's brings one into pleasant social relation with most of the leading Statesmen of the day, such as Lord Curzon, Lord Harcourt, Lord Lansdowne, the Speaker, Sir Alfred Mond, and others, all of whom are great collectors and drop in constantly; and in addition one gets into pleasant social touch with most of the big houses in England, such as Chatsworth, Wilton, Holkham and others in a way which I believe you would appreciate.

I personally did not go into Sotheby's till after I was 40 and I got into the House of Commons the next year, both rather too late, but you are much younger and if you care about it, and choose to work hard at the business for ten to fifteen years I am sure you could then have a good political career. I mention all this because I believe you are quite rightly ambitious, and if you were not I don't think I should be making you the offer I am.

Our business is now splendidly established, and the turn-over this year will be nearly three times what it has ever been before,

Yours sincerely,
C. A. M. Barlow

To Barlow's great chagrin there was no response from Washington. Day after day passed in total silence until in desperation he wrote to Charles des Graz's father to ask 'whether your son has moved from Washington or whether there is any reason for the delay in answering. Although I do not want to hurry your son unduly I feel sure you will realise that the matter cannot be kept open indefinitely'. Maurice des Graz replied to Barlow at once explaining that Charlie had moved to New York, that letters usually took eighteen days to get there, but that he knew that Barlow's long letter had just reached his son.

On the morning of 27 May 1920, Barlow received both this letter from Maurice des Graz and a reply – at long last – from Charles. He wrote to Maurice: 'Curiously enough I received a letter from your son by the very same post, saying he would be glad, in general terms, to accept the proposals I put before him and asking how soon he should come to take up work with us.' Barlow was anxious to meet des Graz Senior and asked him to come to London so that he could show him 'the accounts and position generally and consult with you as to one or two points which it is difficult to explain in writing.[1] I have to

1. These related to the capital sums that would be needed at the time when Charles was to be offered a partnership.

leave England on June 11 to go to Genoa for the Government as the Senior Representative of the Shipping Conference, but I would gladly see you here any day before this if you are in London, and the sooner the better'.

To Charles he wrote: 'I was very glad to get your reply saying that you were prepared to accept our proposal. I have asked your father to come over from Ireland and see me as soon as possible, so that I may go into the whole situation with him as to figures, profits for passed years, etc. Also I should be glad to show him the present methods of working the house, and introduce him to the partners, etc.' He went on to suggest that Charles should terminate arrangements with the Foreign Office and be prepared to start work at Bond Street in September in time for the autumn season. He confirmed the initial salary at £700 per annum, rising by £100 each year until 1923 and reiterated that 'the arrangement must be considered provisional on both sides for the first six months'.

A week later the meeting between Barlow and des Graz Senior had taken place and seems to have created general satisfaction on both sides. Barlow subsequently wrote to Charles:

I have now had the pleasure of seeing your father. He, at first, rather assumed that you had not yet come to any definite decision and, indeed, he told me he had recently been to the F.O. to see what they proposed to offer you. I shewed him, however, your letter to me definitely saying 'Yes' to my proposal and on that he agreed the matter was to be treated as provisionally settled. I then showed him our figures for the last fifteen years or so and answered various queries he put to me. He said he could see his way to providing £10,000 of capital in 1923 but no more, and the rest up to £15,000 must be made up out of your share of profits. There will probably be a considerable readjustment of capital in 1928 and if only £10,000 is brought in by you in 1923, I think a further £10,000 should be brought in by you in 1928. If necessary you might have to borrow it and repay it out of your profits accruing after 1928. We had to borrow capital when we bought the business in 1909. Your life should in that case be insured.

I think now we shall get short provisional heads of agreement initialled and I enclose draft accordingly. If you approve it, will you initial and return to me. If you wish any additions or modifications, will you let me know at once? Time is running on and if by any mischance our negotiations (which I sincerely hope will not be the case) should break down, we have now only a very short time to arrange with anyone else.

I gather you have been going about a good deal in American Society: and our mutual friend, Mrs. Whitridge tells me how much they have all liked you. This may be useful in future years. Since about 1912, I have been going to America regularly every year and have brought off some very big deals in the way of selling libraries and other collections. It would be useful if (without, of course, mentioning the future at all or your possible connection here) you could get on terms with any great collectors you may come across and especially the following:

Mr. Jack Morgan (and his Librarian Miss Belle Green for fine Books and MSS)
H. Widener of Philadelphia (Books, Prints, Pictures)
Henry Huntington (All art objects especially Books and of them early printed English Books and Shakespearian)

    Archer Huntington (Spanish Books)
    Folger (Shakespeares)
and any other collectors you may come across: and of dealers
    Duveen
    Knoedler   } Pictures
and especially Charlie Carstairs in Knoedlers: also
    Rosenbach of Philadelphia (Books)
    White; and Harper, of New York (Books)
    Kennedy; and Keppel; and Max Williams of New York (all prints)
    All these are friends and correspondents of ours: also Safford of Scribners in New York.

    Let me hear on all above points and also as to provisional heads of Agreement as soon as possible.

Yours sincerely,
C. A. M. Barlow.

There is no record of the extent to which des Graz was able to meet these major figures in the American collecting scene at this stage, though certainly he got to know most of them in due course and made regular visits to America on behalf of Sotheby's for many years.

After des Graz's arrival in Bond Street, Geoffrey Hobson at once took him under his own wing. Hobson desperately needed assistance. His secretary, Edith Bourne, recalls that apart from actually taking sales, there was practically nothing in the running of the business for which Hobson did not accept responsibility in one way or another at this time. But he beavered away so quietly that only his closest colleagues were aware of this. While there was remarkable empathy between des Graz and Hobson, the same easy relationship did not develop with Barlow. Des Graz at this stage could be shy to the point of diffidence and he found Barlow's brashness - and occasional vulgarity - a barrier to easy communication.

He very quickly picked up the essentials of book auctioneering and soon found himself dealing with the bulk of the work of the department, though Hobson continued to deal with manuscripts, fine bindings and autograph letters - as well as all sections of the works of art department. The book department put through an enormous volume of business in 1920 and 1921. The Huth, Britwell, Pembroke and Yates Thompson sales of those years were a mere backbone to a host of lesser libraries that came into Bond Street - and des Graz found himself totally immersed in the work. Yet all was not, at this stage, plain sailing. Barlow kept dropping hints and making barbed criticisms. Later these resulted in what must have been agonising interviews. Finally, in March 1922, Barlow wrote des Graz a long letter on House of Commons note paper.

29th March, 1922.

Dear des G.,
    I have had one or two talks with partners since my conversation with you, and I have thought it better to sum the position up in black and white.

(1) I told the partners the points that I had gone through with you; I need not repeat them all, but you will remember they were such things as:

(a) Clients had complained that your manner gave the impression of in-difference and want of interest; there was the small matter also as to dress;

(b) That there was the serious case of indifference or misunderstanding over the Poe autograph, which resulted in a loss to the firm of £60 or £70; clearly this was a matter that you should have mentioned direct to Mr. King and not left to a subordinate; and

(c) Generally you gave us the impression that you did not find the business of interest.

(2) I was very glad to get your assurance in conversation that you were genuinely interested in the business and desired to throw yourself into it and to make a success of it, and I am most glad to recognise that since our first conversation about Christmas there has been real improvement in the points which I discussed with you; your manner in the box is more effective and shows much more real interest in the work you are doing; I gather you are tackling the books with much more effect, and altogether I do feel that the assurance you gave me that you really were interested and desired to make a success of the work was showing definite and effective results.

(3) At the same time, I do not think you quite realise that a business like ours, which you now see running successfully, has only been built up in the last 100 years (and has only been developed by us to three or four times its previous turn-over within the last ten years) by persistent and unremitting attention to the smallest details. We are noted, I believe, for our courtesy and for the great trouble we take in carrying out sales for our clients, and if this unremitting attention flags on the part of the principals, the business will certainly feel the difference and diminish very rapidly. Our business is not like a big finance business or a bank, where –

(a) There is little close contact with clients direct, and

(b) Where the business will stand a large number of high salaried heads of business at £2,000 or £3,000 a year, who can bear the brunt of the detail. With us the principals must come into close daily contact with the clients; and the way the principals earn the not inconsiderable profits in our business is by being responsible for and attending to most of the details themselves.

I most gladly recognise, as I said, the improvement within the last five or six weeks since I spoke to you, but at the same time I was a little sorry to hear of a case mentioned by G.D.H., where you had omitted to put the commissions back in their proper place and asked a clerk to do it instead, with the result that they were not put back and confusion ensued. In our business commissions and reserves are almost the most important pivot in the whole business, and no care is too much in dealing with them and seeing that they are kept in their proper place. Forgive me if I say there is also still some indifference as to dress.

(4) Please do not think I want to make too much of all this, but the issues at stake are serious. We have got a great deal of capital locked up in the business, we have spent a great many years in building it up, and in the years to come the safety of our capital and the future of the business will depend very largely on the new blood which we now take in. In the rival business of Messrs. C. undoubtedly the business is already beginning to suffer from the fact that the juniors they took in a year or two ago are proving to be of very little use. I much hope everything

will go right. I feel sure if you are determined to correct these small matters and to make a career in the business you have got the energy and ability to do it; and what has happened in the last few weeks gives us a very real assurance that there is every prospect of this happening. At the same time, we have so much at stake, and it is so important for you, just as much as for ourselves, that you should not be irrevocably committed to work which you did not enjoy, and consequently would not make a success of, that I think we had better say that we will proceed as at present and then review the whole situation at the end of the present selling season in July. This, I understand, you thought not unreasonable. If, as I hope, by that time we are satisfied on both sides as to the position, we could then consider definite arrangements as originally proposed for a partnership to commence as from the 1st October, 1923.

Lastly, there are two points which you questioned in our second talk last week, viz:

(a) That you understood early in 1921 that the Probationary period was over. We did, I think, have some conversation on the subject, but I have looked up the original letter to you and I find, as I told you I thought was the fact, that the probationary period was to be treated as definitely ended when Articles of Agreement were drawn up, and this was never done, nor did you in fact ask for it to be done.

(b) You suggested you were getting three or four times your present salary when in New York. I do not quite understand this. In your letter at the time you did mention a salary in Dollars which works out at about £900 a year or a little over, with some allowances, but living in New York is notoriously at least 50 to 75 per cent more expensive than in London.

Yours sincerely,

CAMB

Let us have a talk on my return.

Although des Graz pencilled in to the margin of the final page of the letter what he was earning in London and how poorly it compared with what he had been earning in New York, particularly after tax, the tone of the letter certainly made the impact on him that was intended. Various colleagues vividly remember des Graz's attitude of apparent indifference at this stage which often almost approached haughtiness, but they also emphasise that des Graz was intelligent enough to appreciate when the moment had come to change his ways. In July Barlow wrote to him again, as he had promised, offering a ten-year partnership. The terms proposed were to give des Graz one-ninth of the shares in the firm by 1928, two-ninths by 1933 and a full third after that. Barlow emphasised that Hobson and Warre were 'anxious to keep my sister here for the full ten years'. A detailed legal agreement was in due course drawn up and signed by all concerned. It was one of a seemingly endless series of such agreements among the partners that Barlow initiated and which constituted an important part of Sotheby's managerial arrangements for years to come. Such emphatic carping on legal niceties seemed to imply a litigious outlook which the actual day-to-day running of the firm completely belied. No decision was ever taken unless all the partners agreed to it. Communications among them were of the simplest kind. A memorandum would be typed on a scrap of paper and circulated to each of them in turn; each partner simply initialled it if he was in agreement with what was proposed, or added his comments if he was not. It seems to have worked remarkably well even on the odd occasion when a state of friction existed between individual partners, which certainly occurred from time to time. Thus Geoffrey Hobson found Barlow's occasionally overbearing manner, particularly towards the end of Barlow's chairmanship in the late Twenties, highly irritating. The staff regarded the resulting contretemps with detached amusement. One incident, however, remained firmly engraved on everybody's mind. Barlow had despatched a secretary to summon Hobson to his office in rather a peremptory manner. Hobson sent the following message in reply: 'If Sir Montague wishes to talk to me let him come to *my* office'. That dictum echoed through Bond Street for years.

In any case, once des Graz had become a partner things went swimmingly. In due course he became a brilliant auctioneer and expert opinion held that between the wars he had no serious rival in the rostrum. 'The real test of this most exacting of roles,' wrote Tim Munby,[1] 'is not in the selling of works of the very first importance. Long practice made des Graz perfect in the more difficult art of selling secondary material fast without missing a bid. Uncertainty or delay by the seller is soon reflected in lethargy and inertia on the part of the bidders. Des Graz kept the room on its toes. He knew the value of what he was selling and the personalities of the buyers; thus he was able to adapt the pace to the needs of each individual lot. He conducted his sales with dignity and imperturbable good humour which was reflected in an atmosphere of mutual confidence between the rostrum and the floor.'

It is said that des Graz's style of auctioneering survives to this day in the manner taught to all young aspirants to the rostrum at Bond Street, and his rather drier, more precise manner, is what differentiates it from Christie's. Be that as it may, des Graz's career at Sotheby's was a great success story after a rather sticky beginning.

The Backroom Boys

Hobson and des Graz built up a remarkably fine team of cataloguers and experts in the book department during the early Twenties, which was to give Sotheby's continuing supremacy in the field and led to many memorable sales. The progressive deterioration in Phillips's health had led to the arrival of Theodore Perry in March 1919, in answer to an advertisement. Perry had been a classical scholar both at Tonbridge School and at Peterhouse, Cambridge, and then became that great rarity, a properly articled bookseller's apprentice. In his case it was to one of the shrewdest antiquarian dealers in the business, the Reverend P. M. Barnard, an Anglican priest who had fallen out with the Church authorities and had cultivated an astonishingly wide grasp of manuscripts, tracts and early English literature. He ran a truly Dickensian old book business

1. A. N. L. Munby, *The Book Collector*, Summer 1953.

in a large house in Tunbridge Wells where he, his family and his apprentices all lived together. Barnard's learning – and sharp tongue – were widely respected by other dealers and collectors and he had become one of those eccentric figures that gives the antiquarian book trade its very distinctive and delightful flavour. Mrs. Barnard had a particular interest in prints and engravings and started a separate side of the business, which still survives in Museum Street as Craddock & Barnard.

Naturally, Barlow wrote to Barnard for a reference on Perry and received a long and penetrating reply. Barnard described Perry's scholarly interests and quiet conscientiousness. He also asked Barlow to discount Perry's slight stammer. He particularly stressed the young man's 'happy facility in English composition' which was to make itself evident in a long series of catalogues as well as in particularly notable introductions to major libraries.

After a brief spell as a sub-editor on *The Times* and years of wartime work in munition factories, Perry was delighted to get back into the book world and joined Sotheby's for the princely salary of £200 per annum which, Barlow promised, would go up to £250 after a two-month's trial period and then 'with £20 annual rises for five years. After that', Sotheby's chairman continued, 'we cannot guarantee anything in the way of rises and the future must depend upon yourself'. In fact, Perry eventually became head book cataloguer, the last man to hold that particular post, and continued to work for Sotheby's until his death in 1937.

Soon after his arrival he brought another former fellow apprentice from the Barnard establishment, L. M. Irby, into the book department at Bond Street. Irby had been head boy at Lancing College, a classical scholar at Oxford and throughout the war an officer in the artillery. Like Perry, he was of a quiet and retiring disposition and a great scholar. He had considerable private means. During week days, while working at Sotheby's, he lived at his London club and went back to his home town, Cheltenham, where he lived in some style, at weekends. Although supposedly a nervous man he drove about in a Red Label Bentley, usually at great speeds. He was a frequent visitor to Thirlestaine House, once the Cheltenham home of Sir Thomas Phillipps, and eventually in the late Twenties undertook a probate valuation for Sotheby's of some of the most famous manuscripts there on behalf of Phillipps' son-in-law, Thomas Fitzroy Fenwick.

A third new entrant into the book department at about this time was F. S. Ochs. Like Irby he was very tall and an ex-artillery officer. He had been educated at Eton and Zurich University. He had made a name for himself during the war by his constant use of an umbrella in the pouring Flanders rain. An extraordinary experience befell him and the battery he commanded at the time of the Armistice. No authority would acknowledge having this battery on its books, or accept any responsibility for getting them home. As a good officer, Ochs knew that his first duty was to his men, though he himself had no desire to be left alone on the field of battle, so he was driven to forgery – no doubt using his expertise in the writings of ancient manuscripts – to obtain the necessary travel warrants. When he arrived at last at Whitehall, again no one would acknowledge that his 'lost battery' existed. Finally, in desperation, at the Paymaster's office he was forced again to the forger's art to obtain his badly needed back pay. For a long time he lived in dread of the consequences, but was never found out.

Ochs had taken the place of a very live wire, Captain Reggie Haseldon, who had gone to America initially to work for the dealer, Gabriel Wells, and later to become Keeper of Manuscripts at the Huntington Library in California. Haseldon and his wife had run a small antiquarian book shop before the First World War. He came to Sotheby's with a brilliant reference from Sir Stephen Gaselee, the great classical scholar, who attested to Haseldon's genius for finding the rarest of manuscripts in unexpected places.[1]

Shortly afterwards Millicent Sowerby also resigned because it was made clear to her that the employment of women cataloguers had been a wartime expedient. Although she might have been embittered by this attitude, she left cheerfully with the highest regard for Barlow, Hobson, her fellow cataloguers and Sotheby's generally.

Her place was taken by John Cameron Taylor, one of the most interesting and many-sided book cataloguers who ever worked at Sotheby's. His background was very different from that of his colleagues. His father was a self-educated man who became a Baptist minister in middle life. He had been orphaned at fifteen, had brought up four brothers and sisters single-handed in Glasgow while working as a warehouseman by day and studying for a degree in English Literature by night. He also acquired a fine command of Latin, Greek and Hebrew, and felt that no one was properly educated unless they had a good working knowledge of all three languages, which he imparted to all his children. The Reverend Taylor eventually settled in Leeds at an annual stipend of £120. His son, John, was one of the first to enrol at the newly-founded Leeds High School but had to leave at fourteen because there was not enough money to continue his education while educating also his other brothers and sisters. A member of his father's congregation, a manufacturer of dye stuffs, offered the lad a job in his firm's laboratory. Like his father, he worked there by day and studied by night and matriculated in London. Because he was also keen on music he matriculated in that subject at Durham. The boy now wanted to work for a scholarship to Oxford or Cambridge but his father was anxious that he should obtain regular employment, and after moving to London, John was duly enrolled at Hodgson's, once again through the good offices of a member of his father's congregation. Young Taylor became a pupil of Sydney Hodgson's who was an excellent teacher and soon imparted to his pupil a sound knowledge of books. In fact, the two men became close friends and Sydney encouraged Taylor to pursue his academic interests by reading for an extra-mural degree at Birkbeck College. Leaving aside his passionate interest in science for the moment, Taylor decided that his first objective should be a degree in classics; another in

1. Many years later Haseldon was to look back on his time at Sotheby's as a very happy one, and applied to re-enter the book department in 1946.

chemistry could come later. But after two years the war broke out. He enrolled in the Royal Fusiliers and after the usual square-bashing on Salisbury Plain was commissioned and was despatched to the trenches in the autumn of 1915. Only a few weeks later he was wounded when a bursting shell caused a trench to collapse on top of him. A brief period of recovery at home followed which was suddenly interrupted when he was commanded by telegram to appear at the War Office for an interview with General Alexander, one of the founders of I.C.I. A former tutor at Birkbeck College had remembered the brilliant young classicist with a passion for chemistry and Taylor was now asked whether, with the pressing need for more ammunition production, he would work in a newly-built explosives factory in Gretna Green. He soon found himself a fully-fledged member of the Ministry of Munitions in charge of the nitrating chamber in the production of nitroglycerin. Not many people involved in this dangerous work could stand the fumes for more than a few days. Young Taylor, however, lasted some months before becoming ill, but when examined the doctors discovered that his complaint was not due to the usual after-effects of the chemicals. He was suffering from a much more unusual condition. His heart had been displaced by the explosion which buried him in the Flanders trench. He was forbidden to return to making nitroglycerin and was moved instead to a plant where a new process for making sulphuric acid was being developed. His ability was soon noticed and he was transferred to the research laboratory where he developed various major innovations in the production techniques, and indeed published a number of scientific papers on them, the first of many that he was to write later.

At the end of the war he was initially tempted by offers to stay in the chemical industry, but he also resumed work for Sydney Hodgson in his spare time. After producing a particularly good catalogue for the sale of the scientific library of Sir William Crookes, the late President of the Royal Society, Hodgson asked him to come back full time. But Taylor thought that if he was to return to the world of books he would much prefer to work for Sotheby's. He applied for an interview with Barlow who offered him a temporary job. When Millicent Sowerby left it became permanent. Thereafter Taylor continued to work for Sotheby's, with the exception of one fairly protracted excursion to America and his absence during the Second World War, until he retired in 1968. Like his other colleagues in the book department, he was such a quiet and unassuming person that it is difficult to associate the same man with his continuing achievements in many other fields. Thus he wrote some of the first plays ever to be broadcast by Savoy Hill Radio in the Twenties – one, *The Grandfather Clock*, was broadcast a dozen times from London as well as from several provincial stations – and in the late Thirties he also wrote some of the first plays ever to be televised. His interest in music continued and he became an excellent organist. In the scientific field he specialised in the study of micro-photography and particularly photomicrography. Inevitably this scientific expertise within the book department was of the greatest use to Sotheby's, and any cataloguing of scientific and medical material – at a time when interest in the history of these subjects was just beginning – was given to Taylor. He particularly enjoyed this work and made the most of it. Perceptive dealers who nurtured the first glimmerings of interest among collectors – such as J. I. Davis, of the firm of Davis & Oriolo – very much appreciated what Taylor was doing, and as we shall see it led to many important and successful sales. But des Graz took particular notice of Taylor's abilities for quite a different reason. Des Graz had never lost contact with his friends from the First World War in the Censorship Department of the War Office. As the political situation in Europe deteriorated and the threat of another war became a distinct possibility, a shadow intelligence organisation was rebuilt. Des Graz became an important member of MI2B and his job was to recruit others for it. Sotheby's was a natural source of suitable manpower. Two years before the Second World War broke out, Taylor was drafted as a technician to MI2B and received training and lectures in the relevant subjects. More of Sotheby's involvement with Postal Censorship will emerge later.

A few days before the outbreak of the war in 1939 Taylor left Bond Street for 'civilian duties'. At first he was sent to Liverpool, where the Censorship Department had taken over the whole of Littlewood's mail order and football pool business premises. Then the department spread also to Vernon's at Aintree and eventually to the Biochemical Department of Liverpool University as well. Naturally Taylor gravitated to the 'Testing Department' where letters were examined for secret messages, and to the Coding Department in the Cohen Library of the University. Soon he was put in charge of all research work on secret communications involving photographic processes. The high point of his career was the development of the micro-dot, by which a whole page of a newspaper can be photographed down to the size of a full stop. At first he worked in collaboration with an academic colleague but when the latter returned to teaching John Taylor continued alone, although he was far too modest to lay claim to the many 'firsts' attributed to him. He simply said 'many of the secret Intelligence Departments had their own scientific staffs and for much of the war period there was no liaison at all between them'.

He had an exciting time, and at the end of hostilities he went back to Sotheby's – like some latter-day Cincinnatus – and returned to book cataloguing just as if he had been away for a long weekend.

In Taylor's early days, Geoffrey Hobson still kept a tight control over the books which every cataloguer expected to catalogue each day, and every morning he went round with a little notebook to make a check on progress. Hobson also collated the material into suitable sequence for each week's auctions. Great care was taken that important lots should come at the right stage of orchestration within each catalogue. The new team worked with efficiency and speed and the atmosphere within the department was extremely relaxed and cordial. When a tea-room was allocated to the staff, John Taylor became its Dr. Johnson, his words of wisdom being varied by amusing stories of his adventures. He had a remarkable ability as a raconteur and in creating vivid word pictures. At one stage in his life he became friendly with the poet, Edmund Blunden, and described the devastated church at Festupert, the little French village where he had been wounded. Blunden was so taken with what he heard that he turned it into one of his best-known poems (of which he sent a delightfully dedicated copy to Taylor).[1]

When I visited him in 1974 John Taylor said there was really little he could give me in the way of detail in the history of Sotheby's, and then proceeded to talk, virtually uninterrupted with the exception of the odd question, for three hours at a stretch. He repeated this performance several times. Major Warre had gone on record with a comment he once made in the Twenties, for which Tim Munby could never forgive him, 'No expert, however eminent,' said Warre, 'is worth more than £5 a week to this firm'. Inevitably the low rate of pay was one that would only satisfy conscientious men devoid of ambition, and that and the cloistered atmosphere in the book department largely constrained them from involvement, or even interest in, the wider issues of the business. Yet their wholly anonymous but scholarly contribution to the entire field of bibliography was one that deserves a much wider recognition than most of them ever received in their lifetimes. Very few outstanding manuscripts or books or literary autographs ever slipped through their scrutiny without recognition. What limited the full and financial appreciation of their efforts was the relatively small number of collectors throughout the world who wanted to buy what they catalogued so assiduously for the sales held every Monday of the long season, and sometimes on the Tuesday and Wednesday as well when substantial collections or libraries were involved. In the Twenties and Thirties all these catalogues could be obtained for an *annual* subscription of only £2, with 5s. extra for those relating to autograph material.

---

1. In addition to all his other interests, Taylor had always been a keen amateur painter and to make himself more proficient studied art at St. Martin's for five years before his retirement. In his retirement painting abstract pictures was one of his favourite occupations. He died in 1979.

19
Works of Art:
Small Beginnings

WE have seen how under Barlow and Hobson the book department grew from strength to strength, and the vital role of autograph material, historical documents and manuscripts as an adjunct to it. We have touched upon the first beginnings of improved picture sales. It soon became clear to the partners that there could be great expansion in another sphere, which was loosely termed the Works of Art Department. In the Sotheby sense, the phrase 'Works of Art' had a special meaning. It excluded paintings, drawings, prints, coins and antiquities: it included most of the things any enthusiast would find in a good antique shop in the early 1920s. At Bond Street between the wars it covered furniture, tapestry, carpets, needlework, glass, pottery, porcelain, pewter, silver, bronzes, enamels, clocks and watches, stained-glass windows, old musical instruments and all manner of things oriental including again pottery and porcelain, as well as jade, hardstones, lacquer and ivory. In fact, almost anything and everything that had been made by skilled craftsmen in the field of the decorative arts since the time of the Renaissance. The watchword was quality. The nature and standard of what was sold was very much dictated by Geoffrey Hobson's personal taste and outlook. He loved the eighteenth century and what had come before. He was strongly antipathetic to the late nineteenth century and most things Victorian, a taste shared – it must be remembered – with most cultivated Englishmen of that period.

His own house demonstrated this very clearly and was a delight to the eye. He lived in some style in one of the most beautiful of all houses (No. 1) in Bedford Square, that unrivalled pearl of London's West End created by the Dukes of Bedford and designed by Thomas Leverton in 1775. Any sensitive visitor could only gasp as he entered the magnificent hall with a fine dome and decorated ceiling, with a chequerboard marble floor and the most graceful of curving staircases. Its niches were filled with busts by Roubiliac, the finest treen urns and porcelain vases. In the drawing room much of the furniture was in eighteenth-century satinwood. The delicately stuccoed ceiling was decorated with panels painted by Antonio Zucchi. There were magnificent antique Persian carpets on the floors. There was everywhere superb porcelain, both English and Chinese. The walls abounded with eighteenth-century English landscapes. In this setting, away from the office, Geoffrey Hobson became a different personality, expansive and jovial. He loved entertaining. He is remembered as a skilful, amusing host. His deafness here was much less of an impediment. At dinner parties he was literally the life and soul of the party. His conversation abounded in wit and anecdote. He was a confirmed gourmet and thought himself guilty at times of gluttony. He had a talented wife and an excellent cook. Until he had to give it all up at the time of the slump, No. 1 Bedford Square was a place where bibliophiles, collectors and friends loved to spend an evening.

It is not surprising that Hobson wanted to aspire to a similar level of excellence in what passed through the works of art department at Sotheby's. Much of the material would certainly be regarded as of museum standard today, as indeed it was at the time, except that curators had such very limited funds that they could not often avail themselves of what they wanted to buy.[1] Such things required careful cataloguing and a level of expertise that simply did not exist within the house. Hobson was constantly sending pieces to the more erudite dealers and museum authorities for authentication and description. Specialist sales as such did not exist. All works of art were lumped together on Friday mornings (at one o'clock, so that collectors could come along and do their bidding in person). Thus there were particularly memorable Fridays in 1920. The first on 26 March included the Zeiss Collection, at that time the property of an English lady, which had been catalogued originally by the celebrated Dr. Bode of Berlin's Kaiser Friedrich Museum, and other well-known experts. August Zeiss was a German industrialist who had been an active supporter of Bode's museum. His collection was very strong in early Renaissance bronzes. Three were attributed to Donatello himself; others to some of his followers. Then there was a number of German and Italian wood carvings of the sixteenth and seventeenth centuries; a good deal of Italian maiolica; some fine Meissen; various Limoges enamels; elaborately decorated sixteenth-century Italian furniture, and seventeenth- and eighteenth-century Turkish and other carpets. Included in the same sale was a bronze group of *Virtue Overcoming Vice*, only $10\frac{1}{4}$ inches high, by Benvenuto Cellini, which fetched the remarkable price of £1,550.

Another property, that had come from Norfolk, consisted of two pieces of Elizabethan tapestry of a map of Gloucestershire and the surrounding counties. It had been woven at the Sheldon Looms, the earliest tapestry-weaving enterprise known in England. There was particular interest in this at the time and the tapestries fetched £1,010. The Marquess of Lansdowne had sent in a gigantic eighteenth-century gallery table with a mahogany base of ten elaborately carved and boldly designed legs. The top was formed by a single slab of Breccia marble, 16 feet long, 4 feet wide and $3\frac{1}{4}$ inches thick. The porters had groaned as they manhandled this enormous weight into the sale-room. The table fetched £560. Lord Braye had included a mixture of outstanding English and French furniture and many pieces of Flemish tapestry, various seals, some silver and five pieces of late fifteenth-century stained glass with the Royal Arms and effigies of Henry VII and Elizabeth of York. A number of items of seventeenth-century north Italian furniture from Holkham Hall in Norfolk came from the Earl of Leicester, and the sale finished with five outstanding

1. In 1913, for example, and for some years after the Director of the Victoria & Albert Museum could only personally sanction purchases up to £20. For objects exceeding that sum permission had to be obtained from the Board of Education in Whitehall.

pieces of eighteenth-century English furniture and a superb bracket clock, the property of the Dowager Lady Tankerville. The catalogue included twenty-four pages of plates printed by collotype (a photographic printing process) which showed with mouth-watering detail many of the items included.

A not dissimilar sale took place on 16 July in the same year (1920). This included the statuary forming part of the Lord Taunton's heirlooms from Quantock Lodge, Bridgwater in Somerset. There were various busts by Canova, Nollekens, Thorwaldsen, Houdon and Rysbrack. The outstanding item was a late fifteenth-century Florentine bust of Lorenzo di Medici, il Magnifico, 26 inches high. Again this type of bust had been identified by Bode; other copies of it existed in Berlin and in the collection of Lord Methuen at Corsham Court. This example had been bought in the 1840s by Lord Taunton from Professor Santarelli, a well-known Florentine sculptor, through whose hands a good many important pieces of Renaissance sculpture passed into foreign collections. It now fetched £2,050. The Taunton heirlooms were followed by a single anonymous property of a Royal Stuart sword of about 1616 by Clemens Horne of Solingen, elaborately decorated with gilt ornament, and thought to be the only one of its kind outside the Royal Collection at Windsor. It had been used by Charles I as Prince of Wales and was sold for £200. Then followed many lots of fine English furniture of the Queene Anne and Chippendale periods. And, surprisingly, six drawings by Sir Edward Burne-Jones, a grand piano designed by William Morris, a large Morris carpet which had been specially designed and made for the room in which the last lot in the sale was kept. This was a set of twelve tapestries designed by Burne-Jones and woven at the Merton Abbey Works by William Morris. The tapestries depicted scenes from the legend of the Quest for the Holy Grail, and the catalogue stated, in capital letters, that 'this series of tapestries is the finest set of examples of the work of these two great artists which have ever been offered for sale; both gave much time, thought and care to their design and execution and they form a unique record of their work and ideals'. After a long description of all the panels – which varied greatly in size - the catalogue entry concluded, again in capital letters, 'The life-long cooperation and mutual assistance rendered to each other by these two great craftsmen seems to have reached its culminating point in the production of these beautiful tapestries and they must ever remain as a monument to their industry, energy and great abilities.' They were sold by the order of the Trustees of W. K. D'Arcy of Stanmore Hall, Middlesex, and fetched £4,600.[1]

More rare English tapestry from Sheldon came up for sale later in the year on 12 November. No doubt interest had been kindled by the sale earlier in the year and the demand for English tapestry continued to grow.[2] This time there were

1. Three only of the same tapestries came up for sale again at Sotheby's Belgravia on 19 April 1978. They then raised a total of £104,000.
2. The cataloguing of tapestries was particularly good and was the work at this period of A. J. B. Wace, Deputy Keeper of the Victoria & Albert Museum and a former Director of the British School of Archaeology at Athens.

eight panels and they fetched very high prices. The most expensive, at £1,000, eventually went to the Victoria & Albert Museum. The catalogue stated that 'although judicious cleaning and restoration would add greatly to the attraction of these eight panels, it has been thought better to offer them in untouched state, just as they come from the house where they have been for over three hundred years'. There was much other tapestry in the same sale, and an immense eighteenth-century panel in Chinoiserie style fetched £2,000. Flemish tapestry was still much in demand and made good prices, and another Burne-Jones panel had come to light after the hullabaloo in the press following the July sale. The 125 items of furniture in the sale were of a high standard. Outstanding among them were an elaborately carved serpentine, mahogany, Chippendale commode, sold for £2,400, and a walnut harpsichord, exquisitely inlaid with marquetry (on a Chippendale mahogany stand), made by Jacob Kirkman in 1766 for Queen Charlotte,[1] which was sold for only £310.

As similar sales followed in 1921, the load on Hobson continued to increase. Soon after des Graz's arrival in the book department, the works of art department was strengthened in an unexpected form. The old porters had gradually retired, and the enormous ex-guardsmen who had taken their place were more than the sick and ageing foreman, James Hayman, or his brother Arthur, could manage. The partners decided that what was needed was a 'works manager': someone who could be responsible for the porter staff, the mounting of sales, the fabric of the building and who could also act as a relief auctioneer, when one was needed. At some social gathering Barlow met a young woman who mentioned that her brother, after distinguished war service, had landed a temporary job in the Ministry of Pensions and now wanted a permanent administrative post in some sort of business. Barlow's interest was at once aroused and his subsequent interview with the young man in question took place at the Ministry of Labour where Barlow was still Parliamentary Secretary. It turned into a long interrogation about the awards of disability pensions, in which Barlow was extremely interested because of his concern with the demobilisation of the forces. He liked the young man and was impressed by his liveliness and enthusiasm. However, cautious as ever, he wrote off to five of the young man's former Commanding Officers to enquire whether he would be able to maintain discipline among the porter staff. The answers were unanimously reassuring. As a former adjutant who had spent many months cooperating with the little-known Mutiny Breaking Staff, and who had been renowned for his tact and success in this difficult and demanding task, he would have no trouble in handling eighteen porters.

So it came to pass that A. J. B. Kiddell joined Sotheby's in April 1921. After fifty-eight years of unremitting hard work within the firm, Jim Kiddell was Sotheby's for many people. He was the tall, friendly, personable figure who has

1. The Queen was a competent musician. She played both the organ and the harpsichord, and her husband, George III, bought her no fewer than three harpsichords in 1764 at a cost of £278 10s. Two of these were by Kirkman.

greeted them at viewings and sales. He must have had more friends among collectors and dealers than any man in London. He was always about (even at eighty-four) peering benignly over the half-moon lenses of his glasses. He had the alert, quizzical look of the scholar who has strayed into the non-academic scene, though he was more the senior schoolmaster than the absent-minded professor for he exuded benevolent discipline, efficiency and a sense of order. He was just what the partners – and Sotheby's – needed. It was astonishing that such a small head could contain so many facts, figures, a memory for faces and recollections of personalities – and that one mind could have such total recall in the realms of pottery, porcelain, glass, oriental art, furniture, carpets and even of the intricacies and pitfalls of ancient antiquities of all kinds.

When Geoffrey Hobson was on the verge of retirement twenty-five years later he prepared a long paper for his fellow directors (most of whom had been away in the war) to summarise what had occurred between 1939 and 1945. He mentioned some of the firm's many deficiencies, but when it came to works of art it was a very different story. 'Our success,' he wrote, 'is due mainly to the fact that we do our work better than anyone else. We catalogue better, illustrate more, overlook less, advertise more fully, give more facilities for private inspection before the public view – a very important point – show things better and have a better knowledge of values. The success of the department is largely due to Mr. Kiddell, by far the best expert on works of art we have ever had.'

Mr. Kiddell was always a man of total modesty, and – as the trade soon discovered – a man of complete integrity. What he promised, he carried out, even if sometimes it was to the firm's disadvantage. He could be fierce if crossed and certainly he was every inch the disciplinarian that Barlow had hoped for. Nevertheless, 'Cuddles' or 'Uncle Jim', as he became known within the firm, was beloved,[1] where Peter Wilson was respected and sometimes feared.

He set to work with a will in 1921 under Hobson's aegis knowing, in his own words, 'less than nothing about the auction business or what was sold'. Within a week of his arrival he was, unexpectedly, compiling his first catalogue. Antique glass was usually catalogued by a 'Mr. Gould', an outside expert who ran his own antique business under that name and specialised in glass. His real name was Rye and his father, Walter Rye, had been a well-known Norfolk personality and author of the *Index of Norfolk Topography*. One day 'Mr. Gould' failed to turn up when he was expected because – as it turned out later – he had had to undergo an emergency operation. Hobson took young Kiddell down to the glass room, and although it was to some extent a case of the halt leading the blind, they sorted out the various categories of glass which had accumulated and with much checking back to earlier catalogues and the few books of reference then available, they produced a passable catalogue. Gould eventually returned after his operation but he had in the meantime sold his business at such an advantageous price that he decided that he would retire at once, though, because of Jim's obvious interest, he taught the young man everything he knew about glass during the ensuing few months. So within a short while of his

1. Jim Kiddell died on 5 February 1980.

arrival, Sotheby's new 'works manager' had also become the official glass expert. It was an interest he maintained all his life, adding much knowledge to what was known by quiet and patient research. In due course he was invited to join the *Glass Circle*, the principal organisation of glass collectors, and later became one of the Vice Presidents.[1] Under his guidance Sotheby's held an increasing number of glass sales and attracted collectors from far and wide. In later years some of the major collections formed in this way were, in turn, dispersed at Bond Street.

In the furniture field too Jim Kiddell had a first-class tutor. Some time earlier Geoffrey Hobson had made arrangements with a well-known furniture dealer who had shops in Brighton, Eastbourne and Lewes – Thomas Sutton – to supply Bond Street with a regular amount of good antique furniture. This helped to swell the Friday sales and to turn them into regular events. This, of course, was at a time when Sotheby's was still a relative newcomer to this field. Tommy Sutton was a big, burly, handsome man. His commanding presence made him one of the leaders of his trade. He specialised in buying up the entire contents of houses, which were coming on to the market at a prodigious pace after the ravages of the First World War, and hence he seemed to have unlimited material which could be sold at Bond Street. Above all, he really knew his furniture. On one occasion when Jim Kiddell was puzzled by the authenticity of a serpentine Chippendale chest of drawers, Sutton took the entire chest apart, piece by piece, pointed out every component and detail that had been wrongly placed, faked, altered or at best restored. Jim was slightly taken aback by this drastic treatment, but Tommy Sutton simply despatched the sundered remains down to Brighton in a large box where his manager, Mr. Long, re-assembled them in next to no time. He was used to these methods.

This lesson seemed particularly appropriate a few weeks later when another lot of heirlooms, this time from the Townsend family in Raynham Hall, Norfolk,[2] came into Bond Street. They included some really magnificent examples of English furniture and they were being sold 'by Order of the Court'. Lot 40 was a Chippendale mahogany commode, daringly catalogued as 'possibly the finest ever offered for sale, of double serpentine form, beautifully carved with scrolls, flowers and foliage in high relief, every detail showing a master hand; this fine piece seems to be the very perfection of English cabinet making'. Two illustrations were included in the catalogue; one showing the whole piece; the other a detail of the elaborate carving. Among a sale of distinguished furniture it caused great excitement and fetched a record £3,900, a vast sum in its time.

Another Chippendale piece in the same sale, also glowingly catalogued, drew a good many doubting comments from the trade before the sale. It was withdrawn. Jim Kiddell firmly crossed it out in his own marked copy of the catalogue

1. He had already been asked to join the *English Ceramic Circle* (it was initially known as the *English Porcelain Circle*), from which he in 1974 retired as President after holding the office for seventeen years, and was probably the longest surviving member.
2. The pictures – mostly family portraits – had been sold at Bond Street in 1912.

with the laconic comment 'Wrong'. It represented an agonising lesson learned early which he was not to forget.

Another area where outside advice had to be sought was for carpets and rugs. It was a notoriously difficult subject and the trade in it was almost exclusively handled by Armenians. Even Sir Montague Barlow had found that he had to protect himself against the nefarious activities of the 'carpet ring'. He allowed extended credit to one of their countrymen, a dealer named Benlian, a small, dapper, well-dressed man, whose duty it was to bid against the 'ring' on anything he thought was going too cheaply. People at Sotheby's always admired his courage in standing alone against the loudly-voiced, gestured threats of violence that frequently erupted during a sale as each side endeavoured to 'land' a lot on the other. At the fall of the hammer there would be an uproar from the crowd, the named buyer shouting, 'I no bid! I no bid! Dat man bid!' A forest of accusing fingers would point at the slight figure of Mr. Benlian standing near the rostrum. He would look blandly up at Sir Montague and say, 'I no bid. You know my business Sir Montague Barlow'.

Tim Wilder recalls that the carpet ring would appear to start 'settling' almost before they left the premises. Their favourite haunt was the basement of an old ABC Tea Shop in Dering Street, when there would be sudden babbling outbursts, drawn fists and scraping chairs as figures rose in fighting attitudes. Presiding over them all would be a patriarchal figure with a long, white beard, tut-tutting as though to say for the benefit of the other startled customers: 'Heed them not, for they are but children'. But Benlian had retired to less stormy pastures by the time Jim Kiddell came to Sotheby's. In his place he found another Armenian, Mr. Levy of French & Co., who took him in hand and taught him the identification of the many old and beautiful pieces that were then coming on to the market, though they were not much appreciated and demand for them was relatively limited. With the enormous diversity of eastern carpet producers in Persia, Turkestan, the Caucasus, Turkey, Afghanistan, Beluchistan, China and elsewhere, it was not an easy subject to master and the youthful Kiddell did more than anything to win the hearts – and the respect – of the Armenian dealers by occasionally stopping a sale and asking their advice on a particularly difficult rug before the bidding started.

If young Kiddell's second year at Sotheby's saw a steady consolidation of his knowledge and familiarity with the major dealers in the works of art field, one sale stands out because it led to a lasting friendship. Sir Edward Marshall Hall K.C., a distinguished advocate, was an enthusiastic collector and antiquary and also acted as adviser to many important collectors, especially of fire-arms. For years he had explored antique shops all round the country as he moved from court to court. His own particular passion was for French snuff boxes, especially gold ones, *bonbonnières*, needle cases, scent bottles, seals, and also for miniatures. When he put many of these up for sale in May 1922 the *Connoisseur* wrote: 'the collection which bears evidence of having been formed with marked discrimination embodies many pieces of great beauty, but none more so than the magnificent *bonbonnière* of Sèvres porcelain, the paintings of which, though unsigned, are without doubt by Dodin after Boucher. The mounts are of carved and chased gold. The inside rim of the lid being engraved with the maker's name 'FOSSIN ET FILS, Joailliers du Roi à Paris.' The price given for this superb item, £4,000, was far and away the highest in the sale, although there were many other lots comprising articles of charm and distinction'.[1] In fact, the 192 lots fetched £9,026. But to give one a sense of scale, it must be remembered that £4,000 at that time represented the total salaries of five Sotheby secretaries for five years. Hall was impressed by Jim Kiddell's youthful enthusiasm. He came into Bond Street with increasing frequency up to the time of his death in 1929, and often gave wise counsel when difficult problems had arisen and were presented to him.

In marked contrast to the sophisticated bijouterie of the Marshall Hall sale was a single lot in a mixed Friday sale held in the same year. This consisted of a panel of eight medieval picture tiles representing various scenes from the New Testament and Apocrypha in a crude but attractively clear form. The figures and faces had an almost cartoon-like quality about them. It was initially conjectured that they had been made at a Cistercian monastery at Coggeshall in Essex and that they had then been used in the Saxon church at Bradwell-juxta-Mare. They had later come into the possession of the rector of that parish and had been bought at a local sale of his effects for a tiny sum. Durlacher now paid £1,420 for them, and with assistance from the National Art Collections Fund they eventually went to the British Museum, where they were recognised as masterpieces among English medieval tiles, and subsequent research established that they came from Tring in Hertfordshire. It was one of those stories of discovery that stirs the imagination and the press made much of it.

The diversity of works of art sales at that time is hard to imagine today. It is interesting to look in detail at perhaps one of the major sales of the 1922 season, held on 23 June. It started off with Chinese armorial porcelain; moved to 'a remarkable vase, 20 inches high, entirely covered with a design of flowers and foliage, covered in precious and other stones including turquoise, amethyst, lapiz lazuli, cornelian, aventurine, etc., upon a groundwork of mother-of-pearl and seed pearls'. It fetched £50 after spirited bidding. Then followed various items of small sculpture in bronze and terracotta from Italy, France and China. Lot 18 consisted of 'fine boxwood carvings, by Bagard of Nancy (César Bagard 1639–1709), the equipment of a toilet table comprising an oblong casket exquisitely carved . . . a pair of circular boxes and an oblong box similarly carved, a pair of candlesticks of elegant form, and a fine mirror, with arched top, and the frame finely carved with conventional foliage and scrolls'. This had been made for the Duchess of Melfort who, in 1682, married John Drummond, second son of James, 3rd Earl of Perth. It fetched £115. The next lot, the property of another owner, was a fine, old Sèvres vase and cover of campana shape, 17½ inches high, which went for £140. Four more lots of Sèvres followed

1. In his will Alfred de Rothschild left Marshall Hall 'the choice of one of my best boxes'. The *bonbonnière* chosen by Hall had been bought in the San Donato Sale of Prince Demidoff in 1880 for £1,900.

this; then one lot of two Dresden porcelain cups, saucers and covers with dark blue ground, the panels finely painted with subjects after old English engravings, which went for £6; an enamel casket; four Flemish sixteenth-century alabaster plaques (£6); an old Chinese Joey, and a 'carved ivory figure of Christ as the Good Shepherd, curious and interesting' (£3 3s.).

Lot 41 was the first of a number of fifteenth-century vestments from Whalley Abbey, sent to the sale-room by Lord O'Hagan. The collection was described as 'the finest old English embroidered vestments that have come on to the market for many years. It is impossible in a catalogue to give a really adequate description of these examples of "Opus Anglicanum", but it is well to consider the immense regard and value that has always been given to English Medieval Embroideries'. These vestments were thought to have been taken to the Towneley family at Towneley Hall from the neighbouring Abbey of Whalley at the time of the dissolution of that monastery. The first item, a superb fifteenth-century cope of very fine figured velvet, beautifully embroidered with figures of Old Testament prophets and apostles, had been exhibited at the Burlington Fine Arts Club in 1905 and was a well-known piece, but collectors of ecclesiastical vestments were few and far between. The bidding was slow and the piece was bought in at £510. Lot 42, a fine chasuble, embroidered with many scenes from the life of the Blessed Virgin, was bought by Agnew's for £310. So was the dalmatic of the same gold brocade as the previous lot, for £300, and an altar frontal of red silk, for £420. The other eight lots all sold reasonably well, four more of them to Agnew's.

At lot 54 we return to other properties consisting of stumpwork, needlework, embroidery and tapestry. A fine Charles II needlework casket fetched £50. 'A very fine beadwork cabinet, dated 1654, square, with box top, and folding doors enclosing six small drawers; the top worked with a design of Solomon and the Queen of Sheba . . . etc.', found no buyer and was bought in at £22. Lots 62 and 63, consisting of a set of old Spanish coverings worked in bright crewels on white with a scroll pattern of flowers and fruit, for a settee six feet wide, and six chairs and a very fine Spanish coverlet elaborately worked with flowers, fruit and amorini, matching the last lot, were combined and sold for £65.

The property of the Countess of Loudoun of the Manor House, Ashby-de-la-Zouche, starting with lot 72, consisted of English and French furniture and *famille verte* dish. All eight lots sold. The 'king' of London furniture dealers, Mossie Harris, paid £145 for a fine Queen Anne settee, of two chair-back pattern of unusual size, and £390 for an 'early Georgian settee, of bold character, of two chair-back pattern, bell-shaped splats to the piers and carved at the top with scroll foliage, fluted at the bottom and surmounted by five panels of scale pattern, the arms terminating in lion heads, the front of frame carved and the front legs terminating in lion's feet'. Then followed long-case clocks and English furniture. Harris bought some; Mallett others, including lot 93, 'a Chippendale tray-top mahogany table with a pierced gallery border on pillar and tripod stand', for £11 10s.; quite a number of items were bought in. Lots 100 and 101 were two more rare and unusual items. The first was known as the

'Betley Window', 'a remarkable Elizabethan window light of small leaded quarries, twelve of which in four horizontal lines, are enamelled in red, yellow, blue and purple with very spirited figures of characters in the Mayday game and Morris dance and a Maypole across which on a ribbon is the legend "A Mery May" '. The catalogue pointed out that the window had been described and illustrated in various books from 1778 onwards. It now sold for £390. The next item, described as 'an extremely interesting armorial stained glass window, seventeenth century, consisting of three lights with trefoil heads, each light has on it six shields of arms (eighteen in all), all but one embodying two coats according the alliances of a Suffolk family'. This fetched £180.

Then followed a William and Mary marquetry wall-mirror and two important series of Flemish seventeenth-century tapestries, the property of Lord Wharton, removed from Cefn Mably, South Wales. The three items sold for £460. A magnificent Queen Anne four-poster state bedstead was bought in at £160. Lot 108 was a fine Aubusson carpet, 18 feet by 15 feet. Major Warre was infinitely saddened when it had to be bought in at £32, and later bought it himself with agreement from the owners at a higher price.

The total for the sale, including, of course, all the items bought in, came to £9,366. The partners felt that it was an excellent morning's work.

20

Antiquities and Other Sales out of the Ordinary

WHAT Jim Kiddell was not to know, of course, was that the year of his arrival, 1921, had been a particularly good year in financial terms. The turnover of £618,000 was, as far as we know, a record. It reflected the ending of post-war boom, particularly as far as purchasers from America were concerned. Thereafter the economic climate deteriorated for a while and the general depression made itself felt in the sale-room too. Montague Barlow's close involvement with the political scene made him particularly sensitive to this turn of events, although it ought to be said here and now that there was a gradual improvement after the following year right up to the 1927–28 season, when the firm reached a million pound turnover for the first time, and the *annus mirabilis* of 1928–29 when the turnover shot right up to £1,231,000. After that the slump bit hard and long, but that is another story.

1922 was also a landmark in another sense, for during the summer there took place one of the finest antiquity sales ever held by Sotheby's. Broadly speaking, such sales contained objects of the pre-Christian era from Rome, Greece, Persia, Egypt, India and the Far East.[1] The firm had always had a stake in this rather specialist area since the sale of the last Salt Collection in 1835. Henry Salt had been British Consul General in Egypt for many years, and like so many other of our diplomatic representatives abroad had taken a keen interest in the arts – in his case, particularly in the ancient arts. Following upon Napoleon's personal encouragement of archaeological excavation and the study of Egypt's ancient origins there were plenty of treasures available which few appreciated. Salt gathered together a marvellously rich collection of Egyptian jewellery, sculpture, sarcophagi, tablets and vases from the era of the Pharaohs, which he transported back to England bit by bit with all the complications that this entailed. He gave, jointly with Johann Burckhardt, the collo colossal head of Ramesses II to the British Museum, and the pieces the Museum later acquired from Salt's first and third collections form the nucleus of its own outstanding collection in this field.[2]

Dr. Gustav Waagen[3] happened to be in London at the time of the view preceding the Salt Sale and sent an excited account of it home to his wife. He

1. Occasionally, too, collections of early Irish and Celtic material, such as the Robert Day Collection in May 1913, came up for sale.
2. See also page 29.
3. Dr. Waagen (1794–1868), the first Director of the Royal Picture Gallery in Berlin, was an inveterate traveller in search of knowledge of the arts and a frequent visitor to England. His best known work is *Treasures of Art in Great Britain* of 1854.

wrote in a letter: 'I have never yet seen such a treasure of the most beautiful Egyptian ornaments of gold and engraved stones as here', and he spent many hours inspecting, and later describing the 1,270 lots in the sale. He waxed enthusiastic about the mummies and their sarcophagi. 'You know', he said, 'that I once wrote an essay upon such mummies in the Munich Collection . . . and since that time I have examined a great number of such monuments, but I here found some which in splendour and richness of ornament surpass all that I had hitherto seen.' The Salt Sale, which lasted nine days, realised £7,170, of which nearly £4,500 was paid by the British Museum to acquire further items from his collection. In fact, the last ten items in the sale were the property of Madame Belzoni, widow of a fervent archaeologist and adventurer and a close friend of Salt's, who had spent much of his life in Egypt. Not only had he unearthed very rich finds, but it was also he who had invented ingenious devices for transporting some of the vast and immensely heavy sculptures back to Europe. Among the ten lots the diorite bust of Sekmet, the ancient lion-like Egyptian goddess, remained unsold, was bought by the firm and has adorned its entrance both in Wellington Street and in Bond Street ever since.

The increasing interest in archaeology stimulated the collection of Greek, Roman, Persian and Egyptian antiquities during the middle and latter half of the nineteenth century, and with the relatively small amount of genuine material available the dispersal of one collection often led to the formation of another. Unless collectors actually organised their own private excavations, this was often the case. The most important recent collection that had come up for sale and which was still widely remembered in 1922 was the Forman Collection, which was dispersed in a four-day sale in June 1899.[1] Before the sale took place this collection had been virtually unknown. W. H. Forman had collected antiquities from Rome, Greece and Egypt in the 1850s largely through purchases at sales in London and elsewhere. The collection had been housed at Pippbrook House near Dorking, but after Forman's death had passed into the hands of his nephew, a Major H. H. Browne, in the late 1880s. He first built a special, two-storey museum wing on to his house at Callaly Castle and then moved the collection up *en bloc*, showing the vases on the upper floor and the bronzes and other antiquities on the lower floor. He had the collection catalogued by William Chaffers of fame as the author of *Hallmarks on Gold and Silver Plate* and *Marks and Monograms on Pottery and Porcelain*, and printed a private catalogue which Cecil Smith of the British Museum condemned in his introduction to the 1899 sale catalogue as being 'a monument of useless labour and entrusted to a person unequal to the task'. Because of the inaccessible position of Callaly Castle in a remote part of Northumberland, few visitors had ever come to see it. Smith was so impressed by the quality of the items to be included in the sale that he persuaded Tom Hodge to place the cataloguing with Messrs. Rollin & Feuardent, then the leading dealers in antiquities, both in London and Paris. The catalogue was produced in two editions, one in the normal Sotheby format and another in a specially illustrated, folio-sized

1. The second portion of the collection was sold in July 1900.

edition, 'in order', said Smith, 'that some useful record may be preserved of its many treasures before it is dispersed to the four winds, and the United States'. He singled out for particular mention lot 53, a magnificent mounted warrior, 'one of the most important examples which has come down to us of Greek bronze-work of the sixth century B.C.' (it fetched £265); a large mirror supported by a particularly beautiful figure of Aphrodite (lot 68) and a vibrantly powerful 12-inch figure of Poseidon (lot 84), 'three objects which are each in their way a *chef d'ouevre* of a different period of Greek art'. The many Greek vases were also of exceptional quality. The finest was lot 357, a lebes, glowingly described in the catalogue. The entry concludes: 'This magnificent vase may be regarded as one of the finest specimens of Greek ceramography that has come down to us; certainly among the known specimens of the Attic "free-style", it is in its combination of artistic merit and mythological interest absolutely unsurpassed'. Unlike the rest of the collection this was a well-documented piece. It had been excavated at Agrigentum in 1830; then passed into the possession of the Poet Laureate, Samuel Rogers – a great collector – and had been described by Waagen. It was sold at the Rogers sale at Christie's, passed into another collection and was bought at another Christie's sale in 1855 by Mr. Forman for £122. It now sold for £210.

Antiquity sales had continued regularly while Tom Hodge was running the firm. Under the new partners they were the responsibility of Major Warre, being regarded as a natural extension of the rather more frequent coin sales, and Warre called upon Spinks and various museums for assistance in the cataloguing. Later, Professors Ashmole and Beazley, and Howard Carter, also gave a helping hand. An immensely long (eight-day) sale in 1911 of the collection of Egyptian antiquities formed by the Director of the Society of Antiquaries, F. G. Hilton Price, had raised a total in excess of £12,000. The foreword pointed out that there were relatively few collections in this field because it required such close study of a branch of history where knowledge was hard to come by and for this reason most collectors were either practising archaeologists or scholars. In November 1917 there had been a sale of Egyptian antiquities belonging to Field-Marshal Lord Grenfell, and Major Warre conducted at least one or two sales of Egyptian, Greek and Roman antiquities each year. The sale of E. J. Seltman's Roman Standard of the IX Legion and a Roman general's camp chair had caused a great stir in December of 1920. Each item had fetched £200. Again, the sale of the Amherst Antiquities Collection – one of the most famous in England – lasted five days, fetched £14,533 and was widely reported in 1921. It was the first major antiquity sale in which Jim Kiddell took part. It kindled his interest and he got on particularly well with many of the great archaeologists, such as the Egyptologists, Flinders Petrie, Jean Capart of Belgium and Howard Carter, who came to view the items many times before the sale and were delighted to hold forth to him on the more important lots. The great J. B. Beazley (later Sir John) had written a signed introduction to the collection of ancient engraved glass and jewellery formed by Professor Storey-Maskelyne, Keeper of the Minerals Department at the British Museum, which

9

had formed an important part of the Exhibition of Greek art at the Burlington
Fine Arts Club in 1903. A mixture of Chinese, Indian, Persian, Egyptian and
Greek antiquities had even been consigned to Bond Street from Paris in
November 1921, and had done reasonably well.

The remarkable collection of Egyptian antiquities assembled by the Rev.
William MacGregor, that was announced for an eleven-day sale in June and
July, 1922, was unparalleled by any other collection in England, Europe and
America. The firm, usually very careful about expenditure on advertising,[1]
realised the interest this collection would arouse among Egyptologists all over
the world and publicised it widely. The result was an exceptional attendance at
each day's session of the very long sale, which Major Warre took at a spanking
pace. The catalogue had been compiled with particular care by Mr. Knight of
Spinks, and received praise wherever the sale was discussed in print. The collection had, in fact, been the subject of various specialist publications on the
history of Egyptian art because it formed an entire private museum at Bolehall
Manor House in Tamworth in Staffordshire. The Rev. MacGregor supported a
number of important excavations in Egypt and the Sudan and thus had direct
access to unique sources of supply. The sheer volume of what was coming on to
the market all at once tended at first to keep prices to a modest level. There
were, for example, amulets by the hundred, if not the thousand. Thus, lot 22
contained twenty-one, lot 23 fifteen, lot 24 fifteen, lot 25 eighteen, lot 26
fifteen, lot 27 twenty-five, and so on. Ten consecutive lots of them – 160 amulets in all, made of every sort of material including faience, paste, stone of many
varieties, carnelian and glass – fetched £42, or an average of 5 shillings each for
what were beautiful pieces. But on later days there were great and unique works
of art and the competition for them was lively. The *pièce de résistance* was lot
1679 – a 12th Dynasty Head of Amenemmes III in obsidian. But let Mr. Knight's
description speak for itself.[2]

> Contrary to the impression conveyed by the reproduction,[3] this marvellous work
> is not life-size, but 4⅞ in. from the top of the head to the chin. The damage it has
> sustained is slight, but lessens what seems to have been a characteristic of the
> 12th Dynasty period, namely: the size of the large ears placed high up on the
> head. This admirable relic of one of the finest epochs of Egyptian Art gains

1. The total expenditure on press advertising in the 1922–23 season was only £3,633 and
clients contributed about 25 per cent of this outlay. The media used most extensively in
descending order of importance were *Country Life*, *The Times*, the *Daily Telegraph* and the
Morning Post, and much lower down the scale came the *Connoisseur* and the *Burlington
Magazine*. Geoffrey Hobson controlled the advertising budget very firmly and reviewed its
effectiveness at the end of each year. Thus he felt that *Country Life* was not drawing in the
business he had hoped for and the allocation for that paper was reduced from £775 in 1921–22
to £161 by 1924–25. His annual calculation showed not only the cost of the advertisements in
each sale, but also the average cost per day's sale and the total expenditure in relation to turnover. His objective was to keep the latter figure to about half a per cent, but it usually crept
above this.

2. In fact, he expressed indebtedness for it to an article by Charles Ricketts in the *Journal of
Egyptian Archaeology* in 1917.

3. In the Sotheby's catalogue.

additional interest from the fact that the king is represented as an older man than in all other monuments, save that from the Karnak *cache* now in Cairo. The expression is more pensive, more dreamy than in most of his portraits; and there is a striking resemblance to his father Sesostris III. The likeness of the profile to that of a head in schist, preserved in Berlin, is also remarkable, though in the present example the king has perhaps been portrayed when more advanced in years. This superb piece of sculpture conveys a striking impression of sedate and noble calm, and the greatness of the work makes itself felt more and more as one studies it. It was the supreme treasure in last year's Exhibition of the Burlington Fine Arts Club, and is thought by competent judges to be the finest expression of Egyptian statuary art in the world.

The piece was regarded as so precious that Jim Kiddell had to carry it down to the strong room at the end of each day of the viewing and to bring it up again on the next morning. No one else was allowed to handle it. On the day of the sale he was standing next to Howard Carter who started jokingly with a bid of £4,000. He had muttered something under his breath and Major Warre raised his eyebrows questioningly and repeated ' "Fourpence" did you say, Mr. Carter?' Carter was thought to be acting on behalf of Lord Carnarvon, and even though he was slowly driven up to £9,000 the final bid of £10,000 was way above his upper limit and wrested the piece from him. The successful bidder at this record price was the firm of H. Kehyaian and there was much speculation on whose behalf they had bid this vast sum. The mystery buyer was, in fact, our old friend Calouste Gulbenkian who had seen the piece displayed at the Burlington Fine Arts Exhibition the year before and had fallen in love with it.[1] He had already amassed a number of Egyptian antiquities – all of exceptional quality – for in every sphere of collecting he always wanted only the best. The Head of Amenemmes is now displayed in the Gulbenkian Museum in Lisbon. It is probably one of the most outstanding works of art ever to have come up for sale at Bond Street, and would today (1980) fetch well in excess of £500,000.

1922 included some sales of unusual interest which were evidence of Bond Street's increasing reputation in the non-book era. Hobson was clearly beginning to enjoy the success of the collaboration with his young protégé, Kiddell, in place of the ageing Caldecott, in the realms of works of art, just as he enjoyed des Graz's growing stature on the book side, and on a much smaller scale, Bell's improved sales of drawings and paintings. But he was not given to throwing praise about lightly and usually kept his views to himself.

Between March and June a number of sales were planned which broke new ground. March saw the sale of the finest collection of antique fire-arms ever to have passed through Sotheby's. The owner was Herbert Jackson, author of *European Hand Firearms of the Sixteenth, Seventeenth and Eighteenth Centuries*, and a highly respected city merchant known familiarly as 'Head of the Rice

1. He was a master of secrecy and went to great lengths to conceal his identity when buying at important sales. Jim Kiddell recalled that on such occasions several dealers were used, sometimes as many as five. 'A' attended the sale and bought for 'B', 'B' bought for 'C', and so on.

Ring'. He took a great personal interest in the sale of his property and fussed Jim Kiddell endlessly beforehand. The firm cleaned up a lot of the pieces and displayed the whole collection in special glass cases to what was generally regarded as magnificent effect. Jackson himself was so delighted when he saw the collection just before the public view that he exclaimed what became known as a popular refrain: 'It looks much better than at home, Mr. Kiddell'. Yet being himself a member of a ring, he was afraid of what a ring of antique dealers might do at the sale, and reserves were fixed that were decidedly on the high side. A certain amount of armour was included in the sale, for it was felt, quite rightly, that the interest at the time was much greater in armour than in firearms. Jackson had combed Europe for really fine examples of the latter and had found great riches in Italy and, to a lesser extent, in Holland. The catalogue contained a note which stated that the collection, formed over the previous forty years (i.e. from 1880 onwards), was 'composed of pieces carefully selected as being representative examples of the finest quality (*in the best original condition*) of the varying types used in Europe during different periods'. The sale was well attended and widely written up in the press. Prices were regarded as generally satisfactory, and because interest in fire-arms has grown so enormously it is worth looking at them in some detail.

Probably because of the high reserves – and the activities of the ring that Jackson feared – 32 of the 107 lots were bought in. An early seventeenth-century wheel-lock sporting gun, for example, described as '*in perfect original condition*; the stock profusely inlaid with classical subjects in brass, and with brass wire work' was bought in at £18 10s., but the next lot, an early seventeenth-century Italian flintlock rifle catalogued as 'of exceptionally fine workmanship and of beautiful form; the stock inlaid in the best style with buckhorn and mother-o'-pearl; a fine example of the artistic decoration and the graceful lines of weapons of this period' (it came from the collection of Cornelia, Countess of Craven), was sold for £19 10s. Today[1] the value of the first lot would probably approach £6,500, and that of the second £5,500. A little later lot 94, catalogued as 'a unique and exceptionally fine pair of English hand-revolved magazine Flint-lock Pistols, firing three discharges from one barrel', made by an Italian gunsmith working in London during the second half of the seventeenth century, fetched £135, which was regarded as a very satisfactory price. Today they would probably change hands at around £30,000. The best piece in the sale was lot 103. The cataloguer, F. G. Fenton, a well-known arms and armour dealer with a large shop at the British Museum end of New Oxford Street (the stock of which Sotheby's was to sell a few years later), could hardly contain himself with delight in his description of the piece: 'a very elaborately decorated and exceptionally fine and bold example of a German Wheel-lock Pistol of the latter part of the sixteenth century'. It too fetched £135. The price today would be nearer £15,000. Although the singular quality of the sale was widely recognised and commented upon, its total was only £2,589. Today that figure could probably be multiplied by between a hundred and a hundred and fifty times.

1. 1980.

In marked contrast was a sale held a fortnight later. This was a bold experiment and consisted of 'a representative selection of Works of Art by Nelson Dawson Esq., ARWS, RE, RWA (Member of the International Society of Sculptors, Painters and Engravers)'. Dawson was an elderly pillar of the Arts and Crafts movement. He had a charming house in Chelsea called 'The Mulberry Tree', which was also his workshop. He was one of those patient followers of William Morris who had set his heart against the Victorian taste by returning to earlier sources for inspiration, but he was also of an inventive turn of mind, was particularly good at metal-work and enjoyed exploring the potentials of different methods of enamelling and the colour effects he could produce. He had, at one time, a small pottery of his own where he made pieces in conscious simulation of early Chinese as well as traditional English pottery. He was especially fascinated by experimenting with glazes. He painted competently, particularly landscapes. He made decorative, hand-forged ironwork, again looking to medieval examples for inspiration. He also made bronzes and found a ready market for them in schools and universities when combined with the appropriate enamelled heraldic shields. Together with his wife, Edith Dawson, he produced beaten silver work as well as jewellery using both precious and semi-precious stones, and enamelling. A good deal of the jewellery was in gold.

Few of the items in the sale fetched in excess of £5. A 'Nasturtium' cup and cover in beaten silver with a lid of translucent enamel and a ball of crystal forming the knob, 'the whole of very fine design', fetched the highest price. It was £14 10s. The sale was saved from being a complete financial disaster by a final lot added as a last minute makeshift. This consisted of a collection of 151 pieces of Martinware – now one of Belgravia's most sought-after forms of studio pottery – made up 'almost entirely of vases largely derived from vegetable forms, many beautifully inlaid, mottled and glazed with a wide range of colours, and practically all signed and dated'. The collection was sold with two display cabinets and fetched £260. The catalogue explained that 'as the pottery is now closed opportunities of acquiring such a characteristic collection of the highly individual work of the Brothers Martin must be of very rare occurrence'. The very fact that the sale had been allowed to take place at all throws an interesting light on the awakening of a change of taste in Geoffrey Hobson, who was beginning to take an interest in contemporary art. When some years later he moved from Bedford Square to a house in Chelsea, he sold the bulk of his former possessions and furnished the new house afresh in the *art deco* manner and had many of the walls decorated with murals by *art deco* painters.

Six weeks later, at the very end of April and early in May 1922, Sotheby's sold one of those idiosyncratic collections that was wholly memorable. It was the property of two brothers, Max and Maurice Rosenheim. Max had been a wine merchant; Maurice a tea broker. Both men were bachelors; they had shared a house in Hampstead all their lives. Both were fanatical antiquaries and collectors. The Renaissance was the world they revelled in. Their taste was completely at odds with fashion, and judged by today's standards was rather museum-like. They were on the friendliest terms with Charles Hercules Read of the British Museum, and they had been advised when they were younger by Sir Augustus Wollaston Franks who had been Hercules Read's master and mentor. Max, who had died in 1912, and had left all his collections to his brother, 'devoted his time and his means to a miscellaneous kind of collection', wrote Hercules Read in an obituary for the Society of Antiquaries of which he was President, 'which after ranging through the diverse fields of *incunabula*, of foreign heraldry, ornamental engravings and the like, finally took shape in a settled pursuit of the finest *cinquecento* medals, Italian and German, and all bronzes of the same period. In this line of collecting he was singularly successful, while the pursuit was illuminated by an extraordinary power of research and a critical acumen of unusual quality'. Later in his life he had developed 'such a perfection of artistic insight as to constitute him a referee in these matters of connoisseurship, both at the Burlington Fine Arts Club and elsewhere'.[1]

Maurice died eleven years later and his death had brought about the dispersal of the collections. He had shared Max's enthusiasm for Renaissance medals, but took a particular delight in collecting early mathematical and scientific instruments and formed one of the most extensive collections of early engravings and drawings relating to ornament and design used in the decorative arts, as well as book plates, seal matrices, porcelain and pottery and early jewellery. Max was probably the more perceptive scholar and had published a celebrated paper on the *Album Amicorum*, a kind of forerunner of the autograph book, popular among German and Swiss students of the second half of the sixteenth and first half of the seventeenth century, in which they persuaded their friends – and the more distinguished they were the better – to enter their names, with allusive quotations and their coats of arms and other illustrations, often of a heraldic nature. Eventually these albums became so popular that they were, to some extent, pre-printed. Max spent the last few years of his life undertaking the arrangement and cataloguing of the enormous collection of foreign book plates and similar engravings at the British Museum which had been bequeathed to the Department of Prints by Sir Wollaston Franks. It was a drudging labour of love carried through assiduously in memory of a friend for whom Max had immense admiration.

The Rosenheims had a wide circle of friends who called regularly at their house in Hampstead for discussion and elucidation of problem pieces of the sixteenth, seventeenth and, to a much lesser extent, the eighteenth centuries. As Hercules Read wrote in an introductory note to the Sotheby catalogues: 'The conditions under which all these activities were pursued by the two brothers had an almost idyllic aspect, as their more intimate friends realise very well'. Although the Rosenheims were outside the main stream of collecting, they made a considerable impact in stimulating an interest in matters that were to be studied extensively after their own collections had long been dispersed.

1. *Proceedings of the Society of Antiquaries*, 23 April 1923.

While many of their most important items had been left to the British Museum, the prospect of selling the remaining and massive contents of their house was both an auctioneer's dream, and a cataloguer's nightmare. Ultimately, every department within Sotheby's became involved under the fastidious supervision of Hercules Read, who was justly celebrated in his day for the immensity of his knowledge.[1] The catalogues bore strong evidence of his involvement. The most important was for the first sale of 816 lots of 'Medals, Plaquettes and Coins, chiefly of the Renaissance' held over five days from 30 April 1923 onwards. It was a very *technical* catalogue, full of abbreviations and references to the literature in many languages, but the forty pages of collotype illustrations showed a vast array of minor gems of Renaissance sculpture: endlessly fascinating portrait heads and devices, of an almost tactile quality. But once again interest in the sale was limited and it gave a few specialist dealers, a selected band of enthusiastic collectors and a number of museums, superb opportunities to pick up unrepeatable bargains. For prices were universally low, often in shillings rather than pounds, and very rarely in double figures at that. The total for the five days was only £5,355 14s. 0d.

There were further separate sales of the drawings and pictures, the pottery and porcelain, the engraved ornament, the library and works of art – ten days in all. The pottery and porcelain was widely known through articles that had appeared about them in the *Burlington Magazine*. It was a superbly decorative collection of rare and early pieces, mostly of Continental origin. The designs for ornament, in the form of original drawings, loose engravings and books of ornament, were by artists as distinguished as Dürer and Altdorfer and a host of little-known contemporaries of theirs with marvellously improbable names like Wolfgang Meyerpeck, Wendel Dietterling, Vespasiano Amphiareo, Jakob Guckeysen and Friedrich Unteutsch. The work related to jewellery and the goldsmith's craft, weapons, porcelain, needlework and embroidery, lettering and typography, architecture, the abstract and the fantastic. Here too the discerning could find bargains in plenty, many now very valuable items, going only for shillings. Lot 66 was a copy of the first edition of the famous *Kunstbüchlein von mancherley schönen Trinckgeschiren* by Hans Brosamer of 1545. It was the very copy Quaritch had used for the reproduction of a facsimile edition and it included two additional original drawings. It fetched £27. Today's price would not be less than £3,000. Lots 274 and 275 were books of heraldic engravings by Martin Schöngaur that are greatly sought after today. In 1923 Colnaghi's bought them for £76 and £72 respectively, the highest prices in the sale with the exception of a print of a coat-of-arms with a skull by Dürer for which they paid £74.

The library again reflected the Rosenheims' special interest, their love of things visual and their leaning towards Germany in the fifteenth, sixteenth and

---

1. Sotheby's sold his own very wide range of collections for more than £20,000 in a five-day sale beginning on 5 November 1928. There were some startling contrasts as far as prices were concerned. A fine but small piece of fifteenth-century tapestry sold for £4,200 but a collection of 208 very fine Chinese snuff bottles fetched only £111.0.0!

seventeenth centuries. There was a comprehensive collection of tracts by Martin Luther, but they were totally unappreciated. The forty major tracts and Luther's complete works in four volumes – a folio presentation set of 1563–70 with an elaborate inscription to an august member of the princely Coburg family – fetched a total of £7 19s. od. The celebrated collection of *Album Amicorum* did not fare much better. The forty-two lots raised £280. Altogether the 571 lots included in this sale made £2,352 2s. od., a figure which was regarded in its day – and it was, after all, a matter of sixty years ago – as respectable, if unsensational.

There was much wider interest in the final Rosenheim sale of 'Works of Art comprising Seal Matrices, Rings, Jewellery, Cameos, Silver, Ivories, Mathematical and Scientific Instruments, Bronzes, etc.'. No one needed special expertise or knowledge of remote languages to see that here was a unique selection of the finest craftsmanship from the fourteenth to the eighteenth centuries. The frontispiece showed a life-size, bronze bust of Galileo by Pietro Tacca. It was an ingenious choice for the 417 items in this sale, for it epitomised Rosenheims' predilection for the amalgam of the arts and the sciences in their collection of finely decorated astronomical instruments, calendars, many sorts of dials, clocks and watches, gunners' compasses and levels, globes and scales. The bust fetched £140. A conservative estimate of its value today would be £40,000. Other highlights of the sale included lot 226, the Fugger Cup, described as a 'parcel gilt cup with embossed pineapple body and foot with rustic scrolls and fluted stem; in the centre of the bowl is a tower with a hinged lid, which is raised as liquid is poured in and from the tower emerges a hand holding a rose, as if presented to the drinker'. This ingenious device had been given by Mattheus Schwartz, an agent of the Fugger firm in Augsburg, to his principal, Anthony Fugger, on the occasion of the latter's marriage in 1527. It fetched £580, one of the highest prices in the sale, and was bought by William Randolph Hearst, the American newspaper tycoon, to whom this sort of piece appealed beyond measure. Its value today would probably be of the order of £150,000 to £200,000. Two other lots which did well were a pair of sixteenth-century statuettes of Adam and Eve, in pearwood, after Dürer, which sold for £460, and an iron crest for a helmet in the form of a winged, seven-headed Hydra, chased and damascened in gold. This formidable monster was based on the crest of Lodovico Gonzaga, Marchese of Mantua, who died in 1595. It raised an audible gasp in the sale-room when fierce competition pushed the price up to £500. Jom Kiddell watched its sale with amazement. He reckoned the price today would be much closer to £100,000. But among the many bronzes, ivories, cameos, jewellery, seal matrices and miniatures, there were some remarkable bargains for collectors. Twenty-six glass medallion cameo portraits by William Tassie representing George III, Pitt, Fox and other dignitaries fetched only £20; and two fine thirteenth-century German gold rings with Lombardic inscriptions, sold for £39. Two eighteenth-century terrestrial globes, the smaller one in a shagreen case, and a sextant, all combined in one lot, made £9. An early seventeenth-century Italian 'cabinet of walnut wood, of architectural design; with eight columns, four arched recesses containing bronze statuettes and a number of secret and other drawers; the base being a cupboard' – a particularly striking piece – fetched £35. The total for the works of art sale reached £11,903.

One person to whom the sale gave great pleasure was Queen Mary who was an avid collector of antiques. She had acquired a tortoiseshell *bonbonnière* mounted and inlaid with gold, with the initials M R on the lid beneath a royal crest. It had once been the property of William III's wife, an earlier Queen Mary. She had bought it under the *nomme de vente* of 'Geoffrey' for £51. The name she usually employed in her commission bids at Sotheby's was, in fact, 'Dawson'.

The third and final sale of armour from Wilton House; a particularly fine porcelain sale (combined with some splendid French furniture) and a good silver sale (including one of the most beautiful William III toilet sets, the property of Lord Northbourne, ever to pass through Bond Street), brought the season to a close. When all the figures had been added up it turned out that the turnover of the works of art department in the 1922–23 season came to £136,601.

We are so inured nowadays to a perpetual state of inflation that it is quite difficult to imagine that for the next *two decades* after 1923 the value of money remained more or less the same. Of course, fashions came and went; of course, there were boomlets and the worst period of economic disaster of the century; of course, prices rose and fell. But even so, anyone with a genuine love of antiques, and in particular of English antiques, who looks through Sotheby's catalogues of that period, *must* keep thinking that he has been born fifty years too late. The artistic, aesthetic and historic quality of what was sold was as high as has ever passed through the English sale-rooms. What the partners learned from the 1922–23 season in particular was that their insistence on quality of selection gave them just rewards, but what must have disappointed them was the xenophobic and insular nature of contemporary buyers. There was a tremendously strong preference for things English. The most exquisite European antiques of all kinds, furniture and porcelain, always came off a very poor second best. Perhaps this attitude is exemplified to perfection by two items in a mixed furniture sale that appeared early in 1924. Both were very beautiful, probably late sixteenth or early seventeenth century, Italian walnut *cassone* – long, low chests. One was adorned with decorative marquetry and some carving; the other was more elaborately carved but with an austere magnificence. The first fetched £10; the second £7 10s. od. The prices can barely have covered the original cost of transporting them from Italy to England. There was simply no interest in anything that looked so obviously outlandish. But the next few years – as we shall see – were to witness the burgeoning of an interest in something even more alien in its origin, the ancient oriental porcelains, in which Sotheby's were to specialise, which led, many years later, to particularly resounding successes.

21

The Good Years

UNEXPECTEDLY, and contrary to all the early signs, 1924 to 1929 were five good years. While the turnover of the book department remained static (until 1927–28), Works of Art continued to thrive and so did the sale of pictures. Although Charles Bell had left in something of a huff he did, when asked by Evelyn Barlow, recommend a successor and recommended him with some fervour. The man concerned was Tancred Borenius, the Finnish art historian who advised Lord Lascelles. Bell had got to know him extremely well at Oxford, for Borenius had compiled and published a catalogue of the *Paintings of the Old Masters at Christ Church* in 1916. Bell himself had completed the catalogue of the distinguished collection of *Drawings of the Old Masters at Christ Church* two years earlier. Borenius had achieved a considerable reputation as an authority on Italian painting at an early age through his skilful revision of that classic on the subject, Crowe and Cavalcaselle's *History of Italian Painting*, which had first appeared between 1864 and 1871.

Borenius was an altogether remarkable man: highly knowledgeable about the arts with that essential adjunct to art auctioneering – a superb visual memory.[1] He was dynamic to the point of embarrassment, multi-lingual (he could genuinely speak nine languages with complete fluency), he was commercially adept and had an enormously wide circle of acquaintances among artists and art historians, the landed gentry and owners of great collections, even among the Royal Family and the Diplomatic Corps in London. He had been born in Wiborg in Finland forty years previously, was immensely proud of his origins and a passionate campaigner for the independence of his country. He held some form of diplomatic status on Finland's behalf during much of his life, for which he was rewarded with a host of distinguished foreign orders, including a Papal Countship by the Vatican. He had, furthermore, a finely developed, if slightly unorthodox sense of humour. If Tancred Borenius is almost forgotten now it is time to jog posterity's elbow and to bring him back into the realm of the remembered. He remained Sotheby's part-time adviser on pictures from 1924 until the end of the war.

In his early youth his father had frequently taken him on day trips by train to nearby St. Petersburg, because the boy showed a passionate interest in paintings. He was left to his own devices at the Hermitage Museum in the morning with a packet of sandwiches for his lunch, and collected in the evening. Later he

1. A tribute to him in the *Burlington Magazine* at the time of his death in 1948 said, 'His memory was so exceptional, both of the composition of paintings and their location, as well as of the literature of art, that he served as a walking encyclopaedia – a fact of which successive editors of the magazine took full advantage'.

took a degree in the history of art at Helsingfors University; then spent six months at the Kaiser Friedrich Museum as a trainee under Bode and a further year of study at the Prussian Institute in Rome. Afterwards he travelled all over Italy collecting material for his doctoral thesis on the *Painters of Vicenza*. He did, in fact, have an Italian grandmother, and in his chubby, handsome way and with his flamboyant sense of dress he was often taken for an Italian. He completed his studies – and his book – with two years work in London, researching at the British Museum. It was during this period that he had been asked by John Murray, the publisher, to undertake the revision of part of Crowe and Cavalcaselle's long history. On the strength of this commission he decided to get married to his childhood sweetheart – the granddaughter of Finland's foremost poet - and to bring his wife to London and to settle there. The young couple's first house was in Mecklenburgh Square in Bloomsbury and they were soon on friendly terms with some of the intellectuals and artists living there, such as Sir Alan Gardiner the Egyptologist, Lytton Strachey, Clive and Vanessa Bell, Duncan Grant, Vyvyan Holland – Oscar Wilde's son – and the Sitwell brothers, Osbert and Sacheverell. Borenius was particularly impressed by the Englishness of Roger Fry, that versatile art critic, and one has the feeling that for many years he tried to model himself on Fry. Borenius and his young wife were regular guests at the evening parties given by Lady Ottoline Morrell in Bedford Square, a short walk away. He had started writing for the *Burlington Magazine* in 1910 and became a regular contributor from 1913 onwards. This led to a close friendship with More Adey, one of the magazine's editors. Also in 1913 Borenius was appointed Lecturer of Fine Arts at University College, London, and in 1922 he became the first holder of the Durning–Lawrence Chair in the History of Art there.

His membership of the Burlington Fine Arts Club brought him into contact with the world of connoisseurs and collectors. Here he met Sir Herbert Cook (of whose collection of Italian paintings he was to write a catalogue), Sir Eric Maclagan (later Director of the Victoria & Albert Museum), Sir Robert Witt, Laurence Binyon and, above all, Lord Lascelles, who subsequently became the 6th Earl of Harewood and had inherited a great fortune from the Marquess of Clanricarde. The story of how this is said to have come about is worth recounting. Clanricarde was an eccentric Irish absentee landlord who lived in London and was exceedingly miserly and rude to those about him. He wandered into his club in St. James's each day, often unshaven and in down-at-heel clothes, with a parcel of sandwiches wrapped in newspaper. He made himself unpopular – if only because he dropped the newspaper on the floor by his chair – and few members would talk to him. Lord Lascelles, a distant relation, somehow broke through this aura of unpleasantness, chatted to the old man regularly and became quite friendly with him. Clanricarde died suddenly and – completely unexpectedly – Lascelles found himself heir to the Clanricarde Estates. These turned out to be huge and worth something of the order of £6,000,000. With some of this money Lord Lascelles determined to enrich the contents of Harewood House with outstanding pictures, furniture and *objets d'art*. He enquired in the Burlington Fine Arts Club about an adviser on forming such a collection and Borenius was recommended. Thus started a long and fruitful friendship. Even while Lascelles was in the trenches he never stopped corresponding with Borenius about possible purchases of pictures that Borenius had located. After Lord Lascelles's marriage to the Princess Royal, Borenius became acquainted with her mother, Queen Mary. He thoroughly enjoyed the fact that thereafter the Queen constantly sought his advice in her voracious collecting activities.

At Sotheby's he felt at first like a fish out of water. The number of good Italian pictures that came into Bond Street was few and far between. Although initially he knew next to nothing about English pictures he soon formed not only a very good working knowledge but a real sympathy with the art of England which, as Joan Evans was to write much later in reference to him, 'in its strange mixture of provinciality and romantic beauty and its improbable dating is rarely congenial to a foreigner'. Because he was a confirmed monarchist and an ardent admirer of the Stuarts, he became an enthusiastic collector of everything Jacobite – books, engravings, letters and particularly of the fine engraved glass of which Sotheby's had had many major sales since the days when the new partners had taken over from Tom Hodge. Borenius's excellent contacts soon led to an increasing volume of picture sales. The turnover in paintings and drawings alone increased from £33,000 in 1924–25 to £186,000 by 1928–29. Borenius had made an arrangement with Sir Montague Barlow under which he was responsible for all cataloguing of pictures, and though he got a good deal of assistance from Tim Wilder and Archie Russell, who came in to help over drawings, he received a commission on everything that appeared in the relevant catalogues. This swelled his income from £600 in the first year to an optimum figure of nearly £3,000 a year in 1928–29, which was more than some partners were getting. But he worked hard. On one occasion when the head of a rival firm went North to attend an important funeral, he was somewhat startled to meet the Doctor, as Borenius was known in the trade, already coming back. 'He must have been there,' he was heard to complain afterwards, 'to attend at the last rites.' The keen business sense[1] was essential to support Borenius in a stylish way of life, hobnobbing with the grand and the affluent. Thus he spent nearly a month each summer at Harewood House at the Princess Royal's invitation. During the rest of the year he practically lived in his Club and entertained lavishly. It was this very need for money as well as the devotion to the Finnish cause which disturbed his contemporaries. He seemed the ideal candidate for a number of great museum posts, yet he was always passed over. He also tended to quarrel with his fellow art experts. He clashed fiercely with Sir Martin Conway in England and Bernard Berenson in Italy. It was this combination of an uncertain temperament, a number of unlikely romantic attachments and a prolonged final illness which impaired his energy and his mental agility, that led to a lack of recognition of Borenius's talents after his death.

1. Borenius frequently bought at sales both at Sotheby's and Christie's on behalf of clients and certainly during the decade before the war he pocketed an endless series of five guinea payments, his standard charge for giving an authentication of a picture.

The staff at Bond Street doted on him and the partners appreciated the business he brought to the firm, even from abroad. For many years he exuded enormous vigour and the Wednesday afternoons he spent cataloguing were often exciting. He would hold forth on his current problems at *Apollo* magazine which he had founded in 1926 and edited briefly; or on the latest discoveries in his excavations at Clarendon Palace in Wiltshire, which he financed entirely out of his own pocket, or about the goings-on at the Magnasco Society, a select body of collectors of Italian paintings. Both he and his wife were keen Wagnerians and attended every opera that was staged in London and he would comment critically on the finer points of each performance. But he could revert quickly to the matter in hand and dictate catalogue entries at a remarkable speed. Often they showed evidence of this rapid and slapdash compilation. Occasionally he would become deeply interested in a particular picture, undertake a great deal of research about it and then write it up in one of the art journals after the catalogue entry had been completed. On one memorable summer afternoon Tim Wilder was consulting some specialist work in the shelves of the picture director's reference library. Everything in that quiet backwater was peaceful and somnolent, when suddenly the door burst open and there stood the Doctor, arms stretched dramatically above his head. 'Come at vunce,' he shouted. 'I have made the most vunderful discovery!', vanishing down the stairs. Before anyone could recover from their astonishment and follow through the open door he whisked a picture from his taxi, carried it into the room and began a long lecture about it to all who now stood around. The picture turned out to be *An Allegory* by Lorenzo Lotto which had been lost for a century. It was a tribute to the Doctor's scholarship that he had recognised it from an old description. It was sold in May 1934, and is now in the Washington National Gallery. It was one of many fine pictures that passed through his hands at Sotheby's.

Occasionally there were marvellous collections not confined to pictures which came his way through contacts at the Burlington Fine Arts Club or elsewhere in which he would take a burning interest. One such had belonged to Lord Carmichael of Skirling, a former colonial administrator who was a born collector and a man with a superb eye for aesthetic quality in any number of fields. Lord Carmichael had acted as a Trustee of several museums in England and Scotland and had left them generous gifts and bequests at the time of his death. Unusually, he had purchased many of his best items in Italy. His very diverse collection fetched nearly £50,000 in April 1926. It included jewellery, silver, porcelain, fine fabrics and embroidery, Egyptian, Greek and Roman antiquities, particularly outstanding medieval enamels and ecclesiastical metalwork, Italian maiolica and Della Robbia ware. The sale concluded with a number of family portraits by Henry Raeburn. Duveen paid £8,800 for one and Tooth £8,000 for another.

In contrast, the three-day sale of the collection of Vicomte Bernard d'Hendecourt in May 1929 reached Borenius through old friends in the art trade. He had for many years advised the brothers George and Alfred Durlacher who kept one of the most select and magnificent works of art establishments in Bond Street, just opposite Sotheby's. The brothers had been unfortunate in their choice of younger partners, when eventually they realised that they could not carry on the business for ever. The first was drowned in a boating accident in New York. To succeed him they took on the relatively young Vicomte d'Hendecourt, but he had been badly injured while serving in the French Air Force during the First World War and also contracted cancer. Not only did he have to withdraw from the business, but he also decided before his death to sell the family possessions. What now came to Sotheby's included classical and medieval, as well as ancient Egyptian, Asian and African sculpture. But there were also fine early Italian and other Old Masters and an excellent collection of French, Italian, Dutch and English drawings. Tucked away inconspicuously in the catalogue was a signed Renoir painting of a park scene, almost the first by that artist that Sotheby's had ever sold. It fetched £45. A still life of *Two Roses in a Vase* found in Manet's studio after his death was sold for £300 to the Leicester Galleries.

Barlow Out of Politics

During the course of 1924 Montague Barlow had been able to devote much more of his time to Sotheby's, for his role as a Cabinet Minister had come to an end after the general election in December 1923, when there had been a landslide towards Labour and he had lost his seat for Salford. Although the Conservatives regained all that they had lost in a further general election only ten months later, Barlow did not stand for Parliament again. He had been made a baronet in 1924 for his contribution as Minister of Labour.

At the end of each year's sale season, in August, Barlow would call all the staff together and deliver a résumé of how the firm had progressed. In August of 1924 he entered the large gallery armed with figures which showed that there had been a slight decline in turnover each year since 1921 and that increased taxation was having a deleterious effect on trade. He promised, however, to keep salaries up and announced an annual bonus. He asked whether the staff wanted a Works Council and explained how this would work. A stern homily on adhering rigidly to procedures laid down was always included in these pep talks. That year Barlow urged cataloguers not to take outside visitors into their own offices, but in the interests of security to talk to them in the waiting-rooms.

The Works Council did not, in fact, get off the ground until 1926. By 1927, Barlow's penultimate year as Chairman, the results exceeded the 1921 record. That year Barlow thanked the staff cordially for their hard work and raised the bonus. He urged the porters to be neat and smart in their appearance when on duty, and he asked staff who broke items put up for sale to admit having done so at once as otherwise it led to all-round suspicion. There had also been an unusual number of thefts and he asked that porters should watch out for the well-known old lags who specialised in slipping small objects into their capacious coat pockets.

In 1927 he also announced the arrival of a new director – Mr. C. Vere Pilkington, a young man who had come to the firm straight from Oxford, and who was particularly interested in the arts and music. Vere's arrival heralded Barlow's intention of withdrawing from the firm – and, of course, withdrawing his capital as he left. For this reason, as well as for a continuity of management, new partners were sought who could bring new working capital to the business. Vere's father – a wealthy stockbroker – provided £20,000 for this purpose. As always the matter was encapsulated in a complex legal agreement. One of the primary needs for more cash was to pay off a bank loan on the purchase of 5 George Street which the firm had recently bought to cope with expanding business. It was agreed at the outset that Vere, as a junior director, would be paid an initial salary of £500 a year which would rise to £900 a year – a full director's salary – by 1933 when he would also be entitled to 15 per cent of the annual profits. Warre would at that stage draw 35 per cent and Charles des Graz 30 per cent. No one could foresee that, despite these excellent intentions, there would be no profit at all in 1933 and for quite a number of years thereafter. It was made clear in the legal document that Geoffrey Hobson intended to retire in 1933 (but, in fact, the slump forced him to stay on) and that Warre and Evelyn Barlow would go in 1938, but again fate dictated otherwise. The document is an interesting object lesson in showing how difficult it is to make arrangements for anything but the immediate future.

Another major constitutional change in the firm that took place in December of 1924 was that Sotheby, Wilkinson & Hodge, which had been a simple partnership, now became a private, unlimited company with a capital of £150,000. This was being done on the advice of lawyers and accountants as a means of mitigating the increasing demands of taxation.

Napoleon in the Auction Room

Few people can have realised what a protracted saga lay behind the sale announced for 1 December 1924, and the three following days. It represented more than ten years work by Barlow and Hobson, and had involved some of the most delicate and cliff-hanging negotiations they had ever undertaken as auctioneers. A link with the young Earl of Crawford and Balcarres had been forged when Tom Hodge took on the Senior Librarian from Haigh Hall, A. G. E. Phillips, as head cataloguer. Early in 1914 Barlow had been asked informally whether he might, in a personal capacity, find a possible purchaser for the immense collection of manuscripts, printed documents, engravings, caricatures, medals and paper money relating to the French Revolution and the Napoleonic era which the 26th Earl of Crawford and Balcarres (Ludovic, who had recently died) and his father (Alexander, but known as Lord Lindsay for most of his life) before him had put together.[1] The relevant material was so representative and complete that in a memorandum to Barlow (presumably

1. For a magnificent biography of both father and son – but particularly father – see Nicolas Barker's *Biblioteca Lindesiana*, Bernard Quaritch, London, 1977.

aimed at would-be purchasers) the Librarian was able to write: 'The history of the period can be studied from every aspect. Thus often a manuscript or letter (of which there were more than nine thousand) gives the private opinion of the writer to his correspondent; the printed *Bulletin* (broadsheet) conveys to the public the decisions of the government of the day; the *affiche* (poster) represents equal publicity, though it was often unofficial; and the engravings give a pictorial version of the episode – laudatory, satirical or hostile. The *assignats* (bank notes issued by many local authorities) traced the financial history of the French Revolution'. The collection was thus a complete documentary record of the French Revolution, the ascent of Napoleon, his reign and domination of Europe, his life, his death and its aftermath. It showed uniquely the emergence and working of democratic government, civil administration and military organisation.

For a period of many years the manuscript material had been copied out, word for word, by three ladies who were particularly well-versed in the bad handwriting of the period, and whose detailed knowledge of the history of those times enabled them to read the vast number of names of persons and places. It also enabled them to detect relatively easily the forged letters that had increasingly come on to the market, because often the events these purported to describe contained errors of fact. The transcripts prepared in this way were then typed, and the typed copy was in turn checked, corrected and annotated by three Oxford graduates who had made a special study of the period 1789 to 1815. The typed copy was re-typed where necessary and in cases of particular difficulty, documents were photographed and circulated all over the world among acknowledged masters of deciphering such material, though there were marked variations in their readings. Napoleon's famous 'Address to my Soldiers', for example, written just before the Battle of Rivoli in 1797, displayed the almost 'hopeless obscurity of his handwriting' and there seemed little chance of a definitive transliteration.

All this material had been assembled in final form in 1913, just before the older Lord Crawford had died, so that it could be printed as the ninth volume of his library catalogue, the *Biblioteca Lindesiana*, the earlier volumes of which had appeared between 1910 and 1913. It consisted of some fourteen thousand sheets of typed quarto paper, though there were still many boxes of documents more recently purchased that needed to be transcribed and catalogued, and not surprisingly the younger Lord Crawford quailed at the immense cost and labour of turning this material into printed form.

A member of the family had offered to find a buyer for the entire collection, but this had proved abortive. Barlow met him in the summer of 1914 and then wrote to Lord Crawford: 'I had a long talk with your cousin, Mr. L., this afternoon. I am sorry to find there seem to be considerable difficulties. First of all your cousin admitted that the following had been approached already, namely Messrs. Frick, Huntington, Schwab and Reid. This alone is a somewhat serious matter as great collectors are touchy people and after one or two have been approached, others are rather shy'. A dealer had also been asked to help but had not made much progress either. Barlow therefore intimated that he would be prepared to help, but only on condition that Sotheby's had a free and unfettered hand. It seems that Barlow felt that one of the new universities would 'leap at the opportunity of becoming, at one stroke, a centre of international importance for the study of revolutionary France'.[1] Lord Crawford readily agreed 'provided you [Barlow] would be mainly and personally responsible for the work' of selling what was thereafter always referred to as 'the French Collection'. Not long afterwards the whole matter nearly came to a grinding halt. Lord Crawford went off on holiday to Bayreuth in Germany and returned only one day before war was declared. Haigh Hall was turned into a convalescent home and it became difficult to get at any of the papers of the French Collection. In any case, Barlow's mind was elsewhere and Sotheby's temporarily abandoned sales. But by the end of 1915 the matter had come to life again. Lord Crawford's solicitor and his agent had written to Barlow because there had been new enquiries, so Geoffrey Hobson travelled to Wigan to make a detailed examination of the entire material. He was probably delighted to have an opportunity to examine the famous library and discovered that it contained an entire section of books relating to manuscript material which had not previously been mentioned or known about. It was decided that approaches should be made to two possible buyers in France and, because he was known to take a particular interest in the period, to the Russian Grand Duke Cyril. It proved difficult to get the latter's address but the Russian Embassy eventually suggested that a letter simply addressed to him at 'the Palace of the Grand Duke Cyril, Petrograd' would be sure to reach His Imperial Highness. If it did, he never deigned to reply. Nor does there seem to have been any reaction from France. So Barlow determined to make an effort to sell the collection when he went to the United States early in 1916. The minimum price agreed for what was to be sold – and this excluded a good deal of the material – with Lord Crawford's solicitor and agent was £60,000.[2]

Although Barlow encountered many disappointments in New York he eventually found a possible purchaser. But there were to be further complications. Unbeknownst to anyone, Lord Crawford's cousin had approached G. C. Williamson to act in the matter. Dr. Williamson was a well-known authority in his day on everything to do with art and antiques, and had made a particular speciality of portrait miniatures. He had compiled a four-volume catalogue of Pierpont Morgan's collection of these, having played a considerable part in helping to form it. He was the author of some seventy other books and had established a substantial reputation both in the United States and in Britain. A stormy meeting now took place between Barlow and Williamson. The outcome, after much pleading by the latter, was that Barlow agreed that Williamson should be allowed to act for a limited period. Williamson wrote the names of the three possible purchasers he had in mind on the back of his visiting card. They were Mr. Robert H. Dodd, Mr. Sedgwick and Leland Stamford College.

1. Op. cit., *Biblioteca Lindesiana*, page 373.
2. The original material and its transcription had cost his father nearly £90,000.

Barlow was not allowed to see these. The card was placed in a tiny closed
envelope, and enclosed in a further small envelope sealed in wax with an elaborate crest. The whole process was very formal. Williamson then wrote on the
envelope, 'This is the property of Dr. Barlow and Dr. Williamson jointly'.
Although it was carefully preserved it was never opened in Barlow's lifetime.
However, he was subsequently to regret his generosity. Dr. Williamson sent
him an endless stream of prevaricatory letters extending the agreed date of
completion. Whenever a meeting was planned, Williamson wrote to say that he
had asthma, or a cold, or that his medical adviser would not allow him to leave
the house. Whenever Barlow – with Lord Crawford's blessing – grew peremptory, Williamson replied that he regarded the collection 'as good as sold'; that
Americans could never be hurried over a decision; that a lot of money was
involved; that the prospective purchaser was, or was not, on the point of crossing the Atlantic. In the end Barlow went to New York again himself, and called
on Mr. Sedgwick after Dr. Williamson had revealed his name as a possible
buyer. Mr. Sedgwick, it turned out, had 'no definite purchase in view', and
there the matter ended for the time being.

Months later, Sotheby's received a letter out of the blue asking if the collection
was still for sale. It came from M. A. Hughon & Cie, *Libraires-Specialistes*,
of 15 Rue de Surène, Paris. The elaborate letterheading proclaimed that
the firm specialised in historic documents relating to the French Revolution,
the First Empire and Napoleon. Barlow was unaware that Hughon had played a
very active role in the formation of the collection. He at first approached the
26th Earl (Ludovic) in 1902 offering for sale an enormous collection of Revolutionary posters which had been the property of a French deputy who had died
in 1810. At that time Hughon had an office in London where he had acted as
agent for a Lyons fancy paper manufacturer. Ludovic's highly efficient librarian,
J. P. Edmond, negotiated the purchase with Hughon and, in fact, continued to
deal with him for many years. M. Hughon now explained that he had a client
for the collection and, not unreasonably, that the client would like to have sight
of the complete handlist of the material for one week. Barlow tentatively
agreed, on 'your express undertaking that the copy shall only be shown to the
client you have in mind. . . . It is essential in Lord Crawford's interests that
this should be done as you will appreciate that he cannot run the risk of the
handlist being hawked around promiscuously'.

When he received the full details Hughon appeared overwhelmed by the scale
of the collection. At first an assessment of its magnitude and significance seemed
totally beyond his grasp. In a delightfully Gallic manner he kept assuring
Barlow in a series of letters that *any* sum was extraordinary payment for such a
mountain of material, be it £1,000, £3,000 or £5,000. It was quite clear that the
scale of such business was far greater than Hughon had ever tackled before.[1]

Although he always replied instantly to Barlow's letters in charmingly
idiosyncratic English ('as this gentleman's fancy is quite Napoleonic, we have

1. The business of selling historic documents had started as a hobby and a sideline, but
became a full-time occupation on Hughon's return to Paris.

no doubt that he is in a better situation than anybody else to pay a good price for the whole reunion collected by the late Lord Crawford'; or later, 'I must ask you to make the price as smooth as you can'), the French and English approach to making commercial agreements did not gel readily. The principal stumbling-block was that Hughon wanted to know what price Barlow had in mind, and Barlow insisted that it was up to Hughon to make an offer. When, some letters later, Hughon's client at last offered 'a very big sum, £8–£10,000', Barlow countered that it seemed 'a ridiculously small one' to him. There were problems too about a shared commission. Obviously these matters were arranged differently in France because what Barlow regarded as a very generous offer indeed did little to please M. Hughon. But the gallant little man battled on. With what seems remarkable speed he found a new client who was prepared to pay some £40,000. Only two weeks later he writes that 'the purchaser, an important man in the metal trade (A1 references, Bank of France)' had offered '250,000 francs cash down and 100,000 francs every month until complete payment' – 1,250,000 francs in all. 'Kindly write me at once if his Lordship is agreeing, as I have with a lot of palaver reached the amount you suggest of three or four times Mr. Bromwell's offer of £8–£10,000 and I call me lucky to have got such amounts.' Barlow contacted Lord Crawford and although it was less than they had hoped for earlier, a letter went off to Paris agreeing to the principal sum and suggesting terms of payment. M. Hughon replied by return. He named his client as M. Albert Pezieux of 9 Quai de Passy, Paris, managing director of a vast family enterprise in coal and iron.

Only a week later, on 21 June 1919, Hughon sent a hand-written note which the prospective buyer had signed, agreeing to the terms. A first cheque for 149,000 francs (£5,000) followed. Barlow banked it instantly. Hughon also wrote that he and his client would be coming to England, despite the complexities of post-war travel, to inspect the great collection at Haigh Hall and to sign the contract. Sotheby's and Lord Crawford made detailed arrangements to get them passports and to facilitate their journey. There were sighs of relief all round. But the troubles were not yet over. Hughon did indeed reach London with M. Pezieux. Lord Crawford wrote to Barlow in some consternation from his London house in Audley Square, 'Hughon pushed his way in here this morning and had a mysterious conversation. I could not make out what he was driving at, unless it was that he (Hughon) is sceptical as to the power of his friend to pay. . . . He tells me that he is very much impressed by the collection, and that the green catalogue gives a wholly inadequate impression of its value! This at any rate is comforting; because some buyers would take the other view and say that the merits of the collection had been exaggerated'.

Hughon, musing at the Queen's Hotel in London, also wrote to Barlow by the same post. It now appeared that he had the strongest misgivings about his client's state of mind. 'I have seen him only three times, but his talking, his burst of temper last Monday made me suspect that he has not his right mind.' Hughon suggested that Barlow should not cash Pezieux's cheque until all the bank references now being asked for had been cleared.

Thereafter all is silence. Presumably the deal never went through. This failure clearly left Barlow with a strong sense of anticlimax, for he went on referring to these negotiations for many years. They had been an invaluable lesson in the vagaries and uncertainties of the international art market which Hobson certainly never forgot. Other attempts to sell the French Collection privately came to nothing. So in the end the first portion of it was put up for sale by auction in December 1924, and later sales took place in August and November 1925.

The first catalogue contained a preface based on the long descriptive memorandum used earlier. It explained in particular how the late Lord Crawford had formed the collection and his two-part acquisition of the many volumes of manuscripts collected by a Mr. Sainsbury, an enthusiastic admirer of Napoleon, between 1815 and 1830, when such documents could still be found without too much difficulty. The preface added with some justification that the practical value of the collection was greatly enhanced by the typed transcripts which accompanied almost every lot. It drew attention to the twenty odd letters from Napoleon himself which threw light on his early career in Corsica and France; on letters from his father, from Jean-Jacques Rousseau, from Robespierre to Buissard, from Marat, and to the documents relating to the flight of Louis XVI in June 1791. After so much preliminary work the results were extremely disappointing. The total realised was only £9,352, about one-tenth of the original cost, but a considerable proportion of the French Collection was not, in fact, included in the sale.[1] One item of particular interest had been lot 204, an unsigned memorandum by Napoleon concerning the defences of Ajaccio, his home town in Corsica. Maggs bought it for £17. It passed through Sotheby's again, unrecognised, in April 1977 and changed hands for £2,200.

In the meantime, the dispersed Crawford Collection had become an invaluable source to scholars working in the field of Napoleonic studies, and much of the material was used in future biographies of the great French emperor. The sale also provided a host of emerging collectors with raw material for their own collections. When one looks over Sotheby's long history it is astonishing what an important part the firm has played in the circulation of documentary material relating to Napoleon and his entourage. Beginning with the sale of his library from St. Helena on 23 July 1823, a high proportion of material not already housed in some national library or archive appears to have been sold by them. A full survey would almost merit a book on its own.

Following the dispersal of the Crawford Collection, another collection made by Lord Rosebery, who had written a study of Napoleon on St. Helena,[2] was sold

---

1. What in its heyday was one of the greatest family libraries ever assembled in Britain (see also page 66) was slowly dispersed thereafter. Fifty-three tons of books were returned to Quaritch who had played such an important part in its establishment, and after the death of the 27th Earl, there were eight sales of books at Sotheby's between March 1947 and March 1948.
2. *Napoleon: the Last Phase*, London, 1900.

by the order of his daughter, Lady Sybil Grant, in July 1933. Prices were now much higher than they had been at the Crawford sale. The star item was a series of eight passionate love letters which Napoleon had written to Josephine between 1796 and 1800. One postscript read: 'Adieu, adieu. Je me couche sans toi, je dormirai sans toi. Je t'en prie laisse moi dormir. Voila plusieurs nuits ou je te sens dans mes bras, songe heureux, mais, mais, ce n'est pas toi'. Their antecedents were interesting. They had formerly been in the possession of Charles Tennant, a great collector in many fields, and were published by him in facsimile. He had received the letters from a Polish gentleman, who was one of Napoleon's confidential agents. He was believed to have acquired them from a servant at Malmaison who took them from a drawer there after Josephine's death.

Des Graz decided that the series was first to be offered as one lot, but if the reserve of £1,500 was not reached they were to be sold singly. There was fierce competition for them between Gabriel Wells of America, Scheuer, another New York dealer who always attended sales containing Napoleonic material, the Robinson Brothers and Maggs. The last won the day with a record bid of £4,400. Maggs also bought lot 1642, Napoleon's farewell letter to Marie Louise on leaving Elba, for £1,000. In fact, the firm spent £8,118, and bought almost three-quarters of the day's total of £11,163. Scheuer bought fifty-four lots at rather lower prices, and the name Brouwet figured as the buyer of some twenty-seven lots. Finally, an additional item to the sale which had caused much interest, was Napoleon's death mask taken by Dr. Antommarchi on St. Helena and signed by him. It had been bought by the Paris dealers, Susse Bros., on Antommarchi's death in 1839 and sold by them to Prince Demidoff in 1841. It was now sold in a case modelled on the tomb of Napoleon at the Invalides in Paris and was accompanied by two certificates relating to the earlier sales. It fetched £40. A plaster cast (apparently the only recorded duplicate made of the original) was sold in Paris as recently as October 1977.

A further sale devoted entirely to Napoleana took place on 6 December 1933. The first 114 lots belonging to Charles Evan Fowler of New York. Lots 115 to 594 consisted of particularly beautifully bound books from the library of the Empress Marie Louise sold by order of an archduke of Austria to whom they had descended by inheritance. They were, in fact, consigned to Sotheby's by Martin Breslauer, a distinguished German bookseller. Brouwet sent over a number of commission bids but was less successful than at the Rosebery Sale in getting what he wanted.

On 17 December 1934 there was a sale of some 300, mostly unpublished, letters from Napoleon to his second Empress, Marie Louise. They were catalogued as 'the property of a Nobleman to whom they had descended by inheritance'.[1] An addendum to the catalogue said that 'typed transcripts of the letters, so far as it has been possible to decipher them, accompany all the lots in the catalogue', for the question had been asked in the preface: how could Marie Louise have read them? The answer appeared to be that she could not do so

1. The description concealed F. von Montenuovo.

unaided, the handwriting of Napoleon 'being so notoriously abominable'; and that the Duchesse de Montebello owed her ascendancy over the Empress at least in part because of her ability to decipher the Emperor's hand. In the event the sale turned out to be one of the shortest on record. The letters were, in the first instance, offered as one lot. Unexpectedly Maggs came up with a bid that greatly exceeded the reserve and they were sold as a collection for £15,000. It only emerged later that he had bought the collection on behalf of the French Government (the firm had a branch in Paris at 93-95 Rue la Boetie), As a result of this purchase and other similar services to the State, Ernest Maggs was made a Chevalier of the Legion of Honour.

In November of that same year there had already taken place in Paris the first of several sales of the collection of Emile Brouwet. The immensely detailed catalogues had been prepared by the great expert, M. J. Arnna. They contained very full quotations from all the documents and letters included, biographies of all the persons represented as well as detailed indexes. The whole series was titled *Napoleon et son Temps* because M. Brouwet sought to make a permanent contribution to the history of the Napoleonic era with his collection. In contrast to Lord Rosebery, Brouwet had spent thirty years of a passionate collecting career in concentrating on the *early* phase of the Napoleonic epic. A further sale followed in Paris in June 1935. But the third and final portion of the collection was sold at Sotheby's, for M. Brouwet was dissatisfied with the prices he had obtained in Paris at that very difficult time, and hoped that he would fare better in London.

Although it lacked the gold and shiny green covers of the earlier Paris versions, the Sotheby catalogue was identical in presentation and entirely in French, the first Bond Street catalogue for many years exclusively in that language. The most important material in it related to Napoleon's expedition to Egypt and his campaigns there. The letters showed him in many different phases of his versatile genius – as a great military commander, for example, ruthless in upholding discipline, but careful also to maintain the spirits of his troops, and as a colonial administrator signing documents drawn up in Arabic. There were also more than 200 letters from Marie Louise written between 1799 and 1846. Finally, there were a few Napoleonic relics, which always caught the headlines whenever they came up for sale. In this case there were four Sèvres plates used by Napoleon on St. Helena (they sold for £250) and a lock of his hair that had been cut off at Elba and was attached to a letter. The total for the two-day sale (held on 8 and 9 December 1936) was £4,167. The number of bidders was small and about 20 per cent of the 358 lots were bought in. Maggs got a high proportion of what was sold and Dr. Rosenbach bought the occasional lot.

On 1 March 1938 the descendants of Louis-Alexandre Berthier, Napoleon's greatest staff officer, sold a considerable collection of correspondence between the two men. Berthier was a military engineer who had fought in 1778 for American independence and was eventually chosen by Bonaparte as his Chief of Staff, a capacity in which he served for many years. The sale contained a particularly fascinating collection of papers relating to the projected invasion of England. For once Maggs didn't have it all his own way. John Taylor was bidding vigorously under the name of Beckett. This concealed the identity of his great friend in America, André de Coppet. The latter's own protracted sale nearly twenty years later was probably the greatest and certainly the most successful sale of Napoleana ever held by Sotheby's.[1]

Hobson and Barlow: the Parting of the Ways

It was in the good years too that Geoffrey Hobson's scholarly talents in the field of research on bookbindings began to see the light of day. He had become interested in the subject soon after he joined the firm and bought many of the standard monographs on the subject. But as he was to write later: 'It had become obvious even to my innocent mind that the authors and editors of them knew very, very little. But they were men of note in the world of books – officials of great libraries or booksellers at the height of their profession – and I felt that what they did not know, could hardly be worth knowing either ...'. He applied his tireless industry to the detailed examination of bookbinders' work from all over Europe. Almost every lunchtime was devoted to an hour's critical scrutiny of fresh material, for all he ate was an apple and a sandwich. He began to build up an archive of photographs and rubbings which was said to number more than 30,000 examples at the end of his career. Both his cataloguers and the trade made sure that they showed him any and every binding that might be of interest, and he received constant encouragement and stimulation from that erudite bookseller, E. P. Goldschmidt, with whom he had formed a close friendship. Tim Munby later wrote, 'no more striking example can be imagined of the ideal interaction and alliance between bibliography and business' for at Sotheby's Geoffrey Hobson sat literally at the centre of the world's rare book market. His precise mind was a superb tool for assembling a vast accumulation of often unrelated facts and illustrations and then sifting out what was relevant to a particular theme. He combined this deductive flair with a style of writing that was refreshingly clear and vigorous,[2] and his occasional articles in the bibliographical journals attracted increasing attention. The result was that he was asked to deliver the prestigious Sandars lectures in Bibliography at Cambridge for 1926. They were a brilliant exposition of fifteenth-century binding at Oxford, Cambridge and London and were published in book form as *English Bindings Before 1500* in 1929. In 1926 there also appeared his first book, *Maioli, Canevari and Others* which convincingly upset a

1. In the summer of 1939 des Graz and Hobson were engaged in negotiations with Charles Emmanuel Brousse of Paris who had been a frequent buyer at earlier sales of Napoleonic material and had a magnificent collection of Napoleana, including many family relics and pictures, as well as autographs and documentary material. But M. Brousse was undecided whether to sell his collection *en bloc* or at auction. The outbreak of war terminated negotiations.
2. A delightful example is the piece on *Parisian Bindings between 1500 and 1525* (The Bibliographical Society, 1931) in which he describes the flourishing trade in Books of Hours and how these came to be bound in decorated form in order to attract customers.

number of accepted theories on Italian bindings of the early sixteenth century. A. W. Pollard wrote to Hobson after reading the book: 'It is the best bit of work on bindings, which has been done in England ... it is a really fine piece of connoisseurship which takes account of every kind of evidence and lets the conclusion emerge from the facts without any attempt at a pre-conceived theory'.

The indirect consequences of this quest for scholarship were continually increasing standards in Sotheby's catalogues. Hobson never forgot a chance remark by Sir Sydney Cockerell on Sotheby's indifferent cataloguing of illuminated manuscripts, just after the new partners had taken over the business, and the firm took immense trouble to achieve accurate and informative descriptions of what was to be sold. The result was that many of the major sales catalogues became standard works of reference in the bibliographical world. Another change that occurred in 1926 was that printed price lists also giving buyers' names, which had only been produced for exceptional sales in the past, were now produced as a matter of course. But because the compilation of hand-written priced catalogues was a useful form of supplementary income for the young sales clerks (the going rate was two shillings per hundred lots), each of them was now paid a lump sum in compensation, which was why the printed lists were sold at relatively high prices in the first place.

After steady progress in the previous years and the remarkable results of 1927/28 when profits virtually doubled to the highest figure ever achieved, Barlow definitely decided to leave the firm. Most of his ambitions had been achieved. But now that he was done with politics, life at Bond Street did not give him complete fulfilment. Originally he had derived enormous pleasure from his trips to America and widening the firm's trade with that country. Now des Graz went to the States twice a year and devoted himself in particular to the endlessly demanding Dr. Rosenbach. Barlow and Hobson too grated on each other increasingly. The partners' meetings often became a battleground of wits more than a problem-solving institution. On one occasion, after an argument, Barlow suggested that the firm should lay down and stick to a certain policy. 'Policy,' snorted Hobson, 'it's only you Cabinet Ministers who can afford that kind of luxury; we have to earn a living here!'

Barlow's farewell to the firm was a touching and memorable occasion. It was also done with immense style. He invited all fifty-five members of the staff – the cataloguers, the clerical staff, the lady typists, the porters – and his partners, to a magnificent dinner at the New Princess Restaurant in Piccadilly on the evening of 27 April 1929. It was brilliantly organised by H. C. Rham. The eight-course dinner was accompanied by great wines including a 1924 château-bottled Château Margaux and a 1919 Champagne. There were speeches galore: the wittiest by an ex-GLC, House of Commons and Cabinet colleague, Viscount Peel, at that time Secretary of State for India; the most disarming – representing the arts – by Sir Robert Witt. The toast to Sotheby's was proposed by Ralph Blumenfeld, editor of the *Daily Express*, and Felix Warre replied. But the most touching moment of the evening came when Rham read out a letter from Tom Hodge. It said:

My dear Clem,
It is extremely kind of you to ask my wife & me to the dinner you are giving on
the occasion of your retirement from Sotheby's. I wish I could come but I really
cannot. I'm sure you understand me, & you one day may be up against the same
difficulty in a modified degree. That you would like me to be with you makes me
happy & is in keeping with the tradition of perpetual good feeling & regard
between all members past & present, staff & principals alike, of Sotheby's. It is
difficult to believe that you have been twenty years in the firm but its magnificent
increase in fame, power & volume of business helps one to realise it. One now
may well say that my father's & my dream of Sotheby's being the leading
auctioneers of everything in the way of literature & art may materialise. We were
not to see it but he relaid the foundations for the old firm & my friends Barlow,
Hobson & Warre built on them & are building. May they raise a sky scraper that
will attract all the world!
    I am often indeed astonished when I see what the firm is doing & its success is
a deep pleasure to me, for though I am no longer in reality a part of it; its sympathy with & kindness to me make me feel otherwise. Lucky will be the man who
takes your place & so I think will be all those who may follow on in due course:
they will have a comparatively easy job.
    I am very, very sorry you are retiring. It was a joy to have an old friend such as
you in the firm & I counted myself lucky when I found I was no longer strong
enough to carry on my father's work to be able to hand it over to three such
friends as you, Geoffrey Hobson & Felix Warre. Please give my kindest greetings
to everyone present who may remember old Tom Hodge & tell them he forgets
no one who ever worked with him & if any be present who were not actually on
my staff but who were closely connected with me in the natural course of the
business, such as gentlemen of the press, dealers & others, may I ask you to say I
remember with gratitude their patient endurance of my peculiarities.
    All wishes that success may attend your new undertakings, any that comes to
you you deserve & none will be more pleased at it than I. But don't forget the old
firm nor your old affectionate friend.

                                                                        Tom

When Barlow sent him a copy of the menu, the old cobwebs of temper and
conspiracy were finally brushed away, for Hodge wrote again as follows:

My dear Clem,
You are a wonderful man & your steps in life remind me of Moore's angels who
trod from orb to orb!
    Thank you for the souvenirs of the evening, they are delightful & interesting
but melancholy, & truly I am sorry that you have left Sotheby's but none the less
you have my deepest wishes that success may ever succeed your efforts.
    I didn't look for any reports in the papers[1] so missed them but if Roberts
reported for the Times[2] I'm sure he'd do as little as possible; he's never been a
real friend of Sotheby's since he worked with McKay, who was hand in glove
with Christie's, on their life of Romney & after I refused to keep information
from Greig, Carter & others.

---

1. There were many.   2. He didn't.

You are indeed right, pulling together with one object has ever been characteristic of our staff & of course your bonus scheme is magnificent & I'm certain just. I remember many years ago your advocating this principle as a step towards peace in labour. You well deserve those salvers[1] & it's nice for you to have a tangible souvenir of the firm's recognition of what it owes to you. You'll be missed, I'm afraid, for a keen business head is worth more than knowledge even in such a business as this. However, I daresay they'll get on. What a good dinner you gave them, a credit to your taste, experience & knowledge. How you thought of everything – dinner, music, entertainment, dancing & arrangement of speeches & replies – I cannot imagine but as I began so I end, you are a wonderful man.

Ever affectionately
Tom

Barlow now became Vice-Chairman of the Perak River Hydro-Electric Power Company, which succeeded in making an enormous contribution to the economic well-being of Malaya and Singapore and he made the most of yet another career – his fourth – as an industrial magnate. He also took an increasing interest in the well-being of the established Church, for he eventually became Chairman of the House of Laity in the Church Assembly. In 1934, after a fifteen year courtship, he married Doris Louise Reed who had worked as a secretary in Sotheby's for some years after the First World War. Barlow outlived Tom Hodge by eleven years and died on 31 May 1951 aged eighty-three.

---

1. The staff presented Barlow with a fine pair of antique silver salvers.

22

Slump

BARLOW'S departure left Warre in charge as chairman, but Hobson as the dominant force. It became clear to them very quickly that the world was in for another shake-up. Yet initially Tom Hodge's prediction proved right: the sheer momentum of the business led to increasing prosperity even when the financial world outside was under stress. The all-time record net profit of £63,000 in 1927–28 was exceeded in 1928–29 when it rose to over £70,000. But after the Wall Street crash in October 1929, business with America ceased abruptly and almost entirely. The profit for 1929–30 was still a respectable £35,000, but in the following year it had fallen to £12,000 and in 1931–32 it came down to an all-time low (at least since the cessation of sales in 1915) of £4,000, and even that figure was achieved only at the cost of vicious retrenchment and frantically hard work.

Generally, people were very happy in their work at Bond Street, but wages among the lower echelons were low in comparison with other businesses and there was a constant stream of employees who left, albeit reluctantly, because they simply could not make ends meet on what they were paid. A competent clerk, for example, started his employment in March 1926 at £2 10s. a week. This went up to £3 a week after 'he had proved himself' by January 1927. We find him earning £3 17s. in 1936 after ten years' service. Porters averaged 30s. to 35s. a week, though they worked a good deal of additional overtime. A secretary would start at £2 15s. a week in the Twenties and her wage would gradually rise to £3 15s. by the mid-Thirties. Cataloguers earned between £4 and £7 a week. Directors drew a basic £900 per annum.

By 1931 it became clear to the directors that, in common with businesses all round them, they could not carry on without making drastic reductions in overhead costs. In 1930 Jim Kiddell had to undertake elaborate investigations of the cost of electricity, gas, coal and coke consumed in order to reduce them wherever possible. Geoffrey Hobson cut advertising to a minimum and a special watch was kept on minimising expenditure on catalogues. But in the end there was no way of avoiding reductions in the biggest single overhead cost of all – staff. The unhappy task of making the dismissals fell on Major Warre. He also had to negotiate a reduction of 10 per cent of the salaries of all those who remained. There were few objections. Only old Will Edmonds, by now semi-retired, wrote innumerable letters on the subject to Warre. But that was nothing new. He had written letters in a very similar vein to Montague Barlow ever since a special contract had been made with him in 1913. Most others considered themselves fortunate to remain in employment. One can only admire the courtesy and tenacity with which Warre tackled the whole sorry operation. He received a good deal of help from Evelyn Barlow – now looking more like an operatic soprano than ever – though she herself was to become a victim of the slump two years later when her resignation was forced upon her in order to save a director's salary.

It is not easy in our own relatively feather-bedded time, when the state will always provide at least a minimum to support life, just how harsh this period was for those without work. Hobson, Warre, des Graz and Miss Barlow were besieged with letters from former employees asking for any sort of work at all so that they could buy food for themselves and their families for another few days. Many sought money for fares with which to emigrate. Warre and Evelyn Barlow coped as liberally as was possible under the firm's straitened circumstances – paying a doctor's bill here, taking over a pressing debt there, giving occasional part-time jobs to out-of-work cataloguers. Hobson's stern exterior too was often dented by these appeals. Many instances later came to light where he quietly helped some deserving case, saying grumpily, 'Here's a fiver. Don't let it happen again'. Major Warre in particular has often been accused of hard-heartedness – and later in the Thirties he could certainly have become rather more generous about the level of pay – but surviving letters from the slump make it horribly clear what a long heartbreak it was.

All this will explain why prices of what went through the sale-room were low compared to what they had been, and quite unbelievably low by our standards today. The amount of surplus money available for art, antiques and rare books anywhere in the world was minimal. It was, therefore, a marvellous time for the exceptional man with a bit of money to spare and a lot of taste. There were just enough of these rare birds about to keep the trade ticking over and many remarkable collections formed at that time became major sales after the Second World War. But even so, between 1930 and 1934 it required both courage and prescience to invest in the art market, or very determined enthusiasm to keep collecting.

Thoughts of the Unthinkable

Just how serious matters had got by 1933 can be gauged from the fact that the unthinkable actually occurred. After long internal deliberations, Christie's approached Sotheby's about an amalgamation. For years King Street had been the 'big brother' of fine art auctioneering with a turnover vastly greater than the one at Bond Street, and with profits to match. The firm had benefited enormously from the boom immediately following the First World War: in 1919 there had been a profit of £107,000; in 1920 this had shot up to £147,000 (though in 1921 it fell right back to £32,500 – but it was still double Sotheby's. In 1927 Christie's had a surplus after all expenses were paid of £59,000. The comparative figure at Sotheby's was £27,000. But in 1928 the gap narrowed: Christie's figure was £70,000;[1] Sotheby's £63,000. In 1930 both firms were down: Christie's to £29,000; Sotheby's to £35,000. In 1931 and 1932 Christie's made a small loss; Sotheby's were still keeping their head above

1. This included the first, record-breaking portion of the Holford picture sale.

SOTHEBY & Co.

SOME OUTSTANDING PRICES OF 1932-3.

The Winkworth Collection of Chinese Porcelain	£19,330
The Rosebery Library, from The Durdans, Epsom - - - - - -	£49,000
*†Shakespeare, First Folio - - - -	£14,500
Shakespeare, Third Folio - - - -	£2,000
Walton's Angler, 1653 - - - - -	£1,250
The Kilmarnock Burns, with Lord Glencairn's Bookplate - - - - - -	£1,300
A Book inscribed by John Keats - - -	£2,400
A Manuscript written by Jane Austen - -	£2,100
†Eight Love Letters from Napoleon to Josephine	£4,400
Napoleon's Farewell Letter to Marie Louise -	£1,000
†The "De Levis" Hours - - - -	£1,500
†Six Oil Sketches by Peter Paul Rubens - -	£9,200
Portrait of Cecil, Lord Baltimore, by Soest -	£4,600
Portrait of Anne Hyde, by Sir Peter Lely -	£1,050
Portrait of Philip, 4th Earl of Pembroke, by Sir A. Vandyck - - - - -	£1,720
Wheatley's "Cries of London" in Colours -	£1,280
†A Diamond Necklace - - - - -	£5,200
†A Suite of Louis XV Furniture - - -	£1,700
†An Italian Helmet - - - - -	£720
†A Small Panel of German Tapestry - -	£1,200
†A Staffordshire Pottery Figure - - -	£410

* World's Record: Previous Highest £8,600.

† Record for the London Season.

This page from a promotional leaflet in 1933 speaks for itself.

water with small profits. But in 1933 Christie's made a substantial loss, in excess of £8,000, while Sotheby's made a profit of £13,000. Nevertheless, no one at Bond Street could face the future with confidence. Certainly Sotheby's over-heads had been pared to the bone. What still worried the partners was the high cost of advertising. Curiously enough it was the thought of the relatively small saving that could be effected by joint advertising that encouraged merger discussions.

Having consulted lawyers and accountants, Major Warre sent an eighteen-point memorandum to Lance Hannen, the chairman of Christie's. A new un-limited company was to be formed: no name had yet been thought of. The Bond Street premises were to be given up: King Street was to be altered and enlarged to take the extra staff. There were to be seven shareholders from the King Street side and four from the Bond Street side, but there would only be nine directors – five from King Street and four from Bond Street. Warre was to be Chairman. There then followed a proposal which was clearly one of the stumbling-blocks in the negotiations because no management could run a business under such conditions.

> Until such time as a new director is introduced the articles of the Company to provide that both at general meetings and at Board meetings the votes of any of the King Street parties present shall together equal the votes of any of the Bond Street parties present and vice versa. The Chairman not to have a casting vote so that if there is a difference of opinion there will be a deadlock which will be solved by the question in dispute being adjourned to a further meeting to be held within seven days to which meeting an independent party is to be invited and at which such independent party, after hearing all parties will vote as he thinks best with one side or the other, thus solving the dispute.
>
> The independent party can either be named (Sir Lionel Faudel Phillips is suggested),[1] or left to be nominated by the President of the Law Society or the Institute of Chartered Accountants or in some other way to be agreed.

The amalgamation was planned to begin on 1 October 1934 when the transfer to King Street was to take place, though an announcement was to be made six months earlier. 'Details such as the formation of catalogues and the conditions of sale and scales of commission will be required to be settled when general principles are agreed.'

By the beginning of February 1934 the accountants had got out all the figures. One difficulty was that Christie's financial year ended on 28 February and Sotheby's on 30 September. A second was how the valuations of both properties should be allocated to the joint firm when one was to be disposed of, probably at a price which was a long way below its market value in normal times. A third problem was in what ratio the profits were to be divided in the future. Warre wrote to Hannen as follows:

> We are advised that it is inequitable in a proposed amalgamation for one side to pass on its property to the amalgamation at full value and leave the other side to

1. He was chairman of a distinguished city firm and a Trustee of the Wallace Collection.

bear the burden of their property which will be vacated solely for the purpose and benefit of the amalgamation.

We are accordingly advised that it is essential that the amalgamation concerns *take over both properties* at valuation subject to the mortgages thereon. The machinery for doing this can be left to the lawyers but the principle is one from which we cannot see our way to depart.

As to the division of profits:

The figures which I presume you now have before you make it clear that your suggested division of 58% to your side and 42% to us will not do.

The average for the last 5⅓ years shews that we have exceeded your average, the ratio being 51% to us and 49% to you.

The worrying feature however is your figures for the past three years.

We shall be glad to discuss the matter again with you but as I have said we must get the above two points settled before we pass into other topics.

Clearly they didn't, for matters progressed no further, though the merger talks turned out to have been a useful exercise for, as we shall see, the matter was to come up again sooner than anyone could have envisaged.

Credit Control

The cash crisis at the beginning of the 1930s also started a new and much more plaintive round in the gentlemanly struggle to get booksellers to reduce their over-extended credit. Only a few weeks after Jim Kiddell had joined the firm, Barlow had asked him what he thought of the business side of the business. Jim expressed astonishment at the free and easy manner in which Sotheby's was prepared to capitalise some bookseller customers. He took Quaritch as an example. The firm had a negotiated credit ceiling of £20,000. But at the time when the question was put, they owed Sotheby's £34,000. Kiddell was surprised by the vehemence of Barlow's reaction for he could not have known of the protracted struggle between Barlow and E. H. Dring on this very point. It had started as far back as 1918, when Barlow threatened to charge interest on money long overdue. Dring's hurt and masterly reply should be included in any management text book which includes a chapter on credit control. 'Had we been aware', he had written, 'that it was your intention to charge interest on our purchases at the Vernon and Huth Sales we should simply have ignored those sales so far as buying for stock was concerned, and should have confined our purchases to the commissions we held for which we should have paid cash. It is not of paramount importance to our policy to prevent books from fetching less than their value, especially when we have to pay five per cent for the privilege of doing so.' It was a gallant snub. Barlow and Dring had met. New arrangements were agreed very amicably. But the subject was one that kept recurring. Major Warre soon learned to deal with it as efficiently as Barlow, though he was not to know when the slump began that it would take Quaritch nearly a decade to pay off the final instalment of the sum then outstanding. Tim Munby, who worked both at Quaritch and later at Sotheby's, recalls that 'in the deep slump, during which I joined the firm, the paying off of this debt by instalments was, I think, a first charge on Quaritch's tiny profits. I do remember vividly that rather a Thing was made of the final payment about 1938. Old Mrs. Wrentmore, Bernard Quaritch's daughter, decided that she wished to hand the last cheque over in person and this was received with suitable ceremony by Major Warre as Chairman of Sotheby's'.

On a more positive level, particularly in order to replace the American trade, the partners launched various campaigns to get business from new sources. They recognised the increasing importance of valuations for probate, insurance and family division. As catalogues of that period blandly stated, 'Great changes in value have recently taken place and fresh valuations are therefore especially advisable at the present time in order that unnecessary payment of premiums and duties should be avoided'.

Initially this work had been done by Harold Nott, the first porter to attain expert rank. As the work-load increased the firm acquired the services of Norris Davis, a professional valuer who had been with Gurr, Johns & Company. Mrs. Davis, a former pianist with a particularly pleasant personality, acted as her husband's secretary and, like him, she became an expert on furniture. They were never apart and travelled about the country in a tiny car. The procedure would be for a district to be circularised that Sotheby's representatives would be there on a certain date to discuss questions of valuation with anyone interested. Both Harold Nott and Mr. & Mrs. Davis had the knowledge and experience to make a shrewd and speedy appraisal of the contents of a house, and they quickly ascertained the number of different experts as specialists valuers required. The usual payment for a completed valuation was 1 per cent of the contents plus the experts' travelling expenses, but if the owner wanted an on-the-spot figure, the Davis's were quite capable of quoting a suitable fee. By the late Thirties catalogues contained the information that 'recently the demand for Messrs. Sotheby's valuations has so much increased that it has been necessary to open a special valuations department at 35–39 Maddox Street, W.1, where all information and advice will be given'.[1] A further advantage of making valuations was that after the owners had died Sotheby's were often asked to sell by auction the collection which they had valued earlier.

1. The premises received a direct hit towards the end of the war and were completely destroyed: fortunately not during office hours.

23

Country House Sales

MORE and more frequently at this period letters arrived at Bond Street asking if the firm would send someone to look at works of art which owners contemplated selling right away in order to raise money. The young man who acted as Sotheby's roving representative and travelled all over England, Wales and Ireland to inspect such properties was Tom Lumley, who had joined the firm in 1926. Lumley at nineteen was mercurial, ambitious, lively and had an unusually good eye for spotting pieces of quality in unlikely places. He had impressed Barlow by his enthusiasm for the work – and his determination to get into Sotheby's from Puttick & Simpson, a smaller firm of rival auctioneers down Bond Street. After a brief trial period he was taken on as trainee assistant to Caldecott and later as silver cataloguer at £4 a week. The older partners soon found him something of a trial for he was quite unabashed about questioning existing methods of procedure. But although they rarely said so, they were impressed by the fact that he was often right, and he was responsible for many innovations that have survived to this day. It was he, for example, who at that time established a regular routine for the circulation among directors of obituaries of people known to the firm who had recently died. They also found that clients liked him and commented how surprised they were that someone so young should know so much. Tancred Borenius took a paternal interest in the young man and taught him a good deal about pictures. There was one famous occasion which resulted in a major row because Tom was so engrossed in a picture sale – which officially he had no business to attend – that he kept a client waiting until summoned for the third time by porters. It resulted in a severe dressing down by Major Warre. However, the partners were inclined to forgive him when Tom found some of the most valuable paintings – including a Rembrandt, a Frans Hals,[1] a number of Canalettos and a particularly fine Zoffany – which Sotheby's sold in the early Thirties.

It was on a visit to North Wales that Lumley called on an irascible Colonel Hughes at Kinmel Park near Abergele. The old man lived in solitary splendour in a mansion which had no fewer than fifty-seven bedrooms. He consulted Lumley about the best method of disposing of the contents. Back in London, Tom discussed the matter with Jim Kiddell and suggested that the answer would be to hold a sale *on the premises*, except for the silver which would sell better at Bond Street. Jim Kiddell took the idea to Hobson, who eventually agreed. The result was the first of some twenty sales of the contents of a procession of stately and semi-stately houses that Sotheby's undertook during the next twelve years. They were almost equally divided between London and the

1. At £3,600 it was the most expensive painting sold in London in the whole of the 1931–32 auction season.

country, though the country sales remained much more firmly fixed in everyone's memories. Vere Pilkington was put in charge of pioneering this new development and the firm owed a good many of these sales to his contacts. They were not only a useful source of additional revenue but also attracted considerable local and national publicity, which brought new clients to the firm. Most important of all, they encouraged a unique team spirit and flexibility that has been with the firm ever since. All those involved remember the outings with a sense of adventure and enjoyment that more routine matters in Bond Street never quite achieved.

Colonel Hughes was delighted with the £8,164 raised by the ten-day sale held in June 1929. Jim Kiddell took the rostrum during the first five days and a local auctioneer supervised the second five days. This collaboration with their country cousins not only stilled any opposition Sotheby's might have engendered upon breaking into their competitors' home ground, but also gave Pilkington and Kiddell local knowledge that often proved invaluable. A second country house sale at Iwerne Minster near Blandford in Dorset followed in 1930; a third consisted of the 'remaining contents' of the Earl of Harewood's Chesterfield House, in 1932. The real breakthrough came in 1933 when seven house sales took place in the one year. They required meticulous organisation and frenzied effort. Jim Kiddell with his military background was the undoubted leader and organiser. He also identified and catalogued the carpets, works of art, ceramics and objects of vertu. Tom Lumley tackled silver and paintings, and a new, young expert called Temple Williams, who had joined Sotheby's in 1929 from his family firm (Spilman's, antique furniture dealers in St. Martin's Lane), looked after furniture and household furnishings. His historical knowledge and enthusiasm are at once discernible in the catalogues. So effectively did this combination work that the three men became known – both among clients and the trade – as 'The Flying Squad'.

A quick preliminary reconnaissance of a new property would tell Kiddell what he would need in the way of time for cataloguing, and staff. The porters were a most important element. Under their foreman, Bill Carpenter – he of the walrus moustache who appears on every pre-war photograph of Sotheby sales and a legend in his lifetime – moved his ex-guardsmen about with incredible skill. The secret of success was to leave a house looking as if it was still occupied and to avoid the aura of a bankrupt stock sale that country auctioneers often created after they had done their cataloguing. Jim Kiddell recalls that 'the Flying Squad found all the *good* things in servants' bedrooms, guest rooms and attics, and Carpenter had them taken down to the reception rooms, and the poor stuff from downstairs taken upstairs as replacements. *Real hard graft* it was, but it made our name in this line for years to come and established a model that other auctioneers tried to follow'.

Often owners were astonished when they saw their possessions re-arranged by Carpenter in preparation for a sale, for he had a marvellous eye for display. 'We often heard the owners saying, "My God! This room looks much better than when we had it",' is Sam Patch's recollection of Carpenter's skill. Sam, another vital member of the team, acted as sales clerk. He had to make certain not only that all buyers were correctly identified but also that they paid for what they had bought. He was completely responsible for the financial side of the exercise. He had come to Sotheby's as a result of an advertisement the firm placed in the *Telegraph* in 1926 for three vacancies on the clerical side. There were five hundred replies. Barlow interviewed sixty. Sam got one job, and was trained at once as a junior sales clerk under Rham and Lambert, for with his clear memory and remarkable head for figures he had just the capabilities required in that vital sale-room job. Other essential qualifications were quick thinking, total unflappability and the trust of clients. The fact that the name Patch occurred many thousands of times on the printed price lists before his retirement as senior sales clerk in 1973 is evidence of the success which he made of the job, because both dealers and private collectors so frequently asked him to bid for items on their behalf.

The family who gave Sotheby's most encouragement to use their special expertise in house sales were the Cowdrays. In 1932 Annie, the widow of the first Lord Cowdray, one of England's wealthiest men, died. The death duties were swingeing. Lord and Lady Cowdray owned three residences – Dunecht House, Aberdeenshire in Scotland; a fine London house at 16 Carlton House Terrace and a country house – an immense imitation Tudor mansion called Paddockhurst, in Sussex. The next generation of the family decided to keep the house in Scotland and to sell the other two, for they all had splendid houses of their own. Because Vere Pilkington's father knew the Cowdrays well, Bond Street was asked to undertake the sale of the contents. The second Lord Cowdray and his wife, the sister of that great collector, Captain George Spencer-Churchill, undertook the family's side of the arrangements and charmed everyone at Bond Street with whom they came into touch.

For Sotheby's the contents of Paddockhurst and Carlton House Terrace were of a level of magnificence that they had not experienced before. Annie, Viscountess Cowdray, had really enjoyed her wealth. She pursued a level of acquisition in one lifetime which other landed families had only achieved over many generations. 'She was a terrific spender, and an afternoon's shopping just around Bond Street in the Twenties sometimes went into five figures. You can almost hear her saying to "Mrs. G." (her Scottish secretary and A.D.C.), "We'd better make sure there's enough new china to go round," for some big party, and off they'd go to Rochelle Thomas for the best porcelain services, or to Harrod's and Thomas Goode for the more conventional.'[1] Crockery seems to have been one of her passions for there were gigantic storage cupboards and pantries full of it in both houses. At Paddockhurst the catalogue includes no fewer than thirty-one dinner, dessert and tea services; at Carlton House there were only fifteen but they were of the finest quality and the number of pieces went into thousands. At Paddockhurst the cataloguers would be precise about counting a service: one lot for example, included '76 dessert plates, 73 soup plates and 116 dinner plates'. But in London they gave up counting and merely

1. Jim Kiddell in a note to the author.

summarised: 'About 450 pieces' (a Cauldon Dinner Service), 'about 300 pieces' (a Minton Dinner Service), 'about 200 pieces' (a Worcester Dinner and Dessert Service), 'nearly 200 pieces' (a Sèvres Porcelain Dinner Service painted with panels of flowers, figures, pastoral subjects and French châteaux in colours on a turquoise ground within gilt borders). There were also three Dresden services and many pieces (for use) in *famille rose* and, of course, there was glass to match in equivalent quantities. In both houses the furniture – both French and English – the carpets, tapestries and ornamental porcelain tended to conform exclusively to sheer magnificence, though at Paddockhurst a good deal of the furniture was reproduction.[1]

Collectively the catalogues of the house sales are a fascinating commentary on their time, listing as they do the contents of many impressive entrance halls, staircases, libraries, the occasional muniment room, breakfast rooms, morning rooms, music rooms (sometimes with minstrels' gallery), Adam and many other style drawing rooms, saloons, winter gardens, boudoirs (almost invariably full of the finest French eighteenth-century furniture) and dining-rooms. For the men there were billiard and gun-rooms, locker-rooms and studies. At Paddockhurst there was no office but 'His Lordship's Business Room'. Upstairs the bedrooms were often named – for example the Temple of Flora Bedroom, the Tulip Dressing-Room, the Pomegranate Bedroom.

Nurseries, both day and night, and governesses' rooms occurred frequently. People loved looking round these houses before the sale even if they were not going to buy to see 'how the gentry had lived'. Much amusement was caused at 16 Carlton House Terrace by an upstairs lavatory. It was a large room with four different kinds of seats and at least half a dozen different types of toilet paper of extravagant quality (for the benefit of those of maturer years).

Then there was the complex hierarchy of the servants' quarters. At 30 Portman Square, for example, we have the Housekeeper's Room, Butler's Room, wine cellar, Butler's Pantry, Servants' Hall, Housemaid's Sitting Room, scullery, larder, main kitchen, Cook's Office, Chauffeur's Bedroom, room over the garage, Footman's Bedroom, Valet's Room, telephone room. The grander houses included a chef's office instead of a cook's office, and a secretary's room. Other functional variants listed were boot-rooms, brushing-rooms, linen-rooms, store-rooms, still-rooms, bakehouses, seamstress' and sewing-rooms, glass and china pantries. In one house there were nine maids' bedrooms – the more usual number was three or four – and as a rule the head housemaid always had rather more than the sparse furnishings of the ordinary housemaid or footman. One can readily understand that the ladies of these houses had their hands pretty full with the management of such establishments. In addition, of course, there was the outdoor staff. Their accommodation, furnishings and tools were often included in the sales.

Where the owners had died, the Flying Squad usually found senior servants, butlers or housekeepers, still in residence, and out of London the cataloguers

1. This was unusual. Most of the house sales undertaken by Sotheby's contained only genuine period furniture.

often lived in splendour on the premises. At Paddockhurst, for example, the younger Lord Cowdray retained a staff of four, including a cook, to look after them. Sotheby people became very sensitive to house atmosphere. They would be aware within minutes of arrival of an aura of genteel decay, or of highly enlightened culture or care that the generations of owners had lavished on their property and the furnishings. 'At Paddockhurst,' says Sam Patch, 'you could see your face in the floor. There was a two-acre rock garden and lake. The furniture was good. There was a happy atmosphere. The servants' rooms were wonderfully looked after. Thirty gardeners' cottages and every one had a fruit tree on the south wall. Lord C. was very good to us. At the end of the sale he went up to every porter and gave him £5. He was so pleased with the sale.'

By no means all the houses were madly desirable properties. Some were overgrown and overblown Victorian and Edwardian residences, and the atmosphere was depressing. In one instance it was downright evil;[1] in another, memories of the recent suicide of the owner, a financier, affected all concerned. In contrast, some houses were architectural masterpieces in splendid rural settings. These well-loved places had usually been owned by generations of the same family and were plangent with memories. A particularly interesting example of this kind, though sold rather later, in April 1938, was Hartwell House in Buckinghamshire.

The house itself was outstandingly beautiful. The front was still the original Jacobean one: long, low, with fine mullion and oriel windows. The south, east and west sides had been rebuilt in the elegant, classical manner of the mid-eighteenth century under Wyatt's direction. The whole immense pile was set in surroundings gracefully remoulded by Capability Brown. The French royal family had spent their exile there between 1807 and 1814, and it was in the library at Hartwell that Louis XVIII signed the document by which he undertook to accept and observe the new Constitution of France. Many of the rooms were still named after the residents of that party: the Louis XVIII Room, the Duchesse d'Angoulême's Dressing-Room and the Duc de Berry Room. But for much of its four hundred year history the Lee family had held sway in the house and there was a fine collection of family portraits among the pictures. A detailed family tree, included in the catalogue, showed the relationship of the sitters, who had been stylishly portrayed by Lely, Reynolds, Allan Ramsay, Romney and Batoni. There were also particularly good examples of the *genre* by such lesser-known masters as Highmore, Van der Bank, Slaughter, Benjamin Wilson and Hunter of Dublin.

The furniture was outstanding and included supreme examples of the Regency period, much of it designed by Henry Holland in the same style as he used at Southill, the home of the Whitbread family of brewers in Bedfordshire. Indeed, one of the Lees was a friend of, and stood as a Member of Parliament three times with, the first great Samuel Whitbread. It was an exciting sale and

1. The house was burned down soon after the sale. Many of the other country houses vacated subsequently became schools or religious establishments.

was the first to be organised by Fred Rose, a comparatively new arrival at Sotheby's. Vere Pilkington called back Temple Williams (who had, in the meantime, left Sotheby's and joined Blairman's) to help with the cataloguing of the furniture, and the entries describing the best pieces bear witness to Temple Williams' particular *penchant* for Regency furniture. The prices, though seemingly minimal by today's standards, were a long way above the average for the period. Thus, a magnificent upright secretaire (lot 258) went for £210, a figure that would probably be less than one-hundredth of what it would fetch today. A considerable number of other pieces eventually finished up in the Victoria & Albert Museum and museums elsewhere. The three long, mid-day sale sessions were conducted by Vere Pilkington with great verve and style, and the resultant total of nearly £15,000 represented the highest for a country sale of the inter-war period.

Another house with a long family history was one of those sold in 1933, Tythrop House near Thame in Oxfordshire. It included many portraits of the Herbert, Wenman and Wykeham families who had all been associated with the house. The total achieved was £9,237, almost identical with the result of the sale of the contents of 17 Carlton House Terrace, the property of Lady Mount Stephen, literally next-door to the Cowdray's town house. The furniture here – a mixture of French and English, but all unusually sophisticated in taste – was again particularly outstanding. The miniatures, snuff boxes, objects of vertu, gold and silver were sold separately in Bond Street. It was at the first sale 'on the premises' in 1933, at 7 Stratton Street (the property of Mrs. A. M. Salomans) that Kiddell and Pilkington got their greatest fright. Towards the end of the sale the floor in the upper room *began to sag*, and Jim Kiddell had it cleared at the double and sold the remaining contents downstairs. After the sale was over that formidable solicitor, Sir Theodore Goddard, who was acting on behalf of Mrs. Salomans' executors, said brusquely to Kiddell, 'I should have held you responsible for any loss'.[1] After that marquees were erected in the garden if no suitable downstairs room was big enough to contain the crowd that attended such sales.

After 1933 the roll-call continued on its impressive course: 24 Portman Square (Countess di Villamarina), 23 Pont Street (Mrs. George Forbes), Brockhampton Park, Andoversford (Colonel Fairfax Rhodes), Ewhurst Park, Basingstoke (the Duke of Wellington), 38 Portman Square (the Rt. Hon. Feodorowna, Lady Alington), Culham House, Abingdon (Major S. H. Shawe Phillips), 91 Eaton Square (J. P. Heseltine), South Wraxall Manor, Bath (Major Richardson-Cox) probably the most beautiful of all houses on the list, Hartwell House, Aylesbury (Mrs. Benedict Eyre), the Old Court House, Hampton Court, once the home of Sir Christopher Wren (Norman Lamp-

---

1. He may have remembered the famous case that followed upon the sale of Lord Eldin's Collection in Edinburgh in 1833. This was held by the Liverpool auctioneer, Thomas Winstanley, in an upstairs room of Lord Eldin's house. On the third day of the sale the floor collapsed cascading some eighty people into the library below, two of whom subsequently died.

lugh) and – just before the war – Cam House, Campden Hill (Mrs. Evelyn St. George).

The house sales of course generated an unusual number of memorable incidents. Hartwell House is responsible for two. When Sotheby's arrived the whole place was unheated. Someone lit a fire in the enormous entrance hall. Almost at once the chimney caught light. The local part-time brigade tackled the outbreak with kid gloves, rolled back the Chinese silk carpets, moved all the furniture without scratching the floor and were careful to shut the doors wherever they went. Pilkington gave them £10 from the petty cash box. They refused politely. It turned out that they were all local businessmen who knew the house well and were delighted to have been called out. They had not had a fire to deal with for years.

During the cataloguing someone discovered three enormous, locked, metal-banded chests in the basement. They were not included in any inventory. When broken open they were found to be full of manuscripts and seventeenth-century documents, many of Cromwellian origin. They were later sold at Bond Street in three separate sessions and fetched rather more than the entire contents of the house.

When the porters moved a walnut bureau at Lady Alington's house in Portman Square they discovered a secret drawer which was entirely full of resplendent jewellery. They were justifiably excited. It was handed over at once to the solicitors acting for the executors and was included in a later sale at Bond Street. It was in the same house that a crisis of conscience occurred which gave rise to a saga that has survived with a good many variants. A bundle of letters came to light at the very back of a drawer. They bore the royal cypher (of Edward VII) though signed with a well-known *nom de guerre*. They were addressed to a lady friend in passionate terms. After some hesitation they were consigned to the boiler, 'on orders from above'. One cannot help wondering whether any have survived. The quest for secret drawers in the furniture became almost a routine. On another occasion a walnut kneehole desk produced a packet of letters tied up with ribbons. They proved to be from a relative in Western Australia to Col. Sam Browne (of belt fame) in India. The stamps turned out to be Western Australian woodblock swans and were sold to advantage. The letters themselves were included in an autograph sale. Altogether they fetched infinitely more than the kneehole desk. It was later discovered that the owner had bought the desk in another house sale, but had never searched it thoroughly.

At Brockhampton Park a porter found a handbag in an upstairs room. In 1934 its contents of £150 in new £5 notes, and jewellery (later estimated to be worth £6,000) were riches indeed, but it was handed in intact and put away in a safe by Sam Patch. No-one had claimed it for five or six hours when an excited lady rushed up to Sam screaming 'someone's just stolen my handbag'. She was accompanied by a well-known commission agent, Henry Hart, who acted both for private collectors and dealers at such sales. He often advised his clients at Sotheby's sales on prices and the firm had great trust in him. He calmed the lady down and made her check the contents. As nothing was missing she graciously gave the porter who had found it five shillings. Pilkington later made it up to £5 out of the petty cash.

Jim Kiddell always insisted on a really thorough examination of all property when the Flying Squad arrived at a house. He usually found a ladder and made it his personal job to search out-of-reach glass, china and silver cupboards and cabinets, with a strong electric torch. On one occasion he found a set of fifty eighteenth-century Chelsea plates covered in dust; no-one had set eyes on them for generations.

Many of the houses involved were symbolic of an era that had survived beyond its normal span. Once the aged owners had died, the younger genera-tions that followed sought a simpler – and less costly – way of life. The Flying Squad was ushering out this era and giving the earthly possessions of those who had passed on a new and scattered existence as staple for a growing trade, the antique trade. For although such sales were always attended by a multitude of local people, the dealers were there in force, many well-known names (Mallett, Partridge, Spinks, Mossy Harris, Maples, Blairman) buying strongly and for stock, stock which was to last some of them much longer than they had anticipated,[1] though the slow recovery of the American economy began to make itself felt by a marked increase in demand for good English furniture and antiques. The pages of the *Connoisseur* and *Apollo* were full of items that one could recognise from Sotheby's house sales. Dealers loved the outings, both to the views and the sales. 'Rings' were active, of course, but as far as country house sales were concerned Vere Pilkington and Jim Kiddell would always tour the neighbourhood calling on the bigger houses and known collectors and en-courage them to come and bid, and this kept prices at a reasonable and occasionally unusually high level. Sometimes there were unexpected visitors. Paul Getty turned up on the first day of the sale at Cam House and obviously enjoyed it. He bought a superb sixteenth-century Isfahan carpet for £1,550, a pair of resplendent Louis XV *fauteuils* for £58, a Louis XVI kingwood gueridon for £12, a pair of Louis XV *bergères à Joues* for £52, a Louis XV gilt suite of five pieces for £145, a pair of K'ang Hsi pewter blue vases for £20, a Tanagra group of a female figure reclining on a couch for £10, a well-known Beauvais tapestry of Bacchus and Ariadne, woven after a design by Boucher for £2,700 (it illustrated the article on tapestry in the fourteenth edition of the *Encyclo-paedia Britannica*) and a small Louis XV kingwood commode for £110.

From the printed price lists one can recognise the names of the same collec-tors and private individuals who bought steadily at these sales throughout the years, and the wonderful bargains they got among the secondary items. Getting on for half a century later, the most mouth-watering bargains of all these sales seem to have been the multitude of glorious, antique dinner-services that really went for pittances – and the further a sale was from London the lower the

1. For a charming account of an antique dealer's life at this time, his adventures at country house sales (though not often of the quality described here) and a conspectus of prices then prevailing, see *Antique Dealer: an Autobiography* by R. P. Way, 1956.

prices seemed to be. The only major demand was for eighteenth-century Chinese services and this demand came from America and Scandinavia. In many instances, of course, particularly when it came to the simpler furniture from the servants' quarters and to utilitarian objects from the kitchen quarters, these were clearance sales and what was sold realised clearance prices. An early Victorian plain deal kitchen table, 7 ft. long, another smaller one, two large chopping blocks and a screen with sliding panels sold for two shillings, is an example. (The removal of such items after the sale often costs a good deal more than the hammer price.) But by and large, owners and executors were universally satisfied with the results. The good sales fetched between £5,000 and £15,000, the modest ones from £1,500 to £3,500. The firm probably lost money on the latter, but there was to be a pinnacle[1] among such sales in 1937 that more than made good any losses.

---

1. The Rothschild Sale. See page 293.

24

Looking East and Elsewhere

GEOFFREY HOBSON generally enjoyed travel, but one journey he undertook with reluctance in the interests of the business brought nothing but frustration in its wake. The art world had become increasingly aware that the Bolshevik government in Russia was prepared to trade works of art of all kinds for hard currencies. Before the slump the enterprising Armand Hammer was known to have bought great quantities of antique porcelain, icons, church vestments, tapestries and, above all, the bijouterie created in Fabergé's workshops to sell in America. The less publicity-conscious jeweller, Emanuel Snowman, had astonished London with the collection of Imperial Easter eggs by Fabergé he had brought back from his many adventurous trips to Moscow. Francis Matthiessen, a Berlin gallery owner, who later settled in England, seemed in particular to have gained the confidence of the Russian officials who headed the relevant government agency, *Antiquariat*. Though his first experience in this respect was daunting, years later he told Peter Wilson how as a young man he was asked by the Soviet Government to go to Russia to advise them on the sale of major works of art. He prepared a list of twenty pictures in the Hermitage Museum which he regarded as major masterpieces. He also produced a second list of a further twenty pictures which, although fine, were duplicated by the others and, in fact, of far less importance when each one was compared to its counterpart. The Russians thanked him and paid him – and after his departure sold the paintings from the first list, the masterpieces. They simply could not believe that he was not trying to get the better of them and, in fact, advising them to sell the best works in their collection. In collaboration with Knoedler's in New York and Colnaghi's in London, he managed to get superb Old Masters out of Russia, though at high prices. Andrew Mellon had bought a Van Dyck, a Frans Hals and two Rembrandts in this way.

Early in 1931 it was announced that the Russians were selling the works of art confiscated from the Stroganoff Palace in Leningrad at Lepke's auction house in Berlin. Before the sale Princess Sherbatoff, née Countess Stroganoff, protested against the dispersal of what she claimed was her personal property, but the sale went ahead and raised £125,000. At about the same time, C. G. Boerner's auction gallery in Leipzig had been selling duplicates from the Hermitage[1] and other Russian State collections. Boerner's had two sales: one of eighteenth-century French drawings and another of English and French colour prints of high quality. But many of the latter failed to find buyers and were consequently withdrawn. A not dissimilar fate befell a collection of German gold coins that

1. Some of the highlights of the great Von Hirsch Sale in 1978 came from this source.

the Russians had sent for sale to London where the interest in such things then was minimal, and a whole lot of rare French eighteenth-century bindings and literary works had been sent to Vienna where their sale was again a total flop. All this encouraged the belief that if a less haphazard channel between *Antiquariat* and the West could be established, more collectors would know about what was being sold and the Russians would obtain better prices.

Dr. Maurice Ettinghausen, manager of Maggs' branch in Paris, called on Geoffrey Hobson to discuss the matter in March 1931. Hobson sent round a memorandum to the directors proposing a visit to Russia. He wrote: 'Etting-hausen has a new idea for dealing with such sales. He suggests that we should go over not merely as a bookseller and Auctioneer, hoping to get a few sales of government property, but we should put before them a scheme by which we would become their sole or at all events their most important foreign agents for the sale of all the books and Works of Art'. Ettinghausen had gone on to propose the formation of a small company consisting of a representative of the Soviets, of Maggs and of Sotheby's. 'Property would be consigned to this company and it would decide how it should be dealt with. It might be sold privately or by auction; if sold by auction, of course the usual Auctioneer's fees would be charged. The proceeds of the sale, after deduction of expenses including Directors' salaries should be divided into proportions to be arranged between the three partners forming the company.'

After a long discussion of the proposal among Sotheby's directors, Felix Warre took the unusual step of putting his views on record in writing. 'The proposal put forward in the memorandum might prove to be a dangerous departure from the nature of the business as I have hitherto understood it.' He felt reluctant to be too closely allied to any firm of dealers, and he objected very strongly to the point that any director should get a separate fee in whatever form for services rendered to the proposed company. He agreed nevertheless to further exploration of the project. However, neither he nor des Graz were willing to go to Russia, so reluctantly Hobson agreed to represent Sotheby's. He, Dr. Ettinghausen and Ernest Maggs went their separate ways to Berlin. There they met and proceeded to Moscow via Poland. The journey was not without adventures. Ernest Maggs arrived at the Berlin station late and just managed to jump on to the through train to Poland which was already moving out of the station. After changing to another train on the Polish–Soviet frontier, the three men were 'surprised to find themselves in a dining car decorated with elaborate wood carvings and beautifully appointed with original oil paintings. It turned out that it was part of a private train which had belonged to a pre-revolutionary Russian millionaire'.[1] Geoffrey Hobson 'was very thirsty and on seeing a decanter on the table he poured out a tumbler full of what he took to be water; but, unfortunately for him, it turned out to be vodka – absolutely colour-less but not painless!' On their arrival in Moscow they had the greatest difficulty in getting from the station to the hotel where rooms had been booked

1. This and the other quotations which follow are from Dr. Ettinghausen's autobiography, *Rare Books and Royal Collectors*, London, 1966.

for them. At that time there was said to be only four taxis in Moscow, but what was much more discomfiting was a desperate shortage of food. Almost everything was rationed and nothing could be bought without special cards, so during their fortnight in Russia the three men lived on a supply of tinned sardines which Dr. Ettinghausen had thoughtfully brought with him. The only unrationed goods they saw in the shops in Moscow, and later in Leningrad, were coats of armour and outsize French nineteenth-century marble clocks. During his first night in the hotel Ettinghausen was rung up by a feminine voice speaking French who sought his company because she was lonely. He later discovered that 'this matter of the night telephone call was a regular part of the secret police method of keeping a check on foreign visitors through their female accomplices', and it is interesting that Hobson, Maggs and he did not escape this routine surveillance.

While waiting for their appointment in the relevant ministry in Leningrad the three men passed their time with a visit to the museum and picture gallery at the Hermitage and marvelled at its riches. They also called on the local government department which was responsible for the export of books and antiques. They refused to buy some imperfect folio volumes of natural history subjects in colour, but when they were offered a Gutenberg bible at a reasonable price, they sold it at once by cable to Dr. Martin Bodmer, the famous Swiss book collector. A little later they also came across a portion of the *Codex Sinaiticus Petropolitanus* which two years later Maggs' were able to buy on behalf of the British government for the British Museum for the colossal sum of £100,000. Back in Moscow they at last met the Vice-Commissar for Foreign Trade, a tough, successful Quartermaster-General of the Red Army in Turkestan, and negotiations about the formation of a joint company between 'that Section of the Narkontorg of the USSR Government now known as the *Antiquariat*', Ernest Uriah Maggs and G. D. Hobson proceeded sufficiently far for a complex legal contract to be drawn up on their return to London.

The journey back was hell. 'Never leave Russia on a Friday' was the comment that Geoffrey Hobson scribbled on the fly leaf of a Guide to Soviet Russia that he had taken with him.

The consequences of the trip were discouraging too for they brought about the most agonising conflict between Felix Warre and Hobson in their thirty years of partnership. Maggs' had generously paid Sotheby's their share of the profit of the sale of the bible to Bodmer. It came to £1,300. This was on the understanding that all concerned would proceed as if the new company had already come into being. In the same way, Hobson had agreed to give personal guarantees of up to £10,000 for any purchases the company might make. Not unnaturally, therefore, Hobson felt that, having sacrificed a fortnight's holiday and made all the effort, he was entitled to a share of this money beyond his bare expenses. But Warre felt otherwise. To be fair to him he had said so from the outset. In view of the generally depressed circumstances of the times, and the not inconsiderable loss which Sotheby's had suffered over the sale of a collection of Persian carpets and another of Old Masters where Borenius had wildly over-estimated the reserves, Warre wanted to set the money resulting from the Russian trip against these losses. Hobson was very upset by Warre's hard-line attitude. They exchanged carefully drafted memoranda, which were in turn shown to the other directors. Each of the senior partners felt that an important matter of principle was at stake, and righteous men fight more tenaciously when this is the case. It must have been an embarrassing interlude for the other directors. Hobson had not made matters any easier when he had written to Warre: 'You will no doubt show this letter to the other directors. If, after seeing it, a majority of them agree to both your suggestions, I must be bound by their decision: but I shall acquiesce with great reluctance, and I shall be left with a feeling that I have been very ungenerously treated'. Charles des Graz tried to overcome the *impasse* by drafting a compromise agreement under which Hobson would get an extra sum and the rest would go to the firm. Curiously enough he did so on the back of various Cambridge Latin examination papers. There was some delay in finalising the draft because des Graz had to type it himself for reasons of security. Warre then sent it off to Hobson, who was by then on holiday in a German spa, with a rather one-sided and breezy letter ('let us all sink or swim together'). Hobson replied from Germany by return on paper torn out of an exercise book. He was obviously very mortified. Patiently and precisely he countered all Warre's arguments one by one. His skill in legal drafting was being given an unaccustomed airing in this accomplished summary of his evidence. He referred back to a not dissimilar precedent which had occurred over Barlow's pay during the latter's final year. He concluded his case in one sentence, 'If remuneration [additional to my normal salary] is refused to me, Sotheby's will, in my view, be accepting the benefits of the transaction without performing its obligations'. On his return from holiday the discussions continued. Both partners remained obdurate in maintaining their point of view. It was a sign of the times that such a long, drawn-out struggle could be maintained over £300, which was all that Hobson claimed, and also that there was so little subsequent acrimony. In the end Hobson agreed to des Graz's compromise – and Warre apologised. His final letter in the correspondence ran: 'I am sorry that this discussion has caused you to feel a sense of injustice. To me there seemed a danger here that the good of the Company, as a whole, might not be placed first and before that of any individual. But if I have written or acted in any way that was tactless or clumsy I hope you will forgive me ...' It is one of the very few examples of internal correspondence that has been preserved intact. Indeed, it survived in virtually complete form twice over. One copy had been kept by Hobson in his desk and the other by Warre in his private file. One nestled near the other in the same black metal deed box for thirty years before it was opened again.

As to the business from Russia, Maggs' benefited through the sale of the *Codex Sinaiticus*, but apart from the sale of the Gutenberg bible, a change of policy by the Communist régime seems to have put a halt to the export of works of art, and the joint company was never formed.

First Encounter with Goldschmidt

If thoughts of Russia as a source of new business ultimately proved abortive, there were other parts of Europe which did not. Geoffrey Hobson was determined to spread his net as widely as possible. Tancred Borenius had strong links with Paris, and French collections continued to reach Sotheby's right up to the war. So early in 1931 Hobson concentrated his attention on Germany. In the three decades before 1914, Berlin had been a centre of great collecting activity. An immensely affluent generation of mostly Jewish bankers and industrialists had been encouraged by the ubiquitous Bode to spend money on Italian Old Masters and on Rennaissance and, to a lesser extent, on baroque art. He put all the expertise of the Kaiser Friedrich Museum at their disposal in the

---

Messrs. Sotheby & Co. G. D. Hobson, M.V.O. F. W. Warre, O.B.E., M.C.
C. G. des Graz. C. Y. Pilkington

34 & 35, New Bond Street, London Datum...........................

VERKAUFSAUFTRAG

Ich Unterzeichneter, beauftrage hiermit die Firma SOTHEBY & Co., London, meine

.... *zu versteigeren.*

Vor Erscheinen des Kataloges können keine definitiven Limite angenommen werden.

Für den Fall dass ich einzelne Lots limitieren möchte, werde ich nach Empfang des Versteigerungskataloges meine Limite der Firma mitteilen.

(Unterschrift) ....

Adresse ....

Soll das Eigentum versichert werden
  in London? ....
  unterwegs? ....

Kann der Name des Besitzers im
  Katalog gedruckt werden?...

At the time of the slump the firm actively sought business from other parts of Europe for the first time. There were regular visits to Germany, France and elsewhere.

---

hope that many of the collections would eventually find their way there – which they did. After the beginning of the new century, seventeenth-century Dutch painting, fine French furniture, oriental porcelain and Japanese graphic art had also become popular, and the same families were among the first to collect the work of the French Impressionist painters. A love of things English also abounded. Many luxurious Berlin apartments had 'English Rooms' full of Adam and Chippendale furniture and hung with English portraits and landscapes. German art dealers' galleries, antique shops and antiquarian booksellers were among the best in the world. There was no shortage of distinguished auction houses in Germany and they produced sumptuous and memorable catalogues. But after the searing effect of the inflation in the early Twenties those who were prepared to sell works of art very often sought other currencies than the Mark (more so after Hitler and the Nazis came to power in 1933).

Sotheby's appointed a German-speaking English ex-army officer to represent them in Germany, Lt.-Col. R. G. Birch. He was the son of the Keeper of Manuscripts at the British Museum and had a good working knowledge of books and autographs. The fact that he had also been the Allies' Deputy Commissioner of the Rhine after 1919 was an excellent background to knowledge of the German scene. He usually accompanied anyone who came from Sotheby's around Germany – and other parts of Europe.[1] Shrewdly he eschewed direct personal contacts and set up a small network of German dealers and agents who could feed him information about collectors who might want to sell their possessions in England. By the autumn of 1931 Birch had assembled nearly twenty names of possible clients, so Hobson decided to go to Germany. To Tom Lumley's great delight he was asked to accompany Hobson. There were two reasons for this. Tom had proved himself remarkably adroit at speedy appraisals of the fine things in any house full of furnishings. Over and over again owners had asked him to look around and to pick out items that would fetch the most money. His record was a fourteen-day visit to Ireland on behalf of the firm during which he had inspected 126 houses (and worked well into the small hours each night). Hobson also found that he could understand Lumley particularly well despite his deafness. This was no accident. Lumley had taken elocution lessons, having realised that he would have more contact with Hobson than anyone else at Bond Street and that any success he might achieve depended on easy communication with Hobson despite the fact that the latter heard with difficulty.

While Hobson spoke perfect German, Tom spoke not a word. Often this was an advantage for, while Hobson conversed with the owners of the collections they visited or the agent who was showing them round in the owner's absence, Tom could inspect and take notes.

Their first call was on a dealer with premises in one of the most fashionable streets of Berlin, the Wilhelmstrasse. He showed them three magnificent tapestries belonging to the Grand Duke of Sachsen-Weimar-Eisenach. Tom noted that 'the one which is most likely to come over is of very early date, of wonderful quality and in good condition; if anything at all is likely to fetch a high price, this should'. Hobson thought it might fetch as much as £2,000 because the demand for tapestries was still strong. Then Tom went off on his own with another agent who took him to Schloss Eulten, the property of the Grand Duke of Oldenburg. What intrigued him most was a collection of ship models, 'four being very large, with masts and sails, and said to have been made for Peter the Great at Amsterdam'. The same agent also took Hobson and Lumley to meet the Berlin banker, Jakob Goldschmidt. Tom noted, 'he is said to have more fine Chinese porcelain and modern French pictures at his house in town, which was shut up. Bäcke (the agent) was rather mysterious about him,

1. He was later to become the Curator of the Cowper & Newton Museum at Olney in Buckinghamshire.

and we were not allowed to say anything about selling'. Hobson commented 'he is, I believe, the notorious chairman of the *Darmstadter Bank* which crashed in August, so presumably he wants money: he looks clever enough to survive any number of crashes!' The assessment after such a brief encounter was remarkably shrewd. Goldschmidt (who was, in fact, only the senior partner) was a small, rotund man with very bright blue eyes who always had a smile on his face. Having started with relatively little he became a very successful stock-broker with an uncanny gift for successful speculation. Eventually he was invited to become joint managing director of the German *Nationalbank* together with Hjalmar Schacht, who later achieved notoriety as economic adviser to the German cabinet. Schacht soon left for even higher things at the *Reichsbank*. Goldschmidt merged the *Nationalbank* with the much larger but then leaderless *Darmstadter Bank*. There he over-reached himself with in-cautious speculation. Hence the crash Hobson referred to. Goldschmidt was an enthusiastic collector. He had built himself an enormous house in central Berlin in order to display his pictures and porcelain because they looked almost lost in his country house at Neubabelsberg. The premises later became Mussolini's Italian embassy in Berlin. Goldschmidt had been particularly happily married and mourned for years the early death of his wife. His only son became the apple of his eye and was to play a very important role in Sotheby's post-war history.

Some years later Goldschmidt came over to London and called at Bond Street. He asked for Jim Kiddell as the expert on oriental ceramics, but Hobson insisted on seeing him himself. Goldschmidt had decided to sell his collection of eighteenth-century Chinese porcelain but demanded very special terms. Hobson refused to bargain and Goldschmidt left in a huff. He went to Christie's who raised nearly £25,000 in a two-day sale. The most expensive item was a pair of *famille jaune* vases which fetched £1,575. It was a remark-ably high total at what was still a difficult time. When Hobson heard the result he felt very contrite and said to Jim Kiddell 'I've made a bad bloomer. I should never have talked to him myself. You would have handled him far better'. Goldschmidt emigrated to America in the mid-Thirties taking his collection with him, and made a second fortune by shrewd investment in Chrysler shares. Long after Hobson's death the name Goldschmidt was to become one of the major touchstones in Sotheby's post-war history.

Hobson and Lumley continued their tour with a visit to the house of Frau Hermine Feist, accompanied by her lawyer, Dr. von Rogister. They were dumbfounded by what they saw. Tom Lumley wrote, 'this collection is in every way remarkable – for quantity, quality and taste I have never seen anything to approach it'. Frau Feist was probably the greatest collector of works of art, but particularly of porcelain, of her time. Her family was one of the two largest coal merchants in pre-First World War Germany. Her husband made champagne. He died early and she consoled herself with continuing the collection they had begun together. She bought the finest French furniture that Jacques Selig-mann, the great Paris dealer, had to offer. She also regularly attended auctions, mainly in pursuit of rare Meissen figures. Her greatest rival in this field was a lady of similar inclinations, Frau von Pannwitz. Like an early Niarchos and Onassis they waged titanic battles over what they both desired, raising prices to what were then – and are even now – astronomic levels. On one famous occasion she bid 120,000 Gold Marks for a single piece of porcelain, a crinoline group she was particularly eager to possess. It was small wonder that Hobson was astonished. Tom Lumley speculated whether Sotheby's might be able to run the sale in Berlin. But the greater part of the collection was sold privately and the rump later dispersed by a German auction house.

A considerable proportion of what Hobson and Lumley had viewed did indeed come to London and was sold by Sotheby's. For obvious reasons most of these sales were anonymous. One consisted of a small collection of rare seventeenth- and eighteenth-century Chinese figures of birds, the sort of thing which has been enormously in demand during the last four or five years. But there were too many of a kind at one time for the London trade and the results were disappointing.[1] It needed a special cloak-and-dagger trip to Berlin by Jim Kiddell finally to clinch the sale of the fine maiolica belonging to Kurt Glogowski, a businessman with a splendid house at 40 Unter den Linden. Jim travelled in dark glasses; deliberately missed the scheduled cross-Channel ferry; spoke in riddles on tapped telephone lines and was whisked around Berlin in a fast car by Hans Feist, son of Frau Feist, and his beautiful girl friend, a leading German actress. The collection consisted of sixty-six magnificent plates, jugs, tazzas and albarellos. Many of them had been bought not long before from the dispersal of other well-known collections at the height of the mid-Twenties boom, but prices in the depressed summer weeks of 1932 were disappointing in comparison. There were in addition Renaissance bronzes, textiles and oriental rugs. A fifteenth-century Italian terracotta bust of a youth thought to represent Raphael, attributed by Bode to Francesco Francia, and bought on his advice, was withdrawn just before the sale. The Glogowski catalogue made frequent references to a longer established collection of Italian maiolica – probably the greatest of its kind in Germany – which belonged to Professor Alfred Pringsheim, a professor of mathematics at Munich University and a son-in-law of Thomas Mann.

This too was sold at Bond Street but not until June and July of 1939, in two magnificent two-day sale sessions. The collection was widely known because it had been superbly catalogued in 1914 in two volumes by Otto von Falke. But the 400 pieces were dispersed under sad circumstances. They had been acquired by a Nazi gauleiter, and his English wife came to London to make the necessary arrangements.

While in Berlin Hobson had also called on a book collector who shared his passionate interest in bookbindings and was well known to him as the author of the definitive work on the French book in the eighteenth century. This was

1. A few of the birds eventually became the property of Mrs. David Gubbay who bequeathed her collection of porcelain and furniture to the National Trust, where it is displayed at Clandon Park in Surrey.

another, though rather younger, banker, called Jean Fürstenberg, who had at that time contemplated the sale of his very extensive collection of French colour prints. But although the two men remained in touch for many years, Fürstenberg finally donated parts of his collection of books to the Bibliothèque Nationale and retained the remainder in a magnificent Normandy château at Beaumesnil, which he made over to the French State.

Although Hobson continued to visit the Continent regularly, his 1931 trip proved to be one of the most memorable. Tom Lumley left Sotheby's in 1936 initially to join the well-known dealer in antique silver, Commander How. Not long afterwards he set up his own business and is today one of London's most respected silver dealers.

The Grand Deceiver Unmasked

At about this time, in fact in July 1934, there burst upon the astonished world of professional bookmen and collectors a newly published book inoffensively titled *An Enquiry into the Nature of Certain Nineteenth Century Pamphlets*[1] by two antiquarian booksellers, John Carter and Graham Pollard. It proved to be an exposure of crime in the classical tradition, crime that had certainly impinged on the auction room. The laws of libel made direct accusation almost impossible. Instead, Carter and Pollard had adduced objective and completely unshakeable evidence that had been established with great forensic skill and irrefutable logic. They proved that the most eminent bibliographer and book collector of his time and a man greatly respected, Thomas James Wise, had been concerned with the large-scale fabrication of supposed first editions of works by the Brownings, Tennyson, Swinburne, Matthew Arnold, Ruskin, Thackeray, Dickens, R. L. Stevenson and Kipling. He had distributed these forgeries among collectors with extremely ingenious provenances compounded of half-truths based on his intimate knowledge of the authors concerned and their literary output. This mattered a great deal at Bond Street: during his life Wise had played an important role both as a client of the firm and sometimes even as adviser to it.

For nearly half a century he had been cock-of-the-walk of the auction room and the antiquarian book trade. Infinitely knowledgeable – one-time President of the Bibliographical Society, Honorary Fellow of Worcester College, Oxford, Honorary M.A. of Oxford University, member of the Roxburghe Club – his judgement was respected everywhere; indeed, his word was often law.

Wise was seventy-five at the time of the publication of the *Enquiry* and had established a remarkably fine library of seventeenth-, eighteenth- and particularly nineteenth-century literature – the Ashley Library – which he had catalogued with the most detailed annotations in no less than eleven volumes. The

1. The book's half-title contained a quotation from Wise's Bibliography of Swinburne, 'The whole thing proved once more that, easy as it appears to be to fabricate reprints of rare books, it is in actual practice absolutely impossible to do so in such a manner that detection cannot follow the result'.

library was, in fact, bought by the British Museum after his death for a sum of £66,000.

The evidence against Wise was in two forms: that published in the book and more held back by Carter and Pollard, but of which he was made aware. It was so overwhelming that Wise could do virtually nothing to defend himself, and he died three years later a broken man.

Wise came from a simple family background and was in every sense a self-made man, for he appears to have had little formal education. He became interested in collecting books at an early age; haunted the famous book barrows in Farringdon Road and gradually sought out 'the picturesque old book shops up Fleet Street and along the Strand and its very dubious backwaters'.[1] Soon he frequented the better class antiquarian book shops and it was not long before he ventured into 13 Wellington Street. He soon had established a firm friendship with young Tom Hodge, and later was well known to Hobson and des Graz. For nearly fifty years he followed book sales with the greatest interest. From the outset of his collecting days he was prepared to pay unusually high prices for items he wanted badly enough, and his total purchases for his own library, and for other collecting 'friends' must have run to very respectable totals.

He realised quite early in his career that his own expertise could be particularly useful to the many wealthy book collectors in the United States. One such was John Henry Wrenn, a Chicago financier, who met Wise in London as early as 1892. After five years of desultory correspondence, Wise began to supply him with books on a remarkable scale and by the time of Wrenn's death in 1911, he had helped the American to build up a sizeable library of seventeenth-, eighteenth- and nineteenth-century English literature, which was later bought by Texas University. The correspondence pertaining to it also passed to the University but Wise rigorously opposed any part of its publication until after his own death.

A selection from it was finally published in 1944[2] and throws a good deal of light on Wise's involvement with Sotheby's and on his relationship with Tom Hodge in particular. It also establishes quite clearly that, though he labelled his activities as adviser and a 'passer on of duplicates', it was merely an ingeniously camouflaged form of professional dealing.

As long ago as 22 November 1899, Wise was writing to Wrenn, 'I was at Sotheby's to-day, but did not buy the "*Elegy*", although it sold for £58. I want this book for myself, but would not place this copy upon my shelves at any price'. Wise was a great stickler for books in the finest condition; this particular copy did not match up to his exacting standards. With the aid of hindsight one can see that much of the correspondence is pure imaginative humbug because Wise goes to great lengths to write up in the most glowing terms his own forged pamphlets, of which he sold Wrenn no fewer than seventy-five copies.

1. Quoted from *Thomas J. Wise in the Original Cloth* by Wilfred Partington, 1946. Partington was the editor of *The Bookman's Journal* from 1919–31.
2. *Letters of Thomas J. Wise to John Henry Wrenn*, a further Inquiry into the skill of certain nineteenth-century forgers, by Fannie E. Ratchford, New York 1944.

On 26 November 1900, for example, he wrote, 'I have your letter re. the coming sale at Messrs. Sotheby's . . . lot 751 *Pauline*. If this should prove to be a really fine copy it will bring a long price. Browning is, as you say, not everybody's author, but he is one of the "safest" to buy and there are quite enough buyers about to keep his scarcer books up to their value'.

His most celebrated forgeries were Elizabeth Barrett Browning's privately printed *Sonnets*[1] which he linked with a particularly romantic story of their origin first made public by Sir Edmund Gosse in 1894. Carter and Pollard listed thirty-six copies of the forgery known to have been bought by collectors: Wise had also fabricated bogus editions of three poems by Robert Browning – *Cleon*, *The Statue and the Bust* and *Gold Hair* – as well as Mrs. Browning's *The Runaway Slave*. His method of establishing high prices for such items was ingenious. When one came up for sale at auction (and he often placed it there himself) he simply asked two dealers (unbeknownst to each other) to bid for him against each other. Although this would involve him in paying commission both to auctioneer and bookseller, it established a high price. 'He could then produce other copies to collectors – fakes too – and sell them.'[2]

In another letter to Wrenn on 7 March 1901, 'Just a line to tell you the result of the sale at Sotheby's to-day . . . The authenticity of the inscriptions was questioned. Mr. Hodge appealed to me for my opinion to settle the matter. I said I considered that the inscription in *Endymion* was in Mrs. Reynolds's handwriting, and that the inscription in the *Poems* was in Keats's hand, and I am quite certain, absolutely certain, that my judgement was correct'. An interesting demonstration of the power of Wise's bibliographical authority.

On 8 June 1901, Wise used a letter from Tom Hodge to bolster his reputation. He wrote to Wrenn, 'the passage marked in the enclosed letter (from Mr. Hodge of Sotheby's) will interest you, coming as it does from one well able to form a correct opinion, and in a position not to be affected by prejudices. The letter refers to my Browning Bibliography, a copy of which I sent to you'. Tom's letter from 13 Wellington Street read:

Dear Mr. Wise,
I stole a few days holiday which I spent on the Bexhill golf links and on my return I find your kind letter and valuable gifts. You have done me a great honour, and I feel flattered and grateful. The book will be of extreme use to me and unlike many works of the kind I know it is reliable and accurate. It forms another leaf on your laurel wreath to which I sincerely hope you will add many others. Reliable monographs are rare.

I was glad to see you buying strongly again the other day; if we live we shall both see fine copies of early English literature beyond the reach of any except Pierpont Morgan, Bennett and a few other millionaires.

Very truly yours,

1. 'Sonnets from the Portuguese' (*Sonnets* by E.B.B., Reading, 1847).
2. Graham Pollard, quoted from the *Daily Express* on 17 August 1937. The popular newspapers of their day took up the Wise revelations with gusto.

Later in the same year, Wise writes to Wrenn that he could not get to Sotheby's on one particular Saturday, 'so I gave Maggs some commissions'. Maggs bought an imperfect copy of Swift's *Gulliver's Travels* which Wise wanted – as was so often the case – to perfect another imperfect copy he already owned. He had turned increasingly to the eighteenth century both for his own and for Wrenn's collection. Later again he wrote to Wrenn, 'We shall have a good many "finds" in this field before we have done! The natural result of collecting what is coming instead of what has already arrived'. And four years later in the correspondence he glories in the confirmation of his prediction. On 24 March 1907 he writes, 'this sale has vindicated in the strongest possible manner the position we have for some time now been taking up . . . Every item belonging to the eighteenth century in the sale, without one solitary exception, created a new record. . . .' Incidentally, that very same sale also confirmed a prediction that Tom Hodge had made to Wise and many others – that the enormous earlier surge forward in the price of Shakespeare folios and quartos would evaporate. 'In fact,' wrote Wise, 'Shakespeare spelt not merely a "slump"; it was a crash!'

There are many reports of long and intimate conversations with Hodge about what desirable items in forthcoming sales would fetch and how high Wise and Wrenn should allow their bids to go. Often Hodge appears to have been willing to persuade owners to sell privately to the ardent bibliophile. Back in 1903 there had been great excitement when no fewer than three copies of Shelley's suppressed and very rare first publication *Victor and Cazire* appeared at auction within a short spell of time. Wise describes complex machinations to get the third copy for Wrenn at a reasonable price. 'I sent you Mr. Tom Hodge's note regarding the newly discovered copy [the third] of *Victor and Cazire*. This copy has been brought to light by means of the publicity afforded by the sale of the second copy. . . .

'Mr. Hodge has written to the owner of this third copy to go and see him and is going to do his best to purchase it for me by private sale. He will, unquestionably, get it for as low a price as possible. Of course Mr. Hodge will receive his usual commission from the vendor, and if the price should be fixed at £300, his commission would be one-half what it would be were the price to be fixed at £600. Thus it would appear to be to his interest to fix the price as high as possible.' And then follows this touching tribute, 'But Mr. Hodge is my friend; and further he is not only a real good fellow, but he is an English gentleman, and the question of commission would not be of the slightest consideration to him when the question was one of doing a service to a friend'. Ultimately all three copies passed through Wise's hands and he sold the first copy he had obtained to Wrenn.

Wise's stature in the world of antiquarian books and at Sotheby's in particular comes to light in an interesting way. In 1904 he is discussing the possible sale of the Rowfant Library, a collection of books assembled by the poet Frederick Locker-Lampson. It was the first major example of 'cabinet collecting': contained in two small book cases, it included first editions of the supreme examples of English imaginative literature from Chaucer to Swinburne. £50,000 was being asked for it, and though Wise considered this sum excessive, the library was so well known that he felt it would probably fetch that sum at auction. Were he to buy it himself he might get it for less – 'the sum in question would not be prohibitive as I could obtain from Mr. Hodge or from my bankers a sufficient advance to enable me to purchase it'. Later, quoting a Mr. Hadlow, a collector of Elizabethan plays, the latter is reported as having said of him: 'Mr. Wise? Oh, I know him well enough, though not personally. He gets first offer on everything nowadays; at one time I could get good old plays, but now every time I go after a book, I am either told "It's on offer to Mr. Wise", or else "Mr. Wise has taken it!" '

Wise pursued errors in bibliographies or in the catalogues of booksellers and auctioneers (not excluding Sotheby's) with ferocious criticism. The literature abounds with examples of his positively tyrannical observations on this score. On one occasion he summoned a bookseller, who was advertising some Shelley letters, to his presence. Wise thought these were forgeries. He asked the bookseller to show them to him. He did. Wise tore them to shreds and handed them back to the bookseller saying 'Now sue me, if you dare'. No legal action followed! One biographer said 'It is doubtful whether any English book man (Wise compiled no fewer than fifteen standard bibliographies in his life) supposedly unprofessional, has ever attained quite the same eminence and wide reputation, alike for his knowledge and for his boasted intolerance of anything second-rate, shoddy or spurious'.[1]

He was a supreme bibliographical analyst with a prodigious memory and apparently unlimited capacity for painstaking work. One must remember that scientific bibliography as we know it today only came into being as the nineteenth century moved towards its close, and Wise was one of the major figures who helped in its foundation. By the time the First World War was over and book collecting entered a decade of frenzied boom, particularly in the United States, Wise assumed a Napoleon-like stature in that world. Other great bookmen accepted his pre-eminence as readily as did collecting novices. Eleven distinguished authorities wrote flattering introductions to the eleven volumes of his Ashley Library catalogue, which appeared between 1922 and 1936. And yet . . . there must have been stirrings of doubt. Earlier challenges to the Wise supremacy had either been overlooked or quashed, though quite a number were recorded. Was it coincidental then that Arundell Esdaile of the British Museum had written in his introduction to the concluding eleventh volume of the Ashley catalogue, '. . . bibliography is the new tool which the last two generations have forged for the better understanding of books. It is not a small credit that Mr. Wise has played some part in forging the tool and exemplifying in one of the richest fields what use it can be put to . . . ' Or, when C. H. Wilkinson, Dean and Librarian of Worcester College, Oxford, had written in his introduction to Wise's Dryden Library, quoting from The Rambler, 'There have been men

1. Partington, op. cit., p. 123.

indeed splendidly wicked, whose Endowments throw a Brightness on their Crimes . . . because they never could be wholly divested of their Excellence; but such have been in all Ages the great Corrupters of the World'. How Wise must have winced.

One can imagine then the devastating effect of Carter and Pollard's incisive analysis of Wise's earlier crimes of deception. There could be no going back. The methods of investigation brooked no argument. The paper Wise had used for some of his bogus pamphlets was made at least forty years after their supposed publications; some of the typefaces used by his printers were of a much later design, and once there had been a *total* investigation of the sources of the multitude of 'rare, early works', the accusing finger could only point at Wise again and again. His collapse was total. Privately he referred to Carter and Pollard as sewer-rats; publicly, the few attempts at denial he made only dragged him into further disgrace. It was small wonder that Geoffrey Hobson and Charles des Graz were incredulous at the revelations when they first came out, and found them difficult to believe even years later.

John Pashby, a book cataloguer who joined Sotheby's from Hodgson's in 1936, tells a delightful story on the subject. 'Some time after the publication of the *Enquiry* had occurred a whole lot of these Wise forgeries came in and I wrote a Thomas J. Wise Forgery Stock Catalogue. Des Graz came into my room one day and looked at the copy. He said "Tut, tut, Mr. Pashby. We cannot have this." I said, "but the forgeries are now proved". "That is a matter of opinion, Mr. Pashby. I should call them Thomas J. Wise, Privately Printed Pamphlets with fictitious imprints and texts", and walked out.'[1] More positive proof was revealed at Bond Street during the Moulton Barrett sale in 1937, when John Taylor found a letter from Elizabeth Barrett Browning that completely punctured the Gosse legend of the origin of the Portuguese sonnets of 1847, on which Wise had relied so heavily. The letter clearly stated that Mrs. Browning had not shown the sonnets to Robert till 1852. Taylor showed this letter to des Graz. The latter was very upset and totally deflated. 'Well, really', he is said to have commented. 'I cannot believe it. He was such a nice old gentleman. So helpful to us'. But after that occasion des Graz was convinced. He would have been even more astonished had he lived to learn the revelation many years later that Wise had stolen a great number of title pages and other leaves from valuable books in the British Museum.[2] He had used them to perfect copies of the same titles which he owned: many of them were, in fact, bought with the Ashley Library by the British Museum, so they finished up in the same institution but as part of a different set of copies.

The sad saga had an unexpectedly happy ending for Sotheby's. In 1958 that ebullient young literary detective, John Carter, who had by then become a distinguished antiquarian bookseller, joined Sotheby's as an associate director to build up their business in New York. But perhaps it should be said that

1. In a recorded interview with the author.
2. See David Foxon 'Another Skeleton in Thomas J. Wise's Cupboard', *Times Literary Supplement*, 19 October 1956.

detailed scrutiny of the literature of the Wise saga today leaves one with a strong feeling of nausea. The whole episode cast a slur on its era and ultimately it had, of course, done harm to the authority of the book world. Years later Keating might have cocked a snook at the art trade by his pastiches of Samuel Palmer, but at least he did not pose as a high priest among the pundits. Wise did. One must admire Carter and Pollard the more for their courage in denouncing the master forger when he was at the height of his glory.

25

London:
World Centre
of the Art Market

WHILE commentators in Britain in 1936 may still have regarded the art market as in a depressed state, the extraordinary quality of what was passing through the London sale-rooms and the very gentle upward movement of prices had not gone unobserved elsewhere. Europe was in an unsettled state. Many owners of fine collections began to regard possessions as something of an encumbrance that should now be turned into ready money. Where better to do this – they said to themselves – than in London, where the results would be in stable, readily negotiable and prestigious pounds sterling? Sotheby's had, of course, been saying this to potential clients on the Continent for a long time, and the fact that the message had got home became more and more evident from the summer of 1936 onwards.

A collection of twenty-two paintings by Eugène Boudin, for instance, was sent over from Paris by a M. Laffon and was to be included in a sale on 9 July. The owner's father had bought the majority of the pictures from Boudin himself. An exhibition at Tooth's in the previous year had introduced that master of the seaside scene and the open sky to an English audience. The delightful little canvases with their multitude of female figures in long, billowing skirts and parasols, painted at a period when mid-nineteenth-century fashion was at its most impressive, by what was then a virtually unknown artist, had caused wide interest. So did the sale. Continental and English dealers competed to an extent not often seen in London, and M. André Weil of Paris carried off the three most expensive paintings at £1,200, £600 and £600. Such prices were wholly unprecedented. The total for the collection was £7,430 and the elated owner declared publicly that this was half as much again as he had expected in his most optimistic moments. The Duc de Trévise also had sent from Paris French portraits and works of distinguished French painters (Duplessis, Ingres and Quentin de la Tour, and, among the moderns, Gaugin, Monet and Sisley). On the whole he must have been disappointed for, with the exception of an *Execution Scene* and a rather curiously distorted *St. Peter in Prayer*, both by Francisco de Goya, and the Monet (*A Partridge and a Woodcock hung against a wall*), the London trade did not take to his collection and most items had to be bought in. Retrospectively, probably the most memorable bargains of this part of the sale were three sketch-books by Jacques-Louis David (two of which had formerly belonged to Anatole France) which contained numerous studies for David's famous picture of the Coronation of

Napoleon. One page, which one would love to see again, showed Napoleon crowning Josephine, both in the nude. The three items fetched £18, £14 and £8 respectively; and a pair of separate portraits by J. P. Isabey of Napoleon and Josephine at the moment of their coronation had to be bought in at £38 even after being put up for sale together.

All these were included in the same sale as the Laffon Boudins, while some Beauvais tapestries, also sent in by the Duc de Trévise, which the Soviet Government had sold in Berlin in 1928, were included in a furniture sale later on with several other items of his property.

As it happened, a second Quentin de la Tour pastel portrait arrived in London among the collection of M. H. Winterfield of Nice, which was sold at Bond Street in December. This sale too included a number of other French consignments. But the most memorable French collection sold in that month belonged to Mme. Dhainault. She had sent over a great many brilliant examples of the French silversmith's art, miniatures, gold boxes, ormolu, a choice collection of Vincennes and Sèvres porcelain, paintings and Old Master drawings. While prices were well up on earlier years, it was M. André Weil who again bought the most outstanding items at record prices, including a pair of Louis XVI silver tureens by Robert Joseph Auguste. They were made in 1775, weighed 623 ounces and now fetched a record £2,200.

December 1936 was also the month in which the book department sold the last portion of the Brouwet Collection of Napoleana (with its catalogue entirely in French).[1] But it was a sale announced for the following week which really astonished the cognoscenti everywhere. The celebrated Amsterdam auctioneer, Anton W. M. Mensing, had recently died. For nearly half a century he had been associated with the firm of Frederik Müller & Co., who undertook art and literary sales of all kinds but had latterly specialised in picture sales under his guidance. Probably the most celebrated sale Anton Mensing had conducted himself was that of the last portion of the paintings and Old Master drawings from the Six Collection. In 1928 this had fetched £165,000. Mensing's principal delight in life had been book collecting and by using his unique opportunities he had formed a marvellous library of early printed books, particularly block-books, illuminated manuscripts – principally Dutch and Italian ones – and fine bindings. It was decided that all these should be sold in London by Sotheby's.

Now the Dutch had virtually invented book auctions: the earliest recorded sales in modern times were held by the Elzeviers at the beginning of the seventeenth century. The first British book sale, that of the library of Dr. Lazarus Seaman, one-time Vice Chancellor of Cambridge, held in 1676 by William Cooper had been staged at the suggestion of an English Presbyterian minister who had lived in Holland for many years and attended book sales there. Thus, for a major Dutch-owned library, the property of a leading Dutch auctioneer, to be sent for sale to London was a remarkable reversal of historic trends. The press made much of it, and it was indeed a feather in Sotheby's cap. Mensing had often attended sales at Bond Street and their mutual interest in

1. See p. 252.

fine bindings was a strong link between him and Geoffrey Hobson. Some of the Dutchman's most valuable books had come from libraries as renowned as Beckford, Christie-Miller, Hoe, J. E. Hodgkin, Holford, Huth, Crawford, Amherst, Pembroke and Phillipps.

It was one of Dr. Rosenbach's long-standing clients over in America who studied the Mensing catalogue with most particular care. This was Lessing Rosenwald. The slump had severely curtailed his rate of new acquisitions and indeed he had long owed the Rosenbach Company large sums of money, which had only recently been finally paid off. The two lots he now principally desired were the first edition of the *Buch der Weisheit der alten Weisen*, Ulm, 1483 – a collection of originally oriental fables with one of the finest series of woodcuts to appear in the fifteenth century – and a set of thirty-two single, extraordinarily rare, early, coloured woodcuts which Mensing had, in fact, bought at Sotheby's earlier in the Thirties. Rham was briefed and went into action, and the sale-room correspondents all noted with satisfaction that 'the Doctor' was buying again for the first time in ages. Rham obtained the first item for £1,350. For the second he had to pay what seemed the enormous sum of £2,106. The reason for this was interesting. No reserves had been placed on any lots in the sale, but Mensing's son – also an auctioneer – entered the bidding when he thought prices were low. Knowing of the Rosenbach–Rosenwald interest in this particular instance, he competed with Rham for the first of the single woodcuts and pushed it to an unusually high level. This set the pattern for the prices of the remaining items in the same series.

The Continental press took a good deal of interest in the Mensing sale and reported it in detail. The German periodical, *Die Weltkunst*, went so far as to comment that the 615 items would be an event of note *even for the spoilt English market*.[1] After the sale *The Times* stated that the results had greatly exceeded expectations because of competition between continental dealers, cabled bids from New York (Gabriel Wells had been buying as well as Dr. Rosenbach) and spirited bidding from London firms, particularly Maggs and Quaritch. The first portion of the library (a second sale followed in April 1937) realised £21,849.

A 'professional' collection in another area of interest, Chinese porcelain, jades, ivories and enamels, had also caused widespread discussion when it came up for sale on 10 November. This belonged to the New York dealer, Edward I. Farmer. The catalogue stated that he was such a zealous collector in his own right that he kept his personal treasures behind secret panels in one of his galleries, so that he might not be tempted to sell them even to his most cherished clients. But although the catalogue received praise for the beauty of its illustrations, there was regret, as *The Times* said, 'that since pedigree is a big factor in art collecting, the provenances of none of the 66 items is recorded'. A. C. R. Carter was so taken with the Farmer collection that he devoted most of his monthly *Forthcoming Sales* column in the *Burlington Magazine* to it. In contrast to the Mensing policy of no reserves, Mr. Farmer, who wanted to

1. My italics – author.

enjoy the sight of selling his pride and joy during his lifetime, fixed very high reserves. Several major items had to be bought in. Thus, the £7,050 realised by the sale was not as satisfactory as it seemed to appear.

The fact that London had now genuinely achieved a paramount position as an art market was the keynote of sales reviews at the end of 1936. *The Times* had already commented in the summer when the Laffon collection arrived that 'this is an indication that continental collectors recognise the supremacy of London as the art market of the world. High prices are realised in Paris, Berlin and New York but in no capital in the world do prices for fine pictures and art objects maintain such a consistently high level as in London'. The fact brought cheer to Sotheby's, and indeed to Christie's who had made a sensational splash in the summer when they sold the Oppenheimer Collection of Old Master drawings, maiolica and bronzes. Profits all round began to look healthier and seemed to herald the end of a period of seven lean years.

The Sale of Newton's Papers

The Oppenheimer Sale had tended to overshadow a two-day sale at Sotheby's on 13 and 14 July 1936, which may well come to be regarded as one of the most interesting the firm has ever staged. This included the bulk of the handwritten papers Sir Isaac Newton left at his death in 1727. Here were some three million words by one of the world's most powerful and original intellects. They were almost entirely unknown and certainly unpublished, for Newton had done his best to conceal them in his lifetime. They had passed into the keeping of John Conduitt who had married Newton's favourite niece, Catherine Barton, and had then descended to their daughter, the first Viscountess Lymington, mother of the 2nd Earl of Portsmouth. At the time of Newton's death they had been valued at £250. The collection remained intact in the Portsmouth family until 1872 when the then Earl had presented a portion of the strictly scientific papers in Newton's old university, Cambridge.

He retained all those writings dealing with alchemy (some 650,000 words), chronology (250,000 words) and theology (1,250,000 words) as well as all those papers relatings to Newton's thirty years as Master of the Royal Mint. Among enormous bundles of correspondence was a marvellously lively series of letters from Newton's friend Edmund Halley recounting in great detail the history of the publication of Newton's most important work, the *Principia*, for which Halley had been solely responsible. Here too were individual letters from Boyle telling Newton of the appearance of a comet, Locke sending him a refinement of a supposed recipe for making gold, and Samuel Pepys[1] beseeching Newton

---

1. Sotheby's had sold 'the well known Collection of the Relics of Samuel Pepys, the property of the late John Pepys Cockerell (sold by order of his widow)' on 1 April 1931. It included an ivory medallion of Pepys, dated 1688, by Cavalier, his crested silver porringer and salver, three portraits (one of himself) by Sir Godfrey Kneller, his nautical almanack (which had originally belonged to Henry VIII) and two volumes containing Pepys's private correspondence of over 600 letters (there were 100 autograph pages by Pepys, 30 by Evelyn and two or

to put his mathematical talents to some really practical use by computing for him the chances of throwing sixes at dice. There was another section that dealt with Newton's invention of calculus and the extraordinary controversy with Leibnitz over its origination. Finally there was a substantial collection of personal papers which Conduitt (who had been Newton's deputy at the Mint, and later succeeded him) had got together for a biography which he had never completed. Much of what we know of Newton today stems from these documents.

The 1936 sale was brought about by heavy pressure from death duties and, it was later rumoured, by the need of money for a family divorce. The Newton papers had been kept at Hurstbourne Park in Hampshire, one of the Portsmouth family residences. The house itself was now also sold.

When it appeared, the catalogue of the papers was widely praised. It was a brilliant evocation of Newton's temperament and strivings. A detailed scrutiny of it was the equivalent of reading a compact, vivid and revealing biography. It had been compiled by John Taylor. Because of his scientific background he realised better than anyone else within the firm the importance of the yellowing and chaotic assortment of ancient manuscript material that the porters had dumped in his tiny office for cataloguing. He took months to sort it out and to digest its contents. He managed to decipher and to transcribe what was often difficult to read. With his wide background reading of the Newton literature he had grouped the material, and then counted the words. Des Graz became more and more agitated by the delays in the preparation of the copy for the printer of the catalogue. Taylor repeatedly stressed the amount of work involved and the historic significance of the documents. Eventually he showed des Graz his draft for the introduction. Des Graz was convinced and added a final sentence to make the point even more cogently. When the printed catalogue came into the hands of the press there was all-round acclaim – and an amusing sidelight. Des Graz wrote to one paper stating that the firm had, of course, appreciated the importance of dispersing Newton's work and had therefore made special efforts to do the recording of the occasion justice. Taylor, in his patient way, merely smiled.

In the event, interest in the sale was limited to a small circle of dealers and collectors. Among the latter were the brothers Maynard and Geoffrey Keynes, the famous economist and his younger brother, a practising surgeon and distinguished bibliographer. It was Geoffrey who had studied the catalogue and was anxious to buy the items of correspondence between Newton and Robert Boyle. He urged Maynard to go with him to the sale, even though at the outset the economist had little idea of the material that was to come under the hammer. As the sale proceeded he realised the importance of many of the documents in his chosen area of interest – the history of thought. Geoffrey bought his Boyle

---

three by Newton), as well as three bound letterbooks of 940 letters of his official correspondence. They were sold respectively to Gabriel Wells for £1,600 and to Maggs for £800. There was also a letterbook of correspondence between Pepys and the Rev. John Matthews about Pepys's nephew Samuel Jackson, which was then unknown and unpublished.

items and together the brothers purchased 39 lots out of a total of 322. Both were surprised that prices had been so modest. In fact, the sale realised only £9,030: £3,116 on the Monday and £5,914 on the Tuesday. During the rest of the week Maynard Keynes took time off to call on all the dealers who had bought items in order to acquire as many as possible for himself.

Some years later he bequeathed them (together with his library) to Kings College, Cambridge, but not before he had written a paper on Newton,[1] based very much on a reading of these documents, in which he looked upon the great scientist as 'the last of the magicians . . . with one foot in the Middle Ages and one foot treading a path for modern science', and certainly Newton's long pre-occupation with alchemy, transmutation and the abandonment of orthodox belief bore him out. But the material also demonstrated why Newton was 'a wrapt, consecrated solitary, pursuing his studies by intense introspection with a mental endurance perhaps never equalled. . . . His peculiar gift was the power of holding continuously in his mind a purely mental problem until he had seen straight through it'.

As an old man Taylor recalled[2] that his first reading of Keynes's paper had given him as much pleasure as anything he could remember, for the ideas expounded seemed a direct extrapolation of what he had endeavoured to project in the catalogue. Taylor was also fascinated by the growth in Newtonian studies, which had become something of an academic industry in the decades after the war, and their heavy dependence on the exposure of the Lymington papers.[3] (Indeed, the position of Newton has now become so prominent in the public mind that he occupies the back of the current English pound note.)

Three other major items in the sale were acquired by generous donors and given immediately afterwards to the appropriate institutions. Lord Wakefield bought the three volumes of the Mint papers (Taylor had lovingly catalogued them as 529 separate items but they were sold as one lot to Gabriel Wells for £1,100) and presented them to the Royal Mint; Sir Robert Hadfield donated the Halley letters and others to the Royal Society, and Dr. Rosenbach's brother, Philip, passed the Kneller portrait of Newton which had been included in the sale, to the National Portrait Gallery at the price it had cost him.

There had been a sale in the previous year (7 May 1935) in which the published works of Newton had also figured prominently. This was of the library of the Radcliffe Observatory at Oxford, sold by order of the Trustees. Here also John Taylor had done his utmost to stimulate interest. The library had been established in the late eighteenth century but it was mainly Stephen Peter Rigaud, Radcliffe Observer from 1827 to 1839, who had built it up because he was interested in the work of the older astronomers. The 311 lots aroused

1. *Newton, the Man*, published posthumously in the Royal Society's Newton Tercentenary celebrations, July 1946. The text had been prepared for press and read to the Society by Sir Geoffrey Keynes.
2. In a series of interviews with the author.
3. A full scientific appreciation of the documents in the sale is currently in preparation by Peter Spargo of the University of Cape Town.

disappointingly little interest. There were first editions of Copernicus's *De Revolutionibus*; of Newton's *Principia* (and almost all his other works); Hevelius's *Machina Coelestis*, rare because almost every copy was destroyed by fire before publication; Wright's translation of Stevin's *Haven-Finding Art*, a revolutionary book on the science of early navigation, and Halley's annotated copy of Flamsteed's *Catalogue of Stars*. The whole sale raised only £2,422. Today such a sale would cause an enormous stir, and the first edition of Newton's *Principia* alone would fetch five times that sum. While the icy clutches of the slump were still showing little sign of a thaw and the two sales demonstrated an almost universal indifference to the history of science, from that time onwards an awakening of interest in the subject became discernible that finally blossomed twenty-five years later.

The Rothschild Sale

The year 1937 at Sotheby's began well, with the library of Lt.-Col. W. E. Moss, which contained some of William Blake's finest illustrated books, and then the pictures and magnificent library of Lord Aldenham. It was again Dr. Rosenbach who stimulated some of the most spirited bidding in both sales, but this was almost completely over-shadowed by the announcement from Bond Street of an event scheduled to take place in the late spring, an on-the-premises sale of what was virtually an institution.

It seems entirely appropriate that house sales should have progressed from the merely magnificent to the truly palatial in 1937, the year of the coronation of George VI. London was full of distinguished visitors from all over the world, including scores of Indian princes and other Eastern potentates. In mid-April of that year Sotheby's organised what seemed like a lavish exhibition in the very centre of London which these – and thousands of lesser mortals – lapped up with delight. This was at 148 Piccadilly, the residence which Baron Lionel Nathan de Rothschild had built to his own design in 1865. (It was he who had lent the British government of the day £4,000,000 to buy shares in the Suez Canal.) In it he housed furniture and collections mostly acquired between 1830 and 1860, probably the best period of all times to make such acquisitions. His successor, the first Lord Rothschild, had added little to the contents, though his wife, Emma Luise, inherited a number of fine pictures, superb silver and objets d'art, from her father, Baron Carl von Rothschild of Frankfurt after his death in 1886. The house had recently passed to the young Victor Rothschild[1] and the contents were to be sold by his order. The Crown Lease on the property was about to fall due and the family had no alternative house for the elaborate furnishings. They also envisaged that it would be increasingly difficult to inhabit such a mansion in years to come. It cost a small fortune merely to remove the dust sheets and to prepare it for residence each time the family

1. Now Lord Rothschild, Chairman of the English branch of the merchant banking firm, a distinguished biologist, wartime bomb-disposal expert, an enthusiastic book collector and probably best known as Chairman of the Government's 'Think-tank' between 1971 and 1976.

returned to it. The possibility of a second war in Europe was certainly an unspoken threat that added logic to the dispersal of what A. C. R. Carter called so much 'pomp and magnificence in the decorative accessories of a past age'.

The four-day sale was to be held in the ballroom of 148 Piccadilly. The *Observer* described this as 'surely one of the most sumptuous rooms in London', and continued: 'Its decorations include four huge, circular reliefs by the Danish sculptor, Thorwaldsen, and the windows are hung with immense sweeping curtains of satin embroidered with river goddesses and other allegorical and classical figures. In this room stands what is probably the most important piece of furniture in the house, a Louis XVI Secretaire of tulipwood with a marble top and ornamented with ormolu and Sèvres porcelain panels, made by Martin Carlin'.

Another newspaper (the *Morning Post*) reported that formerly it had required three months of intense activity to prepare the house for a ball. Sotheby's had had less than that to prepare the catalogue. The compilation of the furniture section was Temple Williams's crowning achievement at Sotheby's – and his swan song.[1] Relatively little was then known about the makers of eighteenth-century French furniture, though there were old family inventories to help. In addition, Lady Rothschild, Victor's mother, had a fund of knowledge about the virtues of the major pieces and the faults of the minor ones. Temple Williams enormously enjoyed his task, for French furniture of such quality – and in such quantity – hardly ever came on to the market.

The marble walls of the house precluded the hanging of many pictures, but the twenty-odd seventeenth-century Dutch paintings included in the sale were of a charm and grace that had not often come Sotheby's way and almost all the canvases represented major achievements by the artists concerned. Borenius included some of their antecedents in the catalogue where the provenance was known, but a marvellously relaxed *Courtyard Scene* by Pieter de Hoogh, two out of three interiors by Gabriel Metsu (one, though signed, was probably a copy), a Frans van Mieris conversation-piece, an Isack van Ostade and a Jakob Verkolje were catalogued with only the briefest of descriptions.

It was, in fact, the Pieter de Hoogh, the fifth lot in a sale of nearly 800 items, that set the tone of national interest and excitement about the event. The BBC decided to broadcast the sale of the pictures live, something that had never been done before. Henry Rham in his precise, rather dry manner assisted the commentator with explanations of what was happening and in identifying the people making the bids. Both the BBC and listeners were delighted with the results.[2]

The ballroom was absolutely packed for the occasion. Every seat was taken

1. He resigned in May 1937 and joined Blairmans, where almost single-handed he created a taste and a market for Regency furniture, which was then totally unappreciated. After twenty-five years at Blairmans he set up in business on his own.
2. Rham did not get a fee for this, but the BBC presented him with a silver cigarette case inscribed '. . . with many thanks for your assistance on the occasion of the Rothschild Sale'. Another sale was broadcast from Sotheby's in July 1937 where Rham again took part.

and the gangway crowded with late-comers, mostly dealers, who all kept their hats on. Rarely can any ballroom have seen such a fine display of bowlers, black Homburgs and Anthony Edens. Charles des Graz took the sale. Borenius started the bidding for the De Hoogh with £1,000, but within seconds the price had jumped to £10,000. It then became a competition between the great Dutch collector, D. G. van Beuningen (with his friend, Frits Lugt, sitting beside him), the dealer Rosenberg of Amsterdam and Paris, and Colin Agnew. Van Beuningen took the price up to £16,000, Agnew topped it by £500, Van Beuningen nodded again at £17,000, but Agnew countered with a further £500 to win the day. Nobody had expected the record price at the 1928 Six sale of £11,666, or indeed the last De Hoogh interior to be sold in England (by Robinson & Fisher in 1914) at 8,200 guineas, to be exceeded. The reserve had been a mere £6,500. A few moments later Rosenberg received fierce competition in acquiring a Nicholas Maes of *A Maidservant Returning from Market* for £1,100 (the reserve was £600) and Agnew scored again at £2,800 for the first Metsu of *A Woman Cleaning Fish* against the Paris dealer Asscher (and a reserve of £900). The painting had previously been in the collections of Gildemeester, Meulman, the Duc d'Alberg, De la Hante, Beckford at Fonthill – and was sold in 1823 to Higginson in whose sale in 1846 it had fetched 520 guineas. It was mentioned by Smith[1] and again by Hofstede de Groot.[2] It was not often that a work by a minor Dutch master turned up with such a desirable pedigree. The charming interior scene with three figures called *The Letter* by that rare artist, J. Verkolje, a follower of Terborch, was another major surprise. Rosenberg bought it against quick-fire bidding from Legatt and Asscher at £1,800. The reserve had been only £400, but the picture had aroused particular admiration during the viewing.

The total figure for the twenty-one pictures came to £33,620. The papers said 'triumphantly successful', 'far exceeding expectations', 'Bids leap at Rothschild Sale', and though four pictures had been bought in,[3] that part alone of the Rothschild Sale remained one of the highlights of sale-room history in the period between the two World Wars.

Ultimately, five of these paintings were included in the great exhibition of Dutch art held at the Royal Academy in 1952; four found their way to the Mauritshuis Museum in The Hague, including the Verkolje which has since been lent to numerous outside exhibitions. The four paintings acquired by Agnew's were bought on behalf of Lionel Rothschild. Three of these were later in the collection of E. W. Fattorini in Yorkshire.

More, much more was to come, as Vere Pilkington – a close friend of Victor Rothschild's – took over the rostrum for the rest of the first day and dealers

---

1. John Smith, a *Catalogue Raisonné of the Works of the most Eminent Dutch, Flemish and French Painters*, 1829–42.
2. De Groot's work was an almost total revision of Smith's magnum opus published between 1908 and 1927.
3. They were a Kobell, a supposedly dubious Metsu of *An Interior of the Painter's Studio*, an Ostade and a David Teniers landscape.

from all over the world settled down to the buying of the amazing selection of oriental works of art; porcelain and *cloisonné*; the Venetian, German and Arab glass; the carvings in ivory and wood; the rock crystal; the Sèvres and Meissen porcelain (the Sèvres fared badly – an imposing and beautifully decorated dinner and dessert service of 225 pieces fetched only £175), and excitement mounted again for the final item, a rare St. Porchaire Faience 'Biberon' (Henri II ware) Ewer. It had been decided to cancel its reserve at the last moment, for the piece was damaged (a careless butler had dropped it), but Borenius had to pay what was generally regarded as an amazing price, £600, to acquire it for a private client. Earlier on, two remarkable pieces of jade fetched spectacular results. Lot 46, a very fine, dark green jade inkscreen, elaborately carved and with a long inscription in gold, described as Imperial work, Ch'ien Lung, and known to have been brought from the Summer Palace at Peking by Captain the Hon. C. Thesiger of the Inniskilling Dragoons in 1862, fetched £520; and a massive Ming jade buffalo brought £560. It passed into the collection of Sir Bernard Eckstein and was re-sold with his collections at Sotheby's in 1948 for £3,000.

On that first day many people had arrived two hours before the sale was due to start to claim their seats. During the next two days dealers from all over the Continent, particularly from Paris, turned up in numbers which were totally unprecedented to vie for the primarily French furniture and furnishings. Their Gallic tactics of appraisal before the sale caused some consternation and much amusement. Small huddles of them round every major piece noisily refuted the veracity of the catalogue descriptions. Every detail was minutely examined and condemned. To those not familiar with this technique, the effect was more than a little alarming. On a few occasions the deprecation seems to have been warranted. Some pieces were evidently nineteenth-century copies and not eighteenth-century originals as was at first thought. But the presence and competition from Edward Duveen, Wildenstein and other celebrated firms kept prices well up, at any rate by the standards of their own day, bargains though the pieces may seem to us now. Duveen bought the Carlin Secretaire for £8,000 (the reserve had been raised from £1,200 to £2,000 just before the sale); Wildenstein paid £3,100 for a very fine Louis XV commode 'in the style of Cressent' (it had not been considered worthy of a reserve), and a pair of outstanding Louis XV marquetry commodes, made and signed by Jacques Dubois, M.E., for £1,750; M. Helft of Paris bought the widely publicised 'Ceres Table', its top elaborately inlaid in the manner of Boulle, for £670; his countryman, Chalon, acquired a Louis XV rosewood and tulipwood bureau table by Durand, for £1,050 (the piece was both signed and branded with the mark E.H.B.), and Ben Simon, also of Paris, acquired a considerable number of items. A minor Anglo-Saxon triumph was Lady Violet Henderson's purchase at £340 of a splendid Hepplewhite Carlton House writing-table, found in the housekeeper's room. Francis Mallett, Frank Partridge, Mossie Harris and English provincial dealers ultimately all bought shrewdly among the less sensational but often remarkably beautiful pieces.

Considering the vast range of items included from what was after all a family home, very little was withdrawn before each sale session started. The heartache of impending disappearance often causes owners to create last-minute lacunae in on-the-premises sales in this way. In fact, several items of furniture taken from the other Rothschild home at Tring were included in the sale at 148 Piccadilly. But a Louis XV gilt suite of six upholstered *fauteuils* and a settee, and two wider *fauteuils* and another settee *en suite* (Lots 393 and 394) *were* taken out of the sale. The ten pieces subsequently passed to Victor's son, Jacob Rothschild and re-appeared in a sale at Sotheby's in 1967, attributed to Heurtaut. In 1937 such pieces were unremarkable: they existed in quantity. Thirty years later they had become relatively rare. They fetched £26,000, more than half the price of the entire furniture and works of art from 148 Piccadilly. It is an indirect pointer to the history of the art market.

A major disappointment of the sale was the comparative lack of interest in the many magnificent rock crystal and other chandeliers – in Lady Rothschild's boudoir, the library, at the top of the grand staircase, in the West drawing-room and in the ballroom itself.[1] The most important were bought in. The remainder went for low prices. One echo – possibly apocryphal – of this aspect of the sale only reached Temple Williams years later, long after the war. He had cata-logued the chandelier in question as gilt-bronze (the word 'ormolu' was not used in the catalogue). It had hung a long way above the reach of even the tallest step-ladder. It had been bought during the sale by a Paris dealer. One of his forebears had made and sold it to the Rothschild family early in the nineteenth century. The metal used: solid gold.

The quantity of silver in the house was enormous and its quality very much in the Rothschild tradition: massive, well-made early nineteenth-century English table silver for use[2] on the one hand; elaborately sculptural, trophy-like items, made by German silversmiths, for decoration, on the other. Many of the latter had been commissioned on behalf of the German craft guilds in the sixteenth and seventeenth centuries and their symbolism was often connected with the guilds' activities, for they were displayed *en masse* on festive occasions. After the Napoleonic upheavals and the waning of the guilds, this plate and that of the impoverished nobility was dispersed, and Baron Carl had been able to acquire the pick of the great quantities that came on to the market at that time. The diplomatic wording of some of the catalogue entries indicated that not all the magnificent standing cups and covers were in their original condition, but even so, Emma Luise Rothschild's inheritance (she received one-fifth of her father's collection) – for that was how they came to be at 148 Piccadilly – was certainly the largest and most resplendent assembly of late Gothic and Mannerist silver of this sort ever to come into the English sale-room. It caused worldwide in-terest among dealers knowledgeable in this field and many of their purchases on that occasion are now treasured items in museums both in Europe and America.

1. In a pre-sale description of items at 148 Piccadilly, A. C. R. Carter had written: 'The dazzling rock crystal chandeliers throughout the house deserve a chapter to themselves'.
2. There were, for example, 240 solid silver dinner plates and 66 similar soup plates.

It had been decided to move the silver to Bond Street, and during the three-day sale there it realised just short of £40,000, at that time the highest total ever achieved at Sotheby's for a silver sale. Among the buyers on the first day were many private individuals, including Sir Kameshwar Singh, the Maharajad-hiraja of Darbhanga, the head of the Maithil Brahmans in India, who owned nine palaces and was to figure prominently at Bond Street sales during his stay in London for the coronation.[1] On the last day the professionals from all over Europe had it all their own way. Mr. Vecht from Amsterdam bought the Nep-tune Salt by Christian van Vianen (for £1,150); an ostrich egg mounted in silver gilt by Elias Geier fetched £2,900 from S. R. Rosenberg, a prominent buyer throughout every part of the sale. S. J. Phillips, the Bond Street dealer, paid £2,700 for a globe supported on the stooping figure of Hercules, by the Nuremberg silversmith, Abraham Gessner. H. N. Bier of Vienna bought a fine, tall, silver gilt cup and cover with a finial of David standing on the head of Goliath, by Martin Hechel of Augsburg, for £1,550.

Virtually nothing was bought in, though Victor Rothschild bought two of his own small, silver gilt, sixteenth-century *Setzbecher* for £145 on the final day. When the sale was over and the total had been established at £125,262, *The Times* complimented Sotheby's on the success of the occasion and 'the excellent cataloguing and arrangements'. A photograph of Victor Rothschild published in the *Sketch* a few days after the sale showed him striding along a London pavement, taking a cigarette out of his case, his beautiful wife on his arm – looking confident and contented. This, the caption implied, is the young man whose name has been on everyone's lips during the last two weeks. His has been a triumph in the family tradition.

---

1. He also bought a magnificent diamond necklace which had once belonged to Marie Antoinette. It was being sold by order of her direct descendants, the Archduchess Blanca of Austria and her sister, Beatrix Massimo, who had jointly inherited it. It consisted of twenty-nine beautifully graduated, square-cut stones, a single stone snap and thirteen pear-shaped diamonds, all of unusual brilliance. Immediately afterwards a number of rare black pearls belonging to Viscountess Cowdray were offered for sale, but despite the fact that such pearls hardly ever came up at auction, the bidding for them was sluggish and they were bought in. Most unusually Charles des Graz actually stated from the rostrum that they had been with-drawn because 'the owner's price had not been reached'.

26

Another War in Sight

THE summer season of 1937 had finished with a good deal of excitement
that seemed to bode well for the future: a Rembrandt self-portrait sold for
£11,500; thirty-four illuminated manuscripts of rare magnificence and *incunabula* consigned from Clumber, the seat of the Duke of Newcastle, realised
£38,000; a series of paintings by Canaletto originally commissioned by Consul
Smith and sent for sale by the Earl of Lovelace fetched £13,682; a fine collection of oriental ceramics assembled by a wealthy Amsterdam East India
merchant, W. F. van Heukelom, sold for just over £15,000 – and to be
entrusted with this sale was as much a feather in Sotheby's cap as the Mensing
Sale had been in the realm of books. There had been disappointments too, of
course; for example, over the £2,700 realised by a large number of letters by
Elizabeth Barrett Browning about her elopement. The pundits all remembered
the furore over the bidding in the 1913 Browning Sale, but the competition now
was in a much lower key. One of the most interesting items from a historical
point of view which came up for sale in July 1937 consisted of the typescript
depositions taken by the examining magistrate which related to the murder of
the Russian Imperial family at Ekaterinburg in July 1918. They fetched a mere
£100. An illustrated sixteenth-century treatise on mathematics in manuscript
form with the name 'A. Dürer' clearly on the title page, which had been sent to
Sotheby's from Hungary with a whole library and aroused considerable expectations among all who had seen it, fetched £30! Yet taken together with the
Rothschild, Greffuhle and Clumber sales it had been Sotheby's best season
since the boom years in the late Twenties. Sales totalled £840,000 and the firm
proudly announced to the press that as many as eighty-three items had
realised more than a thousand pounds. Reviewing the season in the *Daily
Telegraph*, A. C. R. Carter took up this theme of steady improvement. He had
worked out that all the London auction rooms between them had disposed of
forty-nine pictures and drawings at the magic figure of £1,400 or more in the
first seven months of 1937, compared to only twenty-seven in the whole of the
previous year and only eight in 1932. He remembered nostalgically that 'in that
annus mirabilis of picture sales, 1927, as many as 130 attained this distinction',
and continued, 'Shall we ever see such golden days again'?

It was, therefore, with high hopes that the trade looked upon the beginning
of the 1937–38 season. Sotheby's received an unusual amount of preliminary
publicity for a sale announced for four days early in November 1937. This was
of an immense collection of rings sent to Bond Street by a consortium of London
dealers who had acquired it from the descendants of the late Edouard Guilhou
of Paris. Guilhou had bought actively at the great sales of Spitzer and Baron
Pichon towards the end of the nineteenth century and his collections of

medieval and Renaissance art, and particularly his fine collection of antique jewellery, had been sold soon after his death in 1905 and 1906 in Paris. The rings were, therefore, a remarkable left-over from a previous generation. The comprehensiveness of the collection was unparalleled, except perhaps for that formed privately by Sir Augustus Wollaston Franks, keeper of the Department of Antiquities at the British Museum, to which he had left it in 1897. The two thousand Guilhou rings covered every era from, as Geoffrey Hobson wrote on the title page, 'the Egypt of the Pharaohs to the France of the first Empire'. The beauty of the collection struck an immediate chord of response in all who saw it.

The catalogue was unusually elaborate and clearly the result of long labours. J. B. Caldecott, who should have tackled it in the normal course of events, happened to be overwhelmed with other chores, and an outside academic expert approached by Sotheby's turned the job down because of illness. A young man, Peter Cecil Wilson, who had joined the furniture department as a trainee assistant to replace Temple Williams at the end of 1936, was offered the task during the long summer closure. When Hobson heard about it, he said 'let him try; we'll see what he makes of it'. Peter Wilson had come to Sotheby's through one of those haphazard series of coincidences that were regarded as a perfectly normal method of recruitment forty years ago. Ultimately such appointments depended on the instant recognition of vital though latent qualities in the young, by men like Hobson and des Graz who had been through the same treadmill themselves. Peter Wilson remembers a formidable series of interviews with the partners which followed an initial, chance encounter with Vere Pilkington through a mutual friend over a weekend in Gloucestershire. The first of the interviews was with Felix Warre, who adopted a magisterial manner on such occasions that would frighten away all but the most resolute. The second, with Geoffrey Hobson, was also daunting but there was immediate *rapport* between the older and the younger man. Des Graz proved the most welcoming of the partners despite his reputation for chilliness.

Peter Wilson came to Sotheby's from the *Connoisseur* where, after a short period on the editorial side, he found himself travelling about the country checking that newsagents stocked the paper, and manning the *Connoisseur* stand at the Antique Dealers' Fair at Grosvenor House: it seemed that the editor, Edward Wenham, had resented the young man's arrival and refused to let him continue with editorial work – possibly because the introduction had been through a kindly word from Marion Davies, Randolph Hearst's mistress. Hearst owned the National Magazine Company, which in turn owned the *Connoisseur*. Before that Wilson had spent a short time at Reuter's. But at Sotheby's the immensely tall, young man had quickly made his mark. He applied himself assiduously to the study of furniture. Fred Rose, his immediate superior, was helpful. Outside the office a particularly knowledgeable tutor and close friend was Margaret Jourdain, famed for her books on eighteenth-century interior decoration and English furniture. At the time of the Rothschild Sale, Sotheby's had been deluged with requests from important collectors and visiting dignitaries for specially conducted private views of the Piccadilly Mansion and its contents. Wilson was often deputed to show them round. His charm, courtesy and knowledge had gone down well.

The Guilhou Sale was his first major challenge. It meant weeks of study for long hours in museum libraries and leafing through old records. Seymour de Ricci, who had first catalogued the whole collection, had pointed out some of the most remarkable rings. Now the Sotheby catalogue supplied a vast amount of additional information. Dealers and collectors streamed to Bond Street, and the sale was a considerable success. The young cataloguer had also devoted a great deal of energy to getting the sale publicised. The many fine catalogue illustrations were widely reproduced. Caldecott might make sarcastic comments behind Wilson's back on over-cataloguing, but it had worked and the four days raised over £15,000, a good deal more than anyone had expected.

It was an ironic twist of fate that, following hard on the Guilhou Sale, came a remarkable collection of early English silver which, though sold anonymously, was widely recognised as belonging to none other than William Randolph Hearst, Peter Wilson's late employer, who was divesting himself of some of his vast range of antique property. But his agents had purchased most of the items in relatively recent times, and though the whole sale raised £26,000, this was not much more than half what the American millionaire had had to pay in the pre-slump days. Thus an Elizabethan silver gilt cup and cover which had cost Hearst £3,275 in 1930 (a record at £165 an ounce, as silver was then sold), was now bought in because no one would offer even £500 for it.

Another disappointment was the sale of the library formed by the late Mortimer L. Schiff, a New York banker, which had been been brought to London where it was thought that the French literature and superb eighteenth-century illustrated books in fine bindings would find a better market.[1] But by the spring of 1938 the political situation was not conducive to active collecting in this field, especially by Frenchmen who were not only highly sensitive to the threat of another war, but whose currency had recently suffered serious depreciation in relation to sterling. Not surprisingly, the resultant prices veered from the merely unexciting to the totally disastrous. Thus 75 books which Schiff had bought at the Hoe Sale in 1911 for a total of $24,300 now realised the equivalent of $22,600, a drop of 7 per cent after twenty-six years, which *The Times* regarded as a 'remarkable example of the supremacy of London as an artistic and literary market'. Truly a sign of the times.

In contrast, a third sale from a single source did remarkably well for its time. The Winkworth family played an important role in Sotheby's history. For many years Jim Kiddell had been on very friendly terms with Stephen D. Winkworth, a collector in the old and finest tradition, who devoted his entire life to nothing else. He had bought his delightful house, 'Lovelands', in Walton Heath, Surrey, in 1910, and also had a London house at 13 Craven Hill Gardens. When he came up to London from the country (usually wearing a

1. Once again Christie's sold Schiff's furniture, pictures, statues and other works of art at the same time.

colourful waistcoat and a wide-brimmed, black hat at a rakish angle), he would set out in a taxi on his hunting rounds, starting at Phillips, Son & Neale (at the top of Bond Street in those days); then down to Sotheby's and on to Christie's, Robinson & Fisher, and finally to Foster's. His two houses were furnished from top to bottom with antique English furniture of a very high standard. The enquiring eye would be startled by an endless multitude of fine clocks, English and Irish cut glass and interesting pictures, including an outstanding collection of English glass paintings. More noticeably, every nook and cranny of 'Lovelands' was filled with early Chinese porcelain and pottery, and other oriental works of art. It was indeed in Winkworth's London home that the twelve original 'dragons' met to found the Oriental Ceramic Society in 1921.

Visitors to 'Lovelands' reported that every available shelf and table was covered with antique objects, and Mrs. Winkworth admitted that her husband had to hide the new purchases under sofas, and sometimes even under his bed. One ingenious device he employed which helped to relieve the congestion was to have moulded shelves fixed above every door in the house. This was a marvellous way of showing the outsize *famille rose* and *famille verte* plates which were his particular favourites. Corner cupboards and corner cabinets, fronted with glass, mirror, plain and decorated doors, housed further masses of porcelain and other *objets d'art*. Winkworth also had a weakness for chairs, and fascinatingly rare examples crowded every room. A contemporary wrote: 'In the drawing room one cannot but be even more impressed by the beauty and variety of the furniture, mainly early walnut. Stephen Winkworth bought largely by eye. Only after he had satisfied his aesthetic taste did he look into the question of dates and technical details; and his eye did not fail him. He evidently liked the flowing lines of chairs of the Queen Anne period, and there is a great variety of the most beautiful examples *still* at "Lovelands".'

The use of the word 'still' is interesting, because this particular visitor was writing *after* Winkworth had had a major four-day sale at Sotheby's in April 1933 to relieve the congestion. Winkworth insisted that his friend, Jim Kiddell, should be responsible for the sale, and it was, no doubt, due to Jim's skilful efforts to publicise the sale that the sale-room was crowded even at a time when the slump was at its very worst. The attendance certainly helped prices too, and though the resulting £19,334 for 787 supremely fine lots may seem appalling by today's standards,[1] it was a surprisingly good result then. 611 lots solely of oriental porcelain and works of art occupied the first three days. They included early Chinese wares of the Han, T'ang, Sung and Ming, through to the Ch'ing dynasties, and though the dealers were there in force, many pieces were bought by private collectors and museums. The fourth day was devoted to the cut glass, Chinese and European lacquer, clocks, Chinese paintings on glass and fine walnut, mahogany and satinwood furniture. A great number of items were so well known that Jim Kiddell was able to include a note on the title page of the

1. In the 1938 sale a fourteenth-century bowl with a copper-red flower scroll made £31. It reappeared at Christie's in November 1974 and was sold for £44,100.

catalogue which stated that: 'Many of the pieces have been exhibited at various times and noted and illustrated in the Standard Works and Periodicals on Chinese Art; also in the Dictionary of Furniture'.

After Stephen Winkworth's death in January 1938, a second four-day sale was held at Sotheby's in April of that year. Again it consisted principally of Chinese ceramics and old English furniture, and though also remarkably well attended, the increasingly depressed tenor of the period was reflected in the result of £12,000 for 711 very fine lots. As the *Connoisseur* reported: 'Only four lots reached the dignity of three figures. These were a Küan Yao bottle of the Sung dynasty, covered with close-fitting crackled pale lavender glaze, which realised £180; a Yung Chêng vase decorated in relief with a stork by a willow tree for £140; a K'ang Hsi vase enamelled with a peach, pomegranate and finger citron, the "Three Fruits" symbolic of the three abundances of "Years, Sons and Happiness", £120; and a pair of Yung Chêng saucers of shallow form decorated with figures of lovers, standing on mats, with a table in the background, £145'.

There was a third sale from Winkworth's collection on 20 April 1939. It consisted exclusively of 'old English glass transfer pictures', some 166 lots which fetched £1,483 10s. – once more a seemingly thin price but, one gathers, a very great deal more than Winkworth had paid for them. This collection too was known to a wider public because it had been the subject of a number of articles. One was by Egan Mew in the *Connoisseur* in June 1929, who had written: 'Such a widely ranging collection as that of Mr. Stephen Winkworth is, in itself, a brilliant social history of the fashionable world of the eighteenth century. In sport, Sartorius, Seymour and the rest show us the love of the hunting field and the pleasures of the race course. In the Arts, Houston has a gay series of designs, instinct with the delicate dilettantism of the long days of Horace Walpole. The French interiors and various English conversation pieces and the hundreds of portraits of beauties, professional and otherwise, of aristocratic ladies and their children and of all the famous men of the time in politics, in war, in the liberal professions, form a gallery at once informing, sociologically valuable and of a decorative quality outshining the efforts of much original work'. Although initially produced in large quantities, not many of these beautiful but fragile objects have survived two centuries of social progress, and no other such sizeable collection has ever come up for sale again.[1]

Even though the 1938 season finished with the sale of three collections – all quite unique in their own way – the Damiron Maiolica, the Ham House Library (which included twelve Caxtons) and the Suzannet Dickens letters (there were over a thousand of them), the turnover had plummeted to just short of £500,000, a drop of 40 per cent on the previous year's results. In December of 1938 the *Yorkshire Post* was delighted to note that Mr. Peter Wilson, who 'though he is keenly interested in books and pictures, his special taste is for

1. Stephen Winkworth's talented son, William Wilberforce ('Billy') Winkworth, formally enters our story after the war.

decorative period furniture', had become a director and partner in the firm. The Yorkshire connection was with Peter's father, Sir Mathew Wilson, who lived at Eshton Hall, Gargrave in Craven, and the *Post* recalled that there was a celebrated library at Mr. Wilson's parental home which had been formed by a famous bibliophile, Miss Frances Mary Richardson Currer,[1] when she had lived there early in the nineteenth century, though part of it had been sold years earlier by Sotheby's when the firm was still at Wellington Street.

Once it had been recognised that he had talents beyond the merely social (which was apparently the reason why the older partners thought he might be useful to the firm), Peter had been promoted over his boss's head. The suave manner resulting from an Eton and Oxford education concealed a determination that few had originally suspected. His salary for the following year was to be £400. He had bought £5,000 worth of shares from Major Warre with money put up by his wife. At first the future did not look too bleak, but collections came into the firm in much smaller numbers. Of the few that did, many were limited selections of the very finest quality brought with them by European refugees escaping from the threat of Hitler's growing domain. The turnover shrank again, and by the end of the 1938–39 season it had decreased to £347,000. Despite the sale of the famous Schwerdt collection of sporting books, the book department's turnover was less than £100,000 for the first time since the beginning of the century. The net profit had crashed to no more than £181 5s. 3d. Sales had varied from one extreme to another. There was 'Stoney Jack's' stock-in-trade – a hundred old shoe boxes full of excavated bric-à-brac from the curiosity shop of George Fabyan Lawrence just off the Wandsworth High Street, who had recently died. He was nick-named 'Stoney Jack' in the trade because he liked buying objects found by London navvies employed in excavating for the foundations of new buildings.[2] There was also an unusual sale of musical boxes and a few musical instruments. A huge Swiss, early nineteenth-century 'Grand Format Piece' which rolled out the overtures to the operas of Bellini, Rossini, Weber and Herold fetched £13, and an early Regency square piano of 5½ octaves made a mere £2. In contrast there was a record payment of £6,800 for Goya's superb portrait of the beautiful actress Dona Antonia Zarate from Cam House. The previous highest price for a Goya sold at auction was £3,465 paid in 1916 for a portrait of an *Unknown Lady in Black*. Finally, there had also taken place the first of what became a long sequence of sales – many held *after* the war – of the library of Sir Leicester Harmsworth. Again it was disappointment all the way. A first edition of Goldsmith's *Vicar of Wakefield* in contemporary calf, now raised £340. Only ten years earlier Harmsworth had paid £1,470 for it. On the very same day as this volume was sold to an American visitor, twenty-six works painted by Charles Shannon RA, a great favourite in his day, raised a melancholy total of £158 in another room at Bond Street.

1. See p. 51*n*.
2. Very few people knew that Lawrence also catalogued Sotheby's antiquities sales: his knowledge was far-reaching and only his eccentricity had precluded a more scholarly career.

Hobson and Warre, after a brief post-slump return to relative affluence, were now back on a reduced salary of £500 a year each. It seemed a poor reward for thirty years of very hard work. But they had an even bigger hurdle ahead of them.

27

Wartime

THROUGHOUT the Thirties Jim Kiddell had been on frequent trips to Germany. Latterly an important part of each visit had been to keep informed about the political situation through discussions with Colonel Birch, still actively engaged as Sotheby's agent there. After the Munich crisis Birch had no illusions about the fact that war was now inevitable, despite Chamberlain's assurances to the contrary. It was simply a question of time. Kiddell duly reported each conversation to the partners and by the early summer of 1939 des Graz began to take energetic steps to mobilise the re-establishment of Postal Censorship, of which he was the nominal deputy head.

Deciding on how to plan the future after the end of the July sales was a bewildering business. Certainly in July and August most people went on holiday hoping that the worst would not happen. But Sotheby's and Christie's both left matters vague. Builders were called in to Bond Street to undertake the usual maintenance and routine repair work that was needed at the end of the sale season. Before Munich they had already strengthened the old cellars that had once housed Basil Woodd, the wine merchants (who had occupied the premises before Sotheby's took them over), and converted them into an air raid shelter. On the day war was finally declared they simply upped sticks and departed, leaving their work half completed and a whole lot of gutters blocked. The first war damage at Bond Street was a minor flood when it started to rain!

Des Graz had departed with Vere Pilkington, Peter Wilson, John Taylor and a good many others into the mysterious realms of Postal Censorship, first at Liverpool though eventually most of the organisation moved to Bermuda, Trinidad and New York. Many of the younger porters joined the army, the reservists were called up, the middle-aged went into the police force. All this had been planned months in advance. The remaining partners at once decided to close 'for the duration', a phrase much in vogue at the time. Many members of the staff were paid off. Jim Kiddell, who had remained on the Artillery Reserve for years, found himself a field officer's job under an old Gunner chief in ammunition – at three times the £500 a year salary he was still getting at Sotheby's. Three members of the staff, who had been training in their spare time for months at the nearby headquarters of the Queen Victoria Rifles, joined their unit in Kent. They were Privates Ernie Collman and Charles Dawkins from the clerical staff and Captain Tim Munby, who had joined Sotheby's from Quaritch as a book cataloguer two years earlier. These three became the firm's first victims of the war. In May 1940 their unit was despatched to Calais in frenzied haste to stop the German armoured divisions getting through to Dunkirk where the British Expeditionary Force was waiting for rescue after the German breakthrough. For five days three battalions, including the first Battalion of the

Queen Victoria Rifles, defended Calais against the most intense onslaught of
dive-bombing, heavy artillery and tanks. But the Q.V.R. had had no infantry
training, and most of their weapons and all of their transport had been left in
England. It was one of the war's most harrowing examples of muddling
through,[1] but the three battalions held the Germans for five vital days while the
major evacuation at Dunkirk took place. Though casualties were enormously
high, Collman, Dawkins and Munby all survived to spend the next four years
as prisoners-of-war in Germany.

In the autumn of 1939, the paralysing holocaust that those who had been
involved in the war in the trenches only twenty years earlier expected, failed to
materialise. The lull, as everyone knows, later became known as the 'Phoney
War'. Hobson and Warre begged Jim Kiddell to stay with the firm. After a good
deal of heart searching, long consultations with his family and pressures from
collectors and the trade alike, he returned to Bond Street. A skeleton staff was
re-employed, many called back from early retirement, and an opening book
sale was planned for late November. The press found the fact that Sotheby's
and Christie's planned to re-open a newsworthy item and there was widespread
comment on it. Tom Hodge's death early in December at the age of seventy-
nine was truly symbolic of the end of an era. There was universal flashback to
'the man who *found* a Gutenberg Bible'. This referred to an incident in the late
1890s when Tom was called to Lord Hopetoun's residence in Scotland to
examine the library. While waiting to be driven back to the station he noticed a
cupboard in the hall which he had not inspected. Although he was assured that
it contained nothing of significance, he insisted on looking inside and behind a
great number of empty bottles found two volumes of the Gutenberg Bible, later
sold for a great sum. Although Tom had never set foot inside Sotheby's after
his peremptory departure in the previous war, and despite the amicable
reconciliation with Barlow, Felix Warre had many times observed him from his
office window which overlooked Bond Street, stomping past numbers 34 and 35
on the far side of the road, looking fixedly ahead, clearly lacking the courage to
go back inside. Only a few weeks later, Tom's great *bête noire*, William Roberts,
formerly *The Times* sale-room correspondent, also died, and surprisingly
Sotheby's subsequently sold his formidable collection of books on the arts.

While Tancred Borenius still officially worked for Sotheby's as adviser on
Old Master paintings, he had been devoting more of his energies to the
Burlington Magazine, and when the editor joined the forces, Borenius took over
the editorship in an honorary capacity. The December sales in 1939 had been
relatively stagnant. Dealers were not buying because of a lack of public interest
and the BADA had launched a vigorous advertising campaign to regenerate
that interest, if only as a form of investment. When Borenius suggested to
Hobson and Warre that Sotheby's and the *Burlington Magazine* should jointly
sponsor an exhibition of works of art from all the leading art dealers early in the
new year, it seemed an excellent way of stimulating a trade revival. Frank Davis,

1. The whole sad saga is recounted in detail in the late Airey Neave's book, *The Flames of
Calais*, London, 1972.

who was writing a series on 'The London Art Market in War-time' in the *Burlington*, and was also the magazine's advertising manager, organised the exhibition. From 8 to 26 January the main Sotheby galleries were given over to a remarkable display of paintings, porcelain, furniture and silver which drew some two hundred visitors a day, a figure then generally regarded as very satisfactory. It must be remembered that at that time almost all the London museums were closed. The foreword to the catalogue stated: 'There has been no exhibition at which the public can see at one and the same time a Sienese Primitive, a Chinese painting, a Gainsborough drawing, a seventeenth-century Dutch landscape, an English sporting picture, a Picasso, some good silver and furniture. This lamentable gap in the amenities of civilization we decided to fill'. It had been decided to set an upper price limit of £350, and 10 per cent of anything sold was to go to the Red Cross. Although the organisers apologised for the absence of great names, there were works by Richard Wilson, Van de Velde, Mabuse, Domenico Beccafumi, Sano di Pietro, Van Huysum, Fragonard, Jongkind, Raoul Dufy, John Constable, Boudin, Francesco Bassano, Hendrick van Avercamp, Fantin-Latour, Vuillard, Utrillo, Braque, Picasso, George Stubbs, William Hogarth and Canaletto, and in the idiom of the time, 'almost every painting, drawing and antique was a coconut'. It was a wholly attractive feast for the eyes and senses, and today one can only gasp at the prices. An Irish peer who had looked around very carefully announced to the organiser with emphasis, 'This, my dear Sir, is just like heaven'. The George Stubbs, for example, was an oil painting of some farm labourers in a rural setting unloading a horse-drawn cart. Its price was £350. An enamel painting on Wedgwood biscuit earthenware of the identical subject fetched £300,000 in 1978. Clearly the painting would sell today for a price of the same order. Not all values, however, would have increased in that proportion but anyone brave enough to buy something at the exhibition at that time could now be said to own a piece of rare merit.[1] The double portrait of St. Catherine and St. Barbara by the *Master of Frankfort* was an early sixteenth-century painting of rare beauty for £280. The flower pieces by Van Huysum, Jean Baptiste Monnoyer and Rachel Ruysch (one time court painter to the Elector Palatine) at £250, £100 and £210 respectively seemed eminently reasonable and highly decorative at the price. The antique English furniture was probably relatively more expensive for its day; so was the exquisite Queen Anne and early Georgian silver, but all of the exhibits were of what would be judged remarkable quality today. In the event the number of objects finally sold was small, as the sum handed over to the Red Cross amounted to less than £150.

The exhibition was significant in another respect. It seems to have set a standard for what Sotheby's subsequently accepted for sale throughout the war.

1. Quite a number of the exhibits passed through Sotheby's again later for sale at auction. The Fantin-Latour *Dish of Fruit on a Table* sold for £3,500 in March 1965; the Utrillo *Paris Snowscene* fetched £7,600 in 1970; a very similar Braque fruit still life fetched £48,000 in 1979; Vuillard's *Les Confidences* would be valued at £30,000 today (1980). All four pictures were priced at £350 in 1940.

With reduced facilities for holding sales because of staff shortage and other wartime hazards, it was essential to obtain the maximum turnover by an insistence on optimum quality, and a great deal of what was brought in was referred to other auctioneers. For the next five years 'works of art' completely dominated what passed through Bond Street. The proportion of turnover attributable to it was 72 per cent, books only constituted 15 per cent, and pictures, coins and the rest lumped together 13 per cent.[1] Undoubtedly this was due to the combination of Geoffrey Hobson and Jim Kiddell as the most active members of the small management team. At the end of the war Geoffrey Hobson attributed the lion's share of the responsibility to Jim Kiddell. Certainly the catalogues bear witness to his taste and his skill in cataloguing, whether it was furniture, glass, porcelain, Chinese ceramics or hardstones, medieval and Renaissance art, rugs and tapestries, or arms and armour that were being sold. More often than not there was something of everything in each sale. Because of the limitations mentioned, specialist sales became very exceptional. Almost all the major collections that came Sotheby's way arrived through Kiddell's contacts. The most important of them was actually sold at what was possibly the most fearful moment in English history since Sotheby's began. Nevertheless it still became one of the most famous and outstanding dispersals of its kind. George Eumorfopoulos died on 19 December 1939. His widow and his executors decided that, despite the uncertainty of the times, his collections should be sold without delay and astonished press reports of this decision appeared in March 1940. The catalogue was to appear – and indeed it did – well ahead of the sale so as to give buyers in the United States and in Europe a chance to brief dealers to buy on their behalf.

Eumorfopoulos was born in Liverpool of Greek parentage, and had started collecting in 1891. After a false start with European porcelain, he soon began to collect Chinese ceramics. Like so many of his fellow, oriental ceramic enthusiasts of the period 1890 and 1930, he was a banker. He was Vice President of Ralli Brothers. He had a marvellous eye for beauty and quality. 'To enter my collection,' he wrote in one of his catalogues, 'it was indispensable that [an object] should appeal to me aesthetically in one way or another.' Contemporaries also admired his immense learning and his personal modesty. 'Eumorfopoulos was so modest and unassuming, so entirely free from self-importance, that strangers meeting him for the first time were hardly able to estimate his full worth', wrote Bernard Rackham after his death. If he had turned to scholarship, his fine mind and patient striving would certainly have made its mark in the academic world. He entertained generously, and anyone interested was welcome at his house in Chelsea to study his collections. These included bronzes, gold ornaments, lacquer, jade, glass and other works of art that came not only from China, but also from Korea, Japan, Indo-China and Persia. There were also fine examples of Egyptian, Greek and Roman antiquities, medieval works of art and splendid modern paintings by Gauguin, Matisse,

1. In the previous five years (1934–39) the proportion had been books 30 per cent, works of art 48 per cent, pictures, coins, etc. 22 per cent.

Picasso, Modigliani and Raoul Dufy, and among a wealth of sculptures some by Epstein and Mestrovic. But it was the unbelievable Chinese ceramics amassed by 'Eumo', as he was universally known, which sent a *frisson* down the spine of every like-minded collector. Sotheby's had been at the centre of this market for twenty-five years. The cautious merchant princes who were interested rarely bought at sales in person. They were fortunate in being served by a group of outstanding and knowledgeable dealers. Nevertheless, the collectors constantly turned to Jim Kiddell for advice and information, and it was his catalogues that became the touchstone of opinion. W. B. Honey, Keeper of the Department of Ceramics at the Victoria & Albert Museum, acknowledged in his monumental *The Ceramic Art of China*, that 'I have received much help and information from Mr. A. J. B. Kiddell of Messrs. Sotheby & Co., whose sale catalogues of Chinese and other pottery have set a new standard of accuracy and scholarship'. Though Jim himself in turn acknowledged the unstinting counsel of R. L. Hobson, an earlier keeper of Ceramics at the British Museum.

The organisation that fostered most interest and enthusiasm in the subject was the Oriental Ceramic Society – the twelve 'Dragons' – who had clubbed together under Eumo's presidency in Winkworth's house in 1921, and had grown in number to many hundreds by 1940. The early members soon became aware that there was more to those remarkable wares from China than the blue-and-white export porcelain of the seventeenth and eighteenth centuries. First they learned to recognise the fine classical blue-and-white porcelain of the fifteenth and sixteenth centuries, and more recently the even earlier fourteenth-century wares. There was also widespread enthusiasm for early celadon and other Sung wares.

There had been a steady increase of Chinese porcelain sales in the late Twenties, and throughout the Thirties the collections of early members helped to swell those of later ones and, of course, all the while fresh supplies came from China itself. One of the most unusual figures in this world had been Dr. George P. Crofts who had started life as a fur dealer in London's East End, had travelled to China in search of furs and began to become interested in the vast quantity of battered pottery and bronze ornaments he saw being excavated by workmen engaged in the construction of the new railway line in Tientsin, where the line happened to cross an ancient burial ground. He taught himself Chinese, studied the excavated material, began to buy it up in bulk and eventually sold it to museums and collectors in the United States, Canada and England. He moved to China and ultimately his knowledge of funerary wares became almost unrivalled (Philadelphia University bestowed an Honorary Ph.D. on him). After his death in 1925 a very substantial body of funerary wares was sold at Sotheby's by order of Croft's son. The sale caused a great interest. It was followed by a long series of other such sales where prices, if anything, decreased. Often too the bidding was very limited. Thus at the sale in June 1935 of early blue-and-white wares belonging to Charles Russell, the editor and owner of the magazine *Old Furniture*, and an enthusiastic and very knowledgeable collector in many spheres, no fewer than 82 lots out of 113 were bought by Sparks and Bluett, the two leading dealers in such objects and the principal

suppliers to members of the O.C.S. Eleven were bought in. The other twenty
were divided between Reitlinger, Winkworth, Moss and Spinks and other such
well-known names in that select coterie. The total realised was £3,369. It was
at this sale that the first positively identified and dated fourteenth-century piece
appeared, though there was much controversy about it at the time. In May 1937
the 110 pieces, representing only the cream of a much larger collection, was
advertised as 'The property of a well-known collector, formerly resident in Peip-
ing'. This in fact was Mr. Wu Lai-hsi, one of the few native Chinese collectors
with an extensive knowledge of the subject and the first to recognise the early
wares for what they were. The sale fetched less than £2,000. Gerald Reitlinger
estimated in 1967 that this collection would then have fetched not less than
£200,000, and today the figure would be substantially higher. But a great many
other such collections which originated in considerable part through Sotheby's,
had been given to our national and provincial museums and were to form their
primary oriental collections, and this has continued to be the case until recent
times. Thus Sir Alan Barlow's Chinese porcelain went to Sussex University,
Anthony de Rothschild's to the National Trust, Sir Percival David's and the
Hon. Mountstuart Elphinstone's formed the Percival David Foundation, now
part of London University, H. J. Oppenheim left his to the British Museum,
Oscar Raphael's was divided between the British Museum and the Fitzwilliam
Museum in Cambridge, Ferdinand Schiller left his to his brother Max, who in
turn donated it to the Bristol Museum, and the bulk of Professor C. G.
Seligmann's went to the Arts Council as a circulating exhibition.

Eumorfopoulos himself had sold an immense collection partly to the British
Museum and partly to the Victoria & Albert Museum for the seemingly
enormous sum of £100,000 in 1934, but he had done so at a price infinitely
lower than its true worth at that time.[1] What came to Sotheby's in 1940 was
substantially a *second* collection which he had latterly assembled in the years of
his retirement because he simply could not bear to stop collecting. The attraction of acquiring such wares was the combination of aesthetic judgement and
scholarly discernment, and for Eumorfopoulos this had become a way of life.
Even this second collection was an apogee of its kind. It was of a higher quality
than anything similar that had ever appeared in the auction room. The catalogue
was a real labour of love. It contained an unusually large number of illustrations
and the very detailed references made it clear how many of the pieces had
appeared in the major works of reference on Chinese ceramics, and had also
been shown in the recent great Chinese exhibitions in London, Paris, Berlin,
Stockholm and elsewhere. Above all, when the complete collection was displayed at Sotheby's just before the sale, it demonstrated the subtlety of the
Chinese potter in a way few museum displays had ever achieved. There were
examples from the whole range of manufacture over 3,000 years, from the
simplicity of a bowl and tripod vessel ascribed to the Shang Dynasty in the
second millennium B.C. to the sophisticated intricacy of K'ang Hsi vases of

1. He had also donated individual objects to a great number of other museums, including
particularly the Benaki Museum in Athens.

the eighteenth century A.D. There were certain other pieces that particularly captured the public imagination: a fine model of a prancing T'ang horse (sold for £90), a very strikingly decorated *mei p'ing* vase (tall ovoid body with small neck and everted lip) of the Ming Dynasty (it fetched £195) and a very unusual Khmer female torso in grey limestone of magnificent simplicity (bought by Wildenstein for £1,600 acting on behalf of Robert and Lisa Sainsbury, and now shown with the rest of their superb collection in the University of East Anglia to which they donated it in 1978). Many commentators were moved to write on the collection at length, despite the horror of war going on around them. One used it as a long introduction to the Chinese philosophy of life because he wanted to express his profound gratitude to collectors like Eumorfopoulos who had given the West a glimpse into a very different and often inscrutable culture.

The sale actually opened on the day that Belgium capitulated; nonetheless, the galleries were crowded. Many dealers had received commissions for it from all over the world. Despite what was happening in France almost the last commercial messages to reach London from Paris came to Sotheby's in the form of bids for some of the finest pieces. The Japanese firm, Yamanaka, out-bid the London dealers on many pieces. The manager, Mr. Ino, had actually had the relevant crates made before the sale, so certain was he that he would be able to buy what he wanted, and took them with him only a week later, when the firm's long-established London premises were closed and he sailed back to Japan on the *Hakuni Maru* from Liverpool. The most expensive item on the first day was the last lot in the sale, an exceptional Sung Dynasty Ju Yao bottle with a globular body and a long, slender neck, all covered in crackled pale lavender glaze. Sir Percival David had once written of it: 'This is a remarkable vase, the importance of which, I think, has too long been overlooked'. It was bought for £900 by G. D. Aked. The 135 lots raised £4,985. The second day, on which the evacuation from Dunkirk started, was just as well attended, and Major Warre was quite taken aback by the dense throng that could turn up on such a day. The total went higher to £6,394 10s. Altogether the four days and 520 lots brought just short of £26,000. Perhaps the highest tribute that can be paid to the Eumorfopoulos sale has occurred since 1975 when several pieces from it have re-appeared at Sotheby's sales and have fetched between *five hundred and a thousand times* the prices realised in those memorable days of 1940.

Eumo's other collections that were now sold consisted of Persian and Near-Eastern ceramics, glass, bronzes and other works of art, as well as Greek, Roman and Egyptian antiquities and superb, very early European enamel work; Italian Renaissance sculpture and needlework, and a few exceptional European ceramics. These brought the total raised to not far short of £50,000: a sum that was universally regarded as well nigh incredible. As luck would have it, Sotheby's had another, not dissimilar collection, belonging to Harcourt Johnstone, to sell almost simultaneously. It also contained fine Chinese ceramics, antiquities, modern pictures and sculpture. Many items from the two collections were combined in the same sales. Maynard Keynes and Alexander Korda competed for some of the Impressionists, and thought that they got superb bargains (as indeed they did: Korda bought a fine Dufy portrait for £30). Hobson and Warre were astonished by the results of the two sales, both organised largely by Jim Kiddell. They gave Jim a bonus cheque of £100 to express their pleasure.

When the Eumorfopoulos and Harcourt Johnstone sales were over, however, there was precious little else left in the pipeline. After the fall of France and the horror of Dunkirk, no one's heart was in buying and selling works of art. People were concerned about bare survival, the possibility of invasion from across the Channel, the first intensive bombing raids on Britain, then the Blitz and the Battle of Britain. Once more Hobson and Warre became undecided about the future. No one could find out whether any auctions were to take place at Sotheby's in the autumn. After an interregnum of uncertainty, A. C. R. Carter, pressed by the trade and clients alike, and now an old man himself, though still proudly sporting the biggest handlebar moustache in Britain, decided to call on Hobson and Warre at Bond Street to find out what they had in mind. He drew a charmingly quaint and melancholy picture of the two elderly veterans at the 'receipt of custom', who had just made up their minds once more to carry on, come what may; and indeed they did. What Carter, of course, could not have known was that Hobson and Warre (as well as the partners absent on war duties) had had once more to consider a possible amalgamation with Christie's. The trial run in 1934 had shown all concerned how difficult it was to devise an equitable valuation of the two businesses, both separately and conjoined. The problem now was that while Sotheby's paid a ground rent of a mere £80 per annum for Bond Street, Christie's had to pay a sum of £4,300 for King Street, and in addition they had to service a £50,000 loan to the tune of £2,875 annually. The *average* profits of the two companies in the preceding five years came to £16,477 for Sotheby's and £14,957 for Christie's. If one took the cost of the properties out of the calculations the figures showed Christie's ahead at £23,901 per annum and Sotheby's behind with £19,545. The lawyers had a fine time confusing their clients with a mass of detail and figures, some of which seemed hardly relevant.

However, all were agreed that the new private company to be formed should take over the good will of both Sotheby's and Christie's, plus the furnishings and contents of both premises, plus an agreed amount of working capital. The latter proved one of the most difficult items to assess. Once more it was decided that Bond Street was to be sold and the new company would operate from King Street. The date of amalgamation aimed at was October 1940. The partners of Christie's were unwilling that the combined business should take over some of the long outstanding debts to Sotheby's which stemmed from book sales, or that the new company should give extended credit as Bond Street had done in the past.

Once more the risks seemed high and the possible benefits uncertain. The younger partners, and Peter Wilson in particular, opposed the amalgamation. By the time Carter called on Hobson and Warre they had decided to go it alone.

What no one could have foretold at that stage, of course, was that Christie's premises would shortly be destroyed by enemy action. When the news broke, Warre telephoned the next morning to offer temporary accommodation and shelter, but the suggestion was turned down.

The background to this was interesting. In January 1940 Major Warre had written to Sir Alec Martin suggesting that Christie's and Sotheby's should come to a mutual agreement that if either firm's premises were damaged by bombs, the other would help by taking in for sale any property that was saved, and by providing whatever accommodation was needed. Warre concluded his letter on this topic, 'I shall be glad to know what you and your partners feel about this. If either of our premises were knocked out it would be a good thing to show a united British front if two businesses in competition were to help each other in this way.'

Christie's were delighted to accept this proposal. When their premises were virtually destroyed both Warre and Hobson wrote to Sir Alec Martin to express their sympathy, and to offer space. Sir Alec was evidently very touched by their affection, but in the event he was offered temporary accommodation by his bank manager (virtually next door) and later by Lord Derby, of his own house, just behind Oxford Street. This, in fact, is where Christie's settled for the duration of the War.

So the air raid shelter in the Bond Street basement was refurbished and, raids or no raids, sales continued uninterrupted. The *Daily Sketch* reported that Sotheby's smartly turned-out commissionaire, Sgt. Basson,[1] acted as spotter during the sale of Lady Ludlow's collection of valuable manuscripts on 16 December 1940, standing by the sandbagged entrance and warning the auction room of immediate danger. 'No one has ever left the sales for our underground shelter during a raid,' Geoffrey Hobson was reported as saying, 'We have had three heavy raids since the sales began this season. Everyone stayed in case they missed something.'

There were still remarkable highlights: the early ceramics collection (which also included particularly fine jades and bronzes) of H. K. Burnet of Bradford; the now well nigh unbelievable array of Chelsea porcelain assembled by Dr. Bellamy Gardner; the Phillimore railway collection on everything connected with the early days of steam; the illuminated manuscript dated 1532 in a jewelled binding put up for sale by the executors of Viscount Rothermere, that had once belonged to Dr. Richard Mead, one of the firm's earliest clients, and had then passed to Horace Walpole, the Countess of Waldegrave, Alfred de Rothschild, the Countess of Carnarvon and eventually Lord Rothermere. It fetched £2,400 in March 1942. A vast – and rather mysterious – disappointment in the generally subfusc atmosphere that pervaded the auction room was the result of the sale of 'the biggest diamond ever auctioned', the *Moon of the*

---

1. Geoffrey Hobson frequently used Basson to obtain spare batteries for his deaf aid. It was known that Basson much resented these errands, and there were smiles all round when Basson eventually married Geoffrey Hobson's cook and thus deprived him of an unusually capable culinary artist.

Mountains, at 183 carats, 77 carats heavier than the Koh-i-Noor. Film cameras were installed at Bond Street. The gallery was crowded; the tension, one gathers, terrific. But the bidding began slowly and the stone was sold for a mere £5,200, when a minimum of £15,000 had been expected. That particular diamond was only one item in a big jewellery sale, which for its day was an astounding success. It was arranged and catalogued by D. C. Collins, a part-time adviser, who guided Sotheby's in this field, and also occasionally on silver, for many years.

Prices went up a little at last in 1943. For a long time they had been sitting at a level which many people thought was down to no more than a quarter of what they had been at the time of the apparent recovery in Coronation year. There was a definite reason for this merciful break in the clouds. A new kind of person began to be seen in the auction room. Of all the unlikely individuals it was again Jim Kiddell who acted as a catalyst in a movement that was to make an enormous impact on the entire London art market. Jim exuded an extraordinarily *English* bonhomie that attracted a large number of German and Austrian refugees who had come to Britain. Many had brought over their all in the form of diamonds, rare postage stamps and rose oil which they now began to convert into more conventional forms of capital. Jim Kiddell reassured them when they asked questions in broken, music-hall English; he taught them how to buy and sell successfully at auction. He often stood surety for them when they had to complete forms as enemy aliens at Scotland Yard. He shared with many of the professional art dealers who were earning their livings as waiters, railway clerks, minor entrepreneurs and factory hands in wartime Britain, a perceptive eye for what was rare, beautiful and cheap. Many commented years later that they liked his sense of humour, admired his patience, the twinkle in his eye and his shrewd honesty, and were astonished by the breadth of his scholarship, particularly in European and oriental ceramics. The welcome they received in Bond Street in those difficult days made a deep and lasting impression, which was in stark contrast to the haughty cold-shouldering that met them in other places. Many of these Jewish refugees, who made up an increasing proportion of Sotheby's clientele from 1943 onwards, became enthusiastic collectors as they earned more money, while others set up as dealers soon after the war. It was not long before they began to thrive and prosper. They constituted a particularly important element in the firm's rapid development once international trade had again been put on a proper footing, and later they got on as well with the younger generation of Sotheby directors – Peter Wilson, Tim Clarke and Anthony Hobson – as they had initially with Jim Kiddell.

By the end of the war, Hobson and Warre, and indeed Jim Kiddell, were thoroughly worn out. The two older men wanted to opt out as soon as was prudent. Hobson wrote a brilliant summary of the situation in March 1945 for those directors, des Graz, Vere Pilkington and Peter Wilson, who were returning to civilian life after years of frenzied activity in the many arms of Postal Censorship (and later the counter-espionage side of M.I.6 in Peter Wilson's case) all over the world. 'The two partners,' he explained, 'could not have got through their work had they not had good health. FWW has not been away (since September 1939) for more than a fortnight through illness; GDH had two reprehensible attacks of gout, each of which left him in bed for about a month, in 1940 and 1943; during the second he was able to do a good deal of work from his nursing home.' He paid tribute to the immense efforts by the miniscule staff: Mr. Heaviside who dealt almost single-handed with all the clerical work involved with reservations and commissions; Mr. Lambert who clerked every sale; Rham, who looked after the finances, company secretarial work and took occasional book sales himself; and above all, 'the various young and charming ladies of the secretarial staff, who have helped to brighten our daily toil for periods that have usually been all too brief', but without whom the firm would have ground to a halt. He looked forward to a reduction of government interference – the constant withdrawal of staff into government service, the abolition of coupons[1] and the relaxation of the formidable export restrictions.

Surprisingly, the firm's finances were extraordinarily healthy. Hobson wrote: 'It has been possible to get on without giving more than a small fraction of the usual credit; book debts are lower than ever before; we have not had an overdraft since January 29, 1942, and credit balance has sometimes been over £100,000 for some weeks at a time; on February 16 it was £53,311 after paying Income Tax due January 1945, and providing £15,000 advance payment for Income Tax due January 1946; we have also got £3,000 in Government securities and written £4,000 off the premises. Thanks to FWW's success in raising charges, the ratio of profits to turnover had been improved, and in every way the firm is in a far stronger position financially than in 1939'.

The one department which had suffered during the war was books, not only because the great majority of the expert staff was called up, but also because overseas buying and selling was so important here. Only Ochs, occasionally Irby and a Mrs. Maier remained as cataloguers, though the firm was fortunate in obtaining the part-time services of Dr. H. A. Feisenberger, the manager of Davis & Orioli, a firm of antiquarian booksellers who had long specialised in medical and scientific books. Dr. Feisenberger joined Sotheby's full-time staff after the war. He also married Mrs. Maier. His enormous expertise, particularly in early scientific books, was to be a major factor in re-establishing and consolidating book sales – and encouraging collectors – until his retirement in 1976.

Hobson devoted nearly a third of his report to singing the praises of Jim Kiddell who was made a partner shortly afterwards. He concluded by summarising the work which he and Warre wanted to shed and suggested which of the incoming directors might take over what. Peter Wilson, it was decided, was to look after new appointments and salaries, the area the old partners regarded as the most important for the future.

1. The firm never dealt with 'couponed', i.e. any rationed goods such as household furniture, but this meant that special licences in the form of affidavits had to be obtained from the owners of certain classes of goods such as furniture, rugs, curtains, clocks, watches and smokers' materials – to say that they were exempt.

PART FOUR

The Great Surge

CATALOGUE

OF

SEVEN PAINTINGS

BY

CEZANNE, MANET, RENOIR

AND

VAN GOGH

THE PROPERTY OF
THE ESTATE OF THE LATE JAKOB GOLDSCHMIDT
OF NEW YORK CITY

WHICH WILL BE SOLD BY AUCTION BY

MESSRS. SOTHEBY & CO.

P. C. WILSON	J. C. BUTTERWICK	A. R. A. HOBSON	A. J. B. KIDDELL
T. H. CLARKE	F. ROSE	R. S. TIMEWELL	C. GRONAU
	ASSOCIATE: JOHN CARTER, C.B.E.		

Auctioneers of Literary Property and Works illustrative of the Fine Arts
AT THEIR LARGE GALLERIES, 34 & 35 NEW BOND STREET, W.1

Day of Sale:
WEDNESDAY, OCTOBER 15th, 1958
AT NINE-THIRTY P.M. PRECISELY

On View from October 6th

Catalogue Price 5/-

*A Printed List of all Prices and Buyers' Names
at this sale can be supplied for two shillings.*

The Goldschmidt Sale was a watershed: the first evening sale since the eighteenth century and the most important after the war. It ushered in an era of boom.

28

The Way Ahead

BY 1945, in common with most printed matter then being produced, the firm's catalogues looked like a dog's dinner. Paper was thin and bad, page margins had practically disappeared, only the most outstanding items could be illustrated, and nasty wire staples held the tatty catalogue covers on to the contents. However this austerity could not disguise the fact that much of the material described was still fine, beautiful and increasingly sought after. It was, in a way, the high point of the sale of antiques as furnishings and the average total for each work of art sale had steadily climbed every year since 1942. Indeed, some dealers' long term view of the post-war art market was that prices could not possibly remain at the high level they had reached around 1945. They were soon proved wrong, particularly in the field of porcelain, where prices quickly rose, possibly because the threat of bomb damage and other war damage had been removed from an essentially fragile commodity.

The firm's greatest need now was to enlarge its inadequate expert staff. One of the first new men to arrive was Cyril Butterwick, who, after achieving brilliance as an athlete at Malvern College and Christ's College Cambridge, had gone to Eton as a temporary master. He stayed for thirty years, nearly twenty of them as a noted housemaster. After teaching he had a fervent love for collecting. The son of an impecunious clergyman who was chaplain to the Duke of Portland, he had been brought up as a companion to the Duke's son and had probably acquired a taste for fine things in this way. At first his interest was in books, and for years before the war he and his wife came up to London every second Thursday on the hunt for first editions. Then his enthusiasm changed to silver. So the book collection was sold at Hodgson's and the money raised gradually re-invested in silver. Butterwick regularly attended sales both at Sotheby's and Christie's, and eventually his interest spread to antique English furniture and porcelain. He was gifted with an excellent memory and this helped him to establish a fine collection with relatively limited funds. By the end of the war he had grown tired of teaching, and with his general expertise and wide-ranging Etonian contacts both Christie's and Sotheby's offered him a post. He chose Sotheby's and had twenty blissfully happy years at Bond Street, first in the book department and then as the director in charge of silver. His contribution to Sotheby's growth, if only because of his widespread contacts, was very considerable. He died tragically, shortly after his retirement, while actually attending an investiture at Buckingham Palace.

On the painting side, Tancred Borenius had become increasingly eccentric and had virtually withdrawn some time earlier. A nervous breakdown had eventually forced him to give up all his work, including that at the *Burlington Magazine*. For some years the major part of picture cataloguing had fallen on

Tim Wilder's shoulders, with occasional outside help. Vere Pilkington was the first of the younger directors to return to Bond Street. The strain of secondment to the American O.S.S. in New York led to his being invalided out early in 1945. After a period of recuperation he began to understudy Hobson at manuscript sales, was given the task of rebuilding the diminished valuation department, and took over responsibility for the picture department and picture sales from Felix Warre, who had inherited them from Evelyn Barlow years earlier after her retirement. The need for a new and really experienced cataloguer of Old Master paintings and drawings soon became paramount. At that period the number of people with an above-average knowledge of this most difficult of all the areas of expertise was tiny, and those that had it had been trained principally in Holland and Germany.

Then Pilkington had an extraordinary piece of luck. He went out to lunch one day, with this problem uppermost on his mind, and sauntered down Burlington Arcade in order to get a haircut. He met and chatted to Sir Kenneth (now Lord) Clark, the former director of the National Gallery, and asked him whether he could recommend anyone. Sir Kenneth suggested two names: Hans Gronau and Christopher Norris. The latter had at one time worked in the National Gallery and had been one of the Fine Art Commissioners on the Control Commission in Germany at the end of the war. A little later, when Pilkington put the same question to Colin Agnew, a partner in the famous firm of picture dealers, he received the identical reply. For various reasons, Christopher Norris refused the job. Hans Gronau accepted it with delight, on a three days a week basis. If one wanted to pinpoint one single event that triggered off Sotheby's great post-war expansion, it was this casual encounter.

Hans Gronau was every inch an art historian in the traditional sense: thoughtful, scholarly, gentle, precise, a little afraid of organisation. He had recently finished his stint in the forces, where he had first been in the Pioneer Corps and had then been transferred to the Italian side of Army Intelligence. His particular interest was in Italian art of the fourteenth and fifteenth centuries. In fact, he had specialised in this era so as to avoid conflict with his father, Georg Gronau, a well-known authority on later Italian art who had been Director of the picture gallery at Kassel, one of Germany's oldest and most distinguished provincial museums, from 1914 to 1925. After a major difference of opinion with no less a personality than Von Bode, Gronau Senior had moved to Florence, where he had bought a villa whilst still a student, and had followed his particular art-historical interests and published a number of standard books on Titian and other Venetian painters. The younger Gronau grew up in Florence and, having also decided on an art-historical career, he followed his studies in a relatively leisurely manner and only began working for his doctorate at the age of thirty. In 1934 he published his Ph.D. thesis on Andrea Orcagna and Nardo di Cione. He had already started dealing in pictures as a side line, advising the firm of Bottenwieser in Berlin. In the previous year, on a visit to Göttingen University, he had been introduced to a young student of art history there called Carmen von Wogau, by one of her tutors, Niklaus Pevsner. When she came to Florence in the spring of 1934 to take her doctorate on the subject of Italian architectural drawing of the sixteenth century, with particular reference to Cigoli, she and Hans met again, fell in love and married in June. A return to Germany seemed impossible because anti-Semitic pressures were already daunting, so the young couple moved to London. Hans obtained a job as an adviser to a firm of American art dealers, who had begun buying pictures again for the first time since the great slump.

The arrangement with Vere Pilkington was that for £3 a day Hans Gronau should now come into Sotheby's to see what had been brought into the firm in the way of Old Master paintings, and to catalogue anything worthy of sale. Although Christie's were still completely dominant in the field of paintings, an increasing volume of material was being brought into Sotheby's. At this stage, and for nearly ten years to come, run-of-the-mill Old Master drawings were hardly thought worth cataloguing, except in bundles or portfolios, for they fetched so little unless their quality and provenance were quite exceptional. In fact, one of the first catalogues, dated 27 March 1946, that can now be identified as being mostly Hans Gronau's work, was of drawings belonging to Montague L. Meyer, a wealthy timber merchant who lived in Portman Square. Meyer's drawings made up the first forty-eight lots out of 167. The entire sale realised £1,736, an average price of just over £10 per lot, even though each lot consisted of several drawings.

Gronau devoted the fourth day of the week to continuing his studies at the National Gallery, and on the fifth he worked for Rudolf J. Heinemann, who became one of the world's most discerning and leading dealers in Old Master paintings when he settled in New York. It was an old family connection. Heinemann's father had been a close friend of Hans Gronau's father, Georg, and had frequently sought his advice when he was helping to form the final collection of Heinrich Thyssen-Bornemisza (father of H. H. Thyssen, who has enormously extended that collection in recent years). Gronau's painstaking and more expansive cataloguing soon became noticeable and the volume of work at Sotheby's increased. Three days a week proved insufficient for it and after a couple of years Hans Gronau became a full-time employee of the firm.

Since his demobilisation from the army, Gronau's health had been far from good, and the occasional illness he had suffered since his military service now became more frequent. One evening he collapsed on his return from a visit to Yorkshire, carrying a heavy suitcase full of paintings destined for Sotheby's. The cause was diagnosed as a severe heart condition which at that time it was difficult, if not impossible, to cure. At first on odd occasions, but then more frequently, Carmen Gronau came into Sotheby's to help her husband with cataloguing, correspondence and the hundred-and-one problems that made up the daily routine. With her energy and drive, and her own art-historical training, she took to the work like a duck to water. Sadly Hans Gronau's health deteriorated and in 1948 it was suggested that Carmen, who still had two young children to look after, should join the department part-time. Hans was hesitant, if not downright unenthusiastic, about the suggestion. He remembered all too clearly the example of another husband and wife team in the art-historical field, Hans and Erika Tietze, whose over-emphatic use of the word 'we' had become proverbial among their colleagues. But Geoffrey Hobson, as well as Peter Wilson – now firmly re-established at Bond Street – insisted and so it came to pass that Carmen Gronau was put on the pay-roll.

Some little while later it was decided, at the suggestion of des Graz, that Peter Wilson should take over the picture department – and, of course, picture sales – while Vere Pilkington would look after the thriving works of art department. In the few years they had together, Hans, Carmen and Peter became a most effective, contented and hard-working trio in the art market. But it is difficult to make clear some thirty years later what a generally depressed area the world of Old Masters then was in financial terms. For example, the startling fact which emerges from a close study of the Bond Street fine art sales held between 1945 and 1949 is that in absolute terms the prices were no higher – and, indeed, often lower – than those that had prevailed in the Twenties. In fact, where one can identify identical paintings the prices were sometimes lower than they had been in the 1880s and 1890s, which was, as we have seen, a time of depression. There were people who argued with some justification that Sotheby's had been fortunate in not being over-involved with the market in Old Master pictures, for it seemed so unrewarding financially. The counter to that argument, of course, was that it was a fabulous time for discerning collectors. A little money would go a long way and it needed only a relatively modest sum to establish a really fine collection. One major cause of this depressed state of affairs just after the Second World War was that there were still no buyers from Europe, none from Japan and precious few from America.

Twice, or perhaps three times in each twelve-months season, there would be a sale that really sparkled and exceeded the norm because it contained particularly well-known paintings. But in July 1946, for example, there were five sales averaging 170 lots for which the average price was £24. Many of the paintings included were by perfectly acceptable and competent Italian, Dutch and Flemish masters, or very good examples of the English eighteenth- and early nineteenth-century schools. By the autumn of 1946 the average had climbed to £41. On 11 June 1947, 124 lots catalogued as *Highly Important Paintings of Old Masters*, a phrase then rarely used, which included a portrait of the Duke de Oliveira by Velazquez that belonged to Viscount Cowdray, and pictures from two other well-known collections, Sir Reginald Proctor-Beauchamp and Sir William Bromley-Davenport, fetched a total of £51,624 for 124 lots, an average price of £416. This was ten times the previous autumn's average. It showed what could be done.[1] There was another highlight in December 1947 when a series of twelve Van Huysum flower paintings representing the months of the year were put up for sale by Lord Petre and fetched £13,500.

In the following spring Carmen had an experience that was to impress itself

1. A further sale some years later from the Proctor-Beauchamp Collection was to be a turning point in Sotheby's history (see page 330).

firmly on her mind. She was called to the public counter. A man who looked just like a tramp said he wanted to sell some drawings. He mentioned a Claude Lorrain, a Tiepolo, a Hugo van der Goes. 'Those are very big names,' said Carmen. 'They are very well authenticated pictures, young woman,' came the reply. The man was Alfred Jowett, a retired master spinner from Killinghall, Harrogate. He had known Peter Wilson when the latter was still a boy in Yorkshire and had collected drawings for the last twenty years. Many had been bought at famous Sotheby sales such as that of the Vicomte Bernard D'Hendecourt in 1929 and J. P. Heseltine in 1935. The silver porter, Reg Turner, was despatched to Yorkshire with Jowett and brought back the drawings with him on the following day. They proved as good as he had indicated. The sale was held on 21 July 1948 and caused great excitement. It had a little catalogue of its own and consisted of only seven lots, which fetched a total of £8,910 in seven minutes. Here was another signpost to success. A silver point Ghirlandaio head brought £3,800; the head of a young woman, attributed to Hugo van der Goes, £2,200;[1] a kneeling Magdalen by Fra Bartolommeo, £580. Jowett later produced more pictures which he sold at Sotheby's with some *éclat*. It demonstrated most emphatically to Carmen that one could not judge clients by appearances.

In December 1948 another well-known collection came to the market after the owner's death. Sir Bernard Eckstein had been a collector with a catholic taste in many spheres. After some lively negotiations with the executors, Sotheby's staged a whole sequence of sales of his property. Altogether it was one of the most outstanding series to have taken place since the war.[2] Eckstein's largely English pictures fetched a totally unexpected £62,266: they included a John Constable oil painting of Hampstead Heath which sold for £13,000; two charming studies of children in a rural setting by George Morland were bought by Walter Hutchinson, the publisher, for £5,000 and £5,200; two Gainsboroughs sold for £1,800 and £1,600; a small interior by Jan Steen for £3,800, and a number of flower pieces all raised over £1,000 – a most unusual occurrence.

The Eckstein Sale was an event that gave particular pleasure to Geoffrey Hobson in the first year after he had finally taken over the chairmanship of Sotheby's following Felix Warre's retirement. It boded well for a renaissance of the best of the pre-war tradition. Another event which had pleased Hobson enormously, earlier in the year, was the arrival in London of the cream of the renowned library formed by Baron Horace de Landau. Born in 1824, Landau had entered the Paris House of Rothschild at an early age, and the catalogue preface tells us that he then 'became their representative with the government of the newly created kingdom of Italy in the 1860s at a time when it was raising great sums for railway construction; these projects were mainly financed by the

---

1. The same drawing, with a different attribution, was sold to the Louvre for £20,000 some time later.
2. His collection of jades fetched £20,131; his magnificent gold boxes £18,013; the overall total exceeded £136,000 including further sales of furniture and jewellery.

Rothschilds, the negotiations being carried out by Baron de Landau'. In 1872 he left the firm with the intention of devoting his energies to the formation of a great library and a collection of works of art. With this object in view, he bought a large and beautiful villa on one of the hills of Florence. This had formerly belonged to Lord Normanby, British Minister to the Court of Tuscany from 1854 to 1858, that same Lord Normanby who had devoted so much of his energy to helping the then Director of the National Gallery, Sir Charles Eastlake, to export back to England some of his major purchases of Italian primitives. Eastlake and his wife used to spend their annual leave on such tours of acquisition.

Landau had worked indefatigably for thirty years on the expansion of his collection. He travelled widely to attend the principal sales in various European capitals and bought several libraries *en bloc*. He never married and on his death in 1904 he bequeathed all his property to his niece, Madame Hugo Finaly, who added substantially to the library herself. By her will her son had been given a life interest in it, and on his death it was to be sold. He had died in 1945, and it had taken Hobson and des Graz more than two years of fretful toil and pains-taking negotiations to persuade the various authorities still obsessed with war-time restrictions – including the British Treasury and the Board of Trade – that a selected portion should be allowed to come to London, as London was the natural centre for such a dispersal. The negotiations had begun with Mrs. Finaly's grandson acting as executor of the estate, but they were eventually taken over by Tammaro de Marinis, a renowned Florence bookseller, who had been charged with disposing of the 80,000 volumes that made up the complete library. Only 130 of them were sent to London.

There had been something of a battle at Bond Street over how the sale was to be tackled. Geoffrey Hobson wanted it held as soon as was humanly possible. Des Graz was in favour of taking its preparation at a more leisurely pace. Certain of his colleagues put des Graz's rather lethargic and often negative attitude at this stage down to disappointment over the fact that he had been virtually passed over for the honours conferred upon those who had run Postal Censorship. Des Graz – in common with many others – had fallen foul of Brendan Bracken (who was not only Minister of Information but also a close confidant of Winston Churchill's) and regarded this as the reason why former associates received a peerage and a knighthood while he was fobbed off with a C.B.E. in 1942 for a second long stint in his country's service. Clearly the slight continued to rankle.[1]

So the elderly Hobson now took the organisation of the Landau–Finaly Sale into his own hands. For once he decided subsequently to publish the inside story of what had taken place. He did so in a foreword included in a special limited edition of the priced catalogue which was printed after the sale had taken place and had proved an immense success. 'Whatever the merits or

1. In 1943 he had become the Director of the Western Area of Censorship. As a friend wrote afterwards: 'it was a grief to many that he was not more highly honoured, for in this sphere his name was virtually a legend'.

demerits of the [original] catalogue,' he wrote, 'it was probably produced more rapidly than any other catalogue of equal importance ever issued by the firm. The books were received on Monday, 5th April, and the day was spent in checking them with the owner's representative: work on the catalogue started next day and the illustrations were chosen in the course of the week; the manuscript went to the printers on 3rd May, and the first illustrated copies of the catalogue were sent down by taxi to Heathrow for A. R. A. Hobson[1] to take to America on Friday, 28th May. Two of the lots, the set of De Bry (lot 42), and the Hebrew Bible (lot 56) were catalogued by outside experts; all the other descriptions were written in the house, by one or other of four men.'

Then, one assumes largely for the eyes of the obdurate mandarins in the Treasury and at the Board of Trade, who had opposed the relaxation of import (and export) restrictions for art and antiques every inch of the way, he analysed London's importance as the place to hold such sales:

It has been pointed out in the Preface that foreign libraries have been coming to London for sale by auction for a very long period; the reasons for this flow of business have changed in the course of time. At the beginning of the last century, such foreign libraries as came to this country for sale were sent because the English market was then the most important in the world, and it is safe to say that of Talleyrand's books, for instance (sold in 1816–17), over 90 per cent. remained in England as a result of the sale. By 1880 foreign competition had already become serious; and it is noteworthy that eleven of the chief books in Baron de Landau's collection were bought at Sotheby's in the Crawford sales of 1887 and 1889. With the mass American entry into the market during the 90's the English book trade finally became an entrepôt trade. The extent of this change may be judged from the results of the Phillipps sale in 1946. Out of a total of about £55,000, £12,230 was sold directly to foreign dealers bidding at the sale; £32,640 was either bought on commission for foreign clients by English dealers, or sold to foreigners after the sale; three lots totalling £3,620 went to Eire and Australia; while only five lots totalling £4,330 went to English collectors; another three totalling £2,370 were still in the hands of English dealers when this analysis was made.

In recognition of the vastly increased importance of foreign buyers it was decided for the first time to hold an exhibition of the most important books in New York before the sale. Fifty-two books and manuscripts crossed the Atlantic by air as precious cargo, and by courtesy of those doyens of American collecting, Mr. Philip and Dr. A. S. W. Rosenbach, were displayed for a fortnight on the Rosenbach premises in East 57th Street. Here they were visited by a number of private collectors and booksellers, as well as by officials of the Pierpont Morgan, New York Public and Yale University Libraries. A representative of Harvard had already inspected the collection in England.

After their return to London the books were viewed by a large number of

1. This is the first mention of Anthony Hobson, Geoffrey's son, who had only very recently joined the firm after Oxford and military service. He took over the running of the book department after des Graz's death, and was ultimately responsible for some of Sotheby's greatest book sales between 1958 and 1971.

collectors and experts, including H.E. the French Ambassador, H.E. the Luxembourg Minister, and representatives of the Bibliothèque Nationale, Paris, the Bibliothèque Royale, Brussels, and of various national and provincial collections in this country.

The company on 12th and 13th July included collectors from Italy, Switzerland, Holland, Belgium and France as well as from the United States; members and friends of Madame Finaly's family came from France and Switzerland for the sale. There was also a large English attendance including such veteran authorities as Sir Sydney Cockerell, Dr. Eric Millar, and Professor Bodkin, as well as Mr. A. C. R. Carter of the *Daily Telegraph*, doyen of London art correspondents. The company present at one time numbered about three hundred and formed an international gathering such as had not been seen in London since the great book sales of 1928; the principal lots attracted far more bidding than usually happens with very highly priced books, but each session was completed in just over an hour.

The 1462 Bible (lot 23) was the first copy on vellum, and the second of any kind to appear at auction since the Carysfort sale of 1923. At that time £4,800 was paid for it and £9,500 for the 'Gutenberg' Bible. In view of the extraordinary price given for a single volume of the latter in March, 1947, a great appreciation was expected for the first dated Bible, and at £15,400 it fell to Mr. Williams of Quaritch in competition with Mr. Lionel Robinson as underbidder – the fourth highest price, so far as we can trace, at which a printed book has ever changed hands under the hammer. To C. G. des Graz, the auctioneer, it was of peculiar interest for it was at the same figure that he had knocked down the Lewis Carroll autograph manuscript of *Alice Underground*, with Alice herself sitting beside the rostrum, at the equally crowded sale of 3rd April, 1928.

The highest price of the sale, £16,000, was paid by Mr. Maggs[1] for the Psalter of Bonne of Luxembourg (lot 97), which had fetched no more than 10,000 francs (£400) in the Firmin-Didot sale at Paris in 1882. This compares with £11,800 paid in 1919 by Baron Edmond de Rothschild for Mr. Yates Thompson's Hours of Jeanne of Navarre, the manuscript most closely resembling the Psalter which has passed through our hands within living memory. The underbidder was Mr. C. A. Stonehill at £15,800, both Monsieur Kundig of Geneva and Messrs. Knoedler being close runners-up; £16,000 is, we believe, the second highest price for an illuminated manuscript ever paid at auction.

Next came the vast Froissart (lot 53), lively with countless miniatures, which fell to a Swiss private collector at £8,800 – a great price for a manuscript of so late a date; the underbidder was again Mr. Lionel Robinson.

After the Psalter and Froissart the next highest price for a manuscript (£4,000) was paid against Mr. C. A. Stonehill by the purchaser of the Froissart for the Flemish Horae with miniatures *en grisaille* (lot 60); for this Baron de Landau paid 6,000 francs (£240) at the Firmin-Didot sale of 1883.

The total of £90,982 for 129 lots is, we believe, the highest ever realised by two consecutive days of book sales, though it is run very close by the second and third sessions of that fantastic finale to a great book collecting era, the Kern sale

1. He was buying it on behalf of the Swiss collector, Martin Bodmer, who parted with the manuscript to H. P. Kraus of New York in 1968 and who in turn sold it to the Metropolitan Museum. It is now displayed in the Cloisters Museum.

of 1929;[1] it compares not unfavourably with £110,356 for 108 lots of the Britwell 'plums' (as Mr. S. R. Christie Miller used to call them) on 16th December, 1919. . . .

This is the first sale of a foreign library that we have been allowed to hold since the war; the interest it aroused throughout the book world, and the large foreign attendance at the sale justify us in believing that not only all English collectors, but all book lovers throughout Europe and America, will hope that it may be followed by many others.

After the bustle of disposing of Baron de Landau's treasures was over there was another event which must have pleased both Hobson and des Graz. The very manuscript of Lewis Carroll's *Alice Underground* which Dr. Rosenbach had bought at Sotheby's in 1928 for the momentous figure of £15,400[2] – as Hobson reminded us – among the greatest excitement ever engendered by the sale of a work of literature, now returned to England. The gracious gesture of donating it to the British Museum had been organised by the Librarian of Congress, Dr. Luther H. Evans, and that most munificent of book collectors, Lessing Rosenwald, with a group of fellow countrymen, as a gift from America to the British people. In 1928 Dr. Rosenbach had sold it for some £30,000 to Eldridge Johnson, who had thoroughly enjoyed its ownership. After his death it was offered for sale at Parke-Bernet and the Doctor bought it back for $50,000 (then £12,500). In memory of the fame that the original purchase had brought him, Dr. Rosenbach passed it to the would-be donors at cost price and, in fact, worked hard to help to raise the necessary sum.

At the turn of the year 1948 the Board of Trade announced that the import and export of works of art to 'soft currency areas' was to be relaxed. It was a chink in the armour of restraint of trade: the campaign on the Landau–Finaly treasures had therefore not been wholly in vain, though it was the 'hard currency' areas – America and the Commonwealth – that mattered most in the art market. But Hobson was exhausted. In December he became ill and by Christmas it was clear that he was dying. On 4 January 1949, 'the Bookbinders' Historian', as he was to become known, died at the age of sixty-six. His final year in office had clearly shown the way ahead.

Geoffrey Hobson worked tremendously hard himself and expected everyone else around him to do the same, thus he had always been a stern taskmaster. Carmen Gronau remembers all too clearly how fiercely Hobson had chastised

1. The sale in New York at the Anderson Gallery of the library of Jerome Kern, author of well-known musicals. The strength of his collection lay particularly in eighteenth- and early nineteenth-century English literary manuscripts and association copies. The sale just preceded the Wall Street crash, and prices were astronomical. Dr. Rosenbach, who had expended $25,000,000 on old books in the previous ten years, spent $410,000 out of the total of $1,730,000. Millicent Sowerby wrote later that 'the sale was a most dramatic event and had an influence on book prices for years, and possibly for the rest of time. Everybody lost his head and the prices were fantastic'. Kern invested the proceeds in the booming stock market and lost every penny only a few months later.
2. This was a figure which immediately after the sale Mr. Dring of Quaritch described to the press as 'absurd'.

12

her when she had made a silly mistake with a client. But to the outside world he always backed his staff to the hilt. His fine brain and skilful analysis of intricate problems had given Sotheby's an edge over its competitors throughout a very difficult period. His deafness, the loss of his wife and his unceasing devotion to the study of bindings had latterly made him rather unapproachable and at times very irritable, but the catalogues the firm had issued under his eagle eye for the last thirty years were testimony to his scholarship, his detachment and his integrity.

Charles des Graz now took over as chairman. The vigour quickly returned and his strong personality drove the firm along at a spanking pace. Postal Censorship had taught him the need to be methodical. In the past, partners' meetings, for example, had just been opportunities for discussions. Now the proceedings were minuted with a secretary in attendance, and action specified against the relevant partner's initials. 'Charlie' himself had mellowed and relaxed a great deal. Many thought that his long years in America had filed away the last of the *hauteur*: he could now at times be positively genial. He was in any case a superb and increasingly esteemed auctioneer. In his spare time he devoted himself to collecting drawings and prints of Eton with which he lined his apartment in the Albany, and to the study of heraldry. Very exceptionally he had a vast knowledge of European as well as English armorial matters. During the war he had acquired a house and a host of friends in Bermuda. He looked forward immensely to his one or two lengthy and invigorating holidays there each year.

As des Graz's knowledge was mainly confined to books, the picture department was left increasingly to its own resources. It continued to grow apace. As the work load increased, Hans Gronau's health deteriorated and in 1951 he died. After a good deal of to-ing and fro-ing the board asked Carmen to continue the running of the picture department. Her talents had not gone unrecognised outside the confines of Sotheby's. In 1954 she was offered a senior teaching post in the Fine Art Department of Glasgow University. Her old tutor, Niklaus Pevsner, had had a hand in the matter. She was also offered a directorship by a West End firm of picture dealers with a strong American link. To the board's relief she turned down both invitations. Indeed, they now made her a director.

One lesson learned as a student remained firmly in the forefront of Carmen's thinking: one could not be an expert at everything. The whole subject of identifying Old Master paintings is imbued with pitfalls. The problem of the recognition of copies – contemporary or subsequent – of facsimiles and replicas, of a master's own work or work carried out by pupils and schools, needs a detailed knowledge of a relatively small area – and time for scrutiny, for careful consultation of references and photographs, and time for thought and ultimate judgement. But time is always short in an auction house, when clients want to sell quickly, sales have to be made up many weeks in advance and catalogue entries written at speed. Carmen called in many of her friends for advice and consultation. More importantly, she and Peter Wilson decided that it was essential that the firm should have such experts, trained in museums and in the academic world, on its own staff. The first such expert to arrive was Philip Pouncey from the British Museum, an acknowledged scholar in the field of Italian paintings and drawings. A few years later he was followed by Neil MacLaren, the National Gallery's expert on the Dutch and Spanish schools. Other departments followed suit. John Hayward joined the works of art department from the Victoria & Albert Museum as a leading expert in Renaissance art, and later, Basil Robinson came to the Japanese department from the same Museum.

It was twenty years since Evelyn Barlow had left the firm, and a woman head of department took some getting used to. Carmen's first battle was with her porter. He was used to doing things in his own way and entirely unwilling to compromise. Carmen came to Peter Wilson in tears to offer her resignation after the porter handed in his notice. But there was only relief at his departure: if the firm had not been so gentlemanly he would have gone much earlier. Carmen worked funny hours: she liked to do her cataloguing after the office had closed and the telephones had ceased ringing. She started a small photo-graphic studio in a cubby-hole under the stairs and took on a gifted young photographer, Cecilia Gray, daughter of Basil Gray – the keeper of the Department of Oriental Antiquities at the British Museum – from the Courtauld Institute to tackle the work of recording paintings. She began a proper photographic archive which the firm had never had. She started a serious reference library which she thought essential. After her husband's death she had constantly to travel to look at paintings. Time was the great enemy. With her enormous nervous energy she lost a stone each year between the opening of the auction season in October and Christmas. Altogether this petite, vibrant, determined woman with her astute commercial flair and strong feminine intuition, was a new Sotheby experience. She knew her own mind and stated her views with a forthrightness which sometimes jarred. She fought fiercely when she thought it necessary – and she often did – but she could also charm the birds off the trees. Carmen's presence on the board was in stark contrast to the po-faced old-Etonian tradition. At first she completely lacked the sense of political awareness that inevitably becomes a feature of the board of any major business enterprise. Peter Wilson helped her over a good many hurdles. Soon her department needed regular assistance and she had a gift for picking able helpers – Roddy Thesiger (who later became managing director of Colnaghi's), John Synge, Richard Day, St. John Gore (later in charge of paintings at the National Trust), Charles Maison, Philip Pouncey, Neil MacLaren and, her star pupils, John Rickett and later Derek Johns. She also knew her limitations: she confounded many of her critics by admitting at once when something was beyond her expertise. Above all it was the unique alliance of Peter Wilson's gifts and her own that gave Sotheby's undoubted supremacy as auctioneers of paintings for much of the post-war period.[1]

Among the constant stream of sales of works by Old Masters – there was one

1. After some years Christie's rose to the challenge and fought back vigorously.

virtually every second Wednesday throughout each season every year – a few are particularly memoreble because they triggered off major developments. One such was the sale of a *Nativity* by Nicolas Poussin in July 1956. This was interesting for two reasons: its price represented a major breakthrough in what had been rather a stagnant market, and it showed how complex the problems of ownership can be for an auctioneer, a subject of which the outside world is often completely unaware.

Vere Pilkington had been called to the home of Jocelyn Beauchamp, a retired naval officer who lived at Berghapton House in Thurton, near Norwich. Mr. Beauchamp wanted to sell a certain number of paintings, some porcelain, jewellery and furniture which he had inherited from the Proctor–Beauchamp collection.[1] He explained that death duties had already been paid and all legal liabilities resolved. As soon as Pilkington saw the magnificent Poussin hanging on the stairs he realised that it was something quite out of the ordinary. Although it proved to be virtually unknown, it was signed and had, in fact, once belonged to Sir Joshua Reynolds and had been sold for 205 guineas at auction after the painter's death. It had eventually found its way into the Proctor-Beauchamp collection.

Pilkington left behind the splendid, fragile but immensely heavy Louis XV frame and took the canvas back to London in his car. This was on 12 June. It was decided to include the painting in an important picture sale to be held only four weeks later on 11 July. Carmen and Peter Wilson alerted possible buyers in England, in France and Holland as well as in America. There was a strong and immediate reaction of interest. Then – a bombshell. Jocelyn Beauchamp rang up to say that he had been visited by a mysterious lady, who explained that she was acting on behalf of a London dealer who had heard that the picture was for sale and had offered £10,000 in cash for an immediate sale. Understandably Beauchamp considered the price quite fair. The mysterious lady also offered to pay any commission that he would have to pay because of the withdrawal of the painting from Sotheby's. A few days later she increased her offer to £15,000. Now at that time this was something that had happened on quite a number of occasions after outstanding pictures had been announced as coming up for auction. The London auctioneers regarded it as a tactic in a campaign to stop the finest paintings being sold in the auction room.[2] For it was certainly true that up to the mid-Fifties, outstanding masterpieces were usually sold by dealers behind closed doors. Pilkington and Peter Wilson therefore informed Beauchamp that they felt certain that the Poussin would fetch a much higher price in open competition. Indeed they offered him a guaranteed sum. This was a considerable gamble and something that had never been done before, but seemed the only method of allowing the painting to reach the sale-room. The press took a great fancy to the subject-matter of the painting. Because it was evident that the *Nativity* would look more impressive displayed in its own

1. See page 322.
2. Vere Pilkington felt so incensed about the matter that he hired a firm of private investigators to establish the identity of the dealer in question.

magnificent frame, Jocelyn Beauchamp at once despatched his butler to London with it. The *Illustrated London News* devoted a whole page illustration to it before the sale. Most of the major papers discussed its appearance on the market in some detail.

On the day of the sale it was included as lot 119 out of rather more than 180 paintings and Peter Wilson announced it as '*The* Poussin'. The bidding started rather slowly at £1,000; then moved along much faster. It was eventually bought at £29,000 by David Koetser, a dealer with premises both in London and New York. The underbidder was Geoffrey Agnew. It was soon hailed as an auction record, not only for a Poussin (the National Gallery had recently bought two at much lower prices) but it was also the highest picture price of the season. A small *Winter Landscape* by Hendrik Avercamp, bought by Speelman, also caused surprise by fetching £14,000 immediately afterwards. The two pictures between them accounted for rather more than three-quarters of the morning's total of £57,342. This *seemed* very satisfactory, and Denys Sutton wrote a perceptive review of the event in the *Financial Times* as constituting a genuine breakthrough in the art market where picture prices were now rising generally because more and more private buyers appreciated how undervalued Old Master paintings had been in comparison to other objects. Previously, the major buyers of such works had been museums, and their depressed acquisition funds had kept prices down. In fact, Peter Wilson and Carmen had been led to believe that the price might go even higher and the result was something of a disappointment to them. Indeed there were further shocks to come. Two days after the sale, a letter reached Bond Street from a firm of Norwich solicitors to say that the painting sold was 'settled furniture' and that the net proceeds were to be paid to a trust and not to Commander Beauchamp. Two days after that a further letter arrived from the same solicitors stating that the trustees had now been advised by Counsel that the sale had been 'wholly irregular' because Beauchamp had not previously obtained an Order of Court permitting the sale and that it might have to be annulled. Sotheby's consulted their own lawyers who took the matter in hand. Further legal issues with possibly dire consequences continued to complicate matters almost daily. Not surprisingly, the atmosphere at Bond Street grew extremely tense. But Peter Wilson preserved an icy calm: a quality which was to stand the firm in very good stead for the next twenty years.

An Order of Court was obtained a few days later and the picture eventually released to the vendor by 26 July. He too became involved in unforeseen complications. The painting was refused an export licence and the National Gallery who, according to Commander Beauchamp, had refused to consider its purchase some years earlier, though they might have had it for a mere £300, now offered to buy it for £30,000. They ultimately purchased it for what rumour suggested was a higher price.

Beauchamp sold a few other items at Sotheby's subsequently though nothing approaching the quality of the Poussin. He died in 1958, shortly after his lawyer. But the legal complications continued unabated. New firms of solicitors continued to join the fray. Various counsel were consulted. The matter was not finally resolved until almost five years after the sale. But despite these complications, the exceptionally high price had made its mark all over the world and the Poussin *Nativity* drew a great many other major Old Master paintings to Bond Street.

Less than a year after the sale of the Poussin another event occurred which came to be regarded as something of a milestone. A friend of Anthony Hobson's – whose identity has never been revealed – brought a sketch-book into the Old Master department to discuss its possible sale. Its history was remarkable and the mere sight of it was enough to set all Carmen Gronau's art-historical pulses racing at an erratic pace. The sketch-book consisted of fifty-eight delightfully gentle drawings of the Tuscan landscape on forty-one leaves, that is, in a number of instances there were sketches on both sides of the same piece of paper. The drawings displayed a marvellous economy of line with a minute observation of detail. They seemed the work of a great master. Indeed, a note inside the volume proclaimed them to be the work of Andrea del Sarto, but somehow this did not seem right. They had originally been bought in Ireland in 1925. The owner had recently taken them to the British Museum for an identification of the true authorship. After careful scrutiny, John Gere of the Department of Prints and Drawings identified them as the work of the Florentine painter, Fra Bartolommeo, who had died in 1517.

Carmen undertook extensive researches in Florence to verify the attribution and to establish the provenance. She was remarkably successful in her discoveries. It turned out that the drawings had been included in an inventory compiled at the time of Fra Bartolommeo's death and that they constituted about a quarter of the drawings that remained in the artist's studio. His heir was another monk who later gave the sketches to a talented nun to whom he taught painting and drawing. They remained in her convent in Florence until the beginning of the eighteenth century. It was at that time that Francesco Gabburri, President of the Academy of Painters in Florence and an avid collector, as well as something of a *marchand amateur*, discovered that the reverend sisters were using the precious paper to wrap up parcels and to light their fires. He bought a large collection of drawings from them, including the leaves with which we are concerned. Because the latter were clearly all the work of a single hand, thought to be that of Andrea del Sarto, they were bound into one large volume and Gabburri's coat of arms proudly blocked on to the front cover. Subsequently the volume was sold to William Kent, who presumably brought it back to England for his patron, the Earl of Burlington. What happened to it in the final period of two hundred years was never discovered.

Although the drawings had been preserved in pristine condition, the album itself had become very brittle, and after much heart-searching it was decided to break it up and to sell the forty-one drawings individually. Carmen included a detailed preface to the catalogue in which she described the explanation of the provenance. There was no auction room precedent for the sale of such a series and there was a good deal of speculation beforehand of the likely price. Individual estimates varied between £30,000 and £80,000. On the morning of the sale, the gallery was packed, not only with London dealers but also with an unusually large contingent from all over Europe and America. The prices for some of the individual leaves were generally much higher than had been anticipated: the highest was £8,400 paid by the Matthiessen Gallery for one of the most delightful sketches. Other buyers included Colnaghi, Agnew, Professor Bodkin of Birmingham, Wertheim of Paris and a number of American dealers. In the event the total realised was £100,850, a good deal more than Carmen had allowed herself to imagine in her most optimistic moments. As *The Times* commented with some satisfaction, it was a sale which would be long remembered. In a second session there was also sold a self-portrait of Fra Bartolomineo, fine drawings by Rembrandt, Goya and Claude Lorrain, as well as a pair of wings from a triptych of the Crucifixion by Giovanni Bellini. The overall total for the sale was £174,280, then the greatest such figure ever achieved at Sotheby's.

29

Re-organisation, Specialisation and Increasing Travel

IN 1946 sales had totalled £1,556,700, but they never reached – let alone exceeded – that figure again until 1955 when it went up to £1,703,267. Thereafter there was a steady forward progression: £2,266,827 in 1956, £3,175,212 in 1957, £3,087,918 in 1958, and the £5,809,437 in 1959 was something genuinely to crow about. Such growth brought headaches in its train. The actual number of sales had only increased from 166 in 1946 to 189 in the whole of 1959 but the number of owners of property concerned had shot up much more dramatically from 6,244 to 10,034. This not only meant more paper work and more administrative labour, but it also began to spell out the need for re-organisation. It was necessary not only to improve the service to clients at any particular moment, but also to cater for a steadily increasing flow of goods through the firm. Directors were so busy with their existing work load that a number of outside management consultants were called in from 1958 onwards.

Sotheby's as a functional organisation was a consultant's nightmare, or dream, whichever way one looked at it. After due investigation the consultants' various conclusions and recommendations were usually both apt and seemingly sensible. The problems arose when it came to implementing them. The bottlenecks that had been exposed with great precision after detailed analysis, had a habit of moving up or down the line rather than disappearing. The streamlined paper work seemed to require more staff in operation rather than less, as had been confidently predicted. Later on the installation of reasonably sophisticated accounting machinery led to more problems than it solved, and later still the introduction of the first computer practically brought the running of the firm to a halt. It was only the third generation computer equipment that brought genuine benefits and much greater efficiency.

The most disruptive factor in day-to-day administration as a whole was that each department within the firm had developed its own approach to solving common problems. Those with efficient overlords worked well. Thus Fred Rose's silver department moved on well-oiled wheels, while the painting department – still in the midst of astronomical growth – suffered agonies of frustration over lost files and delayed records. The first consultancy approach did at least make it clear to all and sundry that a common system of clerical procedures and internal communication throughout the firm was essential.

From an organisational point of view, the pattern of change in the last three decades has been interesting. In the late post-war period, the centralisation of administration seemed to be the answer, so all administrative work was taken out of the hands of individual departments and transferred lock, stock and barrel to a central administrative office. This grew like Topsy from an initial staff of three or four in the 1950s to nearer 60 by 1969. Inevitably the introduction of such a large clerical labour force meant the creation of an anonymous buffer, and the relationship between the firm and its clients became alarmingly impersonal. Departments were forced to keep their own duplicate personal files in an attempt to overcome this. Eventually matters got to such a state that departmental heads insisted on a major change of policy. So in 1970 Central Administration was dismantled. Each department now acquired its own administrator who became an integral member of its staff. On this occasion the system was devised and put into operation not by outside consultants (though more of them had recently been in evidence) but by the firm's own administrative management. It worked well from the word go: an interesting example of early recognition of the philosophy of 'small is beautiful', and evidence also that the best solutions often come from within. A further important by-product of the new arrangement was that it recognised, and indeed established, a promotional ladder for administrative staff.

The other major problem was space: space for people, space for storage, space for cataloguing and space for interviews with clients. One consultant's investigation into this came out with a delightfully simple and comprehensive solution: 'we recommend that you should move to new premises as quickly as possible'. But complex and impractical though the growing network of linked property in the area between Bond Street and George Street was, it gave the firm a character and an identity that the partners were unwilling to forsake. Even today (1980) few new entrants to the firm immediately master the labyrinthine and seemingly illogical geography of the premises. In the great boom period of the early Seventies when property development was a phrase with magical (rather than ominous) connotations for many banks and major finance houses in Britain, a grandiose plan was conceived and indeed developed into elaborate and striking sketches by the architect, Sir Dennis Lasdun, which would have converted the mass of higgledy-piggledy property into a contemporary and highly practical piece of architecture for a modern auction house, with all sorts of ancillary shopping arcades and office accommodation. The original estimate of cost seemed high, though within the realms of possibility, but the beginnings of hyper-inflation and economic decline, let alone the obstacles of getting the necessary planning consent, soon rendered such a development out of the question. An imaginative sidelight on the overall rebuilding strategy was the proposal that Sotheby's should rent part of the Royal Academy premises at Burlington House during the actual period of reconstruction in Bond Street.

All this was still far off in the future at the time of the rapid expansion during the late 1950s. Much the most important development after the war had been the increased autonomy of departments. The principal expert in each became its head and usually its auctioneer. This linked responsibility with professional authority. It fostered connoisseurship and scholarship and produced a refreshing totality of control over departmental destiny and success, and finally gave the death knell to the philosophy behind Major Warre's old dictum that no expert was worth more than £5 a week. It also meant that there were far more really competent auctioneers in the firm to take the increasing number of sales, who really knew their clientele both among professionals and private collectors. There was Peter Wilson and John Rickett for paintings, Charles des Graz and later Anthony Hobson for books and manuscripts, the old maestro Jim Kiddell for ceramics and works of art with Tim Clarke for porcelain and glass, and Fred Rose and Richard Came for silver and jewellery. Up to 1964 there were only eight major departments: Old Master pictures, English and modern pictures, prints and drawings, books and manuscripts, silver and jewels, works of art, antiquities and coins, and furniture which traditionally was linked with valuations. For some years there had been a marked shift towards increasingly specialised sales for particular groups of interested clientele, and this trend has continued unceasingly, though on many occasions initial sales were not a financial success and it needed much patience to establish them. After 1967 departments sub-divided enthusiastically like amoebae. The former works of art department, for example, is now a mass of independent units, no less than fifteen of them. One constituent part, porcelain, split into European and oriental; and Japanese was again hived off from Chinese. Perhaps the small Japanese department at Bond Street is an interesting and relevant case history of how the development of such a microcosm took place.

Initially the department had just been one of Jim Kiddell's sidelines, but it really achieved an identity of its own in the early Fifties with the arrival as resident cataloguer of Japanese metal-work and ivories of Billy Winkworth, son of the Stephen Winkworth whom we met on page 301, whose property had been sold at Sotheby's before the war. He came in place of a part-timer who had just retired, G. G. Davies, who had also catalogued for other auctioneers. The younger Winkworth had spent seven years on the staff of the British Museum from 1919 to 1926 under R. L. Hobson, concentrating on the arts of China and Japan. Thereafter he took to collecting, study and occasional dealing. He was particularly fascinated by netsuke. His own principal mentor in this field had been Freddy Meinertzhagen, a delightfully eccentric character who kept a tobacconist's shop just behind Bourne & Hollingworth in Oxford Street. Meinertzhagen was an old-Harrovian who had been left some money as a young man. He dabbled in communism and married a chorus girl. His real passion in life was for some of the then little appreciated Japanese minor arts, netsuke in particular, and he did much to encourage pre-war collectors in this field. He kept a remarkable illustrated index of netsuke and was the author towards the end of his life of one of the first worthwhile books on the subject, the tantalisingly brief *Art of the Netsuke Carver*.

One way or another he had handled the best part of 100,000 netsuke during his lifetime, and had actually bought or sold some 10,000 of them. Hearing about Meinertzhagen from some of his devotees, one carries away an enchanted picture of fabulous glass paperweights and netsuke jostling side by side with tins of St. Bruno and Player's Medium Cut, and our diminutive expert dashing upstairs to his tiny drawing room above the shop to work feverishly on his card index between calls by customers, tobacco company representatives and a small band of collectors. In fact, in Meinertzhagen's latter years the tobacco disappeared and the establishment became an antique shop, pure and simple, specialising in oriental art. Winkworth had taken his mentor's expertise several steps further and his informative catalogues soon began to draw the attention of dealers and collectors towards Sotheby's. At about the same time, Jack Hillier, who had spent a career in insurance but whose all-absorbing hobby had been the collecting of Japanese prints, became Sotheby's expert in this field.

Under its present head, Neil Davey, who had begun his career at Sotheby's in 1958 as a porter, the department now holds separate sales of netsuke and objects in ivory; lacquer-work, including inro; pottery and porcelain; metal-work, including particularly swords, other forms of armour and tsuba (the decorated sword guards so popular among collectors); prints, paintings, illustrated books and scrolls – the latter group also includes Chinese paintings for convenience of administration. The later – that is the late nineteenth- and twentieth-century – carvings (principally Okimono) and ceramics are dealt with quite separately at Belgravia, and a similar section exists, of course, at Parke Bernet in Madison Avenue, New York and another at PB 84.[1] So division can be by subject, nationality, period and location.

Very often the development of a department is directly linked with external circumstances. Neil Davey's department and the Japanese economy have grown, prospered and occasionally faltered on almost exactly parallel lines. After the war, and largely because of the odium of the war, the number of interested collectors was tiny: a mere handful of enthusiasts. Prices were low, very low. Netsuke, for example, or inro were hardly ever sold singly, but mostly in groups to make a viable minimum sales figure. The average number of people attending a sale might be twenty and the print run of a catalogue would be about 250. Slowly an increasing number of bids came in from Japan, and eventually, as the Japanese economy began to thrive, buyers came over in growing numbers. A Japanese girl was employed within the department so that language difficulties for these visitors could be kept to a minimum. The buyers were essentially dealers. In Japan auction sales were generally completely private – by dealers for dealers, with entry by invitation only. Usually there were no catalogues and no private view. Bidding was very quick and required instant decisions. The incursion of dealers used to these methods made a considerable impact on the relevant sales in London, not only those at Sotheby's, but also at Christie's and at Glendining's who had for years specialised in sales of Japanese art. A Japanese collector will tend to have his favourite dealer through whom he buys exclusively both at home and abroad. The result of this invasion was dramatic. The departmental turnover in 1966/67 was £122,000. By the end of the 1978 season it had grown to £1,539,458.

As in the case of so many other specialist departments, it was really the advent of three outstanding series of sales that put Neil Davey's little outfit on

1. Parke-Bernet on 84th Street, always referred to as PB 84.

the map. In the case of netsuke it was the seven sales of the Hindson Collection, widely recognised as one of the most representative of its kind, held between 1967 and 1969. Where Japanese prints were concerned, it was initially the John Mellor Collection sold in July 1963 and the three sales of the Vever Collection in 1974, 1975 and 1976.

Mark Hindson had retired from business abroad as an inspector for the Bank of London and South America to live in London in the late 1930s, a bachelor of modest means. His reason for deciding to concentrate on collecting netsuke was because he liked the liveliness and variety of the carvings and because the question of storing them presented so little difficulty in the confines of a small flat. Hindson bought extensively from Meinertzhagen and later acquired the bulk of Billy Winkworth's own collection. He had a superb eye and loved showing his pieces to other collectors. He was also an excellent scholar and broke much new ground in his reading of the carvers' signatures and in the patient analysis of difficult inscriptions. He took particular delight in teaching Neil Davey all that he knew, and was one of those rare collectors who decided to disperse his collection before he died so that his objects would remain in circulation among fellow collectors. He selected and catalogued the first three sales himself although already a sick man, and was fascinated by the prices these fetched. For although today they already seem very low, they represented a major breakthrough at the time; and it was one of those unusual series of sales where prices increased progressively as the series continued. One of the reasons for the much greater level of competition for netsuke at this time came from American buyers. Many US servicemen had become fascinated by Japanese artefacts and antiques while they were stationed there during the long occupation after the cessation of hostilities in 1945. They took their hobby back home with them and netsuke collecting spread in America. Collectors kept in touch through their own societies and with their own specialist magazine. News of Hindson's great collection had spread over the Atlantic. The sales were fabulously well attended. To overseas visitors, London prices still seemed unduly cheap. Thus Hindson set new trends. By 1969, towards the end of the series, there had been several individual carvings which had each fetched more than £1,000. Established collectors could hardly credit it. Meinertzhagen had rarely sold a netsuke for two figures and £20 was considered a veritable record. By the late-1970s particularly fine individual netsukes were regularly fetching in excess of £10,000. The Hindson series was also an important influence beyond netsuke. Its impact sharpened the interest in things Japanese generally. Its effect, for example, was clearly discernible even in the sale of Japanese ceramics.

The history of the Vever Collection went back rather further. Henry Vever was born in 1854. He became one of the foremost French jewellers of his time and an avid collector in many spheres. He became interested in Japanese art in the late 1880s, twenty years even before 'Hiroshige' (Will H. Edmunds) joined Sotheby's. It was generally reckoned when he sold some of his finest prints to a Japanese industrialist, Kojiro Matsukata, in the early 1920s, that he had disposed of his collection in its entirety because some eight thousand examples are said to have been involved in the transaction. In fact he had still kept back some of the choicest examples of the Japanese wood engraver's art, and indeed, unbeknownst to his fellow collectors, he continued to acquire others throughout his life. He died in 1943 and his collection was carefully hidden during the wartime occupation of France. It was not surprising, therefore, that when Sotheby's first announced its dispersal in a series of three great sales, interest was enormous, and prices seemed astronomical. The three sales realised £1,838,695. Vever's name had become particularly well known in Japan because Matsukata presented his own collection to the Imperial Household Ministry – as it happened, in the year Vever died, 1943 – and from there they eventually passed to the Tokyo National Museum where they form the main body of the collection. For this reason, two separate Japanese dealers had actually chartered aircraft to bring collectors to the last (in fact, the least important) of the three sales, one from Tokyo and another from Kyoto. An interesting sidelight on the Hindson and the Vever collections is that in each case the catalogues have been turned into a major work of reference in their own field.[1]

The emergence of many other departments followed a generally similar pattern. The most immediately dramatic in the Fifties, of course, was the swift rise to total predominance within the firm, and in the art market world-wide, of Impressionist and modern paintings. It was only in the very early Fifties that Peter Wilson had tentatively included a quartet of paintings by Picasso from a Brighton collector in a general Wednesday morning sale. There was some astonishment and then a good deal of interest from several collectors. Great things were expected from one prominent lady in particular, but when it came to the sale itself the collectors' bidding was unadventurous. Dealers stood aside altogether because they did not want the venture to succeed – exactly as had earlier been the case with major Old Master paintings – and the pictures had to be bought in.[2] Similarly, Vere Pilkington was offered a collection of works by Cézanne for a sale at about the same period, but the trade appeared to be totally uninterested and he arranged a private sale instead. The change in attitude thereafter was very rapid. By the mid-Fifties Impressionist sales had become a regular feature, and the Weinberg and the Goldschmidt sales had the same catalytic effect on prices that Hindson and Vever had had on a much smaller scale on Japanese art.

At this stage there was rapid development among the dealers who specialised in buying and selling such pictures, not only in London and New York but also in France, Germany and Switzerland. A number of established galleries had

1. Neil K. Davey, *Netsuke*, a comprehensive study based on the M. T. Hindson Collection, London 1974, and Jack Hillier, *Japanese Prints and Drawings from the Vever Collection*, three volumes, London, 1976; both published by Sotheby Parke Bernet Publications.
2. Only a few years later in May 1955, Picasso's early nude, *La Belle Hallondaise*, was sold by Sotheby's for £55,000, and in the sale of the collection of Somerset Maugham in April 1962, the same artist's *Death of a Harlequin* (with another picture on its verso) fetched £80,000, then the highest price ever paid at auction for a picture by a living artist.

built up considerable stock, which they had put down like good wine, while the prices of the works of the French Impressionists were still low. Others saw the opportunities of a growing market, found an interested clientele in increasing numbers and started new establishments. Once more Sotheby's was called on to provide credit on an augmented scale, and the skills learned on the book side came into prominence again. All this soon meant the establishment of a quite separate departmental division for Impressionists within the realm of the paintings department. For many years Peter Wilson devoted more time to the sale of such collections than any other. This meant constant travel, for they were scattered all over the world, and as Sotheby's reputation in this area grew, owners became increasingly tempted to consign such pictures for sale in London. Travel in search of business was, as we have seen, a long established tradition within the firm, but it took on an altogether different scale after 1953 and this was to have significant consequences. It had become the custom in Barlow's day that each partner or director was responsible for one or more of the many essential administrative chores, and this had continued unchanged in such matters as insurance, finance, advertising, printing, premises, partners' cars and so on. Certainly the habit of always allocating an area of responsibility as soon as it arose was excellent, but it began to work less and less efficiently in the continued absence of partners. The primary method of internal communication was still the weekly partners' meeting, but it was usually a brief and rushed affair, and trivial matters – such as contributions to charity and unusual media for advertising – received as much attention as really major policy decisions.

The first example of prolonged absence by several partners at the same time was the Farouk affair which began in 1952. Neguib and Nasser had recently seized power in Egypt and the revolutionary government decided to sell off the immense riches of the palace collection which the king had left behind after his abdication. He had, in fact, departed in haste with only his collection of jewellery (and the knowledge that he had major bank accounts in Europe). Peter Wilson heard whispers of this decision earlier than most and flew off at once to Cairo in December 1952. Here was what seemed a marvellous opportunity to escape from the strait-jacket of overseas trading restrictions. Initial introductions to the Minister of Justice and to other high-ranking officials were effected by Max Harari. Peter Wilson, Tim Clarke, Anthony Hobson and a supporting cast of fantastically hardworking and loyal colleagues later spent months in the torrid Egyptian heat coping with the legal and political imbroglio in Cairo. Cataloguing the collection itself was a positive delight in comparison with the complexity of making the other arrangements.

During the spring and summer of 1953 it was John Synge and Barbara Hare who held the fort out in Egypt and dealt with the innumerable day-to-day problems and crises over the arrangement of the sales. Cries for help to London often had to go unanswered, because London itself was so frantically busy with another major round of sales. The revolutionary government was still very unsure of itself and touchy to the point of distraction. The slightest adverse comment or clumsily constructed question tended to be interpreted with political overtones. The men in charge, although highly efficient and often charming, were as yet unwilling to accept the responsibility for the most minor decisions. What was worse was that as soon as trust had been established with any one of the senior officials, they tended to be transferred elsewhere. Communication to and from London was almost entirely by diplomatic bag. There were two overriding uncertainties: could Farouk challenge the legality of the sale, and which – if any – of his possessions should be excluded from the sale and retained for the Egyptian national museums? On one occasion Peter Wilson and Tim Clarke actually attended a meeting of senior ministers to explain these matters. In the end the Revolutionary Council was persuaded to enact immediate new legislation to cover the point, particularly of fully authorised sequestration, and to counter the Code Napoleon which had prevailed in Egypt since Napoleon's invasion at the very beginning of the nineteenth century. The consequence was that not only was the king dispossessed of his property and any further claims against the new state, but the same applied to three ex-queens, some fifty-nine ex-princesses and twenty-seven ex-princes, none of whom were prepared to accept the matter without protest.

Withdrawals from the sale (and indeed sudden new inclusions) continued to make the final preparation of the catalogues extremely difficult. No sooner had a major category of items been finally numbered and written descriptions prepared by one or other of the many experts sent out from England, when someone somewhere in the upper echelons of the amorphous hierarchy of the civil service issued an edict that the most outstanding item should be withdrawn. Occasionally this happened after ardent interest in such a piece had already been aroused in London, Paris and New York through advance publicity. The sales of antiquities and furniture, both included in the original contract with the Egyptian Government, had to be cancelled altogether. Furthermore, there was the fiercest rivalry that Sotheby's had ever encountered from other auctioneers. Parke-Bernet tried very hard to become involved, but it was Maurice Rheims, on behalf of a consortium of French auctioneers, whose persistence almost reached a point of open warfare. In the end it was considered expedient to allow Rheims to handle the sales as far as the French market was concerned. All this was marvellous copy, of course, for the newspapers of the world and the publicity for the forthcoming sale reached quite unknown proportions.

It soon became clear that while they would have to tackle all the preliminary work, Sotheby's would not be able to sell the goods in London or outside Egypt, or indeed to conduct the auctions themselves. Specialists had to be called in in any case to tackle the cataloguing of Farouk's magnificent collection of stamps and his little known collection of coins. The relevant work was done by the London specialists, Harmer's for stamps, and Baldwin's for coins, in the closest collaboration with Sotheby's. The scale of the ex-king's acquisitive activities was difficult to fathom even for members of experienced auction houses. When Fred Baldwin was first faced with the coin collection he estimated that there were in excess of 8,500 gold coins and medals and that the platinum coins (there proved to be 164 of them) amounted to five times the quantity of any previous platinum coin sale ever held. In fact, when the coin catalogue eventually appeared it was widely likened to a telephone directory, for nothing of that size had ever been produced for a single series of sales. However, it was what was loosely termed 'Virtue', or works of art in precious metals that caught attention all over the world. As the general prospectus of the 'Palace Collections of Egypt' could justifiably claim, the scope of the sales (but not their quality) invited comparison with those of the Whitehall Palace Collection sold under the Commonwealth in 1653, or of the contents of Versailles disposed of in 1793. The numbers and opulence (and sometimes the vulgarity) of every type of luxury article made by master craftsmen from all countries and periods was simply mind-boggling: the gold boxes often encrusted with jewels, the two thousand magnificent gold watches, the Swiss automata, the enamel pieces by Fabergé including several of his famous Easter eggs, the silver and the glass, all added up to a series of catalogues that caused the greatest excitement wherever they were studied. It was Farouk who almost single-handed had brought about the immense rise in price levels of glass paperweights throughout the world (which dropped as soon as he stopped buying), but his other passion in Gallé glass vases went almost unnoticed at that period.

Farouk's collecting mania, which was often highly tutored and surprisingly disciplined, had expressed itself in many other directions. The Sotheby staff used the ex-king's bedroom in the Koubbeh Palace near Cairo as its base of operations. It still contained his collection of 10,000 ties and hundreds of suits and uniforms. The latter were the cause of one of the most dramatic incidents during the cataloguing. A group of Sotheby experts stood chatting to members of the palace staff in the immense entrance hall of Koubbeh. Suddenly a portly figure in resplendent white uniform, accompanied by three uniformed officers, appeared at the top of the stairs. It could only be Farouk. The Egyptians fell on their knees, while the Englishmen gasped. It was a moment of extraordinary tension, which only relaxed when the figure in white winked. It proved to be an actor who was to play Farouk in a forthcoming film about the deposed king, who had donned Farouk's uniform to see whether he resembled the monarch. The likeness was staggering. It highlighted the prevailing tension of the period.

In other parts of the palace the cataloguers found an immense collection of early aspirin bottles, paper-clips and even razor blades. Rumour had it that Farouk had dispatched agents to find rare examples of such things to remote villages as far away as Persia and Argentina. The most curiosity concerned Farouk's far-reaching and well-known collection of erotica and pornography, housed in some twenty rooms. Even the British Museum expressed a strong interest in the purchase of the former, though only a small part was ultimately included in the sale. The Egyptian authorities made an astonishing offer that anyone spending more than £5,000 at the sales would be allowed free access to this special collection, but very few buyers availed themselves of the opportunity to do so. Those who did tended to be disappointed.

In the earlier stages of negotiations and surveillance of the royal property,

Tim Clarke's wartime experiences came in useful. For some years he had headed an army intelligence unit in Aleppo in Northern Syria, keeping a careful watch on the traffic crossing the border. This had given him an unusual insight into the workings of the Levantine mind. Indeed, on one occasion when he and Peter Wilson called on the British Ambassador in Cairo to be introduced to the Military Attaché, the latter looked Tim over quizzically and said, 'Not Clarke of Aleppo?'

The first obstacle that had to be surmounted was to persuade the new Egyptian Government actually to sign the very complex contract (in both English and Arabic) which appointed Sotheby's official advisers to the sale that finally resulted after months of negotiation. Peter Wilson and Tim Clarke attended an official ceremony in the Ministry of Finance in Cairo for this to be done on the morning of 26 February 1953. In the late afternoon the news was made official at a press conference. The local BBC correspondent in particular gave the matter tremendously wide coverage throughout the Middle East and in Europe. No one was more delighted when he heard the news than Charles des Graz, who sent a congratulatory telegram. Back in London the firm was deeply engrossed in the preparation of three major sales for the summer: the Emile Wertheimer sale of objects of virtue (on a smaller scale, they were the sort of possessions beloved by Farouk); the Alan P. Good eighteenth-century pictures, furniture and porcelain, and – most memorably – the magnificent contents of Ashburnham Park which were having to be sold because of the immense death duties following on the death of Lady Catherine Ashburnham. Des Graz was in the thick of all this. Peter Wilson reported in a long letter the events leading up to the signature of the contract, and how one Egyptian official had described the collections as 'a modern day Aladdin's Cave which was thrown open to the world'. But des Graz was never to receive the report. He died, totally unexpectedly, of a sudden coronary thrombosis, in his Albany apartment. His charlady found him dead there in the morning. It was a dire reminder of mortality in the midst of so much activity. For des Graz, then sixty, had planned to retire to the life he loved in Bermuda in the autumn of the same year. Sotheby's received a large number of letters of condolence. It was astonishing to what an extent des Graz's commanding presence had come to be regarded as irreplacable. Vere Pilkington seemed the natural successor and he at once became chairman.

The Farouk sales were planned for February and March 1954. The catalogues were issued many months in advance so that dealers could make their plans about going to Egypt. The Egyptian Government waived the normally complex export restrictions and set up a whole new banking and customs department to deal with the occasion.[1] BOAC offered a specially reduced return fare from London to Cairo for £162. The actual sales were conducted by a local British auctioneer who had been resident in Egypt for some forty years, Maurice George Lee. A dapper figure with a genial personality who was highly

1. At the time, the value of the Egyptian pound equalled £1 0s. 6d. sterling, 11.95 Deutschmarks, 1800 Italian lire, 12.52 Swiss francs and 2.88 US dollars.

regarded throughout Egypt, he not only knew the local customs and was acceptable to the authorities, but was also able to accept bids and to converse in no less than seven languages. The stamp sales set the pace. Prices were much higher than had been expected, despite the fact that lawyers, acting on behalf of Farouk, made continual threatening noises right up to the moment of the first sale. Bids and orders to buy came in by telephone from all over the world as many potential buyers were still unwilling to hazard a visit to Egypt in the uncertainties of the political climate, for it was known that Nasser and Neguib were in the midst of their struggle for power, though a surprising number did: Mr. Mark Fitch for example, a wealthy Essex businessman and stamp collector who carried off a single lot he had come specifically to buy – eight albums of Austrian stamps – for the seemingly enormous sum of £4,100; and Mr. Jack Minkus of Gimbels in New York.

The Koubbeh Palace looked its best for the occasion. Outside on the neatly trimmed lawns and among the flower beds and banks of blazing bougainvillea blossom, guests strolled around discussing their purchases or pausing to sip cool drinks from glasses tinkling with ice, served by courteous servants in the familiar tarboosh and white galabaiya. A brass band played military music and Viennese waltzes in the gardens throughout the sales. For the Sotheby staff who had toiled to make it all possible, it was merely a more exotic country house sale with its garden party atmosphere in the old tradition. Yet no one could escape the impression that the event had a much deeper significance – the end of a dynasty.

The remaining sales were not without incident. An elderly Scottish lady antique dealer, Mrs. Esta Henry of Edinburgh, objected vociferously to the way the Egyptian authorities instructed George Lee to sub-divide lots that had been catalogued as one, or to start the bidding at prices vastly higher than Sotheby's had advised or estimated. Even Victor Hammer, who attended the sale from New York, was moved to comment that the Egyptian Government 'was crazy' when pieces he had sold to Farouk were put up at starting prices four times as high as the ex-monarch had paid him only a few years earlier. In one sale session, ninety-four out of 144 lots were withdrawn. As Kenneth Snowman of Wartski's wrote in the role of acting correspondent for the *Sunday Times*: 'With admirable tact, suave representatives of Sotheby's steered situation after situation to calmer waters. It was not a bit like Bond Street'.

The total for the sale was in excess of £750,000, a figure which the revolutionary government found disappointing. They later accused Sotheby's of having publicised the sales insufficiently: an astonishing claim when hardly a family in the western world that read a newspaper can have been unaware of it. What was disappointing, and certainly contributed to some poor prices in the innumerable and interminable sales sessions (as well as the constant withdrawals), was the almost total absence of local Egyptian buyers, who in the prevailing political climate felt that it might be unwise to be seen to be buying former royal property for large sums of money. The result was that after the most unstinting efforts, Sotheby's were not paid.[1] The under-secretary at the Finance Ministry, to whom they had put their case for payment soon after the conclusion of the sale, was arrested. The wrangling went on for some time. Vere Pilkington launched a spirited offensive to get the money. Then Suez intervened and Sotheby's had to write off their investment in time and travel to experience. It was to stand them in good stead.

One immediate consequence of the work on the Farouk sales and des Graz's death was further internal reorganisation. Vere Pilkington initially took on a number of additional administrative responsibilities, but soon found he had to shed them again for lack of time. The consultants advised that the firm should appoint a new overall administration manager to solve the problem once and for all. It was to be twenty years or more before this piece of advice was finally implemented. In the meantime, however, Peter Wilson was asked to find someone to help in the re-styling of the sales galleries. John Fowler, later to become one of London's most renowned experts in the field of interior design, accepted the challenge – for a fee of fifteen guineas. He advised that the uniform colour for the walls should be crimson. After a great deal of thought and many months of discussion this was changed to the green that has now become so well established.

1. Early expenses and the commission on the stamp sale *were* paid. Further payments initially ceased when the Egyptian Ministry of Finance demanded tax payments from Sotheby's of which no mention had been made earlier. In fact, the taxes were eventually paid in order to clear the way to settlement, but in vain.

30

New York:
Beginnings and Breakthrough

SOTHEBY'S permanency on the American scene is due to the combined teamwork over many years of four men – Peter Wilson, John Carter, Peregrine Pollen and Jesse Wolff. There was, of course, a long tradition behind them initiated by Barlow and consolidated by Charles des Graz. Peter Wilson had spent part of the war in the States engaged at the British end of a joint Anglo-American Intelligence operation bent on the destruction of the Japanese war machine.[1] As soon as was decently possible after the end of hostilities and his return to Bond Street, he went frequently to New York to establish contacts and to search for business for Sotheby's, despite the constrictive grip of Board of Trade and Treasury regulations.

In this connection a visit in May 1947 was particularly memorable. Nominally he had gone to probe the possibility of getting the sale for Sotheby's of the enormous stock of the Brummer Corporation. Its owner, Joseph Brummer, had been one of New York's foremost dealers. He dealt not only in antiquities of all kinds, especially medieval works of art, but also, unusually, in modern paintings. He had died intestate at the beginning of 1947 and his widow and brother, who had finally inherited the business, were still uncertain what to do with it. The stock was said to run to some two hundred thousand items. Peter Wilson seriously contemplated holding the sale in New York but the Brummers decided to bide their time.[2]

Under the pretext of pursuing Brummer, Peter Wilson had in fact made a first tentative approach on behalf of Sotheby's to acquire Parke-Bernet. He was encouraged in this by the banker and collector, Robert Lehman, and the lawyer who had been instrumental in setting up Parke-Bernet in 1937, Louis Levy. Major Parke, now over seventy, had little capital other than that invested in the firm and was anxious to make provisions for his wife, who was many years younger than he. He owned one-quarter of the shares in Parke-Bernet and felt he could persuade the other shareholders to sell at a reasonable price. At the first meeting with Peter Wilson and Levy, the Major remained totally impassive but he did make it clear that he considered Sotheby's a suitable purchaser. Within a few days he provided Peter Wilson with all the financial details of

1. Peter Wilson was, in fact, asked to remain on the staff of MI6 at the end of the war and for a time felt tempted to do so. He rejoined Sotheby's in June 1946. It is interesting to speculate what would have happened to MI6 – and to Sotheby's – had he done so.
2. A good deal of the property was sold by Parke-Bernet in April and May 1949 and some at Sotheby's in 1964, the year in which Ernest died. His widow sold his personal collection of classical and medieval antiquities in October 1979 at a sale in Zurich organised jointly by Spinks and Galerie Koller which achieved considerable *éclat*.

Parke-Bernet's assets ($325,000 in cash plus $75,000 for the firm's library and its furnishings), turnover ($6,000,000) and profits ($125,000) respectively. He also suggested a formula for arriving at a purchase price (assets plus three times the current year's earnings – a maximum of $750,000 in all) and a five-year plan for payment. The most likely obstacle was that the British Treasury would be unwilling to grant permission for the export of funds to buy an overseas business.

Peter Wilson hurried back to London and reported to his partners. Curiously, his return coincided with yet another approach from Christie's about a possible merger. The partners, deeply immersed in the growing volume of the day-to-day running of the business, decided to set aside a whole day for a special meeting to discuss these matters. As usual, Geoffrey Hobson's written summary of the salient facts was a *tour de force*. Despite his age and growing weariness, he still looked into the future with unclouded vision, though he dreaded the prospect of an increased work load at a time when he was particularly anxious to withdraw from the business. As it happened, it was one of the last major memoranda he prepared. Des Graz, after initial hesitancy, came out wholly in favour of attempting to acquire Parke-Bernet. Though he saw many difficulties ahead, he felt it would be an insurance against the uncertainty of Britain's impoverished position after the war. Like so many people engaged in running businesses at that time he was depressed and discouraged by the total lack of understanding of commercial needs by officialdom and felt that this would be unlikely to change in the near future, if at all. Although the board's decision was neither clear-cut nor unanimous, it was decided not to continue discussions with Christie's and to pursue the establishment of a base in New York, even if the acquisition of Parke-Bernet itself did not go through. It didn't. Parke-Bernet not only moved into magnificent new premises at 980 Madison Avenue but continued in business strongly and independently, though by no means always profitably, for another seventeen years. Major Parke's own shares, as well as many of those belonging to his colleagues, were bought by a consortium of American businessmen who were also collectors.

It became clear towards the end of 1953 that the strict control on the export of sterling and the import of goods was likely to be relaxed at long last, and that this would pave the way to re-establishing London as a centre of the international art market. The matter had been the subject of frequent memoranda prepared at Bond Street for submission to government departments. On 7 December 1954 under the heading of 'Freeing the Dollar Import Restrictions' the British Embassy in Washington proudly announced that 'Non-fiction books, antiques and works of art, wool tops, nephelene syenite and wall board of flax waste are to be added to World Open General Licence'. Sculptures and rare books were provisionally excluded because the civil servants concerned had had 'definition difficulties'. Nevertheless, the edict was music to Sotheby's ears and, of course, to Christie's and the art trade generally.

Some time earlier Vere Pilkington, now chairman of Sotheby's, had already approached an old school friend about acting as the firm's representative in the

States when restrictions were relaxed. The man concerned was John Carter, a celebrated figure in the world of rare books. From 1927 to 1939 and again from 1946 to 1953, Jake, as he was known to his friends, had built up the antiquarian book business of the New York publishing house, Scribner's. During the war he had worked for the British Information Service in New York and, in fact, at the time of Pilkington's approach, because of his unrivalled knowledge of the States, he had been seconded from Scribners to be personal assistant to Sir Roger Makins (now Lord Sherfield), the British Ambassador in Washington. Carter's principal claim to fame though was as joint author with Graham Pollard of the book which had led to the unmasking of the book forger, Thomas J. Wise.[1] Carter's wife, Ernestine, was an American, who had formerly worked for the Museum of Modern Art (as Curator of Architecture and Industrial Art) and was now a distinguished journalist. Jake enjoyed meeting people and to many hundreds of American acquaintances this erudite, stylish old Etonian of haughty mien and impeccable manners, represented the personification of the typical Englishman. Although his qualifications seemed so eminently suitable for the post of Sotheby's man in America, Jake was concerned about his lack of expertise in fields other than books. After so many years of full-time employment, he also had ambitions about acting as both free-lance adviser to collectors and consultant to specialist dealers. He was therefore hesitant to commit himself exclusively to one firm. After some lengthy correspondence and many visits to and from Vere Pilkington, Peter Wilson, Anthony Hobson and Cyril Butterwick, a formula was at long last devised that suited both parties. Jake became Sotheby's 'Associate' in New York. It had been Tim Munby who had first suggested John Carter's name to Pilkington for the job, and Munby watched with amazement and delight how swiftly Jake took to it. The combined role of scout, scholar, man of business and, above all, diplomat suited his talents to perfection. Not many of his contemporaries were aware of Jake's brilliance (and determination) as an individual who planned his activities down to the last detail. He was also an astute judge of other men's talents and had few rivals in motivating them to do as he wanted when circumstances demanded it. His letters, with their elegant turn of phrase and indestructible logic, were the result of endless drafts and revisions. His seemingly casual phone calls and chance visits were calculated with the greatest precision. But Jake was a wholly dependable friend and an extremely efficient person. In his ten-year stint for Sotheby's in the States the two matters that upset him most were the occasional periods of neglect by Bond Street when his contacts there were swamped by overwork, and the fact that Pilkington had not made it possible for him to become a full shareholding partner at the outset.

The idea was that every year he should undertake two 'sweeps' of six weeks each round America, with a permanent office and secretarial help in New York. As luck would have it, only a month before he was due to set out for New York after a period of indoctrination at Bond Street, Christie's took a series of full-page advertisements in a number of collecting journals. These announced that

1. *An Inquiry into the Nature of Certain Nineteenth-Century Pamphlets* (see page 280).

Sir Alec Martin, their managing director, would be visiting the United States and Canada and would be available there for consultation to owners of works of art who might want to dispose of them, throughout the whole of October. It was the best thing that could have happened. Jake launched a series of announcements of his own presence, and where, without this direct competition from England, he might have stepped into action rather gingerly, it gave him an immediate aggressive edge that he never lost.

His principal weapons were the low commission rates in London compared to those charged by Parke-Bernet. He himself described his early efforts as 'two gruelling years of preparatory exploration and the renewal or establishment of useful connections, of physical reconnaissance, above all of persistent propaganda'. At first he concentrated on New York; eventually he covered most major cities across the American continent. His tiny office in the suite of his friend, the lawyer and book collector, Donald Hyde, at 61 Broadway, traded under the bold banner of SOTHEBY'S OF LONDON. Jake's twin objectives were to find properties that could be sent to and sold in London, because wider interest in Europe aroused greater competition, and also to find putative buyers in the States for major items that were coming up for sale in London. Inevitably the prime target for competition was Parke-Bernet and that firm soon began to feel the results of his presence in New York. Jake called endlessly on collectors, lawyers, bankers, dealers and museum directors many of whom he knew already. 'Everyone who could possibly be of use to Sotheby's,' Jake himself wrote,[1] had to 'be made aware that the firm's services were now available to them on their own doorstep, and not only to themselves but to others who might seek their advice for the most advantageous disposal of a collection or a single valuable item. To back up what soon became a well-polished spiel I always carried a brief-case full of the most impressive Sotheby catalogues (and price lists) to document the thesis that we could get higher prices in every department at a commission rate less than half Parke-Bernet's and even further below those ruling in Paris, which was sometimes in the mind of picture and furniture people. "Take", I would say, "a Cézanne or a Chardin which you know (as of course an alert professional would know) will bring the same $100,000 under the hammer whether it is sold at Parke-Bernet or Sotheby's or the Hotel Drouot, because the same half-dozen people, whether in New York or Los Angeles or Chicago or Paris or Basle will be the high bidders. What does the owner pocket *when the dust dies down?* In London, $90,000; in New York, perhaps $75,000 or $80,000 (Parke-Bernet's scales were flexible); in Paris, after commission *and* taxes, (none in London), about $65,000" '. Jake was also able to propound the advantage of the protection of reserves, a system which American *buyers* had always regarded with suspicion.

An unexpected invitation from the English Speaking Union's headquarters in London to lecture to their mid-Western branches on 'Sotheby's and the international fine art market' was a unique opportunity to spread the word. 'It seemed', wrote Jake, 'that the E.S.U.'s audiences were getting worn out with

1. In 'Sotheby's of London, New York: the Early Days', in *Art at Auction, 1970–71.*

addresses on "Whither Africa?", "Britain and the Commonwealth" or, worst of all, "Anglo-American Relations" and would like something friskier. This, we thought at 34 New Bond Street, was an opportunity too good to miss: expenses paid, all arrangements made and captive audiences under impeccable non-commercial sponsorship for an itinerary which I stipulated on controlling myself. The first tour was sufficiently successful to lead to two more, and by 1962 I had preached the Sotheby gospel in pulpits flanked by the Union Jack and the Stars and Stripes in Louisville, Indianapolis, St. Louis, Memphis, Cleveland, Toledo, Detroit, Chicago, Cincinnati, Richmond, Raleigh (North Carolina), Charleston and Palm Beach. Branches liked to be offered a choice of subjects and I always offered several: for example, "Behind the Scenes at Sotheby's", "Bull market at Bond Street", "Sold to the highest bidder", "Going, going, gone"; a later set was "Art in the Market Place", "Blue chips and painted canvas", "A Renoir is a girl's best friend – or is it?". Whichever title they selected, they actually got the same speech, naturally with suitable local or original trimmings, and it was always ten minutes shorter than the prescribed length so as to allow plenty of opportunity for questions, for I was there to learn as well as to expound.' Jake was a superb lecturer and with his slim figure, his immaculately cut suits, his monocle (which he always referred to as his eyeglass), his pipe and his irreverent wit he was an enormous success with most of his audiences. By the 1956–57 season American consignments were already responsible for more than 20 per cent of Sotheby's then record turnover of £3,168,476.

Much of this great influx was also due to Peter Wilson's own repeated visits to America. His colleagues bear testimony to his magnificent stamina in dropping everything in London if the possibility of the 'capture' of a major collection of pictures seemed likely. It was Peter Wilson who trained Jake's eye in the realm of Impressionist paintings. Often Carmen Gronau came too and Jake was always grateful for her guidance in the field of Old Masters. On one occasion the three of them travelled together out to Scarsdale, N.Y., early in 1957, to inspect a collection of Impressionist paintings, drawings and sculpture that had belonged to a Mr. William Weinberg, a banker of German extraction who had recently died. They were accompanied on the trip by John Walker, Director of the National Gallery in Washington and an old friend and neighbour of Jake's, who had never seen the collection and wanted a chance to inspect it, and Chester Dale who came for the ride (in the rented Cadillac). The contents of the house were under dust sheets, the lighting negligible as in so many affluent residences in America, so the whole delicate operation of inspection had to be conducted mainly by means of hand torches supplied by the caretaker in charge. 'Despite these handicaps,' Jake wrote, 'my brilliant colleagues came up with a remarkably prescient estimate for a dazzlingly name-studded but somewhat off-beat collection, and the deal was consummated.'

Although the cognoscenti might argue the point, it now seems abundantly clear that the sale of these fifty-six pictures by modern French masters from the Weinberg Collection thrust Sotheby's from a gentle upward trend into full orbit. The preparatory work for the sale, the promotion and publicity, its staging to a massive audience informed for the first time by closed circuit television, the gusto and control of the whole operation – and its enormous and resounding success – changed Sotheby's character overnight. Weinberg started the most astonishing decade in Sotheby's history. Primarily it established the brilliance of Peter Wilson, the auctioneer as impresario. At forty-four, with twenty years' experience of Sotheby's behind him, and on the verge – as it turned out – of becoming chairman, he was able to see ahead with a clarity and a degree of assurance that gave the firm an immeasurable advantage over its rivals. Behind the traditional discretion and the suave exterior of an almost placid mien, an imaginative mind and thrusting iron will came to the fore that made even Barlow's vision seem restricted. Suddenly Sotheby's burgeoned. The very name became a household word. The national interest in things old and beautiful was given a totally different complexion. A post-war hunger for art became manifest. Art sales were merely one, but probably the most immediately arresting, facet of this phenomenon. The financial rewards obviously mattered too. Owners came to Sotheby's to consign objects for sale, in unprecedented numbers. Books did well, works of art did well, but it was the picture department that really soared ahead. And among the paintings it was the works of the French Impressionists and Post-Impressionists that consistently made star sales and what then seemed to be astronomical prices. Weinberg ushered in the dizzy days of growth. Jake had sown the seed. Peter Wilson reaped a bumper harvest.

William Weinberg was a German financier who had settled in Holland soon after the First World War. In 1940 he was on a business trip to Paris when the Germans invaded Holland. He had already despatched his possessions, including his pictures, to America. He was now unable to return to his wife and three children. Despite frantic efforts to do so he never saw them again. They were arrested by the Nazis and perished in concentration camps. Weinberg emigrated to America but this loss left him inconsolable. Collecting pictures became the passion of his life. He had started in a small way long before the war under the aegis of J. B. de la Faille as adviser. De la Faille's name will live as compiler of one of the great modern *catalogues raisonnés*. He had spent his life tracking down the works of Vincent van Gogh (and of his imitators). It was not surprising, therefore, that Weinberg should have bought ten paintings, drawings and watercolours by that remarkable artist. One of the reasons why the whole collection was not unknown was that these Van Goghs had been used in the filming of *Lust for Life*, based on the novel by Irving Stone. With no immediate family to leave them to, Weinberg had stipulated in his will that his three executors – his attorney, his accountant and his secretary – should sell the collection by auction and that the proceeds should go to charity.

This poignant background certainly helped to interest the press and it was the reaction of the world's press that made the sale. There had never been coverage like it. It was at all levels: popular, serious, specialist. It started five weeks before the sale with an enormous press conference, reached a crescendo in its coverage of the event itself and shimmered on for months afterwards. No reader of any national morning, evening or provincial newspaper can have remained in ignorance of the sale. Radio and television gave it constant full news coverage. *Panorama* devoted most of a programme to the forthcoming event. Nor was the interest by any means purely British. The Italian, French, Dutch, German and American press took it up very quickly and continued to hammer away at the event. It was reported fully as far away as India, Rhodesia, Canada, Australia and New Zealand.

There were particular factors that fuelled the interest. The first had been the sale at the Galerie Charpentier in Paris of the collection of the American, Mrs. Margaret Thompson Biddle, where a still life by Paul Gauguin had been bought by the Greek shipping magnate, Mr. Basil Goulandris, for £104,000. This figure may seem unremarkable today, but it has to be set in the context of the £31,000 paid by Knoedler's for Weinberg's Van Gogh of *Les Usines à Clichy* which was then the highest figure for a painting ever paid at auction in London. Secondly, to everyone's amazement, on the day before the sale, the Queen came to look at the pictures, accompanied by Princess Margaret and Prince Philip. She was shown round by Anthony Blunt (then Sir Anthony), who was Keeper of the Queen's Pictures at that time. She met the three executors of the Weinberg Estate.[1] It was rumoured – and the rumour was confirmed by one of the press secretaries from Buckingham Palace on the next day – that the Queen would have liked to buy the Degas painting called *At the Races: the Wounded Jockey*.

Some months before the sale, Peter Wilson had obtained the Sotheby board's consent to considerable additional expenditure on publicity and public relations for the Weinberg sale. After much cogitation the P.R. side was placed with J. Walter Thompson, the famous advertising agency. For the surprising fee of £100 they planned and carried through an astute two-part campaign based on the fact that the pictures were being sold in London (and *not* in New York), and then on publicising the sale itself. The work was handled by Raymond Baker, who had simply sent an invitation to Buckingham Palace. When the directors had seen 'The Queen' on the list of invitations to be sent out, they had assumed that the reference was to *Queen* magazine.

It was the staid *Times Educational Supplement* who put the éclat into proportion. Speculating long before the sale about possible prices, it hazarded a guess that 'it would be no surprise to see the five-figure mark passed more than once', and then continued, 'the pictures themselves are so remarkable and so unknown, that one hopes that at least some will find their way into museums so as to widen the experience of art lovers, whose only collections must be public and not private. Drawings by Seurat, bronzes by Daumier, a self-portrait by Degas – things that are hardly known to exist, are emerging, perhaps only briefly, from obscurity. Most remarkable of all is the large batch of Van Goghs . . . A special

1. From a file relating to the Royal visit, it is interesting to learn how carefully organised even such an apparently informal occasion had become since the earlier Royal visit of Queen Mary in 1917.

effort has been made to bring these outstanding works to the attention of the public, and perhaps those responsible for handling such precious merchandise feel a responsibility to let the art-loving public know what there is in private keeping'.

While the American *Christian Science Monitor* stated plainly that 'London has become the centre of the art market', the *Sunday Times* put the point of view that 'what may be overlooked in the general excitement is that this is not in the strict sense an American collection. It is a collection which was formed largely in Amsterdam, where Weinberg was advised by J. B. de la Faille . . . in a great many cases the pictures came to Weinberg from Dutch collections. Theo van Gogh, for instance, owned Cézanne's portrait of his wife; the Monet of Zaandam had never previously left Holland. Most of the Van Goghs had been kept in Van Gogh's own country. A great part of the collection is, in fact, a tribute to enlightened Dutch taste'.

There was much guess-work about the probable results. The *Daily Express* hazarded an estimate of 'upwards of £200,000'. The *News Chronicle* reported Carmen Gronau as saying that the total might be more than £200,000. Only the *Glasgow Herald* drew attention to the fact that Weinberg's library of art books was being sold a few days before the pictures. 'Several of the items are of considerable rarity. They include annotated catalogues of early exhibitions in Paris of post-impressionist artists whose canvases were then ridiculed.' The gossip columnists took enormous interest in the preparations for the sale. They attended rehearsals and marvelled at the wonders (not previously seen in the sale-room) of the closed circuit television which would enable buyers in different overflow rooms to follow the auctioneer on the rostrum, and to make their bids however far they might be from the main gallery.

The coverage of the sale itself was more extensive than anyone could remember. *The Times* and the *Daily Telegraph* each devoted rather more than a whole page to it. The anonymous *Times* sale-room correspondent gave a charmingly detailed account of the proceedings:

> The flower of the intelligentsia, divided fairly evenly between the opulent and the impecunious, crowded Sotheby's rooms yesterday in such numbers that business had to be dealt with in three rooms at one and the same time by means of closed T.V. circuit. Dealers and collectors from Europe and across the Atlantic were naturally present in force, including Lord Rothschild and Baron Elie de Rothschild, and there was an unusual amount of spirited bidding from private individuals. The scene was extraordinarily animated, adorned by half a dozen feminine hats – perhaps chosen to vie with the charming confection worn by the Renoir lady of one of the paintings – and if any pins were dropped during the more tense moments of the morning, the sound did not reach the ears of your correspondent.
>
> Nor surprisingly did the perpetual comings and goings of television operators and press photographers, present in greater numbers than ever before seen in an auction room, distract the attention of the company or mar its obvious enjoyment – an enjoyment which occasionally found expression in delighted ripples of laughter as the hammer was about to fall and a further bid of £500 or so came at

the last moment. . . . The total for the 56 lots was £326,520. It was a memorable occasion, not merely because it made auction room history or because it will be many years, if ever, before a small personal collection of nineteenth-century masters of comparable quality comes on to the open market, but also because it would appear to provide overwhelming evidence that London has fully regained its position as a highly efficient world centre for the disposal of works of art from either side of the Atlantic.

The C.B.S. radio network in Washington noted with wonder that the *Financial Times* had made the event its leading story on page one, 'including that rarest of all things in the *Financial Times*, a photograph'. The *New York Times* had a long piece headed 'U.S. ART OBJECTS LURED TO LONDON: high prices at Sales cause Americans to send their Treasures to Britain'.[1] *Le Figaro* in Paris ran the story under a bold headline 'Vente Fabuleuse à Londres'. Probably the most perceptive commentary on the whole sale was in the *Birmingham Post*. It took the form of another whole page article by Professor Sir Thomas Bodkin, Keeper of the Barber Institute. 'In many respects,' he wrote, 'it was a most unusual auction. In a few it was quite unprecedented . . . I have attended two fabulous auctions in the past. The first was that of the collection of Rembrandt's friend, the Burgomaster Six, held about thirty years ago in Amsterdam. The second was that of the contents of John Sargent's Studio at Christie's soon after his death. As a fashionable occasion, as an exciting and exhausting experience, the Weinberg sale surpassed them both.' As a professional art historian Bodkin was particularly impressed by the catalogue. 'It is admirably compiled and presented, and the innovation of stating measurements in both inches and centimetres is one that must be highly commended.' Earlier he had commented that 'the handsome catalogue is illustrated by no fewer than 41 plates, including a coloured frontispiece[2] and was sold at five shillings which could not have gone far towards covering the cost of its production'.

The journalists who were present at the sale took particularly to Peter Wilson's restrained manner in the rostrum. The most memorable account of it occurred in a long piece on the sale and its implications for the future by Mollie Panter-Downes in the *New Yorker*. 'After every seat was occupied and people were standing jammed at the back of the gallery, the empty rostrum began to dominate the attention of the audience. . . . At two minutes past eleven, Mr. Peter Wilson . . . climbed up into it, smiled deprecatingly in response to a playful burst of clapping from some friends in the front row and asked for an opening bid of £100 for three small figures by Honoré Daumier. (They finally brought £1,400.) Below him stood an alert-looking man with bristling grey hair [it was Sam Patch] whose business it was to cast a hawk-like glance over the

1. Much of the material in this piece had been supplied by John Carter, as always making brilliant use of his opportunities to plug the firm.
2. It was an interesting reflection of the time, that in order to save costs, Sotheby's borrowed the blocks of the colour plate (of Van Gogh's *Les Usines à Clichy*) from the Museum of Modern Art in New York. They had, in fact, been made at Mr. Weinberg's expense two years earlier for inclusion in John Rewald's *History of Post-Impressionism*.

room and pounce on any bid the auctioneer might fail to see, but his assistance was rarely needed, for Mr. Wilson, a man with a gentle but remarkably carrying voice and a way of pausing almost affectionately to wait for the gentleman on his right – or left – to advance another thousand pounds, is known in the art world to have the sharpest pair of eyes in London.' When the bidding for the portrait of Madame Cézanne paused uncertainly for a moment 'Mr. Wilson imperturbably surveyed the room with the air of being prepared to give anyone a second, third or even fourth chance'.

Punch too gave the sale its attention – with remarkable prescience in the light of later events. 'Who were the mystery bidders?' it asked. 'I have my own views. One gentleman looked like a top-brass representative of the Transport and General Workers' Union; another may have been acting for the Iron and Steel Trades Federation; and the man who signalled his attentions by touching his nose with the *Daily Worker*[1] could have been an agent for the Union of Shop, Distributive and Allied Workers. Fanciful? Yes, I suppose so. But the unions, according to tradition, do not invest in industrial stocks, and it would be perfectly reasonable in the circumstances if they decided to lock up their members' funds in a few Van Goghs, Seurats, Manets, Cézannes and Picassos. After all, nobody in the country knows better than the union leaders how vicious the inflationary spiral is going to be.'

Many of the more popular papers commented on the fact that more than three hundred seats in the main gallery had been reserved for dealers from all over the world – and what 'hard-faced', 'inscrutable', 'calculating', 'determined' chaps they were. There were two delightful interludes of collectors buying for themselves. One was the American film producer, Sam Spiegel, who bought a pen-and-ink Odalisque by Toulouse-Lautrec for £300, the Degas painting of the Wounded Jockey, in which the Queen had expressed interest, for £5,800, two figure studies in black chalk by Camille Pissarro for £180 and a Vase of Flowers painted by Maurice Utrillo (signed and dated May 1939) for £3,200. The *Washington Post* reported that after the sale was over Spiegel had 'strolled up to the clerk's table' and, in the best Hollywood tradition, asked him 'to arrange for these little items to be sent home. "Just a few things for my own collection", he told a reporter'.

The fact that another person, a totally unknown stranger, universally described as 'the mystery buyer', took away a lovely little Renoir portrait of a young lady in a red dress, by outbidding the dealers to £22,000, that was what really startled the press – and, indeed, Sotheby's. *The News Chronicle* reported that when asked about his identity, the firm said 'we've never heard of him. As a matter of fact, one of our girl ushers tried to push him out because he didn't seem to be a buyer and had no ticket' (or catalogue either, it transpired later). Peter Wilson commented, 'I don't know him personally but I have every confidence in him, and hope the picture will be taken'. It didn't take the press long to track the buyer down. He was Mr. Sydney Reuben Bright, who had a flat in Portland Place and was Chairman of a group of South coast department

1. Who reported on the sale in great detail.

stores. He was a little taken aback by the public interest in his spur-of-the-moment venture into art collecting. He commented that he had not known 'about the picture until I got to Sotheby's and bought it. I seemed to have fooled the dealers'.

The purchaser of lot 14, a view of the Seine by the pointillist, Charles Angrand, painted from exactly the same spot at Courbevoie as Seurat's *Esquisse pour la Grande Jatte*, lot 39 in the same sale, was H. M. Robinow. He was an investment banker who had become interested in collecting paintings, and Peter Wilson had advised him to buy this picture. For Mr. Robinow it was the beginning of a long and close association with Sotheby's, for not long afterwards he became one of the firm's financial advisers, and later still its financial director.

At the end of the sale the executors of the Weinberg Estate declared themselves delighted with the result, though they never did confide in the press about which charities were to benefit. Only three days before the sale they had felt very differently. Following upon the notable sale of the Cognacq Jay Collection of Impressionists in Paris a year or so earlier, and then the results of the Biddle sale there only a few weeks before, it was easy to be over-optimistic about pre-sale reserves. Executors and Sotheby directors found themselves completely at loggerheads. Peter Wilson indulged in one of those highly theatrical gestures for which he has become famous (though he is sparing in their use). At a moment of complete *impasse* he picked up all the papers spread before him, threw them high into the air and scattered them all over the room. Then he stood up and said, 'Obviously we cannot go on', and stalked out of the board room. Richard Netter, one of the executors, stopped him, realising that they had pressed their case too far. Sense prevailed and reasonable reserves were agreed upon, though as the meeting broke up, Netter could not help remarking to Peter Wilson, 'You'd never have made a good actor, Peter'. Sotheby's owes Netter a debt, for it was he who had insisted on the introduction of closed circuit television for the sale, which was soon to become standard equipment for major auctions, and indeed he who had pressed for the maximum public relations effort on both sides of the Atlantic.

What, in retrospect, did the Weinberg sale achieve? In the light of what followed it was simply a stepping stone in post-war developments. It came at precisely the right time, when there were enough men about with money who enjoyed adding to their collections in a public jousting such as this. Fiscal policies were another vital factor. In America the government now positively encouraged collectors to invest in art by dint of legislation which allowed them to set a portion of the current value of such purchases against income tax if they were left to a public museum on the owner's death, and even in Britain the Chancellor of the Exchequer had recently ruled that valuable works of art would be accepted separately in lieu of death duties, instead of only as part of the contents of some stately home.

It showed that specialist sales of Impressionists (of which this was the first in London) not only worked but worked wonderfully well. The appeal of the

French masters involved, with their radiant colours and dazzling images which had been so deprecated in their own day, now achieved a maximal appeal for a vast public which was constantly fed with art books on the subject. The Weinberg prices were regarded as good, if not sensational, even though the total of £326,000 had only been exceeded once before at a London sale of paintings – in the 1928 two-day Holford Sale of Old Masters at Christie's. The profits of the sale – if the truth were told – were not momentous, but its value in terms of press reaction and publicity was incalculable and nowhere more so than in America. Now Jake really had something to talk about.

In terms of administration it had, without doubt, been the most complicated sale the firm had ever had to arrange. The overheads, particularly in terms of management time, were very high. Carmen Gronau and Peter Wilson had worked at it practically to the exclusion of all else for weeks on end. The three executors wanted the best possible result for their estate and were demanding in their terms. They were fully cognisant of the risks they ran in sending the pictures to London instead of to Parke-Bernet, who were bitterly disappointed at this turn of events and did not hesitate to say so. For three weeks during the final stages of negotiating the contract and making the definitive arrangements for the sale, Richard Netter was writing Peter Wilson as many as three letters a day – and they all required answers. It was marvellous training in the complexities of what was involved, and in perfecting Bond Street as the ideal arena for similar events in the future. The legal conditions, the niceties of complex commercial arrangements, the elaborate requirements of the Bank of England, the insurance, the air and sea freight of the pictures from various locations (including the panic when the principal consignment was 'lost' for forty-eight hours on its way from New York to London), the establishment of provenance and the production and distribution of an unusually elaborate catalogue, the constant press enquiries – and sniping from New York – the technicalities of installing closed circuit television at the height of the sales season, encouraging a host of prospective purchasers that the prices would still be within their reach despite the ballyhoo, and the sheer nervous strain of the sale itself with its multitude of unseen bidders: all these seemed as nothing when success was certain. How different it might have been in the light of failure. That is why Weinberg was in every sense a breakthrough.

Of course, there was some backlash. Quentin Crewe wrote a withering piece in the *Evening Standard*, which was widely syndicated to the provincial press, in which he forecast that the high prices in Impressionists would not last and that the new owners of the Weinberg pictures would live to regret their extravagance. Denys Sutton, the editor of *Apollo*, also wondered whether the forward surge in values could continue. He pointed to earlier fashions – such as the Barbizon school – that had not lasted. When the House of Lords came to discuss the purchasing grants of the National Gallery and the Tate (£12,500 and £10,000 respectively) for 1957, which seemed ridiculous in the light of Weinberg prices, some of their lordships suggested that such pictures should be bought at a later date when prices would certainly have fallen.

31

Heady Days:
The Westminster Rubens

THE importance of sales of Old Master paintings appeared to have reached a climax in the summer of 1958. Although there was a sound supporting cast, it was in fact on a single, truly outstanding picture that the blaze of excitement was centred. This was the magnificent and gigantic altar-piece representing the *Adoration of the Magi* which Peter Paul Rubens had painted in a mere eleven days of intense activity for a Flemish convent in 1634. The very speed of execution had given the picture a degree of vigour and immediacy of impact which the many other variants of the same subject executed by Rubens (but often completed by his assistants) lacked. The convent was suppressed a hundred and fifty years later and the picture was moved to Brussels where it was sold by auction. Subsequently it entered the collection of the Marquis of Lansdowne and when this was sold up in 1806 it was bought for 800 guineas by Lord Grosvenor. The Grosvenor family at that time were already well on the way to becoming one of the wealthiest in Europe. Their fortune was founded on property. In 1677 an earlier forebear, Sir Thomas Grosvenor, had married as a child bride the twelve-year-old daughter of an ingenious young legal draughtsman who had managed to accumulate several hundred acres of adjoining farmland which was eventually to become the heart of London. Successive generations of the family had developed great tracts of townscape which later became known as Mayfair, Belgravia and Pimlico. When the 2nd Duke of Westminster died in 1953, his London estates still covered 285 acres and his executors were faced with paying the most sizeable sum in death duties ever levied. Six years after the Duke's death they had already remitted £7,000,000 to the Treasury. They had to find another £10,000,000 before the authorities at the Estate Duty Office declared themselves satisfied.

As the interest in the purchase of major works of art expanded and the auction room became an increasingly important factor in the art market, Sotheby's found that the work done on earlier insurance and probate valuations and their expertise in dealing with the Revenue authorities represented an expanding part of their business. When the Trustees of the Grosvenor Estate decided that major works of art would have to be sold, it was this and the long-standing friendship between their legal adviser, Sir William Charles Crocker, and Jim Kiddell that came into play. Peter Wilson and Carmen Gronau inspected a number of suitable paintings and these were moved to London. The Rubens had hung for many years over the main staircase at Eaton Hall near Chester, the family's country seat, an enormous, turreted Victorian mansion which had been used as an officer training centre by the army during the war. The Rubens

Ia. Nicolas Poussin's *Adoration of the Shepherds* (which once belonged to Sir Joshua Reynolds) was the first important Old Master painting to be sold by auction after the war (in July 1956), for a record £29,000. It was refused an export licence and was eventually bought by the London National Gallery.

Ib. *The Adoration of the Magi* by Peter Paul Rubens was painted for a Flemish convent in 1634. In 1806 it was bought by Lord Grosvenor for 800 guineas and it hung for many years over the main staircase at Eaton Hall. It had to be sold for death duties when the second Duke of Westminster died in 1953 and reached a record £275,000 in June 1959. The buyer subsequently presented it to King's College Chapel in Cambridge.

IIa. Rembrandt's *Aristotle Contemplating the Bust of Homer* was sold at Parke-Bernet in New York at the Alfred W. Erickson Sale on 15 November 1961 for £821,000 – almost exactly the same sum as that expended by the London National Gallery on all the paintings it purchased in the first century of its existence (from 1824–1924).

IIb. Andrea Mantegna's *Christ's Descent into Limbo* was bought for £490,000 by Colnaghi's in July 1973 and later passed into a private collection.

was a familiar sight for more than 16,000 officer cadets who had passed through Eaton Hall during the war years. It was a wonder that it was not damaged during many a high-spirited evening.

Its very size was to add substantially to the acute nervous tension which every aspect of the sale involved. For it soon became evident that it was going to be impossible to get the 12ft 9¼in by 8ft 1¼in wooden panel with its monumental frame into the principal Bond Street Gallery through the existing doorways and staircases. In the midst of considering alternatives, Carmen Gronau suddenly remembered that the Rijksmuseum in Amsterdam had had similar problems in getting Rembrandt's vast *Night Watch* into the correct gallery. She discovered that the Rubens could be got into the yard by Sotheby's back entrance and devised an ingenious plan of breaking a long slit into an outside wall and then winching it through a slit expressly made in the floor of the smaller West Gallery. The picture was moved from a storage depot late in the evening when there was a minimum of traffic, and twelve men manhandled it into Sotheby's courtyard. In Carmen's words, she was 'as taut as a bowstring during the proceedings', and it was only an old friend, Herbert Lank, who had often worked as a picture restorer for Sotheby's, who helped to preserve her composure. A crisis arose after the builders had broken the hole in the wall. Despite the most careful measurement, everyone had forgotten about the fact that there were a number of pipes inside it. Eventually the picture, cocooned inside an immense padded wrapping and protected by wooden struts, was winched through with a mere quarter of an inch to spare. The whole operation took five hours and there was immense relief when the picture suddenly emerged inside the gallery. Carmen was astonished that a journalist from the *Daily Express* and his attendant photographer had insisted on staying throughout the entire proceedings. When she asked them why, they explained that they had been waiting for the painting to fall down! Once in the West Gallery, another wall was broken through so that the picture could be manoeuvred into the main gallery. After its safe arrival there, the porters removed the wrappings, but as soon as Carmen saw the painting a fresh crisis dawned. She discovered that there was a small crack in the panel that was *new*. In her own graphic description, Carmen says 'I went berserk, and spent all my time boiling kettles in the very dry main gallery in order to achieve the correct level of humidity'. The relatively unheated atmosphere at Eaton Hall over 150 years had been ideal for preserving the painting.

While these preparations for the sale were proceeding, the public interest in it had grown enormously, although there was widespread concern that such a rare treasure might have to leave Britain. While there were few private buyers for such a colossal work of art, it was obviously a highly suitable purchase for museums all over the world and many of their directors came to London to inspect it. James Rorimer of New York's Metropolitan Museum insisted on being given a step-ladder and inspecting the picture in solitude. He was suspicious about the fact that the dimensions given in a nineteenth-century catalogue were greater than those printed in the sale catalogue. He suspected that the picture had been cut down in size, possibly overlooking the fact that formerly sizes were often measured inclusive of the frame. If he had been open about his suspicions, Sotheby's could readily have explained that this was a known fact. Probably because of his fears he decided against the purchase. John Walker, Director of the National Gallery in Washington, examined it also but declared that it was a case of purely personal interest. The enthusiasm of other transatlantic buyers continued unabated.

Repeatedly questions were asked in Parliament whether the picture could be bought in lieu of death duties for the nation. The ministerial answers tended to be evasive, but the pressure on this theme continued without interruption, particularly after the comment in *The Times* that because, 'thanks to the enthusiasm of earlier collectors, England was exceptionally rich in paintings by Rubens, no objection will be raised if this magnificent example leaves our shores'. This was so forcefully but unofficially contested by the National Gallery that Sir William Crocker felt compelled to write a carefully worded letter to *The Times* in which he indicated that while indeed there had been an approach to the Westminster Trustees by the National Gallery, the price suggested had been so derisory that it would have constituted a considerable sacrifice on the part of the executors, which they were not inclined to make in the light of the enormous death duties they had to find. Lord Robbins, Chairman of the National Gallery, responded with a letter in *The Times* of his own on the next day. He mentioned two tentative earlier approaches to the family and the National Gallery's enthusiasm to acquire the picture and their determination to stop it leaving the country. Despite its mild manner, the letter was dynamite. Leaders in *The Times* and the *Daily Telegraph* immediately stressed that here was a test case and it was up to the government of the day to act in order to lay down a generous policy for the acquisition of such national treasures in lieu of death duties for the future.[1] The government merely responded when Lord Hailsham, as President of the Council, informed a fellow peer in the House of Lords that 'potential purchasers from abroad had already been warned by the National Gallery Trustees that they would seek to prevent export if the picture was sold to a foreign buyer'. Because of the long interval between the granting of probate and the sale of the picture, Lord Hailsham also had some difficulty in assessing exactly what estate duty would have to be paid on the eventual auction price. At home there was instant reaction: various other papers commented that Lord Hailsham's intervention was 'a monstrous imposition by the National Gallery to jeopardise in this way the price that might be reached by auction'. The Westminster Trustees conferred endlessly with Peter Wilson and Carmen Gronau. Further letters to *The Times* were drafted, but ultimately it was decided that silence would be the better option.

It was quite clear that, despite the possible obstacles, particularly as far as exporting the picture was concerned, the number of interested buyers remained considerable. No doubt most of them felt reasonably certain that the sale price would be a long way above the £100,000 which Sir Philip Hendy was said to

1. Twenty years later no really satisfactory policy has emerged.

have offered for the painting on behalf of the National Gallery. Certainly it was true that the unceasing press comment had raised excitement to fever pitch once again, when a very pale Peter Wilson mounted the rostrum at 11 a.m. on 24 June 1959. He had had enough excitement in the previous few days to make the sale a record-breaking event in terms of nervous strain alone, whatever the financial outcome might be.

Much later, George Ridley, one of the executors of the Westminster Estate said, 'The Rubens was never highly thought of by the late Duke or his advisers. Otherwise he would never have left it on the staircase at Eaton Hall' – or insured it for only £7,000, he might have added. The most recent turmoil about the picture had been over what reserve to put on the painting. The press had many stabs at guessing the figure. The favourite one was £100,000. The initial thought inside Sotheby's had been £120,000. Then, because of the widespread interest, the executors indicated that they thought £150,000 would be nearer the mark. In this context one must recall that only a year earlier a magnificent Rubens design for a tapestry had fetched a record-breaking £33,000 and was sold to a New York dealer. Just a few days before the sale Peter Wilson and Anthony Hobson had had what was supposedly a final meeting with the Trustees to discuss the matter of the reserve. Sir William Crocker, who had not been previously involved but whose decision in such matters was final, now insisted that he was not interested in £150,000 (there had been an offer at this level from New York), or £170,000, £180,000 or even £190,000 which had been tentatively put forward as alternatives that might be within the bounds of possibility, but £200,000 – and not a penny less. In 1959 this was *vastly* greater than any Old Master painting had ever fetched. In order to make quite certain that there had been no misunderstanding and that he had made his point with sufficient force, he dictated a letter which was immediately delivered to Sotheby's by special messenger in which he wrote to Peter Wilson:

> When I agreed with George Ridley that the picture should be put up for auction by Sotheby's it was on condition that the reserve price should be fixed at £200,000. On mentioning this as the reserve price when you, Mr. Hobson and Mr. Ridley called upon me a few days ago you made no comment but I thought you displayed momentary surprise. This evening in conversation with Ridley I was astonished to learn that he had overlooked my condition [to this effect] but he promised to put this right with you. This letter is my personal confirmation that the reserve price is, as I have said, £200,000.

Special and highly elaborate arrangements had to be made for the presence of the press in the principal gallery at the sale, as all the world had wanted to send representatives, including what *The Times* called 'the most formidable array of photographic apparatus yet seen in the auction room'. The arc lights added to the normally high summer temperature. There was hardly a dry brow among the enormous number of people attending the sale. Admission was by ticket only and the great and the famous were there in unprecedented numbers. Many sat on the floor of overflow rooms which were linked by closed-circuit television.

The press concentrated their attention on Paul Getty and photographs showed him looking positively boyish compared to the image of the wizened gnome to which the public became accustomed towards the end of his life. They also shadowed the Dowager Duchess of Westminster, the widow of the late Duke, who attended various sales of Westminster property and wore an impressive range of striking hats.

The Rubens was lot fourteen out of 89 paintings to be sold that morning. The first eighteen were all the property of 'The Most Noble Hugh Richard Arthur, Duke of Westminster (dec'd), G.C.V.O., D.S.O.'. The first major item was a delightfully peaceful river scene by Albert Cuyp which Agnew's bought for £25,500. The second (lot 7) was a *View of Emmerich from across the Rhine* by Jan van Goyen. It was bought for £24,000 by a Dutch dealer long resident in London called Leonard Koetser. Then came two well-known Claudes – the *Sermon on the Mount* and the *Worship of the Golden Calf* – which realised respectively £35,000 and £36,000, a good deal more than had been expected. The *Adoration of the Magi* was the next major picture. Peter Wilson glanced round the packed gallery. He had noted in his catalogue that seven major contenders were likely to enter the bidding: Dr. Heinemann, Leonard Koetser, Geoffrey Agnew, Paul Getty, possibly James Rorimer of the Metropolitan Museum, Rosenberg, and that particular wizard among shrewd dealers in Old Masters, Julius Weitzner – the last two both from New York. Peter Wilson coughed slightly and began, 'Shall I say £20,000?'. A strong voice from the back of the audience yelled '£100,000'. This was Martin Asscher, another London dealer. The bidding rose rapidly in steps of £5,000 with nods from Paul Getty, Weitzner and Agnew. At £130,000 Leonard Koetser entered the fray. There was a momentary pause of fifteen pregnant seconds at £200,000. There was a slight gasp when Peter Wilson, immeasurably relieved to have passed the danger point of the reserve, raised the price at one sweep to £215,000. The contenders now were still Paul Getty, Mr. Asscher, Agnew and Leonard Koetser. After another brief pause at £250,000 Getty and Asscher dropped out. Geoffrey Agnew bid £270,000 and Koetser £275,000. No one would offer any more. Peter Wilson brought down the hammer after exactly 120 seconds, at 11.23.

Leonard Koetser had not done. He paid £72,000 for a small portrait of *the Apostle St. James* by El Greco and £48,000 for a portrait, by Frans Hals, of the painter Frans Post, who spent much of his life in South America, as well as buying four lesser paintings. The entire room applauded him loudly at the end of the sale when he had bought the final lot – a Saloman van Ruysdael for £10,500 – and fellow dealers congratulated him vociferously. He stood up to leave quickly but took a gentle bow instead. The total for the morning's sale was £740,780. Out of this total Koetser had paid a staggering £505,000. Now the press would not let him go. Questions poured upon him. 'Who', everyone wanted to know, 'was the new owner of the Rubens?' All that Koetser would say was that he was English, that he had a large house where the Rubens would hang in the company of a sizeable collection of other fine paintings; that the new owner would certainly keep the painting in Britain and would probably be lending it for public exhibitions, possibly at the National Gallery.

There was hardly a paper that did not carry lengthy comments on the price of the Rubens on the following morning. The *Daily Herald* took the trouble to ask the National Gallery for its comments on the figure. 'Has this mystery Englishman – who casually signed away what for most people is a small fortune – wasted his money?' the paper asked. 'It certainly was not worth that sum', a spokesman replied. 'Even if we could have afforded it, we would not have paid it.' So much for the correspondence in *The Times*! Sir Gerald Kelly, on the other hand, a former President of the Royal Academy, thought it was worth every penny. 'It's a magnificent and wonderful picture', he said. Leonard Koetser confessed that he had been prepared to bid more: 'The value of the painting was much more than the price'. The Duchess of Westminster commented astutely: 'I feel it was very courageous for an English private collector to buy the painting, and I am extremely glad that we gave collectors in this country the chance of acquiring it. Both the result and the price are quite splendid'.

At least eight wealthy collectors were put forward by the press in the next few days as possible purchasers. All of them denied it. While there was general relief that an Englishman had bought the painting, and incredulity that anyone within the United Kingdom could still have afforded such a price, the fact that the buyer preferred to remain anonymous rankled, particularly as it soon emerged that Koetser had also bought the El Greco and the Frans Hals on his behalf. *The Times* was moved to say, 'Perhaps we may be permitted to comment that while the desire for anonymity in the world today is understandable, to spend nearly £400,000 in a single morning on these pictures, is hardly the way to achieve it'.

There was a momentary distraction on the following day. A jewellery sale at Bond Street included another famous property of the late Duke, the Westminster Diamond Tiara, which contained the two enormous pear-shaped stones known as the Arcot diamonds (they were detachable) as well as 1,240 smaller stones. Fred Rose took the sale. The response to his tentative question, 'Can we start the bidding at £40,000?' was a loud and assertive 'Yes' from a New Orleans visitor to London, Mrs. Nat Greenblatt. The elegant Mrs. Greenblatt dropped out of the bidding at £60,000 and a professional Hatton Garden dealer, Mr. Levi Cohen, entered the bidding at £90,000 and won the day at £110,000, nearly twice as much as any piece of jewellery had ever fetched before at auction. On this occasion the Chancellor of the Exchequer had been positively helpful. Just before the sale he had announced that second-hand jewellery would *not* be liable to his newly introduced purchase tax. This certainly encouraged the bidding. It soon became clear that Mr. Cohen had not bought the tiara, which the Duchess had worn only a few years earlier at the Coronation of Queen Elizabeth II, for himself but for the celebrated New York diamond dealer, Harry Winston, who had sat just behind Levi Cohen and instructed him on the bidding.

As soon as this furore had died down, the press returned to their guessing game on the identity of the purchaser of the Rubens. It never emerged until the permanent location of the painting became public knowledge. There was much talk of exhibiting the picture at the National Gallery. The mystery owner was, in fact, anxious to donate it to the Gallery. Twice he arranged a time for an interview with the trustees. Unbelievably, twice it was cancelled. It was not surprising therefore that he became exasperated. Others in the know encouraged him to channel his generosity elsewhere. It was only when King's College at Cambridge formally announced that they had been given the painting to place in their chapel that the identity of the donor finally emerged. He was Major A. E. Allnatt, owner of a long-established property company that specialised in industrial and commercial buildings around London. It was Michael Jaffé, a leading Rubens scholar and now director of the Fitzwilliam Museum, who had persuaded Major Allnatt to give the painting to Cambridge. The El Greco Leonard Koetser had bought for him at the same sale, he donated to New College, Oxford for their chapel. In both chapels considerable rearrangement of the immediate surroundings was necessary before the pictures were finally settled in their permanent resting places. The whole story of Major Allnatt's magnificent gesture of generosity is an interesting demonstration of the problems that can beset a would-be donor.

Another aspect of the Westminster sale of Old Masters only came to light thirteen years later. In fact, it involved lot 13, a large dirty canvas depicting a scene from the First Book of Samuel of Abigail making her offering of loaves to David. Edward Speelman, a prominent West End picture dealer, had looked at the painting and had come to the conclusion that, although it was simply catalogued as 'by Rubens', implying that it was a work after or in the style of the master, it was indeed by Peter Paul Rubens himself. In order not to alert any other dealers to his discovery Mr. Speelman asked a fellow dealer, Steven Pollock, to bid for the picture on his behalf. Pollock bought it for £1,500 and is recorded as the purchaser in the printed price list. The picture was cleaned and revealed as an astonishing masterpiece. In the first instance Dr. Ludwig Burchard, one of the great Rubens scholars of his time, and later Michael Jaffé, confirmed its authenticity. It was initially sold to a private collector in Germany but was later brought back to England.

From Sotheby's point of view, the Westminster sale finally put paid to the post-war blues in the Old Master field that had lasted much longer than had been considered likely. It was now five years since all currency restrictions had been relaxed and free trading had started. Only in this year (1959), however, had the last essential of truly untrammelled international trade become possible, when the Treasury allowed vendors to take out the proceeds of sales at auction in any currency of their choice.

32

Watershed:
The Goldschmidt Sale

THE flow of properties from America to London after the Weinberg Sale proceeded vigorously. John Carter was able to report that 'during this acorn period' Belle da Costa Greene's early Italian pictures had been consigned to London by the Pierpont Morgan Library; so had the Landau Collection of Rowlandsons from New York, the Flesh Group of Barbizons from Ohio, Gerald Oliven's noble Frans Hals from Beverly Hills and, most remarkably, the famous Irwin Laughlin Collection of French eighteenth-century drawings and prints, consigned by Mrs. Hubert Chanler of Washington D.C. – this last with much assistance from Peter Wilson. In the field of books, Jake could later look back with some pride on the immense sale of the Herschel V. Jones Collection of Americana from Minneapolis, the Auerbach Collection of early Mormon literature, the fine Otis T. Bradley Library from New York and, most exciting of all, the famous White–Emerson Collection of William Blake, from Brookline, Massachusetts. After a preview in New York – a device that came to be used more frequently – the seven illuminated books brought £40,800 in May 1958. Later there followed the Dr. Eli Moschcowitz medical collection from New York (which reached Sotheby's because the executors had found some learned notes by John Carter inserted in the author-corrected copy of the first edition of Browne's *Urne Buriall*),[1] the John F. Neylan Library from San Francisco, and the very substantial Archer M. Huntington's Collection of autograph letters and documents consigned by the American Academy of Arts and Letters – to outraged protests from Parke-Bernet in the New York press.

In November 1957, four months after the Weinberg Sale, Parke-Bernet staged the Lurcy Sale. It was a sensation, a triumph and a major comeback. For fifty years George Lurcy had been a Frenchman. He emigrated to America just before the Second World War. He brought with him his American wife, his wealth and a marvellous collection of outstanding Impressionists. He left behind a brilliant career at the Banque Rothschild and a million memories. A small, slim, bird-like man with a film star moustache, he exuded nervous energy, always did the unexpected, and never quite found the nirvana he sought. On arrival in America he enrolled at the University of North Carolina as a candidate for a master's degree in political economy, which he indeed received – with honours – in 1943. Then he moved to New York and back into business, making millions. He liked to be surrounded by opulence, and photographs of his residence at 813 Fifth Avenue bear ample evidence of this. He really doted on the pictures he collected. Alfred Frankfurter, editor of *Art News*, wrote in his preface to the Lurcy Sale Catalogue: 'The collection as a whole is a tribute

1. Which Jake had, in fact, edited.

to his remarkable taste and innate sense of quality. It is that which distinguished him, in this critic's view, as one of those rarer patrons of art who discern as well as collect'. People garnered his astonishing sayings: 'The priceless temptation of art gives one everything, delectable stings, a hint of pepper and sun, the effortless crush of the teeth into a morsel of cantaloupe.... Especially in impressionism, the periphery is as important as the focal point. If you have ever seen Monet's wall of waterlilies, then you know what I mean. What you see is gorgeous eternity – an immortality so lovely . . .'. He died in 1953. Speaking of his paintings he had said 'what a beautiful auction they will make'. There were six *great* canvases, and a mass of lesser works which revealed what a good eye Lurcy had had for landscapes that gave great pleasure to the viewer. But there were delays. Mrs. Lurcy objected to a quick sale. It was only after a long legal battle that the executors were able to send the collection to Parke-Bernet. Leslie Hyam, Parke-Bernet's chief executive, realised that this was an opportunity to outshine Sotheby's at glamorising a major auction. The publicity stirred art lovers in America to fever pitch. 1,700 people were given tickets to the sale: more than 5,000 were sent polite apologies. There had never been such a sale audience at 980 Madison Avenue. Words almost failed the purveyors of society gossip. Bill Latimer, Parke-Bernet's celebrated commissionaire, was heard to say that he never knew there were that many Rolls-Royces in New York. Parke-Bernet had installed closed circuit television for their overflow galleries for the first time. All seats were taken up by seven o'clock, though the sale was not due to start until eight. Richard Netter had obtained two tickets: one for himself; the other for Peter Wilson. It was a night of ideas.

The firm's principal auctioneer, Louis Marion, took the rostrum. There were mishaps,[1] but the result was a triumph. The sixty-five paintings raised a total of £610,000.[2] Lurcy's favourite Renoir, *La Serre*, of a woman in front of massed banks of flowers and a greenhouse, was bought by Henry Ford II for $200,000. Alexander Goulandris bought Gauguin's *Mau Taporo* for $180,000. Paul Mellon bought a Toulouse-Lautrec for $95,000. There had never been prices like it. The total was the highest ever recorded for an auction of fine paintings in the USA.

At about this time a curious thread of history was being unreeled at Sotheby's. It had its beginnings in 1955. The banker, Jakob Goldschmidt, that same Goldschmidt whom Hobson had met in 1931 and again in 1937, had died in New York. His very considerable estate passed to Erwin Goldschmidt, his son, who had in the meantime become a leading New York insurance broker. Goldschmidt Senior had only been able to take part of his art collection out of Germany. The Nazis seized the rest and sold the greater part at a special auction organised by their Ministry of Finance in 1941. After his father died Erwin

1. There were disputed final bids for two pictures from the galleries served only by television and they had to be put up for a second time. Such repetition was the one thing that Louis Marion cavilled at, but he agreed under pressure to allow it and good humour prevailed.
2. The French furniture and other decorative items later brought the total (for all 414 lots) to £793,341 ($2,223,358). The rate of exchange was about $2.80 to the pound in late 1957.

battled for years seeking restitution of the canvases that had been seized and dispersed, and in many instances he got them back after fearful legal wrangles. In one instance Peter Wilson had been involved as an arbitrator. By the terms of Jakob's will the paintings which he owned at the time of his death had to be sold and the proceeds divided between the three heirs – his son and his two grandsons, Marc and Anthony. The will specified that the property was 'to be sold at such time and times and by such means, as my executors may determine in their sole discretion'.

Erwin decided to see whether the pictures could be sold more advantageously in Europe than in the States. At first he had been tempted by Paris and had entered into negotiations with Maurice Rheims, but he was daunted by the expenses which could at that time swallow up to 35 per cent of the proceeds. Eventually he came to London with his beautiful Canadian wife, Madge, and his attorney and co-executor, Jesse D. Wolff. He brought with him a selection of fourteen paintings in heavy, wooden cases. He took rooms in the Savoy Hotel and made arrangements to see representatives from both Christie's and Sotheby's. Neither firm knew that the other was being interviewed simultaneously (in separate suites). Erwin could be exceedingly difficult and at that preliminary meeting he gave Peter Wilson and Carmen Gronau a very rough ride. He showed them lists of pictures and asked for their reactions on possible prices. Then he left them alone for a while. As he returned he was heard to say to a companion outside the door, 'Die hier gefallen mir viel besser'.[1] It suddenly dawned on Peter Wilson and Carmen that Goldschmidt had been talking to Sir Alec Martin of Christie's in another room.

Erwin's ill-temper was explained by the fact that the Customs authorities at Southampton would not release his pictures. He had been given the wrong clearance form by the British Consul-General in New York. Carmen offered to organise their release. When they eventually arrived in London, they were too big to go into Goldschmidt's room and the Savoy offered to store them in the basement, but there they were dangerously close to a central heating boiler. Peter Wilson suggested sending them to Sotheby's – on one condition: that Goldschmidt would be free to show them there to any interested outside party. It was a delightfully typical gesture, and despite Jesse Wolff's opinion that it was too subtle by half, Goldschmidt agreed to the proposition.

So it came about that these pictures were included right at the end of an Old Masters' sale scheduled for 28 November 1956. There were 131 lots in the sale: the last fourteen were catalogued as 'The property of the Estate of Jakob Goldschmidt'. Among the most important was a striking nude by Corot, *Venus au Bain*; *A View of the Maas* by Aelbert Cuyp; two canvases by Eugene Delacroix; an El Greco *Virgin*; *Two Heads of Negroes* by Sir Anthony van Dyck; *A Young Girl Lifting her Veil* by Murillo (a companion piece to the same artist's much loved *A Peasant Boy leaning on a Sill* in the London National Gallery); a fifteenth-century *Adoration of the Magi* in the Flemish tradition, attributed to the Master of Sainte Gudule; a street scene by Camille Pissarro; a

1. 'I like this lot much better'.

female head by Renoir and a rather mysterious Daumier of a blacksmith at work.

The press reported the forthcoming sale as 'the most important group of such paintings to be offered in London since the war' and marvelled that it was being sold in London and not in New York. Those in the know realised the importance of the breakthrough. There were many other important pictures in the sale and it attracted much wider attention than usual. But in line with its policy at that time, Sotheby's refused to commit itself to any guess at the final result, despite constant prodding. This, of course, led to much greater speculation in the press. It was the time of one of the most vicious post-war credit squeezes and no one could say with certainty before the sale what effect this was going to have.

In the event the sale itself exceeded everyone's best hopes. There were some early surprises. The greatest was a price of £15,000 for an altar-piece of the Crucifixion by an early seventeenth-century Dutch master, Hendrick Terbrugghen. It had been discovered by a young art historian who had paid a mere £100 for it. It was bought by Harry Sperling and is now in the Metropolitan Museum in New York. The Goldschmidt Corot fetched £27,000 and was bought by Frank Partridge for the Maharanee of Baroda.[1] It had cost the collector £12,500 in Paris. The Murillo was bought by John Carras, a Greek ship owner, for £25,000. Goldschmidt had paid £6,300, and it had fetched 5,600 guineas (£5,880) at the Holford Sale in 1928. The El Greco was bought under a *nom de vente* for £14,000. It had cost £1,350. The Van Dyck – also bought by Carras for £7,800 – had become Goldschmidt's for only £900. The total for the whole sale was £224,411; the highest such total at that time since the Holford Sale. The *Daily Telegraph*, in a moment of excessive enthusiasm, said 'it must be regarded as one of the greatest sales of all time'. The fourteen Goldschmidt pictures alone had realised £135,850. In fact, three had been bought in: the Cuyp at £9,000 (against a reserve of £12,500), the Master of Sainte Gudule at £3,800 (the reserve was £6,500) and a Van Beyeren still life at £2,000 (its reserve was £4,200).[2]

Erwin Goldschmidt was well pleased and returned to New York a firm friend of Sotheby's. It was indeed he who had later brought the possibility of selling the Weinberg collection to Peter Wilson's attention, as he was responsible for its insurance and had known Weinberg well while he was alive. In a letter to one of Weinberg's executors, in which he outlined his own recent experience in the course of selling his father's pictures, he wrote: 'Had I known at the beginning what I know today I would not have shown my paintings to any dealers or to any private individuals and would have dealt straight off with Sotheby's and relied on their judgement about the value of the paintings. . . . Both Mrs. Gronau and Mr. Wilson, who are the partners in charge of the sale of paintings, see and

1. It was said that she hung it in her bathroom. She sold the painting in Paris in 1961 where it fetched £51,700 at auction. It came up for sale again at Bond Street in April 1979 and realised £240,000.
2. It was eventually bought by Dr. Hans Wetzlar and sold again by Sotheby's at Mak van Waay as lot 119 at the sale of his collection in Amsterdam in June 1977. Curiously enough, it was bought in yet again: this time at £18,500.

observe the market in both Old Masters and French Impressionists every day in their own auctions and are very capable of evaluating the pictures and anticipating the prices which they can reach'.

It was merely the first of many instances when he pressed Sotheby's cause. He never accepted any introductory commission, and it was only some years after Sotheby's had bought Parke-Bernet that he eventually became responsible for that firm's insurance. More important, he had already mooted in London the fact that the first sale was only in the nature of an hors d'oeuvre. There was a great deal more to come. Eventually, some time after the Weinberg and the Lurcy sales, Peter Wilson and Carmen Gronau were shown the seven great paintings which really cemented the Goldschmidt connection. After lengthy negotiations in Geneva their sale was planned for the autumn of 1958. There was a self-portrait of Edouard Manet, and a portrait of Madame Gamby *Au Jardins de Bellevue* by the same painter, as well as the famous street scene of a public holiday, *La Rue Mosnier aux Drapeaux*; Vincent van Gogh's *Jardin Public à Arles*[1] with two figures of lovers in the shade of an immense cedar tree (he had described the canvas in detail in a letter to his brother Theo); a Cézanne still life, *Nature Morte: Les Grosses Pommes*, as well as Cézanne's portrait of a young Italian boy in a red waistcoat; and, finally, Renoir's *La Pensée*.[2]

Each picture was great in its own right: collectively the seven were a sensation. Peter Wilson realised that they would prove irresistible magnets to the thirty or so collectors in the world with the necessary resources who had already emerged as the ultimate masters of the auction room's destiny. Goldschmidt, his lawyer Jesse Wolff, Peter Wilson and Carmen Gronau formulated a long and complex contract in New York. Back in London it was translated into simple terms that any layman could understand. The final document contained three characteristics that were of great importance in the future of Sotheby's. It demonstrated a new flexibility on commission rates. Sotheby's were prepared to back their judgement by predicating reserve prices below which only a tiny commission would have to be paid. Once that barrier had been broken, they stood to receive a much greater share of the proceeds than was usually the case.

It was really this acceptance of a new level of risk by Peter Wilson, his sense of adventure, or his blind gamble as many termed it, that led to the firm's great surge forward in the decade following the first Goldschmidt sale. It attracted sellers of major properties in Great Britain, in Europe and, most important of all, in America. With an element of generosity, Goldschmidt and Wolff, seeing the risk that Sotheby's were carrying, wrote a new clause into the contract – a sort of sandwich filling – which mitigated the uncertainty. After a minimum had been reached, 100 per cent of the proceeds would go to Sotheby's. In Goldschmidt's case it amounted to $30,000, after the first $1,700,000 had been

1. The Lurcy Renoir, *La Serre*, and the Goldschmidt Van Gogh, *Jardin Public à Arles*, had both been acquired by Henry Ford II and were sold at Christie's in New York in May 1980 for $1,200,000 and $5,200,000 respectively.
2. The artist himself objected to this title. He had written: 'I wanted to portray a lovely, charming, young woman. . . . That girl never thought; she lived like a bird and nothing more'.

reached. Someone in Sotheby's must have had brilliant actuarial flair, for the final result yielded a commission rate of 9.2845 per cent.

The preparations for the sale were long and painstaking. Lessons learned from Weinberg were scrupulously followed, but there were new elements of cliff-hanging suspense. Just after final arrangements had been made in the late spring of 1958 to hold the sale in October of that year, Goldschmidt rang Peter Wilson from New York. 'Are you sitting down?' he opened the conversation. 'I have just had a very good offer for the collection.' He explained that a Greek ship owner had offered just over £600,000 for it, an immense sum by any standard. Even so Peter Wilson had the courage to counter that the offer would only have been made because it was thought that the pictures would go for even more at auction. There had already been an earlier attempt by a London consortium of well-known businessmen to buy the pictures – or a share in them – before the sale, but this too had come to nothing.

When Peter Wilson, on a visit to New York, had finally agreed the terms of the contract with Goldschmidt, news of the event leaked out prematurely in London and hit the press. Erwin was furious and threatened to withdraw the pictures from sale. At first he had said to journalists in New York, 'The sale is off – it's finished'. But a few hours later this was modified to, 'I have been waiting since 1955 for the best moment to sell and the best place. In the meantime I have been warding off hundreds of art dealers who pester me without ceasing[1] . . . now I think I probably will decide after all to sell my pictures in Sotheby's. They may be hazy about who is going to sell what and where but they are still the best auctioneers in the world'. The storm blew over. There were sighs of relief.

Cautious to the end, Erwin never actually signed the contract, although Jesse Wolff, his co-executor, did. Goldschmidt felt it gave him the freedom to back out till the very last minute. At one stage he quipped to Wolff, 'If anything goes wrong I'll hold you responsible and sue you'. Mr. Wolff was quite unmoved. He replied, 'Go ahead and sue me. It won't do you any good, because I haven't got that sort of money'.[2]

The promotion of the sale was again handled by an outside firm. This time it was Pritchard Wood & Partners. After the sale was over *Advertisers Weekly* analysed 'how the build up was organised' for its readers. One ingenious device had been to ask journalists at the press view to choose which they considered was going to be the most popular and expensive picture. The great majority chose Van Gogh's *Jardin Public à Arles*. A major public relations objective was to continue the promotion of London as the art centre of the world. A month before the sale it had been written up extensively in no less than twenty-three countries as an event readers should keep an eye on. The Central Office of Information had helped enormously. But, in fact, for some time after the Weinberg

1. Goldschmidt's pictures were well known to a wide audience in America as he had frequently allowed them to be shown at exhibitions.
2. Under American law a contract with the estate of someone who has died is binding if it is signed by one of two executors, as long as the signatory is prepared to accept responsibility.

Sale, journalists everywhere had regarded what Sotheby's did as news.

At Erwin's own suggestion it had been decided early on to hold a special sale, just for the seven pictures, at 9.30 p.m., the first evening sale in London at that point since the eighteenth century. Those attending were asked to wear evening dress, which in itself was news, but more than anything else, the seven canvases were their own best advocates. One London paper that mattered, which at first did little to cover the event, was the *Daily Express*. Unabashed, Peter Wilson rang up Lord Beaverbrook who had been a great friend of Peter's father, the delightfully eccentric Yorkshire baronet, Sir Mathew (Scatters) Wilson.[1] Peter Wilson explained that the sale would be the making of London as the art centre of the world. Beaverbrook acted at once: the *Daily Express* and the *Evening Standard* gave the sale maximum attention.

By the evening of 15 October Erwin had become something of a folk hero. His passion for collecting vintage cars, his crinkly hair, his father's career, his certainty of success, the beautiful and relaxed Madge had been written up end-lessly. Again a rehearsal for the sale, to test the lighting and closed circuit television equipment (two tons of it) made news everywhere, particularly when Peter Wilson sold Carmen Gronau ('poor Mrs. Gronau') for £42,000. Inter-viewed afterwards Peter Wilson had commented, 'I shall be accepting bids from three galleries and praying hard that everything will go smoothly'. The pictures had been on view much longer than usual and thousands of people had queued to get a glimpse of them. The police had to be called two hours before the sale itself to control a huge mass of people who wanted to gain admittance. Fourteen hundred had been allocated tickets, including Somerset Maugham, Dame Margot Fonteyn, Anthony Quinn, Kirk Douglas, Lady Churchill and a great multitude of art dealers from all over the world. Probably the most excited – though he never showed it – was Francis Matthiessen, who had advised Jakob Goldschmidt on many of his purchases. He had transferred his Berlin gallery to London in the early Thirties. It was right opposite Sotheby's front entrance in Bond Street.

For once Peter Wilson mounted the rostrum a little late – delayed by yet another episode that would have tried the most resolute of temperaments. A man, well known to Sotheby's and to Goldschmidt, made an offensive remark which Erwin overheard as he and Madge struggled to their seats through the crowd, ten minutes before the sale was due to start. Erwin was livid. 'Unless this man is banned from Sotheby's at once, the sale is cancelled', he clamoured. With suitable tact – and force – Tim Clarke ejected the trouble-maker.

'At 9.35', wrote the *Express*, 'tall, dinner-jacketed Mr. Peter Wilson, Chair-man of Sotheby's and auctioneer of the night, climbed the steps of the pulpit-like rostrum in the green-walled main sale-room. Chubby-cheeked Wilson blinked in the glare of the massed T.V. lamps, ran his eye over the mink and diamond-dappled audience, rather like a nervous preacher facing his first

1. And of his maternal grandfather, Lord Ribblesdale, who had been a Trustee of the National Gallery and the National Portrait Gallery (and incidentally, the subject of Sargent's well-known portrait now in the Tate Gallery).

congregation, and rapped firmly with his ivory gavel. The sound, amplified by
the microphones, stilled the chatter. Then to a great movement of anticipation
and craning of necks, the first picture was carried in by two cerise-coloured
attendants. It was Edouard Manet's self portrait.'

For once the specially marked catalogue in front of the auctioneer in which he
enters the successful bid and bidder (and sometimes the under-bidder) as each
lot is sold, contained the reserves written in red ink in ordinary figures in view
of the fever pitch state of excitement before the sale. Normally they are in code,
as obviously they are highly confidential information before a sale. Obviously
too the auctioneer can tell at once how successful a sale is from the margin by
which the final bid exceeds the reserve figure. In the first Goldschmidt Sale and
at the Weinberg Sale it had been touch and go, but after five minutes of this
momentous occasion, Peter Wilson knew that his great gamble had succeeded.
In those five minutes he had sold the first three paintings.

The Manet self-portrait fetched £65,000 against a reserve of £45,000;
Manet's portrait of Madame Gamby made £89,000 against a reserve of
£82,000; Manet's *Rue Mosnier* sold for £113,000 against a reserve of £90,000.
The *Daily Express* reported that at £100,000 'the grey head of Somerset
Maugham shook slowly in amazement. Dame Margot Fonteyn, in an off-the-
shoulder, eau-de-nil dress, stood on her famous toes craning with excitement.
An iron-grey man dropped his monocle under foot'.

The bidding for the Van Gogh started at £20,000 ('by this time the uproar
was rising higher than the temperature. Again the gavel rapped for order').
There was slight hesitation at £120,000. Very slowly – it took the longest time
to sell – the figure rose to a final bid of £132,000 from Rosenberg and Stiebel,
art dealers from New York. Sotheby's reserve had been £118,000. Knoedlers of
New York bought Cézanne's still life of apples in seventy seconds for £90,000
(against a reserve of £68,000 and a bid 'on the book' of £60,000).

The climax of the sale was lot 6, Cézanne's *Garçon au Gilet Rouge*. It must
that night have become one of the most photographed paintings in the world.
Its subtle red tones looked superb against the greens and browns of the huge
Brussels tapestry used as a back drop behind the rostrum. Peter Wilson stared
at his reserve of £125,000. The bidding again started at £20,000. The *New York
Times* wrote: 'Scuttlebutt on Bond Street and 57th Street had it that the
Cézanne would surely bring the highest price, since today Cézanne is respected
as the greatest of the post-impressionists . . . the bidding quickly became a
contest between two New York art dealers. One was Georges Keller of New
York's Carstair's Gallery, a suave man who looks and speaks rather like Charles
Boyer; the other was Roland Balay of Knoedler's, a short, moon-faced man
(they were, interestingly enough, once business partners). The man for whom
Keller was bidding was not present'. Keller and Balay fought out their duel
virtually without interruption. When Keller's final bid had been taken and
Balay remained silent, Peter Wilson intoned, '£220,000. £220,000. What, will
no one offer any more?' His tone of voice was that of a man genuinely astonished
that a group of experts of such distinction would let a painting of this quality

go for so paltry a sum. A roar of laughter relieved the tension. The price was by a long way (since the Biddle Gauguin sold at £104,000) the highest ever paid for a modern picture at auction – and almost £100,000 above the reserve. There was a momentary pause while people took in the significance of what they had just witnessed. Lot 7 was the wistful female head by Renoir. It was the only picture bought by an English dealer, E. Speelman (for the Birmingham property magnate, Jack Cotton). At £72,000 it had topped the reserve by a mere £1,000. The disappointed under-bidder was Stanley Wade of Frost & Reed: his last bid had gone unnoticed.

The whole sale had taken only twenty-one minutes. Every record in the book had been broken. The whole audience stood on its chairs and cheered and clapped. 'It sounded', said the *Western Mail*, 'like a Covent Garden great occasion.' It was a scene that had not previously occurred at Sotheby's.

George Keller had also bought Manet's Madame Gamby and the *Rue Mosnier aux Drapeaux*. He had spent a total of £422,000, and rushed back to New York the same night to report to his client. There was frenzied speculation about who this might be. John Carter was in Los Angeles at the time of the sale, with one ear on the telephone to London, reporting on another line to Edward G. Robinson, who had declined Jake's advice 'to put his shirt on his one favourite lot instead of spreading, and consequently got nothing'. A week later Jake lunched with Paul Mellon at the Metropolitan Club in Washington. He later recounted the conversation that took place. 'Would he, he asked, be right in congratulating Mr. Mellon on buying a certain wonderful picture – the *Garçon au Gilet Rouge*? "Did I," Mellon asked by way of reply, "pay too much?" Before I could say no, he added, "You stand in front of a picture like that, and what is money?" I warmly applauded this admirable sentiment and have often cited it when people talk about "inflated" prices for really great works of art as the ideal attitude for any serious connoisseur'.

Even the Weinberg Sale was dwarfed by the press coverage that cascaded across the world on the morning after the Goldschmidt Sale. It was a magnificent tonic in the face of the anti-climax that inevitably follows the scaling of every such major peak. No one now doubted that London had become firmly established as the centre of the art market. The weeklies carried on where the dailies left off. In its day, the greatest triumph was a major article in *Life* illustrated in colour throughout. *Newsweek, Time* (twice), *The Economist, The Listener, Illustrated London News, New York Times Magazine, Jour de France, Epoca, Apollo, Sphere, Queen, Die Weltwoche* and dozens more all gave the sale the most detailed coverage with a great welter of illustrations. There was bewilderment as well. Just where were prices going from here? *Art News* had put its finger on the answer even before the sale: 'The prices fetched,' it said, 'will be indexes for the market in this most-prized luxury for some time to come.' The nicest comment came from Erwin himself. Talking to the press after the sale he said: 'No, I don't know what I'm going to do with the money. All anyone can do is eat three meals a day'.[1]

1. He spent £48,000 of it on a strange, distorted Braque, painted in 1946 and titled *La Femme*

Truly the second Goldschmidt Sale opened the floodgates from outside Britain, and particularly from America. Jake became busier than ever. Between October 1958 (the sale had opened the new season) and July 1959, Sotheby's sold property worth more than £5¾ million. It was the highest total ever achieved in the history of the art market and 'virtually double that of any other Fine Art Auctioneers in the world'. This quotation, taken from the fourth annual review of Sotheby's activities to be published,[1] could have referred either to Christie's or to Parke-Bernet. The siren voices of Richard Netter, Erwin Goldschmidt and other friends from across the Atlantic kept calling. Peter Wilson, Carmen Gronau and the younger picture expert, John Rickett, continually had to go to New York. It gradually became clear that a fully staffed office there was essential.

Peter Wilson's choice for a full-time emissary fell on a young man who had joined the picture department in 1957 and who had then acted as his personal assistant. Peregrine Pollen was twenty-nine, tall, slim, presentable and very quick on the uptake. He had been educated at Eton and Christchurch, Oxford. He had done his National Service in the Green Jackets; become a schoolmaster; then bummed around the world for a year as pantry boy on a ship, aluminium smelter, filling station attendant, market researcher, chauffeur and nursing orderly in a mental hospital. He had even played the organ in a night-club in Chicago when he was completely broke. His travels had taken him to Canada, to the United States, Honolulu and the South Sea Islands, Australia, New Zealand, South Africa and the Canaries. Peter Fleming had once written a piece in the *Spectator* in which he related how at Oxford the Vice-Provost of Worcester College described at a dinner how a century earlier Henry Kingsley, brother of the author Charles Kingsley, had performed the feat of running a mile, riding a mile and rowing a mile consecutively, all within a space of fifteen minutes. 'No one has been able to beat that although a great many undergraduates have tried' he commented. 'I'll beat that time,' said Peregrine. And along the banks of the Isis he ran, and he rode, and he sculled on the river. After weeks of practice he did it in fourteen minutes flat. At the time when the *Spectator* printed the story the record still stood.

After his travels the young man became ADC to Sir Evelyn Baring (later Lord Howick), Governor of Kenya. At the end of Peregrine's tour of duty,

---

au Miroir, at the Jaques Sarlie Sale held on the evening of 12 October 1960. On that occasion 51 pictures and drawings (including 29 by Picasso) fetched £429,700 in 1¼ hours.

1. John Carter had produced an unassuming little pamphlet with a two-page introduction and twenty-seven illustrations to summarise what had passed through Bond Street during the 1956/57 season, largely as something to put into the hands of prospective American clients. By 1958/59 under Peregrine Pollen's editorship this had become rather more elaborate and by 1959/60 its extent had grown to 256 pages and had a long review of the season's sales by that doyen among saleroom correspondents, Frank Davis. In the following year the format again increased in size and the *Review* was now transmogrified into *The Ivory Hammer: the Year at Sotheby's*. It was published by Longman's at 45 shillings and edited by Michel Strauss. In the 1966/67 season the title changed again to *Art at Auction* (under a new editor, Philip Wilson) in which magnificent form it has been continued and has flourished to the present day.

Evelyn Baring had written to Lord Crawford to ask him for an introduction to Christie's for his ADC. Peregrine's grandfather had been Robert Benson who, with his wife, Evelyn (sister of the Sir George Holford, whose pictures Christie's had sold with such record-breaking *éclat* in 1928), had formed a magnificent collection of Italian paintings from the fourteenth to the sixteenth century. In 1927 this had been bought for the staggering sum of £620,000 by Duveen. Robert Benson had also catalogued the Holford Picture Collection at Dorchester House (later demolished and now replaced by the Dorchester Hotel). In his introduction to that huge catalogue he had written 'pictures are the big game of collecting'. It seemed entirely appropriate therefore that with this background, having been turned down by Christie's (where his cousin, Patrick Lindsay, holds sway over the Old Masters Department), Peregrine should have finished up in the rival establishment. Everything he had done seemed excellent training for the rough, tough, hurly-burly of the New York art world.

Peter Wilson was a little worried how Jake would react to the appointment. He sent him a carefully worded, hand-written note stating that Peregrine was 'going to be asked to report to London direct'. Jake responded with characteristic gusto and generosity. 'I was greatly surprised to receive your "hands off Peregrine" memo,' he replied. 'Pray reassure any of the partners who share your apprehension that no such warnings were necessary. Peregrine himself, I think you will find, knows that I have no wish to breathe down his neck or jog his elbow. He also knows that I am entirely at his disposal for any help or advice he may feel the need of. Neither will be proffered unasked. So please let all concerned relax.'

Peregrine went to New York on 15 March 1960. Peter Wilson had also recognised the extraordinary gifts of Jesse Wolff whom he had got to know so well as Goldschmidt's attorney. Wolff was a partner of the New York law firm of Weil, Gotshal & Manges who were now appointed Sotheby's official lawyers in the States. Jesse Wolff found Peregrine an office in the Lincoln Building which he could use initially. Peregrine lived in the Yale Club and for weeks he walked up and down New York every day, taking a different avenue each time from 86th Street to Wall Street and back. When he knew the city really well, he decided that the best venue for Sotheby's office would be in the brand new Corning Glass Building (on the corner of 55th Street and Fifth Avenue). Jake retained his office at 61 Broadway, in the 'downtown' financial district.

From this tiny (400 square feet) outpost in his glass tower Peregrine began to consign things back to England. Jake helped mightily. An early struggle was to get a collection of Impressionist paintings, on loan to the Cleveland Museum, to London. They had been the property of the curator, Ralph Coe's father. They included canvases by Renoir, Gauguin and Cézanne and were successfully sold in London. Peregrine gradually became familiar with New York's huge host of antique and art dealers. Like Jake, he became acquainted with museum directors, bankers and, of course, collectors. An unrecognised stranger whom he had kept waiting in his tiny office for more than twenty minutes while taking one telephone call after another, turned out to be Paul Mellon, who later spent hours there studying London catalogues. Ebulliently Peregrine and Jake would stroll into Parke-Bernet with Sotheby's catalogues ostentatiously displayed under their arms to see what was being sold. After the war and probably up to the mid-Sixties 'being British' still had a great cachet in the States. Both Jake and Peregrine benefited considerably from the advantages this mood of anglophile devotion conferred.

At times, of course, it could prove a positive handicap. It became known that the collection of Old Masters assembled by the advertising magnate, Alfred W. Erickson, was likely to be sold following his widow's death. It included not only Rembrandt's great picture, *Aristotle Contemplating the Bust of Homer*, but two smaller Rembrandts, a Crivelli, a magnificent Perugino, and portraits by Cranach, Holbein, Van Dyck, Frans Hals, Fragonard, Nattier, Romney, Raeburn and Gainsborough. It was a collection, formed with the help of Duveen, which would create the same stir in the world of Old Masters that Lurcy and Goldschmidt had initiated for the Impressionists. Peter Wilson came over to assist Peregrine in the negotiations to land the sale, but although the battle was hard and long drawn out, the executors, the Bankers Trust Co., eventually opted in favour of Parke-Bernet. A month or so before the sale Peregrine made an appointment with Leslie Hyam at 980 Madison Avenue to introduce himself. They got on well.

The Erickson Sale was the greatest challenge to Parke-Bernet in the first twenty-five years of its existence and the firm rose nobly to the occasion. The twenty-four paintings were of such supreme quality that success was assured as long as the greatest possible number of major collectors and museums all over the world knew about them in sufficient time to study their available finances (and add to them where this was possible). The promotion for the sale lasted from June until mid-November of 1961 and was brilliantly orchestrated. The advertising budget was unusually high and the catalogue looked sumptuous. Twenty thousand people flocked to Parke-Bernet while the pictures were on view. On the evening of the sale, even people with tickets waited patiently in the street for over an hour before getting to their seats. Four galleries were crammed with bidders, linked to the main gallery by closed circuit television.

The first five lots in the sale went for satisfactory but not sensational prices. The real excitement began with lot 6, a beautiful portrait of *Princess Sybille of Cleves* by Cranach. Agnew's bought it for $105,000. Lot 7 was what everyone had been waiting for: Rembrandt's magnificent *Aristotle Contemplating the Bust of Homer*. He had painted the picture as a commission from a Sicilian nobleman in 1653. The sombre mood of the large canvas, the absorbed look on the model's face (known for years as a portrait of the poet P. C. Hooft), and the mystical nature of the subject-matter all added up to making the painting every museum curator's dream. Its recent antecedents helped. Joseph Duveen had bought the picture in 1907 from the Rodolphe Kann collection in Paris and sold it to Mrs. Collis P. Huntington, widow of the railroad king, who had recently married her nephew, the great collector – already so well known to us – Henry Huntington. Twenty years later, after her death, Duveen bought the picture back and sold it to Alfred W. Erickson, co-founder of the renowned advertising agency, McCann-Erickson, for $750,000. When the stock market collapsed in 1929 Erickson needed cash and sold it back to Duveen for $500,000. As business gradually recovered he re-purchased the portrait in 1936 for $590,000. Although he had died soon afterwards, his wife retained it until her own death in 1961.

Lou Marion was in the rostrum on the evening of 15 November 1961. Sanka Knox of the *New York Times* commented: 'As Aristotle was brought on stage, the spotlights transformed the flowing sleeves of the robe into gold, the audience seemed to catch its breath, then broke into applause'. The occasion offered Lou Marion an opportunity he had always longed for – to start the bidding for a single lot at a million dollars. He got a bid for that figure almost as soon as he had mentioned it. By leaps of $100,000 the price soon rose to $2,300,000 and stopped. The purchaser was James J. Rorimer, Director of the Metropolitan Museum. The applause now turned into an ovation. At that figure 'Aristotle' had become the most expensive picture ever sold at auction at that time. Translated into pounds sterling, the figure at £831,000 was slightly in excess (by £7,000) of the total cost of all the pictures the London National Gallery had purchased in the first one hundred years of its existence.

The second highlight of the sale was the $875,000 paid for a charming family portrait by Fragonard known as *La Liseuse*, by Chester Dale on behalf of the National Gallery of Art at Washington, which he did through a complex system of disguised bids arranged before the sale with Lou Marion's son, John. The total for the sale was $4,679,250 – a record that was to stand for many years.

An interesting relic from the sale survives at Sotheby's in London. Peter Wilson had gone to the Erickson preview with a colleague who asked him to have a shot at estimating the sale's total. He scribbled some sums on the back of an envelope. His estimate turned out to be a mere $65,000 less than the actual total.

If Sotheby's lost the Erickson Sale they gained a long concatenation of others: the Impressionists of Walter P. Chrysler Junior, Mrs. T. G. Kenefick,[1] and George Goodyear;[2] John Rewald's marvellous drawings; Martin J. Desmonis' Renaissance jewellery;[3] Jaques Sarlie's twenty-nine Picassos and other modern paintings. Almost more important than these landmark sales was a steady stream of single pictures and smaller collections of the decorative arts that American clients, who had seen the name Sotheby's more and more frequently in their newspapers, brought to the cramped office of 'Sotheby's of London'. Great interest had also been aroused by the firm's presence at the British Exhibition held in the New York Coliseum in June 1960. Thirty thousand visitors streamed through the stand, many attracted by the genuine works of art (as well as reproductions) displayed there with seemingly slight security. They included a Modigliani portrait from the collection of the late Ernest Duveen, later sold for a then record of £24,000.

1. Her well-known Cézanne portrait, *Paysan au Blouse Bleue* (of which several versions exist), fetched £145,000.

2. His Gauguin, *Te tia i na ve i te rata* ('I await the letter'), was sold for £130,000 at the same sale.

3. An exhibition of this jewellery in aid of a charity was held at a time of recess between sales and this proved very popular with the public.

33
Fribourg

A TURNING point in Peregrine Pollen's presence in New York occurred very early in 1963 with the death of the great collector, René Fribourg. He was of Belgian origin and his very considerable fortune was based on a large grain merchanting firm in Chicago, founded as long ago as 1813. Before the Second World War he had lived in Paris. He abandoned his beautiful house there very shortly before the war and moved to America. After the war he transported its entire contents to a fine, six-storey house in Manhattan quite close to the Metropolitan Museum (to which he later made various donations and bequests). Here he lived with a staff of seven, including a notable French chef and two French butlers. The language spoken in the house was almost invariably French, although Fribourg spoke English perfectly. He had rarely missed a major art sale in the last fifty years (though he almost always bought through agents) and the house contained a collection of French eighteenth-century furniture, porcelain and faience, pictures and drawings, carpets and tapestries, bijouterie and gold boxes, of a consistently high quality that had few rivals in America, where a love of the finest examples of the French pre-revolution period is widely spread. Peter Wilson and Richard Timewell had visited Fribourg on several occasions and knew the contents of the house well, because the collector had taken great delight in showing off his treasures to them and expounding on his passion for the very finest French craftsmanship of his favourite period. After the old man had passed his eightieth birthday he had even discussed with them the dispersal of his collection after his death.[1] Like Lurcy, he was determined that this should be done by auction, but he was advised that a specific reference to Sotheby's in that context in his will could lead to complications.

His final illness had been noted by major auctioneers throughout the world. Peter Chance of Christie's attended Fribourg's New York funeral. So did Leslie Hyam and Lou Marion. Peregrine Pollen had merely sent flowers. Peter Wilson wrote to Madame Fribourg from London. Only a few days later the executors invited various firms to discuss a possible sale. One invitation went to 'Sotheby's of London' New York office and Peregrine cabled Peter Wilson to come over. They met the executors, Fred Meyer and Charles Gutwirth, at 11 East 84th Street and generally looked around the house. Peter Wilson's detailed knowledge and obvious delight in the contents made a considerable impression. Ways and means of arranging a sale were discussed. The two Englishmen then left for a cup of coffee in what Peregrine remembers as 'a greasy spoon restaurant nearby' and worked out the details of a contract which the executors had asked for.

1. He had had similar conversations with Lou Marion of Parke-Bernet.

Only a week or so later the latter's choice of auctioneer was announced publicly. It was Sotheby's. Interviewed by the *New York Times*, Peter Wilson commented, 'I think we got the sale because we convinced the executors that we could obtain the best prices'. He rejected the suggestion that Sotheby's ten per cent commission might be lower than that of competitors. 'If you went to one doctor who said his fee was $100, another who said it was $50 and a third it was $10, you wouldn't necessarily go to the $10 man. You'd go to the one you thought would cure you.'

Because of the great wealth of material it was decided to stage one series of sales towards the end of the summer season of 1963 and another in October of the same year. This meant the most frenzied activity in order to prepare the catalogues in good time for the June sales, particularly as it had been agreed that these should be produced in a more elaborate and more fully illustrated format than Sotheby's had ever previously undertaken.[1] Richard Timewell and Tim Clarke flew over to New York to start the cataloguing of the furniture and the porcelain. Fortunately this was aided by detailed inventories which had been compiled by René Fribourg himself, though they were by no means complete. The New York office had to move a veritable mountain of administrative paperwork. The problems of insurance alone were monumental; in fact, for an enormous fee the house was guarded day and night by a detective agency until the contents were cleared.

It was decided to charter an aircraft to bring the smaller items over to London[2] and to send the bulkier furniture by sea. No sooner had the cargo been loaded when the press became aware of what was going on and clamoured for photographs. In particular they were intrigued by René Fribourg's own bed which had once, so it was alleged, been Napoleon's. The Emperor had had it made for his second wife, Marie Louise, and inscribed with their wedding date.[3] Interest in the sale was particularly strong in France (Maurice Rheims had been one of the strongest contenders for it) and the two French art magazines, *L'Oeil* and *Connaissance des Arts*, competed fiercely for exclusivity to cover the collection. In the end one concentrated on the June sales and the other on the ones held in October.

There was general relief when, after a multitude of crises, the magnificent sales catalogues finally reached New York. The executors were delighted with them and both dealers and collectors were impressed by their unprecedented elegance. Interest in the collection was enormous and dealers from all over the

1. They are particularly distinctive in any collection of sale catalogues because they were the first ever to be given striking, full-colour dust jackets.
2. The charge for this by BOAC at £2,858 was not as prohibitive as one might think in relation to the total raised by the sale.
3. Part of the catalogue description read: 'Lot 710, the marriage bed of Napoleon I and the Empress Marie Louise, in mahogany and magnificently mounted with ormolu. The panelled head and foot of slightly arched form with rectangular columnate uprights, the foot centred by bas relief plaques of the Emperor and Empress standing at either side of an altar of love, one side with interlaced wreath of laurel and marguerites joined by ribbons and inscribed 1 Avril 1810. . . .' It fetched £3,800.

world asked to inspect particular objects – often accompanied by their distinguished clients – long before the whole was put on view.

The three sales came in the midst of an unbelievable season: the June sales alone in 1963 included a very fine collection of Old Masters belonging to Lt.-Col. William Sterling of Kier; the second part of the collection of gold snuff boxes, watches and objects of vertu belonging to Sir A. Chester Beatty; the Chinese porcelain of Mrs. Nellie Ionides, a particularly adventurous and persevering collector, an inveterate supporter of the firm between the wars and friend of Queen Mary's; English silver belonging to Lord Rothschild; jewellery belonging to Lady Brownlow and Mrs. Vere Harmsworth; a distinguished collection of modern French illustrated books that had belonged to Nicolas Rauch of Geneva, and an anonymous but remarkable collection of glass ('the property of a lady'; in fact, Mrs. Harrison Hughes). Frank Davis described this as a 'nine-day wonder', for the eighty-two items changed hands for nearly £30,000, then one of the highest totals ever for a glass sale. Lot 82 was one of the very few undisputed pieces in existence made by the Italian, Jacob Verzelini (to whom Queen Elizabeth I had given a monopoly for glass manufacturing), in 1583 in his Whitefriars 'glass house'. It was sold for a record £6,500. Two engraved bowls, five inches high, by the glassmaker George Ravenscroft, to whom similarly Charles II had granted a seven year patent to make his specially toughened lead glass (the formula for which is not known), and which traditionally rejoiced in the name 'the Butler Buggin Bowls' after one of their former owners, were sold for another astonishing sum, £6,800. They had been bought by a perceptive dealer for a few shillings among a collection of Victorian finger bowls at a country house sale near Tring in Hertfordshire in 1937.

Also in June there occurred the sale of the 'immensely important' collection of Impressionists of the late William Cargill of Carruth, Bridge of Weir, Scotland. In his collecting he had progressed cautiously from an early interest in Fantin-Latour (there was a group of eight flower paintings) and Corot, to Monet and Renoir, who were both still regarded as rather an advanced obsession in the 1920s. A Degas pastel, *Danseuse Basculante*, for which Cargill had paid £4,200 in 1928, now fetched £105,000, and Pissarro's *Charing Cross Bridge* of 1890, which had cost £2,600 in 1937, sold for £47,000. There were also four fine Renoirs, a Brittany Gauguin, two Monets, two Seurats and a Van Gogh.

One of the finest properties, mixed into various sales towards the end of the same season, was a whole gamut of modern and Old Master paintings and *objets d'art* belonging to Mrs. Derek Fitzgerald, the daughter of Mrs. Meyer Sassoon. The most spectacular among her twenty-two pictures were a little predella panel painted by Raphael which fetched £95,000 and the handsome and much admired portrait of *La Belle Strasbourgeoise* by Nicolas de Largillière,[1] for which the City of Strasbourg paid £145,000. The preliminaries

1. As so often happens in the art world, another – possibly earlier – version of the same portrait appeared for sale at Frank Partridge & Sons just after the Sotheby sale. The price was said to be £70,000.

to the sale were interesting. Mrs. Fitzgerald arrived at Sotheby's to see Peter Wilson. She discussed the matter with him in a waiting-room for ten minutes and everything was settled. This brief informality was in stark contrast to major American properties, where there were often negotiations going on for weeks, even months, which resulted in long and complex contracts. The results in this case were every bit as successful.

The Fribourg contract ran to some fifteen pages. The terms were tough. Sotheby's undertook to pay the expenses for the sale up to $120,000. No commission was payable unless the total for the sale exceeded $1,500,000. Between $1,500,000 and $3,000,000 it was 15 per cent. Beyond that it reverted to 11 per cent. It was even laid down that cataloguing should start within five days of the signature of the contract and that the printed catalogues would be generally available forty-two days before each of the relevant sales. The executors reserved the right to call in a valuer of their own choice if Sotheby's estimates seemed low to them, and they did, in fact, call in Edward Fowles, Duveen's old old partner, in one or two instances just before the goods were all shipped to London.

The first three sales were scheduled for the last week of June. There was general astonishment when the porcelain, the furniture and the works of art came on view. London had not often seen so many eighteenth-century French objects of such quality. Tim Clarke took the first sale of the porcelain. The room was crowded and *The Times* reported that 'prices can be described without exaggeration as unprecedented and the £180,950 realised (for 68 lots) is far and away the highest sum yet recorded for ceramics of this character on a single morning. The sale was also remarkable for the number of private individuals bidding in person, several of them remaining anonymous. An unnamed American gave the highest price of the morning for a single item – £20,000 for a pair of Meissen groups of horses and grooms by J. J. Kaendler on Louis XV ormolu mounts. The Antique Porcelain Company paid £19,000 for a pair of Louis XV ormolu candelabra with figures of cockatoos by the same gifted modeller', but it was Kaendler's figures of various harlequins that aroused the most interest. One superbly sinuous example, in a red coat, sweeping his hat off with one hand and holding a silver tankard with the other, was sold for a record £9,000.

While some of the paintings and drawings were decorative and full of charm, the quality generally was not of the standard of the furniture and porcelain. One paper described the drawings as 'the sort of thing that will always be in demand, but irritates the really discerning'. The paintings had seemed just right on the walls of René Fribourg's apartments, but seemed less sure of themselves in the limelight of the sale-room. The portraits fared moderately well, though a number of them had to be bought in. A pair of views of Venice by Francesco Guardi sold for £12,500 and £9,000 respectively, under one of those complex bidding arrangements when a dealer, buying under a cover name, continued in the running while his glasses were on and had reached his limit when he took his glasses off. In fact, he got the first painting, but the auctioneer's clerk bought the second on behalf of an anonymous client.

The furniture was sold on 28 June 1963, and eighty-four items realised £324,520 in a single session. Once again the galleries were really packed. No fewer than eleven people had decided to bid under a *nom de vente*, a headache for the auctioneer's clerk. The sale started with some thirty items all elaborately mounted on ormolu. Such decorative objects had covered every plain surface in Fribourg's residence. From the very first, they went with a bang. Prices were often three times or more as high as the reserves, and such consistently high prices were almost unprecedented. Fribourg's own dream of 'an auction of the century' seemed to be materialising.

His possessions were the sort of thing that particularly appealed to a large body of wealthy collectors all over the world in the early Sixties: they were not unique items for museums or for the super rich, but works of art of a quality rarely available on the market, that exuded luxury and sophistication. Few collectors could afford such things in the vast quantities that Fribourg had assembled, but a scattering of them under one roof or in one apartment or even in the state room of a resplendent yacht was quite enough to indicate *ton*. Very little was bought in, and despite the express rate of cataloguing there were few disagreements. A small Louis XV marquetry *secretaire* and *poudreuse* containing the original glass and porcelain fittings made by the great *ébéniste*, Roger Vandercruse, fetched the highest price of the day at £28,000. A small, delicate Louis XVI marquetry writing table attributed to J. H. Riesener was bought for £20,000 by Seligman, one of the many Paris dealers attending the sale. Five assorted oval and circular *gueridons* (little ornamental working tables) fetched enormous prices.

There had been some concern whether this pace could be kept up in the second series of sales after the long summer break in the following October. The first of them, on 15 October, consisted exclusively of Fribourg's gold and enamel boxes and they realised £142,187. There were some superb examples of bijouterie and these fetched prices that were virtually unprecedented even in the Chester Beatty sale a little earlier. Interestingly enough, some of the same items reappeared in the New York sale at Parke-Bernet in the collection of Henry Ford II fifteen years later in February 1978 and afford some comparison into the appreciation of such objects in the interval. In 1963 a brilliant red enamel and gold snuff box, made in Paris in 1765, with a finely painted miniature (of a young woman opening her bodice invitingly for her student lover, who points to his watch and sits surrounded by books, with a dog at his feet), was sold for £1,000 (then $2,800) to a New York dealer against a reserve of £575. In 1978 the same box fetched $19,000 (£9,900). The increase in another ex-Fribourg Louis XVI gold, red enamel and diamond rectangular box was not quite so great. In 1963 it fetched £2,900 ($8,120). In 1978 the same piece was sold for $26,000 (£13,542). In 1963 the highest price of the sale for a superb gold and enamel snuff box by Jean Moynat decorated with sprays of botanical flowers was £14,000, and no fewer than 41 of the 108 lots sold for prices in excess of £1,000.

More porcelain and faience, more drawings, and two further long sales of furniture concluded an entire week of Fribourg sales. The total by now was well in excess of the magic figure of $3,000,000. The whole affair – risky for Sotheby's, as so many major sales of that period were and a subject of divided counsel within the firm – had been a resounding success. The executors of the Fribourg estate expressed themselves completely satisfied, but the sale demonstrated the sophisticated commercial approach and the sheer complexity of the physical organisation that such events now demanded. Because of the immense volume of items that Fribourg had left, it took another four years to tie up all the loose ends and to present the final accounts. One lesson learned then was that the overhead expenses had been much higher than estimated, but even so with a net yield of £48,000 the sale was very profitable and brought in much more business of the same kind.

34

The Acquisition
of Parke-Bernet

WITH Fribourg behind them, a resounding success, Peter Wilson and Peregrine Pollen agreed that the New York office should be housed in more impressive and commodious accommodation. In fact, it remained in the same building, on the same floor even, but it now occupied 2,200 square feet in place of the cramped 400. For some time already Peregrine had led the prolonged campaign that now began to engulf him more and more. This was nothing less than the acquisition of Sotheby's great rival in New York, Parke-Bernet itself.

The event which precipitated the transformation of what had seemed a pipedream for a decade and a half into reality was the sudden and unexpected death on 10 September 1963 of Leslie Alexander Hyam, Parke-Bernet's English-born president and chief executive. Hyam at sixty-two had been a tall, commanding, rather remote figure who was something of an autocrat and very much in the mould of the old Bond Street Titans. After leaving Cambridge University with a degree in physics he went to America in 1923. Almost by chance he had got a job in the cataloguing department of the American Art Association, then New York's leading auction house. Always a perfectionist, before starting work he devised for himself a crash course of self-education in the decorative arts at the Metropolitan Museum. In six weeks of intense, uninterrupted study he filled three notebooks with a self-compiled encyclopaedia in tiny script and minute sketches, of every facet of man's creative genius. Under C for the Church, for example, there were thirty pages on how to identify saints and twenty-five on religious symbols – the iconography of candlesticks, the hierarchy of crosses, the habits of monastic orders. But the letter C also stood for Chinese Art, the bronzes, the porcelain and its marks, motifs and shapes of vases (drawn and labelled), the embroidery, the typical products of various dynasties. Coupled with that quintessential quality of the outstanding fine art auctioneer, a superb visual memory, this was the beginning of his connoisseurship and the foundation on which Hyam built his career. 'The direction of cataloguing then,' he had said in reference to American practice in that field years later, 'was to present the object with a description corresponding to the most optimistic expectations of the owner.' By degrees Hyam introduced objectivity and scholarship into the firm's catalogues, and his was one of the most valued skills which Hiram Parke and Otto Bernet took with them when they broke away from the ailing AAA with much of its staff in the autumn of 1937 to set up their own business, which they called Parke-Bernet Galleries Inc.[1] Great success

1. For the record, the name Parke-Bernet Inc. came into being in 1953. It was designed to

soon crowned their endeavours and by the time the two founding partners had retired from the business, at the height of its quite astonishing success some twenty years later,[1] its management was left in the hands of a remarkable triumvirate: Leslie Hyam, Louis Marion and Mary Vandegrift. Marion was the auctioneer and an expert on jewellery, Miss Vandegrift looked after administration and promotion and Hyam was the driving force as planner and principal expert. He and Lou Marion were also the firm's primary business-getters. Right to the end, Hyam's passion for fastidious cataloguing remained undiminished and he continued to insist on the supervision and correction of every detail. It was reported that he died of a heart attack. In fact, he committed suicide. It was not so much overwork or despair about the inroads made into the business by the challenge from Sotheby's that were the causes of his death, but more the realisation that he was not holding his own in a changed world and – the final blow – rejection in a late love affair.

At the time of Hyam's death there were some twelve shareholders in Parke-Bernet. Only three worked within the firm. A minority of the outside directors had for some time been in favour of selling the business. Approaches had come from a number of prospective purchasers, including Sotheby's, Christie's and a consortium of Paris auction houses headed by the ubiquitous Maurice Rheims. Negotiations of a sort had been going on for more than a year before September 1963. Alex Hillman, a New York businessman and collector, had approached Sotheby's about making a joint offer for Parke-Bernet in 1962. There had been inconclusive meetings between Sotheby directors and Parke-Bernet directors both in New York and in London. They had foundered over Parke-Bernet's insistence on total equality (described by Peter Wilson as the creation of a dragon with two heads), although Sotheby's was already much the bigger business. Even earlier, in February 1961 – after the death of Arthur Swann, a famous bookman and one of the founders of the firm with Parke and Bernet – Col. Richard Gimbel, a relatively new major outside shareholder, had actually approached John Carter about coming to Parke-Bernet as head of the book department in order to help restore the firm's fortunes. Jake enjoyed this boost to his ego, and he certainly enjoyed his exchange of letters with Gimbel which gave him a remarkable opportunity to express his opinion of the opposition with fierce candour. 'You will understand, that you are inviting me (and don't think that I underestimate the compliment) to sever all my connections here [i.e. in England] in order to lead a forlorn hope, in uncongenial company, over a very

---

serve a subsidiary company that undertook auction sales of war surplus material. One such sale held on the premises of the United States Naval Supply Depot at Bayonne, New Jersey, took place on 4 November 1953. It included 'a tremendous quantity of valuable electronic tubes of many types, a 16-ton Manitowoc crane and a 6000 h.p. Generator'. But the sale was not a success. The appellation 'Parke-Bernet Inc.' came into full-time use after the acquisition of the firm by Sotheby's in 1964. On 19 April 1972 the company's official name was changed to Sotheby Parke Bernet Inc., and the hyphen between the names of the two founding partners finally disappeared for good.

1. Otto Bernet died in 1949; Major Parke 'retired' at eighty-five in 1957 and died a year later.

ON SATURDAY, NOVEMBER 13, 1937, a company was organized to conduct public sales and to prepare appraisals of art and literary property, with a personnel entirely composed of the former officers, executives, and technical staff of the American Art Association-Anderson Galleries, Inc.

This corporation, known as the Parke-Bernet Galleries, Inc., announces its intention of bringing to the conduct of its sales the same high principles which were initiated by the late Thomas E. Kirby, co-founder of the old American Art Galleries, and his son Gustavus T. Kirby, who has joined the new Board of Directors. These principles have been maintained by Mr. Parke, Mr. Bernet, Mr. Swann, and their associates during their conduct of public sales for three decades.

The extraordinary record of their work includes the personal management of vastly the greater part of the outstanding auctions of art collections and libraries in America, some of which are set forth in the following pages. The men responsible for this achievement will need little introduction to those who have bought and sold confidently under their direction for more than a quarter of a century.

HIRAM H. PARKE has been prominent in the art and literary auction world of Philadelphia and New York for forty years. His connection with the old American Art Association commenced in 1915, when Gustavus T. Kirby brought him into the Company to conduct

---

PARKE-BERNET GALLERIES
Bulletin

VOL. 1   FEBRUARY - MARCH 1938   No. 1

PUBLIC SALES
February 17 - March 26

FEBRUARY 17, AFTERNOON
Americana. *The Walker Collection.*

FEBRUARY 18 AND 19, AFTERNOONS
Furniture and Objects of Art. *Property of Mrs William Platt and Other Owners.*

FEBRUARY 24, EVENING
Paintings. *Property of Mrs William Platt and Other Owners.*

FEBRUARY 25, AFTERNOON
Sets, Manuscripts, Drawings, Americana. *From the Looram and Other Collections.*

FEBRUARY 26, AFTERNOON
Firearms of the XVI-XIX Century. *From the Pareto, Boss, et al. Collections.*

MARCH 3, EVENING
American First Editions. *Property of Morris L. Parrish and Another Owner.*

MARCH 4 AND 5, AFTERNOONS
Furniture and Decorations. *From the Eben J. Knowlton Estate and Other Sources.*

MARCH 10, AFTERNOON
Americana. *From the Estate of P. K. Foley and Other Sources.*

MARCH 11 AND 12, AFTERNOONS
Art Property. *From the Collection of the late Mr and Mrs Percy A. Rockefeller.*

MARCH 15, MORNING AND AFTERNOON
At the Residence 18 East 68 Street.
Furnishings and Decorations. *Property of the Estate of Henry T. Sloane.*

The First Sale—Over $150,000

THE OFFICIAL opening of the Parke-Bernet Galleries, Inc., took place on Friday, January 7, with the exhibition of the collections of the late Mr and Mrs Jay F. Carlisle. On that day, a distinguished crowd of over 2,000 persons, among which were many of the city's leading art collectors, thronged the spacious exhibition rooms of the first, second, and third floors; by closing time on Monday, January 10, after but three and a half days of exhibition, over 9,000 visitors had viewed the collections. The handsome quarters provided for exhibitions and sales were generally admired, and the officers of the company, well-known to collectors in their former capacity as executives of the American Art Association, received many valued expressions of congratulation.

ATTENDANCE at the various sessions of sale was almost unprecedented. On the first day of
[Concluded on Page 4]

MARCH 17, EVENING
MARCH 18 AND 19, AFTERNOONS
Paintings, Art Objects, Furniture. *Estate of Marie Louise Paterson.*

MARCH 24, AFTERNOON
First Editions, Autographs. *From the Eittinger, Gutterman et al. Collections.*

MARCH 24, EVENING
Paintings. *From the Rockefeller, Sloane, Union League Club and Other Collections.*

MARCH 26, AFTERNOON
Furnishings from Elmhurst. *Home of Mr and Mrs S. S. Bloch. Wheeling, W. Va.*

PARKE-BERNET GALLERIES · INC · 742 FIFTH AVENUE · NEW YORK

PARKE-BERNET GALLERIES · INC
Public Sales & Appraisals of Art & Literary Property

HIRAM H. PARKE, *President*
OTTO BERNET, *Vice-President*
ARTHUR SWANN, *Vice-President*
EDWARD W. KEYES, *Secretary and Treasurer*

AUCTIONEERS
Hiram H. Parke   Otto Bernet   H. E. Russell, Jr

742 FIFTH AVENUE · NEW YORK
PLAZA 3-7573

Subscription to Catalogues

ALTHOUGH catalogues of the Parke-Bernet Galleries may be purchased singly for each sale, clients will find it both a saving and convenience to subscribe to the full series of catalogues on a yearly basis at $3 for art catalogues and $3 for catalogues of the book department, occasional de luxe catalogues not to be included in this low subscription rate. A sample art or book catalogue will be sent free on request.

"ART" catalogues include paintings, furniture, textiles, porcelains, silver, rugs, other objects; "book" catalogues include autographs, manuscripts, first editions, and other books and etchings, engravings, prints and drawings.

THE TEXT of Parke-Bernet Galleries catalogues is written with a view to supplying accurate information as to period, history, and physical details of the objects described. Furthermore, the typography and illustration of these catalogues is directly supervised by the Galleries with the purpose of producing books which will be worthy records of the various collections dispersed under its management.

REQUESTS for catalogues from libraries and museums both in this country and abroad are constantly being received, in addition to the large number of catalogues supplied to private subscribers. The great demand for the Carlisle catalogue necessitated a second printing.

Art Property of the Late
Mr and Mrs Percy A. Rockefeller

ON MARCH 11 and 12 tapestries, rugs, and other art property collected by the late Mr and Mrs Percy A. Rockefeller will be dispersed at public sale at the Galleries. Until their removal in preparation for public sale these objects comprised the furnishings of *Owenoke Farm,* the Rockefeller residence at Greenwich, Conn., which is now to be demolished. The group of about twenty-five choice tapestries include: an Enghien *choufleur* of the 16th century, a rare Louis XII small Brussels tapestry depicting *Jacob and Esau,* a set of four Aubusson 'Teniers' examples, a small 16th century Brussels medallion specimen depicting *Psyche and Cupid,* and a Flemish Renaissance example of about 1540. The rugs have the character of collector's specimens and include a number of 18th century Ghiordes and Kulah prayer rugs, also examples in silk and an 18th century palmette carpet. French salon suites in tapestry, Renaissance walnut furniture, Chinese porcelains, and table appointments are included in the sale.

THE PAINTINGS from *Owenoke Farm* collected by the late Mr and Mrs Rockefeller will be dispersed at public sale on March 24 together with paintings from the collection of the late Henry T. Sloane, the Union League Club, and from other collections.

Delivery and Shipping

PACKING AND SHIPPING to distant points and local delivery of purchases at the Parke-Bernet Galleries may be arranged for on the premises. Mr Gustave E. Meyer of the firm of Day and Meyer, Murray and Young, Inc., a well-known company with long experience in the packing and transportation of furniture, art objects, and books, has an office at the Galleries and may be consulted in person or by telephoning Plaza 3-1064.

Two pages from the original announcement of Parke-Bernet's foundation (*top*) and two pages from the first issue of *Bulletin*, a preview of sales to come and a record of notable sales already held.

difficult terrain, in a direction flatly opposite to the course I have pursued, energetically and not without blowing of trumpets, for the past five years. Such an invitation can obviously be sincerely considered, in my position and at my time of life, only if it is so heavily weighted with gold as to make it irresistible.' And in response to a further plea he had written, not without a touch of venom, 'I have decided that you and Parke-Bernet would have to get along without me in your campaign to put Sotheby's in their place . . . I shall be much interested to see what you can do, both in the matter of personnel and of policies to rehabilitate PB, and although I cannot exactly wish you luck I hope you have yourself a good time doing it'. Robert F. Metzdorf, a well-known American bookman, was eventually appointed to the post. Not surprisingly he became a fierce opponent to the possibility of a merger with Sotheby's and, in fact, was the only principal to resign when it was clear that the two companies would join forces.

Hyam's demise was a stunning blow for Parke-Bernet and prompted a new and more insistent round of approaches. Peter Wilson was in Japan at the time. Peregrine phoned him and he came at once to New York. Following a long and stormy board meeting at Parke-Bernet a discussion took place between Ralph Colin, Parke-Bernet's attorney (and a minority shareholder),[1] Peter Wilson, Peregrine Pollen and Jesse Wolff in order to sound out Sotheby's on the terms of any offer they might be prepared to make. This was to be followed by a proposal in writing from London. When this was sent, admittedly couched in rather cautious terms, the response at first seemed totally negative.

What had become clear by now was that the whole future of Parke-Bernet hinged on the conditions of the lease of their premises at 980 Madison Avenue. The building had been specially constructed for the firm in 1949 with all the necessary facilities a fine art auction house needed. At that time the management of Parke-Bernet had agreed to terms with its landlords which stipulated an annual rental of only $85,000, but on top of this it had to pay a further 2 per cent of gross income after a turnover of $6,000,000 had been reached. This was fine when business was brisk and profitable, but at a time when the company had to cut its commission rates in order to maintain turnover – and cut them to the very bone, for example, in the case of the great Erickson Sale as an answer to the challenge from Sotheby's – it represented an immense burden on overheads and thus an erosion of profitability. In the years between 1960 and 1963 in particular the proportion of rental to income had shot up alarmingly from a proportion of 12 per cent to 20 per cent of the gross income. There seemed no way out of this constrictive spiral. It spelled out very clearly the single word, *disaster*. But the matter was one over which both the directors and shareholders of Parke-Bernet had very little control. Only a new owner of the business could re-negotiate the terms of the lease, and that posed complex and indeed

1. He was a considerable collector in his own right: see *The Colin Collection*, 1960, an extensive catalogue of post-impressionists and modern paintings, watercolours, drawings and sculpture, brought out by Knoedler's to coincide with an exhibition of the family collection at their galleries.

interlocking problems in both the process and the tactics of making the acquisition, for any offer could only be contingent on bringing about the necessary change by re-negotiating the terms for the future. Indeed such negotiations could only proceed if Parke-Bernet were agreeable to a sale, at least in principle.

The lease was controlled by Antiquities Inc., which in turn was a wholly-owned subsidiary of the City Investing Company, headed by Mr. Robert Dowling. While Parke-Bernet was hesitant to commit itself to a decision, it was difficult both for Sotheby's and Mr. Dowling to come to any definite understanding. Negotiations proceeded at a snail-like pace and decisive action had to be delayed again and again. After many weary months of meetings, correspondence and legal discussions on the one hand, and endless probing by the US press, frequent leaks and alarming rumours on the other (which sapped the morale of Parke-Bernet's staff and began seriously to damage the business), Jesse Wolff received a letter from Ralph Colin that seemed to bring all the parleying to a shattering halt. It stated categorically that 'all negotiations have been terminated and the galleries are NOT for sale'. It followed hard upon a long internal board meeting at 980 Madison Avenue which had culminated in a public announcement that Parke-Bernet had decided to resist all suitors and to carry on on its own. However, there was a sentence in the letter which seemed to indicate that the door was not slammed completely. 'If at some time in the future,' it said, 'Sotheby's is prepared to make a new and *unconditional* offer, it may be considered at that time and on its merits.' Jesse Wolff asked for clarification by return but the answer was not reassuring. It rather seemed as if the chapter was closed.

Unexpectedly it was the lawyer acting as executor for the estate of Leslie Hyam (he also acted on behalf of two other sizeable shareholders) who came to the rescue a week later with a suggestion for a new approach that could be made unconditionally. Jesse Wolff analysed it from all possible points of view and suggested that the London directors should chew it over. A board meeting was called and Peregrine Pollen went back to London especially for the occasion. He had recently been made a director, and it was the first such meeting he was to attend, but now another major hurdle seemed to present itself.

The long negotiations were certainly the most important in Sotheby's 230 years of existence. It required vision, optimism and a good deal of self-confidence to see that the ailing Parke-Bernet could become not merely profitable again but a pre-eminent bastion in the world's art market, without taking business away from Bond Street. The style of the two businesses was essentially different. In contrast to Sotheby's sober presentation of what it had to sell, Parke-Bernet had evolved a unique tradition of auctioneering which involved a much greater element of the theatrical. It was, in fact, relatively restrained and low-key compared to most other forms of auctioneering in the United States. After the experience of country house sales in the early Thirties, a style of arrangement in the Bond Street galleries had come about that substituted harmony for the calculated clutter of long ago. Parke-Bernet took matters much further. They employed a professional interior decorator for the display of the objects prior to each sale. Old photographs show that there was a wonderful sense of spaciousness, clever use of lighting and masses of floral arrangements to help each setting. Even though a sale might be made up of properties from a host of different sources, this re-arrangement gave them a unity which resembled the contents of a single spacious home. So much so that pre-sale visits to 980 Madison Avenue became a regular social feature on Saturdays where New York collectors and the merely curious met their friends and admired the displays. The benefit, of course, was a very much higher proportion of private bidders at sales than in London. Again, during an auction each item was displayed on a specially-built stage and could be revealed by the drawing back of stage curtains. Indeed the very manner of the auctioneering in the rostrum was totally different in London and in New York. Instead of Bond Street's calm, quiet, unadorned progression of rarely repeated bids, Parke-Bernet effected an unceasing staccato repetition of increasing bids, with comments, quips and occasional pleas for higher totals as constant interjections, and all this was complicated by shouts from a host of bid-tellers scattered round the auction galleries. The end result might be identical, but the method was as different as chalk from cheese.

The standard of production of catalogues too was infinitely higher than anything known in the UK. They were beautifully printed, in the case of book catalogues often on laid paper. Others were printed on coated paper with illustrations right beside many catalogue entries. Certainly the overall effect could be rather bookish but then Mitchell Kennerley, who had originated the style at the old Anderson Galleries, had started life as a publisher. Such catalogues provided a sense of dignity where none had existed before. All this was accompanied by a highly effective programme of public promotion which in England was still slightly frowned upon.

With the early demise of the combined Anderson Galleries and AAA,[1] Parke-Bernet had relatively little local competition and after two difficult years it burgeoned into a magnificent and virtually unique institution. But latterly it had suffered not only from greatly increased opposition; there was also a wide disparity between the quality of the constituent parts of the firm. Hyam, Mary Vandegrift and Louis Marion had concentrated their style and panache on business-getting, on producing good-looking catalogues, and on brilliant publicity. They lacked London's expert connoisseurship and concomitant strength on the financial side. It was this that let them down. Few people in the firm realised how far the decline had gone, or indeed how to get over it.

It soon became apparent that Sotheby's board was divided about going ahead with the acquisition. Some members had serious doubts about taking such a major step so far from base. Where was the money going to come from? Who was going to run the firm? Supposing things went wrong? Obviously Peter

1. The two firms had merged in 1929, but after Parke and Bernet had departed it soon went into a decline. They purchased the rump of their former employers' business for a pittance some years later.

Wilson was strongly in favour. He felt convinced that the United States still represented a huge, relatively untapped source of business which Sotheby's initiative and know-how could exploit the more readily through an existing business. Carmen Gronau strongly backed him up. Peregrine supported the idea passionately after his long, first-hand experience in New York.

The debate went badly. Anthony Hobson, who was one of the first partners to have negotiated major London sales that had originated in the States, but who was also on the point of selling his own shares in Sotheby's, voiced misgivings. He considered the acquisition a foolhardy venture. Richard Timewell vigorously opposed the idea as well. He had done so when the matter was first mooted soon after the war. Fred Rose, who shared Timewell's view, but was away at the time of the meeting, had left his proxy vote with Timewell. Peregrine, after months of daily conferences with Jesse Wolff, after far-reaching tactics of every kind, began to see a unique opportunity for Sotheby's future slipping away. He pushed his chair back and stood up. He didn't so much address his partners as make a speech. It was a passionate appeal to have a go. 'And if we can't find anyone else to run PB, I'll run it myself', he concluded. Years later, Peter Wilson still described that moment as 'Peregrine's finest hour'. Surprisingly, John Rickett and Tim Clarke remained neutral. Peter Wilson turned to Jim Kiddell. 'What do you think, Jim?' Kiddell replied 'I believe the young people in the firm want it and it's their future we should be thinking of. Though I'm nearly seventy, I believe we should do it too.' His view tipped the balance. A vote was never taken. The board concurred with a proposal that negotiations should continue.

There were still serious problems in New York: the threat of the US Anti-Trust laws; should Sotheby's negotiate for Parke-Bernet's assets or its shares; the conflict of tax considerations between a wholly owned and a partially owned American corporation; the fact that a New York auctioneering license could only be granted to an American citizen; and most difficult of all, that Parke-Bernet considered Sotheby's offer inadequate. There was still total uncertainty about settling more favourable terms of a new lease with Robert Dowling; understandably he was reluctant to accept a lower income from the premises at 980 Madison Avenue, but had to set this against the possibility of Parke-Bernet going out of business; furthermore, Dowling had to satisfy other mortgage holders that Sotheby's would be an acceptable, and more successful tenant. It was only the fierce determination of Peter Wilson and Peregrine Pollen, coupled with the brilliant advocacy of Jesse Wolff, that overcame these intractable issues one by one. Letters flew across the Atlantic daily. The telexing and telephoning never ceased.

By June 1964 it seemed that agreement in theory at least had been reached, but it gradually became clear that one of Parke-Bernet's shareholders would not sell out, whatever the rest and the overwhelming majority might do. This was Colonel Gimbel.

A complex plan had to be devised to overcome these difficulties. Even the firm's ancestors were called from the shadows to assist the consummation

IIIa. This little masterpiece of 15th-century painting had been attributed to both Hubert van Eyck and Rogier van der Weyden, but because of its size ($5\frac{5}{8}$in. by $4\frac{1}{8}$in.) was not thought to be particularly valuable. To the owner's delight it fetched £220,000 in 1966. It was sold as a Van Eyck and now hangs in the National Gallery, Washington, ascribed to Rogier van der Weyden.

IIIb. The work of the Venetian vedutists has increased steeply in value during the last decade. This Canaletto was sold for £280,000 in December 1973.

IVa. Vincent van Gogh's *Le Cyprès et l'Arbre en Fleurs* from the W.W. Crocker Collection was sold in New York on 25 February 1970 for $1,300,000. Two versions of this composition are in the London National Gallery and the Bührle Collection, Zurich.

IVb. Kandinsky's marvellously colourful *Dorfstrasse* which was sold in London for £165,000 on 2 April 1979.

of the most important development in its history since the eighteenth century. A nominee company called Baker, Leigh and Sotheby was formed purely to take over Parke-Bernet. The crunch date seemed to be 29 June 1964. Robert Dowling had at last agreed to acceptable terms though only after a memorable meeting in which Peter Wilson deliberately lost his temper, once again with devastating effect. The Sotheby board had agreed to a greatly increased offer that topped another known to be in the offing.[1] The terms were presented at a Parke-Bernet board meeting, but after all-day discussions the meeting was still unable to reach a decision. Shareholders representing 54 per cent of the stock were in favour of selling to Sotheby's but the rest – and they included the vital executive directors – felt obliged to reconsider a tenuous earlier commitment.

A great deal of newspaper interest had been generated by the negotiations. Colonel Gimbel made his own views known in fiercely xenophobic terms. On 30 June Jesse Wolff wrote at length to one of the Parke-Bernet shareholder's attorneys on various aspects of Sotheby's offer. He concluded his letter by saying, 'As you and the other directors and shareholders can readily understand, in view of the recent newspaper publicity on this matter our client is being besieged by English and American newspapers for some statement in the matter, including a request for a clarification of Sotheby's plans for the United States in the event that it does not acquire Parke-Bernet'. There had been an earlier undertaking by Sotheby's not to make any press announcement about the proposed acquisition, and indeed, to preserve complete silence and security about the deal, but the US papers appeared to get hold of every aspect of the negotiations 'almost before we knew the facts ourselves', as Peter Wilson was to write at the time. The exception to this were the vital negotiations with Robert Dowling, of which no whisper ever leaked out. It was the ace in Sotheby's hand.

Now Stanley Clark, that maestro of public relations, went into action in London. Clark is undoubtedly one of the principal architects of Sotheby's fame and fortune and deserves a brief introduction into the story. There was a long tradition of skill in promotional matters at Sotheby's. Interesting press releases on major sales had certainly been a regular feature even at the beginning of the century.[2] Tom Hodge knew all the sale-room correspondents as personal friends and uttered fiercely as and when he wanted a particular point made. Montague Barlow had regarded close relations with the press as one of his own primary functions. Geoffrey Hobson, because of his deafness, concentrated more on the written word. In the early Fifties Sotheby's appointed 'Tomorrow's News' as public relations consultants. This was a small firm run by two ladies, Margaret Bean and Mollie Seton-Karr, who had for many years worked on the *Illustrated London News* under Sir Bruce Ingram. Soon after the Goldschmidt

1. Once again it came from Alex Hillman, and not from a consortium of Paris auctioneers as many people thought.
2. We know this if only because three or four of the major sale-room correspondents would always write up forthcoming sales in virtually identical terms.

14

Sale a new appointment had to be made. Peter Wilson saw a host of applicants. He chose what seemed to many the most unlikely candidate among them, a very unmilitary looking brigadier. Stanley Clark had started life as an apprentice to the British India Steam Navigation Company and had then become a journalist. 1939 found him at Odhams Press. Then he joined the army as a subaltern. During the war he had survived the long siege at Tobruk, and later had helped to organise the 'Aid to Russia' line from Iraq. After demobilisation he joined Reuters and became features editor both there and later at the Press Association. He had also written a biography of De Gaulle and the story of the Queen's working life, entitled *A Palace Diary*. Early in 1958 he had started his own public relations firm, Clark Nelson.

From the moment of his appointment Stanley Clark added a new dimension to Sotheby's public relations. When asked by Peter Wilson what he would do for Sotheby's as publicity consultant he had stated with disarming modesty, 'I would make you the most famous auctioneer in the world and would make Sotheby's the place where everyone would come to buy and sell'. When Peter Wilson retorted that the first suggestion was fine but that the firm relied substantially on wealthy clients for their business, Clark said, 'I am not trying to teach you your business, Sir, but one should remember that for every ten people in the world with £100,000 to spend there are a hundred million with £100 to spend'. The diversity of the clients who bring in goods to sell at Sotheby's sales counters and the range of those attending sales shows that over the years Stanley Clark has proved his point. A high proportion of Sotheby's business still stems from lesser objects that sell below £300. The first big sale that Clark had to handle was the Duke of Westminster's Rubens, the *Adoration of the Magi*, and the Westminster Tiara, and since that time the short, stumpy character with a slight limp and a face like a friendly bloodhound has become a legend in his own world. Apart from the common touch, three things have contributed to his success: a quite remarkable *rapport* with Peter Wilson, a great devotion to the firm and a strong imagination for original aspects of promotion.

Clark had been chafing to counter the extraordinary stories that appeared in the world's press about the possible acquisition of Parke-Bernet, but the embargo on comment had been absolute. Now it was to be lifted. He seized his opportunity with what has become a classic case history in the use of public relations. On 5 July the *Sunday Telegraph* in London published a piece under the heading 'Sotheby's Looks West' (written by Edwin Mullins). It stated:

> Sotheby's struck the most humiliating blow last week at their American rivals in art auctioneering, the Parke-Bernet Galleries in New York. After a £1,000,000 sale on Wednesday[1] they blandly announced that their season's turnover for works of art sent from the United States alone already exceeded Parke-Bernet's entire takings in the year – approximately £3,800,000. Sotheby's is likely to be £13,000,000. It has been no secret for months that Parke-Bernet was on the way

1. A mixed sale of French Impressionists and modern paintings on 1 July 1964 which included the collections of Mrs. Leo M. Glass and Mrs. Edward F. Hutton had set a world record for such sales at £1,031,250.

out, and that substantial holdings in the company were up for sale. The only question was, who would step in? Would it be Sotheby's themselves?

Ten days ago a report from New York said that Sotheby's bid had failed and the gallery had gone to a private buyer. I understand that this report and all others like it are substantially incorrect. There is no doubt that, under certain conditions, the London firm could still obtain a majority interest in the Parke-Bernet if they wanted it. The undisclosed bidder would at best be a minor partner.

The article went on to say that if Sotheby's failed to acquire Parke-Bernet, they planned to set up an auction gallery in New York of their own which would begin functioning in the next season, that is in the autumn. The effect of this news was electric. On the following day, the Monday, the rest of the press took up the story. It did not take long to reach New York, as was intended. The *New York Herald Tribune* commented, 'In view of Sotheby's announcement yesterday, a strong feeling persisted in auction circles that the London house with its prodigious profits, had finally managed to thaw out the New Yorkers and that the company flag would wave at Madison Avenue and 76th Street in the next fully bracing breeze'. Certainly that breeze helped to resolve matters at Parke-Bernet's next board meeting, which had been postponed several times because of the absence on business elsewhere of some of the major shareholders and Colonel Gimbel's ingenious delaying tactics. On 16 July Jesse Wolff was able to report to Peter Wilson at long last that on the previous day the owners of 78 per cent of the outstanding shares had agreed to sell their shares – 3,003 of them – to Sotheby's for a total of $1,525,000.

Now the press got really excited. Colonel Gimbel was quoted as saying that 'the American flag has been sold down the river'. When a reporter cited this to Peter Wilson he replied 'I am sure you would find people in my country who said the same thing when Ford bought into England. One-way traffic in any business is undesirable'. Sotheby's issued a press statement which said: 'It is Sotheby's intention to preserve the identity of Parke-Bernet. Louis J. Marion, President, and Mary Vandegrift, Executive Vice President, and their entire staff will be retained in their present capacities. Parke-Bernet and Sotheby's feel that the combined resources and international prestige of their organisation will ensure that the best possible results are obtained in the New York and London markets. Their joint actions will be to strengthen the New York art auction market for American clients – museums, private collectors and dealers alike. An exchange of experts between the two firms is envisaged as one of the first steps to be taken'. It was Peregrine Pollen who summarised the future – and the past – with a delightfully typical touch to another reporter: 'For a long time we have been looking at each other at a distance – rather balefully, I must admit. Under the new management we will be able to get a glimpse inside both operations and decide what, if anything, we want to alter'.

One great advantage of the timing of this final stage – or nearly final stage, for there were more surprises to come – was that so many people were already on holiday or just on the verge of going. Jesse Wolff had to break his own because of the unending delays over Parke-Bernet's decisive meeting. In a whirligig of hostile press comment deploring the fact that an interloper had seized a piece of national heritage, one New York columnist was able to put the news across in a relaxed and understanding way. This was Earl G. Talbott, who reported regularly about the auction scene in the *New York Herald Tribune*, and happened also to be an officer in the U.S. Air Force Reserve. Having paid a visit to 980 Madison Avenue he wrote:

> We had just returned from performing a stint of military duty, guarding the ramparts against all enemies of the republic, foreign and domestic, only to discover that in our absence the British had landed and made off with Parke-Bernet.... Majestic in defeat, that outpost still kept proud vigil at Upper Madison Avenue, its turrets empty but its battlements unscarred; a mute testimonial to the potency of a great alien weapon, the ten per cent commission. Nonchalantly whistling 'God Save the Queen', to throw any lurking enemy troops off the track, we negotiated the post portcullis without incident and rounded the almost empty corridors.
>
> Someone remarked that most of the garrison had gone on leave, a piece of intelligence that we weighed with slight scepticism. Inwardly scoffing, we could only offer a fervent prayer that Sotheby's, the new seneschal, subscribed to the Geneva Convention prescribing the treatment of prisoners of war.
>
> Still at her post, Mary Vandegrift, Parke-Bernet's Executive Vice President and normally vivacious chatelaine, presented a brave smile.... Nervously fingering huge keys to the fortress that dangled from a cincture encircling her slender waist, Miss Vandegrift said, 'We have negotiated a clean-cut, firm and satisfactory agreement with Sotheby's. There will be no mass exodus of merchandise for sale in England. Where and when his property will be disposed of is up to the consignor. Since Sotheby's now controls both galleries its people will be interested in assuring successful sales in New York as well as in London'.

What nobody knew, of course, was that the final signing of the contract of purchase and the payment for the shares was still some weeks off. There was a major problem over the agreed warranties and indemnities, for example, and at one stage Jesse Wolff was beginning to wonder whether some of the shareholders were going to renege on the deal. Some feverish, last minute negotiations and compromises over wording went on. On the condition that they remained with the firm, Sotheby's had offered a $100,000 bonus to be shared amongst senior personnel of Parke-Bernet on top of the purchase price. It was a gesture that was rapidly agreed to. This in turn required the drafting of separate employment agreements. Because of considerable uncertainty over outstanding monies due to Parke-Bernet, and thus the value of the assets being acquired, $150,000 of the purchase money was put into an escrow fund, that is, an account held by an outside party and frozen until all such matters were satisfactorily resolved. The purchase money had to be in New York at the right time. There were hitches about that. In fact, the method by which the necessary funds were raised was a brilliant stratagem in its own right. London sent over only £70,000 or just short of $200,000. It was decided to borrow the remainder. Peregrine's wife was friendly with the wife of a junior Vice-President at Morgan

Guaranty Trust. Would they, they were asked, advance $1,500,000 to Sotheby's so that they could buy Parke-Bernet? There seemed no obvious difficulties. When Peregrine called to discuss the matter with the bank's officials he was shown to the wrong department and astonished looks met his request for funds. In the right one it all seemed childishly simple. Then came the snag. Someone would have to put up a guarantee for the money. Even collectively the Sotheby directors were in no position to do so, but for some years the firm had formed a close relationship with an outside finance house in London, Barro Equities. The intention behind this arrangement had been to reorganise the capital structure so as to allow young partners to acquire shares, and to make some savings on the crippling taxation which impeded the conversion of earnings into capital.

Barro Equities, a public company controlled by H. M. Robinow and Clifford Barclay, a merchant banker and an accountant, had a substantial financial interest in Sotheby's at that time. After much discussion they and the Sotheby partners agreed to guarantee the loan jointly. It was that element of risk which had so disturbed some members of the board. So confident, however, did Peter Wilson feel about reviving Parke-Bernet's fortunes that it was intended to repay the loan out of earnings in New York over the next three years, which is, in fact, what happened.

By 14 August 1964, eleven of the twelve shareholders in Parke-Bernet had signed the contract. Colonel Gimbel, with his 22 per cent of the equity, decided to sit it out. He did so for three months. It appears that during this period he was instrumental in initiating an enquiry by the Justice Department's Anti-Trust division to see if the merger of Parke-Bernet with Sotheby's constituted a violation of Section 7 of the Clayton Act: whether, in other words, it genuinely lessened the degree of competition within the art market. The matter caused some considerable anxiety at Parke-Bernet, but Sotheby's vigorously defended itself against such accusations, and although the enquiries dragged on for a long time, no charges were ever made. Gimbel found himself if not in a precarious, certainly in a very uncomfortably isolated position once the new regime at Parke-Bernet held sway. He managed to raise and oppose no fewer than eighteen mainly procedural motions during the course of the one board meeting held on 5 October 1964 which he attended jointly with the new directors, having done his utmost to declare their earlier election null and void. Although he had doggedly stated that he would never resign of his own free will or sell out, Jesse Wolff persuaded him to give up his holding only a few weeks after the completion of the merger. Gimbel had bought 909 shares for $132 in 1961. He parted with them now for $375 per share. He also obtained a number of privileges that other shareholders had not been granted. No part of his settlement was locked into the escrow account and he continued to receive a variety of sale catalogues that would be of help to him as a book collector and librarian of the Aeronautical Library at Harvard. Although his brief 'martyrdom' became something of a *cause célèbre*, by dint of Jesse Wolff's tactful and patient negotiations the eventual parting was reasonably amicable and finally sealed the end of a fateful episode quite painlessly.

35

New Era

PEREGRINE POLLEN'S role in New York now changed dramatically: the poacher had turned gamekeeper with a vengeance. All his diplomatic skills were needed to preserve and construct, rather than covertly to take away.

He had two able, young assistants from London to help him: Hugh Hildesley and David Nash; both have remained in New York ever since. Richard Timewell came over to look after the works of art department for a period. Later Marcus Linell settled in New York for a four-year spell to reorganise and to strengthen departmental expertise.

Peregrine drew up plans and notional financial projections. Clifford Barclay, a master of budgetary control and cash flow management, flew over to New York to help. In a room in the St. Regis Hotel he and Peregrine analysed the existing situation and reviewed the immediate and long-term objectives. The overall strategy was to increase turnover by a factor of three, to something of the order of $35,000,000.[1] The most urgent tasks were to seek the co-operation of the staff, to collect an enormous number of outstanding debts and to boost the sales for the coming season.

Then Barclay and Pollen went to Parke-Bernet, having made a date with Lou Marion. They met in Parke-Bernet's boardroom. It had previously been agreed that Peregrine would become chairman of the executive committee. Barclay broke the ice, defined the problems and listed the priorities. 'How', he asked Lou Marion, 'do you reckon to right the situation?' Marion was understandably touchy. He called in Mary Vandegrift. She soon smoothed the ruffled feathers and the discussion settled down on a positive tack. It was to be the first of an endless number of such meetings. Mary Vandegrift became the pivot between the old and the new. After forty years in the business there was nothing she did not know about it. Her vitality, her (now maternal) charm, her ability to create order out of chaos, and most important, her genius for nipping disputes in the bud and her inviolable integrity were God's private gift to Sotheby's. 'Without her,' Peregrine mused a decade later, 'the take-over of Parke-Bernet by Sotheby's would have been impossible. She was the nub of the business.'

It was Mary Vandegrift who, years earlier, had personally hired the red-headed lad in short trousers, of Italian ancestry, who was now president of Parke-Bernet. Lou Marion's breathless energy had taken him from the mail department to the accounts department, then to be sales clerk and eventually – trained by Otto Bernet himself – he had become the firm's leading auctioneer. Marion had a genius for making friends, but this peppery, barnstorming, all-American businessman did not find the Bond Street brigade easy to get on with as colleagues. Although he had signed a three year contract, he asked after only a

1. This target was reached after only five years, in the 1968/69 season.

year if he could step down to start his own appraisal business. 'It's not a glamorous pursuit', he said to the press, 'but it lies at the heart of all sales.' Parke-Bernet, he confessed, had not been the same since August 1964. 'I didn't make final decisions; I didn't like a job where I was not doing that.' But close business links with Sotheby's would continue in a collaboration that would bring sales to the galleries and appraisals to Lou Marion. He left behind at 980 Madison Avenue his most precious asset, his son John. The latter had worked in the business full-time for five years and part-time for ten years before that. Clearing the accumulated junk out of the basement had been one of his first jobs. He probably appreciated better than anyone else just how much ill-will there was when Parke-Bernet had been taken over and what a difficult assignment Peregrine had taken on in trying to re-establish morale. For some time the younger Marion had been uncertain whether to stay. Peregrine realised even before the acquisition had taken place how vital this quietly-spoken young man with his enormous determination would be to the business. There was immense relief when, despite his father's going, John decided to stay. Since 1972 he has been the firm's president. He has achieved for it a remarkable level of independence and very great success.

Peregrine, Hugh Hildesley and David Nash saw very quickly that from the inside, and particularly coming from London, every aspect of Parke-Bernet seemed strange and different. The manner in which private clients and members of the trade were treated was a good example. They did not arrive in endless streams as in London. They had to be sought. When they did come, they did not always seem to be made welcome. Hildesley, responsible for Old Master paintings, innocently asked to see all the Old Masters there were in the building on consignment. There were virtually none, and it took time to appreciate that the interest in Old Masters in New York at that time was negligible when compared to the fervour they aroused in London. In general, collectors felt safer about buying them in London or in Paris.

Americans rarely sold anything because they were short of money. Chattels – and works of art after all are chattels – did not so often form a major part of a well-heeled man's possessions. Yet in contrast, when the Englishmen visited great American houses and collections, these illustrated just how effectively the antique exporters from England in particular, and Europe in general, had done their job in the era between 1870 and 1930 when America had become wealthy and Europe had become poor. Only the best had been good enough. The one factor that fed a great auction house like Parke-Bernet was death. Magnificent American collections do not often survive from one generation to the next. They are usually broken up as soon as a collector dies; sometimes even before his death when an interest has waned or changed. This impermanence spells trade.

To the numerous visitors from Bond Street to Parke-Bernet the most striking fact in 1964 seemed in certain subjects to be a lack of consistency in expertise, a feature of the major English auction houses that was taken for granted. Nor did experts take their own sales as in London. One of the first edicts that Peregrine had to issue was that Parke-Bernet should refuse to accept any Impressionist or

later painting for sale if there was any doubt whatever about its authenticity;
even if on occasion this might mean the loss of good will from the consignors.
Under the existing conditions of sale at Parke-Bernet it was virtually impossible
to withdraw a painting once a contract of sale had been signed, without exposing
the firm to the risk of a suit for breach of contract. On the West Coast, for
example, where experienced picture dealers were few and far between and the
art market was correspondingly less sophisticated, mis-attributions abounded.
When, some years later, Parke-Bernet began to hold occasional sales in that
part of the world, an Impressionist expert who had gone to see paintings that it
was thought might be included in the sale, telexed London in answer to an
enquiry on how he had fared: 'Have just seen $10,000,000 worth of superb
Impressionists. Not one of them genuine'.[1] It was not surprising that in general
art auctioneers were held in low esteem; that they were even widely regarded as
dishonest and that the bulk of important sales in the art world were made
privately through dealers. For the same reasons, unlike in London, museums
shunned relations with the auction room. If Parke-Bernet was to share
Sotheby's reputation for integrity, Peregrine would have to bring about a major
shift of public attitude. Such matters were the very cause of his and Jake
Carter's earlier success in attracting important goods to London. On top of all
this he soon found that the bread-and-butter business, the multitude of small
but attractive lots selling up to $1,000, was lacking. This area had once been the
purview of Otto Bernet, but with his death such business had been neglected in
favour of more glamorous attractions. Peter Wilson, more than any other person,
insisted that such items were essential for the future. So successful ultimately
were the efforts to regain this market that an additional auction room, PB 84,
was opened at 171 East 84th Street in 1968 specifically to cater for it.

One thing that surprised visitors to Parke-Bernet, and indeed initially the
staff there, was the apparent youthfulness of the English invaders. What everyone had expected was a host of middle-aged professors. Certainly the energy and
long working days of the newcomers was another surprise. The post-war
reputation for British sloth and phlegm was already deeply rooted.

Peregrine found the compactness of the Parke-Bernet buildings of great
benefit after the higgledy-piggledy character of Bond Street. It encouraged a
much closer liaison between departments and assisted speedy internal communications, and this was essential in the circumstances. It was also much
easier to make structural alterations to the premises.

Making procedural changes was often very difficult indeed. What seemed the
most natural appurtenances to fine art auctioneering in London, were regarded
with the gravest suspicion in New York. There was the matter of reserves, for
example. These are essential protection for the owner against selling below true
value, either because of the activity of 'rings' or simply because there are not
enough interested bidders in the auction room at the time of the sale. The New
York press took up at once the question of whether Sotheby's would introduce

1. He returned to London with the old story of how Corot painted 500 landscapes, 10,000 of
which were in America.

reserves universally at Parke-Bernet. Many writers considered that they were against the interest of buyers because they took the bargain-hunting element out of sales. It was the period of the memorable *Sunday Times* exposé of dealers' rings in England and news of this had crossed the Atlantic. Reserves were not illegal in America. The old management at Parke-Bernet had used them, but infrequently. Rings certainly existed in New York and the overall absence of reserves increased the riskiness of selling by auction. This militated against the sale-room as a means of disposal, though it was often overcome by the presence of the owner in the room who would bid up the price himself. The alarmist attitude against reserves was merely a useful expedient with which to express the very understandable and deep-seated anger against Sotheby's for acquiring a famous American business. This attitude seemed the more perplexing in Europe at a time when American corporations were buying up European companies on such a scale that whole industries seemed threatened.

There were, however, more immediate internal problems that needed attention. The secretary and treasurer, Max Bartholet, departed. The organisation of the accounts department was chaotic. Peat Marwick Mitchell arrived as consultants to devise a reorganisation. The book department was without a director. Jerry Patterson was appointed at its head. Parke-Bernet's board needed to be strengthened. After an interval of some months Peter Wilson became chairman. Peregrine Pollen, John Carter, Tim Clarke, Carmen Gronau, Jim Kiddell and Jesse Wolff were appointed new directors in mid-November 1964. Commission rates were so high that a lot of business still went direct to Bond Street because they were lower there. In February 1965 lower commissions on paintings came into force[1] and in May 1966 they were reduced for almost everything else. This was a major factor in improving relations with the New York trade. Above all it was a slow, agonisingly slow business to get collaboration going between staff in England and America. As soon as the merger had been completed there had been an instant and charming exchange of letters between Carmen Gronau and Mary Vandegrift as the two women directors in the combined set-up, but it was only as the two-way traffic of directors and experts across the Atlantic increased, and people got to know and trust their opposite members, that the essential all round co-operation began to get under way. The campaign to counter the Anti-Trust accusations absorbed an enormous amount of management time. There were constant demands for complex statistical information. Sotheby's had remarkable allies. In London the US Ambassador, David Bruce, went out of his way to be helpful. In New York the British Ambassador, Lord Harlech, provided invaluable assistance. Edward Heath took up Sotheby's cause with the Board of Trade and Douglas Jay responded. Above all, Peregrine continued to learn the hard way that the New York atmosphere was altogether more pugnacious than the West End of London, and that ownership of a company demanded familiarity with local corporate legislation at every turn. Under the well-cut suits and the elegant fur coats, under the charm and urbanity, the pioneering spirit lingered on – and expressed itself in a

1. Against vociferous internal opposition.

love of litigation. Every detail agreed to had to be buttoned up in writing. In a
nation where people could understand the law because it was written in plain
English, they used it at the drop of a hat to protect their interests. The lawyers
too were a tougher breed and did not hesitate to hit below the belt if that hurt
more. Thus increasingly Peregrine's greatest support in the corporate life was
Jesse Wolff of Weil, Gotshal & Manges. Jay[1] was always in the background,
taking the kicks in the most expert manner and hitting back with a hundred per
cent effectiveness. His astute mind, his forensic skill and his breadth of vision
steered Sotheby's safely around the needle-sharp rocks of a litigiousness that
was a new experience for them. The entire American fine art auction scene
owes Wolff a great debt. It was he who advised so sanely on courses of action
against the legal hawks who wanted unendingly to impose restrictions on Parke-
Bernet that would have stifled all enterprise, and it was he too who eventually
advised congressional committees on the drafting of fair-minded and acceptable
legal constraints.

Above all what Parke-Bernet needed was more and better sales. An outstanding,
four-star event was planned for the spring of 1965; something that would start
people talking and would demonstrate that the Sotheby skill had been implanted
at Parke-Bernet. A combination of luck and good judgement provided the
answer: an enormous double sale on a single evening combined with a stun-
ningly festive social occasion. Stanley Clark came over to help to make the
event known. On 14 April 1965 there was to be a sale of fine Impressionists and
modern paintings at 6.30 p.m. It seems scarcely credible fifteen years later that
so many collectable paintings could have been got together in such a short time.
Many of them had been sent from Europe to New York, emphasising the new
'other way' traffic. There were two Bonnards, four canvases by Marc Chagall, a
truly memorable pastel of a ballet rehearsal by Degas, a Gauguin, eight sculptures by Maillol, six by Matisse, two by Henry Moore, two paintings by Monet,
four by Picasso, four coincidentally similar Renoir portraits, a Van Gogh and
five gentle Vuillards. There was even a French canal scene by that distinguished
London bricklayer, Sir Winston Churchill, sent for sale by his daughter.[2]

The audience was in evening dress; Parke-Bernet's staff were tense. There
was a hard brilliance about the occasion. Peter Wilson had at long last obtained
the necessary licence to conduct auctions in New York. It had required a
personal affidavit from the American Ambassador in London to vouch for his
integrity. Both he and Peregrine suggested that on this occasion Lou Marion's
son John should start the evening's auctioneering. John found the necessary
rostrum manner with uncanny skill. The excitement became more and more
good humoured. Prices were phenomenal. The original plan – that Lou should
take over half way – was abandoned. Father tapped son on the shoulder at the

1. As he has affectionately been known within Sotheby's now for twenty years.
2. It was the first of Sir Winston's canvases to appear at auction. By some quirk of fate, or
perhaps as a deliberate ploy, it was placed in the sale to follow the Van Gogh. It fetched a
very respectable $26,000.

agreed moment and asked him to carry on. Thus John took the first sale in its entirety. He sold the eighty-seven lots for a prodigious total of $2,345,000. The Degas ballet scene formerly in the collection of Mrs. H. O. Havemeyer realised $410,000; one of the Bonnards $155,000; and the Van Gogh painting, *Les Dechargeurs*, $240,000.[1]

Such success marvellously set the tone for the social occasion that followed; a richly elaborate benefit dinner on the third floor of 980 Madison Avenue. The whole area had been transformed to resemble the interior of a Parisian bistro of the 1870s frequented by the Impressionist painters. The scene was based on the interior of the Café de la Nouvelle Athènes on the Place Pigalle where Degas and Manet had drunk together and discussed their problems, and where in 1876 Degas had painted one of his most famous paintings, *L'Absinthe*. The two interior decorators, Buford Chisholm of Parke-Bernet and Kenneth Partridge from London had worked for weeks to recreate the setting. John Rewald had helped with authentic detail and a large collection of contemporary sepia photographs of all the Impressionist painters, which were projected life-size on to the walls. Among the four hundred guests was Robert Lehman, the banker, delighted that after an interval of seventeen years his suggestion of a merger between Parke-Bernet and Sotheby's should have been finally consummated; also Robert Dowling, Parke-Bernet's landlord and now a firm friend of Sotheby's, the months of grumpy negotiation happily forgotten as the sense of occasion took over.

After the dinner Peter Wilson took the second sale. It was the first time that his gently coaxing style of auctioneering had been heard in Parke-Bernet's great gallery. The Philippe Dotremont collection of forty-three works by modern, mostly contemporary, French and American artists had been brought over from Brussels. A good many of the paintings and sculptures had never previously changed hands. Many were only between five and ten years old. Rauschenberg's *Gloria* of 1956, for example, was only the second picture by that artist ever to have been offered at auction. The *pièce de résistance* was Pablo Picasso's *Femme au Corsage Bleu* painted in 1941 which fetched $115,000. A Jackson Pollock brought $45,000; an Alexander Calder mobile $10,000; a Mark Tobey $8,000. The total came to $510,000. There was long applause at the end of the evening. The ice had been well and truly broken, but there was yet another surprise to come. While the second sale was being held, the third floor had been transformed again to reveal a further remarkable collection of contemporary painting and sculpture belonging to Mr. and Mrs. Charles Zadok which was shortly to be sold in London. It included a superb sculpture of a horse and rider by Marino Marini. As the party finished John Marion staggered home to bed totally exhausted. Peter Wilson returned to London, confident that Parke-Bernet's star was now firmly in the ascendent.

For some years after the merger it was primarily the sale of important Impressionist and modern paintings that restored Parke-Bernet's fortunes. One

1. It had been bought in when it came up for sale with other paintings of Mrs. Derek Fitzgerald's in London.

of the most memorable moments occurred when Cézanne's *Maison à L'Estaque* was sold for a record $800,000 on 14 October 1965. Edward Beck, then Clark Nelson's man in New York, had come across the picture when he had gone to dinner at a house in Greenwich, Connecticut. While he was there he saw what he thought to be a particularly fine reproduction of a Cézanne. He commented on this when he returned to the office and when he and Peregrine together looked through the literature they discovered that it was in fact a well-known original. The owner, they subsequently discovered, was the widow of a Spanish art historian who had written one of the best early books on primitive art. He had also given a considerable collection of pictures to the Prado, and had obtained the Cézanne and a famous Gauguin from Wildenstein in 1916 together with a number of other pictures. His widow had kept them without realising their worth. She was more than delighted to sell them at Parke-Bernet and they were soon included in a sale. No one had expected anything quite so sensational. It made a good story for the press.[1] In March 1966 the collection built up over twenty-five years by a Pittsburgh industrialist, J. David Thompson, sold for $2,416,000, and that was after a substantial portion had already been sold privately, and a remarkable assembly of Paul Klees had been bought by the West German state of North Rhein-Westphalia. In April 1968 twenty-eight pictures from the Allan Bluestein collection made $1,292,000 and further sales from many other sources on the two following days brought the total to nearly $4,000,000.

When a famous New York picture dealer was asked how Parke-Bernet had fared by the end of the first season under Sotheby's management, he remarked acidly that 'Parke-Bernet was seen to survive'. A year later the story was very different. Just after Christmas 1965 it was announced that Peregrine Pollen had become Parke-Bernet's fourth president. By the end of July 1966 the galleries were able to announce the highest turnover in their history, $23,520,000. There had been ninety sales as compared with seventy-three in the previous season. Peregrine was able to comment with some pride: 'We have held many more sales for specialist[2] collectors. Authoritative cataloguing by an increased staff of experts has given confidence to consignors. The result has been an increased flow of important properties through the auction room. We have achieved a turnover more than $9,000,000 higher than that on any previous year in Parke-

1. A Gauguin, sold in the same sale for $275,000, three canvases by Braque, two drawings by Cézanne and one by Ingres, as well as a number of antiquities of exceptional quality eventually reached Parke-Bernet from the same source.
2. The magnificent collections of jewellery of Mrs. Hamilton Rice and Helena Rubenstein laid the foundation for another form of specialist sale that was to have an increasing impact on Parke-Bernet's fame and fortunes. The publicity attracted by the purchase of some of the world's most famous diamonds by Elizabeth Taylor and Richard Burton at 980 Madison Avenue was immense. In 1970 Sotheby's held its first jewellery sale in Switzerland and in the first six years sold jewels there to the value of £23,000,000. In the same period in New York the jewellery turnover was £13,560,000. Sotheby's global turnover of jewellery in a single season in 1977–78, amounted to almost the same sum, no less than £22,235,000, making them the premier auctioneers of jewellery in the world.

Bernet's history. This has helped to increase the influence of New York as a world centre of the art market and Parke-Bernet has become the most important source of works of art of every category available to collectors in America.'

Inevitably there was some change of staff after Peregrine Pollen had taken over the reins, but one stalwart personality who stayed on was John Marion's former college contemporary, Tom Norton. Tom had acted as Hyam's right hand for some years and had now taken charge of the painting department with Hugh Hildesley and David Nash as his assistants. Later he specialised in American painting and later still he was to take on responsibility for all the many facets of Sotheby Parke Bernet's public image, which embraced everything from catalogue production to press releases. Similarly Tom P. Clarke, who had started in the firm's mailroom in the days when Parke and Bernet had set up on their own, and had soon moved to the book department, played an increasingly important role there, eventually specialising in American manuscript material. He was on terms of close friendship with many collectors, including Frank W. Streeter and Philip D. Sang whose collections he helped to build up and also eventually catalogued when it came to their dispersal.

Vital from Peregrine s point of view was the body of salesfloor assistants collectively known as the 'union men', because many of them had entered the firm through the relevant trade union. They were the porters and bid-callers and handlers of property. They were in constant touch with the buying public and there was often a strong element of affection between them and Parke-Bernet's clients. They included such memorable figures as Al Bristol, Walter Stovall and his brother Percy, and Tommy Roberts. Their benevolent autocracy at various levels gave Parke-Bernet sales a sparkle and efficiency which few other auction rooms were able to emulate. Both Tom Clarke and the Stovalls represented a second generation at Parke-Bernet: their fathers had worked for the old American Art Association.

The fact that the two-way traffic really was working as Peter Wilson had predicted that it would, was borne out by the fact that the volume of books and works of art sent over *from* America represented nearly one-third of Sotheby's London receipts, while American buyers in London continued to be the largest purchasers after the British, accounting in direct sales for 23 per cent of the London turnover. The actual percentage was probably very much higher because so many London dealers at that time were buying almost exclusively for the American market. Because London itself was doing so well, Sotheby's profit by 1968 reached the highest total it had ever been, just over £652,000.

36

In All Directions

LONDON and New York, Bond Street and Madison Avenue, were now working on a fixed pattern of immense activity. The old dream of twin centres on either side of the Atlantic had at last become a reality, but that still left vast areas of the civilised world untapped where art was strongly in demand. Sotheby's phenomenal growth in the sixteen years between 1964 and 1980 was the result of establishing a presence in new locations, while nurturing their two principal centres of activity. During this period, sales increased from £13,350,000 to £186,000,000. These were figures – even when allowing for inflation – that went wildly beyond any ambitions ever harboured by Sir Montague Barlow or even Geoffrey Hobson. Management might not have had a fixed plan to conquer the world: that nevertheless emerged as the apparent ambition. While success was important it was sometimes slow in coming, and there was often strong division within the firm whether it was worth having at all. There were influential voices who said 'Enough is enough: let us be satisfied with what we have', but the momentum was now unstoppable. The skill came in keeping mistakes to a minimum. It called for initiative leavened with caution, and for powers of innovation which could be harnessed to a tradition. The most difficult prerequisite was that management should recognise its own areas of weakness, and then strengthen them.

In the first three years after its acquisition, Parke-Bernet fully occupied all the spare management and expert talent that Bond Street could muster. Then during the 1967/68 season there began quite unprecedented development overseas. The first move in 1967 was literally only just across the border when the first ever of the now well-established sales of eighteenth- and nineteenth-century pictures took place at Gleneagles in Scotland. A fully manned and particularly successful office opened in Edinburgh in 1969. Later in 1967 a large consignment of pictures, porcelain, furniture and silver was flown across the Atlantic by Air Canada for a series of five sales to be held at Simpson's large department store in Toronto, Canada. Everyone was completely taken by surprise when 35,000 people attended the viewing and some 10,000 people actually came to the sales to bid a total of $767,475. Sotheby's of Canada opened a permanent office within Simpson's in the following year.

Only a month after the first Canadian sale, Sotheby's opened an office in Paris at 8 Rue de Duras. Valentine Abdy became Sotheby's first French representative. He had owned a fine art business in Paris for some time and was well known in French art circles. His father, himself a distinguished dealer/collector, had been a long-standing client of the firm before the war. In April 1968 the first outpost was set up in Melbourne, Australia, under Reg Longdon and Bruce Rutherford, and at the beginning of May Sotheby's opened an agency

in Beirut for the Near and Middle East, and only three weeks later it started off
another in Florence. The suggestion for a strong presence in Italy had come
from a friend of Carmen Gronau's. He was a famous wartime partisan and
subsequently a leading antique dealer, Dr. Augustino Chesne Dauphiné. The
laws on exporting antiques from Italy were particularly stringent and it was an
early decision that the agency there should deal with purely Italian material.
Thus Sotheby's wisely obtained permission to hold sales anywhere in Italy very
soon after the Florence office opened its doors. This was a precaution
Christie's, who started selling in Italy a little later, had overlooked which was to
cause them very considerable difficulties. As luck would have it, a major Italian
sale soon came Sotheby's way. It consisted of the Villa Demidoff at Pratolino
outside Florence, a property which belonged to Prince Paul of Yugoslavia. He
had inherited it from an aunt, Princess Abamalek-Lazaret, a direct descendant
of the incredibly wealthy Russian Demidoffs, in 1953. As he only spent six
weeks a year there, and the cost of its upkeep was becoming an increasing
problem, the Prince had approached the Florence office for advice on selling it.
The Italian antique trade was not pleased at this English invasion of its home
ground and there was considerable opposition to the sale. Stanley Clark went
to Florence and promoted it in his most brilliant and persuasive manner.
Important buyers flocked there in totally unexpected numbers. Tim Clarke
took the sale with great verve – and in fluent Italian. Despite the fact that Italian
taxes and duty added almost 30 per cent to the hammer price, prices for what
was a very mixed property were high. One Florentine dealer grumbled about
them with justifiable chagrin. A table he had sold to Prince Paul only two years
earlier for £5,000 now fetched £17,000. The *pièce de résistance* was a mid-
eighteenth-century presentation commode of inverted bombé form inlaid with
staghorn and rare woods, bearing the monogram of Catherine the Great and the
Imperial Crown and Eagle, which was sold for 52,000,000 Lire, or £34,666, at
that time the highest price ever paid for a piece of furniture. It was purchased
by an anonymous private buyer, but there was strong speculation that he was
acting on behalf of the Russian government. The sale grossed more than
£300,000 and firmly established the Florence office, which later moved to the
Palazzo Gino Capponi with its own impressive auction gallery. After Dr.
Dauphiné's retirement in 1971, John Winter took over its running, and Carmen
Gronau, who retired from Bond Street some years later to the villa at San
Domenico da Fiesole just outside Florence which her father-in-law had bought
many years earlier, still maintains an active interest as its picture consultant.

1969 was another adventurous year of global expansion. Offices were opened
in Johannesburg, Zürich and Munich. The people appointed to run them were,
as usual, forceful characters of an independent cast of mind, ambassadors of the
firm in every sense, who would play a considerable role in the local community.
Thus, in Johannesburg Reinhold Cassirer was married to Nadine Gordimer,
the distinguished South African novelist. Dr. Jürgen Wille who started
Sotheby's office in Zürich, joined the firm on the direct recommendation of
Robert von Hirsch, an old friend of Peter Wilson's. Sotheby's had undertaken

the periodic revaluation of the Von Hirsch collection for insurance purposes for many years. Valentine Abdy was again the first incumbent of the Munich office but this was soon taken over by Kate Foster. She had come to Bond Street twelve years earlier (there was a family link with the Winkworths) and under the tuition of Jim Kiddell and Tim Clarke she had become a pillar of the porcelain department. Indeed, a little earlier the firm had agreed to send her on two months study leave, during which she toured museums and private collections throughout Europe on both sides of the Iron Curtain. After the revelation of the riches of Vienna, Berlin, Hamburg, Dresden, Prague and then Switzerland and France, she realised that in London one saw only a fraction of the world's great ceramics. She learned German rapidly and after her transfer to Munich she imbued that office with enormous zest, though she took great care to ensure that the informality of the Bond Street atmosphere was preserved in a very different environment. Her principal objective was to counsel and to advise the growing number of active German private collectors and the younger dealers. After Kate's departure, Dr. Ernst Behrens, whose earlier career had been in Goethe Institute, expanded activities in Germany even further and eventually moved the firm to magnificent premises in the Odeonsplatz and started branch offices in various other parts of Germany.

In October of 1969 Sotheby's agreed to take part in a different sort of adventure, which in its way broke even more fresh ground. Arguably 1969 could be regarded as the high point in the post-war boom in the arts, which the press at that time found a fascinating and evergreen topic of discussion. The Times/Sotheby Index of art prices in particular gave them food for thought. Old Master drawings were seen to have increased in price by twenty-two times between 1951 and 1969; Old Master prints had similarly increased overall by thirty-eight times, with the price of Rembrandt prints up forty times, Canaletto prints up thirty times, Piranesi prints up $33\frac{1}{2}$ times and post-Bruegel up ninety-seven times. Stirring increases were also recorded for Impressionist paintings ($17\frac{1}{2}$ times) and twentieth-century paintings (up 29 times overall). Less attention was paid to Old Master paintings where the average increase had been very much smaller at that time. The index was based on statistical information evaluated through a complex mathematical formula and it aroused very mixed feelings on publication. The apparently finite nature of these calculations seemed appealing to many financial pundits, but both dealers and art lovers protested vociferously that to put a mere numerate gloss on what were often supreme human achievements debased art generally. The index lasted only two years but it created greater public awareness not only of what was happening in the art market itself but it also drew attention to the vast number of people who were now involved in it. At a time when export achievements by British industry were not all that impressive, the strength of the British achievement in the international art market was something of a triumph.

When the Board of Trade, therefore, began to organise a British Week for the sale of British goods in Tokyo, over twenty leading dealers in art and antiques

63. Regular Sotheby sales held outside London have become a feature of the auctioneering round. The photo shows the first of many sales at Gleneagles in Scotland.

64 & 65. As the firm has grown it has had to seek more and more space both in Bond Street *(top)* and St. George Street *(below)*. These photo-montages show the extent of the spread. In 1980 Sotheby's moved to the other side of Bond Street when it began to convert the old Aeolian Hall in order to house the book, coin and jewellery departments.

66. A model prepared under the direction of Sir Dennis Lasdun, the architect, to show how the site of the Bond Street complex could be redeveloped. Soaring costs put paid to the plan.

67. A relaxed study of Peter Wilson and Mr. Dent, a picture dealer well known in the trade because he would never pay more than £300 for any lot. It was taken in the early 1970s.

68. After 1970 it became clear that there was an increasing market for Victoriana and nineteenth-century works of art of all kinds. There was no space for this at Bond Street so the old Pantechnicon building in Motcomb Street was converted into a new auction room which became known as Sotheby's Belgravia.

69. The first sale on view at Belgravia. This sort of material was not to everyone's taste, but nineteenth-century art and artefacts existed in prodigious quantities. A certain degree of selectivity soon established a new stylishness. Belgravia became a great success.

70. The Belgravia porters taking a break before a sale of mechanical musical devices in 1975.

71, 72 & 73. Behind the scenes at Belgravia: glass and pictures in the storeroom *(above)*; properties in the porcelain department waiting to be catalogued *(left)*; the picture department *(below)*.

74. Sotheby's most memorable house sale since the last war was at Mentmore. There was vigorous lobbying to persuade the Government to acquire the contents with which Baron de Rothschild had furnished the house in the mid-nineteenth century. When officialdom said no, the sale went ahead. The photograph shows Lord Rosebery, Mentmore's owner, repairing a temperamental microphone just before the sale was due to begin in June 1977.

75. The year after Mentmore the most valuable collection ever to reach the auction room arrived at Bond Street from Switzerland, the property of the late Robert von Hirsch. The sales session devoted to medieval antiquities totalled over £6,000,000, as much as the eighteen sales sessions at Mentmore. Peter Wilson is here taking bids for an enamel arm ornament from the coronation vestment of the Emperor Barbarossa, which was sold for £1,100,000.

76. After 1977 Sotheby's began to acquire a number of provincial auction rooms. This is 'Rainbow', home of Sotheby Bearne in Torquay. Other sale-rooms that joined the group are in Pulborough, Taunton and Chester.

77. One of the many European offices of Sotheby's at 24 Rue de la Cité in Geneva.

78. Direct contact with the public in New York. An 'Heirloom Discovery Week' attracted over 10,000 people with objects for appraisal to Parke Bernet. At times the patient queues stretched right round the block.

79. Two veterans who never retired. Tim Wilder *(left)*, print expert, who joined Sotheby's in 1911, with the late Jim Kiddell, porcelain director, who had come to the firm in 1921. This book owes much to the phenomenal memories of both these men.

80. Where it all started. John Carter *(right)* inspecting an exhibition of the literature of collecting organised by the author *(centre)* at the National Book League in 1972. Martyn Goff, director of the NBL, is on the left. It was at lunch afterwards that John Carter asked Frank Herrmann to undertake the writing of the history of Sotheby's.

were invited to participate and Sotheby's was asked to stage a series of art auctions there to coincide with the event. It was being organised on behalf of the government by George Whyte, then associated with Maples of Tottenham Court Road, at that time the largest furniture store in the UK. The complexity of earlier overseas sales organised from Bond Street paled into insignificance in comparison with what was required for Japan. For one thing – as we have already seen – the concept of a public auction was something new for the average middle-class Japanese, so that what was required was a whole process of education, as well as immensely detailed organisation. In Tokyo, as in Canada, it was decided to hold the sale within a major department store, Mitsukoshi, and to do so with the assistance of a large force of their sales staff led by a small Sotheby contingent. John Cann, with many years' experience as sales clerk and Bond Street administrator behind him, was given a force of twenty-four store managers and an excellent female interpreter (who happened to be Japan's Olympic high-diving champion in her spare time) to undertake all the necessary preparations. With much help from the London and European trade, a large collection of material, carefully selected to appeal to Japanese taste, was shipped to Tokyo. It included Far Eastern and Greek antiquities and sculpture, Persian and European pottery and porcelain, a wide range of paintings from the Victorian era to the almost contemporary, with a strong element of well-known Impressionist names, arms and armour and, of course, a large quantity of Japanese and Chinese antiques and porcelain.

A magnificent, very fully illustrated catalogue was produced with all the text in both English and Japanese. Peter Wilson and Julian Thompson took the actual sales, assisted by Japanese interpreters, while Neil Davey and Michel Strauss took phone bids from all over the world. Initially the going was very slow despite the constant explanations. During the six days of public viewing it had been difficult to make it clear to intending buyers that the winning bid on any object actually constituted a sale. In fact, the buyer of the very first lot changed his mind about it immediately after the hammer had come down, and shook his head violently when it was explained to him that he was the new owner. The piece was put up for sale for a second time after further explanations – and the same buyer bought it back, among smiles, at a higher price. Thereafter things became easier and the proportion of items which had to be bought in because they did not fetch their reserve prices was not much higher than it would have been in a difficult London sale. So the occasion could be rated a success, and certainly the widespread publicity within Japan itself gained a new credibility for auction sales which led to greatly increased buying at Sotheby's and Parke Bernet as the Japanese economy prospered.

With the growing activity of the firm in so many directions, the staff increased by leaps and bounds. Clearly the necessary experts were not always available from within the antique trade or elsewhere and in the early 1960s a whole new generation of young men began to arrive at Bond Street. They mostly started on their careers as porters, graduated to cataloguers and experts, often eventually rose to head their own departments and finally took an important role in management: there was Michel Strauss and David Nash in the Impressionist department, Michael Webb in furniture, Paul Thomson in English painting, Derek Johns in Old Master paintings, Julien Stock in Old Master drawings, Adrian Eeles in prints and engravings, Kate Foster and Marcus Linell in porcelain, Howard Ricketts in works of art (particularly arms and armour), Julian Thompson in Chinese ceramics, Neil Davey in the Japanese department to name just a few. It was this very combination of youth and expertise that gave the firm a new image in the Swinging Sixties. Strangers who arrived at Bond Street for the first time – particularly from overseas – were astonished to see young men who seemed barely out of their teens holding sway in the rostrum. Yet these same young men would discuss matters before and after a sale with a maturity and judgement seemingly ahead of their years. The fame of Mr. Wilson's 'Academy of Youthful Auctioneers' spread far and wide. I remember hearing about it in astonished terms within the space of a few weeks from an elderly millionaire collector in Geneva, an antiquarian bookseller in Edinburgh and a recently bereaved widow of a porcelain collector in New York. What was less apparent outside was that the young also had drive and ambition that was not always easy to control. Dealers began to use the word 'ruthless' when they thought of Sotheby's, and there was a period when Peter Wilson was forced to rule the boardroom with a rod of iron. There were stormy scenes and inevitably these were followed by departures. It was sad to see such talent go after years of training. Those who left rarely joined rival auctioneers: much more frequently they set up as dealers on their own where there were opportunities to earn much more money than the rather meagre salaries which still prevailed within Sotheby's at that period. Usually time mellowed the bitterness, if the parting had not been amicable – as sometimes it was not – and disgruntled young men returned to Bond Street as active, and indeed important, clients.

After the acquisition of Parke-Bernet, others spent extended periods in New York. Distance not only lent enchantment; the widening of horizons enabled those who crossed the Atlantic to see Bond Street with a new perspective. The unrest was merely a symptom of enormous and continuously expanding activity and a hectically frantic way of life.

The need for new talent in the late 1960s had increased even further. The intake through the porter training system, where young men started at the very bottom of the ladder like policemen on the beat, began to be seen as inadequate. An alternative and interesting development of its kind, had its tiny and highly informal beginnings in a Bond Street waiting-room in the autumn of 1969. The idea was devised by Peregrine Pollen, Howard Ricketts and Richard Day. They had persuaded Derek Shrubb to come to Sotheby's to start a properly planned training scheme for young entrants to the firm. The original contact with Shrubb was through Richard Day's wife who had gone to a lecture course at the Victoria & Albert where Shrubb had spent ten years in the education department. The initial plan was that nine carefully selected young people should each be paid £800 per annum for ten months' concentrated training and tuition ending with a three week trip to some European city of major artistic importance – the first choice was Venice – and that some of them should then be offered employment by the firm. The scheme worked reasonably well, though it was re-thought in its second year. The students were now to pay a fee for the course, so that it could become self-financing. New premises were found; a detailed syllabus was devised which concentrated on combining a strong visual training through the study of colour slides, with practical research work, visits to museums and London dealers, judging objects while they were on view before the sales to make accurate assessment of their quality and worth, and attending sales to study auction techniques and finally to discuss the results with the auctioneer afterwards.

By the third year the demand for the course was such that even larger premises had to be found and the number of students was limited to fifty. Requests to attend came from all over the world, for under Derek Shrubb's guidance the course soon became not only a useful recruiting ground for Sotheby's, but an effective educational adjunct to the fine art trade generally. Because the course is relatively short (it lasts nine months), students have to work extremely hard, but those with a natural aptitude for the subject seem thoroughly to enjoy it. The design of the practical work is ingeniously contrived to combine the various aspects of the art world. In one exercise for example, six students are told that they are museum curators with limited budgets in specialised areas; another six pretend to be dealers in the same field. The two groups then get together for mock selection of objects and negotiations for their purchase. The membership of the course reflects the internationalism of the art trade. Thus, of the forty-nine students in the 1980 course, twenty came from the United States, seven from the UK, six from Italy, five from Germany, three from Austria, two from Switzerland and one each from Argentina, Canada, Finland, France, Iran and Lebanon. A second course linked with Sotheby's Belgravia intended for those who want to specialise in European decorative arts of the nineteenth and twentieth century came into being in 1978.

That phrase, 'Sotheby's Belgravia', heralded the most interesting development in the history of the firm since the acquisition of Parke-Bernet. Despite occasional sales of Victoriana and *art nouveau* objects held in Bond Street, it had been clear for some years that there was a huge area of what the Americans termed 'collectibles' which largely by-passed Sotheby's. There simply was not the time, the space or the will to deal with it. Demand was not always certain and prices seemed fickle. There was too a dearth of the expertise essential for good cataloguing. The necessary research work had not at that stage been tackled and there was a general lack of useful up to date and scholarly reference books. It was only under the gently persistent and persuasive tuition of Sir John Betjeman, and a host of like-minded and articulate art historians such as Sir Nikolaus Pevsner and John Steegman,[1] that there had been a gradual shift in

1. The author of *Consort of Taste: 1830–1870*, London, 1950, an astute pioneering study of Victorian art (re-published as *Victorian Taste* in 1970).

taste towards an appreciation of the merits of many forms of nineteenth-century art. As eighteenth-century and earlier antiques became scarcer – and prices rose accordingly – dealers found a growing demand for things Victorian and even Edwardian. The terms *art nouveau* and the later *art deco* became as familiar as baroque or Regency. People suddenly looked at such things, where before there had been an unseeing gaze. It was as if an impenetrable veil had been snatched away from examples of these forms of art, design and craftsmanship; a veil which had firmly settled since the time when the original generations had produced and bought them. The result was that more and more people were now ready to accept the product of these periods into their homes again, and also into their collections. Furthermore, such material – much of it produced in a machine age – existed in enormous quantities.

It is already difficult a mere decade later to see what a bold move it was to set up Belgravia as we now know it. The conception right from the start was *not* to have a mere secondary auction room with a rapid turnover in lesser quality goods, but an outlet for the best things from the later, largely uncharted fields of collectable material. The intention was to set a standard of stylishness and quality that would generate its own demand.

The original idea had first come to Howard Ricketts, who was responsible for the whole works of art department in the late 1960s. He had been commissioned to write a book on *Objects of Virtue*,[1] and during the course of his researches on the subject, particularly while studying the long run of back numbers of that great Victorian periodical *Art Journal*, it occurred to him that while much of the material discussed must still exist, hardly any of it ever came near a sale-room. During this period an executive committee of senior Sotheby directors, such as Peregrine Pollen, Graham Llewellyn, Carmen Gronau, Herman Robinow and the much younger Howard Ricketts himself, would occasionally take themselves out of the office for a day and meet elsewhere in order to think about long term objectives and new ideas: a sort of auctioneering think-tank. One of the ideas to emerge at such a meeting was the training scheme. At a meeting early in 1969, Howard put forward the notion of a separate sale-room that would concentrate on the cream of what had been produced in the nineteenth century and after. He subsequently prepared a long paper to develop the idea. A copy in letter form went to Marcus Linell, a close friend as well as a business associate. Marcus had been picked out by Jim Kiddell among a host of aspiring entrants to the firm in 1956, had started as a porter, had then undergone a rigorous training under Tim Clarke and Jim Kiddell in the porcelain department, had become the firm's youngest director ever at twenty-three and had more recently been seconded to Parke-Bernet to head the works of art side in New York under Peregrine Pollen. Marcus was immediately fired with enthusiasm for the idea, and he and Howard developed it rapidly in correspondence thereafter.

The question of finding a suitable venue never posed a problem. For many years Sotheby's had stored any excess of goods coming up for sale at the old-

1. Barrie & Jenkins, 1971.

established 'Pantechnicon' in Motcomb Street. It had belonged to the Seth-Smith family since Thomas Cubitt had developed Belgravia for the Grosvenor family in the 1830s. The Seth-Smith of the time had been a West country builder working under Cubitt's direction. The Pantechnicon was intended to house the carriages of the families living near-by and also as a furniture store when people moved away temporarily. Later it also contained an enormous strong room and stabling for over a hundred horses. Despite a number of serious and damaging fires, its Parthenon-like façade was always preserved and became a well-known landmark. In 1962 when the future of the Pantechnicon as a furniture depository and its use as a minor auction room seemed uncertain, there had been long discussions with Sotheby's about a proposed merger. The plan had been that the principal building and a number of adjacent sites also belonging to the Seth-Smiths should be redeveloped into a new, enlarged auction gallery and a modern block of offices into which Sotheby's might move from Bond Street. The negotiations eventually came to nought and a property developer became involved instead. There was, however, such a public outcry at the proposed demolition of the old and highly attractive group of buildings that the plan for 'total redevelopment' was dropped and it became possible instead, some years later, to modernise the Pantechnicon and to adapt the interior for use by Sotheby's.

The colour scheme of the refurbished interior was an ingenious return to the original nineteenth-century style designed by Michael Raymond (down to such detail as restoring and then reproducing the one remaining lamp in the hall). Howard Ricketts masterminded the building transformation in London; Marcus Linell devoted himself to planning the organisation of the sale-room from afar in New York. The intention was that he should return to London permanently to take over responsibility for it in January 1971, and to hold the first sale there in October of that year. When the Tokyo sale at Mitsukoshi was over, Peter Wilson suggested to John Cann that he might like to return home via New York in order to see Marcus who had one or two new ideas on systems that might help administration in London. When Marcus and John met over dinner, Marcus outlined the plan for Belgravia and invited John Cann to be its principal administrator – a key job in the new enterprise. There were indeed a number of novel features in New York's administration that could be used in Belgravia. John Cann accepted the challenge with delight. It was an opportunity to devise and to implement innovations which auction room administrators had been dreaming about for several lifetimes.

There was a multitude of problems over getting the building work done and choosing the staff to launch the new operation; also over security, because it was felt that if any rival heard of the new concept of operation and launched a similar one, the impact of Belgravia would be seriously dented and would inhibit its chance of success. In the event Belgravia's activities, once revealed, were difficult to imitate and there was little direct competition for three or four vital years. The hardest nut to crack by far was in getting agreement from some of the existing departments at Bond Street to 'release' some of their sales to Belgravia. This was quite understandable. With increasing specialisation, departmental turnover had become a yardstick by which progress, success and profitability could be judged, and removing two or three dozen sales to the new premises which was to have its own local management meant a great bite into existing turnover that might not at once be easy to replace. As a general guideline it had been agreed that objects made after 1840 should be sold at Belgravia. The most difficult area in which to apply such an arbitrary segregation was in the realm of pictures, and yet pictures were probably the most important element in the future of the new sale-room. Michel Strauss agreed at once to send all Barbizon paintings and minor Impressionists to Motcomb Street. Richard Day, who looked after prints, offered nineteenth-century sporting prints and topographical material, but the transfer of sales of Victorian and later English paintings to Belgravia was only achieved after a great deal of internal wrangling.

Yet it was these very paintings sales that gave Belgravia its own particular character from the day it opened and which brought it almost instant success. The new style catalogues with their distinctive red covers showed illustrations of almost every item sold, and demonstrated the good sense of a policy of photographing everything that passed through the sale-room.[1] As more and more people came to view the sales in Belgravia and appreciated the wealth and scope and varied achievements of nineteenth-century fine and applied art in a suitable setting (the aim had been to reconstruct the interior of the Pantechnicon very much as it was in the 1830s), the former derision and one-time almost universal vilification of things Victorian soon died down. Buyers arrived from many countries with which the firm had never had dealings. Here were markets that no one had ever suspected, where a profusion of ornament and flamboyant complexity of design were positive magnets. The initial turnover in all sectors was gratifying. Goods poured in for sale, particularly furniture. There had been a feeling at one stage that where furniture was concerned Belgravia might well poach on the preserves of Bond Street, but what arrived was completely different in character and the demand for this was a pleasant surprise to all concerned. The careful and painstaking research of the catalogues soon established them as valuable points of reference in a largely uncharted area of interest. In the second season, printed price estimates were introduced as a guide to new buyers. These proved so popular that they were soon included in all catalogues published by Sotheby's, and other auctioneers all over the world followed this lead. Sales too gradually achieved a new level of specialisation as a better understanding of market needs developed. Thus in 1971 a single ceramics sale had contained English and continental porcelain, studio pottery, glass, Chinese and Japanese porcelain and all kinds of oriental works of art. By 1975 there were regular separate sales for each of these categories. By the third

1. It was only in the early 1960s that the longstanding prejudice among the trade against the circulation of photographs of objects that had passed through the sale-room began to die down.

season Belgravia was so firmly established that the trade only wondered how they had ever got along without it. Today Belgravia's principal problem is lack of space as it reaches a turnover of nearly £10,000,000 per annum, and its English painting department under Peter Nahum completely dominates the field in the prolific period of 1870 to 1925.

As soon as it had become apparent that the Pantechnicon was to be a sale-room and not a repository, the firm had to find itself a new warehouse, where bulky goods sent for sale, particularly furniture, could be stored until they were actually needed at Bond Street. After a long search the ideal premises were found in South West London. But there was a hitch. The extra staff, the new sale-room, the overseas offices, a more powerful computer had all meant more investment and by the time Belgravia was well on the way to opening, Sotheby's suddenly found itself strapped for cash. Herman Robinow and Tony Holloway constantly reiterated the need for caution – in a general economic climate that veered from the merely depressing to the downright disastrous. Though up to that moment the art market had certainly not suffered the buffeting which almost all sectors of the financial world had undergone.

There then occurred an event which was to give the firm as great a jolt as any that had taken place since the war. It started as a proposal from outside that seemed, at least temporarily, to solve a lot of problems. £100,000 seemed available just for the asking at this time of acute cash shortage at Bond Street. Major tobacco companies were expanding too. W. D. & H. O. Wills was looking for a new brand name, already familiar to the public, that reflected an established image and were willing to pay well for it. A market research firm had come up with the idea of using Sotheby's or Fortnum & Mason; it didn't really matter to the Imperial Tobacco Company which name was chosen. It also involved a long campaign of free advertising linking the new cigarette brand name with the activities of the company after which it had been named. The auction room seemed to offer an ideal setting.

When the proposal was put to Sotheby's London board it aroused immediate resistance. There then followed three weeks of agitated contemplation of the matter internally which catalysed a level of discord among the directors that had been dormant for some years. When the New York board agreed to the proposal a number of London directors resigned. Both Marcus Linell and Howard Ricketts felt very strongly about the matter but agreed to wait a year to see what would happen. If the cigarette did well they would go. If it failed they would stay. In the event, Howard Ricketts, who had felt himself at loggerheads over a number of other recent decisions, went anyway and set up a highly successful business on his own. When the cigarette failed to make an impact, Marcus Linell stayed to launch Belgravia with enormous éclat, and as we have seen, to make a great success of it. It is today run by another one-time porcelain porter, David Battie, while Marcus has become Managing Director of Sotheby's. Another director who had resigned stayed as an expert consultant: the links with Bond Street were hard to break after a lifetime's work there. The capital sum acquired did not, in the end, make much difference one way or another.

The cash situation soon remedied itself,[1] and with the benefit of hindsight it might be said that the shock of the near schism probably improved the health of the firm in the long term. Those in charge re-thought their objectives and saw what action was needed. The strain from the permanent dissenters was reduced as they departed. The cigarette affair was a cogent demonstration of the fact that in business the corporate entity is stronger than the individual. An interesting postscript was that when six years later the Sotheby board had another proposal put to them to the effect that an enormously powerful firm in the consumer field wanted to use Sotheby's name linked with their advertising, the board turned them down without even bothering to ask the identity of the other party concerned.

For the book department – in contrast to the general pre-occupation with the future – the period 1971–72 saw three cogent reminders of links with the past. In March 1971 there was a single memorable two-day sale of all that was left of the Britwell Court Library.[2] Contrary to general belief, there had not been a clean sweep in the Twenties and it still contained a good many items of outstanding importance which realised a total of £174,866. A hand-coloured copy of William Blake's *First Book of Urizen* fetched £24,000 and his slim *Poetical Sketches* of 1873, £3,800. A truly magnificent hand-coloured copy of Ptolemy's *Cosmographia* printed on vellum in Ulm in 1482 was sold for £34,000, and Charles I's travelling library containing fifty-eight works of the classics for £6,500. One item which stirred memories of the Wise era was a unique advance copy of the first edition of Keats's *Endymion* with an unrecorded state of the title page and four corrections to the text in the author's own hand. It sold for £6,200.

In June 1971 the Pierpont Morgan Library of New York decided to sell twenty-nine important duplicates and sent them to London. They included two Caxtons: Chaucer's translation of Boethius' *De Consolatione Philosophiae* and Caxton's own translation of de Cessolis' *The Game and Playe of the Chesse* (there were now only eleven known surviving copies). The first fetched £25,000 and was the only copy offered at auction in this century, and the second realised £44,000. These were remarkable return tickets, among a total of £115,214. 6 February 1972 was the centenary of the death of Sir Thomas Phillipps. The great man's library was still selling as strongly as ever at Sotheby's. There had been a sale of manuscripts on papyrus, vellum and paper in 1971, and other sales both of manuscript material and printed books followed roughly at the rate of two a year. Every one of them still caused a minor sensation. The meticulously detailed cataloguing alone would have given Phillipps enormous pleasure: the prices would have staggered him. The last series of Phillipps sales continued up to 1978. The architect of its success was Anthony Hobson, who

---

1. It was barely known, even among Sotheby directors, that when one of them saw Tony Holloway's drawn face at the time of this crisis and offered to loan the firm his life savings until the crisis had passed, the offer was gratefully accepted.
2. See page 194.

finally left Sotheby's in that year. H. P. Kraus who had bought so many of the major Phillipps items since the war, acquired the tail end of the collection in November 1977 from the trust created by Lionel and Philip Robinson. There still remained some 2,000 volumes of manuscripts and more than 130,000 letters and documents. Kraus wrote laconically, 'It will take time to catalogue this huge mass of material'.[1] The price he is said to have paid for it is £1,000,000. Kraus had been one of the dealers who had wanted to buy what was left of the Phillipps collection in 1944, but the brothers Robinson had sealed their bargain at £100,000. It is a sobering thought that they subsequently offered the collection to William Jackson, then the rare book librarian at Harvard, for £110,000. To Jackson's everlasting disappointment his trustees refused to sanction the purchase. This must rank as one of the greatest missed opportunities in the realm of rare book acquisitions in the present century.

The book department had plenty to do apart from selling volumes associated with Britwell, Pierpont Morgan and Phillipps. It is true that there were now very few of the great country house library sales of John Wilkinson's time or the inter-war period, but instead an increasing number of institutional libraries began to sell duplicates or volumes outside their special areas of interest in order to raise funds for other acquisitions. As always, great, recently formed collections came under the hammer when their owners grew old or died. Since 1965, for example, Sotheby's had been dispersing the remarkable library of C. E. Kenney and the magnificent bindings, manuscripts and topographical books assembled by Major Abbey. There were as many specialist collections as ever on cookery and gastronomy, on the history of science and medicine, on botany and astonomy, on travel and navigation, on the theatre and circus, on specific authors and places. The sale of manuscripts continued unabated too. Indeed illuminated medieval Books of Hours and major illustrated manuscripts of Middle Eastern origin had almost taken over the star quality that used to pertain to Impressionist paintings in the early 1960s, and a strong revival of interest in autograph material became discernible through a formidable series of catalogues in the late Sixties which continued to grow throughout the Seventies. For nearly fifteen years the book departments had grown in status and prospered under Anthony Hobson's guidance and more than kept pace with Sotheby's general expansion. In 1965 he handed it over to Lord John Kerr whom he had persuaded to come to Bond Street two years earlier. Lord John had undergone a rigorous early training as a cataloguer for the celebrated E. P. Goldschmidt, and had then bought and run one of Oxford's famous antiquarian bookshops, Sanders, in the High Street. It was an excellent way of learning to appreciate the importance of holding regular Monday sales, week in, week out, as staple for the book trade. Under Lord John's aegis, Sotheby's also acquired the premises of Hodgson's of Chancery Lane, in 1967, then being run by Mr. Wilfrid Hodgson, the grandson of one of the brothers Hodgson to whom Tom Hodge had tried so hard to sell Sotheby's some sixty years earlier. It was a noteworthy reversal of roles. Hodgsons in the interval had marvellously retained

---

1. In his autobiography, *A Rare Book Saga*, New York, 1978.

its Dickensian atmosphere (the building was, after all, especially designed for them as a book sale-room in 1863) and its regular sales had maintained a strong following, not only among dealers, but also among enthusiastic private collectors who could not afford the higher prices usually, but not always correctly, associated with Bond Street.

There were gentle changes in the style of cataloguing and in the nature of the sales (more specialisation in such areas as private press books, children's books and modern literature). They also became more frequent. Wilfrid Hodgson continued to take the majority of sales, and the august Fred Snelling continued to 'clerk' them. Even the initial and inevitable misunderstandings over which books were to be sold at Bond Street and which at Chancery Lane soon resolved themselves when a general break at 1830 was decided on, and with sensitive refurbishing of the premises, Chancery Lane soon settled down as an adjunct to Bond Street book sales while completely retaining its own identity. Both Tom Hodge and the two Hodgson brothers, John Edmund and Sydney, would certainly have approved of this belated coming together.

While Lord John kept a paternal eye on the proceedings in WC2, for which direct responsibility went to Michael Heseltine, he grew in stature at Bond Street manifesting a remarkable physical likeness to his predecessor, John Wilkinson, with his pink-cheeked, infinitely genial countenance, magnificently Victorian with its striking white sideboards. Like his predecessor he also took snuff. He is the quickest caller of bids in the business, very quiet in voice (which helps to rivet attention) yet infinitely authoritative. It is a style of auctioneering for professionals; indeed, many of the firms dealing in antiquarian books today still bear the same proud names that were represented at Sotheby's sixty, seventy and eighty years ago. The amateur has to keep on his toes – in every sense of the phrase. As soon as Lord John senses that a collector is genuinely involved in the bidding, the pace slows down, he cocks his head gently to one side, smiles expectantly and waits for the more hesitant reaction of the untrained cerebral processes of the amateur. Here is a total master of his calling. A fascinating example of his facility in action occurred during a sale in July 1977. The prize items were the Beckford Archive (consigned for sale by the present Duke of Hamilton), a series of Wordsworth letters and a Jane Austen manuscript in the author's own hand. Lord John took the event at a spanking pace. The bidding for the Beckford papers, which consisted of a vast quantity of hand-written documents and letters in twenty-four boxes, took exactly thirty-eight seconds and reached £120,000 in a minimum number of bids. It was bought by Blackwells of Oxford against strong competition from the United States. The next item (lot 273) took a few seconds longer and went for £52. The group of Wordsworth letters made £35,000 and Jane Austen's manuscript of *Volume the Second*, £40,000. It was a day's work wholly in a tradition now 244 years old.

37
Action and Reaction

THE global encirclement continued unabated. Between 1974 and 1978 further new offices were opened in Amsterdam, Stockholm, Milan, Brussels, Dublin, Rome, Frankfurt and Geneva. Each opening inspired its own dramas. For there was tremendous variation in the attitudes of mind, the commercial practices, the legal system and the very auction room terminology between one country and another.[1] It was, therefore, something of a challenge for each Sotheby representative to work to an identical pattern in such different environments. In November 1974 all the firm's overseas representatives met together for the first time under the benevolent superintendence of Graham Llewellyn, for some years one of the firm's three Vice-Chairmen, the architect of Sotheby's real breakthrough in the sales of fine jewellery in Europe and a tower of strength in the general management at Bond Street. The meeting was called in order to discuss common problems and ways and means of solving them so that clients could have the best possible service. A major headache was the high and indeed escalating cost of packing and freight to and from London, which might well eat up a substantial proportion of the value of a fragile object such as a piece of porcelain or a clock (particularly if it did not reach its reserve and had to be returned to its source). In an endeavour to keep these costs down, Sotheby's had bought the old established firm of fine art packers and shippers, James Bourlet, in 1973. A further series of problems were posed by the constant fluctuations in the relative value of international currencies.

This representatives' meeting took place in Amsterdam, a city with an auction room history that went back almost a century further than London's, for the Dutch have always been great collectors and were, as Geoffrey Hobson used to say, the inventors of auction sales. It was natural, therefore, that Sotheby's should want a base there at a time of general expansion. One or other of the firm's directors had gone over almost every month to meet clients at the Krasnapolsky Hotel since the mid-Sixties. The most active local competition came from Mak van Waay, the city's leading auction house that had been founded at the turn of the century. There was generally surprised delight, therefore, when its owner approached Peter Wilson to ask if Sotheby's would be interested in acquiring the business: it seemed the perfect gateway into Europe. The early Seventies was the time when nineteenth-century Dutch romantic pictures were most actively in demand, their prices sometimes even higher than their original seventeenth-century counterparts, and the art trade in Holland was booming. After a great deal of thought the actual negotiations were remarkably brief, and Sotheby's found itself the owner of Mak van Waay

1. The words 'limit' and 'reserve', for example, are used with quite different connotations in German auction houses compared to English ones.

in exchange for a cool eight million guilders (then about £1,000,000) in August of 1974. The business was in two parts: the offices at Rokin 102 and a former tobacco warehouse just behind where property could be stored and put on view. The Dutch staff remained under Jan Pieter Glerum – whose father had been active in the running of the firm before him – and Derek Johns became responsible from the London end. The organisation of sales was essentially different from Bond Street's. Instead of brief, specialist sales on regular days during the week, there were protracted marathon affairs, covering every sort of object, that went on uninterruptedly for several days at a time, and there were much longer intervals between sales. This habit was so deeply rooted that although efforts were made to change it to the English system, it has remained virtually unaltered and has generated a very useful profit contribution for the whole Sotheby Parke Bernet group. Even the occasional sales of collections of international importance that drew the limelight to Amsterdam from London made little ultimate difference to local custom.

The first of the outstanding collections sold under Sotheby's aegis consisted of the magnificent Old Master drawings of Bernard Houthakker in November 1975, but the sale that really caught the headlines was that of the Dutch paintings belonging to Bas de Geus van den Heuvel in April 1976. The auction was staged in the Round Lutheran Church in Amsterdam, and Jan Pieter Glerum took it in his stylish manner with the great eighteenth-century organ just behind him. Almost a thousand people attended and buyers came from the Netherlands, the UK, Belgium, France, Germany, Switzerland and the United States. The total of Fl.14,400,000 (then £1,800,000) was the highest ever realised in Holland. Fifteen months later the Round Lutheran Church was the scene of another memorable Mak van Waay sale of paintings: this time of the collection of Dr. Hans Wetzlar. Wetzlar had started to buy paintings along conventional lines in the early 1930s, concentrating on the seventeenth century, Holland's 'Golden Age', but the collection had been broadened to reflect a remarkable sense of earlier history in collaboration with the German art historian, Max J. Friedländer, who had moved to Amsterdam just before the war. Interestingly enough, both Van den Heuvel and Wetzlar were determined that their collections should be dispersed at auction after their death so that a new generation of collectors should benefit from their possessions. A number of major sales also took place in Amsterdam which originated in London. Among them was the distinguished cabinet of Dutch, Flemish and German drawings started by Alfred Gathorne-Hardy with help from his uncle, John Malcolm, which later passed to other generations of the same family.

At about the time when the acquisition of Mak van Waay was first becoming a possibility, Sotheby's established its firmest link yet with South East Asia. About the beginning of the 1960s there had been a readily discernible increase of attention by the Japanese to Chinese porcelain. It was probably at the two-part sale in 1963 of the private collection of H. R. Norton, before his death himself a dealer in Chinese ceramics, that prices began to move upwards more speedily. Despite a hesitant period in 1970 they continued to do so until they reached what were virtually boom proportions early in 1974. As had so often been the case in the past, it was a single, very active buyer who became the focal point of what was a broad front of interest. In this instance it was a little, elderly lady of German origin called Mrs. Helen Glatz, who owned two small antique shops that faced each other across the road in the backwater off Baker Street where antique shops jostle cheek by jowl. Any observant passer-by would have noted a particularly fine display of armorial Chinese export ware in both her windows. Mrs. Glatz had come to England soon after her release from a concentration camp, and had been patiently assembling these Chinese wares since the early 1950s, a period when they were little appreciated. Firstly the trade, and after a surprisingly long time the press, began to sit up and take notice when Mrs. Glatz started to take a much wider interest in Chinese porcelain of all kinds and to out-bid all-comers on the finest pieces in every relevant sale. It was rumoured that in a single season in 1973–74 she had spent a sum exceeding £3,000,000 at Bond Street alone, and much guesswork was devoted to the identity of her major clients throughout Europe, one of whom, at least, was known to reside in Portugal. The most spectacular of the upward surge of prices occurred in April 1974, when in a two-day sale an early Ming blue-and-white 16½ inch bottle, decorated with a single dragon, became the most publicised piece of Chinese porcelain in the world when it fetched £420,000. Two other lots in the same sale were sold for £160,000 and £170,000, and a hexagonal *famille rose* bowl broke all records for Ch'ing pieces at £95,000. The principal buyer in this sale was again Mrs. Glatz. But the revolution in Portugal led to her absence at the following sale in July, and the beginning of a major financial recession and growing misgivings about the speculative nature of the market led to a rapid shake-out of prices. Among the most enthusiastic buyers, there had been many who hailed from Hong Kong. As it happened, a little earlier Mrs. Mamie Howe, an interior decorator who worked for Lane Crawford, Hong Kong's leading department store, had approached Sotheby's about holding occasional sales of Chinese porcelain and antiquities in Hong Kong. Julian Thompson welcomed the idea enthusiastically, and the first sale of material which originated in Hong Kong almost in its entirety had taken place in November 1973. A second sale was planned for November 1974. Someone should have studied the Chinese astrological calendar for the days concerned and heeded its warning, for every sort of disaster was predicted – and indeed took place. It was the time when the market hit rock bottom in a manner reminiscent of the early 1930s, which naturally discouraged many buyers who had been active previously, but it also coincided with a devastating typhoon which brought the airport to a complete standstill. Yet despite these disastrous circumstances, there were still significant sales and it was decided to carry on. Sotheby's and Lane Crawford did so in partnership. The market recovered. In 1975 a major local collection was included in the November sale and sold well. Collectors in Hong Kong regained their confidence and enthusiasm, and liked the way in which the sales were organised to suit their life style. Thus, the twice-yearly series of sales held at the Mandarin

Hotel, which now also attract items from London and New York, have become a regular and very successful feature of the Sotheby calendar.

After all the developments in the decade 1964 to 1974 anybody might have been forgiven for suggesting that the moment was now at hand for a period of quiet consolidation, but, if anything, the pace of growth quickened. In January 1975 the firm issued a brief press statement to announce that 'The Government of S. A. S. The Prince of Monaco has agreed that Sotheby & Co., by an agreement just signed with the Societé des Bains de Mer, will be granted facilities to sell fine art at auction in the Principality'. This announcement, it must be remembered, was issued at a time when Britain's economy was in a state of parlous disarray that had not been equalled since 1930. Only a few weeks earlier the Bank of England had actually been forced to deny that it had had to support the National Westminster Bank to keep it going. The Stock Exchange had reached an all-time low. The *Financial Times* Index stood at 146. There was serious doubt in many quarters whether the capitalist system would survive in the UK. The whole of British industry could have been bought then and there by one or other of the oil-rich Middle Eastern states without making a serious dent in their resources. *The Times* printed a three-column leader – an indication of the gravity of the situation – headed 'Fear itself'. Those who remembered it recalled the black gloom of May 1940 and the fall of France. Yet here was Sotheby's – in fact clobbered by the crisis as much as every other sector of commerce and industry – carrying on as if nothing had happened and calmly projecting its image into an area traditionally attractive to the very rich from all over the world.

Soon the first sale in Monte Carlo was announced. It had all the makings of a major auction event and its presentation was pure theatre. All the material belonged to Baron Guy de Rothschild and his close friend, the Baron de Redé. The reason for the sale was that Baron Guy and his wife, Marie-Helène, had bought the Hotel Lambert on the Ile St.-Louis in Paris where de Redé had had a magnificent apartment and he was moving upstairs to a much smaller one. For many years the Baron de Redé had been the financial adviser and close friend of the Chilean millionaire and great collector in his own right, Arturo Lopez Willshaw,[1] and had indeed inherited part of the latter's fortune and many of the finest items in the Willshaw collection. Alexis de Redé had formed a superb collection of his own in the intervening twenty years and was thus in constant touch with dealers and fellow collectors all over the world. The Rothschilds in turn were in the process of handing over their Château de Ferrières (just east of Paris and designed by Sir Joseph Paxton in 1857) to the French State, and it proved a useful moment to dispose of some of its contents. What was being sold, therefore, was the amalgam of the tastes of three great connoisseurs, the Rothschilds, de Redé and Lopez Willshaw. It was a powerful magnet and it

1. Sotheby's had sold a selection of Willshaw's Rennaissance jewellery and decorated hard-stone cups for very high prices in October 1970. The quality was so outstanding that it seemed as if some minor branch of the Habsburgs had discovered a secret cabinet of late medieval treasure which had remained undisturbed for centuries.

drew an immense crowd to Monte Carlo. The particularly lavish catalogue set a standard of its own (that has been maintained in subsequent Monte Carlo sales). Dealers and collectors filled the hotels to capacity, and when Peter Wilson opened the bidding on the first item in the sale – an Indian silver and enamel rose-water sprinkler – he faced no fewer than 1,200 people in the vast, gilded, art deco hall of the Winter Casino, possibly the finest auction room in Europe or America. They had come from France, from Switzerland, from the Middle East, from the United States and wherever the very affluent sojourn. One of the principal advantages of holding a sale in Monte Carlo was the fact that what was sold was not liable to the full customs restrictions if it remained within France itself. The Paris auctioneers were not at all pleased at this invasion of their territory and the French government put a slight damper on the proceedings by forbidding the export of some of the most distinguished items of French origin, such as a magnificent mechanical desk made by David Roentgen for Catherine of Russia, and a suite of furniture made for Versailles. However, the excitement was intense, the competition ferocious and most of the prices above – some substantially so – the high estimates. The prize item of the sale, a Florentine bronze figure of an anatomical study of a horse, three-feet high, from the Bologna-Susini workshops, was sold for 1,500,000 francs (the estimate had been 400–700,000 francs) to an Iranian collector living in Paris, Habib Sabet, against fierce opposition from both English and Italian buyers. Local rules stipulated that the sales should be supervised by a responsible *huissier* or licensed auctioneer, and it had taken a fair amount of rehearsal for M. Marquet and Peter Wilson to learn to conduct the bidding in harness. At the first sale there was occasional confusion. The three sessions of the collectors items, the furniture and the silver, however, fetched a spectacular total of 17,224,600 francs and not only assured the future of Sotheby sales in Monte Carlo, which have taken place there at increasingly frequent intervals ever since, but did much to cheer up and to re-establish confidence in the entire international art market at the time.

1974 was also important for quite another reason. The signs of galloping inflation and of distress in the world economy had soon begun to make themselves felt in the fine art auction field. It became clear to the board that this was the moment when their own financial management needed to be strengthened. It had really not kept in step with the skill, drive and entrepreneurial development of the firm in other directions. To some extent it was still an enlarged version of the post-war traditional accounting set-up when a single, competent cashier had kept control of most matters connected with money, and now the machinery squealed and groaned at every turn. Tony Holloway, in charge of finance generally since the departure to Rothschild's of Herman Robinow, performed miracles of improvisation and worked at an unbelievable pace to keep the wheels turning. What was needed, however, was a radical overhaul and a totally new organisational approach; above all a man used to controlling this scale of operation.

Lord Jellicoe, one of Sotheby's outside, non-executive directors, mentioned to colleagues in his own firm, Warburg's, the merchant bank, that Sotheby's were looking for a Group finance director. Peter Spira, a vice-chairman at Warburg's, was asked to deal with the matter and after a long search he recommended a suitable candidate, ripe with experience and already in his sixties, who was willing to come to Bond Street on a three-days-a-week basis. But Peter Wilson wanted and needed someone full time. He looked thoughtfully at Peter Spira and suggested that the post might suit Spira himself. It was not for nothing that Peter Wilson had acquired a reputation for being an excellent picker of men. After Eton, National Service, three years at Cambridge and three more at the accountants, Cooper Brothers, Spira had joined Warburg's in 1957. He had worked closely with Sigmund Warburg himself in that financial genius's almost single-handed, post-war creation of London as an international capital market; he had then become head of Warburg's corporate finance and international departments, and had reached the stage of his career in the City where a change began increasingly to engage his thoughts. After a few days of agonised and concentrated cerebration he rang Peter Wilson and said: 'If you meant it, the answer is yes'. That was in June. He moved to Bond Street in October 1974, remaining a non-executive director of Warburg's.

In the period since then he has given a firm foundation to what was Sotheby's principal area of weakness. It was uphill work; and his early efforts within the firm probably caused more resentment than anything since the cigarette affair, but then not everyone understood what he was trying to do, or how vitally necessary it was. From Spira's point of view, it was not easy for an outsider to grasp at once just how sensitive and finely balanced much of Sotheby's administrative management was. After Holloway's premature and unexpected death he began recruiting the senior staff for an entirely new Group financial division, and inevitably, as staff cuts became necessary elsewhere, there was universal muttering about all those 'bloody new accountants'.

The lesson that Spira succeeded in teaching Sotheby's is that there is nothing so sweet as success – in the form of consistent profitability. A company that is making good profits can afford more readily to be adventurous, constructive and bold – and this breeds further success in its turn. A company that always sees retrenchment round the corner has to tread warily and is forced to think small rather than big. In order to achieve consistency in profitability a company has to have good controls – of overheads, of capital investment and, above all, of communication. It was the introduction of these, after long periods of successful departmental free-wheeling, that was most painful and the cause of much resentment, though it soon became clear how beneficial they could be. Improved financial reporting also gave the small units a chance to see their own achievements – and ultimately the departmentalisation of Sotheby's means that it is a large number of small units working in concert. The resultant extra confidence enabled management to function more effectively, to encourage where encouragement was needed, to move staff about as circumstances dictated and

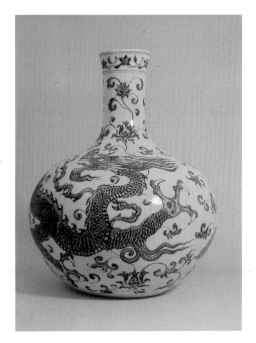

Va. An early Ming blue and white bottle with a single, superbly drawn dragon, Yung Lo, 16¼ in. high, sold for £420,000 in London in April 1974.

Vb. The star item from the Malcolm Collection sold on 29 March 1977, the 'K'ang Hou *Kuei*', a ritual bronze food vessel made in 1010 BC, fetched £110,000. It is now in the British Museum. A contemporary inscription inside gives the piece an unusual documentary importance.

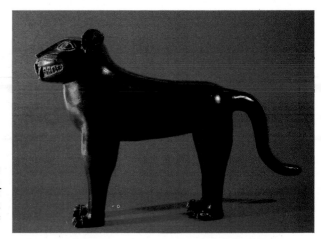

VIa. A Benin bronze aquamanile in the form of a leopard from the George Ortiz Collection of primitive works of art sold in London in June 1978. This piece fetched £150,000.

VIb. One of the finest Lower Niger bronzes known, from the same collection, which was sold for £120,000. The sculpture lay forgotten in a cupboard for many years until brought to light by the researches of the collector.

VIc. A Raratonga figure, possibly of a Polynesian god, brought back from the Cook Islands in 1836 by a member of the London Missionary Society, also in the Ortiz Collection. Its thirty-four items were sold for a total of £1,598,000. The collection was put up for sale to compensate for the £1 million ransom the owner had to pay in the previous year for the release of his kidnapped daughter.

occasionally to kill a project when it had not proved its long-term worth.

One of the most difficult and far-reaching decisions which Spira had to face soon after his arrival was how to increase revenue in order to cover escalating overheads at a time of peak inflation. The Post Office had, for example, *tripled* telephone charges in a single step; and vastly increased postal rates suddenly rendered the daily despatch of thousands of catalogues all over the world a punitive business. Printing and paper costs too had rocketed. Christie's felt the pinch as much as Sotheby's and announced a sizeable staff lay-off. Little Mak van Waay in Amsterdam was virtually creating a larger financial surplus than everything that the whole huge London operation was doing collectively and no one regarded Mak van Waay as even middling profitable at that stage, even though they charged the buyer a premium as well as the vendor commission. Likewise, the first, single sale in Monte Carlo had realised more profit at that particular period than all the other Sotheby locations put together. A good deal of internal rationalisation was planned by Marcus Linell to reduce expenditure at Bond Street and Belgravia.

The general consensus was that to increase commission rates beyond the average of fourteen per cent would be punitive for sellers and would frighten them away from the auction room. It would also have blunted the edge which London had over the Continental auction houses. The alternative was to follow their method of introducing a charge to buyers and to reduce commission rates, but it was felt that the trade would bitterly resent the idea. There were endless meetings to discuss the pros and cons of the matter. Eventually a decision was taken to go ahead, but its implementation awaited Peter Wilson's return from a long trip to Tehran and Monte Carlo. Then John Floyd, the chairman of Christie's, rang up one evening as a matter of courtesy to say that his firm was to announce the introduction of a ten per cent buyer's premium on the following day.[1] That announcement hit the press on 31 May 1975. The plan was to introduce the premium at the beginning of the autumn season in September. Sotheby's made a similar announcement on 2 June. Commission rates were reduced simultaneously and the firm offered a five-year guarantee against forgery to all buyers.[2] Although there was some concern at Bond Street that their great rivals had introduced the innovation first, in fact it drew some of the resultant fire away from Sotheby's. Subsequently there were charges of collusion between the two houses, but these were quite unfounded. Dire circumstances had dictated the premium as a vital means of survival. There was one interesting reaction: Phillips' announced that they would reduce their commission rate to ten per cent but would charge no premium. It attracted a tremendous amount of business their way initially, but three years later Phillips' came into line by introducing the premium; it was no longer economically possible for them (or for any other major auctioneer) to survive without it.

The reaction from the trade was spearheaded by the silver dealers, who

1. Though not at Christie's, South Kensington.
2. Christie's did not follow suit in this respect.

15

decided to boycott silver sales, but in a thoroughly gentlemanly way – by missing the first few minutes of each sale. Surprisingly this still left a large number of eager buyers.[1] Richard Came, Sotheby's silver director, was probably one of the firm's auctioneers who could face belligerent opposition with most equanimity. He turned what could have been a nasty confrontation into an occasion where laughter triumphed over resentment. There was no noticeable drop in total prices, though there was a lengthy period of confusion about what price to record as the authentic sales price. In the end, what became known as the 'hammer price' was quoted *without* the premium. The inclusion of ten per cent on purchase invoices was always something of a shock to buyers, but eventually it became accepted – albeit with reluctance – as a norm.[2]

Of course that was not the end of the matter. A number of trade associations took the matter to the British Office of Fair Trading, and pursued their campaign to have the premium annulled the more vigorously when it was seen that it had not only restored the financial good health of the auction houses, but had made them more generally profitable than had been the case for generations.[3] In fact, despite the economic gloom, matters improved to such an extent that by the early spring of 1977 Peter Spira was able to recommend to the board with confidence that the oft considered step of 'going public' should be taken. It was a bold decision at a time when no other major company had offered its shares on the market for nearly three years, but like so many other of the firm's bold moves, it came off. Despite a last minute postponement of the public offer of shares because of an immense release of new shares by British Petroleum on to the market, the Sotheby shares were over-subscribed by twenty-six times and the price immediately rose above the issue level. Eighteen months later it had increased from 150p to 380p per share.[4] The three largest shareholders now emerged as Peter Wilson, Peregrine Pollen and the Rothschild Investment Trust. The latter had been a substantial shareholder in Sotheby's since 1966.

The offer document had forecast a profit for the year 1977 of £4,600,000. In fact, this was comfortably exceeded, and in the following year when sales increased by 30 per cent to £161,097,000, the pre-tax profit increased to £7,024,000. Precisely 50 per cent of the volume of turnover came from sales held outside the UK. Of that 50 per cent, Parke-Bernet contributed the lion's share of 72 per cent and Switzerland was in second place with 12½ per cent. The American end of the Sotheby Parke Bernet Group – as it was now increasingly referred to since a further official change of name in February 1975 – had had an

1. And as emerged later, a number of the boycotting dealers were, in fact, bidding through agents.
2. The situation was complicated further when from 1 January 1979 H. M. Customs and Excise insisted on the payment of VAT on the premium following a decision to this effect by a VAT Tribunal.
3. Surprisingly, the matter of the legality of the premium eventually reached the courts in the spring of 1979, some four years after its introduction, over the matter of collusion at the time it originated between Christie's and Sotheby's.
4. In mid-June 1980 it exceeded 500 for the second time.

exciting time since 1974. Offices had been opened in Boston, Chicago, Houston, Philadelphia, San Francisco, Hawaii and Palm Beach. Los Angeles had had a full-blown auction house since 1971, which had been launched on its career with a sale of the 'props' from the nearby studios of 20th Century Fox, and now had regular and well-attended sales of paintings and every kind of antique. In 1972 Peregrine Pollen had handed over the presidency of Parke-Bernet to John Marion, and returned to London.

In his period of stewardship at Parke-Bernet since Sotheby's had taken over, the turnover had increased fivefold. In New York, as in London, Impressionists and modern paintings had, during much of that period, been the most dynamic sector of the art market. After 1973 the buoyancy attached to such works could no longer be taken for granted. Fortunately, by then Parke Bernet had consolidated its position in most other sales areas. John Marion's most testing moment was to come in 1977 when Christie's finally decided to turn what had merely been a highly active office into a fully-fledged auction centre. They acquired space in the old Delmonico Hotel Building on Park Avenue, and opened their doors for sales in May of that year. Furthermore, Christie's decided to import the 10 per cent buyer's premium into the United States and were thus in a strong negotiating position when it came to fixing the vendor's commission on any major item or collection.

For anyone who makes a study of such matters it is quite clear that Sotheby's and Christie's are of extreme importance to each other. Between them they virtually constitute the core of what gives London its reputation as the centre of the international art market. Yet the competition between them is fierce and each firm – while vigorously denying it in public – watches the other's activities with more than passing interest. Each has maintained its own quite individual character, and internally each regards itself as totally supreme in its own line of business. Peter Wilson and I. O. Chance became chairmen of their respective companies in the same season in 1957,[1] and each man gave his firm a renewed sense of identity. But for almost three decades now, Sotheby's turnover has been running at roughly twice Christie's. Quite early on in this period Sotheby's opted for internationalism; to cover the whole broad spectrum of fine art auctions; and a readiness to try out new ideas and innovatory techniques. This meant taking formidable risks, a much greater capital investment and a higher rate of overhead expenditure. Christie's, it seemed, took a cautious decision to concentrate on what were known to be the most profitable areas, to cultivate their superb and long-standing connections with old established, landed families and to move only to markets where the cream was thickest, as in Geneva. In this context it is interesting to quote *The Times* sale-room correspondent, Geraldine Norman. She wrote in 1978,[2] 'Sotheby's have turned into the dominant art wholesaling operation worldwide, a type of international operation that had not previously been conceived of in this field. Christie's, their closest competitor,

1. Mr. Chance joined Christie's in 1930 and retired from his position as chairman in 1974. He was succeeded by John Floyd.
2. In *Time and Tide*, October 1978.

are of course running a very similar organisation but that is because they followed Sotheby's lead'.

Curiously, although there were extreme jitters at 980 Madison Avenue at the time, the Christie's opening helped Parke-Bernet by giving New York extra muscle as a centre of the world's art market. With more sales to view and to buy from, European dealers were that much more prepared to bear the cost in money and in time of going to New York. The added competition – and Phillips also decided to open up actively in New York that year – seemed to concentrate the mind wonderfully at Parke-Bernet, and a good deal of thinking went into ways and means of expanding and improving the business. The result was spectacular. Parke Bernet has never had seasons as good and successful in financial terms since Christie's opened their own establishment at 502 Park Avenue; and when it was decided early in 1979 that Parke-Bernet would also lower its commission rates and introduce a buyer's premium, profitability increased by leaps and bounds.

For some years a number of special factors had made considerable impact on Parke Bernet's activities throughout the United States. One was the concentration on 'Americana', antiques of American origin, and as the interest grew prices ascended steeply. The firm's name too became more widely known by dint of 'Heirloom Discovery Days', which were introduced in 1974. These were simply the old Sotheby 'clinics' held in different towns all over the States, when anyone could bring anything they considered old or precious to be scrutinised and identified by the firm's experts. A good deal of what was inspected naturally made its way to the sale-room. In one memorable week in 1974 in New York itself, this 'gold at the end of the rainbow' philosophy attracted a staggering 18,000 people to Madison Avenue, and there were queues of over a thousand people waiting outside the building at one stage. These innovations were a great success. One that was not and caused a good deal of resentment was the decision by the firm to make outright purchases of goods from clients who wanted their money instantly and refused for whatever reason to go through the slow process of valuation, cataloguing and the arrangement many months ahead of a specific sale. Initially, both entire collections and single, important items were acquired in this fashion. There was ample precedent for the idea – in previous centuries, in the coin trade and as a standard practice in many parts of the Continent. But the concept dented the image of the auctioneer as an agent and there was an outcry against it. The trade hated it, particularly in the UK, and read signs of double-dealing into it which even the most reasonable of explanations could not dispel. Such business was therefore quickly terminated, and though it left scars, there was relatively little comment some years later when Sotheby's acquired such collections as the archive of Cecil Beaton's photographs or the Honeyman collection of scientific books, and subsequently sold them clearly identified as their own property.

1977 saw a revival of a form of sale that Sotheby's had abandoned in 1919 against increasing competition – the auctioning of postage stamps. Seven sales took place in New York that year, and London started a stamp department under John Michael in the following year. The US venture was in the charge of Andrew Levitt, a practising stamp dealer and auctioneer, and was launched as a separate company, the Sotheby Parke Bernet Stamp Auction Company, with headquarters in Danbury, Connecticut. One of the first series of sales was devoted to the dispersal of the well-known Homan-Krassa collection which included a large European and British Empire element, and it was thus entirely logical that part of it should be sold in London. John Marion explained that the essay into philately had been under consideration for some time largely at the request of executors of estates, still the principal source of an auctioneer's business. The late Bill Homan's collection had, in fact, come to the firm by order of his executors, our old friends the Morgan Guaranty Trust Company of New York.

The previous year, 1976, had seen the establishment of another new enterprise that had altogether different development potential. It had come about as a direct consequence of what had to date been the dispersal of the biggest single collection ever handled by Parke Bernet. Mrs. Geraldine Marcellus Hartley Dodge was the daughter of William Rockefeller, the President of Standard Oil. When she married Mr. Dodge in 1907 they were referred to as 'the richest young couple in the world', for her father left $200,000,000 in trust for his four children. Her husband's grandfather, an arms maker, left $50,000,000. Mrs. Dodge's own estate was estimated at around $85,000,000 after her death in 1973. By order of the Fidelity Union Trust Company of Newark, New Jersey, and St. Hubert's Giralda Inc., acting respectively as executor and legatee, Sotheby Parke Bernet was charged with the dispersal of her collection and the furnishings of her town house at the corner of Fifth Avenue and East 64th Street in New York, and 'Giralda', Mrs. Dodge's country home at Madison, New Jersey. The town house had been constructed by demolishing a total of ten brownstone houses in 1922 and erecting a luxurious modern town house with spacious grounds in their place. For several decades Mrs. Dodge stayed there only on Thursday nights before a day of business and shopping in central New York. The space it occupied was considered to be one of New York's most desirable residential plots, and offers for it running to many millions were turned down over the years. Geraldine Dodge was much happier at Giralda, fifty miles outside Manhattan. It had been her principal home for sixty-two years after she purchased the Giralda estate of 455 acres in 1911 and had the house built for her. It was renowned not only for the size and style in which it was maintained (there was a staff of 125 at one time), but also as the scene of the world's largest one-day dog show during the years 1927 to 1953. Animals of any kind, but dogs in particular, were Mrs. Dodge's consuming interest in life. There were 300 dogs resident in the kennels at Giralda for many years, and the annual meat bill was said to total $50,000. Mr. Dodge, who had first been President and later Chairman of the Remington Arms Company, was a passionate breeder of horses and lived on an even larger estate adjoining Giralda, called 'Hartley Farms'. From its dining room, the dining room of his wife's Giralda was visible down a long vista of carefully planted trees.

Sotheby Parke Bernet devoted eight complete sales to the Dodge property, and items from the collection were included in half a dozen more. By the end of the season the sale of 7,950 lots had totalled over $7,000,000. It was a sale of superlatives: 'the largest number of objects belonging to one collector ever sold by Sotheby Parke Bernet, the largest house sale ever held by the firm and the largest amount ever realised by the sale of an estate in the United States'.[1] House sales, of course, were as much in the tradition of Parke-Bernet and the earlier companies, American Art Association and the Anderson Galleries from which it took its roots, as they had been at Sotheby's in the UK, though they had become comparatively rare in the Sixties. In fact, the tradition went back further: to the Yerkes Estate, in 1910; the collection of Catholina Lambert's (despite the odd name, a male silk manufacturer) Old Master and Impressionist paintings in 1916; the collection of John Quinn in 1927 and that of Judge Elbert H. Garry in 1928. Sotheby Parke Bernet house sales had again become a much more frequent occurrence in the 1970s.

The two Dodge residences contained material at a level of abundance that took even hardened cataloguers by surprise and they toiled away for months on the preparation of catalogues. Mrs. Dodge had started collecting in the 1920s and was still adding pieces after the Second World War. Records of her purchases were carefully entered into a series of book-keeper's ledgers. Above all they showed her passion for *animalier* bronzes (particularly by Barye) which she was buying as early as 1920 and as late as 1961. Among her favourite painters were Landseer and Rosa de Bonheur, and she was buying their work at a time when it was at its most unfashionable. More than 50,000 visitors came to view the sale at Giralda and 12,000 people attended the sales. Prices were consequently high.

The two houses that had belonged to Mrs. Dodge were disposed of by another firm after the contents had been removed. What shook some of Parke Bernet's management was that the sum raised for the town house exceeded the entire contents total by a considerable margin, and yet the deal was done remarkably smoothly in a very short time. It was in painful contrast to the auctioneer's wearying toil over many months. When, therefore, an acquaintance well versed in all aspects of the property market approached Edward Lee Cave, at that time New York's director in charge of the sales of Decorative Arts, to ask if the firm might be interested in entering the property market, the idea was received with unusual interest. So it came to pass in early October of 1976 that the Sotheby Parke Bernet International Realty Corporation came into existence with the energetic Charles H. Seilheimer at its helm. It soon became clear that there were many wealthy Europeans who were interested in purchasing outstanding country houses in the United States if someone brought them to their attention. By April 1977 the sale of five major properties had been finalised to two Germans, a Brazilian and a Danish nobleman residing in Monte Carlo, as

1. Quoted from Jerry E. Patterson's article on the Dodge Sale in *Art at Auction*, 1975–76.

well as to a lone American. 'Realty' concentrated on dream houses at high prices and soon a steady stream of colourful leaflets showing remarkably lush, luxurious estates, mansions and apartments began to circulate among a clientele that the firm could reach through its wide-ranging network of contacts. The illustrations showed traditional American farmhouses, stately 'period' residences, ultra-modern seaboard houses, tucked away in obscure and deliberately isolated locations, as well as sizeable, beautifully furnished and infinitely exclusive New York apartments. Famous names soon added lustre to the organisation. Rockefeller, Dupont, Heinz, Ken Lane sold: Lisa Minelli and Billy Joel bought. By 1978 property to the value of $17,000,000 had been sold in the previous season and increasingly the sale of houses brought with it furniture and works of art that came up for sale both 'on the premises' and in Parke Bernet's New York galleries. In England, estate agency work and auctioneering had gone hand in hand within the same firms for generations. It was unexpected that such a development had come about in the USA in the 1970s simply because someone had espied a need for it.

38

A Story with No Ending

WHILE New York had been pre-occupied with the arrival of Christie's, with Dodge and the potential of real estate, London had had its hands full with a re-awakening economy and with the biggest house sale the firm had ever undertaken. It was yet another instance of the history of the Rothschilds and of Sotheby's crossing each other's paths. Mentmore was a huge, strangely winsome stone pile erected in the rolling Buckinghamshire countryside in the 1850s. It had been designed by Sir Joseph Paxton in a 'Jacobethan' style, flanked by four formidable towers, at the behest of Baron Mayer Amshel de Rothschild who, as the youngest of four sons, was much more active as a connoisseur, collector and lover of the turf than he was in the traditional family banking business. The style and richness of the interior of his new residence became something of a prototype for housing the great Rothschild art collections of the nineteenth century elsewhere in England and in France. But after 120 years Mentmore had spent itself. It had been designed for a lifestyle that was almost totally extinct in Britain, and by 1977 the house had become a majestic white elephant. Yet in its death-throes Mentmore became a *cause célèbre* which epitomised the conflict between conservation and dissolution during a period when the State had taken over almost every form of patronage.

The 7th Earl of Rosebery had inherited the property, and a number of houses elsewhere, on his father's death in 1974. This faced him with the payment of death duties of £4½ million. Realising the artistic significance of Mentmore as a symbol of the height of Victorian opulence, he had been negotiating with the government since February 1975 to sell the house and most of its contents for possible use as a museum or country house open to the public. The price asked, £3,600,000, was a market valuation that clearly represented a bargain for the authorities, but for three years there had been endless bureaucratic procrastination. In the meantime the cost of upkeep was mounting and the place and its contents deteriorating. A decision had eventually to be forced. Sotheby's had to remain on the sidelines while the discussions continued. As a preliminary it had been decided in October of 1976 to start cataloguing the contents. There were large parts of the house that were not lived in or heated, and the decorative detritus of several generations of the Roseberys (Baron Rothschild's only daughter had married the 5th Earl of Rosebery who was to become Prime Minister in 1894) had accumulated in some of the larger downstairs rooms that were kept permanently shuttered. Some of the greatest treasures had already gone in sales or been sold privately both before and after the war. To anyone who had seen the house before it was prepared for the final sale, it seemed something of a miracle that the cataloguing had been as thorough as it was under such conditions.

The Department of the Environment at last decided in January of 1977 that it would not make an offer for Mentmore and its contents. Thereupon, Lord Rosebery's mother, the eighty-two-year-old Dowager Countess, helped to conduct parties of journalists around the house, and long articles on Mentmore, its contents and the forthcoming dispersal by Sotheby's planned for May 1977 were featured prominently in leading newspapers and journals. Letters of protest, inaugurated by the editor of the *Connoisseur* appeared in *The Times*, and in a matter of weeks the public expressed dismay and concern, and the outcry reached giant proportions. Late in February Lord Rosebery therefore approached the Department of the Environment for a second time so that they might reconsider the purchase of Mentmore. But he set a deadline for an official decision by 5 April, the last day on which the provisional arrangements for the sale – which was still planned for May – could have been cancelled. A further date, 30 May 1977, was of paramount importance. Up to then the death duties were payable on the probate value only; thereafter they would be based on the price realised of anything sold, and values in general had increased substantially in the intervening three years since his father's death.

Despite intense pressure from many quarters, including a strong conservationist lobby, the government announced early in March that it would *not* come to the rescue of Mentmore: it was, said a spokesman, 'politically and economically impossible'. Whatever the rights and wrongs of the case might have been (and there were telling arguments on both sides) or the outcome of the spirited debate on the aesthetic merits of the art collection within the house, in the eyes of the public Mentmore had become a test case of whether the government cared about the nation's heritage or not; and the government of the day clearly and lamentably failed the test. The implications of this slowly burned themselves into the public conscience. It was obvious, for example, that taxation was now so excessive that it was endangering not only the upkeep but also the future preservation of the stately homes of England. So despite a host of further nerve-racking rumours to the contrary, the sale of Mentmore was on.

In the superbly beautiful setting of the Vale of Aylesbury in a late, seemingly reluctant spring, the ten days of actual auction after the months of frenzied organisation and preparation were like a long outing into cloud cuckoo-land. There was a tremendous disparity between the portent-laden brouhaha preceding the sale and the reality of the occasion itself. The preview of the thousands of lots that were to come under the hammer demonstrated to many the difficulties of turning Mentmore into a permanent public showcase. Years of neglect were visible everywhere, and such neglect in the long term was simply a sentence of death. It became obvious that the sale would re-circulate a lot of magnificent objects that might otherwise have just rotted away. One American visitor when asked what he thought of it all remarked pensively that in his eyes 'it was all a load of high-class junk'. Few people had ever seen so much French eighteenth-century furniture – Baron Rothschild found it cheaper than buying furniture new at Maples – in the form of seemingly unlimited numbers of marquetry commodes, boulle desks, throne-like chairs, elaborate candelabras, decorative clocks, Gobelin tapestries and Venetian mirrors – or so much ornamental silver from every part of Europe, or so many racing trophies, or so much sixteenth- and seventeenth-century enamelware, or carved ivory figures, or rock crystal, or objects made of amber, or Vincennes and Sèvres porcelain, or, for that matter, so many paintings of battle scenes by Van Blarenberghe. It was all on a majestic scale that positively dwarfed the accretions of Mrs. Dodge. Here after all were the possessions accumulated by several generations of one of the most affluent families in England. Few people had ever been allowed a glimpse into this special world except favoured visitors and members of the family; and those visitors who could express themselves readily on paper, such as Lady Eastlake or Benjamin Disraeli or Matthew Arnold or Henry James had reacted with astonishment. Lady Eastlake – and goodness knows she was accustomed to inspecting palaces all over Europe when her husband had been director of the National Gallery – wrote in 1872 after her first visit: 'It was like a fairyland when I entered the great palace . . . I don't believe the Medici were so lodged in the height of their glory'.

Sotheby's had given Mentmore a festive dress for the occasion of its end as a Rothschild–Rosebery preserve. There were marquees outside the house for refreshment, for the despatch of goods and an enormous striped, draped and decorated affair for the sale itself which could seat 2,000 and house also a great battery of reporters, photographers and TV camera crews from all over the world. Entrance was by ticket only. The catalogues had a special magnificence about them, and though 11,000 sets of the five volumes were printed, and sold at £30 a set, they had gone out of print three weeks before the sale started and sets were said to be changing hands at up to £300. A special paperback edition – devoid of colour – had to be rushed through the press.

Lord Rosebery and his family were in attendance throughout. His Lordship himself, an enthusiastic expert on stage lighting and sound reproduction since his days at Oxford, came to the rescue when, just as the first sale was about to start, it was found that the principal microphone was not working. It was not surprising that anyone who saw Peter Wilson strolling around behind the scenes half an hour before the opening furniture sale was about to begin on that sunny May morning, should find him tense and nervous. The firm had never had a build-up of such proportions for any sale. The very antagonism of the conservationists had made Mentmore a household name. The eyes of the world were focused on the sale and most British morning newspapers gave it front page treatment. The delay over the microphone lasted twenty-five agonising minutes and added enormously to the pre-sale tension. But when the bidding started at long last, it became clear within minutes that the occasion was going to be a success. Prices were much higher than the estimates and the bidding was vigorous and widespread. With forethought typical of the whole undertaking the firm had brought a number of New York staff over for the occasion who acted as additional bid callers (a normal feature at Madison Avenue), because the auctioneer could not see every deliberate movement in the vast sea of faces in front of him. There were gasps when lot 26, a Louis XIV ormolu-mounted marquetry secretaire *en pent* stamped BVRB JME was knocked down for £280,000 – then the highest price ever paid at auction for a piece of furniture – and even more astonishment when it was reported in the papers on the following day that it had been bought in. Lord Rosebery had fixed a very high reserve on it. It was one of several pieces marked with an asterisk in the catalogue to indicate that it had been 'designated by the Government as being of Pre-Eminent importance'. A number of such pieces were eventually acquired by national museums, but only because their respective directors fought ferociously for the acquisitions in the face of Treasury lethargy. Thus the National Gallery of Scotland bought the superlative portrait of the ageing Madame de Pompadour by Francois-Hubert Drouais and the *Portrait of a Scholar* by Maroni. And the grandest piece of furniture at Mentmore, the immensely elaborate Augustus Rex bureau, went to the Victoria & Albert Museum together with a number of lesser pieces which had been bought as a sop to Cerberus not long before the sale was due to begin.

The most amusing part of the proceedings was the sale of the household goods, pedestrian perhaps by Victorian standards, but historically fascinating as well as being quaintly useful in the 1970s. There was enormous competition for the old but elegant wooden coat-hangers and towel rails, the brass and copper hot water jugs and laundry baskets, and fire irons and coal-scuttles (catalogued as purdoniums), the kitchen china and the maids' plain chests of drawers. All had been displayed in the long stables behind the house, among busts of ancestors and famous politicians and live chickens pecking away at ancient ears of wheat. The nursery cradle fetched £400 and even the butler's desk made £950. The sale had demonstrated to the thousands who came, more out of curiosity than any intense desire to bid, the value not only of what was ornate and spectacular but also of the social left-overs of a former generation. In general the concensus of comment on the spot agreed with Lord Rosebery's sixteen-year-old daughter, who had made a moving contribution to the long correspondence in *The Times*. She had written, 'For several generations, Mentmore was lived in, in that incredibly dazzling life-style, and now that it has to go – can it not die in some semblance of the dignity in which it lived?' The total sum raised by the eighteen sale sessions came to £6,390,000 – the highest ever figure by far for any house sale. For Marcus Linell and John Cann who had been responsible for the organisation, and those who had toiled with them, it had been the most enormous job of work, at times in dreadfully dispiriting conditions because of the initial uncertainties and political overtones. Their greatest achievement was that an event which might have been funereal or merely unprepossessing, had, in fact, been imbued with an enormous sense of fun and style and was crowned with great success.

Mentmore was merely the high point in the most active summer season than anyone at Sotheby's could ever remember. It stretched the staff in all departments to extremes but there seemed to be few who did not enjoy such accelerated activity. In fact, it was reflected elsewhere: there were great sales in

Monte Carlo, Amsterdam, Florence, Zürich, Hong Kong, Johannesburg and New York. There had been an understandable reluctance by owners to sell art and antiques during the depressed period after 1974. Now it seemed that the floodgates were open and there was genuine surprise that so many things of such quality should appear for sale simultaneously from famous collections of all kinds. The catalogue department worked marvels in giving permanence to much that was about to be scattered. Over a thousand sales were held, collectively, in the year ending in July 1977. It was a fine crescendo for the season in which the firm was to become a public company, a fact which Peter Wilson announced, in the best Sotheby tradition initiated by Sir Montague Barlow, to the assembled staff in the great gallery at Bond Street, and John Marion to his staff in Madison Avenue, just as it was released to the press all over the world.

And yet, and yet . . . it would be misleading not to mention that what was a triumphant season had been bedevilled by those complications that were now a regular staple in an auctioneer's life. First there had been the seemingly insoluble uncertainties over Mentmore. Inevitably a lot of *flak*, particularly from the conservationist lobby, had been directed at Sotheby's, usually in the person of Peter Wilson, though as the full facts emerged the press itself began to point out that the firm was merely acting as Lord Rosebery's agent. The fusillade was then turned on to the Treasury and the various ministers responsible. Elsewhere the French government contributed its share of alarm by refusing to grant export licences on three of the finest pieces of black lacquer furniture made by Riesener for Marie-Antoinette's apartment at Versailles, which were sold at Monte Carlo. The Italian authorities actually stopped the sale of the contents of the Palazzo Serristori in Florence, on the day it was due to begin, by reference to a seemingly ambiguous law of 1911 on historical buildings. In Zürich the most outstanding jewel sale of the season was affected when someone walked off with the two prize pieces, despite stringent security precautions, by the classic method of substituting perfect plastic copies of the gems concerned, resulting in the biggest insurance claim the firm had ever made. A little later in New York John Marion had to call in the district attorney when two men attempted to extort $100,000 from the firm in exchange for not releasing damaging information, which turned out to be wholly spurious. The men were arrested and charged after an exchange of briefcases, supposedly containing money, that had been organised by the police. Someone had been reading too much crime fiction.

If this book had been completed in the summer of 1977, Mentmore would have seemed a good, record-breaking climax with which to conclude the story, but the following year saw the sale of another collection which was genuinely epoch-making. The circumstances surrounding it could not have been more different. It was a well-loved private collection, formed in one very old man's lifetime, mostly during a period when what particularly interested him was not widely sought after. It had been assembled in Germany, moved to Switzerland and was now to be dispersed in London. There was nothing in the Swiss legal system that would bring about any complications. Although the collection ranged widely over paintings and drawings from the fifteenth to the twentieth century, and included furniture, silver, porcelain and decorative works of art of many kinds, it was the contents of a single glass display cabinet that stirred the acquisitive imagination of scholarly collectors and curators all over the world, and which was to have a monumental impact on the entire art market.

Von Hirsch

Robert von Hirsch had been a regular visitor at Sotheby's for many years. He had met Peter Wilson at the time of the Pringsheim maiolica sale in 1939 and had remarked to Geoffrey Hobson then that here was a young man with a remarkably discerning eye. At that time Von Hirsch had already been collecting for forty years. From 1905 onwards his mentor had been Georg Swarzenski, a distinguished medievalist and the director of the Städel Museum in Frankfurt. With Swarzenski's help, Von Hirsch built up an unrivalled collection of medieval and Renaissance works of art: each a jewel-like example of the finest craftsmanship of its period. The majority of pieces had been acquired between 1925 and 1935 at some of the most important Continental sales and dispersals of that period: from the Guelph treasure in Brunswick; from the Hermitage Collection; from the collections of Prince Karl Anton von Hohenzollern-Sigmaringen, and from other collectors such as Figdor of Vienna, Trivulzio of Milan, Passavant-Gontard of Frankfurt-am-Main and Rütschi of Zürich. In their turn these collectors had bought them from celebrated collections of an earlier generation such as Lanna, Spitzer and Baron von Rothschild at Grüneburg. Thus everything came with impeccable provenances. The items acquired included the early bronze aquamaniles and candlesticks, the enamels, the Venetian glass, various reliquary caskets and an incomparable series of ivory carvings. Most stemmed from between the eleventh and the fourteenth centuries. They were not only old: most were exquisitely beautiful. Well over a hundred such pieces were kept in the glass cabinet in Von Hirsch's library. For many years he had harboured the desire to leave his entire collection to some major museum, but his expulsion from Germany under the Nazis and his later rift with various museum authorities in Switzerland deterred him from this course of action. He died in 1977 at the age of ninety-four. In his will he stated that though he wanted a general dispersal by auction (he did not – contrary to belief – stipulate that this should be carried out by Sotheby's), he laid down that the medieval collection should, in the first place, be offered as a single entity to a Swiss foundation. In the event this foundation was only prepared to acquire some of the objects. A shrewd middle-Western museum in America also applied to the executors to purchase the collection, but the offer they made of £4,000,000 was not considered adequate. As we have seen, Sotheby's had been responsible for a periodic valuation of all Von Hirsch's artistic property for insurance purposes for some years and therefore had a particularly detailed knowledge of it. The old man had frequently challenged the valuations attached to individual pieces, and as recently as 1969 he had been appalled when

John Hunt, who often undertook such work for the firm, as far as Romanesque and medieval works of art were concerned, valued two of the most important examples of Mosan enamel ware at £30,000 each, which Von Hirsch thought was much too high a figure. In view of the possible direct sale of the medieval collection, the executors took the unusual precaution of asking Sotheby's to evaluate the effect its removal would have on the sale of the remainder of the collection. The resulting assessment was discouraging. It was therefore with some pride, and not inconsiderable apprehension, that Sotheby's announced in due course that, with the exception of certain specific bequests, they were to sell the entire corpus of the Von Hirsch collection in June 1978. 190 of the 800 objects were sent to Frankfurt, Zürich and the Royal Academy in London for special exhibitions well before the sale. It was at Frankfurt at the Städelsches Kunstinstitut itself, where the collection was exhibited for a few days, that events occurred which were to be of particular importance when it came to the sales. It became apparent to a number of German museum directors that the supreme quality and rarity of much of the medieval material, and of some of the most important drawings, were virtually unique in private hands. Twelve of them therefore clubbed together and set about raising the necessary funds and working out a common purchasing strategy. This was co-ordinated under the direction of Dr. Herman Abs, the retired (but still active) head of the Deutsche Bank and for many years Adenauer's confidant and adviser on financial and economic affairs. After lengthy negotiations a sum said to be in excess of DM.15,000,000 was made available by the German Ministry of the Interior from a frozen federal endowment fund, and dealers from Hanover, Hamburg, Cologne, Zürich and London were then briefed to act in London.

The final viewing before the sales was slightly longer than usual and the number of visitors that streamed into Bond Street was prodigious. What impressed both commentators and the interested public alike was that almost everything was on an intimate scale that any lover of the arts could instantly understand and appreciate. This applied equally to the bronze aquamaniles in the form of horses, the enamel arm ornament that came from the coronation vestment of the Emperor Frederick Barbarossa, the Limoges enamel eucharistic dove, the north-Italian glass plaque of the Crucifixion, the Romanesque walrus ivory draughtsman and the south-Italian ivory chess piece of a young king seated on his throne; the many small marble, wood and bronze sculptures, the illuminated miniatures on vellum, the particularly striking Urs Graf drawing of a man setting his timepiece by the sun, the rapidly sketched watercolour drawing of a church in front of a large rock by Albrecht Dürer, the Rembrandt and Jan Bruegel drawings of townscapes, the Francesco Guardi painting of San Giorgio Maggiore in Venice, two fine drawings by Van Gogh and the many Cézanne watercolours.

The opening sale was an evening session at 9.30 p.m. on 20 June. It consisted of the medieval miniatures and the Old Master drawings. By this time the media had spread the message of the importance of the sale around the world on a scale that surpassed even Mentmore. The atmosphere was tense when Peter Wilson in evening dress climbed into the fiercely lit rostrum. The estimates were quickly left behind. Breslauer paid £45,000 for a Spanish illuminated miniature of *c*. 1200, a long lost leaf from a Beatus on the apocalypse in the Bibliothèque Nationale in Paris, and H. P. Kraus paid £90,000 for two miniatures of the crucifixion by the Veronica Master who was active in Cologne around 1400. The Urs Graf drawing was bought by the Swiss dealer Segal, for an amazing £122,000. (It turned out later that this was for the Basel Museum.) The Dürer drawing shot up from an opening bid of £50,000 to £640,000 in bidding so rapid it took only just over thirty seconds, and it was bought by the veteran Swiss dealer, Mrs. Marianne Feilchenfeld, for a German museum. She also paid £105,000 for a coloured chalk portrait of a man in a soft hat by Wolf Huber dated 1522 and £300,000 on behalf of the Karlsruhe Museum for a brilliant, though unfinished Dürer pen-and-ink drawing, *Christ on the Mount of Olives*. A head of a rather soppy young man looking upwards by Pintoricchio fetched £65,000. A sheet of studies for the *Martyrdom of St. George* by Veronese fetched £75,000. The Bruegel sketch of Heidelberg was bought by a bidder in an adjacent room who had been watching the sale on closed circuit television, for £50,000. A rare Rembrandt nude seemed very reasonable at £52,000, but there were some who questioned its authenticity. But there was no doubt whatever about Rembrandt's wash drawing of Shah Jahan, one of the twenty-one known copies that Rembrandt had made of Indian miniatures of the Mogul school. It was bought for £160,000 by the Cleveland Museum. When it had made an earlier appearance at Sotheby's in the Lord Brownlow sale in 1926, Duveen had paid £680 for it.

The paintings by Old Masters were sold on the following morning, though all were not of the same level of excellence. The Branchini Madonna by Giovanni di Paolo, a picture in the great fifteenth-century Sienese tradition, was bought by Speelman for the Norton Simon Foundation for £500,000. Many had thought the price would go even higher. Bernhard Strigel's Annunciation fetched £120,000. A Hans Baldung Grien *Madonna* which Von Hirsch had bought fifty years earlier from the Hohenzollern Collection, fetched £235,000. Both these pictures were bought for European private collectors.

The high point of the series began at 11 a.m. on the Tuesday morning with the sale of the medieval antiquities, the contents of the display cabinet in Von Hirsch's library, in front of a largely professional but smaller audience that did not throng the overflow galleries as densely as in the previous two sales. The session started quietly enough, though Peter Wilson took the bidding at an unusually brisk pace. The first piece that caused something of a stir was a thirteenth-century Lower Saxon bronze aquamanile in the form of the bust of a youth. It was bought at £62,000 by that shrewdest of buyers, David Carritt. The third of the aquamaniles in the form of a horse was bought by Rosenberg and Stiebel for £45,000. Then it came to the turn of a quaintly primitive kneeling figure of a naked woman. For many people this unsophisticated eleventh-century Italian bronze with its bulging haunches was one of the most memorable medieval objects in the collection and it was known that several museums were anxious to acquire it. But a number of private collectors, who had anticipated fierce opposition from institutional buyers or dealers acting on their behalf, wisely left their bidding to Malcolm Barber, the young auctioneer's clerk on whom the mantle of Sam Patch had finally come to rest. It was fascinating to watch Peter Wilson taking alternate bids from the room before him and the sales clerk on his right. Barber brought off some brilliant buying by perfect timing: he bought the kneeling woman, for example, for £100,000. His flicking silver ballpoint pen was often the strongest opposition to the German museums who had now come into the open and were bidding fiercely. An interesting fascicle of sale-room history was attached to lot 210, a large English gilt altar candlestick base of elaborate twelfth-century workmanship. It was bought in just thirty-five seconds by Eskenazi for £550,000, but the atmosphere grew truly electric when it came to the twenty-second lot in the sale, the wonderfully luminous enamel armilla which had once belonged to the Emperor Barbarossa. Peter Wilson started the bidding at £100,000. In nineteen curt bids the price had risen to £1,100,000 – the highest ever paid at auction for an antique object that was not a painting. A few minutes later that figure was exceeded when a circular Mosan enamel medallion was bought by Rainer Zietz, a dealer from Hanover, for £1,200,000. These were the very pieces on which Von Hirsch had disputed Sotheby's valuation at £30,000 each less than a decade earlier. By the time this altogether remarkable sales session was over, those who had attended it were left limp with excitement. The ninety-seven lots had raised no less than £6,368,150, almost as much as all eighteen sessions of the Mentmore sale in the previous year put together. The remaining Von Hirsch sales took the total to a completely unprecedented figure of almost £18,500,000.

While the German museums were preparing to take their many purchases across the Channel, it emerged on the morning following the antiquities sale that Eskenazi had bought the English medieval candlestick base on behalf of the British Rail Pension Fund. The story of that Fund's activities in the art market aroused as much interest as anything with which Sotheby's had ever been associated. On its office door the nameplate 'Lexbourne Co'. seemed innocuous enough as a name for a commercial undertaking. In fact, it concealed an organisation which was the brain child of Christopher Lewin, an enthusiastic collector of antiquarian books in private life who happened to be an actuary by profession: indeed as such he was one of several people responsible for the enormous annual investment on behalf of Britain's railwaymen through a number of superannuation funds. As a book collector Lewin had seen a rise in the prices of antiquarian books that out-distanced other purely financial capital investments. Why not, he pondered, use a small proportion of the sums available for investment in something similar on behalf of the pensioners[1] of British Rail?

1. At the end of 1978 there were 231,000 workers paying contributions and 123,000 receiving pensions.

VIIa. A Limoges copper gilt châsse decorated in champlevé enamel with scenes from the martyrdom of St. Thomas à Becket, *c.* 1195 (possibly made for Peterborough Abbey). The piece came from the collection of Ernst and Marthe Kofler-Truniger of Lucerne and was sold on 13 December 1979 for £420,000. It had been sold previously at Sotheby's in July 1930 for £3,150.

VIIb. A Byzantine ivory relief of *Christ in Majesty*, probably made in Constantinople in the 11th century, from the Robert von Hirsch Collection fetched £630,000 on 22 June 1978. The ninety-seven items, mostly of medieval antiquities, sold in that morning's session, raised no less than £6,368,150.

VIIIc. A Carolingian ivory relief with a figure of St. John the Evangelist was probably carved in Aachen around A.D. 800 as the cover for a manuscript gospel. Originally brought into Sotheby's as 'an old piece of wood', it was sold for £255,000 on 15 December 1977.

VIIIa. A selection of works by Picasso and Braque from the collection of the Paul Rosenberg family, on display in Bond Street before its sale on 3 July 1979 for a total of £3,206,700.

VIIIb. Two Bond Street porters carrying Turner's view of Venice, entitled *Juliet and her Nurse*, the property of Mrs. Flora Whitney-Miller, before its sale in New York in May 1980 for an astonishing $6·4 million. In the background are some of the major paintings from the collection of Edgar William and Bernice Chrysler Garbisch, also sold in New York.

It took a good deal of time to persuade others to his way of thinking. Eventually, as a first move, there was an approach on behalf of the trustees of the
Funds to Sotheby's to sound out their views and to see whether the firm would
act as the Funds' advisers. Why Sotheby's? people asked. The answer given was
that they were known to be the most prominent firm of fine art auctioneers, the
most internationally based, with the largest number of experts on their staff,
and the biggest turnover. The very multiplicity of departments, in fact, militated against prejudices in favour of any particular sort of object at any given
moment, be it Old Master paintings, primitive art or ancient atlases. Many
months passed in which the objectives of buying suitable articles were considered and established, and the procedures for so doing were laid down. The
person appointed to manage the selection process was Annamaria Edelstein,
who had worked in the antique trade for some years before editing *Art at
Auction* for several issues. The combination gave her a useful insight into the
art market internationally. She worked completely independently though in
consultation with the firm's experts. Before suggesting specific acquisitions
there was the most scrupulous vetting process which included a detailed
comparison with similar objects displayed in museums or recently sold elsewhere. A completed proposal form with the suggested price tag was then put to
a progression of committees. Such suggestions might be for objects coming up
for sale at Sotheby's itself, at Christie's, in Paris, Zürich, Monte Carlo, New
York or from dealers, and even occasionally from private collectors. A budget
was fixed at about three per cent of the annual funds available, and in November
1974 the British Rail Fund made its first purchase, an English translation of a
seventeenth-century illustrated Italian book on architecture. It had once
belonged to Thomas Wentworth, Earl of Stafford, and later to none other than
Sir Thomas Phillipps. As it happened, the early purchases could not have
occurred at a more opportune moment. Prices were depressed and there were
few buyers for really important objects in the market. Some of the items bought
in the first two years already looked like considerable bargains two or three
years later when similar pieces again came up for sale. The Fund operated for
something over five years. By the time it closed in 1980 it had bought in excess
of 2,000 objects at a cost of £40,000,000 (out of a total investment portfolio
worth well over £1,000,000,000). The primary aim had been to establish a
representative art collection of what had been some of the finest pieces to come
on to the market. It included classical and medieval antiquities, Old Master
paintings and drawings, Impressionist pictures, Chinese ceramics, silver,
carpets and tapestries, furniture and *objets d'art*, manuscript material and books,
and a particularly good selection of primitive art from Africa and Asia. It
excluded glass, coins, icons and contemporary paintings. The Fund's managers
had expressly stated that they would not dispose of any piece for at least a
generation – many of their known liabilities would not, in fact, arise until well
into the next century. A considerable proportion of the things bought were, in
the meantime, put on display at Britain's principal museums. Thus, the Von
Hirsch candlestick went on loan to the British Museum; a portrait bust of

Benjamin Franklin by Houdon, a gilt bronze of a lion from the T'ang Dynasty, Pablo Picasso's portrait of a *Young Man in Blue* are on loan to the Victoria & Albert Museum; Matisse's *Deux Negresses*, a bronze of 1908, is at the Tate Gallery, and Tiepolo's *Miraculous Translation of the Holy House of Loreto* is at the National Gallery.

For a time the Fund was perhaps the world's biggest single purchaser of art, probably surpassing the Paul Getty Museum in Malibu (not yet in its stride) and rivalling the Norton Simon Foundation in Pasadena. For obvious reasons, in a competitive world the Fund's managers had to move with great discretion and the inevitable secrecy that cloaked their activities stimulated an immense amount of probing by the press and a good deal of hostile public comment from members of the art trade. Only time can tell whether this adventurous exercise will have fulfilled its purpose and whether the four per cent investment in art matches the monetary accretion in real terms of the ninety-six per cent invested in industrial shares, property and mutual funds. But already there are clear pointers ahead. One can also, for example, look back some thirty years. One of the critics of the scheme in a letter to *The Times* was George Levy of Blairman, a distinguished and long-established firm of antique dealers who have been buying at Sotheby's for many years. Mr. Levy, who was President of the British Antique Dealers' Association at the time, was writing in 1978. Let us suppose for a glorious moment that Blairmans had suddenly discovered a store room full of the goods Mr. Levy's firm had actually bought at Bond Street in the 1940s, a generation earlier, and that these included the fine Sheraton mahogany sideboard for which they had paid £34; the rare and remarkable Adam mahogany pier table (illustrated in Macquoid & Edwards *Dictionary of English Furniture*) for £60; the Yung Cheng tea service of eleven pieces, painted with reserve panels of exotic birds and flowers, for £19, or the Chün wine ewer of double gourd shape in lavender glaze with three gold repairs of the Sung/Yuan Dynasty, for £13, or the three outstanding *inro* for £19, or the pair of eighteenth-century jade table screens 14in. high, decorated in various coloured hardstones, for £12, or the fine 16in. high 'Chelsea' white bust of George II, for £56. What would the price tags be on such items now? A conservative answer must be at least fifty to a hundred times the original cost price. If the British Rail Pension Fund, which, of course, paid high prices for the best in quality that was available, achieves only a reasonable fraction of this, its pensioners will have been well served, despite all the tax advantages a pension fund enjoys because of its charitable status when it invests in equities or gilts.

Though there was nothing quite to match a Von Hirsch collection in the following season, that too had its memorable highlights: the sale of the Sonnenberg Collection in New York, the collection of eighteenth-century French furniture much of which had once belonged to Wildensteins and was now put up for sale by Mr. Akram Ojjeh in Monte Carlo, the firm's first house sale in Spain at El Quexigal, the Paul Rosenberg family collection of Picassos and Braques, and the Constable–Maxwell collection of ancient glass.

New developments continued unabated. In recent years the firm has joined forces with and acquired the chattel auction business of a number of English provincial estate agents as the importance of that market has grown: Bearne's at Torquay, Beresford Adams in Chester, King & Chasemore in Pulborough, Humbert's in Taunton. It has developed a tax advisory service for clients in the face of the increasing intricacies and ferocity of the fiscal system. A scheme was started to sponsor the arts through exhibitions and by helping artists and musicians. It acquired a long lease on the Aeolian Hall in Bond Street as yet another measure to counter the perpetual shortage of office and selling space as a new home for the book department, as well as for coins and jewellery. In New York the purchase of the former Kodak building at 1334 York Avenue was an even bolder and more fundamental step: it meant that after the autumn of 1980 the New York business would be literally split in two. Paintings, coins and jewellery would remain at Madison Avenue. Everything else would come up for auction in York Avenue. Tom Hodge would have been totally baffled by the incredible complexity of the organisation that now existed in order to achieve the same simple ends which he had managed almost single handed.

The growth of the firm is one of the really great success stories since the Second World War. It would be foolish to pretend that this success has been accepted universally with delight and acclamation. There are many people who do not like Sotheby's. One thing that has frequently caused resentment is the firm's remarkable ability to turn adversity to their advantage. This is one of Peter Wilson's many formidable attributes, for more than any other man he has been the architect of the Sotheby's that goes on into the 1980s and towards the 250th anniversary of its foundation.

It is not often that a major commercial enterprise has at its head a man who is so completely devoted to the business and is so totally convinced that the future can only hold prospects of even greater triumphs; and has been right in predicting them for over twenty years. Two abilities in particular have helped him: one is to think big, and always to opt for the more ambitious of any two alternatives; and the second is to give his undivided attention to anyone with whom he is in conversation to a degree so convincing that the other person is left with the firm impression that to Peter Wilson he is the most important person in the world. Throughout the years Peter Wilson has demonstrated that he has a truly remarkable eye for quality. He cares passionately about great art, but equally it would be fair to say that he cares passionately about great artists as creators of outstanding objects which he can sell, usually to someone who will appreciate them. It is with his dual appreciation of real worth in the artistic sense and value in the financial sense that he has helped create an environment where great works of art can be bought or sold at will. Art collecting need no longer be looked at merely as an expensive form of self-indulgence, for the size and internationalism of the present art market mean that works can be converted into money and back into other works of art more swiftly and more easily than ever before. It is this 'liquidity' of works of art that makes them an increasingly viable form of alternative investment. Enjoyment can be equated with sound commercial common sense: the guilty conscience of the puritan ethic has been put to flight.

Wilson is at his best in the rostrum, some twenty minutes into a major sale when the ever-present anxieties of a sticky beginning are behind him. He is a past master of the pregnant gesture, the momentary pause, the head tilted left and come-on smile, the raised eyebrow, the deprecatory look that says 'you really should have made another bid'. His facial expressions convey concern, humour, encouragement and a special form of instant communication with a hesitant bidder that generates confidence. The tempo can be agonisingly slow or move at the speed of lightning. Peter Wilson is always firmly in control. That is why, until his retirement as Chairman, for any major painting or other sale he was Sotheby's ultimate weapon. The training as an auctioneer has given him the ability to think at an enormous speed, and if need be, to take instant decisions. He is one of the few people who will always say 'let us decide it now' rather than 'let's think about it tomorrow'. Inevitably he has had to learn the skills of a diplomat, resilience in the face of public controversy, a ready charm, a certain sense of guile, a diffusion of bluntness. But he has few equals in being devastatingly direct in analysis when the occasion permits – or demands – it. With the iconoclastic wit goes a puckish sense of humour, a saving grace in the constant crises which the management has to face as a matter of routine. He also has a finely developed sense of showmanship and one of his strengths is that his tall, distinguished, urbane and rather conventional appearance masks a distinctly unconventional and very agile mind.

It is difficult for the public, strolling through the leisured calm of the galleries in Bond Street or Madison Avenue in order to inspect the goods displayed before a sale, to appreciate that the studied elegance around them is simply the visible pinnacle of a vast iceberg of an immensely active organisation. An auction house such as Sotheby Parke Bernet today, combines the varied scholarship of a major museum with the commercial prowess of a large department store. It has all the problems of a multi-national corporation and needs the financial skills of a merchant bank. It must have flair not only for attracting public attention, but must also learn to collect money from recalcitrant debtors without resorting to strong arm methods. The perpetually increasing length and complexity of the conditions of sale printed in each catalogue only reflect the growing litigiousness of commercial life today. The company must appear to know all the answers, and yet the very essence of its business is perpetual uncertainty. Its most successful employees show a strong streak of the *entrepreneur* and yet a multitude of independent departments must be welded into a compatible whole conforming to entirely uniform methods. It requires a very special brand of leadership that needs to be proof against unending self-criticism from inside and informed sniping from outside. It must learn to deal as courteously with the greatest in the land, with millionaires and governments, as with the proprietor of a modest family heirloom wrapped in crumpled brown paper. Most important of all, the firm has continually to build up and to maintain a position of trust and total integrity with sellers and buyers alike. It is its finest asset in an era where the pressure of competition is likely to grow.

Take the scene on any one morning around the public counters. This is where it all starts. This is where those with something to sell first come into contact with Sotheby's and where the expert's ability for instant judgement matters most. Here at one and the same moment John Hayward can be seen inspecting a nineteenth-century copy of a medieval ivory brought in by a French client; while Tim Clarke is studying a rare du Paquier porcelain snuff box that reminds him of one in the famous Blohm sales; Graham Wells is looking at a violin, in fact an only-just-above-average instrument. On the opposite side of the George Street entrance, Richard Came is tut-tutting over the damage to a piece of beautiful eighteenth-century English silver, while Christopher de Hamel is explaining in the most courteous terms that although it is certainly five or six hundred years old, there is little demand for the Court roll on vellum brought in by the young man who has just inherited it from his grandfather.

In the 'Com. box' the morning's auctioneer is familiarising himself with the latest bids that have been recorded on the marked copy of the catalogue he will take with him into the rostrum in two minutes at precisely eleven o'clock. Two members of the valuation department are scrambling into a taxi. They are on their way to Euston Station in order to start an urgent probate valuation. Later that day on the other side of the Atlantic John Marion is taking a particularly important jewellery sale, while in another part of New York John Block is looking with astonishment at a huge consignment of Victorian gilt candlesticks that someone has just brought into PB84. Back in Bond Street the finance committee has gathered in Peter Spira's office: plans for the future, profit from the past, problems for the present. The catalogue production department has a crisis over late deliveries; the press office ... the cashier ... the business continues. There are four more sales tomorrow.

Sotheby's

Founded 1744

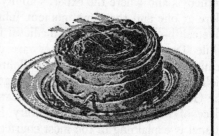

TODAY, MONDAY, 12th MARCH
HIGHLY IMPORTANT JOINTS OF BEEF
AND MUTTON
from the collection of Mrs. Enid Norris
and others, including a very wonderful
spare rib and a unique assortment of lamb
chops (slightly foxed)

TUESDAY, 13th MARCH
HIGHLY IMPORTANT SAUSAGES
by Walls and Son, Bowyers, Balon's Kosher
Butchers and others, including original
fourteen foot very rare Liverwurst, hand-
tied and wrapped in wax by Buxtehude of
Dresden; a complete set of finest Italian
chipolatas commissioned by the Count
Lamborghini di Neasdini from the Master
of Pisa; a very wonderful British pork
sausage by Josiah Knibbs (extremely rare)
with maker's name clearly marked in gold
inlay on navy blue and maroon; highly important Polish garlic-sausage by Topolski
(slightly chewed); rare unopened early tin
of Frankfurters sealed and labelled
"Momma's Real-Beef Frankfurters Dontcha
Love 'Em? (Reg Trade Mark) Ingredients:
Wheat Husk, Soya Flour, Monosodium
Glutamate Salt Colouring, Flavouring" manufactured by Seifert Sausage Co. Boston
Mass; exceptionally fine pair of English
hand-made cocktail sausages in perfect
condition, uncooked, by John Wells of Piccadilly, with matching carved oak sausage-
sticks, both mounted on mint doily and
disposable cardboard plate; a unique and
extraordinarily wonderful black-skinned
Furtwanglerwurst (3 feet long and 6 inches
thick), the property of WILLIAM DAVIS
Esq.

WEDNESDAY, 14th MARCH
VERY FINE CONTINENTAL AND ENGLISH
BREAD AND ROLLS
including a unique and very exceptional pair
of Bridge Rolls (prob. 20th cent), a highly
important very fine-sliced white loaf by
Sunwheat of Wealdstone, beautiful condition
in polystoxyphenalyne wrapper untouched
by human hand; a unique and highly desirable stoneground full wheatgerm wholemeal
large "tin" by Livelong Bakeries of Roberts-
bridge; and a very rare French 'bagotte'
by Marcel du Pottinger (slightly fixed).

THURSDAY, 15th MARCH
HIGHLY IMPORTANT CUPS OF TEA AND
COFFEE
including an extremely rare plastic beaker
containing coffee solubles and hot water,
the property of British Rail; a highly unique
tea-bag (v.g. condition) containing Finest
Darjeeling Tips by Pricenice Supermarkets
very fine white enamel mug with blue rim
and handle (slightly chipped) containing
steaming hot very exceptional "Kwik-Cuppa"
Indian blend, very important powdered
milks and quite exceptional matching pair
of refined sugar lumps by Trust Houses
Forte Ltd, the set made especially for Mr.
Patrick "Paddy" O'Lawless by Jox Cafe of
Kentish Town.
Catalogue £15. 3 plates. 2 saucers.

Sotheby & Co., 34-35 New Bond Street, London W1A 2AA

Auction activities have not escaped the censorious antennae of *Private Eye*.

APPENDIX

Hints for a Young Auctioneer[1]
of Books[2] *1828*

I   Consider your Catalogue as the foundation of your eminence and make its perfection of character an important study.

II   In common collections uniformly arrange by cataloguing by alphabet; taking the titles of books as they promiscuously [*sic*] occur, for naming one 'and six', is a plan never to be indulged in by the regular book auctioneer. It may serve for a furniture sale attended by the rig and knock out crew. If a sale is compounded of the property of fifty proprietors make fifty alphabets, or if the character will not allow that arrangement make alphabet classes. The public cannot have anything to do with your proprietors, or your convenience, and always recollect your best friends, in fact your patrons must ever be that same public, to whom your standard duty is to communicate what you have to offer by a true description, in the most intelligent and customary manner possible.

III   In collections of notoriety, if that notoriety is reputedly founded on any particular subject, class assuredly, alphabet the class and lot every work singly. Never in the sale of a good library depend on either your own judgment or even that of a bookseller (who may be sufficiently interested to mislead) in forming large miscellaneous lots, if above the character of old almanacks and Court Calendars or Guides. It were better expend a day in the exertion of detailing than sacrifice a single article by want of due attention.

IV   Being intrusted with Commissions is of vital importance to your public character. Never put in but at one fourth of your Commission if a single Commission, a confluence of them falling on one lot, dictates the lowest to put in at, by just covering the highest commission but one. Without that guide force biddings from the audience, unless you act upon a reserve then take two-thirds as the rule for putting in. Two-thirds may appear on a higher scale than is before suggested as to commissions: if so it must be recollected the character of a reserve differs materially from a commission and is too commonly founded on an assumed value which will not justify the auctioneer in trespassing too long on the

1. S. Leigh Sotheby.
2. The author of these hints was Joseph Haslewood (1769–1833), a solicitor who was also an enthusiastic antiquary and book collector. He was a member of the Roxburghe Club and a friend of Dibdin's. He attended auctions regularly and Samuel Leigh Sotheby describes him as 'my excellent friend'. Haslewood made something of a speciality of perfecting imperfect books and selling them at a considerable profit. His interests included *incunabula*, Elizabethan poetry, as well as books on angling, hawking and field sports. A substantial collection of his books was sold by King and Lochee in 1809 and Evans sold his library after Haslewood's death.

time of his audience by a drawling advance. A reserve is little varying from a mock auction and to give sauce the appearance of validity should be worked in person, i.e. a puffer.

V Your private or Sale accounts are of serious and material importance. That is serious to yourself and material to both the purchaser and employer. As to being serious to yourself needs no explanation, for even were you independent of your business and made same a recreation it would by neglect of the finances plunge you into difficulties. It is material to the purchasor (particularly the trade) to know from time to time, at least once a month, in what amount the account stands to prevent similar difficulties and stimulate a regular prompt payment in order to keep your own capital ever at command. This is on the presumption of the account increasing some 10£ or 20£ every month. With the employer it is still more important to have the account always ready within a certain period, say six days after the Sale, and the balance should be paid over immediately on request or punctually as agreed upon, according to debtors. In a recent instance, the auctioneer retiring, well appointed, was attributed more to his punctuality in paying proceeds, than his merits – which were slender, or his industry. The usual remark was no man called twice for his account and balance.

VI Lots uncleared, or returned imperfect, and pilferings, are serious drawbacks in an auctioneers business, as it forms a loss that cannot well be calculated against or provided for. To meet same liberally is most adviseable for eight out of ten employees will give credit for such a system if not meet the loss half way and the too less liberal will have no foundation for complaint. Crush in its birth discontent by every means possible.

VII You are young, exertion is no other labour than what Society has a right to demand which promptitude of accounts is the stable part, or ought to be, of your character: and is most important. By attending to No. 3 you establish a proof of assiduity and attention as an auctioneer: by like attention to No. 4 may be obtained and retained the confidence of the proprietor as well as the purchaser, and that it may be expected, favoured by the common events of life in a fair proportion of business, place you among the most honourable of your compeers.

Trade sales are too intolerant and otherwise objectionable in the mode of conducting them, to offer any suggestions upon.

Index

Compiled by Douglas Matthews